None Dare Call It Treason...
25 YEARS LATER

John A. Stormer

Liberty Bell Press
Florissant, Missouri

ALSO BY JOHN STORMER

None Dare Call It Treason
The Anatomy of a Smear
The Death of a Nation
Growing Up God's Way

None Dare Call It Treason...25 YEARS LATER

LIBERTY BELL PRESS
Post Office Box 32
Florissant, MO 63032

Library of Congress Cataloguing-in-Publication Data
John A. Stormer
None Dare Call It Treason...25 YEARS LATER
Includes index.
1. Communism 2. Soviet Union 3. United States - Politics and Government I. Title
E743.5
ISBN 0-914053-10-8
PRINTED IN THE UNITED STATES OF AMERICA
Hardcover Edition - January 1990
First Paperback Edition - February 1992

ABOUT THE AUTHOR

None Dare Call It Treason said that John Stormer, "...like most young Americans who grew up during the Depression, was the product of a conservative home and a liberal education. In the late 1950s he gradually came to realize that the political candidates and philosophies he was asked to support in the voting booth did not reflect the standards and principles he tried to apply in his business and personal life."

In 1962 after an intensive study of communism, he left a successful career as editor and general manager of a leading electrical magazine to devote full time to writing and conservative political activities. His first book, *None Dare Call It Treason*, was a runaway best-seller in 1964. His four books have sold over 10-million copies.

As a best selling author, pastor and Christian school superintendent, John Stormer has encouraged many to fulfill their responsibilities to their families, the Lord and America. He was president of the Missouri Association of Christian schools for ten years. Since 1978 he has conducted a weekly Bible study in the Missouri Capitol for members of the legislature.

He publishes *Understanding The Times*, a periodic newsletter analyzing significant news developments in foreign policy, politics, education, religion and economics. He speaks regularly in Bible conferences and *Understanding The Times* seminars.

A native of Altoona, Pennsylvania, he attended the Pennsylvania State University and graduated from California's San Jose State University after Korean War service as an Air Force editor and historian. He is a member of the American Legion and the Council For National Policy. He has honorary degrees from Manahath School of Theology (1965) and Shelton College (1976). He and his wife, Elizabeth, are 35-year residents of Florissant, Missouri, a St. Louis suburb. Their daughter, Holly, is married and the mother of four small children.

DEDICATION

The original *None Dare Call It Treason* was dedicated to my daughter, Holly, with the hope that her future might be as bright as mine was at age five. Holly is now in her thirties. She and Steve have given my wife and me four grandchildren for whom we have the same hope—even though they are growing up in a world that is even more decadent and threatened than Holly's was at their age.

PREFACE TO THE 1992 PAPERBACK EDITION

Those who refuse to learn from the mistakes of the past are bound to repeat them.
                                    —*George Santyana*

SINCE WRITING the introduction for *None Dare Call It Treason—25 YEARS LATER* in 1989, much of the world has appeared to turn upside down.

Experts say communism is dead. The media has declared that the Cold War is over. Thousands of Bibles and hundreds of Christian missionaries are flooding into Eastern Europe and Russia. Christian videos, even though barred from America's schools, are shown openly in public schools in the Soviet Union. Christian broadcasts are heard on government radio and TV stations. These dramatic and unprecedented changes are all reasons for hope and rejoicing.

At the same time, there are reasons for caution. As 1991 ended, communism, while appearing to wither in the Soviet Union, is alive and on the march in much of the rest of the world. Communists openly control or work from the underground in China, in Southern Africa, in Central and South America, in Iraq, Libya, Syria, Vietnam and Cambodia and in the Philippines. In much of Eastern Europe and the republics of the Soviet Union, power is still wielded by "former" communists whose conversions need the test of time. Their entire training and experience has shaped and equipped them to be "masters of deceit." Deceptions, coups and sudden reversals of hopeful trends have marked all of recorded history and continue to be a danger.

Even if changes in the Soviet Union should be real and communism there has really died, anti-communists and freedom-loving conservatives in America still face major challenges.

The leftists of various persuasions who have dominated America's schools, churches, press, labor unions, State Department, etc. for over 70 years are still in power. They are the "liberals" who have aided, supported and apologized for the Reds in China, Russia, Cuba, etc. while they were murdering at least 100-million people. In 1964, the original *None Dare Call It Treason* (reprinted completely in this edition) documented the role these liberals played in aiding the followers of Marx, Lenin and Mao Tse-tung in extending their rule over nearly 25% of the earth's land mass and one-third of the world's people.

That these American "liberals" still cling to the dream of a one-world socialist state was made plain in a September 8, 1991 column by William F. Woo. He's editor of the *St. Louis Post-Dispatch*, a newspaper with a leftist slant much like that of *The New York Times*, the *Washington Post* and other major newspapers. Woo, in a lengthy column, reviewed the 45 years of the cold war conflict and said:

> And now, almost miraculously it seems, communism has evaporated as a serious alternative to capitalism and democracy.

> A certain humility here is advised. Historians 1000 years hence may possibly regard the U.S.S.R. as a failed experiment in communism that awaited a much later flowering—even as we see Periclean Athens as a brief attempt at democracy that served as an inspirational example for the system's eventual fulfillment centuries later.

Woo's words reveal an attitude typical of so many liberals and apologists for communism in the last 75 years. While perhaps abhorring some of the bloodshed and brutality, they more often have excused or overlooked the violence and repression as a necessary evil to be tolerated because they believed (or hoped) that the perpetrators were seeking to establish a "more just," socialist world order—a dream shared by communists, socialists, and secular humanists.

Even if communism should be dead in the Soviet Union, these dreamers and their disciples still hold positions of influence in America's schools and colleges, the press, the trade unions, the liberal churches, the U.S. State Department and many levels of government. For example, the original *None Dare Call It Treason* documented how Dr. George Counts, an influential educator of the 1930s, returned from a time in the Soviet Union as an admirer and apologist for the communist system. He wrote a widely circulated monograph in 1932 calling teachers to be the vanguard of the revolution. In *Dare The Schools Build A New Social Order?* Counts said:

> That the teachers should deliberately reach for power and then make the most of their conquest is my firm conviction. To the extent that they are permitted to fashion the curriculum and procedures of the school they will definitely and positively influence the social attitudes, ideals and behavior of the coming generation.

Counts made it plain that the changes he envisioned would result in...

> ...a coordinated, planned and socialized economy...a new age of collectivism.

Some would say that's ancient history, an isolated example from 60 years ago. However, Counts, although now dead, still speaks. His revolutionary call to teachers, exposed in the original *None Dare Call It Treason* is being used now to indoctrinate another generation of future teachers. Counts 1932 monograph *Dare The Schools Build A New Social Order?* is included in the book, *Philosophical Foundations of Education*, a widely used text in schools of education for the last 15 years. In introducing Counts article, the authors tell today's teacher trainees:

> Counts calls educators to "reach for power" and initiate changes in society. The words still have a decidedly contemporary ring.

Obviously, the warnings *None Dare Call It Treason* published 25 years ago are still relevant.

This new edition has the same purpose as the original. It is not intended to forecast the future. It simply presents and documents some of the factual history of this century.

The true record of the last 70 years is vitally important. Individuals and organizations which developed policies which resulted in communist advances in the past are now frantically trying to rewrite history to cover their tracks while claiming credit for the "victory" over communism. If they succeed in keeping Americans confused about what really happened in the past, leftists of various persuasions can continue working to move the United States and the world toward their long held goal of world socialism and a "new world order." True history can unmask and thwart them.

If enough Americans are brought to see the tragic fruit of the failed policies of the past, they will never again be deceived by the liberal, humanist, Marxist philosophies which led to 100-million tragic deaths and the enslavement of almost two-billion other human beings, many of whom still live in Red bondage.

It's hard for most Americans to realize that U.S. policies and programs have produced one defeat after another since 1917. However, as the original edition of *None Dare Call It Treason* documents, it wasn't Red military might or "the will of the people" that caused China to fall to communism. The suffering in China, which continues today, resulted from policies shaped and implemented by traitors and one-world dreamers in the U.S. State Department. Russian tanks didn't conquer Cuba for the communists. The Cuban tragedy was orchestrated by people with names and faces in Washington, D.C. The original *None Dare Call It Treason's* 7-million copies awakened multitudes to the sad but factual record.

Several generations of other Americans have accepted at least some facets of the socialist one-world philosophy. They were brainwashed, not by the official communist newspaper, *Pravda,* or short wave radio programs from Russia but by influential individuals in the American news and entertainment media which consistently push and promote a leftist agenda. They received further indoctrination in the schools of America. If communism should actually be withering in Eastern Europe and Russia today, American parents and grandparents must ponder a strange paradox: More than 10,000 dedicated and committed Marxist professors who have already indoctrinated a generation of Americans still teach in America's universities today!

To insure that new tragedies are not piled on top of the old—or that traditional American freedoms are not traded for socialist dreams or communist deceptions—Americans must realize both what has happened in the past *and how and why it happened.*

Never before has the statement, "Those who refuse to learn from the mistakes of history are bound to repeat them" been more important. All Americans must fully understand the true history of these past decades so that their "mistakes" are never repeated. It's vital for our children, our grandchildren, our country and all mankind. It is for this purpose that I send forth this paperback edition of *None Dare Call It Treason—25 YEARS LATER.*

John A. Stormer
Florissant, Missouri
February 1992

CONTENTS

Treason doth never prosper, what's the reason?
For if it prosper, none dare call it treason.
—SIR JOHN HARRINGTON, 1561-1612

INTRODUCTION

DID COMMUNISM REALLY DIE?

Can the Ethiopian change his skin, or the leopard his spots?
then may ye also do good, that are accustomed to do evil.
— *Jeremiah 13:23*

FIVE YEARS OF DRAMATIC EVENTS in Eastern Europe and the Soviet Union culminated in August 1991 with the failed coup and the supposed dissolution of the Soviet Union and its Communist Party. Many of the world's most knowledgeable anti-communist leaders jumped on the bandwagon of those proclaiming, "Communism is dead!"

Could it be so? English author G.K. Chesterton once observed, "The cleverest thing the devil ever did was to induce people to believe that he did not exist."

Is the reported death and burial of communism for real? Or could the dramatic events of 1986-92 be a clever deception designed to advance the longtime communist goal of world domination as a former KGB strategic planner predicted with amazing accuracy eight years in advance? Could the heralded changes be a ploy to quiet unrest in the Soviet Union while getting desperately needed aid for the bailout of a failed socialist system and inducing the west to disarm?

In light of these questions, consider these facts about the supposed "changes" in the Soviet Union:

In the aftermath of the failed coup of August 1991, the Communist Party and its role in government was supposedly abolished.[1] However, eleven of the twelve new "independent" republics were headed by "former" top communists whose "conversions" had not yet been tested by time. Most of the key spots in the "reformed" and reorganized bureaucracy were also held by former communist functionaries.[2]

Western leaders and headlines declared that the Soviet Union was "dead."[3] However, the former U.S.S.R. was immediately replaced by Boris Yeltsin's new "Commonwealth of Republics, formed by leaders of eleven of the twelve "independent" republics.[4]

When the anti-communist president of the republic of Georgia refused to join the commonwealth "voluntarily," immediate armed action was started to depose him. He also quickly became the target of a world-wide media propaganda campaign branding him a dictator.[5] There were other important warning signs that Red rule in the Soviet Union was not being replaced by true democracy:

> Russian president Boris Yeltsin, *by personal decree,* took control of the former Soviet intelligence and security services (the KGB), the press, radio and TV, the foreign ministry and the Kremlin.[6] Overnight, the Soviet embassy and personnel in Washington, D.C. became "the Russian embassy."

The mayor of Moscow, apparently a sincere reformer, announced his resignation to protest Yeltsin's dictatorial actions and blockage of true economic changes.[7]

The new "Commonwealth of Republics" was to be governed by a council composed of Yeltsin and the heads of the other republics. All of them ruled by decree with their decsions rubber stamped by their parliaments in traditional communist fashion. Among their first "agreements" was action to dismantle the Soviet military. However...

> ...the leaders of the "independent" republics quickly agreed to unified control of the former Soviet Union's 29,000 nuclear weapons and warheads. Boris Yeltsin's Russian finger was placed on the control button. The former Soviet defense minister, Gorbachev-appointed Yevgeny Shaposhnikov, was named the commonwealth's military commander.[8]

As all the changes were made, the independence claimed by the Baltic states of Latvia, Estonia and Lithuania was recognized and approved by the "dissolving" Soviet Union. The Baltics and the world rejoiced.

However, a week later the Soviet defense minister Yevgeny Shasposhnikov informed Latvian Prime Minister Ivars Godmanis that 80,000 Soviet troops in Latvia and like numbers in Lithuania could not be withdrawn from the Baltics until at least 1994. The Soviet defense minister explained that troop withdrawal was impossible because housing would not be available for them back in Russia.9

How free, therefore, were the "independent" Baltic states? To get the proper perspective, realize that the 80,000 Soviet troops stationed in (occupying) Latvia (population two-million) would be comparable, percentage-wise, to having a force of nine-million Soviet troops stationed in the United States. Wouldn't Americans feel free and secure standing on street corners, grasping copies of the Declaration of Independence, while nine-million occupying Soviet troops watched? (Similar explanations were given for keeping 300,000 Soviet troops in what had been East Germany.)

Against the background of these facts, the Winter 1991 *Democracy Bulletin* of the American Foundation for Resistance International gave a sobering analysis. Under the headline, "The Soviet Union Died, But The Communists Live On," the report said:

As 1991 draws to a close, what do we see? Old guard communist leaders suddenly professing anti-communism and a commitment to democracy. In republic after republic incumbent presidents, never elected, but appointed to office by the Supreme Soviet, now use communist methods to rig presidential elections to ensure their continued power. They deny opposition candidates access to media and television time. Violent harrassment of campaign workers is prevalent. Power shut-downs, transportation stoppages, unavailability of newsprint and ink are the order of the day [for challengers]—but not for incumbents.

Using classic totalitarian methods, the old guard exploits popular pressure for democracy, independence and self-determination to re-install old-style communist dictatorship. They establish their legitimacy in the eyes of the world by holding referendums on independence, while at the same time conducting fradulent elections designed to maintain the old-guard system intact. We are witnessing not the creation of new democratic republics, but many new Soviet governments.

The west has so far not questioned these practices and is in danger of accepting the new governments and their elections as legitimate.

In early 1992 skeptics could look at the widely heralded changes in the former Soviet Union and ask, "Has anything but the name really changed?" In answering that question and in trying to understand events in the communist world (or almost anywhere else), first remember: "Never trust the obvious" and then ask, "Who benefits from the event?"

The dramatic events which followed the failed coup of August 1991 accelerated what *None Dare Call It Treason— 25 YEARS LATER* said in 1989 were the five goals of the KGB/Gorbachev/Communist Party combine. Their five goals for the *glasnost* and *perestroika* "reforms" were:

1. Calm unrest by giving the Soviet people hope that things will change (while at the same time identifying real dissidents for possible future elimination).

2. Obtain another wave of desperately needed western economic aid to bail out the failing socialist system for the fifth time since 1917.

3. Give the west the confidence to disarm.

4. Communists are great magicians and masters of deceit. Dramatic events in Eastern Europe and the Soviet Union have drawn attention (like the magician's hand in the air) while communism's "other hand" continues to advance and solidify its influence and control in China, Vietnam, southern Africa, Central and South America, Cambodia, Afghanistan, Korea and the Philippines.

5. Gain respectability for Russian leaders to enable them to be full partners (and perhaps the ultimate ruthless rulers) in the New World Order's coming world government.

As 1992 began each of these five long range communist goals for deceiving the west were being accomplished more rapidly and successfully as a result of the failed coup and the seemingly dramatic events which followed. That should stimulate caution. Serious questions should be asked before

America's military establishment is dismantled and floodgates of aid are opened for those whose recent "conversions" from communism need the test of time.

Most of the dramatic changes in the Soviet Union including the supposed dissolution of the Communist Party and the Soviet Union were triggered by the failed coup of August 1991. Therefore, the coup needs to be examined.

Dr. David Funderburk, ambassador to Romania in the early years of the Reagan Administration (until he resigned to protest the coddling of Ceaucescu's hard core communist regime), raised questions which are still unanswered. Among them are:

> If there was a real coup why was Yeltsin not arrested or killed immediately? Why were conscript troops *led by Yeltsin supporters* used to surround the Russian Parliament building? Why were crack KGB troops not moved to Moscow until fourteen hours after Gorbachev's arrest? Above all, why was the media not shut down (as in the Chinese Communists massacre at Tiananmen Square?)

Those are all vital questions. Others are: Why didn't the coup leaders cut the communication lines, particularly those through which Yeltsin rallied supporters and world opinion? Why were water and electricity never cut off to the Parliament building?

PIZZA HUT DELIVERS DURING THE COUP

Not only was the water and electricity not cut off, the "embattled" Yeltsin and his supporters were even well fed during the days that they were under siege in the Parliament building. *The Washington Times* had this story:[10]

> It may be true that Domino's Pizza delivers, but does it deliver during a coup? Pizza Hut does.

> When supporters of Russian President Boris Yeltsin were guarding the Russian Parliament building during the coup in the Soviet Union, Pizza Hut delivered 260 pizzas, 20 cases of Pepsi and gallons of hot coffee to tide them over.

> Roger Rydell, chief spokesman at Pizza Hut international head-

quarters, quoted Mr. Yeltsin as calling the Moscow Pizza Hut after the craziness settled down. "Thanks for your support," Mr. Yeltsin said.

Coup experts expressed amazement at the inept grab for power. As a student at the leftist London School of Economics in the late '60s, Edward Luttwak wrote a definitive do-it-yourself guidebook for staging coups. The book, *Coup d'Etat: A Practical Handbook*, became a guidebook for leftist rebels seeking power in third world countries and colonies. The author, now a military analyst with Georgetown University's Center of Strategic and International Studies, summed up his analysis of the failed coup this way:[11]

> For people who are creatures of the Leninist Party, which seized power through a successful coup d'etat in Petrograd [Leningrad] in 1917, the technical errors were so gross that they beg an explanation.

Skepticism about the failed coup spark doubt and questions about the validity of the dramatic changes which followed. Questions which deserve answers include:

> Is communism really dead in the "former" Soviet Union?

> Have changes in the U.S.S.R. actually reduced the military threat to the United States—or is America being setup for a military disaster—a nuclear Pearl Harbor?

> Are the Soviet reformers for real—or could all of the changes in the Soviet Union be part of a carefully planned deception as a former KGB planner claims?

Any reasonable analysis should also ask:

> If all the changes in the Soviet Union are for real, will government attempts to create a "market economy" from the top down create such economic turmoil and suffering that people will look to old-line communists hoping they will again put some bread and sausages at the end of the food lines.

IS COMMUNISM REALLY DEAD IN RUSSIA?

Amos Perlmutter is a political science professor at American University in Washington and editor of the *Journal of Strategic Studies.* Perlmutter evaluated the so-called demise of the Communist Party and cautioned:[12]

> Now that the party has been dissolved by the new transitional state, the political police, the KGB, the institutions, governments and bureaucracies of the republics are still dominated at or near the top and in the middle echelons by former members of the party with the exceptions of the municipalities of Leningrad and Moscow.

As communism "died" there were still up to 15-million communists in the USSR—whatever name they may chose to use. They are skillful at using power, blackmail, etc. to advance their cause. The Party itself may be reorganized under a new name as the Communist parties in Eastern Europe have done, continuing under a new name to wield power and influence policy.

A somewhat similar delusion followed the supposed defeat of the Communist Sandinistas in Nicaragua's 1990 election. After Mrs. Violetta Chammorro's anti-communist coalition won the election, she permitted Communist Humberto Ortega (brother of dictator Daniel) to continue to head the army. The Ortega brothers boasted that through their control of the army, the unions, etc. "We will continue to rule from below." Because of threats of Communist violence and disruption, Mrs. Chamarro regularly vetoed measures passed by the National Assembly which would have cut appropriations for the communist-controlled military and returned property expropriated by the Sandinista communists to the rightful owners. The communist minority in the legislature sustained her vetoes.[13] The major change as a result of the election "victory" for anti-communism was to transfer Nicaragua from Soviet welfare rolls to America's.

The Communist cadres, rejected by the people at the ballot box, are still a dominant force in Nicaragua "ruling from below"—and they could remain so in the Soviet Union and its "independent republics as well.

ARE THE REFORMERS FOR REAL?

Most citizens of a communist nation genuinely want

freedom. Some of them risk their lives in standing for freedom, as they understand it, or in trying to escape from the tyranny of their communist homelands. They are among the many reformers who spent years in jail, "psychiatric hospitals" or Siberia for their stand for freedom. These are not, however, for the most part those who led the "reform" movements in Russia or the other "independent" republics. And they were not among the leaders of the Commonwealth of Republics Boris Yeltsin formed to replace the Soviet Union. Only Zviad Gamsakhurdia who was overwhelmingly elected president when the Soviet republic of Georgia gained its independence had valid credentials as a longtime reformer. Gamsakhurdia was arrested and jailed in 1978 for protesting Soviet violations of the Helsinki human rights agreements. After Gamsakkhuria was elected president of Georgia in 1991 he was driven from office by Moscow supplied and supported troops when he opposed Georgian entry into Yeltsin's commonwealth and attacked the Yeltsin "reformers" as phonies and part of the "Communist mafia."[14]

Once he was overthrown, his opposition proposed that Eduard Shevardnadze might be a suitable successor. Ironically, Shevardnadze had been the Communist Party boss and head of the KGB in Georgia in 1978 when Gamsakhurdia was arrested and jailed.

Former U.S. Senator Thomas Eagleton (D-MO) gave a realistic appraisal in his regular column in the January 12, 1992 *St. Louis Post-Dispatch*. Eagleton wrote:

> Politically, the communists are as dead as our old Whig Party, but the party's thugs still permeate the Russian structure. Hangover communism by whatever name frustrates the creation of something new.

> Into it all comes Boris Yeltsin....The best that can be hoped for is that he has experienced some sort of miraculous conversion. In phases he's been transformed from Jimmy Hoffa to Huey Long to Thomas Jefferson. The erstwhile heavy-handed bully now has the velvet touch....It is possible that Yeltsin is a democrat by convenience and an authoritarian by experience. Russia will suffer extraordinary pain.

....History teaches that, just as Russia was unfit for communism, it is today equally unfit for democracy. Nothing in the Russian past justifies any optimism about a democratic future in a land that has never been even slightly inclined toward it.

For these reasons, the statements, actions and activities of former communists who become leaders of reform movements must be closely watched. They make strong statements about failures caused by former leaders of the bureaucracy. They condemn roadblocks erected to reform by entrenched bureaucrats and speak out strongly about past human rights violations by Stalinists in the Party, etc. The real test is how far they will go in denouncing socialism as a philosophy and as an eventual basis for the organization of society.##

ARE CHANGES IN THE USSR REDUCING THE MILITARY THREAT TO THE U.S.?

Since "reformer" Mikhail Gorbachev came to power in 1985, the Soviets, while smiling and talking peace, have out-produced the United States in most weapons areas by margins of four or five to one.

During 1988-90, for example, the Soviets had a 12 to 1 advantage in ICBM's, producing 415 new long range missiles to 33 produced in the U.S. Similar disparities existed in almost every category of weaponry. Soviet bomber production totaled 215 to 33 for the U.S. The Soviets launched 29 nuclear attack submarines while the U.S. built 14. The Soviet edge in sub-launched ballistic missiles was 215 to 103. The Reds outproduced the U.S. in tanks 6500 to 2190 and in armored vehicles 15,950 to 2325.[15]

Has the failed coup, the death of communism, supposed elimination of the military hard-liners, etc. made any dif-

---

##Chinese and Russian "reformers," including a key Yeltsin associate, admitted during lengthy face-to-face meetings with the author in 1989-90 that the market economy was being introduced so capitalism would come to its full corruption *after which* true socialism and communism could develop. The author's October 1991 *Understanding The Times* newsletter reports in detail on the meetings. Copies are available for $2 from Liberty Bell Press, P.O. Box 32, Florissant MO 63032.

ference? On September 10, 1991, the Associated Press reported:

> Despite reforms underway in the Soviet Union, Pentagon analysts say they expect production of some of the Kremlin's most lethal weapons systems to continue because the Soviet economy is so dependent upon military construction.[16]

Even so, President Bush in a dramatic late September speech announced major unilateral steps to reduce U.S. nuclear capability—in hopes the Soviets would reciprocate. The President announced that the U.S. would bring home and destroy all short-range nuclear weapons, cancel the around the clock alert status of the Strategic Air Command and reduce strategic long range weapons. He said, "If we and the Soviet leaders take the right steps, we can dramatically shrink the arsenal of the world's weapons."[17]

Even if the "former" Soviets should respond in a dramatic way, what assurance would there be that they would fulfill any new commitments they make? Before the U.S. acts on changes in the Soviet Union, reformers should fulfill all the treaties made and broken by Communist regimes for the past seventy years. There is evidence they won't. In the closing days of 1991, after the Communist Party and the Soviet Union had both supposedly been dissolved, U.S. Defense Secretary Dick Cheney announced that the former republics of the Soviet Union were continuing to produce and deploy nuclear weapons despite their commitment to reduce those arsenals. Cheney said:

> One of the things I'm concerned about is that even with their economy in a state of utter collapse we still see efforts inside the former Soviet Union to produce more nuclear weapons—to deploy new ballistic missiles targeted against the United States. It's going to be difficult for the American people to feel a good deal of confidence that things have truly changed over there until we see an end to that kind of activity.[18]

IS THE UNITED STATES BEING SETUP FOR DISASTER?

Could the seemingly dramatic changes in the Soviet Union and the U.S. responses be setting the stage for a long planned

Soviet move to either smash the U.S. or force America to capitulate to nuclear blackmail? Dimitri Manuilsky gave the blueprint to his students at the Lenin School of Political Warfare in Moscow in 1930. One of the students, Zack Kornfeder, later broke with the Communist Party and told the story in sworn testimony to a Congressional committee in 1951. He reported that Manuilsky, who served later as Russia's UN representative said:

> War to the hilt between communism and capitalism is inevitable. Today, of course, we are not strong enough to attack. Our time will come in 20 to 30 years. To win, we shall need the element of surprise. The bourgeosie will have to be put to sleep. So we shall begin by launching the most spectacular peace movement on record. There will be electrifying overtures and unheard of concessions. The capitalist countries, stupid and decadent, will rejoice to cooperate in their own destruction. They will leap at another chance to be friends. As soon as their guard is down, we will smash them with our clenched fist.[19]

Manuilsky's quote is no longer "politically correct" in Washington. A May 1990 directive from the U.S. Air Force Director of Public Affairs to Air Force public affairs officers banned its use in Air Force officers' speeches as being "counter to Air Force, DoD, and U.S. Government policy."[20]

COULD IT ALL BE PLANNED DECEPTION?

In 1982, a former top KGB planner who had defected to the west wrote a book outlining long range Communist plans for world conquest. The book, titled *New Lies For Old*,[21] was published in 1984. In it Anatoli Golitsyn predicted a coming false liberalization in the USSR, spurious independence for the Communist nations of Eastern Europe and the possible demolition of the Berlin Wall. Amazingly, he predicted it all years in advance. In 1982 Golitsyn wrote:

> ...communist strategists are now poised to enter into the final, offensive phase of their long-range policy...for the complete triumph of communism. (Pg. 327)

> ...the communist strategists are equipped in pursuing their policy, to engage in maneuvers and strategems beyond the imagination

of Marx or the practical reach of Lenin and unthinkable to Stalin. Among such previously unthinkable strategems are the introduction of false liberalization in Eastern Europe and, probably, in the Soviet Union and the exhibition of spurious independence on the part of regimes in Romania, Czechoslovakia and Poland. (Pg. 327)

[In Poland] the communist strategists probably are planning the reemergence of Solidarity and the creation of a quasi-social democratic government (a coalition of the communist party, the trade unions [Solidarity] and the churches.) (Pg. 329-337)

"Liberalization" in Eastern Europe would probably involve the return to power in Czechoslovakia of Dubcek and his associates. If it should be extended to East Germany, *demolition of the Berlin Wall might even be contemplated.* (Emphasis added) (Pg. 340)

Pressure could well grow for a solution of the German problem in which some form of confederation between East and West Germany would be combined with neutralization of the whole and a treaty of friendship with the Soviet Union. (Pg. 341)

Everything Golitsyn predicted in 1982 (and published in 1984) had been fulfilled by 1989 *including the changes in Poland and Czechoslovakia, the demolition of the Berlin Wall and the reunification of Germany!* What about changes in the Soviet Union itself? Golitsyn wrote:

The "liberalization" will be spectacular and impressive. Formal pronouncements might be made about a reduction in the communist party's role; its monopoly would apparently be curtailed....The KGB would be "reformed." (Pg. 339)

Dissidents at home would be amnestied; those in exile abroad would be allowed to return, and some would take up positions of leadership in government. *Sakharov might be included in some capacity in the government.* [Emphasis added]....Leading dissidents might form one or more alternative political parties. Censorship would be relaxed; controversial books, plays, films, and art would be published, performed and exhibited. (Pg. 339)

...the "liberalization would be calculated and deceptive in that it would be introduced from above. It would be carried out by the party through its cells and individual members in government, the Supreme Soviet, the courts, and the electoral machinery and by the KGB through its agents among the intellectuals and scientists. (Pg. 339-340)

Golitsyn's book, *New Lies For Old,* was published in 1984. It attracted little attention and few sales until 1989 when it was discovered to have accurately predicted all the amazing and dramatic events that were unfolding in Eastern Europe and the Soviet Union *including the demolition of the Berlin Wall.* The predictions were accurate. Rather than being hailed as a hero, however, Golitsyn (and his mentor and protector, the late CIA counter intelligence chief James Jesus Angleton), became the target of ridicule by liberals and even some pseudo-conservative leaders and columnists.[22] Of course, they were careful not to tell their readers what he wrote or the accuracy of his predictions.

That's all history, of course, but Golitsyn continued to analyze and write *and warn.* Because his continuing assessments of perestroika for the CIA apparently did not influence American policymaking, Golitsyn reportedly requested clearance to publish his memoranda in book form.

While the book was not issued, a dynamite 30-page summary of the unpublished manuscript started circulating in intelligence circles around the world in 1990.[23] It reads like a blueprint for the events which unfolded in the Soviet Union a year later after the August 1991 coup. Golitsyn's predictions, warnings and observations in the 1990 summary include:

Long-time preparation by the KGB and the security forces in other communist nations of controlled "political opposition" makes possible the deployment of this political opposition to create deceptive "non-communist" and "democratic" structures...it is the new form for developing socialism. (Pg. 7-8)

The communists have succeeded in concealing from the West that the "non-communist" parties are secret partners, not alternatives or rivals and that the new power structures, though they have democratic form, are in reality more viable and effective structures introduced and guided by communist parties with a broader base. Because of this communist control, they are not true democracies and cannot become so in the future. (Pg. 8)

A leading reformer seemed to confirm Golitsyn's charge that the reformers were either secret partners or being used by the communists. In a February 11, 1990 report, *Washington Post* columnist David Broder quoted Soviet reformer Arkadij Murachev as saying of Gorbachev in a Washington meeting:

"He often speaks one way and does the opposite," Murachev observed. An example was the Soviet president's backstage role in the largest Moscow demonstration since the 1917 Revolution, the march of at least 100,000 people demanding an end to one-party rule the day before the Central Committee meeting began.

"We knew for two weeks," Murachev said, "that Gorbachev had a plan for this march." Six days before the march, he said, Anatoly Lukyanov, Gorbachev's vice president and ally [later charged with supporting the coup] met in the Kremlin with one of the march organizers and word went out that Gorbachev wanted the demonstration to be very big.

Murachev, a leader of the "reform" group in the Supreme Soviet and a key supporter of Boris Yeltsin was named to head the 125,000 member Moscow police force after the coup.

Since 1985, Golitsyn has been warning that *perestroika* and all that has followed is a cleverly devised deception. Golitsyn wrote that the reformers...

...are not true democrats and never will be. They remain committed to socialism and communism. They are a new generation of revolutionaries who are using "democratic" reforms as a new way to achieve final victory. (Pg. 15)

Meanwhile, the communist party is apparently relegated to the shadows. The communist party, however, has not surrendered its real monopoly of power....Although the end of the party's monopoly is proclaimed, the party apparatus remains in being and is still being run by the same old-timers. The party apparatus, though less visible, will continue to provide guidance to party members in the reformed institutions. (Pg. 15-16)

After predicting the relegation of the Communist Party to the background, (which happened) Golitsyn also foresaw the supposed dissolution of the Soviet Union. He wrote:

> The communist strategists are concealing that it is they who are now creating "independent" republics, repeating on a broader scale Lenin's experience with the Far Eastern and Georgian republics and also Stalin's deceptive dissolution of the Comintern in 1943 [when seeking U.S. aid in his battle with Hitler]. (Pg. 12)

> The strategists are concealing the secret coordination that exists and will continue between Moscow and the "nationalist" leaders of these "independent" republics...the fragmentation of the Soviet Empire will not be real but only fictional. This is not true self-determination but the use of "national" form in executing a common communist strategy. (Pg. 12)

Golitsyn's anticipation of a phony dissolution of the Soviet Union was written more than a year before it happened. It appears to have been a virtual blueprint for Yeltsin's "Commonwealth of Republics."

Golitsyn also anticipated a year in advance that reformers, in the aftermath of the coup, would call for the removal of Lenin's embalmed remains from public display in Red Square for burial elsewhere. Golitsyn wrote:

> The [Kremlin] strategists no doubt realize that they cannot march to victory under Lenin's banner or even use the word "convergence" while Lenin remains unburied. They may therefore finally bury him with full honors while in practice they follow his ideas in their final assault on the capitalist West. (Pg. 18)

Within weeks after the August 1991 coup attempt, Soviet lawmakers started discussing the proper time and way to bury Lenin next to his mother in Leningrad.[24]

GOAL IS GETTING WESTERN AID

Golitsyn speculated on how the reformers using supposedly "democratic" structures and institutions would proceed. He said:

> The innovative application of Lenin's New Economic Policy approach to revive the Soviet economy through trade, credits,

technology and the help of western specialists will help transform the communist regimes into attractive models of "socialism with a human face." (Pg. 4)

The goal of all the deception, the deployment of a controlled "political opposition" and creation of "democratic" forms, structures and institutions is the creation of...

...favorable conditions for a convergence (merging) of the two systems into a new world order which will eventually be controlled by the more brutal, ruthless communist participants. (Pg. 4)

Golitsyn, the former KGB planner summarized the paralysis which would result in the West as the works of the controlled "political opposition" were accepted as genuine. He wrote:

As these misconceptions have accumulated in western foreign ministries, intelligence services and "think tanks" they have created a vicious circle of bureaucratic vested interests which makes the correction of the misconceptions difficult if not impossible. (Pg. 20)

As a result, Golitsyn observed and wrote:

Conservatives [in the West] are confused....Their old assumptions are upset. They are out of ideas. They have lost perspective....For this reason, the major strategic objectives of Soviet political warfare are:

First, to neutralize anti-communist influence, especially the conservative parties, as an important factor in the political life of the United States, West Germany, France and Britain, and *Second,* to secure the victory of the radical left in the next presidential elections in 1992 in the United States and the victory of the socialist and Labour parties in the national elections in West Germany, France and Britain in the 1990s. (Pg. 22-23)

Golitsyn's comments even though prepared a year or more in advance read as though they were written day-by-day in the aftermath of the failed coup. In view of his validated ten year record of accurately predicting the future maneuvers of the communist deceivers his warnings must be taken seriously.

WHAT IF ALL THE CHANGES ARE FOR REAL?

If changes in the Soviet Union should be real, anti-communists and freedom-loving conservatives still face major challenges.

Even if communism dies in the Soviet Union, the Communists and their secular humanist liberal allies, those who have controlled America's schools, churches, press, labor unions, State Department, etc. for over 70 years, are still in power here. They are the "liberals" who have aided, apologized for and kept in power the Reds in China, Russia, Cuba, etc. while they were murdering at least 100-million people during the last 75 years.

Syndicated columnist Cal Thomas put the situation into perspective in January 1992.[25] He wrote:

> Before Soviet communism is allowed to slip gently into the night, a full accounting is required of those who offered it political life support without which it might have died much more quickly. A non-judicial forum on the scale of the Nuremberg war crimes trial should be held to indict those in the academic, financial, political, artistic and religious communities, past and present, who gave aid and comfort to Marxism-Leninism.

Thomas detailed how American liberals for decades admired and idealized political systems in highly repressive communist countries, ignoring flagrant human rights abuses, even as they denounced comparatively minor infractions in the United States and other Western nations. Thomas said:

> Whether it was Nicaragua, El Salvador, Grenada or Cuba in our hemisphere or Angola, Afghanistan, Ethiopia or South Africa, the script was the same. Whether the communist leader was Mao Tse-tung or Fidel Castro, Ho Chi Minh or Leonid Brezhnev, he could do no wrong. Many liberals saw these leaders as near gods and the freedom fighters who opposed them as repressive louts. To those on the left, communists were liberating heroes who had the best plan for the transformation of mankind and society.

> The list of apologists, "fellow travellers" and dupes is book length. Every editorial writer, every author, every artist and every university professor who defended the horror of communism should be

brought to the people's court of public opinion. Those who wrote and spoke in favor of communism should be given a chance to recant or lose, not their rights, but whatever credibility remains.

Thomas very correctly concluded, saying:

This is the only way history and the future can be fairly served. By remembering and judging those who betrayed truth we help preserve, protect and defend coming generations from making similar mistakes.

That these "liberals" still hold their positions and to their dream of a one-world socialist state was made plain in a September 8, 1991 column by William F. Woo. He is editor of the *St. Louis Post-Dispatch*, a newspaper with a leftist slant much like that of *The New York Times*, the *Washington Post* and other major newspapers. Woo, in a lengthy column,[26] examined the 45 years of the cold war conflict and said:

And now, almost miraculously it seems, communism has evaporated as a serious alternative to capitalism and democracy.

A certain humility here is advised. Historians 1000 years hence may possibly regard the U.S.S.R. as a failed experiment in communism that awaited a much later flowering—even as we see Periclean Athens as a brief attempt at democracy that served as an inspirational example for the system's eventual fulfillment centuries later.

Woo's words reveal an attitude typical of so many liberals and apologists for communism in the last 75 years. While perhaps abhorring some of the bloodshed and brutality, they more often have excused or overlooked the violence and repression as a necessary evil to be tolerated because the perpetrators were seeking to establish a "more just," socialist world order—a dream shared by communists, socialists, secular humanists—and even some who like to be regarded as conservatives.

Even if communism should be dead in the Soviet Union, these dreamers (with the help of a relatively small but dedicated cadre of actual Marxist-Leninists) still control most of America's schools and colleges, the press, the trade unions, the liberal churches, the U.S. State Department and many levels of government.

Even if communism should be dead in the Soviet Union, it is alive and well in Southern Africa where Mandela and his fellow Reds control the terrorist African National Congress. In Central America Sandinista-aided communist guerillas in El Salvador are being added to the police forces as a "peace" move. In Peru Maoist Shining Path guerillas terrorize the countryside. In Columbia, the "former" M-19 guerilla terrorists have taken off their battle fatigues, donned business suits and participate in government. In Afghanistan the Red war against the Mujahideen is maintained with massive supplies of Soviet weaponry. In North Korea a high ranking defector revealed that the hard-line communist regime will be producing nuclear weapons at a secret facility by 1993. In Cambodia and Vietnam Communists still rule. In China the butchers of Tiananmen Square still reign and are blessed with Most Favoured Nation trade status by President Bush. In the Philippines the Communist New Peoples' Army terrorizes the countryside, mudering Christian pastors and people. Their allies in the Philippine government and media in September blocked the renewal of the lease on the American naval base at Subic Bay. The Reds rejoiced worldwide.

KNOW YOUR ENEMY

Because communism is alive and well in many areas of the world and communists could still be working deceptively in what was the Soviet Union and Eastern Europe, it is vital to understand how they work.

That understanding is essential because the supposed reforms under *perestroika* and *glasnost* and Yelstin's "Commonwealth of Republics" could be an implementation of Leninist teaching that to advance you must know how to make strategic retreats. Lenin taught that progress toward the ultimate goal of communism is made through the *dialectic process* of "one step forward and two steps back." (Chinese Communist theorists use the term "three steps forward and two steps back.")

Dr. Fred Schwarz, in his classic work, *You Can Trust The Communists (to be Communists)*, described Communist "dialectical progress" which proceeds in a deceptive way and pattern. Dr. Schwarz said that Communists never move directly toward their ultimate goal. He explained:

> The dialectical pathway [to progress] is different. It consists of a resolute forward advance followed by an abrupt turn and retreat. Having retreated a distance there is another turn and advance. Through a series of forward-backward steps the goal is approached.

> To advance thus is to advance *dialectically*. The Communist goal is fixed and changeless, but their direction of advance reverses itself from time to time. They approach their goal by going directly away from it a considerable portion of the time...If we judge where the Communists are going by the direction in which they are moving, we will obviously be deceived.[27]

In the book Dr. Schwarz gives a very perceptive and helpful illustration of "dialectical progress." He wrote:

> The Communist method of advance may be likened to the hammering of a nail. It is a very foolish person who brings the hammer down with a crashing, resounding blow and then keeps pushing. When the first blow has spent itself, back must go the hammer in preparation for the next blow. A person seeing the reverse movement of the hammer as an isolated act in time and not understanding the process of which this was a part, might find it difficult to believe that this hammer was driving in the nail. When he sees the backward swing as a portion of a complete process, he realizes that the withdrawal is as important as the downward thrust to the realization of the objective.

> For those not trained in dialectical thinking, it is very difficult to understand that Communists have a fixed and changeless goal, but that their method of approach reverses itself all the time [as in hammering a nail]. The tendency is to judge where they are going by the direction in which they are moving.

"Glasnost" and "perestroika" and the Gorbachev "reforms" were *dialectic* rather than fundamental. Understanding Gorbachev, the "father" of the "reforms" is essential to evaluating the supposed death of communism and dissolution of the Soviet Union. It is important therefore to know what Gorbachev was actually planning (and could be accomplishing.)

Gorbachev is a master of the dialectic. In a 3-1/2 hour speech[28] marking the 70th anniversary of the Revolution he subtly wrapped himself, perestroika and the future progress of the Communist Party in the mantle of the dialectic. Early in the speech he warned:

> Those who treat Marxism dogmatically and pedantically cannot understand its central point: *its revolutionary dialectic.* (page 6)

In doing so he subtly instructed the Soviet Communist Party's Central Committee and Supreme Soviet that the perestroika and glasnost reforms were to be dialectic in nature. His speech reviewed the 70 years of Soviet history—its triumphs and its failings. He spotlighted Bukharin, a hero of the Revolution and a longtime stalwart supporter of Joseph Stalin, who was executed in 1936 on Stalin's order. Gorbachev said that Bukharin's approach in the early 1930s "was based on a dogmatic approach *and a non-dialectic assessment of the concrete situation.*" Bukharin wanted to press forward unwaveringly toward socialism—rather than take the dialectic approach Stalin was using at the time. (Stalin had introduced limited free enterprise and other "reforms" to get western aid for the failing Red economic system.) Gorbachev told the Supreme Soviet (and communists all over the world who read his speech):

> In this connection it is appropriate to recall Lenin's opinion of Bukharin. "Bukharin," he said, "is not only a most valuable and major theorist of the Party; he is also rightly considered the favorite of the whole Party, but his theoretical views can be classified fully Marxist only with great reserve, for there is something scholastic about him (he has never made a study of dialectics, and, I think, never fully understood it)." The facts again confirmed that Lenin had been right. (pages 13-14)

Gorbachev's recounting of this sordid bit of Soviet history confirms that he regarded a failure to understand and apply dialectics as a capital offense for which Bukharin did get the death penalty.

Gorbachev was, of course, not the first Communist leader to implement seeming "reforms" which were, in fact, "dialectic withdrawals." David Wigg, a one-time deputy assistant secretary of defense for policy analysis, in a paper on Soviet strategic deception pointed out (as have others) that Soviet founder V.I. Lenin used the term "glasnost" 46 times in his writings in the early 1920's.[29] Then, as now, the purpose was to lure Western businessmen into bailing out the ailing Soviet economy.

Lenin *dialectically* turned to capitalism and limited free enterprise briefly in the early 1920s in what was called "The New Economic Program." In his 70th anniversary speech, Gorbachev said of Lenin's temporary retreat from socialism and supposed move to capitalism:

> The decision to launch a new economic policy, which substantially widened the notions of socialism and the ways of building it, *was imbued with profound revolutionary dialectics.* (page 7)

Wigg said that Lenin's successor, Joseph Stalin, suggested in the mid-1930's that the Soviet Union should restructure the economy along capitalist lines. Stalin, like Gorbachev, called his program "perestroika."[30] Western businessmen responded but the perestroika "restructuring" was shortlived. With the beginning of the massive purges and reign of terror in 1936, Wigg said...

> ...the entire program of perestroika proved to be a total sham.

Even so, twenty years later, Stalin's chief hangman during the purge of the '30s, Nikita Khrushchev won acclaim from Western media and politicians for his "de-Stalinization."

In both his speech marking the 70th anniversary of the revolution and his book, *Perestroika*,[31] Gorbachev pointed with admiration to an early dialectic move of Lenin. The emphasis Gorbachev made may give real insight into his apparent willingness to grant a measure of freedom to Poland, Hungary, East Germany, etc. in late 1989. In his book, Gorbachev identified perestroika with Lenin saying:

The works of Lenin and his ideals of socialism remained for us an inexhaustible source of *dialectical creative thought*, theoretical wealth and political sagacity. (page 25)

Gorbachev went on to illustrate how turning to Lenin "stimulates the Party and society in their search to find explanations and answers to questions that arise." He said:

It would be appropriate to recall how Lenin fought for the Brest Peace Treaty in the troubled year of 1918. The Civil War was raging, and at that moment came a most serious threat from Germany. So Lenin suggested signing a peace treaty with it.

The terms of peace that Germany peremptorily laid down for us were, as Lenin put it, "disgraceful, dirty." They meant annexing [to Germany] a vast tract of territory with a population of fifty-six million. It seemed impossible to accept them. Yet Lenin insisted on a peace treaty. Even some members of the Central Committee objected...

Lenin, however, kept calling for peace *because he was guided by vital, not immediate, interests*, the interests of the working class as a whole, of the Revolution and the future of socialism. To safeguard them, *the country needed a respite before going ahead*. Few realized that at the time. Only later was it easy to say confidently and unambiguously that Lenin was right. And right he was, because he was looking far ahead; he did not put what was transitory above what was essential. The Revolution was saved. It is the same with perestroika. (pages 52-53)

It was in discussing Lenin's "disgraceful, dirty" March 1918 Brest Peace Treaty that Gorbachev warned the Central Committee and the Supreme Soviet:

Those who treat Marxism dogmatically and pedantically cannot understand its central point: its revolutionary dialectic.

It is in this context that Gorbachev's seeming relaxations in Eastern Europe should be understood. Much of the territory and the countries he supposedly released from some of their ties to the Soviet Union and the world communist movement were the same peoples Lenin dialectically agreed to give up in March 1918 "to save the Revolution." Interestingly, Lenin and the Soviet Union dialectically broke the Brest Peace Treaty eight months after it was signed.[32]

Gorbachev's 70th anniversary "Perestroika" speech to the Central Committee of the Communists Party was heralded by the world's leaders and media. Because they didn't understand the concept of dialectic progress, Gorbachev's calls for reform were seen as hopeful signs that the Soviets were changing. His closing words were not so well publicized. Gorbachev recommitted himself and the Communist Party "to the great Leninist cause." He closed the three hour speech with the words...

> In October 1917 we parted with the old world, rejecting it once and for all. We are moving towards a new world, the world of communism. We shall never turn off that road![33]

This is not an isolated quote. Whenever smiling propaganda statements are made to deceive the West, the Party faithful are always informed that there is to be no deviation from the long range goal of world communism.

While smiling at Americans, Gorbachev regularly called for communists to rededicate themselves to the Leninist cause of world conquest and communism. In his 800,000 copy bestseller, *Perestroika: New Thinking For Our Country and the World,* Gorbachev asked:

> Does perestroika mean that we are giving up socialism or at least some of its foundations? Some ask this question with hope, others with misgiving....Perestroika is closely connected with socialism as as a system. (Pg. 36)

To fully comprehend Gorbachev's words one must understand that when Communists use the term "socialism" they are referring to the present system which Americans call "communism." For instance, the Communists called their nation, the Union of Soviet *Socialist* Republics. They believed that they had *socialism* which is the transition stage to *communism.* They teach and believe that communism cannot be achieved until the entire world is socialist and the evil influences of the poisoned class, the bourgeoisie (those who own any private property, believe in God, and practice free enterprise, etc.) are eliminated.

Gorbachev answered the question, "Are we giving up socialism?" with this declaration:

> To put and end to all the rumors and speculations that abound in the West about this, I would like to point out once again that we are conducting all of our reforms in accordance with the socialist [communist] choice....Every part of our program of perestroika— and the program as a whole, for that matter—is fully based on the principle of more socialism and more democracy[##]. Those in the West who expect us to give up socialism [communism] will be disappointed. (Pg. 36- 37)

Gorbachev repeats the theme throughout the book. A few pages after the above statement he reemphasizes this way:

> We are not going to change Soviet power, of course, or abandon its fundamental principles, but we acknowledge the need for changes that will strengthen socialism and make it more dynamic and politically meaningful....Perestroika requires Party leaders who are very close to Lenin's idea of a revolutionary Bolshevik.

Gorbachev's widely publicized (and acclaimed) "Perestroika" was simply a sugar-coated "restructuring" *to make the communist system more efficient*—while making it appear more democratic, humane, etc.

So, Communists regularly make progress toward socialism and communism through the dialectic process of "advance and retreat." This must be remembered in evaluating on-going changes within the Soviet Union and Eastern Europe.

[##]When Communists use the word "democracy" they understand it to mean "communism." Friedrich Engels, co-author with Karl Marx of the *Communist Manifesto* wrote "Communism today is democracy." Contemporary Communists still use the Engels definition.[34] Communist "democracy" is achieved by permitting free and open discussions of the true meaning and correct application of Marxism-Leninism at all levels of the Communist structure after which the supposed will of the people is announced and implemented from the top down through the Communist Party. Once the "democratic" decision is made at the top, it is binding on all lower levels of the party structure. That is "democracy"— Communist-style.

Gorbachev's speeches, his writings, his smiles and his appeals to the crowds on his trips to America were all part of a carefully orchestrated program of Soviet Strategic Deception.

Dr. John Lenczowski examined the Soviet program of deception and the reason why deception is so necessary for the Red cause. Lenczowski was Director of European and Soviet Affairs in the National Security Council before Iran-Contra. In a 1987 book titled, *Soviet Strategic Deception,*[35] he explained strategic deception this way:

> The objective of strategic deception is to paint a false picture of the entire political climate in which the Soviet Union operates among both friend and foe alike—disguising their objectives and ultimate ambitions.[36]

Lenczowski told why Red deceivers and their deceptions have been so successful. He said:

> Soviet strategic deception succeeds not so much because of the ability of Soviet propagandists and agents of influence to deceive us, but because of our tendencies to deceive ourselves. Thus...Soviet strategic deception efforts are geared toward exploiting existing Western tendencies of thought....Soviet strategic deception also attempts to take advantage of our inclination to engage in wishful thinking or psychological denial. This manifests itself principally in our reluctance to admit the possibility of certain ugly realities.

Soviet strategic deception plays upon what Alexander Solzhenitsyn has termed "the desire not to know." Ambassador Jeane Kirkpatrick called it "the will to disbelieve the horrible." People don't like to hear disturbing news. Americans would like to believe that communism and the Soviet Union are no more—that their longime threat to peace and freedom has ended. Soviet strategic deception plays upon both that fact and an almost total lack of knowledge of Communist philosophy and tactics by America's leaders, scholars, media, exchange students, etc.

Even if much that is happening in the Soviet Union should be real, the dedicated communists still at every level of Soviet life can produce economic, social, ethnic and political chaos.

As the chaos permeates the society of the republics, dedicated communist cadres can capitalize on it and regain control. Indeed, if the chaos becomes bad enough, a desperate hungry people may look to the communists to restore order and return the nation to the "good old days" when there was some bread and sausage at the end of the food lines.

IF IT IS A CLEVER COMMUNIST DECEPTION?

If the changes in the Soviet Union are part of a cleverly planned and executed deception, what might be expected in the months and years ahead?

If the ploy succeeds in getting enough U.S. and western aid and investment to ease some of the tension and defuse citizen unrest, the "reformed" communists can be expected to consolidate their forces and power and snuggle up close to western Europe and the United States as they move to the left. The leftward move in Europe and the U.S. could be accelerated by a recession or total economic collapse in the west. The Red goal?—Gradual step-by-step economic and political merger of east and west into the one-world socialist system envisioned by Karl Marx 150 years ago. It might be carried out by Boris Yeltsin. If he doesn't succeed (or maintain control) he can be replaced by another in the long series of "reform" heads of the Soviet Union, each one of which the media has promoted as different from the bad leaders they succeeded. (A fuller understanding of the long range plan and the philosophies underlying it is spelled out in the chapters titled: "Internationalism" and "Why Are Our Leaders Betraying Us?")

If the communists don't succeed (or if the reformers are real) expect on-going ethnic violence, lots of turmoil and ultimate bloodshed and civil war. (Always remember that even a cornered, dying dog can attack—and these dogs have nukes).

COMMUNIST INFLUENCE IN AMERICA

While most Americans were being enthralled by the Communist "hand in the air" in Eastern Europe (or the game of the week on TV), what degree of influence and power were the Communists achieving in the United States?

There are no longer any official answers for that important question. America was spending $300-billion annually for military defenses against the Communist threat during the 1980s. However, it had no agency charged with protecting the nation internally from Communist influence and manipulation.

Communist subversion in America was once observed and evaluated regularly by Congressional investigating committees and the Federal Bureau of Investigation under J. Edgar Hoover. Through the work of these agencies Communist penetration of American government in the 1930s and 1940s was uncovered. *None of these agencies compile information on the domestic activities of the communists today.*

The Congressional committees which once investigated Communist activity were abolished in the mid-1970's. Since then, the FBI has been forbidden to investigate domestic communists or keep them under surveillance unless there is evidence that a crime has been committed. As a result, on-going FBI investigations of communist activity in America dropped from 24,414 in 1973 to 51 in 1983.[37]

So there is no official evidence or evaluations on which to base answers to the question, "Do communists have real influence and power in America today?" (For the full story on the destruction of America's internal security system, see Chapter 19.)

However, there are other important indicators that the Communist Party USA has developed the ability to manipulate public opinion, administration policies and the United States Congress *almost at will*. Communist Party leaders have regularly been able to announce major legislative goals and see them adopted even when they directly conflict with policies of the President of the United States.

Shortly after the November 1986 elections, Gus Hall, the head of the Communist Party USA, addressed the Party's Central Committee. He rejoiced that liberal Democrats had won control of the U.S. Senate from the somewhat more conservative and anti-communist Republicans. His speech was printed in the January 1987 issue of *Political Affairs*, the party's theoretical journal. Hall ordered the comrades to capitalize on the change and lead the struggle in Congress to...

1. End all nuclear testing.

2. End aid to the Contras [the Nicaraguan freedom fighters].

3. Stop Star Wars [the communist name for SDI (Strategic Defense Initiative) which would protect the United States from a surprise Soviet attack if the communists cheat on their treaty commitments in the future as they have in the past].

4. Ratify the SALT II disarmament agreement.

Those familiar with recent history will recognize that Gus Hall's 1987 legislative agenda was also the agenda of a majority or near majority of the U.S. Congress and about 90% of the news media. As a result, the Communist Party's four legislative goals were largely achieved by Congressional action or Executive Order by early 1988.

Aid to the Contras was on-again, off-again through 1987. It was finally killed by an eight-vote margin in the Democrat-controlled House of Representatives on February 3, 1988 under the leadership of House Speaker Jim Wright.

SDI? The left came within one vote of killing the entire project in the U.S. Senate in September 1987. Vice President Bush cast a tie-breaking vote to keep SDI alive.[38] Even so, the hope of ever deploying the system which would protect Americans from a sneak attack by communist missiles was dashed a few weeks later when Congress cut the appropriations for the SDI system by 40%. In addition, Congressional leftists inserted provisions against testing SDI components into the 1988 Appropriations Bills and made further cuts in research funding in 1989.[39] As a result, even though restricted research could proceed the system can't be fully tested to see if it works.

Other Congressional votes placed budget restrictions on nuclear testing and required the Reagan administration to adhere to the unratified SALT II treaty.[40]

Each of the communists' four legislative goals were implemented— either directly or by a back door approach.

COMMUNISTS REJOICE

The communists were jubilant. The headline on James Steele's 1987 Christmas Eve column[41] in the official communist newspaper, *People's Daily World*, read:

> 1987 was a very good year; 1988 can be even better.

Steele served as secretary of the Legislative and Political Commission of the Communist Party. His column detailed ten events that made 1987 "the year that was" for communists. Steele's list of communist victories included the achieving of Communist Party Chief Gus Hall's four 1987 legislative goals plus...

  * The Iran-Contra inquiry which resulted in many hard line anti-communists leaving the administration and put the brakes on much of the administration's anti-communist activity,

  * The launching of the Arias peace plan in Central America which stopped the contra offensive which was pressing for victory over the Communist Sandinistas in Nicaragua,

  * Senate rejection of Robert Bork's nomination to the Supreme Court,

  * The reelection of Mayor Harold Washington in Chicago,

  * Jesse Jackson's early victories in race for the Democrat presidential nomination,

  * The signing of the Reagan-Gorbachev INF treaty banning short-range nuclear missiles from Europe,

Steele's *People's Daily World* article cited the ten events as communist "victories" and said:

> Well, one could go on and on, but the above examples give a good account as to why 1987 has been a vintage year [for the communists].

(The organization and tactics U.S. Communists used to stop contra aid, orchestrate the anti-Bork drive, and win their other victories are examined in detail in Chapter 21 and 22.

The apparatus is still in place and a real threat to American freedom. Their plan for exploiting and using the coming economic crisis to transform America into a socialist state is detailed in Chapter 23.)

AN OVERRIPE FRUIT

Communist influence in America is great. An even greater threat—moral decay—could destroy America even if there were no Communists. The Reds recognize and expect to exploit the deepening decadence when the final showdown comes. It's all in their plan.

Communists have been working to win the world following a blueprint laid down by Lenin early in this century. Summarized and paraphrased, Lenin's plan stated:

> First, we will take Eastern Europe, then the masses of Asia, then we will encircle the United States which will be the last bastion of capitalism. We will not have to attack. It will fall like an overripe fruit into our hands.

Since 1960 the United States has lived through a "revolution." The "revolution" has transformed America and her population. A people in rebellion against the traditional values on which America's greatness was built have become violent, sex-crazy and drug-dependent. America has become much like the "overripe fruit" Lenin said would one day fall into Communist hands.

People under 40 have a hard time comprehending the changes. They haven't known any America other than today's violent, sex crazy, drug dependent world. Because many of the changes the Revolution has produced have happened little by little, even older Americans who lived through them didn't notice what was happening—but the Revolution has produced a different America than that which existed before 1960.

Jeremiah Denton was a man who saw the change the Revolution produced. Commander Jeremiah Denton was a Navy pilot. He was shot down over North Vietnam on July 18, 1965—during the first days of America's open participation in the Vietnam War. He spent seven years, five months and 25 days in the Communist prison camp known as the "Hanoi Hilton."

He was tortured and forced to go before Communist propaganda TV cameras. He was forced to tell how well the Communists treated the prisoners. He condemned America's involvement in the Vietnam war. Jerry Denton spoke the words the Communists wanted. But even as he was reciting the words the Communists forced him to say, his eyes squinted and blinked—seemingly blinded by the bright TV lights.

When the Communist propaganda films were shown on the world's TV screens, Jerry Denton's message got through. The blinking was not caused by the TV lights. Denton was blinking his eyes to spell the Morse Code message: T-O-R-T-U-R-E. Jerry Denton was a genuine American hero.

When he came home in February 1973, he found a different America than the one he left seven-and-a-half years before. In the book, *When Hell Was In Session,* Jerry Denton told of the shock he experienced when he returned home and pinpointed some of the changes he found. He wrote:

> In the first weeks [home], unhappily I began to note some dark corners in America. I saw the evidences of the new permissiveness, group sex, massage parlors, X-rated movies, the drug culture, that represents to me an alien element. I also noted a mood of national political disunity which has damaged the foundations of the most powerful but compassionate nation on earth.

> The seven-and-a-half years I spent as a prisoner of the North Vietnamese convinced me that America's strength depends on the values of morality and patriotism that come from her families. When I returned from Vietnam, I was shocked at the deterioration in our society. It quickly became obvious that the basic problem was a deterioration in our national attitude towards the family and family life. The personal values of spousehood and parenthood stand too far down the hierarchy of society's values relating to individual responsibilities, accomplishments, and vocations.

> The consequences are manifest in our inability to respond effectively to all the major challenges of our society, our economy and even our national defense.[42]

Jerry Denton was elected to the United States Senate by the people of Alabama in November 1980. He waged an often thankless battle in Washington to return America to the political and spiritual foundations which made her great. The internal demoralization of America Jerry Denton saw continues. It can cause America to become the "overripe fruit" which Lenin said would drop into Communist hands without a fight.

In fact, the "revolution" America has lived through since 1960 can destroy America even if there were no Communist threat.

What caused the changes Jeremiah Denton saw in America? What has happened in America since Jerry Denton came home in 1973 from the Communist prison?

SINCE PRAYER WAS BANNED

In his book, *America: To Pray or Not To Pray,* author David Barton documents America's decay in 40 key areas since the U.S. Supreme Court banned prayer and Bible reading in America's schools. The subtitle describes Barton's book as: "A statistical look at what has happened since 39 million students were ordered to stop praying in public schools."

In 1962, the U.S. Supreme Court banned a 22-word prayer recited in the schools of New York. The prayer the Supreme Court declared "unconstitutional" said:

Almighty God, we acknowledge our dependence upon Thee, and we beg Thy blessings upon us, our parents, our teachers and our Country.[44]

Barton's book uses official government statistics to examine what has happened to the children of America, their parents, their teachers and schools and the nation since the simple 22 word prayer was banned. Barton's research documented the decay in each of the four areas the students were forbidden to ask God to bless. The first was "upon us." After school prayer was banned in 1962...

...SAT college entrance exam scores dropped sharply for 16 consecutive years after holding almost steady for the previous ten...the percentages of teen-age girls who engaged in pre-marital sex almost tripled in 14 years...pregnancies of girls in the 15-19 age bracket increased 550% in the 20-year 1963-83 period...pregnancies to girls under 15 went up 400%...sexually transmitted diseases increased 350% between 1963 and 1975...suicides doubled in the 15-24 age bracket.[45]

The shocking decay started as soon as the Supreme Court banned the prayer in which students asked God to bless them. Government statistics show a similar tragic pattern after student prayer asking for God's blessings "on our parents" was banned:

The divorce rate in America *doubled* between 1963 and 1980 after having declined slightly in the years 1948-63...single parent families jumped 250% in 22 years...there was a 400% increase in the number of unmarried couples living together...incidence of adultery and unfaithfulness in marriages tripled.[46]

What happened in America's schools after the Supreme Court banned the prayer in which students asked God's blessings "upon our teachers?"

...SAT college entrance exam scores as indicated previously dropped sharply for 16 consecutive years after holding almost steady for the previous ten...illiteracy rates tripled in 15 years...the number of students dropping out of high school and taking GED tests to get high school diplomas increased 775% between 1963 and 1982...before prayer was banned the top discipline problems listed by public educators included talking in class, chewing gum, running in the halls, wearing improper clothing, etc. By 1985, educators ranked drug abuse, pregnancies, rape, robbery, assault, absenteeism, vandalism, arson, etc. as the major school discipline problems. [47]   A U.S. Senate committee reported that 70,000 teachers were being assaulted annually in schools[48]

Prayer for God's blessings "upon our country" was the final area in which the Supreme Court said "Nyet!" Since then...

...the rate of violent crimes (rape, murder, assault, etc.) has increased 422%...the *number* of violent crimes has jumped 525%...crimes against property (burglary, robbery, etc.) increased 11 times faster than growth in population...prosecution of government officials for corruption increased five fold...sexually-transmitted disease rates for the population as a whole increased 313% in the 12 years from 1963 to 1975...per capita alcohol consumption jumped 29%...the number of high school seniors who had tried marijuana increased 15 fold in the 20 years between 1962 and 1982...child abuse and neglect cases tripled and reported cases of sexual abuse of children increased ten fold.[49]

There were other indicators of the decay in America which resulted from the "revolution" the nation has lived through since 1960. In 1960 there were...

...no legalized abortions in America...no X-rated or R-rated movies...no coed dorms on college campuses...gays were called "queers" and hid their sin rather than parading it openly and proudly in demonstrations and on TV...there was also no AIDS problem...and a radio or TV station was in danger of losing its operating license from the Federal Communications Commission if it permitted the words "Hell" or "Damn" to go out over the air waves.

SEX SYMBOL APPALLED BY DECAY IN STANDARDS

How different things have become in 30 years. One person did notice and speak out. Mae West was the movie star sex symbol of the 1920s and early 1930s. Her name was almost a dirty word which would not be spoken in polite company. In 1933 she murmured, "C'm up 'n see me sometime" to Cary Grant in the movie, *She Done Him Wrong*. Furor over that "suggestive" scene precipitated a wholesale revision of the film industry's censorship code. After a double-meaning remark in a skit on the Charlie McCarthy show in 1937 she was banned from radio for 12 years. However Mae West spoke out against the decadence in America on her 80th birthday. The Associated Press said:

Perhaps surprisingly, Miss West deplores the current trend toward sex and nudity in films. "I don't approve of it, it's just not right," she declared. "Now they have no stories. They've run out of plots. They simply throw naked bodies at the audience. And showing the sex act, I think that's terrible!

"When I was making pictures I couldn't even say 'hell' or 'damn' on the screen. The church people watched me like a hawk. Where are the church people today? How can they allow such things as you see on the screen?"[50]

Where are the church people? Too often representatives of traditional "mainline" churches have contributed to the decay and defended the decadence. In 1975 newspaper front pages carried the headline, "Lesbian to be ordained Episcopal Deacon."[51] Two weeks later the ordaining bishop responded to critics of the ordination. The Associated Press reported:

> The Rt. Rev. Paul Moore, Jr., the Episcopal Bishop of New York, believes the ordination of a lesbian as a deacon in the church is a sign of a healthy change in attitude toward homosexuality, he said Tuesday.
>
> "Homosexuality is a condition which one does not choose; it is not a question of morality," Bishop Moore said in a statement about the ordination of Ellen Barrett as a deacon on December 15.
>
> "Historically many of the finest clergy in our church have had this personality structure," he said, "But only recently has the social climate made it possible for some to be open about it."[52]

Leaders like Moore no longer challenge people to higher standards of decency. Too often they undermine traditional values. For example a woman judge in New York city dropped prostitution charges against a 14-year-old girl. She ruled that sex for a fee is a "recreational business" and therefore could not be prosecuted.[53] Public sensitivity to decay and decadence is dulled when public figures show tolerance for sin. That which is first tolerated will eventually be embraced.

TAX-FINANCED PERVERSION

By the 1980s the most gross forms of perversion were being paraded publicly *and were frequently financed and subsidized with tax dollars.* For example, in 1986 and 1987 federal grants of $734,717 and $239,962 were made to the "Gay Men's Health Crisis, Inc." of New York City. The money was used, not just to fight AIDS, but to promote homosexuality. They were the first in an on-going series of ever increasing federal grants to "fight AIDS." Among the goals of the funded projects were:

...to deal with...homophobia and fundamentalist religious belief that AIDS is God's curse...to promote low-risk sexual and drug-taking behavioral practices among gay and bisexual men which decrease their chances for acquiring AIDS...generating gay consciousness and a positive sense of gay pride among participants.

Among the federally-funded class activities and homework were...

...meeting someone new at a bar and letting him know you are interested in having sex...Writing a personal sex advertisement for publication in *The New York Native* [a homosexual publication]...listing satisfying, erotic alternatives to high-risk sexual practices...a survey questionnaire which described 24 different perverted sex practices with participants checking those they enjoyed and would be willing to participate in.

These projects were not financed through a sneaky misapplication of federal tax dollars. They were spelled out in advance in the grant applications and award notifications using gutter language and graphic detail.[54] The grant requests which were pornographic in content carried glowing personal endorsements by liberal Democrat Congressmen William Green and Ted Weiss of New York.

Other federal grants financed perverted "art." "Artist" Andres Serrano got a $15,000 National Endowment for the Arts grant for his display of a crucifix in a jar of his own urine. It was called "Piss Christ." The NEA also provided $30,000 in tax money for a traveling display of homo-erotic photographs. The unbelievable display included a picture of one man urinating into another man's mouth. The rest of the display showing perverted homosexual acts was so pornographic and sick that it can not be described.[55] Congressmen opposed to further financing of such "art" were prohibited from bringing the photos into the halls of Congress—even though the "art" had been paid for with tax money. Senator Jesse Helms (R-NC) attempted to have the 1990 appropriation bill...

...prohibit use of federal funds for the distribution, promotion, and production of obscene and indecent materials, including but not limited to depictions of sadomasochism, homoeroticism, the exploitation of children or individuals engaged in sex acts....[56]

Helms effort was defeated by a 264-153 procedural vote in the House of Representatives.[57]

In a column commenting on the tax-financed obscene exhibits, columnist Pat Buchanan wrote:

> In the '60s, the children of the counter-culture wanted to be free to curse "Amerika," and to use "filthy speech." Now, in middle age, they wish to be subsidized, even as they do so. Truly, they have never grown up; and a showdown is coming.[58]

Perverted and subversive art forms, much of it tax-financed, flooded the nation in the late 1980s. A filthy play, *The Normal Heart,* built tolerance for homosexuality. It was presented over 600 times—frequently on college campuses financed with tax dollars. Thirteen of the play's 14 characters are "men"—ten of whom are openly homosexual. Most of them have AIDS. There are 17 instances of embraces or kissing on the stage between the "male" characters with open discussion and invitations to perverted sex. The language is unbelievably crude, vile and often blasphemous. The four letter "F" word is used 26 times—and there are countless other three, four and five letter gutter words used for various parts of the male anatomy. Actors use the Lord's name in cursing.[59]

A courageous lady state representative challenged use of tax money to present the play in the heart of America's Bible-belt at Southwest Missouri State University in November 1989. She and her position were attacked by the university president, the school's law firm, six of seven members of the board of regents, the faculty senate and the Springfield, Missouri newspaper.[60] After the opening night's performance the college president, Marshall Gordon, was asked if he liked the play. He said:

> I'm very proud of our students and our faculty. This is another example of the outstanding work they do—in this case, under a great deal of pressure.[61]

In a guest editorial in the Springfield newspaper another

state legislator tried to put the controversy into perspective for parents of students. He wrote:

> With the extremely high cost of a college education, most of the student body probably attends taxpayer-supported SouthWest Missouri State through a combination of grants, scholarships and money from mom and dad.
>
> I often hear from parents who lament the fact that they send their children off to college at great financial hardship to themselves and seem to get back a complete stranger, void of morals and espousing a liberal philosophy foreign to that of their upbringing.
>
> If anything good can be said about the exposure given to *The Normal Heart*, it is that now, mom and dad know why.[62]

Strong penalties were not enacted when the decay and degradation first appeared on college campuses in the 1960s. Tolerated then, it has since spread its tentacles into every area of American life.

Lenin said that by the time the final showdown came between capitalism and communism that the United States would have become so rotten from within that it would drop into Red hands like an overripe fruit. America is in deep peril.

WHAT CAN BE DONE?

Any sober, realistic survey of Communist successes—both around the world and in putting America to sleep—can only lead the concerned citizen to a cry of, "Can anything be done? Can America be saved?" Those questions are not new. May Craig, the longtime lady member of TV's *Meet The Press* panel, tried to find answers in a column she wrote for the Portland, Maine *Sunday Telegram* on February 9, 1964. Mrs. Craig, long since retired, wrote:

> Unless there is a change, deep-down in the American people, a genuine crusade against self indulgence and immorality, public and private, then we are witnesses to the decline and fall of the American Republic.

She looked at the first signs of a sickness she was seeing develop in America 25 years ago—a sickness in America's people and government—and warned:

Death on the highways...cheating from top to bottom in our society, get rich quick, break-up of the family, faltering foreign policy, reckless debt—these have destroyed nations before us. Why should we think we should take that path and change history?

In a stinging indictment of America's "faltering foreign policy" Mrs. Craig detailed Washington's failures this way:

Round the world they think they can take our money with one hand and slap us in the face with the other...Because it is unpleasant to think of unpleasant things, we say the Soviet Union is changing its determination to bury us. Red China is bad, of course, but maybe Russia is not.

Half-heartedly we send American men to die in jungles, where we do not have the guts to go in and win or stay out. We sell wheat to Russia to save her from a demonstration that Communism cannot produce enough food for its own people.

We sign test-ban treaties with known enemies, known defaulters on treaties, that we will not test as we may need to. Why should we rest our defense on such agreements?

Mrs. Craig offered a two-point program to prevent the "decline and fall of the American Republic." She wrote:

First, everyone of us has to clean out weakness and selfishness and immorality of all types. *Then*, choose leaders who with strength and principle and intelligence will lead us to where we can have self respect and the respect of others.

Before that can happen great numbers of Americans must be (1) awakened to the danger, (2) given an understanding of the true nature and tactics of the Communists and their many allies, and then (3) trained and organized to effectively oppose evil philosophies and forces (political and moral) at work in America and the world. In the process they must find the spiritual strength and develop the character to persist in the longterm battle which can often turn vicious.

DEFENSE ALONE CAN'T WIN

As important as opposing humanism and its communist and socialist offspring is, it is not enough. Defense alone can't win. To go on the offensive Americans must rediscover the source of America's greatness—the unique concept spelled out in the Declaration of Independence that rights do not come from government or a constitution but from God. That message must be given to those seeking freedom all over the world.

There are reasons for deep concern—but not for despair. There are reasons to hope. Millions of Americans responded, however briefly, to Oliver North's TV testimony during the Iran-Contra hearings. Without a follow up to broaden the understanding and give a call to action the initial excitement soon died out. But the amazing response to North's testimony and his efforts against communism, however short lived, gives reason for hope—real hope and a challenge to action. A similar resurgence of patriotism and pride in country was experienced during the Desert Storm effort in the Middle East.

When Americans have the facts they respond. The over-whelming majority of Americans—whether black or white—rich or poor—Catholic, Protestant or Jew—oppose communism and its cousins, socialism and secular humanism. Unfortunately they don't get enough information to recognize the dangers. If even one percent of them could be awakened and given a foundational understanding of the true basis of freedom and the forces at work opposing it, freedom can be safeguarded. The God-given blessings of liberty can be extended around the world.

This 25th anniversary edition of *None Dare Call It Treason* is a tool for the battle. This new edition republishes the original without change (history is history) before presenting 350 pages of new material. What has gone before is the key to understanding today's headlines. It foreshadows what will be happening tomorrow.

THE ORIGINAL CHAPTER I

HAVE WE GONE CRAZY?

As long as capitalism and socialism exist we cannot live in peace; in the end, one or the other will triumph—a funeral dirge will be sung over either the Soviet Republics or over world capitalism.

—V. I. Lenin[1]

THE COLD WAR is real war. It has already claimed more lives, enslaved more people, and cost more money than any "hot" war in history. Yet, most Americans refuse to admit that we are at war. That is why we are rapidly losing—why America has yet to win its first real victory in 18 years of "cold" war.

Within the framework of the "cold" war there have been "hot" wars in China, Malaya, Indonesia, Algeria, the Congo, Cuba, Iraq, the Gaza Strip, Hungary, Korea, Angola, Burma, Tibet, and Egypt. In 1963, there was fighting in Laos, Viet Nam, and on the Indian-Chinese border, renewed skirmishing along the 38th parallel in Korea, and terrorist activity in Africa. The forces of freedom have lost or will lose them all.

There has been no "big" war because the Communists are winning without one.

In 1945, the Communists held 160-million Russians in slavery. They controlled a land area smaller than the Russia of the Czars. Soviet industry had been largely destroyed by the Nazi war machine. Communism was a third rate power, militarily, industrially, and economically.

Today, after the United States has spent $600-billion to fight communism and sacrificed the lives of 50,000 of its youth to thwart Red aggression, the Kremlin has grown to become the absolute slavemasters of one-billion human beings. The Communists openly control 25% of the earth's land mass. Their puppet, Fidel Castro, has been installed in Cuba, just 90 miles from our shores. The hidden tentacles of the Communist conspiracy exert unmeasured influence over the rest of the world.

Where have we failed?

Almost unnoticed by most Americans, Congress while appropriating billions for defense *against* communism, has at the same time given over $6-billion in direct military and economic aid *to the Communists.*[2] Here are examples:

> Radar-equipped F-86 jet fighter planes worth over $300,000 each have been sold to the Communist dictator of Yugoslavia for $10,000. This "sale" to Tito has been defended because both the Eisenhower and Kennedy Administrations approved it. The planes were said to be "obsolete." Yet, during the Berlin crisis, reactivated U.S. Air National Guard units flew to possible battle against Communists in Europe *in even more* obsolete F-84 jets.[3]

Nikita Khrushchev has said that peaceful coexistence involves peaceful economic competition. Our leaders agree, and place great emphasis on this aspect of the cold war in urging disarmament. Why then has the United States...

> ...supplied nuclear reactors to the Communist government of Czechoslovakia, railway equipment to Bulgaria, chemical plants to Yugoslavia, and synthetic rubber plants to Soviet Russia? Why has America given Russia the machinery to produce the precision ball bearings used in the guided missiles they "rattle" during every international crisis?[4]

> Why has America built the world's most modern, most highly automated steel finishing plant for the Communist government of Poland? Constructed in Warren, Ohio, the plant was dedicated as the *Lenin Steel Works* by the U.S. Ambassador to Poland in July 1961. The American people "lent" the Communists $ 2.5-million to pay for it.[5]

The examples are endless. The failure of Russian agriculture has historically been communism's weakest "link." So, in 1961...

> ...officials in the U.S. Department of Agriculture and the Commerce Department agreed to sell surplus wheat to the Soviet

Union for $.62 per bushel less than the baker who bakes your
bread pays for it. Only quick action by an awakening public
stopped this folly which would have supplied wheat to ease food
shortages and the resultant unrest against the Communists in the
Soviet Union. The officials who initiated the program are still
holding responsible government positions.[6]

Much American aid to Communists is hidden in U.S. grants
to the United Nations and its specialized agencies. For example, the United Nations Special Fund is giving Castro, the
Communist dictator of Cuba, funds to bolster his agricultural
programs. The American who heads the fund, Paul Hoffman,
approved the grant, and the U.S. taxpayer is paying 40% of
the total bill of $1.6-million.[7] The grant was made just after
the attempted invasion of Cuba failed in April 1961.

Is it any wonder that Nikita Khrushchev predicted confidently in a speech in Bucharest, Rumania, on June 19, 1962,
that:

 The United States will eventually fly the Communist Red
 Flag...the American people will hoist it themselves.

The Communists have sworn to bury us. We are digging our
own graves.

Does aid to communism make sense? If, during World War
II, anyone had suggested sending food or industrial materials
to Nazi Germany, they would have been tried for treason, or
carted off to a mental institution. Today, favoring aid to
communism is, to some, evidence of good *mental health*.

After years of such folly, where do we stand today in the
battle from which, Lenin, first head of Communist Russia,
said there could be no coexistence, that either capitalism or
socialism would emerge triumphant?

Senator Thomas Dodd (D-Conn) is a former FBI man. He's
vice chairman of the Senate Internal Security Subcommittee,
and a member of the Senate Foreign Relations Committee.
Speaking in Los Angeles, California, on August 28, 1961, just
seven months after President Kennedy was inaugurated,
Senator Dodd said:

There is a developing mood of anger and frustration in this country and there ought to be for we are losing round after round in the Cold War and our people do not like it.

At the close of World War II, our forces stood triumphant on the land and sea and in the air. We had at our command the mightiest array of military power in all history. Yet, the last 16 years have witnessed a calamitous retreat from victory. During all these years we have suffered defeat after defeat at the hands of international communism. We have retreated from position after position and committed folly after folly.[8]

Senator Dodd explained that because such defeats and retreats took place in faraway lands such as Latvia, Poland, Hungary, Czechoslovakia, China, Korea, and Indo-China, Americans were inclined to feel smug and secure. Then, he continued:

But in December 1958, what many people had considered impossible came to pass. While we stood by in confusion and disarray and apparent helplessness a Communist dictator was installed on the island of Cuba, only 90 miles off our own shores. In 1959, Tibet was brutally annexed by the Chinese Communists despite again, the anguished protests of free men throughout the world.

Since the beginning of this year (1961) alone there has been the sealing-off of East Berlin, the disaster in Laos, the fiasco in Cuba, and only last week, the victory of Cheddi Jagan and his Communist-dominated Peoples Progressive Party in British Guiana elections. Everywhere we are on the defensive. Everywhere we find ourselves being pushed back. We have retreated so far that we now stand perilously close to the brink of total disaster.[9]

How close are we to this disaster, the total enslavement of the world? Senator Dodd gave this evaluation:

Last December, I was privileged to speak in the City of Paris and at that time I said if there were another 15 years like the last 15 years there would be no more free world left to defend. In the light of what has happened over the intervening eight months since I made that observation in Paris, I feel compelled to revise that timetable.

I do not believe we have 15 years left. The next five years will contain a series of decisive battles which will determine for centuries to come whether mankind is to live in freedom or live in slavery. We stand now, my friends, with our backs to the precipice. We have no more ground to give, no time to lose, no margin for error.[10]

Since Senator Dodd issued that warning in August 1961, America has yielded further ground. The Congo, Algeria, Dutch New Guinea, Laos, Viet Nam, Cuba, Brazil, and the Dominican Republic have had the tentacles of communism drawn more tightly about their throats.

Senator Dodd was not the first to speak out. The warning has been issued many times. Several years ago, General Albert C. Wedemeyer, chief of strategic planners during World War II, appeared before the House Committee on Un-American Activities for a consultation. Wedemeyer was asked:

Based on your background and experience, and current studies of the operation of this conspiracy, how late is it on the Communist timetable for world domination?[11]

Richard C. Arens, staff director of the Congressional committee, reported that Wedemeyer dropped his eyes to the floor, looked up, and said:

Sir, my humble, honest judgment is, that it is too late.[12]

Before it was printed, Wedemeyer edited his testimony. He struck out those words and wrote:

I am not completely a pessimist, but it is very, very late. If I were the senior planner in the Soviet hierarchy, I would advise Khrushchev, "Continue to do exactly what you are doing now. Do not involve the Soviet Union in major war, but employ the satellites in brush fires or limited wars against our enemies, the capitalist countries."[13]

That is just what has happened. Khrushchev has threatened nuclear war to get his way. He has employed the satellites in brush fires in Tibet, Laos, Viet Nam, Algeria, the Congo, and most recently, on the Indian-Chinese border.

Consider the sobering implications of Cuba in the perspective of the following words. Written in 1951, they were based on a study of Communist sources:

> Communist strategy teaches that there can be no successful revolution followed by the creation of Soviets in any Latin American country unless an internal revolution has been effected with the United States. The Comintern views the Western hemisphere as an integral unit in which the United States must first be *rendered helpless* before a Soviet-type government can be established in any other of the 20 republics in the hemisphere.[14]

Part of a study on Latin American Communist activities, this analysis was published by the House Committee on Un-American Activities in a volume entitled, *Soviet Total War*. It was issued on September 30, 1956, *almost two-and-a-half years before Fidel Castro established the first Soviet-type government in the western hemisphere.*

Could the American government possibly have been rendered helpless in the struggle against world communism or is this official analysis wrong?

In 1961, the Senate Internal Security Subcommittee issued a 12-volume study entitled, *Communist Threat To The U.S. Through The Caribbean*. It showed conclusively that Castro could not have brought communism to Cuba *except for the continual aid and assistance of the U.S. State Department.*[15]

Even so, the State Department personnel implicated by the Senate study as being directly involved in Castro's rise to power still held important State Department jobs two years later. William Wieland, a man branded as "either a damn fool or a Communist," before the Senate committee has been promoted to the highest foreign service rank and pay.[16]

As head of the State Department Caribbean desk, Wieland received and "buried" continuing intelligence reports which indicated that Castro was a Communist.[17] After the U.S. Senate revealed this and other derogatory information, Wieland was promoted and named to the State Department committee studying a revision of *security practices*.[18] He was still employed in the State Department as of February 23, 1963.

Wieland is not an isolated case. John Stewart Service, a

career diplomat, was arrested by the FBI on June 7, 1945, for passing secret documents to Soviet espionage agents. He was deeply involved in the Communist-influenced web in the State Department which lost China to communism. In the early 1950's, Service was dismissed, but the Supreme Court, without questioning his guilt ordered him reinstated in 1956. The Court's decision was based on the technicality that proper procedures had not been used in firing him.[19] At first assigned to the menial task of handling baggage for diplomats, Service started working his way back up the State Department ladder. By 1961, he occupied a key diplomatic post in Liverpool, England.[20] In 1962, he retired, and is now drawing a pension from the American taxpayers. Owen Lattimore was deeply involved in the betrayal of China to the Communists in the late 1940's. In 1952, the Senate Internal Security Subcommittee found him to have been "a conscious articulate instrument of the Soviet conspiracy"[21] for 15 years. In May 1961, he was granted a passport to go to Outer Mongolia, a Communist satellite.

When questioned by newsmen, the State Department said, "He's not there as an official representative, of course, but we are anxious to get his impressions."[22] Four months after Lattimore's return to America, the U.S. agreed to admit Outer Mongolia to the United Nations.

No one denies these facts. They are just ignored.

Is it possible in view of these facts that the United States government has been rendered helpless in the struggle with communism? It did happen once. The grave question which few appear willing to face today is, "Could it happen again?"

Twenty years ago, similar warning signs were uncovered by the FBI and Congressional investigating committees. In the eight years which passed before the alarms were finally heeded, Alger Hiss had reached a high State Department post and sat at FDR's side. He was there at Yalta when decisions were made which ultimately committed 700-million human beings to Communist enslavement.[23] Harry Dexter White, as assistant secretary of the U.S. Treasury, controlled all fiscal matters in which foreign policy was involved.[24] Nathan Witt, as secretary of the National Labor Relations Board, was the Board's top executive officer.[25] He controlled board proceedings and all hiring and firing of NLRB employees. Board actions, under Witt's direction, were the deciding factor in many labor-management negotiations across the country. Lee Pressman was General Counsel of the Works Progress Administration (WPA).[26] John J. Abt was special assistant to the Attorney General.[27] Lauchlin Currie was executive assistant to President Roosevelt.[28] All were identified before Congressional committees as Communist agents.

High government officials ignored authoritative reports that these men, and others in equally high places, were Soviet agents. Some warnings came as long as eight years before the conspirators were publicly exposed.[29]

Could such infiltration of American government happen again? Has it happened? We can't know.

In 1954, an order by the President who had pledged to "clean up the mess in Washington" reiterated earlier "gag" rules which placed security files of executive department employees (about 98% of all federal employees) firmly "off-limits" to Congressional investigating committees.[30] The job of uncovering future security risks was thus made nearly impossible.

In a nutshell, America as a nation, and you as an individual, are in trouble. A look at the shrinking map of the free world confirms the warnings of responsible leaders. The future of Americans as a free people is threatened. The continued refusal of elected officials to rid the government service of the Wielands, the Services, the Lattimores, for whatever reason, tells why. What can we do?

A responsible person must first gather information on which to base his judgments and actions. Motivation without knowledge produces fanaticism. J. Edgar Hoover, director of the Federal Bureau of Investigation has told us:

> Attributing every adversity to communism is not only irrational, but contributes to hysteria and fosters groundless fears. Communism is, indeed, our paramount adversary, and it leans on its credo of invincibility to accomplish its ends. The way to fight it

is to study it, understand it, and discover what can be done about it. This cannot be achieved by dawdling at the spring of knowledge; it can only be accomplished by dipping into thoughtful, reliable, and authoritative sources of information.[31]

The study of communism must be approached objectively. For too long Americans have been "paralyzed by politics." They have seen only the mistakes, errors, and omissions of the opposition political party. Leaders of both parties have been at fault. Members of both political parties have blindly supported their own party leadership—and nothing has been done about the very real menace which threatens America.

It is not enough to assess blame or point an accusing finger at past or present political leaders. The guilt also belongs to those apathetic Americans who have ignored warning after warning and let this chain of events continue. The past mistakes, and they are many, must be spotlighted so similar errors can be avoided in the future.

CHAPTER II

THE ORIGIN OF COMMUNISM

Communists everywhere support every revolutionary move-
ment against the existing political and social order of things.
The Communists disdain to conceal their aims. Let the ruling
classes tremble at a Communist revolution. The proletarians
have nothing to lose but their chains. They have a world to
win. Working men of all countries, unite!

—Karl Marx, The Communist Manifesto

THE STORY OF COMMUNISM is a story of contradictions.
Despite Marx's call for the workers of the world to unite,
communism has never been a working class movement. Its
strength is in the intellectual and thought centers of the
world.

Communism is commonly believed to rise out of poverty.
Yet, Fidel Castro was a product, not of the cane fields of Cuba,
but of the halls of Havana University.[1]

Joseph Stalin was not a simple peasant rebelling at the
oppression of the Czar. He became a Communist while studying for the priesthood in a Russian Orthodox seminary.[2]

Dr. Cheddi Jagan, Communist premier of British Guiana,
became a Communist, not as an "exploited" worker on a
plantation of a British colonial colony, but as a dental student
at Chicago's Northwestern University.[3]

The membership of the first Communist spy ring uncovered
in the U.S. Government was not spawned in the sweat shops
of New York's lower east side or the tenant farms of the South.
Alger Hiss, Nathan Witt, Harry Dexter White, Lee Pressman,
John Abt, Lauchlin Currie and their comrades came to high
government posts from Harvard Law School.[4]

The Senate Internal Security Subcommittee's *Handbook*
For Americans delves into why people become Communists.
It says:

A trite explanation offered by the ill-informed is that communism is a product of inequalities under our social system. Hence, these people argue, if we will alleviate these conditions, we will never have to worry about communism...The misery theory of communism runs contrary to actual facts in our country. New York State, for example, has approximately 50% of the total Communist Party membership. Yet it is second in terms of per capita income and per capita school expenditures... Conversely, Mississippi is lowest in the scale of Communist Party membership but is also lowest in per capita income.

The Senate committee comments on these facts, saying:

The misery theory of communism does not jibe with these figures nor with the fact that such wealthy persons as Frederick Vanderbilt Field, and prominent members of the Hollywood film colony, have been found to be members of the Communist Party. Indeed the misery theory of communism is exactly what the Communists would have us believe, in order to mislead us.[5]

According to John Williamson, then organizational secretary of the Communist Party, USA, writing in the Party's top theoretical journal, *Political Affairs*, for February 1946, "71% of the Party in New York City consists of white collar workers, professionals and housewives.[6]"

Communism is a disease of the intellect. It promises universal brotherhood, peace and prosperity to lure humanitarians and idealists into participating in a conspiracy which gains power through deceit and deception and stays in power with brute force.

Communism promises Utopia. It has delivered mass starvation, poverty, and police state terror to its own people and promoted world-wide strife and hatred by pitting race against race, class against class, and religion against religion. Treason, terror, torture, and Moscow-directed wars of "national liberation" spread Communist "brotherhood, peace and social justice" around the world.

Communism is frequently described as a philosophy—but it is not a philosophy in which intellectually honest men can believe for long. It is a conspiracy in which hate-driven men participate.

Lenin confirmed this. In his important and authoritative work, *What Is to Be Done*, written in 1902, he set forth his views on the structure of the Communist Party, and said:

Conspiracy is so essential a condition of an organization of this kind that all other conditions... must be made to conform with it.[7]

In other words, the philosophy of communism must be bent and twisted as needed to fit the conspiratorial needs of the situation.

There is much first-hand evidence that Communists quickly see through the fallacies of Marxism-Leninism but continue in the Party as blind believers, as conspirators against the established order, or for the personal power and privilege Party membership gives the select few.

Colonel Frantisek Tisler, former military and air attache in the Czechoslovakian Embassy in Washington, D.C. defected from communism in 1959 and sought permanent asylum in America. A few months later he told his story to the House Committee on Un-American Activities. Tisler said:

I have not been a believer in communism for a long period of time, although in the early days of my association with the Communist Party of Czechoslavakia I was an ideological believer.

My initial disillusionment with communism in practice began to take place while I was attending Military Staff School in Prague. It was at this school that I witnessed many incidents which proved to me that communism in practice was greatly different from theoretical communism. I was exposed to numerous incidents where members of the Communist Party who were high-ranking officers in the Army took advantage of their position in order to obtain personal advantages and job security. The disillusionment which set in as a result of the excesses...began to shatter my faith in Marxism-Leninism.[8]

This realization that communism was not an idealistic philosophy came while Tisler was still a relatively young student officer. He continued as a conspirator for ten years before he defected, rising in that time to a high ranking position in the Party and its international intelligence network.

What is the "philosophy" which traps the student intellectual and transforms him into a conspiring, conforming, never-questioning tool of the Communist Party? How are brilliant young minds twisted to swear that "slavery" is "freedom," "dictatorship" is "democracy" or that "war" is "peace"—*and actually believe that it is so?*

Karl Marx compounded the theories which "explain" all the contradictions. He called it dialectical materialism. Marx, the 19th Century father of communism, was not a worker but a university-trained intellectual with a doctorate in philosophy. Although his ideas have had a deep impact and lasting effect on the intellectual world, he was not an original thinker.

Marx concocted dialectical materialism by blending Feuerbach's atheistic materialism with Hegel's theory that everything in nature is in a state of constant conflict. In its simplest form, dialectic materialism teaches:

> All people and things in the universe and the universe itself are simply matter in motion. As matter moves, opposites attract. When the opposites come together, conflict results and from the conflict comes change.

With this theory, Marx explains the origin and development of the universe, everything in it, and all life. Man, plants, animals, and their world are all products of "accumulated accidents." Ignored is the creative force which produced the first "matter" and made it "move" and develop in an orderly way. This First Mover and Great Planner, we know as our Creator, God.

Marx applied his theories of conflict and change to society. Human beings were arbitrarily divided into two classes (opposites). The bourgeoisie (propertied classes) were considered the degenerate class. The proletariat (unpropertied wage earners) were the progressive class.[9]

Communism teaches that a state of continual conflict or class warfare exists between the two groups. In this conflict, according to dialectical materialism, the bourgeoisie will be destroyed. This *change* is "inevitable" and is defined by Marx as *progress*.

SCIENTIFIC SOCIALISM

Marx was a self-proclaimed scientist. His "scientific" theories explained the entire history of man and determined his future. They are to be used to transform man's nature. Being "scientists," Communists have certain basic "scientific" laws which underlie their beliefs and teaching. They include:

> There is no God. When Communists deny God, they simultaneously deny every virtue and every value which originates with God. There are no moral absolutes, no right and wrong. The Ten Commandments and the Sermon On The Mount are invalid.[10]

Accepting this concept of "morality," the Communists teach that all is right which advances the cause of socialism. All is wrong which impedes its progress. For the Communist, to lie, cheat, steal, or even murder, is perfectly moral if it advances communism. Conversely, a Communist who would refuse to lie, cheat, steal or murder to aid the socialist movement is immoral. In the words of Lenin:

> We do not believe in eternal morality—our morality is entirely subordinated to the interests of the class struggle.[11]

The second "scientific" law of communism follows the first logically. It is:

> Man is simply matter in motion. As such, he is without soul, spirit, or free will and is not responsible for his own acts.[12]

Marx taught that man was entirely an evolutionary animal, the highest animal form, without significant individual value or eternal life. Man is a body completely describable in terms of the laws of chemistry and physics.

The third "scientific" law, economic determinism, is to be the means for *transforming* man. It states:

> Man is an economically determined animal. Qualities of human intelligence, personality, emotional and religious life merely reflect man's economic environment. The evil a man does is just a reflection of his environment.[13]

After coming to this conclusion, Marx taught that the only way man could be improved or changed would be to change or eliminate the evil-producing elements in man's environment. He reasoned that the one common influence in man's life was the economic environment. Mid-19th Century Europe's predominant economic system was a rough-and-tumble combination of feudalism, mercantilism, and free enterprise. Marx called it *capitalism* and blamed it for all the evil in man and the world. He concluded that the only way to eliminate evil and improve man was to destroy capitalism. Marx taught that this was both desirable and historically inevitable because the continued conflict between the classes had to produce *change*.

The inevitable outcome of the class war, according to Marx, was the triumph of the proletariat in a revolution which would destroy a decaying capitalism and replace it with socialism. Under socialism, the dictatorship of the proletariat (Communist Party) would work towards the establishment of communism.

Marx taught that once the material needs of man were satisfied, greed, profit-taking, avarice, and hate would disappear. The State would wither away. There would be no laws or need for a police force. A heaven on earth would result. Man's nature would be magically transformed. Each would work according to his ability. Each would desire to receive only according to his needs.

To reach this goal, the proletariat must achieve control of the entire earth, Marx taught. All poisoning traces of capitalism must be eliminated. In practice, as the Communists conquer a country, and if they conquer the world, they are left with those people raised in a capitalist environment. It has formed their character and personality. They will transmit the illness to their children.[14]

Being materialist "scientists," the Communists do not hesitate. All the "animals" infected with the "disease" of capitalism and freedom must be exterminated. To the Communists, this is not murder. Murder means killing for bad reasons. They will kill the bourgeoisie class for a "good" reason, the establishment of world communism. This "end" justifies the "means."[15]

The Communists, therefore, are not interested in converting you, the reader, to communism, particularly if you are over 30 years of age. *If you can be lulled into doing nothing to oppose the triumph of world communism, that is enough.* Once the takeover comes, you, like millions of others, who believe in God and man's responsibility for his own life and actions, can be slaughtered like diseased animals or worked to death in slave labor camps or brothels for the Red Army.

The Communists are after your children or grandchildren who can still be molded into obedient slaves of the State.

Gus Hall, General Secretary of the Communist Party, USA, told Americans what to expect when the Communists take over. Speaking at the funeral of Eugene Dennis in February 1961, Hall said:

> I dream of the hour when the last Congressman is strangled to death on the guts of the last preacher and since the Christians love to sing about the blood, why not give them a little of it.[16]

WHO WAS MARX?

What sort of man could dream of Utopia, and yet advise, even command his followers to lie, cheat, steal, and commit individual mass murder to achieve it?[17]

Marx was born in 1818 of scholarly Jewish parents in a Germany which was just becoming a nation. His early life was torn as his family left the Jewish faith and adopted a more "accepted" Protestantism.

His radical ideas, even as a student, caused his ejection from several universities, and he toured the intellectual and political capitals of Europe associating with a varied assortment of revolutionaries and "free thinkers."

The Communist Manifesto, written in conjunction with his friend, Engels, was published before Marx was 30. His major work, the first volume of *Das Kapital*, was completed before Marx was 50.

His marriage resulted in six children. Marx, however, was so engaged in formulating theories to "uplift" the downtrodden masses that he never bothered to accept a job to support his family. Three of his six children died of starvation in infancy. Two others committed suicide. Only one lived to maturity.

Marx, at one point, was so taken up with his concern for "humanity" that when a gift of 160 pounds (about $ 500) arrived from a rich uncle in Germany, he used the money for a two-month drinking spree with continental intellectuals. His wife, left penniless in London, was evicted from their apartment with the infant children.

During these years, Marx's ideas and philosophy were accepted only by the radical fringe groups which comprised the First International, and his friend and collaborator, Friedrich Engels. Engels, a rich man's son, was Marx's chief source of income. When Marx died, his funeral was attended by only six persons.

THE FABIANS AND THE COMMUNISTS

Following Marx's death in 1883, his theories were made a world force by two developments. They were the rise of the Fabian Society in England and Lenin's Bolshevik movement.

In 1884, a small group of English intellectuals formed the Fabian Society. It was their goal to establish the same classless, godless, socialistic, one-world society envisioned by Marx.[18] Leadership of the group was assumed by Beatrice and Sidney Webb and the Irish author and playwright, George Bernard Shaw. Shaw described himself as a "Communist"[19] but differed with Marx over how the revolution would be accomplished and by whom. He spelled out these differences in 1901 in his, *Who I Am, What I Think*, when he wrote:

> Marx's *Capital* is not a treatise on Socialism; it is a jermiad against the bourgeoisie...it was supposed to be written for the working class; but the working man respects the bourgeoisie and wants to be a bourgeoisie; Marx never got hold of him for a moment. It was the revolting sons of the bourgeoisie itself, like myself, that painted the flag Red. The middle and upper classes are the revolutionary element in society; the proletariat is the conservative element.[20]

On this basis, Shaw and the Fabians worked for world

revolution not through an uprising of the workers but through indoctrination of young scholars. The Fabians believed that eventually these *intellectual* revolutionaries would acquire power and influence in the official and unofficial opinion-making and power-wielding agencies of the world. Then, they could quietly establish a socialistic, one-world order.

Webb formulated the highly successful method these future rulers would use to change the world. He called it the "doctrine of the inevitability of gradualness." In practice, it has meant slow, piecemeal changes in existing concepts of law, morality, government, economics, and education. Each change is so gradual that the masses never awaken in time to stop the "inevitable."

Shaw, in the preface to the 1908 edition of *Fabian Essays*, stated the goal, which was...

> ...to make it as easy and matter-of-course for the ordinary Englishman to be a Socialist as to be a Liberal or Conservative.[21]

Shaw, in his *Intelligent Woman's Guide To Socialism*, explained what life would be like once the new order was established:

> I also made it clear that Socialism means equality of income or nothing, and that under Socialism you would not be allowed to be poor. You would be forcibly fed, clothed, lodged, taught, and employed whether you liked it or not. If it were discovered that you had not the character and industry enough to be worth all this trouble, you might possibly be executed in a kindly manner; but whilst you were permitted to live you would have to live well.[22]

The Fabian Socialists rejected all suggestions that they form a political movement of their own. They planned to spread their influence by penetrating existing educational institutions, political parties, the civil service, etc.

As a starting point, the Webbs established the London School of Economics on the first floor of 10 Adelphi Street in London. The upper floors were occupied by Shaw and his wife, Charlotte, who financed the venture. It was from this humble beginning that the intellectual center of the Fabian Socialist movement has grown. Today, it has world renown as a branch of the University of London. Its influence has been spread around the world by such faculty, students, and supporters as Harold Laski, Bertrand Russell, Joseph Shumpeter, John Maynard Keynes, H.G. Wells, and Nehru of India.

Down through the years, the Fabians, while masquerading under all sorts of "respected" labels have achieved power and influence far out of proportion to their numbers, which have never exceeded about 3000. By 1889, when the Society was only six years old and had fewer than 300 members, two of the group were elected to the London School Board.[23]

When the British Labour Party came to power in 1924, Fabian leader Ramsey MacDonald was Prime Minister. Fabian founder, Sidney Webb was Minister of Labour. When the party regained power in 1929, MacDonald was again Prime Minister and 20 Fabians held high positions. Eight served in the Cabinet.[24]

FABIANISM IN AMERICA

The seeds of Fabianism were planted in the United States before the start of the 20th Century. Leading English universities exchanged professors, scholars and writings with top American colleges. Sidney Webb himself came to America in 1888. The following year, his *Socialism In England* was circulated at Harvard and other schools by the American Economic Association.[25] By 1905, American Fabians had formed the Rand School of Social Science in New York and incorporated the Intercollegiate Socialist Society.[26] Within three years, chapters were formed at Harvard, Princeton, Columbia, New York University, and the University of Pennsylvania.[27]

Early adherents of this socialist movement in America included such later day leaders as John Dewey (education), Walter Rauschenbusch (theology), Walter Lippmann (government and press) and Supreme Court Justice Felix Frankfurter. Other equally skilled but lesser known theorists and conspirators operated in other fields. Their beliefs, their careers, their methods, and the influence they have exerted on American life will be explored later.

THE COMMUNISTS

Meanwhile, the other movement which was to make Marxism a potent, dynamic world force developed on the Continent in 1903. Nicolai Lenin, a Russian revolutionary and an ardent student of Marx, came to believe, like George Bernard Shaw, that it was neither possible nor desirable to sell Marx's theories to the masses.

Lenin and about seven followers split away during a meeting of socialist radicals in London, forming the Bolshevik "splinter group."

Lenin's major contribution to the world struggle, and the development which made Marx's theories a potent force, was his plan for organizing the Communist Party along conspiratorial lines. Lenin said:

> The only serious organizational principle the active workers of our movement can accept is strict secrecy, strict selection of members, and the training of professional revolutionaries.[28]

Lenin's plan called for a small, highly disciplined, well-schooled, and fanatically-dedicated core of revolutionaries. They would "combine illegal forms of struggle with every form of legal struggle."[29] Their power would be multiplied through infiltration and penetration of existing governments, organizations and groups. Thus, they would redirect the influence, prestige, and power of capitalistic institutions for the benefit of world communism. In the labor field, for example, Lenin advised his followers:

> ...to agree to any and every sacrifice, and even—if need be—to resort to all sorts of devices, maneuvers, and illegal methods, to evasion and subterfuge, in order to penetrate the trade unions, to remain in them, and to carry on Communist work in them at all costs.[30]

Another of Lenin's strategies for "multiplying" the power and strength of the small, dedicated group of revolutionaries was to exploit the differences between non-Communist groups so as to "incite one against another."[31] Stalin later spelled out Lenin's theory in detail in the book, *Stalin On China*. He said:

The most powerful enemy can be conquered only by exerting the utmost effort, and by *necessarily*, thoroughly, carefully, attentively and skillfully taking advantage of every, even the smallest "rift" among enemies, of every antagonism of interest among the bourgeoisie of the various countries and among the various groups or types of bourgeoisie within the various countries, and also by taking advantage of every, even the smallest opportunity of gaining a mass ally, even though this ally be temporary, vacillating, unstable, unreliable, and conditional. Those who do not understand this do not understand even a particle of Marxism, or of scientific, modern Socialism.[32]

A classic example of such modern socialism in practice was Fidel Castro's takeover of Cuba. Of Castro's followers, about 98% were non-Communists. The Cuban people would not have tolerated the bearded fanatic had they known he was a Communist. Yet, by exploiting their differences with another anti-Communist, Batista, Castro was able to get the temporary support he needed to establish a Communist regime in Cuba.

In America, Communists inspired the student riots against the House Committee on Un-American Activities in San Francisco on May 12-14, 1960, using the same tactics. A small group of trained, dedicated Communist agents fanned the differences between the students and a committee of Congress. Several thousand non-Communist students were stirred, first to demonstrate, and then to riot against lawful authority.[33]

An excellent example has been the implementation of a special Moscow Manifesto issued December 5, 1960, which ordered the destruction of the growing free world anti-Communist movement.[34] American Communists alone could not neutralize the fast-growing grass roots anti-Communist movement in the United States with a frontal attack.

Instead, the comparatively few Communist agents in America and their more numerous fellow-travelers in liberal movements, the press, and other opinion-making positions have worked to pit sizable segments of the American people against other Americans dedicated to fighting Communists.

The methods and tactics used are documented in a fascinating study by the Senate Internal Security Subcommittee[35] which is discussed at length in Chapter IV.

Teaching these and equally devious methods, and by restricting their recruits to only the most fanatical and dedicated, Lenin and the seven followers who formed the Bolshevik movement, swelled their ranks to 17 in the first four years. They returned to London in 1907 and searched for a suitable meeting place.

The Fabians came to their assistance. Ramsey MacDonald, later a three-time prime minister of Great Britain arranged for Lenin's Bolsheviks to use the Brotherhood Church in London's east end.[36] The conference was financed by a grant of 3000 pounds from Joseph Fels, a wealthy American soap manufacturer and a leader of the Fabian movement.[37]

Just ten years later, Lenin's 17 followers had become 40,000. They subverted and seized the Democratic Socialist Republic established by Kerensky in Russia after the fall of the Czar in 1917.

The early cooperation between the Communists and the Fabians, without which Lenin might have faded into oblivion, has continued as a united "anti-capitalistic front" down through the years. The Fabians abhor the "aggressive nature of communism" but cannot attack communism's godless, classless, socialistic one-world concepts because the Fabian creed is based on the same goals and beliefs.

Fabians flock to the defense of the accused Communist, as did Eleanor Roosevelt, Dean Rusk, Adlai Stevenson, and Felix Frankfurter when a top State Department official, Alger Hiss, was exposed as a Communist agent.

"He can't be a Communist," the Fabian reasons, "he believes the same as I do." When Hiss and Lauchlin Currie, executive assistant to President Roosevelt, were exposed as Soviet agents, Mrs. Roosevelt's outburst was typical. In her syndicated column, *My Day*, for August 16, 1948, she said:

> Smearing good people like Alger Hiss and Lauchlin Currie, is, I think, unforgivable.

Currie later fled the country rather than answer questions about his activities. Hiss served five years in the Federal Penitentiary for perjury after denying his participation in a Soviet spy ring.

Fabians are frequently found working in the Communist camp under the mistaken belief that *they* are "using the Communists." To a degree this accounts for the long lists of Communist-front affiliations accumulated by many leading "liberals." The mutual goals of the Communists and socialist "liberals" often lead to false accusations against "liberals" by those who assume "if he waddles like a duck, quacks like a duck, and is found in a flock of ducks, he must be a duck."

Indeed the loudest praise for the Russian Communist "experiment" has come, not from Moscow-directed Communists, but from Fabians. Fabian founder George Bernard Shaw, on a trip to Russia in 1931, stated in a speech in Moscow:

> It is a real comfort to me, an old man, to be able to step into my grave with the knowledge that the civilization of the world will be saved...It is here in Russia that I have actually been convinced that the new Communist system is capable of leading mankind out of its present crisis, and saving it from complete anarchy and ruin.[38]

Shaw, after an earlier trip to Russia, had praised Lenin as the "greatest Fabian of them all." Shaw helped formulate the Fabian concept of eventual control through infiltration, permeation, penetration, and piecemeal acquisition of power. He strongly admired Lenin and Stalin. He said they publicly championed Marx and his principles of world revolution while quietly working to communize one country after another. They used, Shaw said, the *Fabian methods of stealth, intrigue, subversion, and the deception of never calling socialism by its right name.*[39]

THE PLAN

After only seven years at the head of the world's first Communist state, Lenin died in 1924. Before he died, he formulated a plan for world domination. Summarized and paraphrased, Lenin's plan stated:

First, we will take eastern Europe, then the masses of Asia, then we will encircle the United States which will be the last bastian of capitalism. We will not have to attack. It will fall like an overripe fruit into our hands.

CHAPTER III

THE GROWTH OF WORLD COMMUNISM

I do not believe in communism any more than you do but there is nothing wrong with the Communists in this country; several of the best friends I have got are Communists.

—*Franklin D. Roosevelt*[1]

USING LENIN'S PLAN, the Communist followers of Marx and Lenin have moved "step-by-step" until today they hold 40% of the world's population in absolute slavery. With the capture of Cuba in 1959, the Kremlin bosses started on the last phase of Lenin's plan, the encirclement of the United States.

How has this been done by a nation which has never completed one of its highly publicized *Five Year Plans*? The Soviets have had police state control of their people, 44 years of centralized economic planning, and some of the world's richest natural resources. They have produced nothing but economic failure.

How has a nation which cannot feed its own people while employing 55% of its total working force on the farms come so close to conquering the world?[2]

The Communist world revolution has been largely financed from its start in 1903 until the present day by American wealth, public and private. Lenin and his heirs have had the sometimes knowing, sometimes unknowing, cooperation of the United States State Department every step of the way.

Every Communist country in the world literally has a "Made in the USA" stamp.

Look at true history and prove for yourself what has happened.

The part an American soap manufacturer played in financing Lenin's early career has been detailed.[3] In 1916-17, Leon

Trotsky was in exile in America.[4] In New York, he recruited, financed, and trained a cadre of gangsters and hoodlums. Transported to Russia, this hard core of cutthroat shock troops was used by Lenin and Trotsky to seize control of the shaky Kerensky Republic.

Immediately following World War I, economic chaos developed in Russia. Lenin's attempt to make the big leap into communism had failed. The toppling of the socialist experiment was imminent.

Millions were starving when American relief, food, medicine, and other supplies eased the pressure. Lenin had time to consolidate his strength.[5] This well-meaning, humanitarian gesture of the United States solidified the power of tyrants whose heirs in the succeeding 40 years have murdered at least 60-million human beings and enslaved one-billion others.

During the 1920's, American oilmen, technicians, and their machinery opened Russian petroleum fields. Other American engineers, scientists, and production experts assisted the Communists in building steel plants, assembly lines for tractors, trucks, and autos.[6]

Even so, by 1933 the Communist state was again faltering. Then, the USSR was recognized by the United States. With U.S. diplomatic recognition came world-wide prestige, and access to the credit and money markets of the world. In return for recognition, the Communists promised, in writing, that Russia would not interfere in the internal affairs of the United States.[7]

While the agreements were being signed, Alger Hiss, and other young Communists were infiltrating the New Deal. Soviet intelligence officers were busy in Washington setting up elaborate spy networks in government agencies.[8]

Six years later, Stalin made another agreement which was to have an equal impact on the course of history. In 1939, he and Hitler entered into a non-aggression pact. Together they carved up Poland in a blitzkrieg "war" which set records for its lightning speed, and the savage butchering of the Polish people. The attack on little Poland started World War II.

The Hitler-Stalin pact was short-lived and in 1941 Russia came under Nazi attack. The Kremlin, now an ally, received more than $11-billion in American lend lease aid. It was all supposedly war material to bolster the USSR in the fight against Germany. Actually, Russia received non-military supplies and materials worth billions. Stockpiled until the war's end, they were the foundation on which the Communist industrial machine of today was built.

Deluded U.S. officials and actual traitors, exposed later, arranged these shipments, in knowing defiance of laws passed by Congress prohibiting such non-military aid.[9]

In 1943, Congressional investigations later revealed, before the United States had itself assembled the first atomic bomb, half of all American uranium and the technical information needed to construct a bomb were sent to Russia.[10] Is it any wonder that the Communists became a nuclear power years ahead of "expectations?"

At the same time, a Communist agent, Harry Dexter White, became Assistant Secretary of the U.S. Treasury.[11] He sent the Soviet Union engraving plates, paper, and ink to print occupation currency which was redeemable by the U.S. Treasury.[12]

In actual conduct of the war, military decisions were made, not according to the tactical needs of the day or to capitalize on the weaknesses of the enemy, but for the long-range political advantage of the Communist conspiracy.[13]

For instance, at the wartime conferences, Roosevelt agreed to Stalin's demands for a "cross-channel" invasion of Europe, over Churchill's objections. Churchill urged an attack on Europe's soft "underbelly." Such an offensive, aimed at the Balkans, through Yugoslavia, would have defeated Hitler, *and* prevented Communist occupation of eastern Europe.[14]

At Yalta, Roosevelt, with Alger Hiss at his side, gave Stalin the eastern half of Poland, and the Baltic states of Estonia, Latvia, and Lithuania. He agreed to coalition governments for Yugoslavia and Poland, with Communists holding all the key posts. Stalin's occupation of the 11 eastern European countries was approved. Stalin promised to permit free elections in these Communist-occupied countries.[15] The U.S. government has never demanded that the agreements be fulfilled as a condition for further negotiations.

Thus, at Yalta, the first step of Lenin's master plan was accomplished. In addition, the foundation was laid for the completion of the second phase. Our Chinese ally, Chiang Kai-shek, was excluded from the Yalta Conference. Roosevelt and Churchill acceded to Stalin's demands for increased influence in postwar Asia.[16]

When the war ended, the United States demanded that Chiang Kai-shek give the Communists representation in the government of China. He refused. On orders of General George C. Marshall, all American aid was withheld from Chiang.[17]

With Marshall's embargo enforced, Chiang had tanks and planes, but no gasoline. His troops had guns, but no ammunition. By 1949, the Communists, supplied by Russia, were overrunning China. Chiang evacuated the remnants of his army and his government to Formosa.

In 1951 and 1952, the Senate Internal Security Subcommittee under the late Senator Pat McCarran (D-Nev) unraveled the sordid story of China's betrayal.

A quasi-official agency, the Institute of Pacific Relations, was found to have held a near controlling influence over American far eastern policies for 15 years. The IPR, as an unofficial State Department recruiting and training agency, had planted Communists and pro-Communists in sensitive diplomatic posts in Washington and China.[18]

IPR-oriented State Department officials in China deliberately falsified reports to Washington on the status of Chiang's government. Chinese Communists were depicted as "agrarian reformers."[19]

The Chinese people's confidence in Chiang's government was shaken by runaway inflation. It was planned in Washington by IPR officials in conjunction with Assistant Secretary of the Treasury Harry Dexter White, a Communist agent. White's plan to destroy China's currency was implemented by the U.S. Treasury Department's representative in Chungking, Solomon Adler. He was also a Communist.[20]

In its report, the Senate Internal Security Subcommittee concluded that...

...the Institute of Pacific Relations was a vehicle used by the Communists to orientate American far eastern policy toward Communist objectives.[21]

Owen Lattimore, an influential member of the IPR and sometime government official and State Department adviser, was found to have been "a conscious articulate instrument of the Soviet conspiracy" for 15 years.[22] Two years earlier, a young Senator from Wisconsin, Joseph McCarthy, had warned that Lattimore and the IPR were serving the Communist conspiracy. McCarthy's charges were regarded by some as "red herrings" and "unfounded smears."

Lattimore's activities were not limited to influencing State Department policies and placing his proteges in key diplomatic posts. As a best-selling author and book reviewer for the *New York Times*, Lattimore and a handful of pro-Communist and pro-Soviet writers flooded the book channels with anti-Chiang, pro-Communist books. Objective, anti-Communist books on the Far East were "killed" when Lattimore and his pro-Soviet colleagues in the book review trade "panned" them.[23]

The *Saturday Evening Post, Colliers* and other influential magazines were flooded with articles glorifying the Chinese Communists as "agrarian reformers" and other Soviet-inspired materials. During the 1943-49 period, the *Saturday Evening Post* published over 60 articles which promoted the Communist line.[24]

The American people were mislead. About 600-million Chinese were betrayed into Communist slavery. It was all done by a handful of American traitors and their liberal dupes.

With the fall of China, the second step in Lenin's plan for world conquest, was nearly accomplished.

Dean Acheson, one of the diplomats who participated in the

series of decisions and actions which ultimately lead to the fall of China in 1949 announced to the world in a speech on January 12, 1950 that Korea was "outside our defense perimeter."[25] Within six months, the North Korean Communists accepted the invitation and attacked South Korea on June 25, 1950. President Truman responded by committing the meager American forces in the Far East to the defense of South Korea. Once action was started the United Nations was asked to assume the responsibility for the "police action."

General Douglas MacArthur, in fighting the delaying action down the Korean peninsula, showed the same brilliance he displayed in playing for time against overwhelming odds in the Bataan Campaign at the start of World War II. Within two months, the Communists controlled all of Korea except for the small perimeter around Pusan. Meanwhile, MacArthur received minimum reinforcements.

In one of the greatest displays of military genius in history, MacArthur attacked the enemy's rear with an "impossible" amphibious assault at Inchon, far up the Korean peninsula.[26] Within eight weeks, the Communists had been driven pell-mell north to the Manchurian border. Six days later on November 26, 1950, hordes of Chinese Communist "volunteers" swarmed across the border and entered the fight. Even while under savage attack, MacArthur was forbidden to bomb the Red supply bases and lines of communication north of the border. The Yalu River bridges across which Communist supplies and re-inforcements flowed were also "off-limits."[27]

With the enemy operating from this sanctuary, the war was thrown into a stalemate. American casualties mounted in the hopeless effort. MacArthur protested the restrictions placed on his military operations by the diplomats and the United Nations.

He was "muzzled" by Presidential order on December 5, 1950.[28]

MacArthur maintained a discrete silence until April 1951. Then, in answer to a written inquiry from Congressman Joseph W. Martin (R-Mass)[29] MacArthur alluded to how military efforts in Korea were handcuffed on orders from

Washington. His letter indicated agreement with Martin's suggestions for using Chinese nationalist troops. He expressed the view that the battle against communism around the world would be won or lost in Asia. It was read to Congress on April 5, 1951. Five days later, Truman fired MacArthur.

The significance of MacArthur's dismissal was not understood by most Americans. Ostensibly, he was replaced for violating the "gag" imposed by President Truman on December 5, 1950. Much of the world understood, however, that future U.S. policy was to be one of "containment" of communism and not victory. Wanting victory, not stalemate or defeat, was the real crime for which MacArthur was punished.

When it was too late to correct the tragedy, Congress investigated. Top commanders in Korea, MacArthur and his successors, testified.[30] General Mark Clark, one of MacArthur's several successors said:

> I was not allowed to bomb the numerous bridges across the Yalu River over which the enemy constantly poured his trucks, and his munitions, and his killers.

General James Van Fleet, another Korean commander, told Congress:

> My own conviction is that there must have been information to the enemy [from high diplomatic authorities] that we would not attack his home bases across the Yalu.

General George Stratemyer, Air Force commander in the Far East, said:

> You get in war to win it. You do not get in war to stand still and lose it and we were required to lose it. We were not permitted to win.

General MacArthur told the Congressional committee:

> Such a limitation upon the utilization of available military force to repel an enemy attack has no precedent, either in our own history, or so far as I know, in the history of the world.

The American plum, which Lenin predicted would one day

drop into Communist hands without a fight was beginning to ripen.

AMERICA REBELS

America, however, was learning of some of the treachery in high places. There was an awakening. The story of Yalta and Alger Hiss unfolded. Harry Dexter White, John Abt, Nathan Witt, and other agents who reached top spots in at least six cabinet departments before, during and after World War II were exposed. The role of the Institute of Pacific Relations in the betrayal of China was disclosed. The web of subversion which reached into dozens of executive agencies unraveled. The White House Staff itself had been infiltrated as Lauchlin Currie became executive assistant to President Roosevelt.

As the Communist agents were exposed by Congressional committees, aroused Americans demanded action. They were in a fighting mood, ready to root out the conspirators. They'd had enough and were ready to stop the international cancer of communism.

Dwight Eisenhower appeared on the scene.

Eisenhower campaigned on his victorious war record, a winning smile, and the slogan "Let's Clean Up the Mess in Washington." He promised "peace with honor" in Korea. He piled up a landslide victory in the 1952 Presidential elections. Most Americans, whether they voted for him or not, believed and hoped that Eisenhower would clean up the mess.

The hero was elected. The Korean War ended. A public tired of conflict and controversy settled down to approve $40-billion annual military budgets. More billions were appropriated for foreign aid to keep the world "safe." Disturbing thoughts that communism might be more than a vague threat which required higher taxes were carefully ignored.

In short, the mess in Washington wasn't cleaned up. The public never noticed.

The first disturbing signs came with the signing of the truce agreement in Korea on July 26, 1953.

Eisenhower's "peace with honor" abandoned at least 400 American soldiers to rot, forgotten in Chinese Communist prison camps. Few people at home, except for the mothers, wives, and children of the forgotten few even noticed. Today, after 100 "polite" requests in negotiations with the Chinese Reds at Warsaw, Poland, these Americans are still in Communist captivity.

Even the "official" and sympathetic biographer of Eisenhower's first years[31] in the White House, Robert Donovan, admitted in *Eisenhower, The Inside Story*, that the Eisenhower truce made even more concessions than Truman had offered. The 1952 Republican platform had labeled the Truman plan "ignominious bartering with our enemies."[32] Few Americans noticed, but some Republicans were themselves critical.

Senator William Knowland (R-Cal) was asked in a radio interview, "Is this a truce with honor that we are about to get?" Knowland replied, "I don't think so."[33] On the Senate floor, Senators William Jenner (R-Ind) and George Malone (R-Nev) traded these remarks:[34]

MALONE: Does the distinguished Senator remember any change in State Department policy...by Mr. Dulles since he has taken office?

JENNER: I have noticed no change.

The venerable Senator Robert A. Taft (R-Ohio) said prophetically that Eisenhower's acceptance of a divided Korea would spark further wars by freeing the Chinese to attack anywhere in Southeast Asia. Within a year, the Communists had moved into Indo-China.[35] Using the Korean precedent, John Foster Dulles negotiated a settlement which split Indo-China into North and South Viet Nam along the 17th parallel. Today, American boys are paying for that appeasement with their blood in Southeast Asia's undeclared war.

Senator Joseph McCarthy (R-Wis) called attention to the "mess which remained." On a nationwide radio and TV broadcast on November 23, 1953, he charged Eisenhower with failing to liquidate the "foulest bankruptcy" of the Truman Administration. He asked that foreign aid to Great Britain be withheld as long as the English traded with Red China,

"the jailers of American soldiers captured in the Korean War."
McCarthy said:

> Are we going to continue to send perfumed notes? It is time that
> we, the Republican Party, liquidate this blood-stained blunder.
> We promised the American people something different. Let us
> deliver—not next year or next month—let us deliver now. We can
> do this by merely saying to our allies and alleged allies, "If you
> continue to ship to Red China...you will not get one cent of
> American money."[36]

Seven days later, the Administration said that McCarthy's
proposal "attacks the very heart of U.S. foreign policy."[37] It
was sometime before even astute Americans fully understood
this cryptic statement. Then it became obvious that it would
be ridiculous to cut off aid to the British for *trading* with Red
China when Eisenhower was readying a program of expanded trade with and foreign aid direct to the Communist
nations![38] British trade with the enemy and their aid continued.

Criticism of Eisenhower soon grew weaker. Eisenhower
planned it that way. The American people elected Eisenhower in 1952 to "clean up the mess in Washington." He did
not see this as his primary goal. According to both Sherman
Adams, assistant president under Eisenhower, and the "official biographer" of his first term, Robert J. Donovan, Eisenhower saw his mission this way:

> When Eisenhower took office in 1953 he had hoped that in four
> years the Republican Party could be reformed from its role of an
> opposition party and invigorated with more progressive leaders.
> He had hoped for the rise of what he called "positive" Republicans
> as opposed to "negative" Republicans.[39]

The "negative" Republicans were the "hard" anti-Communists in the Senate who pointed out that Eisenhower's
foreign policy differed little from the appeasing actions of
Roosevelt and Truman. They had been outspoken critics of
subversion in government under Roosevelt and Truman and
continued their warnings with Eisenhower in the White
House. Before Eisenhower left office they were all gone. Taft

and McCarthy died. Bricker, Malone, Welker, Potter, and others were beaten at the polls. Knowland and Jenner left Washington disgusted and discouraged. In all, Republicans lost 80 Congressional seats and 15 Senatorial positions in Eisenhower's eight years.

AID TO COMMUNISTS

With the critics gone, Eisenhower initiated foreign aid programs for the Communist enemy in Poland and Yugoslavia. Before he left office in 1961, Poland and Yugoslavia were to receive nearly $3-billion[40] in American food, industrial machinery, jet fighter planes, and other military equipment. The aid continued even after Tito, Yugoslavia's dictator, repeatedly pledged his allegiance to Moscow.

For example, in June 1956, Tito went to Russia for a state visit and said:

> The spirit of Lenin's principles of collective leadership are such that I am sure there never again will be misunderstanding among the nations of the socialist camp...In peace as in war, Yugoslavia must march shoulder to shoulder with the Soviet Union.[41]

Two weeks later, John Foster Dulles warned that if Congress stopped aid to Tito, we would drive Yugoslavia back into the Soviet camp. The few skeptics asked, "When did they leave?" But no one listened.

By the fall of 1956, Khrushchev and Tito had exchanged two more warm visits. Eisenhower then announced that Yugoslavian aid would continue because Tito had *clearly demonstrated his friendship for the west.* When a month later, in November 1956, the Soviets raped Hungary and butchered Budapest, Tito publicly branded the Hungarian patriots as "bandits" for rebelling against Moscow.[42] His American aid continued. In December 1956, President Eisenhower invited Tito to the U.S. for an official visit. After public opposition developed to the visit in America, Tito refused to come.

In 1957, Tito and Khrushchev met in Rumania on August 1 and 2 and pledged mutual cooperation.[43] On August 15, President Eisenhower announced that U.S. aid had "broken Tito away from Moscow." On September 17, Tito announced full support for Soviet foreign policy.[44] On December 9, 1957, Tito announced rejection of further U.S. military aid.[45] On December 23, American diplomats went to Belgrade and asked that he reconsider. He did, and military and economic aid has continued.

Since 1956, American aid has provided about half of Communist Yugoslavia's national income. In 1961, they instituted their own foreign aid program to spread communism to under-developed nations of the world.[46]

Poland and Yugoslavia were not the only Communists to benefit from Eisenhower's generosity. Achmed Sukarno received the planes, tanks, and guns he used to crush the last anti-Communist resistance in Indonesia from Eisenhower's mutual security program.[47] Since 1955, Sukarno's Indonesian government has received $479-million from the United States.[48]

Patrice Lumumba was widely known as a Communist terrorist in 1960 when he became Premier of the newly independent Congo in Africa. Eisenhower and the U.S. State Department gave Lumumba's prestige and his treasury a big boost with a Washington welcome and $20-million in American foreign aid.[49] Even so, he was deposed and later killed by the anti-Communist forces in the Congolese government.

By the time Eisenhower's two terms ended, direct economic and military aid to Communist and "neutralist" nations totaled over $7-billion.

CULTURAL EXCHANGES

Eisenhower's Administration developed the "cultural exchange" idea jointly with the Communists. Under this experiment, Americans go to Russia and return to tell other Americans about the "progress" they see and the friendly Russians they meet. In return, the Communists are supposed to come to America and learn about our superior system.

Congressman Walter Judd (R-Minn) told how it worked in practice:

Who goes over from our side? Anybody who wants to go. He may be the most ignorant and naive person...totally unequipped to deal with them:

Who comes over from their side? Any Russian who wants to? No; only those who are "reliable," which means so thoroughly indoctrinated and tested that their bosses are sure they can trust them. And further, they are skilled in presenting Communist ideas, trained in the dialectic—that is agents.

Who goes from our side? Farmers. Whom do they send? Agents. Who goes over from our side? Journalists—to get information. Who is sent from their side? Agents— to sell their ideas. Who goes from our side? Professors. Who comes from their side? Agents.

From our side, clergymen. Their side, agents. From our side, students. Their side, agents. From our side, businessmen. Their side, agents.[50]

What effect will this Eisenhower-conceived "people-to-people" program have? Congressman Judd tells us:

We will lose, not win, in this exchange of persons if the Americans who go over and see that the ordinary Russian people are friendly and conclude that therefore we can relax and trust the Communist rulers.[51]

In April 1960, the House Committee on Un-American Activities became so concerned about the misinformation tourists were bringing back from Russia and Red China that two special hearings were held.[52] Witnesses told how tourists are shown "model" showplace prisons—not slave labor camps. Visitors to China are shown special "show" cities, housed in special hotels with excellent food and service at very low prices. Churches are refurbished to impress important visitors. Visitors who return and report their experiences help to further break down the anti-Communist attitudes of the American people.

THE CLEANUP IS BLOCKED

In the 1952 campaign, Republicans had promised to uncover security risks in government who escaped detection in the hectic 1948-52 period when Hiss, Lattimore, White and others were exposed.

Three Eisenhower actions in his first term vetoed fulfillment of that promise.

The appointment of Earl Warren as Chief Justice of the United States was to have an impact in destroying the security laws of the United States not fully felt for several years. In the meantime, two Eisenhower executive orders effectively closed the door on congressional investigation of Communists in government.

After Warren's appointment to the Supreme Court, in the first eight cases involving communism in which he participated, he supported the Communist position five times, the government's case on three occasions. *After that, Warren supported the Communist position in 62 cases without deviation.*[53]

In the three year, 1956-58 period, the Supreme Court decided 52 cases involving communism and subversion in government. The decisions supported the Communist position 41 times, the anti-Communist position only 11 times. Warren's consistent pro-Communist votes were the deciding factor in the many narrow 5 to 4 decisions.[54]

By contrast, in the ten years before Warren's appointment by Eisenhower, the court decided 37 cases involving communism and subversion. Of these, 23 were decided *against* the Communists.[55] The Communist position was upheld 14 times.

Under Warren's leadership, the Court voided the longstanding sedition laws of 42 states. Communists convicted under them were freed.[56] The government was denied the right to fire federal employees who were proved to have contributed money and services to Communist organizations.[57] Schools and colleges were denied the right to fire teachers who refused to answer questions about their Communist activities.[58] In the Watkins decision, later modified, the Court questioned the right of Congress to inquire into and publicize communism and subversion suggesting that this "involved a broad-scale intrusion into the lives and affairs of private citizens."[59]

Apologists for the Supreme Court's decisions justify them as "leaning over backwards to protect the rights of the individual." However, when the *individual* was a Yugoslavian *anti-Communist* refugee, the Court denied his right to political asylum. Andrew Artukovic, who lived with his wife and children in California, was forced to submit to an extradition hearing based on political charges made by the Communist government of Yugoslavia.[60]

The Court set aside the discharge of John Stewart Service by the State Department. As was noted in the opening chapter, Service, a career diplomat, had been deeply involved in the loss of China but held his job. He was finally fired, eight years after an FBI arrest for violation of the Espionage Act. Without disputing his guilt, the Supreme Court ordered Service reinstated in 1956 with back pay of over $30,000. The Court's action was based on the technicality that proper procedures had not been used in firing him.[61]

The decisions of the Warren Court stirred thoughtful, earnest criticism from highly reputable authorities. In August 1958, the Conference of State Chief Justices, the highest judicial officials of the then 48 states, adopted a scorching appraisal of the Supreme Court and its actions by a 36 to 8 vote.[62]

The same month, the American Bar Association Committee on Communist Strategy, Tactics, and Objectives prepared a special report on communism and the Supreme Court decisions.[63]

J. Edgar Hoover testified before a Congressional committee that 49 top Communists convicted of advocating the overthrow of the U.S. government had been freed by the Supreme Court. Hoover said that a top Communist had described the Court's decision in the Smith Act case as the greatest victory the Communist Party had ever received.[64]

The New York *Daily News*, largest circulation newspaper in America, suggested impeachment of justices whose decisions consistently favored the Communists.[65]

EISENHOWER'S ROLE

Actually, effective Congressional investigations of subversion in government has been quietly stymied by executive order before the full impact of Warren's appointment to the Supreme Court was felt. On March 5, 1954, President Eisenhower in a "Personal and Confidential" letter ordered his cabinet to "shield" executive department employees from Congressional investigations into their loyalty, actions, and background.[66]

In practice, Eisenhower's order has meant that when Congress questions the loyalty or conduct of a government employee, the department head, and not the person under investigation, answers the committee's questions. Had this principle, known as the "executive fifth amendment," been used in 1948, Alger Hiss could not have been exposed, convicted and jailed.

The Eisenhower-ordered "executive fifth amendment" stymied congressional investigations but left one embarrassing loophole. In screening security files, Congress turned up employees who were "cleared" by department heads despite unfavorable or derogatory FBI reports. When the department heads were subpoenaed and asked "Why?" in open hearings, a public clamor for corrective action resulted.

This last "loophole" through which subversives in government might be detected was plugged nine months after Eisenhower's original order. On December 29, 1954, all security files of executive department employees were placed "off-limits" to congressional committees *by Presidential Order*. Congress then couldn't learn if an employee was cleared despite FBI warnings.[67]

Was there a real threat and danger from Communists hidden in government in 1954? Was there still a "mess" to be cleaned up in Washington? Or were Senators McCarthy and Jenner, Congressman Harold Velde and others simply "witch-hunting" in search of headlines?

Elizabeth Bentley, a former Communist, exposed the two Soviet spy rings in which Harry Dexter White, Lauchlin Currie, and about 80 others had participated. On May 29,

1952, she testified that at least two other Soviet espionage rings were operating in government. She had learned of their existence from her Soviet superiors, but never knew who was in them, or in what branches of government they operated.[68] Whittaker Chambers, the man who exposed Alger Hiss, gave collaborating testimony.[69]

Neither of these groups has been exposed to this day!

There are other proven threats which the Eisenhower Administration refused to correct.

On May 26, 1953, Senator William Jenner, Chairman of the Senate Internal Security Subcommittee, notified key officials *including President Eisenhower* that the American Communications Association, a union so heavily dominated by Communists that it was expelled from the CIO, was servicing communications lines to and from key defense installations in the United States and the cable facilities to overseas defense installations.[70] The warning was ignored.

Four years later, the Senate Internal Security Subcommittee conducted a study on the *Scope of Soviet Activity In the U.S.* Eisenhower's Secretary of the Army, Wilbur Brucker, testified. Committee counsel Richard Arens asked Secretary Brucker about the serious security situation:

> ARENS: Are you conversant with the fact that the North Atlantic Cable which carries important messages vital to the security of our nation is now serviced by the American Communications Association, a Communist-controlled labor organization?
>
> SEC. BRUCKER: I am aware of that.[71]

Neither Congress, nor Secretary Brucker, nor President Eisenhower acted to correct the situation. It still exists today.

It was in trying to uncover trails leading to the unexposed spy rings about which Elizabeth Bentley testified that Senators Jenner and McCarthy ran afoul of the Eisenhower Administration. The first major scrape came in August 1953, just seven months after Eisenhower took office.

McCarthy's subcommittee learned that a Government Printing Office employee was given a security clearance even though 40 FBI sources had reported on his Communist activities. This was before Eisenhower placed security files off-limits to Congressional committees. Administration officials did not deny the employee's Communist affiliations. Instead, they attacked McCarthy, saying that the security file contained *nothing like 40 derogatory FBI reports.*[72] This was a typical tactic. McCarthy's charges were rarely denied. Instead, the critics would engage in a "numbers game." In the resultant controversy, a smokescreen would be created around the uncontested fact that derogatory information did exist.

McCarthy investigated the Voice of America and the U.S. Information Agency. His finding that Communist literature and authors were being used to "sell America" were not denied. Instead, McCarthy was denounced by Eisenhower as a "bookburner." Attacks were directed not at the facts uncovered, but at McCarthy's investigators and their alleged activities in Europe.

McCarthy finally met his doom when he tried to find out how and why a man *known* to be a Communist, Irving Peress, could be promoted to the rank of Major in the Army Dental Corps. Before his promotion, Peress had refused to answer questions about his Communist Party membership on Army Security Forms. He attempted to set up a Communist cell on the Army base at Camp Kilmer, N.J. and tried to recruit military personnel into the Communist Party. The Korean War was underway at the time. The Army knew these things and promoted Peress.[73] McCarthy wanted to know why.

It was that simple, in the beginning.

McCarthy wrote to Army Secretary Robert Stevens requesting that the Army court-martial Peress *and* make an investigation to find out *who* promoted him and *why*. Was it a simple case of bureaucratic bungling, or were subversive influences at work? With foresight, McCarthy said in his letter to Stevens:

I realize that this letter will be interpreted by the left wing elements of press, radio, and television as a "fight with Army Secretary Stevens." Therefore, let me try again to make it clear that I have great respect for you both as an individual and as Secretary of the Army. I feel that you have served tremendously well in a most thankless job.[74]

In reply, the Army gave Peress an honorable discharge three days later.

McCarthy summoned Brigadier General Ralph Zwicker, the commanding officer of Camp Kilmer, N.J. Zwicker had issued the formal orders promoting, and then honorably discharging the Communist, Peress.

On the witness stand, Zwicker was evasive. He first said that when he promoted Peress and then discharged him he didn't know Peress was under investigation. Then he admitted that he had known. Under questioning, his answers became contradictory. He agreed that he *could* have stopped both actions but then said he *couldn't*. Finally, he said that he *couldn't* stop Peress' promotion and discharge because of *orders*.

McCarthy tried to clarify the cloudy situation with a hypothetical question. McCarthy was more smeared over the result than over any other incident in his stormy career.

Read the actual hearing transcript, reproduced here. Then check newspaper accounts of the incident.

MCCARTHY: Let us assume that John Jones is a major in the United States Army. Let us assume that there is sworn testimony to the effect that he is part of the Communist conspiracy, has attended Communist leadership schools. Let us assume that Maj. John Jones is under oath before a committee and says, "I cannot tell you the truth about these charges because, if I did, I fear that might tend to incriminate me." Then let us say that General Smith was responsible for this man receiving an honorable discharge, knowing these facts. Do you think that General Smith should be removed from the military, or do you think he should be kept on in it?

ZWICKER: He should by all means be kept if he were acting under *competent orders* to separate the man.

MCCARTHY: Let us say General Smith is the man who *originated* the order...directing his honorable discharge.

ZWICKER: I do not think he should be removed from the military.

MCCARTHY: Then, General, you should be removed from any command. Any man who has been given the honor of being promoted to general and who says, "I will protect another General who protected Communists is not fit to wear the uniform."[75]

Lionel Lokos, author of *Who Promoted Peress?* the authoritative and comprehensive book-length study of the Peress-Zwicker-McCarthy case, said of those few words:

Those words were to haunt McCarthy to the end of his life. Completely lost sight of was Zwicker's shocking answer to McCarthy's question. All that the public could, or would remember was that McCarthy had said Zwicker was "not fit to wear that uniform"—not why he said it or what provoked it.[76]

Why did the public lose sight of McCarthy's question and Zwicker's answer? From the *New York Times* here are a series of four typical news stories showing the distortion and falsehoods in the reporting of the event:

On that occasion, the Senator told the Camp Kilmer commander, who has been decorated 13 times during his Army career, that he was "shielding Communist conspirators" and was a "disgrace to the uniform." (NY Times, Aug. 2, 1954, pg. 7)

The *New York Times* use of quotation marks denotes, falsely, that they were reproducing McCarthy's exact words. Note the "hero" build-up for Zwicker. Three months later when the Senate was considering the resolution censuring McCarthy, the *New York Times* said:

Called to testify in the case, General Zwicker declined to answer some security questions about Dr. Peress because he said he was prohibited by Presidential order. *Thereupon*, Senator McCarthy denounced the General as unfit to wear the uniform. (NY Times, Nov. 8, 1954, pg. 13)

Note how two completely unrelated incidents are tied together. The real provocation for McCarthy's outburst is deleted. Who, upon reading this in the "reputable" *New York Times* could conclude that McCarthy was other than a complete cad? Who wouldn't look upon Zwicker as a poor, persecuted victim of McCarthyism? Two months later, the *New York Times* repeated the lie:

> Senator McCarthy denounced General Zwicker, commanding officer at Camp Kilmer, N.J. as unfit to wear his uniform because he said he would not answer questions on the Peress case before a hearing of Senator McCarthy's subcommittee. (NY Times, Jan. 6, 1955, pg. 14)

Two years later, the *New York Times* was still painting the image of the "monster" McCarthy brow-beating a dedicated soldier:

> Senator Joseph R. McCarthy, Republican of Wisconsin, charged during the hearings that General Zwicker was "not fit to wear that uniform." General Zwicker had refused to tell Senator McCarthy who ordered an honorable discharge for former Army Major Irving Peress, an Army dentist. (NY Times, Jan. 15, 1957, pg. 20)

The much distorted Zwicker episode, more than any other, crystallized public opinion on McCarthy.

In succeeding years, several Senate committees restudied the issue. Subsequent testimony showed that General Zwicker had committed perjury during the several hearings. The Justice Department, however, refused to prosecute.[77] To have done so would have vindicated McCarthy.

McCarthy's "trial", the harrowing eight weeks of televised Army-McCarthy hearings, was staged in an atmosphere of untrue, twisted, and slanted news coverage. In addition, McCarthy's gruff, cold, business-like manner, his deep, booming voice, and heavy bushy eye-brows were not made for TV.

His mistakes were magnified. His staff, if the reports were true, abused the committee's prestige and power, not an uncommon practice in Washington. McCarthy stood by them. His booming, "Point of order, Mr. Chairman," was ridiculed. The conflicting testimony and procedural violations McCarthy tried to question were ignored. Later study showed that Army Secretary Stevens was regularly guilty of conflicting statements which bordered on perjury.[78] But in the planned confusion they were ignored.

The basic issue "Who Promoted Peress?" was also ignored. The magnitude of the furor the question provoked leaves a lingering suspicion that more than bureaucratic bungling had to be hidden. Even Defense Secretary Charles Wilson admitted this possibility.[79]

However, by the end of 1954, McCarthy was censured and silenced. By 1957, he was dead. The liberals cheered. The Communists breathed a sigh of relief. Dwight Eisenhower's delight at the destruction of McCarthy is chronicled in Donovan's book, *Eisenhower, The Inside Story*,[80] and the memoirs of Eisenhower's assistant, Sherman Adams.[81]

The tragedy of the McCarthy story is that McCarthy was essentially right. What he said and tried to prove was rarely denied. It was simply buried in the controversy his charges provoked.

His targets were unsuitable for government service, if not by reason of treason, then because of gross negligence and complete naivete about the Communist conspiracy. That is all McCarthy tried to prove. His critics discredited him by disputing, not that guilt existed, but his presentations of the facts. The Communist-conceived slogan, "I like what McCarthy is trying to do, but I can't stand his methods." was parroted by millions. The inherent unfairness of such criticism is underlined by the fact that after McCarthy was destroyed those who "liked what he was trying to do" never completed the job by more acceptable "methods," or at all.

What were McCarthy's "methods?"

He drew unprovable, although logical conclusions from accumulations of damning and uncontested facts. In the resulting controversies, the facts were ignored or brushed aside and forgotten. It would do an injustice to Dwight Eisenhower, the Communists, and the fellow travelers in our society, the liberals, and the press to say McCarthy was his own worst enemy. He only provided the weapons they used against him. The case of Philip C. Jessup was typical.

Jessup was the State Department's influential ambassador-at-large and chief troubleshooter in the Dean Acheson period following World War II. In a Senate speech on March 30, 1950, McCarthy charged Jessup with...

> ...having pioneered the smear campaign against China and Chiang Kai-shek, and with being the originator of the myth of the democratic Chinese Communists.[82]

For liberals, this attack on Jessup was to become both the symbol and proof of the evils of McCarthyism. McCarthy could not prove that Jessup had *pioneered* the smear against Chiang, or that he *originated* the myth of the "democratic" Chinese Communists. His conclusions were based on a damning collection of provable and largely uncontested facts.

For 13 years Jessup was an influential member of the Board of Trustees of the infamous Institute of Pacific Relations, which was later to be cited by the Senate Internal Security Subcommittee as "a vehicle used by the Communists to orientate American far eastern policy toward Communist objectives."[83] Jessup headed the IPR's American Council for two years, and was chairman of the Pacific Council for another three years.[84]

In 1944, when the anti-Chiang drive started, Jessup headed the IPR's policy-making Research Advisory Council. If this group did not *originate* the anti-Chiang smears, it at least implemented their dissemination.[85] The same year, Jessup helped block the investigation requested by several IPR members who charged that the organization was becoming Communist-oriented.[86]

Jessup associated with 46 Communists and eight others in the IPR, including Owen Lattimore, who were cooperating with Soviet intelligence. He knowingly worked closely with an open Communist, Frederick Vanderbilt Field. Field was secretary of the IPR's American Council in 1939 and 1940 when Jessup was its head.[87]

McCarthy charged that Jessup accepted $7000 of Field's "Communist money" to finance IPR projects. It was later proved that the total actually exceeded $60,000.[88] McCarthy charged that Jessup belonged to and/or sponsored five Communist front organizations.[89] Four such affiliations were finally proved.[90]

Finally, Jessup appeared as a character witness for Alger Hiss. After Hiss was convicted, Jessup said:

> I see no reason to alter the statement which I made under oath as a witness in that case.[91]

The Tydings Committee, formed to investigate McCarthy's "unfounded smears" called Jessup to testify. He denied Communist Party membership.[92] Of this, he had never been accused. He also denied Communist sympathies. The committee accepted the statements as true. Senator Tydings refused to permit McCarthy to cross-examine Jessup. All the provable evidence was ignored, and the committee "cleared" Jessup with this statement:

> The subcommittee feels that the accusations made against Philip C. Jessup are completely unfounded and unjustified and have done irreparable harm to the prestige of the United States.[93]

To many, the whitewash of Jessup and similar "clearances" of others by the Tydings Committee *proved* that McCarthy was a sadistic, irresponsible, headline-seeking smear artist. The public retains this impression even though the U.S. Senate vindicated McCarthy to a degree 18 months later by refusing to confirm President Truman's appointment of Jessup as the U.S. Ambassador to the United Nations.[94]

Today, McCarthy is dead. Jessup is the United States representative on the International Court of Justice (World Court). His election by the United Nations General Assembly in the closing days of the Eisenhower Administration provoked little or no public dissent. Editorially, the *New York Times* on November 16, 1950, said about Jessup's selection:

> It is hard to conceive of a better selection than that of Philip C. Jessup for the International Court of Justice at the Hague, made by vote of the United Nations General Assembly on Wednesday.

The McCarthy story plays up the striking double standard and inconsistency in our society. A murder suspect can be convicted and executed on the strength of circumstantial evidence. It is extremely difficult or impossible, however, to remove an alleged Communist, fellow traveler, or incompetent from a government post using the same rules of evidence.

THE IRON CURTAIN CRACKS

By the end of President Eisenhower's first term, concern about communism was almost non-existent. Then, suddenly, Americans warmed again. The first possible break appeared in the Iron Curtain.

Aroused by American campaign oratory and Voice of America broadcasts about "rolling back the Iron Curtain" and "freeing the captive peoples," the Hungarians revolted and drove out their Russian captors.

During their five days of freedom, Imre Nagy's Freedom Fighter government appealed in vain for help. U.S. diplomatic recognition was requested. It was never given. The U.S. announced that it couldn't get involved.

The Hungarian affair was referred to the United Nations.

Americans sat up through the nights in early November 1956, listening to the stirring oratory of Ambassador Henry Cabot Lodge in the UN. They didn't know that it had no real meaning. When President Eisenhower sent the Hungarian affair to the United Nations, he was, in effect, telling the Soviet Union to do as it pleased. The Communists had the veto in the UN Security Council and could stop any action.

Finally, on November 4, 1956, the Hungarian Freedom Fighter Radio Station broadcast these last words:

> People of the world, listen to our call. Help us not with words, but with action, with soldiers and arms. Please do not forget that this wild attack of Bolshevism will not stop. You may be the next victim. Save us...Our ship is sinking. The light vanishes. The shadows grow darker from hour to hour. Listen to our cry. Start moving. Extend to us your brotherly hands...God be with you and us.[95]

The Hungarian Freedom Fighters conducted their rooftop vigils in vain, watching and waiting for American planes which never came.

Most Americans didn't understand what it meant when the United States referred the Hungarian affair to the UN. Is it possible that President Eisenhower and his State Department didn't know what they were doing?

They did know. They meant for the Hungarian revolt to fail. After four years of silence, Congressman Michael Feighan (D-Ohio) released the text of a State Department cablegram to Tito, the Communist dictator of Yugoslavia. Dispatched on November 2, 1956, the telegram to Tito read:

> The Government of the United States does not look with favor upon governments unfriendly to the Soviet Union on the borders of the Soviet Union.[96]

It was no accident, Congressman Feighan charged, that just 36 hours later Soviet tanks re-invaded Hungary. The Kremlin butchered Budapest, secure in the knowledge that America would not oppose them. The U.S. State Department had given its approval.

Would aid to Hungary have provoked war? It is unlikely. Khrushchev and the Kremlin have one overriding fear, the *simultaneous* revolt of the enslaved peoples. In November 1956, the satellites were restless. Localizing rioting had erupted even in Russia. The Red troops in Budapest deserted their officers and joined the Freedom Fighters.[97] For this reason, Khrushchev could not risk war.

He hesitated five days in Hungary. Finally, savage Mongolian troops were imported from Asia to crush the uprising. Even these forces were not committed until Khrushchev had tacit U.S. approval.

Three years later in a speech in Budapest, Khrushchev himself admitted the Kremlin's indecision on using force in Hungary.[98] Had the United States made a show of force, or even granted diplomatic recognition, the Kremlin would have abandoned Hungary. The United Nations, if the U.S. feared to intervene, could have sent observers into Hungary the instant the Russians were driven out.

When the Hungarians were condemned to die alone, the hopes and faith of millions of the world's most dedicated anti-Communists died with them. Our staunchest allies, the enslaved people behind the Iron Curtain now believe they cannot expect help from America. If Americans lose their freedom, the beginning of the end came in Hungary.

Any hope remaining behind the Iron Curtain was erased forever in July 1959, when President Eisenhower invited the Butcher of Budapest, Nikita Khrushchev, to America.

To protest Eisenhower's action, the House Committee on Un-American Activities scheduled hearings on the "Crimes of Khrushchev." The distinguished editor of the *Reader's Digest*, Eugene Lyons, testified. Lyons, a long-time student of international communism, said of Eisenhower's invitation to Khrushchev:

> It amounts to a body blow to the morale of the resistance forces in the Communist world. It's a betrayal of the hopes of the enemies of communism...The announcement of the invitation was a day of gloom and despair for nearly the whole population of every satellite country and for tens of millions inside Russia itself. What has been underway in the Red orbit, ever since 1917, is a permanent civil war between the rulers and the ruled...we have not merely been neutral in that civil war, but we have constantly by our policies sided with the Kremlin against its victims.[99]

Khrushchev accepted Eisenhower's invitation and toured American cities. Proper "precautions" were taken so that irate friends and relatives of the dead of Budapest, the refugees from Poland, and patriotic Americans could not get near enough to the Communist dictator to cause "tensions." It was to the credit of most Americans that, outside of government circles, Khrushchev was greeted with stony silence.

Before Khrushchev arrived, the House Committee on Un-American Activities completed its documentation of Khrushchev's bloody record as Stalin's most trusted killer. In seven volumes, it showed:

> Khrushchev personally conceived and executed the mass starvation and liquidation of six to eight million Ukrainians in the early 1930's.[100]

Khrushchev was the chief executioner for the bloody Moscow purge trials in 1936. He supervised the killing of thousands.[101]

Khrushchev, during a second two-year reign of terror in the Ukraine in 1937-38, slaughtered another 400,000 people.[102]

Khrushchev's post war Ukrainian purge liquidated or exiled hundreds of thousands to slave labor camps.[103]

Even after that bloody record had been starkly documented, Eisenhower entertained Khrushchev at Gettysburg, had his grandchildren photographed on the killer's knee, and announced to the world:

> This was the kind of heart-warming scene that any American would like to see taking place between his grandchildren and a stranger.[104]

This was the statement of the man elected six years before to "clean up the mess in Washington." Pictures of the event and Khrushchev's triumphant tour of 20 American cities were published in every Iron Curtain country. They carried the unwritten message, "Forget your hopes that America will rescue you. The Kremlin bosses and the American president are allied against you."

Of the entire visit, the Catholic prelate, Richard Cardinal Cushing of Boston said:

> For the past 25 years the United States has by and large been pursuing a policy of appeasement before Soviet Russia...if we are to save our country, it is clear we must halt this process which came to a new high point with the invitation to Nikita Khrushchev to visit the United States in 1959.[105]

CUBA

By the time Khrushchev came to America, the Kremlin puppet, Fidel Castro, had already been installed as the Communist dictator of Cuba. His rise to power was largely the work of the U.S. State Department.

Castro was supported by but a few dozen bandits and a handful of Communists in May 1957, when a career diplomat with a questionable record was named to head the Caribbean Desk in the U.S. State Department. His name was William

Arthur Wieland. Nineteen months later, Castro was Cuba's Communist dictator.

Castro's rise to power is documented in a series of reports issued by the Senate Internal Security Subcommittee in 1960-61. William Wieland's actions are prominent in the story. Here is a digest of Wieland's record:[106]

Before joining the Foreign Service during World War II Wieland lived in Cuba under the alias "Arturo Montenegro" (pg. 746). Wieland entered the Foreign Service when its Latin American Department was headed by a Soviet agent, Laurence Duggan. As a reported "protege" of Sumner Welles, Wieland "earned" four promotions in nine months and was assigned to Brazil in 1947 as press attache. The American ambassador to Brazil, William Pawley, filed reports on Wieland's "leftist" ideas and activities with Washington (pg. 736), after which Wieland was promoted again and transferred to Bogota, Columbia as vice consul. (pg.756)

While in Bogota in 1948, Wieland engaged in strange activities. The Senate report disclosed:

While the American vice consul in Bogota, Wieland knew a young Cuban revolutionary, Fidel Castro (pg. 806). Castro was a leader of the Communist-inspired riots at the time of the Foreign Ministers Conference in Bogota in 1948. During the riots, Castro captured a radio station and U.S. officials heard him broadcast, "This is Fidel Castro. This is a Communist revolution." (pg. 725) Both Wieland and Roy Rubottom, Assistant Secretary of State and Wieland's superior during the Castro era were in Bogota during the riots.

Former Ambassador Pawley testified that he was shocked when Wieland was appointed to head the State Department's Caribbean Desk. Pawley contacted high State Department officials and President Eisenhower to tell his story, but no action was taken. The Senate committee disclosed that *after* the State Department and President Eisenhower were warned of Wieland's background, the career diplomat's activities included:

From the time of his appointment to the key State Department post in May 1957, Wieland regularly disregarded, sidetracked or denounced FBI, State Department, and Military Intelligence sources which branded Castro as a Communist and showed that his associates were Moscow-trained (pg. 793, 797-800). In August 1959, Wieland "wrecked" an intelligence briefing given to Dr. Milton Eisenhower by the American Embassy staff in Mexico City when it became obvious they were going to prove that Castro was a Communist (pg. 798). For this action, Wieland was denounced to his face, with Eisenhower present, as "either a damn fool or a Communist" (pg. 798). Milton Eisenhower chose to ignore the incident (pg. 798).

Despite all the warnings from reliable sources, Wieland was continued in control of American policy toward Cuba. The Senate study concluded:

> Wieland is considered author of the fatal arms embargo which cut off munitions shipments to the anti-Communist Batista while Castro was being liberally supplied by sources in Florida and by Russian submarines surfacing off the Cuban coast (pg. 738). Similar State Department action ten years earlier had crippled Chiang Kai-shek's Army and permitted the Communists to come to power in China.

Wieland managed to remove all anti-Castro diplomats from influential positions. The American ambassador to Cuba, Arthur Gardner, who forwarded continual reports to the State Department which exposed Castro as a Communist, was replaced. He was prevented from briefing his replacement, Earl T. Smith. Instead, Wieland sent Smith to Herbert Matthews, a *New York Times* reporter and Castro's principal "press agent" in the United States.[107]

Ambassador Smith did not fall for Matthews' pro-Castro "briefing" and was also replaced as the U.S. representative in Cuba. Smith in testifying before the Senate committee exposed the role Matthews played in Castro's rise to power:

> Three front page articles in the *New York Times* early in 1957, written by the editorialist Herbert Matthews, served to inflate Castro to world stature and world recognition. Until that time, Castro had been just another bandit in the Oriente mountains of

Cuba, with a handful of followers who had terrorized the campesinos, that is the peasants, throughout the countryside.[108]

Matthews' articles likened Castro to Abraham Lincoln. At the time, Castro's small force of trained terrorists were committing horrible atrocities against the peasants to force their "support" in the characteristic Communist tactic used by the FLN in Algeria, the Mau Mau in Kenya in East Africa, and the Chinese "agrarian reformers." However, typical of Matthews' "reporting" at this time was a front-page story in the February 24, 1957, *New York Times*, which described Castro as...

...the most remarkable and romantic figure to arise in Cuba since Jose Marti, hero of Cuba's wars of independence.

Even though Matthews had used similar praise in describing the Communists in the Spanish Civil War in 1936,[109] a majority of the American press fell into line after his articles appeared, just as they had in depicting the Chinese Communists as "agrarian reformers" ten years before. The usually reliable Jules Dubois of the *Chicago Tribune* said in his friendly biography of Castro:

...Castro was to become the Robin Hood of the Sierra Maestra and was to pursue the same policy of taking from the rich to give to the poor.[110]

Edward R. Murrow of CBS-TV staged a highly complimentary "documentary" on Castro. Ed Sullivan made a brief, but spectacular trip to Cuba and returned with a filmed interview. Thirty million TV viewers saw Sullivan ask Castro such leading questions as:

You are not a Communist are you, Fidel? You are a devout Catholic, aren't you?[111]

Sullivan capped off the whitewash with this statement to the bearded Castro:

The people of the United States have great admiration for you and your men because you are in the real American spirit of George Washington.

Eighteen months later, Sullivan retracted his statement, but by then it was too late. Religious magazines, the book publishers, all communications media pictured Castro as a romantic rebel, a Robin Hood leading a fight for social justice. Even with all the press build-up, however, if President Eisenhower and his State Department officials had heeded the warnings of reliable intelligence sources, Castro could not have come to power.

Castro did come to power. He proceeded, in classic Communist fashion, to execute thousands of Cubans in bloody firing squad marathons. Even so, he continued to receive the praise of liberals in press and government.

In April 1959, Castro was brought to America and given a hero's welcome. He had well-publicized audiences with Secretary of State Christian Herter and Vice President Nixon. Nixon, to his credit, tried without success after the interview to convince Eisenhower that Castro was a Communist.[112] Assistant Secretary of State Roy Rubottom arranged the prestige-building appearance Castro made before the American Society of Newspaper Editors. The State Department announced that Castro was being welcomed as "a distinguished leader."[113]

The rise of Castro was as inexcusable as it was tragic. The State Department was warned that Castro had a long Communist background, that his supporters were Moscow-trained, that he was promoting a Communist revolution.

Eisenhower and high State Department officials were warned in 1957—18 months before Castro came to power that William Wieland was "leftist" oriented, and unsuitable for his high post.[114]

All the warnings were ignored.

Thus ended the eight years as President of the man who promised to "clean up the mess in Washington."

CHAPTER IV

WORDS VS. ACTIONS

Look at the means which a man employs; consider his motives; observe his pleasures. A man simply cannot conceal himself.

—*Confucius*[1]

UNLIKE THE ELECTION CAMPAIGN OF 1952 when Communist infiltration of government and appeasement of world communism were key issues, these crucial topics were largely ignored in the 1960 presidential campaign.

Tragic handling of the Hungarian revolt was given passing mention by the Democrats, but only in areas with high concentrations of immigrants from Eastern Europe. Castro's rise to power was discussed in a partisan way. The sordid story of the State Department's direct responsibility for hiding the bearded dictator's Communist affiliations, as disclosed by a Senate committee, was not mentioned.

Why?

Richard Nixon was not likely to dredge up the record of failure and appeasement of the Administration of which he was part. Under pressures for "party unity" anti-Communist Republicans remained silent.

The few knowledgeable anti-Communists in the Democratic Party were paralyzed by politics also. They knew that any loud voice raised against the dismal record of Modern Republicanism would have provoked only partisan replies, such as, "Well, we don't have an Alger Hiss in our party."

Candidate John F. Kennedy didn't turn the spotlight on the tragic actions of the William Wielands in government. Instead, when Kennedy became President, William Wieland was promoted to the State Department committee charged with revising security procedures. As was noted in the opening chapter, President Kennedy denounced the woman reporter who described Wieland as a "security risk" during a televised press conference and questioned his appointment. Kennedy stated that Wieland's record, cleared by the State Department, qualified him for the highly sensitive post.[2]

The party in power in Washington changed on January 20, 1961. The basic direction of American foreign policy remained the same.

JUDGMENT

John F. Kennedy himself set the standard by which his administration must be judged. On November 8, 1961, he wrote the foreword for *To Turn The Tide*, a published collection of the speeches and statements he made in his first ten months as President. He said:

> Strong words alone, of course, do not make meaningful policy; they must, in foreign affairs, in particular, be backed both by a will and by weapons that are equally strong. Thus a collection of Presidential statements cannot convey their true perspective unless it is realized or recalled precisely what they signified in committing the power and majesty of the American people.[3]

To evaluate President Kennedy's Administration using the standard he suggested required a careful analysis of his words and actions in crisis after crisis.

LAOS

In a widely publicized talk with Congressional leaders on March 26, 1961, President Kennedy promised that Laos, then under attack from Red China and North Viet Nam, would not be permitted to fall.[4]

After Kennedy's strong words, U.S. and Soviet diplomats agreed on a "peaceful" solution in Laos. The "coalition government" they proposed was the same "peaceful solution" which led to the communization of Poland, Czechoslovakia, and China. Prince Boun Oum, legal head of the anti-Communist government of Laos, was ordered to give Communists key positions in his cabinet.[5]

When Boun Oum refused, his monthly allotment of $4-million in American foreign aid was stopped on February 16, 1962.[6] Without money to pay his army, which was under Communist attack, Boun Oum was helpless. Within four months he bowed to joint American-Soviet pressures and a coalition government was formed. The Communists and the "neutralists" named 13 of the 15 cabinet ministers.[7] The pro-western, anti-Communist, Boun Oum, was out.

President Kennedy and Nikita Khrushchev praised the "peaceful" settlement in Laos.[8] Once the Communists were firmly established in the coalition government, American foreign aid payments were resumed.[9] U.S. military forces were withdrawn. The 10,000 North Vietnamese Communists and Red Chinese troops stayed in Laos in violation of Khrushchev's pledge.

President Kennedy's actions directly contradicted his promise to keep Laos from going Communist. They repudiated the sharp condemnation of "coalition government" he expressed on January 30, 1949, when as a young Congressman from Massachusetts, he said:

> Our policy in China has reaped the whirlwind. The continued insistence that aid would not be forthcoming unless a coalition government with the Communists was formed, was a crippling blow to the Nationalist government. So concerned were our diplomats and their advisers, the Lattimores, and the Fairbanks, with the imperfections of the diplomatic system in China after 20 years of war, and the tales of corruption in high places, that they lost sight of our tremendous stake in a non-Communist China.
>
> There were those who claimed, and still claim, that Chinese communism was not really communism at all but an advanced agrarian reform movement which did not take directions from Moscow.
>
> This is the tragic story of China whose freedom we once fought to preserve. What our young men have saved, our diplomats and our President have frittered away.[10]

In 1961, the diplomats whom Kennedy condemned in 1949 were named to run his State Department. They used the same methods in destroying the anti-Communist Laotian government as had been used against Chiang Kai-shek and China 15 years before.

Dean Rusk, who served in the State Department's Far Eastern Section during the tragic China period, became Kennedy's Secretary of State.

Rusk was a long-time affiliate of the Institute of Pacific Relations.[11] In 1952 while the IPR was being branded "a vehicle used by the Communists to orientate American far eastern policy toward Communist objectives," Dean Rusk, as head of the Rockefeller Foundation, was recommending a $2-million grant to the Communist-influenced organization. Two years later, Rusk defended Rockefeller support of the IPR to a Congressional committee.[12]

In 1949, Congressman Kennedy voiced scorn for "those who claimed, and still claim, that Chinese communism was not really communism at all but merely an advanced agrarian movement."

Dean Rusk was one of them. A full 18 months after Kennedy made his speech in 1949, and after Chinese Communists had murdered millions, Dean Rusk, speaking at the University of Pennsylvania, compared Mao Tse-tung to George Washington and indicated that the Chinese revolution did not aim at dictatorship.[13]

Even so, in 1961, President Kennedy appointed Rusk as Secretary of State.

To the post of Assistant Secretary of State for Far Eastern Affairs, Kennedy named W. Averell Harriman. It was Harriman who conceived and executed the policy of cutting off aid to Laos when the Laotians refused to put Communists into their government.[14] While President Kennedy was pledging support for Laos, Harriman at a critical point in the negotiations told members of Congress:

> It doesn't matter much to us, one way or the other, what happens in Laos.[15]

Instead of being fired for his handling of the Laotian situation, Harriman was promoted to the number two post in the

State Department. In July 1963, he was sent to Moscow to negotiate the nuclear test ban treaty on which the survival of America may depend.

Harriman is a long-time Soviet apologist. He was ambassador to Moscow during World War II. He was one of FDR's top advisers during the tragic Teheran-Yalta period when the groundwork was laid for the betrayal of China. As late as July 1951, after the Communists had completed their conquest of Eastern Europe and China, Harriman still defended the Yalta agreements.[16]

CUBA

As a candidate, John F. Kennedy's criticism of the Eisenhower Administration's Cuban policy led many Americans to hope that under his leadership, the United States would topple Castro. On October 20, 1960, for example, Kennedy said:

> We must attempt to strengthen the non-Batista democratic anti-Castro forces in exile, and in Cuba itself who offer eventual hope of overthrowing Castro...thus far, these fighters for freedom have had virtually no support from our government.[17]

On the morning of April 17, 1961, three months after Kennedy's inauguration, a task force of 1400 anti-Castro Cubans invaded Communist Cuba at Cochinos Bay—the Bay of Pigs.

The invasion was planned, financed, and controlled by the U.S. State Department and the Central Intelligence Agency.[18] President Kennedy approved the plan and promised air cover to the invaders. Two U.S. carriers, including the *Boxer*, were in the task force of five World War II Liberty ships and other supporting vessels. The carriers stood by, within easy striking distance during the invasion. Their decks were loaded with fighting planes. *U.S. News and World Report* in its September 17, 1962 issue summed up what happened. It said in part:

> Secure in this assurance of air support, the invaders went ashore...1400 armed men reached the beaches...In the battle that followed Castro's troops suffered heavy casualties...Castro's

tanks, coming up to the battle were sitting ducks for attack by air. Confidently, the little invading force waited for its air support to arrive. Its leaders had assurance of that support. It was provided in the pre-invasion planning.

Hours before, on Sunday evening, a small but potent force of B-26's was sitting in readiness on an airstrip 500 miles away, waiting to take off for the Bay of Pigs. Those were planes of the invasion force with Cuban pilots.

But those planes didn't take off. The reason: President Kennedy forbade their use.

That was the fateful decision President Kennedy made on that Sunday evening. He decided that the anti-Castro Cubans could not have the support of their own air force during the invasion. Without that support, the invasion failed.

PLANNED FAILURE?

Absence of air cover was not the sole factor in the failure of the invasion. Many other fatal "blunders" doomed the attempt to topple Castro. For example:

A near impossible supply problem was created when the CIA armed the 1400 man invasion force with weapons requiring over 30 different types of ammunition. The guns were purchased in second-hand stores "to avoid identifying the invading force with the U.S."[19]

Weapons and ammunition were supplied to the underground in Cuba by the CIA in such a way as to insure that they could never be used:

Some guerrilla groups were supplied with 30.06-cal. ammunition and "grease guns" which fired .45-cal. bullets. In other areas the CIA supplied .45-cal. ammunition to accompany BAR's (Browning Automatic Rifles) which shoot 30.06-cal. bullets.[20]

Planned coordination of an underground uprising with the Bay of Pigs invasion was so mismanaged as to indicate deliberate sabotage. To be successful, even with air cover, such a small invasion force had to be supported almost immediately by uprisings all over Cuba. Some of the reasons

why the uprisings did not occur were uncovered later. They
included:

> The underground was never advised of the landing date and did
> not know whether the Bay of Pigs operation was a real or diver-
> sionary invasion. Radio SWAN, the CIA's mysterious short wave
> broadcast station which blankets the Caribbean, failed to broad-
> cast the pre-arranged signals to trigger the underground into
> action. Instead, the station broadcast one conflicting and false
> report after another of uprisings in Cuba.[21]

> U.S.-based coordinators of the nearly 100 underground organiza-
> tions in Cuba were rounded up several days before the invasion
> by CIA agents and were held incommunicado by U.S. authorities
> at a secluded spot in Florida. They were not advised that the
> invasion had started—until it had already failed. By then, it was
> too late to alert their contacts in Cuba.[22]

Some details on why the invasion failed became clouded in
official accusations, admissions, denials, and contradictions.
The controversy over whether or not air cover was planned—
and then withdrawn from the invasion—raged for 18 months.
Then, the Senate Internal Security Subcommittee released
testimony given by Whiting Willauer three months after the
invasion attempt failed.[23]

Willauer, former ambassador to Honduras and associate of
Flying Tiger chief, General Claire Chennault, had directed
the *only* successful overthrow of a Communist dictatorship
anywhere in the world, the Guatemalan revolution in 1954.

On December 10, 1960, after President Kennedy's election
but before his inauguration, Willauer was recalled from Honduras and placed in charge of plans for an invasion of Cuba.
Working with the CIA, Joint Chiefs of Staff, etc. he formulated the overall blueprint for the invasion. He planned air
cover, both low-level close support to be provided by Cuban-
flown B-26 bombers and high level cover for the B-26's to be
provided by carrier-based Navy jets.[24]

Willauer held the title, Special Assistant to Secretary of
State Christian Herter. After Kennedy's inauguration, Dean
Rusk asked him to continue in this capacity. Within two

weeks, however, he was "frozen out." His CIA contacts were ordered not to talk with him. He was ignored in the State Department. For 30 days, Willauer's immediate superior, Chester Bowles, refused to see him. He was never consulted or "debriefed" by a successor for the background information, suggestions, etc. that Willauer could have passed on.[25]

Finally, on April 16, 1961, the day before the Bay of Pigs invasion, Willauer received an informal telephone call dismissing him from the State Department. He had been in "isolation" for nearly two months.[26]

Because the monstrous story has unfolded bit by bit, much of it largely ignored by the press, the American people have never faced the full implications of the first Cuban fiasco. Was the Bay of Pigs invasion planned to fail? Were young Cubans deliberately sent onto the beaches to die, with no hope of success?

The father of two of the boys who were missing in the invasion attempt wrote a letter to the Superintendent of Culver Military Academy in Indiana where they had gone to school. He said:

> This letter is to inform you that my two sons, Jorge (Culver '59) and Mario (ex-Culver '61) together with other Cuban men, were in the US-endorsed invasion attempt in Cuba during the past week. Jorge is a captive and Mario is missing. I want you to know and the world to know that all of us who once believed in the greatness of the United States feel that they and all of us have been the victims of gross, high official treason.

> I allowed them to go because they had an ideal...and we were told that they would be backed to the end by the United States government and its armed forces if necessary. We believed this because we know that this fight is not for Cuba or the Cubans. It is a fight for the very life of all Americans.[27]

AID FOR CASTRO

Just weeks after the disastrous Bay of Pigs invasion failed, the United Nations Special Fund, headed by an American, Paul Hoffmann, voted to give Castro, the Communist dictator of Cuba, a $1.6-million grant to improve his agriculture.[28]

The U.S. taxpayer is paying over 40% of the bill. The grant was one of 10 the United States is helping to finance in Cuba.

Within four weeks after the failure of the Cuban invasion, the Kennedy-Johnson Administration asked Congress for authority to give economic aid to the Communist nations of Hungary and Czechoslovakia—and broaden aid given to Yugoslavia and Poland under programs started by President Eisenhower.

Even though Czechoslovakian arms had been used to repel the attempted invasion of Cuba less than 30 days before, the U.S. Senate voted 43 to 36 to give the aid to the Communist enemy.[29] Of the 36 Senators who voted against the bill, 18 were Democrats and 18 were Republicans. A few months later, the Senate killed by a 45-43 vote another measure which would have barred foreign aid to countries selling arms and strategic goods to Communist countries.[30]

MISSILES IN CUBA

In the aftermath of the Bay of Pigs fiasco, recurring reports from Cuban underground sources indicated that Russian Communist troops, missiles, and jet bombers were being moved into Cuba.

After nearly a year of official denials, evidence of the buildup in Cuba became so overwhelming it could not be ignored. President Kennedy acknowledged the presence of Soviet troops and missiles in Cuba in September 1962—but assured Congressional leaders that they were "defensive types."[31]

Concerned Americans and Congressional leaders refused to be appeased. "Weapons are weapons," they answered, "and troops can be used offensively as well as defensively." As President Kennedy campaigned for Democratic congressional candidates in Cincinnati, Chicago and Detroit, he was greeted with signs, placards, and posters asking, "What about Cuba?" and demanding "Less Profile, More Courage."

Senators Kenneth Keating (R-NY), Homer Capehart (R-Ind) and Barry Goldwater (R-Ari), Charles Bacon, national commander of the American Legion, and others called for a naval blockade or military invasion of Cuba to remove the missiles and Russian troops.[32]

Such demands were labeled "irresponsible warmongering." President Kennedy applied this term to Senator Capehart on October 16, 1962, in Indiana. In a speech in Albuquerque, New Mexico, Vice President Lyndon Johnson said that Americans who advocated a blockade of Cuba have "more guts than brains... stopping a Russian ship is an act of war."[33]

Five days later, as public pressure continued to build-up, President Kennedy admitted that Castro did have offensive missiles and jet bombers. He ordered a naval blockade.[34] The American people rallied to his support. Khrushchev quickly agreed to remove his troops and missiles. Democrat losses in the Congressional election were held to a handful of seats.

To win the election, President Kennedy paid an appalling price. In the pre-election excitement and tension, few Americans read the full text of Khrushchev's agreement. The Communist dictator in his message to Kennedy, which the *New York Times* published, said:

> I regard with respect and trust the statement you made in your message on October 27, 1962, that there would be no attack, no invasion of Cuba, and not only on the part of the United States, but also on the part of other nations of the Western Hemisphere as you have said in the same message of yours.[35]

President Kennedy had given Khrushchev a personal guarantee that the U.S. would not attempt to liberate Cuba— and would not allow other forces to do so.

This part of the agreement was later denied by the Administration—even as it moved to uphold its guarantee to protect Castro.

Anti-Castro refugee groups in Florida were subjected to harassment and weapons were confiscated from groups training for raids on Cuba. Exile groups were refused time on radio stations in Florida for anti-Communist broadcasts to Cuba. Remarks derogatory to Castro were deleted from Spanish-language newscasts on Miami radio stations WGBS, WCKR, and WMIE.[36]

American naval forces were deployed in the Caribbean, not

to stop Castro's Communist agents from spreading out across
Latin America, but to prevent anti-Castro raids against the
Cuban coast. Under pressure from Washington, Great
Britain stopped Cuban resistance groups from using bases in
the Bahamas for raids against Castro.[37]

The President's shocking action in creating a sanctuary for
the Communists in Cuba—the unbelievable use of American
military forces to protect a Communist dictator from attacks
by freedom loving Cubans prompted many concerned
Americans to ask, "Which side is our government on?"

NO INSPECTIONS

For committing the Cuban captives of communism to permanent slavery, for betraying his campaign promises to the
American people, President Kennedy received no real
guarantee that the Soviet missiles were removed. He received
and accepted Khrushchev's promise. U.S. inspections were
limited to surveillance by low-flying aircraft which observed
"missile-like shapes" on the decks of several departing Soviet
ships.

Within 30 days after Cuba was declared "free of Soviet
Missiles," Carlos Todd, editor of the Cuban Information Service, released maps and a detailed statement showing dozens
of locations in Cuba where Soviet missiles were installed
underground in caves, hidden from aerial reconnaissance
flights.[38] Todd's evidence was ridiculed, just as his original
reports about Soviet missiles and troops in Cuba had been
denied by the Kennedy Administration.

Similar documented reports by other Cuban underground
groups were publicized by Senator Kenneth Keating (R-NY)
and other Congressmen. They were ridiculed by the Administration until finally the Senate Preparedness Subcommittee estimated, and the Administration confirmed, that a
minimum of 17,500 Soviet troops were based in Cuba,[39]
10,000 more than Kennedy admitted were in Cuba before his
pre-election "victory" over Khrushchev.

The surrender was not limited to the Western Hemisphere.
When Khrushchev "agreed" to remove his missiles from
Cuba, rumors circulated that President Kennedy had made

a "deal" to remove U.S. missiles from Turkey and Italy. The Administration vehemently denied the reports. In January 1963, after the "crisis" was over, the Defense Department declared U.S. missile bases in Turkey and Italy "outmoded." The bases were closed.[40]

The influential chairman of the Senate Armed Forces Committee, Senator Richard Russell (D-Ga) recapped the disgraceful chain of events in a television interview on December 5, 1962. He said:

> Three months ago we were pledged to see that Castroism in this hemisphere was destroyed. We have now been euchred into the position of babysitting for Castro and guaranteeing the integrity of the Communist regime in Cuba.

> We don't know for a positive fact that the missiles and bombers have been removed. I assume they have, but all we have seen is a box they said contained a bomber and a long metal container that they said contained a missile. We have not had on-the-spot inspection.

> The Communists start out on a course of action they know is wrong, and then when you call their hand they say, "All right, we'll stop this if you'll give us something over here," and they know they have no right to it whatever. And that is what they did to us in Cuba.[41]

BERLIN

In June 1961, President Kennedy, meeting with Nikita Khrushchev in Vienna, became the fourth American President to go to the "summit." He returned for a TV report to the nation, and said:

> No new aims were stated in private that had not been stated in public on either side...Neither of us were there to dictate a settlement...There was no discourtesy, no loss of tempers, no threats or ultimatums by either side.[42]

A week later, Khrushchev revealed that he had given Kennedy a three-pronged ultimatum at Vienna. He demanded that Kennedy get Western forces out of Berlin by fall, recognize East Germany, and conclude a peace treaty with it.

After six weeks of silence, President Kennedy appeared on nationwide TV on July 25, 1961. He confirmed that his original TV report to the people had been untrue. He admitted that Khrushchev had issued the Berlin ultimatums at Vienna. He made a firm promise that American rights in Berlin were not negotiable.[43] The President asked for expanded defense spending, increased size for the regular Army, and the power to mobilize reserve forces. He summed up the meaning of the crisis saying:

> If we do not meet our commitment to Berlin, where will we later stand? If we are not true to our word there, all that we have achieved in collective security, which relies on these words, will mean nothing. And if there is one path to war, it is the path of weakness and disunity.[44]

Seventeen days later, the Communists built the Berlin Wall, dramatically sealing off East Berlin in a flagrant violation of Western rights. Despite Kennedy's pledge, and a stirring speech by Lyndon Johnson in West Berlin, the United States did nothing.

Shrewd observers had anticipated that the U.S. would not stand firm. Within days after President Kennedy made his pledge to stand firm in Berlin, Senator William Fulbright (D-Ark), chairman of the influential Senate Foreign Relations Committee and sometime administration spokesman, suggested that perhaps some "accommodation" could be arranged. Fulbright believed the source of the problem was the mass exodus of refugees from East Germany to the West which was "embarrassing to Khrushchev."[45]

While the President was asking for "sacrifice on the part of many citizens" to meet the threat of communism in Berlin, his administration was approving a 600% increase in export licenses for shipment of goods to Communist countries. During the two weeks when the Berlin crisis was "hottest" the administration approved shipment of such "nonstrategic" items as $2.5-million in railway equipment to Communist Bulgaria, $1.5-million in synthetic rubber to the Soviet Union, and $700,000 worth of iron and steel scrap to Communist Yugoslavia.[46]

At the same time mobilization of 100,000 National Guardsmen and reservists was being considered to "meet the Communist threat," the American ambassador to Poland was officiating at the dedication of the world's most modern, most highly automated steel finishing plant. It was built for the Communist Polish government in Warren, Ohio, and American taxpayers "lent" the Communists $2.5-million to pay for it.[47]

Many concerned Americans asked, "Can these be the actions of a government which considers communism an enemy, which means to stand firm in Berlin, or anywhere?"

THE CONGO

The story of the Congo, like that of Cuba, Laos, and other crises of the Kennedy Administration, had its roots in the Eisenhower era.

The Congo received its UN-ordered independence from Belgium on June 30, 1960. The first prime minister was the Communist terrorist, Partice Lumumba. Although supported by the United States and the United Nations, Lumumba's regime let the Congolese Army degenerate into marauding bands of terrorists.[48]

Murder, mayhem, rape, and pillaging spread through the rich jungle land. At Lumumba's invitation, hundreds of Soviet "technicians" swarmed into the country. Racist "black only" policies were instituted. Cannibalism resumed. Fiscal policies which were to lead to runaway inflation were adopted.[49]

After 11 days of such strife and turmoil, President Moise Tshombe proclaimed Katanga province of the Congo an independent country. He said, "We are seceding from chaos."[50]

During the following 30 months, Tshombe and the people of Katanga were subjected to diplomatic pressures, economic coercion, and UN-conducted, US-supported military actions to force Katanga to rejoin the Central government which even after Lumumba's death was Communist-dominated.

Cyrille Adoula, the UN-US supported premier of the Central Congolese government, is labeled a "neutralist" but as a participant in Tito's Belgrade Conference in 1961, he voted for the vicious anti-American resolutions and announced he would follow the policies of the Communist puppet, Patrice Lumumba.[51]

Adoula's cabinet was riddled with Communists and pro-Communists. Soviet-backed Antoine Gizenga was vice premier. Gizenga is a Prague-trained Communist and successor to Patrice Lumumba. The Interior Minister, Christphe Gbenye, also trained in Communist Czechoslovakia, controlled the police. Gizenga supporter, Reny Mwamba, was Minister of Justice.[52]

Reporters covering the Congo named three other cabinet ministers as pro-Communists. The newspaper, *Uhuru*, in Stanleyville, the capital of the Communist province in Congo, boasted that Lumumbists won a majority of 23 of the 44 seats in the August 1961, elections.[53]

Tshombe rejected the US-UN ultimatum to join the Adoula government in September 1961, knowing that coalition government with Communists leads to eventual Communist control. This was his "last chance." The United Nations, with logistical support of the U.S. Air Force, attacked Katanga on September 13, 1961, to start an on-again, off-again war which was to last 18 months.

The UN action violated the Security Council's own directives on the Congo and Article 2, Section 7 of the United Nations' Charter, which provides:

> Nothing contained in the present Charter shall authorize the United Nations to intervene in matters which are essentially within the domestic jurisdiction of any state.

Even so, the U.S State Department defended the invasion as necessary to prevent Communists from taking over the Congo. *However, Egide Bocheley-Davidson, a vicious pro-Communist follower of Patrice Lumumba, was named as the Central Congolese government's administrator for Katanga.*[54] Michael Tombelaine, assistant UN director for Katanga, is a French Communist.[55]

Senator Thomas Dodd (D-Conn) protested on the Senate floor and declared that it...

...is not the business of the UN to go about overthrowing anti-Communist governments...It is difficult to believe that this action was taken in simple innocence.[56]

Congressman Donald C. Bruce (R-Ind) gave this evaluation:

I charge that the U.S. State Department...is acquiescing in the Communist takeover of the Congo. I fully realize the seriousness of that statement...I make no charges of treason. I cannot prove any. I simply say that over a period of years the tragic growth of communism and its victories in one area after another of the world forms a consistent pattern. What is wrong with our State Department?[57]

During the 18 month on-again, off-again war against Katanga, the United Nations committed unbelievable atrocities. At one point, uncivilized and untrained bands of Congolese soldiers, including Communist supporters of Antoine Gizenga were transported to Katanga by the UN in US planes and unleashed. The two-week orgy of mass murder, rape, pillage, and cannibalism they carried out under the UN flag with the United States paying the bill is unequaled in modern times.[58]

Hospitals, schools, missions, and homes were made targets for UN bombs and mortar fire on December 7-8, 1961. UN troops fired on ambulances; bayoneted helpless infants; and slaughtered women and children, both black and white.[59] Senator Dodd, who was in the Congo at the time, returned to report to the Senate:

The UN has brought the chaos and bloodshed of the North Congo into areas where there was complete public order so long as they were administered by the Tshombe government.[60]

Most UN members refused to pay special assessments for the actions which violated the UN Charter and could only aid the Communists. The UN ran out of money to wage the costly war and a truce was negotiated. Thomas J. Hamilton, UN correspondent of the *New York Times*, explained the situation in his March 11, 1962, report:

It is to be suspected that U Thant, the Acting Secretary General of the United Nations, is not moving against Mr. Tshombe at this stage for fear of jeopardizing Congressional authorization of $100-million of United Nations bonds by the United States.

Hamilton's speculation was correct. Once the U.S. Congress approved the "bond" purchase in September 1962, the UN again moved into action. In a surprise "defensive action," UN forces destroyed the Katanga Air Force *on the ground* in early December 1962. Adlai Stevenson, U. S. ambassador to the United Nations, announced continued U. S. support for the UN Congo operation. He said that the people of Katanga had "no right to self determination." Over Christmas weekend, the uncivilized butchering of helpless children and civilians which marked United Nations action a year earlier was renewed. In Elizabethville, Katanga, officials of the Red Cross reported:

> ...United Nations soldiers moved into the hospital after being fired on from the building and machine-gunned patients in their beds.[61]

The UN-US action to crush Katanga was challenged by the world-renowned Dr. Albert Schweitzer, 87-year old medical missionary, philosopher and once staunch supporter of the UN.

Schweitzer, who has worked in Equatorial Africa for 50 years, called for Katangan independence, saying that the people of Katanga and North Congo have no common language, cultural background, or anything to make them a nation except having been under Belgian rule for hundreds of years. Of the UN-US action to force Katanga to "unite" with the Congo, Schweitzer said:

> One wonders how a civilized state can undertake such a thing...The mission of the United Nations is not to make war. Reason and justice demand that this foreign state (U.S.) and the United Nations immediately withdraw their troops from Katanga and acknowledge and respect in the future, the independence of this country.[62]

Schweitzer's call went unheeded. Tshombe's government was crushed and Katanga was placed under the rule of the Communist-dominated Central Government headed by Adoula.

Tshombe was the one native leader in Africa with the personality, intelligence, and diplomatic skill *plus* the respect of both whites and blacks to bring peace, progress and civilization to much of Africa. The Communists, the U.S. State Department, and the United Nations denied him the opportunity to try. The final chapter of the operation which the U.S. State Department said was necessary to prevent a Communist takeover in the Congo appeared on page 11-D of the *St. Louis Post-Dispatch* three months after Tshombe was finally subdued. It said:

> Premier Cyrille Adoula formed a new "government of national reconciliation" yesterday...Adoula brought a broad sampling of opposition members into the cabinet. Representatives from Katanga received four important posts. However, the nationalists who had strongly opposed Katanga's secession also gained strength. The National Congolese Movement, the party formerly led by the late Patrice Lumumba, picked up three new ministries to become the strongest single party in the cabinet.[63]

The Associated Press dispatch did not point out that the "late Patrice Lumumba" was a Communist terrorist nor that the National Congolese Movement is the Communist-dominated political party in the Congo.

THE DOUBLE STANDARD

The campaign which crushed Tshombe and the anti-Communist Katangan government was not limited to military attacks and economic and diplomatic pressures. After a lengthy study, the Senate Internal Security Subcommittee found that the U.S. State Department had conducted a systematic crusade of smears, harassment, lies and intimidation against Tshombe and his press representative in America, Michel Struelens.[64]

The committee's official report found that high State Department officials had...

> ...conspired to revoke Struelens' visa and deport him to prevent the Katanga story from being told in America.[65]

> ...released untrue stories to the press which accused Struelens of

offering a $1-million bribe to a Latin American country in exchange for diplomatic recognition for Katanga.[66]

...made public speeches smearing Congressmen who opposed the State Department's Katanga policy.[67]

...pictured all opposition to the UN brutality and atrocities in Katanga as the work of "ultra-conservatives" and those with financial interests in the Congo.[68]

The Senate committee questioned why the State Department denied the anti-Communist Tshombe a visa to visit America while granting royal welcomes to numerous Communist dictators and pro-Communist puppets. At the time when Tshombe was denied entry to the U.S., the State Department granted visas to Holden Roberto, leader of the Angolan terrorist movement, and Mario de Andrade, leader of the Communist faction among the Angolan terrorists.[69]

The Senate committee learned that de Andrade, as a Communist, was ineligible for a visa, until the State Department and Attorney General Robert Kennedy ruled that his visit was in the best interests of the U.S. and granted a waiver.[70]

In commenting on the double standard under which the State Department welcomes Communists and persecutes anti-Communists, the Senate committee in its report said:

> There is unjustifiable inconsistency in a policy which arbitrarily excludes friends of the U.S. who are not excludable under the law, while granting visas to known Communists and mass murderers, who are sworn enemies of this country, and whose exclusion is called for by law.[71]

Holden Roberto and Mario de Andrade were not the only enemies of the United States who were welcomed to America during the time when Tshombe was being persecuted and finally crushed by the joint UN-US action. Others were:

Dr. Cheddi Jagan, Communist premier of British Guiana, received a royal welcome in Washington and a promise of $200-million in American foreign aid in August 1961. The press and TV buildup of his Washington visit equaled that given Fidel Castro in 1957-58.[72]

After Ben Bella, the FLN terrorist, established himself as dictator of Algeria and concluded economic, political and military alliances with Moscow and Peking, he was invited to Washington. President Kennedy greeted him on the White House lawn, honored him with a 21-gun salute, and promised him American aid. Ben Bella flew to Cuba the following day and was pictured kissing Castro.[73]

Americans who contrast the crushing of Tshombe, the harassment of Cuban freedom fighters, the destruction of the anti-Communist government of Laos with the coddling of Communist dictators in all parts of the world should recall a brief paragraph from President Kennedy's inaugural address and wonder at its meaning. He said:

Let every nation know...that we shall pay any price, bear any burden, meet any hardship, support any friend, oppose any foe to assure the survival and success of liberty.[74]

In his first speech to Congress, President Johnson repeated these words of his predecessor—and pledged to continue the Kennedy's policies.[75] Will President Johnson follow President Kennedy's words—or his actions? Less than 40 days after Johnson took office, the *St. Louis Globe-Democrat* reported on December 30, 1963, that U. S. customs officials had siezed a boat carrying bombs that anti-Communist refugee groups planned to use against Castro.

INTERNAL SECURITY

Newspaper headlines were mainly occupied by Cuba, Laos, Berlin, and the Congo during President Kennedy's first two years. The rapid deterioration of safeguards against infiltration and subversion of the U.S. by Communists, domestic and foreign, went almost unnoticed.

The return to government of the old "IPR crowd" alerted some Americans to vigilance. Close observers and careful students of communism watched apprehensively during the first year of the Kennedy-Johnson Administration as:

President Kennedy appointed Dr. James Killian, Jr. to coordinate and monitor the most important government intelligence agencies including the CIA, FBI and 30 other military and civilian security agencies.

Killian's "qualifications" to supervise the agencies which are America's front line of defense against Communist infiltration and subversion include: (1) In 1947 he favored absolishing the Massachusetts legislative committee which investigated Communist activities and protested listing of organizations as subversive by the Massachusetts attorney general (2) In 1948, Killian opposed a Massachusetts law which would have banned identified Communists from teaching positions (3) He defended J. Robert Oppenheimer in 1954 when the Atomic Energy Commission withdrew his security clearance for close association with Communists (4) As President of Massachusetts Institute of Technology, Killian rehired Professor Dirk Struik who had been fired from the MIT faculty because he was a Communist (5) As President Eisenhower's chief scientific adviser, Killian was a major influence in having U.S. nuclear tests halted in September 1958.[76]

Another top security post was given to Salvatore Bontempo, a New Jersey politician. He was named to head the State Department's critical Bureau of Security despite a complete lack of any security experience—and a record of being indicted for criminal actions in disposing of surplus government property after World War II.[77] Bontempo finally resigned when Congressman Francis Walter (D-Pa) planned an investigation.

The State Department Bureau of Security budget was slashed, however, so that 25 security agents and investigators had to be fired. John W. Hanes, a former CIA official and one-time head of the Security Bureau, labeled the cutback in the vital force as "either incompetence or a deliberate attempt to render the State Department security section ineffective.[78]

In November 1963, the several years drive to destroy the last remnants of a security program in the State Department culminated with the firing of Otto F. Otepka, chief of the Division of Evaluations in the Office of Security.

Otepka was a veteran security employee and dedicated anti-Communist. He was fired by the State Department after he furnished the Senate Internal Security Subcommittee evidence to show that high State Department officials had lied under oath about the security matters when they testified before the committee.[79]

Dozens of actions breached normal security procedures. Among them:

Security investigations were waived on President Kennedy's orders for appointees to over 200 highly sensitive State Department positions.[80]

Fingerprinting of alien nationals entering the U.S. was abolished. The State Department explained that the procedure had been "an affront to Communist newsmen and UN employees."[81]

Dean Rusk ordered a Polish Communist admitted to the U.S. under the "cultural exchange" program, even though the Immigration Commission presented evidence that the man had been trained in Moscow to gather industrial intelligence information in the U.S.[82]

A return to the news of two names from the past, Lauchlin Currie and J. Robert Oppenheimer, along with the story of Owen Lattimore, related earlier, typify the approach of Presidents Kennedy and Johnson to security matters.

Lauchlin Currie had been FDR's Administrative Assistant for Foreign Affairs during World War II. In 1949, Currie left the United States and relinquished his citizenship to avoid testifying about his participation in a Soviet spy ring while on the White House staff.[83]

In 1961, the *Chicago Tribune* revealed that Currie was in South America administering the Alliance for Progress dollars the U.S. was providing to help "fight communism" in Columbia. The *Chicago Tribune*, after detailing Currie's participation in the World War II Soviet spy ring, said:

This is the man who is planning how the dollars provided by a country which has stripped him of citizenship are to be employed in Columbia. It will be surprising if President Kennedy doesn't find out he has made an alliance for Communist progress in that country.[84]

In 1954, the Atomic Energy Commission withdrew the security clearance of Dr. J. Robert Oppenheimer, the scientific director of the World War II A-bomb project. The AEC determined that Oppenheimer had contributed large sums of money to the Communist Party during World War II, that his brother, his wife, and his mistress were Communist Party members, that Oppenheimer had recommended an identified Communist for a job on the top-secret A-bomb project, and that he had lied to security investigators about Communist attempts to obtain nuclear data.[85]

In June 1961, the Organization of American States, of which the U.S. is the largest and most influential member, arranged to send Oppenheimer on a lecture tour of five Latin American countries. The State Department offered no objection even though Oppenheimer had no security clearance.

In fact, following the tour, Oppenheimer was a guest of honor at a formal White House Dinner. After this preliminary buildup, in December 1963, President Lyndon Johnson gave Oppenheimer the 1963 Enrico Fermi award of $50,000 in tax-free government funds. The award was granted by the Atomic Energy Commission in April 1963, with President Kennedy's approval.[86]

The *St. Louis Globe-Democrat* quoted administration officials as saying privately that the award was a first step in rebuilding Oppenheimer's "public image" and as a "test" of public reaction in preparation for his eventual return to a sensitive government job.[87]

One of President Johnson's earliest appointments was that of Abe Fortas as one of his top personal assistants. Fortas, a New Deal figure in the 1930's won fame in the late 1940's as a lawyer for loyalty and security risks such as Owen Lattimore.

Another of President Johnson's acts which caused dismay among concerned anti-Communists was his appointment of Chief Justice Earl Warren to head the commission investigating the assassination of President Kennedy by a Communist killer. The appointment of such a commission, headed by Warren, was suggested in the November 26, 1963, issue of the official Communist newspaper, *The Worker*. Three days later, President Johnson appointed the commission, so loaded with "liberals" as to build suspicion of a planned coverup of any leftist involvement in the killing.

The New York *Daily News*, the nation's largest circulation newspaper, was quoted in the January 3, 1964, *Time* as calling for...

> ...An all-out attack on Chief Justice Earl Warren's commission to investigate the Kennedy murder, plus a drive to persuade Congress to give Warren & Co. the heave. The *Daily News* editorial said:
>
> In view of the Earl Warren Supreme Court's long-standing tenderness toward Communists, any report this commission may give birth to will be open to suspicion of pro-Communist and anti-conservative bias."

OPINION SUBVERSION

The return of the Oppenheimers, the Lattimores, and others to the fringes of government service creates an atmosphere which encourages further disregard of security procedures.

In addition, and very importantly, it tends to demoralize active anti-Communists while conditioning the great majority of less informed Americans to believe that earlier actions in security cases were unjust "witchhunts," that the internal threat of communism has been exaggerated.

For example, the *St. Louis Post-Dispatch* criticized Senator Thomas Dodd (D-Conn) for questioning Owen Lattimore's visit to Outer Mongolia. The newspaper implied that Dodd was continuing an unjust persecution of the one-time State Department adviser. The editorial said, "Professor Lattimore was *stigmatized* by the *McCarthyites* a decade and more ago." It adds about Lattimore, "It was *alleged* he influenced the State Department to regard the Chinese Communists as agrarian reformers."[88]

The editorial ignored the Senate Internal Security

Subcommittee's verdict on Lattimore, which branded him "a conscious, articulate agent of the Soviet conspiracy."

Such twisting of facts and truth, the rewriting of history, has been termed "Opinion Subversion" by J. Edgar Hoover. It is one of communism's deadliest weapons in the battle against free men. Other actions of the Kennedy-Johnson Administration have similarly contributed to the subtle conditioning of the American mind to believe that "maybe communism isn't all bad." For example:

> A long-time ban on the importation of the products of slave labor was lifted by the Administration. American stores were thereby open to Russian crab meat, Polish hams, Yugoslavian and Hungarian baskets, Czechoslovakian glassware and Christmas tree ornaments. In the first year, Communist products worth over $100-million were imported into America.[89]

The trade was a two-way proposition. Through sales of woven baskets, clothes pins, and other non-essentials in America, the Communists earned the money to buy strategic goods here.

MORE TOOLS FOR THE ENEMY

As an example, in 1961 officials in the Commerce Department overruled Defense Department protests and issued export permits to allow the Soviet Union to buy machine tools in America for grinding the precision ball-bearings for missile guidance systems.[90]

Alert Congressmen stopped the sale on five separate occasions but the units were finally shipped even after the Senate Internal Security Subcommittee proved the machines were available no where else in the world.[91]

When patriotic Americans tried to learn which companies were trading with the Communist enemy, Commerce Secretary Luther Hodges, classified such lists "confidential" to protect the firms from "harassment."[92]

On March 17, 1961, with the approval of Secretary of State Dean Rusk, Treasury Secretary Dillon, Postmaster General Edward Day, and Attorney General Robert Kennedy, the President lifted a ban on importation and distribution of

Communist propaganda into the United States. The ban against *free* distribution of Communist propaganda through the U.S. mails had been imposed by President Harry Truman 13 years earlier.[93]

In nine months, an estimated 8-million *packages* of Communist propaganda materials from Russia, Poland, Czechoslovakia, and Red China were imported into the United States. Placed in the U.S. mail, *American taxpayers paid the postage* for delivering the Red propaganda to schools, churches, homes, and libraries all over the nation.[94]

When Congress moved to take action to bar importation of Communist propaganda, the U.S. State Department encouraged U.S. printing firms to produce the official Soviet propaganda materials in this country. Haynes Lithograph Co., Rockville, Maryland, for example, with the full approval of the State Department publishes the official Soviet propaganda publication, *USSR*, which is sold on American newsstands.[95]

ANTI-ANTI-COMMUNISM

Alarmed by the disregard of internal security safeguards, Cuba, Laos, and the dozens of other "incidents" during the early months of the Kennedy-Johnson Administration, citizens in all parts of America started intensive anti-Communist study programs.

Schools of anti-communism and cold-war forums, which sprung up in the last years of the Eisenhower Administration, were held in increasing numbers. It was at one of these schools, held after eight months of Kennedy leadership, that Senator Thomas Dodd (D-Conn) made the speech quoted in the first chapter of this book.

Unsolicited mail to Congress from the "grass roots" reached all-time proportions as awakening and angry citizens protested free distribution of Communist propaganda through the mail, trade and aid to Communist countries, and the other actions of appeasement.

The unrest spread, until, suddenly, the Administration accelerated what had been a quiet crackdown on anti-Communist information programs. The government's actions

were accompanied by a coordinated onslaught of highly inflammatory and grossly distorted attacks on the military,
anti-Communist leaders, and conservative groups in much of
the nation's press.

CENSORSHIP

In Congress it was revealed that speeches of military
leaders such as Admiral Arleigh Burke, chairman of the Joint
Chiefs of Staff, were being censored to delete anti-Communist
remarks. Use of hard-hitting anti-Communist films in
military education programs was discouraged.[96]

A military officer was removed from his command for showing *Operation Abolition*, a filmed documentary of Communist-inspired riots in San Francisco. The film had been
produced by a Congressional committee.[97]

Cold war anti-Communist seminars at which military officers were scheduled to learn about the Communist menace
were canceled at Indianapolis, Fredericksburg, Glenview
Naval Air Station, San Antonio, Shreveport, and the Panama
Canal Zone.[98]

THE FULBRIGHT MEMORANDUM

The isolated incidents began to form a pattern which indi-
cated a planned suppression of anti-Communist information.
Then, in late July 1961, it was disclosed that Senator William
Fulbright (D-Ark) had prepared a highly secret memoran-
dum earlier in the year which was the basis for the
Administration's drive against anti-communism.[99]

In the memorandum, one of the most extraordinary documents ever distributed in Washington, Fulbright voiced such
views as:

> Fundamentally, it is believed that the American people have little,
> if any need to be alerted to the menace of the cold war.[100]

Alerting the people is a dangerous step, according to
Fulbright, for...

> ...the principal problem of leadership will be, if it is not already,
> to restrain the desire of the people to hit the Communists with
> everything we've got, particularly if there are more Cubas and

Laos...Pride in victory, and frustration in restraint, during the Korean War, led to MacArthur's revolt and to McCarthyism.[101]

The Fulbright memorandum was a cynical appraisal of the ability and right of the American people to be informed on U.S. foreign policy. It brought charges that the Kennedy Administration had a "no-win" policy toward communism. The charges were to grow louder in the 12 months after disclosure of the memorandum.

Congress tried to investigate. The Senate Armed Services committee showed in testimony, which totaled over 3000 printed pages, that speeches were being censored, that military training programs on communism were being "softened," and that military officers were persecuted for tough anti-Communist views.[102]

The committee assembled over 200 printed pages of the anti-Communist remarks which had been deleted from just a few of the 1500 speeches which were censored during the last part of the Eisenhower Administration and the first months of the Kennedy regime. Senator Strom Thurmond (D-SC) cited ten speeches prepared by Lt. Gen. Arthur Trudeau from which anti-Communist phrases were deleted or softened by censors.[103] Deleted phrases included: "the steady advance of communism"..."insidious ideology of communism"..."the Soviets have not relented in the slightest in their determination to dominate the world and destroy our way of life."

Congress was unable to learn specifically who ordered the censorship because the Administration and its spokesmen took the "executive fifth amendment."

State Department and military censors were ordered not to answer questions about the censorship of specific speeches. Names of censors actually responsible for deleting anti-Communist remarks from individual talks were withheld from Congress by Presidential order.[104]

Censorship continues and it is not limited to military officers. Even Agriculture Secretary Orville Freeman, an ultra-liberal, was muzzled by the State Department. A speech he planned compared the failures of the slave system of agricul-

ture in the Soviet Union with the successes of the relatively
free farms in America. These references were censored.[105]

Other government employees felt the sting of the anti-anti-
communism drive.

Don Caron, a forest ranger employed by the Department of
Agriculture, was forced to resign from his $8000 a year
forestry service job rather than stop writing a column on the
menace of communism for a weekly newspaper.[106]

Caron's superiors in the forestry service stated that...

> ...the editorials reflect a zealous and almost fanatical patriotism
> and an active effort to awake the public to the dangers of com-
> munism...regardless of all else, the whole subject matter is surely
> controversial.[107]

Ordered to stop writing the column, which he based on
Congressional sources and FBI reports,[108] Caron resigned
from the forestry service.

Five months before, President Kennedy in his first State of
the Union message to Congress had said:

> Let every public servant know...that this Administration recog-
> nizes the value of dissent and daring, that we greet healthy
> controversy as the hallmark of healthy change.[109]

Under his Administration, words had no relations to action.
Those who dared to dissent to condemn communism or defend
America were censored, muzzled, or driven from government
service.

MOSCOW-DIRECTED

Concerned by the government attacks and the almost total
commitment of the press, radio, and TV to the drive against
anti-communism, the Senate Internal Security Subcommittee scheduled hearings. Edward Hunter was invited to testify.

Hunter is one of the world's leading experts on psychological warfare, and the author of the authoritative book, *Brainwashing From Pavlov To Powers.*

Referencing his remarks to the Communists' own publications, Hunter reported that the development of a healthy,

vigorous grass roots anti-communism movement in the United States was of serious concern to the Kremlin. Hunter showed that the vicious attacks launched against anti-Communists in the United States during 1961 were...

> ...a Red anti-anti-Communist drive, that was openly initiated, under orders issued to the Communist forces of the world, especially to those in the United States, through the Red manifesto of December 5, 1960.[110]

The Red Manifesto Hunter exposed was issued December 5, 1960, in Moscow at the conclusion of the strategy conference of the 81 Communist parties of the world, including the Communist Party, USA. After acknowledging the growth of the anti-communism movements, the Moscow manifesto ordered:

> To effectively defend the interests of the working people, maintain peace and realize the Socialist ideals of the working class, it is indispensable to wage a resolute struggle against anti-communism—that poisoned weapon which the bourgeoisie uses to fence off the masses from socialism.[111]

Hunter introduced articles from domestic Communist publications in which Gus Hall, general secretary of the Communist Party, USA, relayed the Moscow directive to Party members for implementation.

Hall proposed a "unity of the left"—a coalition of Communists, liberals, and progressives—to defeat the "fascist network" responsible for the anti-Communist movement in America. In Communist jargon, "fascist" is the label for all *active* anti-Communists. Hall called for unified attacks by the left on the leadership of the "fascist network" including Senator Barry Goldwater (R-Ari), the John Birch Society, Congressional committees which investigate communism, military officers, and those labor union officials who actively oppose communism.

The Communist Party chief disclosed the role that the Kennedy-Johnson Administration could play in killing the anti-Communist movement. Hall's article, published in the official Communist organ, *The Worker*, criticized some Kennedy actions, but advised the comrades...

> ...it would be a serious mistake to consider the Kennedy Administration as embarked at present on the fascist road.
>
> If the tactical problem is solved correctly, it will be possible to slam the door on the ultra-right, defeat it, and force a shift in policy upon the Administration itself in the direction of peace and democracy.[112]

Hunter analyzed the article for the Senate committee, pointing out that Hall employed "peace" and "democracy" in their dialectical materialist sense. "Peace" indicates a state which arrives when all sides accept communism. "Democracy" is the police state form of dictatorship existing in the Soviet Union.[113]

Within days after Hall triggered the attack on the "ultraright" the campaign spread rapidly. The "unity of the left" against anti-Communists which Hall proposed developed almost immediately. Hunter showed that within a week after Hall's orders went out, similar attacks appeared in major magazines, "liberal" newspapers such as the *Washington Post, New York Times*, and the *St. Louis Post-Dispatch*, and on the wire service of the Associated Press.[114]

In short, the tremendous smear campaign by government officials, the press, radio, and TV against anti-Communists followed the exact line put out by Moscow.

As a result of his study, Hunter predicted that the Communist effort to smear The John Birch Society would be followed by a campaign linking every other effective conservative anti-Communist organization to it. He pinpointed a book, *The Fascist Revival*, published by the Communist Party, USA, which purports to tell "the inside story of the John Birch Society." Hunter said:

> The virulent tone of the booklet, indicates that the Communist Party would like to create a new Pavlovian trigger word for this period in it psychological warfare, and believes "Birchite" might be put into the language this way, replacing "McCarthyite"...the Communists now seek to create a new scare word.[115]

Tactics of the press, leftist organizations, and the Communists in the 24 months after Hunter made his prediction attest to his skill at foreseeing Communist strategy.

KENNEDY ATTACKS ANTI-COMMUNISTS

The Administration's attack against those opposed to communism reached a peak on November 18, 1961. Despite Hunter's warning that the anti-anti-communism drive was inspired in Moscow, President Kennedy himself joined the assault. In a speech in Los Angeles, California, Kennedy said of anti-Communists:

> Now that we are face to face again with a period of heightened peril...the discordant voices of extremism are heard once again in the land. Men who are unable to face up to the danger from without are convinced that the real danger comes from within...They look suspiciously at their neighbors and their leaders...they find treason in our finest churches, in our highest court.

> But you and I and most Americans take a different view of our peril. We know that it comes from without, not within. It must be met with preparedness, not provocative speeches.[116]

FBI DIRECTOR RESPONDS

Just 20 days after President Kennedy made his attack on conservative anti-Communists, FBI Director J. Edgar Hoover set the record straight. In a speech on NBC-TV, he said:

> The Communist threat from without must not blind us to the Communist threat from within. The latter is reaching into the very heart of America through its espionage agents and a cunning, defiant, and lawless Communist Party, which is fanatically dedicated to the Marxist cause of world enslavement and destruction of the foundations of our Republic.[117]

Ironically, just two years and four days after President Kennedy denied the existence of an internal Communist threat in his speech in Los Angeles, he was cut down on the streets of Dallas by a sniper's bullet. It was fired by Lee Harvey Oswald, a self-admitted Communist.

President Kennedy's speech was full of contradictions. He ridiculed as "fanatics" those who say "peace conferences fail

because we were...deceived by the Russians." He voiced scorn
for those who attribute the Communist hold on Eastern
Europe to "the sellout at Yalta" and the loss of China to
"treason in high places." Yet, 13 years earlier on June 6, 1948,
this same John Kennedy made a speech which the *Boston
Globe* reported under the headline, "Kennedy Says Roosevelt
Sold Poland to Reds."

A year later, in the speech quoted in the opening pages of
this chapter, young John Kennedy said of the loss of China,
"What our men have saved, our diplomats and our President
have frittered away."

As President, Kennedy labeled those who voice the same
ideas "fanatics"..."discordant voices of extremism"...and
"sowers of seeds of doubt and hate...fear and subversion."

NATIONAL DEFENSE

In ridiculing Americans who believe that communism is a
threat internally, President Kennedy said that the real
danger "comes from without" and that "it must be met with
preparedness...to make more certain than ever before that
this nation has all the power it will need to deter any attack
of any kind."

Few Americans would disagree with the need for maintaining military superiority, yet, less than 60 days before making
his statement in Los Angeles, President Kennedy had
proposed a plan for the general and complete disarmament
of the United States.

The offer was made in Kennedy's speech to the opening
session of the United Nations on September 25, 1961. It was
formalized a few days later by publication of State Department Document 7277, entitled, *Freedom From War: The
United States Program for General and Complete Disarmament in a Peaceful World.*

Under the official, published, three-stage disarmament
plan, nuclear tests would be banned, production of nuclear
weapons and their delivery systems (manned bombers, missiles, etc.) would be halted, existing stocks of weapons and
atomic warheads would be transferred to the United Nations,

development of anti-missile missiles and similar *defensive* weapons would be abandoned.[118]

Use of outer space for other than peaceful projects would be prohibited, conventional armed forces and weapons would be reduced by transferring control over U.S. and other troops to the United Nations so "no state (including the U.S.) would have the military power to challenge the progressively strengthened UN Peace Force."[119] Even shotguns and hunting rifles owned by private citizens could be affected.[120]

Senator John Tower (R-Tex) took issue with the entire disarmament concept. In a speech on the Senate floor on January 29, 1962, he said:

> At a time when Western civilization is confronted by an extreme militaristic threat looking forward to world conquest, I think it is naive and unrealistic to be preoccupied with the question of disarmament. We know that the Communist conspiracy has no intention of co-existing with us. We know that they are bent on domination of the whole world.[121]

Senator Tower quoted an editorial from a Dallas, Texas, newspaper which labeled the disarmament document one of the most incredible proposals ever to emerge from the "foggy corridors of the State Department." The editorial concluded:

> As skeptical as I have always been of the measure of good sense and loyalty within the State Department I never would have believed that these people we call our diplomats could so completely and unabashedly advocate the surrender of American rights and sovereignty until this bulletin appeared...if more of the American people knew about this scheme there would be a nationwide uproar that would make the reaction to the Alger Hiss scandal look like another era of good feeling by comparison.[122]

Most Americans haven't known what is happening—and many of those who do laugh off the entire disarmament proposal. A typical reaction to the disarmament proposals has been, "Don't worry, they're just talking."

In the face of such disbelief, Senator Joseph Clark (D-Pa) attempted to "set the record straight." Clark "refuted" Senator Tower's statement that the Communists were not interested in co-existence. He denied that the disarmament plan was "dreamed up in the foggy corridors of the State Department." Clark said that State Department Document 7277, with its proposal for complete disarmament of the United States, is...

> ...the fixed, determined, and approved policy of the Government of the United States. It was laid down by the President of the U.S., John Fitzgerald Kennedy, in a speech he made before the United Nations on September 25 of last year.[123]

Six weeks after Senator Clark's statement, the Administration offered the Soviet Union a formal treaty incorporating the disarmament proposals in Document 7277.[124] Clark further stated that the proposal for total and complete disarmament is not only the policy of the Kennedy-Johnson Administration but...

> ...is also the kind of program which Congress envisioned when, last summer, it passed the statute creating the Arms Control and Disarmament Agency.[125]

Congress passed Public Law 87-297 creating the agency one day after Kennedy made his disarmament proposals to the United Nations. It is charged with managing disarmament negotiations, conducting technical research in the disarmament field, and instituting a public relations campaign to "condition" the American people to accept disarmament.[126]

During its first year of operation, the Agency reported that it was unable to fill all requests for information on disarmament, but...

> ...Agency officials did participate in over 100 meetings, panel discussions and study groups in 1962. In addition, such informational materials as articles for commercial journals, scripts for educational television programs, network and local TV and radio programs were prepared and briefings and interviews were arranged with agency officials for correspondents of public information media.[127]

The degree of danger inherent in the operation of the Disarmament Agency, apart from its propaganda function, is a subject of controversy even among conservatives. Buried in the routine "enabling" provisions of the Act, Section 47 (b) grants authority to the President to transfer to the Disarmament Administration *any activities or facilities of any Government Agency.* Many believe that under this provision, and subject only to the cumbersome Congressional veto, American weapons could be placed under the control of the Director of the Disarmament Agency.

That such fears are not completely unfounded was shown on March 9, 1963, when Senator Barry Goldwater (R-Ari) disclosed that the Disarmament Agency was considering a massive American-Soviet "bonfire" in which 30 American Air Force B-47 bombers and 30 Soviet Badger bombers would be destroyed. The Agency denied Goldwater's charge. However, two days later, Secretary of State Dean Rusk admitted that such a project was being "considered."[128] Such destruction of weapons is provided for in Section A, 2c of Stage I of the Draft Treaty on disarmament submitted to the Soviet Union at the Disarmament Conference in Geneva on April 18, 1962.[129]

The "bomber burning" incident is one of many indications that the disarmament proposals of State Department Document 7277 are being implemented unilaterally by the United States government. The actions are taken surreptitiously with each step given a logical justification. Only by carefully evaluating the erosion of the overall U.S military position over a several year period does the pattern become obvious. In the 1961-63 period, the Kennedy-Johnson Administration took these actions:

> ...refused to spend money appropriated by Congress for a speed up in the development of the high-flying, supersonic RS-70 nuclear bomber.[130]

Defense Secretary McNamara justified his defiance of Congressional mandates by explaining that the RS-70 was unnecessary *because missiles and conventional jet bombers equipped with the Skybolt air-to-ground missile would do the job cheaper.*

This rather logical explanation was poked full of holes when the Administration stopped all production of long range manned bombers and canceled production of the Skybolt missile, over the objections of competent military authorities.[131] In addition it was announced that...

...manned bombers (B-47's and B-52's) stationed at air bases in Morocco, France, England and Spain would return to the U.S. and these bases would be closed.[132]

At about the same time in the spring of 1963, 45 American missile launching bases in Turkey and Italy were declared "obsolete" and closed.[133]

Each of these decisions—cancellation of the Skybolt missile project, the halt in production of manned bombers, the closing of bomber and missile bases in Europe—were justified by the Kennedy-Johnson Administration on the basis that soon to be available Minuteman missiles and the nuclear missile-firing Polaris submarine provided adequate deterrents against Communist attacks. There were three major discrepancies in these comforting words:

Planned deployment of Minuteman missiles was reduced from 2000 to 950; negotiations for Polaris submarine bases in Spain and Italy bogged down; loss of the one known Polaris base in Northern Scotland is likely when the Labor Government takes power in England.[134]

And so it goes. The RS-70 was abandoned for the manned bomber and the Skybolt missile—the bomber and the Skybolt are canceled to be replaced by Minuteman missiles and the Polaris submarine, which are in turn cutback.

Conventional armed forces and purely defensive weapons systems have not been immune. Defense Secretary McNamara admitted to Congress that his plan to "streamline" the National Guard and Organized Reserves, in effect, eliminated eight National Guard divisions and 750 units of the Organized Reserve.[135]

The Nike-Zeus anti-missile missile was designed to seek out and destroy enemy missiles high in outer space before they could reach American cities. The Nike-Zeus had its first successful tests in November 1961.[136] Since then, it has been shelved.[137]

Defense Secretary McNamara explained to Congressional critics that a more sophisticated defense system against missiles, the Nike-X, was on the drawing boards. However, the Nike-X, if it works, won't be operational until 1969. Meanwhile, American cities are defenseless against possible Soviet missile attacks.

While the U.S. Defense "high command" was debating whether to proceed with development of the Nike-Zeus or the Nike-X, the Communists developed their own anti-missile missile (or stole the design of the tested Nike-Zeus). On April 17, 1963, the Defense Department admitted that the Soviet anti-missile missiles deployed around Leningrad have the capability to intercept and destroy American Polaris missiles.[138]

Once the Soviet Union protects its cities against retaliatory attacks by American missiles, it can, at any time, issue the ultimatum, "Surrender or Die." That is the trap into which the Kennedy-Johnson Administration is leading America. Khrushchev expects that America will surrender. Robert Frost, the American poet, interviewed Khrushchev in 1962 and reported:

> Khrushchev said American liberals were too soft to fight.[139]

Senator Barry Goldwater (R-Ari) summed up what has been happening. On March 14, 1963, he said:

> Not one new weapons system has been proposed under the present Administration. The RS-70 has been abandoned. Skybolt has been dropped, manned bombers are being phased out. Nike-Zeus is being delayed, the Dyna-Soar is being re-examined for possible junking. This is not only stagnation, *this is Disarmament*.

While it was all happening President Kennedy was denouncing anti-Communist "extremists" who look suspiciously at their leaders. He was telling the American people that the real Communist threat "comes from without" and "must be met with preparedness...to make more certain than ever before that this nation has all the power it will need to deter an attack of any kind."

President Johnson appears committed to continuing the dismantlement of the American military establishment. Among his first acts as President were approvals of the complete abandonment of the B-70 and the Dyna-Soar. Within ten days after he took office, Johnson's administration announced the closing of 30 military bases in the United States and overseas—and the strategic navy shipbuilding and maintenance yards in Philadelphia and Boston. By the end of 1963, Johnson ordered withdrawal of the last strategic bombers based in Japan—and a return to the U. S. of other strategic Air Force units in the Far East.[140]

NUCLEAR TEST BAN

While American striking forces were being dismantled, American superiority in nuclear know-how was also being eroded away at the nuclear test ban talks in Geneva. While the United States talked for five years, the Communists tested.

In the talks, under both Kennedy and Eisenhower, there were massive concessions to the Communists, a continual erosion of the American position. For example:

> In a series of concessions, the U.S. agreed to accept fewer and fewer "monitoring stations" to detect possible nuclear test cheating. Over a five year period, demands for control stations were reduced from 180 to 8.[141]

After reducing the number of monitoring stations far below the minimum "safe" level, further concessions were made:

> The U.S. agreed that checks in the Soviet Union could be made by "tamper-proof" black boxes—scientific instruments *which the Communists would be trusted to install and maintain themselves.*[142]

Under the original proposals, whenever control systems detected radio-active fallout, or suspicious earth tremors, an international team of experts would make an on-site inspection of the area to determine whether an illegal nuclear explosion had occurred.

The U.S. agreed that the inspections could be made by teams of "experts" from Ghana, Outer Mongolia, or other Communist satellites, without American or western representatives participating. The most serious concession involved the administration of whatever inspection and control organization might ultimately be established:

> A Communist request for veto power over the budget and personnel of the international control and inspection organization was granted by the U.S., making any final agreement worthless because the Soviet Union could stop *any* spending for inspection.[143]

The implications of these and other concessions became so ominous that on February 21, 1963, Senator Thomas Dodd (D-Conn) made a lengthy speech in the Senate outlining the dangers. He said:

> We have made these concessions piecemeal, so that our position at any given moment has never been too different from our position three months previously. It is only by going back to the beginning and laying our concessions end to end that the terrifying scope of our retreat becomes apparent.[144]

The negotiations and concessions continued even after the Communists showed their bad faith by breaking the three year "gentleman's agreement" not to test while the talks were proceeding. On September 1, 1961, in the midst of negotiations, the Communists embarked on the most massive series of tests in history, climaxing on October 20, 1961, with the explosion of a 58-megaton bomb. Experts said the preparations for the tests had been underway for at least one year— while Soviet diplomats sat at the conference table "negotiating" a test ban. On November 8, 1961, President Kennedy told the American people:

> The Soviet Union prepared to test (nuclear weapons) while we were at the table negotiating with them. If they fooled us once, it is their fault, if they fool us twice, it is our fault.[145]

On March 2, 1962, Kennedy told a nationwide television audience:

> We know enough about broken negotiations, secret preparations, and the (Soviet) advantages gained from a long test series never to offer again an *uninspected* moratorium.[146]

Despite the President's words, the talks and concessions continued. Even so, the Communists, strangely, wouldn't accept a treaty in which they, in effect, would determine whether or not they were cheating. They held out for a no-inspection system at all. On March 8, 1963, Senator Barry Goldwater (R-Ari) in a Senate speech asked whether...

> ...the Administration is engaged in an attempt to arrange a test ban without any inspections...when you look at the concessions we have already made in this area, you can see we are certainly headed in that direction.[147]

Eight months before, Senator Strom Thurmond (D-SC) predicted the ultimate outcome. He said:

> ...we should have learned long ago in trying to negotiate with the Communists—that the Soviets never accept our initial offers of appeasement. They know we will be back again, with hat in hand, making further concessions toward their position.[148]

Senator Thurmond was right. In July 1963, the United States agreed to a *no-inspection* nuclear test ban treaty which prohibited tests in outer space, under water, and in the atmosphere.[149]

The treaty was hailed as a "great break in the cold war." President Kennedy called it "the first step toward limiting the nuclear arms race."[150]

Actually, the treaty was nearly identical with one proposed by the Communists 18 months earlier. On November 27, 1961, the Soviet Union offered the U.S. a treaty providing that...

> ...all testing in the atmosphere, in outer space, and under water should be banned indefinitely. No international detection system is required because enough countries have systems adequate to detect all nuclear explosions.[151]

U.S. experts rejected that pact, contending that not all atmospheric tests could be detected, that detection of underwater tests was "extremely difficult," and that nuclear blasts in outer space could be effectively shielded by using test rockets with lead "wings" to absorb radiation.[152]

American Secretary of State Dean Rusk assailed the Soviet plan for an uninspected test ban as a...

> ...transparent propaganda gesture put forward in a vain hope to mislead and deceive world public opinion.[153]

Eighteen months later, all the earlier technical objections were brushed aside, and Dean Rusk asked the U.S. Senate to ratify a nearly identical no-inspection test ban treaty, saying:

> If the promise of this treaty can be realized, if we can now take even this one frail step along a new course, the frail and fearful mankind may find another step and another until confidence replaces terror and hope takes over from despair.[154]

The drastic change in Rusk's position—and that of the Kennedy Administration—was in accord with the strategy proposed by Paul H. Nitze, who was Kennedy's Assistant Secretary of Defense for International Affairs and President Johnson's first Secretary of the Navy. In an essay published just before his appointment in 1961, Nitze indicated that many believe that continuing negotiations with the Communists are vital to survival. Having accepted this viewpoint, Nitze said, the only logical corollary is that...

> ...if we cannot get them to agree to our viewpoint, we must accept theirs if we are to survive.[155]

That's what Averell Harriman did in making a no-inspection test ban agreement in Moscow in July 1963. The test ban is only the first step. A few days before that agreement was made. William C. Foster, director of the Arms Control and Disarmament Agency, said:

> Everyone feels that if we can't negotiate a test ban—when we are so close—that we can't negotiate any other part of the disarmament program.[156]

The Administration looked upon Khrushchev's agreement

and his apparent willingness to discuss other parts of the disarmament program as a "hopeful sign." President Kennedy said:

> There is hope that it may lead to further measures to arrest and control the dangerous competition for increasingly destructive weapons.[157]

Careful students of communism were not so hopeful. They recalled the prediction made by Dimtri L. Manuilski at the Lenin School of Political Warfare in Moscow in 1930. A student, Zack Kornfeld, later broke with the Communist Party and told the story. He reported that Manuilski, who later served as Russia's UN delegate, told the class:

> War to the hilt between communism and capitalism is inevitable. Today, of course, we are not strong enough to attack. Our time will come in 20 to 30 years. To win, we shall need the element of surprise. The bourgeoisie will have to be put to sleep. So we shall begin by launching the most spectacular peace movement on record. There will be electrifying overtures and unheard of concessions. The capitalist countries, stupid and decadent, will rejoice to cooperate in their own destruction. They will leap at another chance to be friends. As soon as their guard is down, we will smash them with our clenched fist.[158]

THE "NO-WIN" POLICY

As appeasement followed appeasement, Senators in both political parties, some military leaders, and a few syndicated columnists raised charges that the Kennedy-Johnson Administration's foreign policy was based on a "no-win" concept.

A few more aggressive critics of the Administration charged that the President and/or his State Department were actually engaged, knowingly or unknowingly, in a planned program of surrender to communism.

Most newspapers ignored the charges, or ridiculed those who spoke out.

Finally on May 3, 1962, a high administration official, Walt Whitman Rostow, in a speech in Minneapolis, said:

> It is sometimes asked if our policy is a no-win policy. Our answer

is this—we do not expect this planet to be forever split between a Communist bloc and a free world. We expect this planet to organize itself in time on principles of voluntary cooperation among independent nation states dedicated to human freedom. It will not be a victory of United States over Russia.[159]

At the Special Warfare School at Ft. Bragg, N.C. Rostow expressed the same "no-win" idea, and added:

It will not be a victory of capitalism over socialism.[160]

Under Secretary of State George Ball, in testimony before the Senate Armed Services Committee, explained why the Administration believes freedom will prevail. He said:

I think one cannot rule out, looking down the long course of history, that changes may take place in the individual nation states which make up the Communist bloc which will transform them from being dangerous, because they are exponents of a militant, aggressive, international communism, to the adoption of postures which will make them easier to live with in the the world.[161]

Is such an outcome possible? Will Communist leaders "mellow?" Years ago, Lenin foresaw this outcome for the world struggle:

As long as capitalism and socialism exist we cannot live in peace: in the end one or the other will triumph—a funeral dirge will be sung over either the Soviet Republic or over world capitalism.[162]

Is it possible that present day Communists have forsaken Marxism-Leninism and are "mellowing?" Here's what Khrushchev says:

Anyone who thinks we have forsaken Marxism-Leninism deceives himself. That won't happen till the shrimps learn to whistle.[163]

Even so, the Kennedy-Johnson Administration based nearly every foreign policy decision—in Laos, Cuba, Africa, Geneva, Berlin—on the assumption that Communists have "mellowed," despite all the evidence to the contrary. If American leaders persist in refusing to pursue a victory goal while the Communists base their actions on the premise that either capitalism or socialism must triumph, then surely America will lose.

Senator Barry Goldwater (R-Ari) in his forthright book, *Why Not Victory?* says of the "no-win" policy:

> I doubt if this nation ever before has found itself in a battle for her very existence where any public official or group of officials automatically foreclosed the possibility of victory...the opposite of victory is defeat—not coexistence or compromise. For the first time in our history that glorious word victory seems to be slipping out of our national vocabularly. [164]

Willard Edwards, the distinguished Washington correspondent of the *Chicago Tribune*, pieced the story together. He revealed in a two-part article that a top-level staff working under State Department Policy Planner, Walt Whitman Rostow, had formulated a 285-page policy draft as a guide for cold war decisions. [165]

The Rostow master plan is based on the assumption that the Soviet Union is "mellowing" and that the way is open for meaningful agreements between the Communist and non-Communist world—*if we can convince the Communists that we mean them no harm!* [166]

Basically, Rostow's manifesto evisions that Communist leaders have abandoned their goals of world conquest. It is essentially an updated version of the misguided strategy and advice Roosevelt accepted from Alger Hiss, Averell Harriman, and Harry Hopkins at Yalta, Teheran, and Cairo.

Those "mistakes" placed 800-million Poles, Hungarians, Chinese and Czechs in Communist slavery. The world situation has reached a point where the next "mistake" won't enslave more Czechs, Cubans, or Viet Namese, but Americans.

The Rostow Manifesto, as exposed by Willard Edwards, admits that the evidence, in the form of words and deeds by Communist leaders, directly contradicts the assumption that Communists are "mellowing." It proposes, therefore, a massive program of "indoctrination" to "educate" Congress and the people to the new "approach" using planted news stories, appearances before Congressional committees, speeches and articles by Administration officials.[167]

The propaganda department established within the framework of the Arms Control and Disarmament Agency is a prime example of the policy in practice. Rostow's own speeches and those of State Department officials George Ball and Harlan Cleveland are part of the "educational effort." Others can be cited. Dr. Ralph K. White, for example, is head of the Soviet Division of the United States Information Agency. Speaking to the American Psychological Association in September 1961, Dr. White said:

> ...the avowed goals and values of the Russians are pretty much the same as ours...the U.S. must understand that the Russians genuinely look upon the United States as an aggressor...the Soviets fear the U.S. because it is allying itself with the Germans who attacked Russia during World War II.[168]

Senator Thomas Dodd (D-Conn) demanded that White be fired for equating the goals and values of murderous Communist leaders with our own. Nothing was done.

NEWS MANAGEMENT

The propaganda effort to indoctrinate the American people to accept the Rostow dream that the Communists are "mellowing" is part of an unprecedented effort to "manage the news," which started early in the Kennedy-Johnson Administration.

Contradictions between President Kennedy's words and Administration actions on Laos, Cuba, Berlin, the need for military strength, and the right of government employees to speak their minds have been recounted. The completely false and untrue stories government officials released to smear friends of the United States such as Moise Tshombe and his press representative in America, Michel Struelens, were exposed by a Senate committee.

Much of the news media accepted the Administration efforts to "manage the news" but finally became "restless" over the provably false statements released officially during the Cuban crisis. Criticism of the press grew until finally on

December 6, 1962, the Assistant Secretary of Defense for Public Information, Arthur Sylvester, blatantly proclaimed that government had "an inherent right to lie." In a speech to New York newsmen, he said:

> ...it would seem basic, all through history, that it's an inherent government right, if necessary, to lie to save itself.[169]

Administration spokesmen hedged on whether President Kennedy sanctioned the concept of "Government by lie" which Sylvester proclaimed, but Sylvester retained his high position.

Sylvester's pronouncement confirmed what many Americans already knew. Statements by any government official mean nothing. The American people can have no faith, no trust in anything told them by their government leaders.

An official policy of "government by lie" is in itself serious. The implications it holds are frightening when coupled with other indications that the Administration had rejected all traditional concepts of morality as the basis for its rule.

Kennedy's assistant, Arthur Schlesinger, Jr., in an article in the *Partisan Review* in 1947, gave an insight into the morals of liberalism. He said that liberalism...

> ...dispensed with the absurd Christian myths of sin and damnation and believed that what shortcomings man might have were to be redeemed, not by Jesus on the cross, but by the benevolent unfolding of history. Tolerance, free inquiry, and technology, operating in the framework of human perfectibility, would in the end create a heaven on earth, a goal accounted much more sensible and wholesome than a heaven in heaven.[170]

Liberal standards of morality, as enumerated by Schlesinger in 1947, were reiterated by another high government official in 1962. Assistant Secretary of State for International Organization Affairs, Harlan Cleveland, on a TV interview said:

> ...we find that in trying to figure out what to do next, that general codes of ethics, prescriptions that is to say, that have been written down by someone else, by our church or our parents, or the books

we read, or scripture, that these general prescriptions really aren't awfully useful in deciding what to do next.[171]

William Penn warned early Americans of the pitfalls in such a policy. He said:

The nation which refuses to be governed by God will surely be governed by tyrants.

CHAPTER V

HOW HAS IT HAPPENED?

Yes, we did produce a near perfect Republic. But will they keep it, or will they, in the enjoyment of plenty, lose the memory of freedom? Material abundance without character is the surest way to destruction.

—Thomas Jefferson

WHAT HAS HAPPENED to that intangible something called the American spirit? When Barbary pirates on the north coast of Africa tried to blackmail our nation when it was less than ten years old, Americans rallied to a cry of "Millions for defense, but not one cent for tribute."

Today, we grovel before a bearded dictator and offer tractors, drugs, food, and money in tribute. Our leaders tell us they will lie to us to stay in power—and we do nothing.

What has happened to the bold young nation which fought a war in 1812 against the world's mightiest power to protect a handful of its citizens from harassment on the high seas?

Today, 400 American boys rot in Red Chinese prisons, deserted after a war which ended in 1953. Thousands of other Americans are in the hell of Russian slave labor camps. Is it a sign that America is too apathetic or decadent to care when those who protest such injustice to fellow Americans are labeled "crackpots" and "extremists?"

What has happened to the noble American breed which was personified in the legend of Nathan Hale? He was a 21 year old school teacher who volunteered to go behind British lines and collect information for George Washington in the Revolutionary War. When caught, he faced death with a rope around his neck and these words on his lips:

I only regret that I have but one life to give for my country.

Today, we hear news speeding around the world from a Communist courtroom in Moscow, where another young American accused of espionage says:

I didn't know what I was doing. I know now I was risking world peace. My superiors were responsible.

Released several years later from his Russian prison, U-2 pilot Francis Gary Powers returned to America. Central Intelligence Agency officials announced that he had "carried out his mission." A "grateful" American people paid him $45,000 in back salary for his *heroism* and Powers said:

One thing I always remembered was that I was an American.

Who is this new creature who calls himself an American? Gary Powers is not an isolated case. Why is he tragically typical of his, and my, generation? Are these the young men who should be leading the fight to protect ourselves, our children's future, and our heritage from godless communism?

Here is a professional, and very unflattering, evaluation of a typical American. Written by the Chief of Intelligence of the Chinese Peoples Volunteer Army during the Korean War to his superior in Peiping, it fell into American hands:

The American soldier has weak loyalty to his family, his community, his country, his religion, and to his fellow soldier. His concepts of right and wrong are hazy and ill-formed. Opportunism is easy for him. By himself he feels frightened and insecure. He underestimates his own worth, his own strength, and his ability to survive.

There is little understanding of American political history and philosophy, the federal, state, and community organizations, state and civil rights, freedom safeguards, checks and balances and how these things allegedly operate within his own system.

He fails to appreciate the meaning of and the necessity for military or any other form of organization.[1]

It would be easy and reassuring to pass this capsule indictment off as Communist propaganda. However, without use of physical torture, drugs, intensive psychological treatment, coercion, or any of the other tactics usually associated with brainwashing, the Chinese Communists made collaborators of one-third of all American POW's who fell into their hands during the Korean War.[2]

This shocking record so astonished and concerned military authorities that a full-scale inquiry was conducted. One thousand of the 4000 prisoners returned from Korea were studied. Investigators found that some Americans had broadcast anti- American propaganda, informed on other prisoners, wrote articles, letters and stories praising life under communism, confessed to "germ warfare" and other atrocities and generally cooperated with their captors in every way.[3] With others, the "collaboration" was not so complete.

For the first time in American history, of the 7000 POW's in captivity in Korea, not one escaped, even though security measures were lax.[4]

In the early months of captivity, four out of every ten Americans died. This was the largest death rate for any group of Americans in any kind of captivity since the American revolution. A frightening number died, not from maltreatment, battle wounds, or starvation, but from a new disease Army psychiatrists termed, "Give-Up-Itis." A 20-year old American would refuse to eat, tell the others to leave him alone, pull his blankets over his head, and be dead in 48 hours.[5]

Without personal responsibility for their own lives, they had no thought of helping their fellow prisoners when they were sick or in trouble.

Deaths occured when fellow Americans, objecting to the stench of a "buddy" weakened by dysentary, picked him up bodily and threw him out to freeze to death in the snow and 30-below zero weather. Questioned after release, other prisoners who witnessed the event but did not participate were asked why they didn't stop the murder. "It wasn't our affair," was a typical answer.[6]

These products of a supposed Christian nation had lost all concepts of decency, all sense of concern for their fellow man.

The record was so untypical of American prisoners in previous wars that the Army searched for answers.

In contrast to the disquieting performance of the Americans, all of the 229 Turks captured in Korea and subjected to the same treatment and conditions as American POW's, survived to *march* back through the gates at Panmunjon. Not only did they survive—but not a man among them collaborated in any way with the Communists![7]

Major William Mayer, U.S. Army Psychiatrist, who participated in the lengthy and detailed study of American collaborators in Korea has described the techniques used to produce the sorry record.

Simple rewards were offered to the prisoners by their Communist captors for seemingly "unimportant" types of collaboration. Soon, many were "going along." "Why not," they'd say, "everyone else is doing it."[8]

"Indoctrination and re-education" was accomplished in simple "discussion periods." American-produced books and texts were used which emphasized all that was bad in America. The 12-page course "outline" given each man was prepared in America, at a Communist-operated school, the Jefferson School of Social Science in New York City.[9] If the "student" didn't have a solid foundation in American history, government, and economics, much of the material made sense and sounded reasonable.

There were no drugs, physical torture, or highly developed hypnotic techniques—just subtle pressures for *conformity.*[10]

This was the "brainwashing" to which one-third of the American POW's in Korea succumbed. Major Mayer said:

Frankly, it did everything the Communists wanted it to do. It didn't turn anybody into a Communist because it wasn't designed to turn anybody into a Communist. A small percentage of the people in the world are Communists. The great majority are acquiescors. The great majority are simply cowed and somehow pushed along by this system *which doesn't look like something*

you can fight; it's not very dangerous looking; *it just controls you.*
You don't have to be a coward to give in to it. The majority of
Americans (in Korean prison camps) in a sense did give in to it.[11]

Mayer continued his summation of the activities of
American POW's:

> The majority of Americans, more than half in these camps never
> did anything they could really be criticized for. But just doing
> nothing has never been the way that America in 168 years got the
> work done which produced this fabulous society. When we get to
> the point where we just do nothing and enjoy it, maybe we've
> become an old country and not a new one and maybe we are well
> on the way down the western slope. This is a valid question for
> us to debate: whether our own success can destroy us?[12]

The Army study found that Americans who fought in Korea
were a fair cross-section of young American males and slightly better educated than the troops who fought in World War
II.[13]

However, they were a strikingly different group of human
beings than those who fought in that earlier war less than 10
years before. They fit the evaluation of them written by a
Chinese Communist intelligence chief to an alarming degree.

This change in the American male, and his sister, had
occurred in a very short time in the history of a nation. The
collaborator in Korea had a brother five, eight, or ten years
older who distinguished himself on the battlefields of World
War II, and in prison, if captured. Actions of the Communists
substantiate this conclusion. Ignoring men over 30 as "hopeless reactionaries," they concentrated their indoctrination
program at men in the 18 to 30 age group.[14]

In civilian life, the counterparts of the Korean collaborators
have been responsible for the doubling of the crime rate since
World War II. Since 1957, the crime rate is increasing five
times faster than the population. Juvenile delinquents now
commit 43% of all crimes.[15] With their sisters, they have been
responsible for tripling the rate of illegitimate births in the
20 years between 1940 and 1960.[16] They have provided a
market for an unprecedented volume of filthy and indecent

literature—and permit much of it to be displayed openly in newsstands, family drug stores, and distributed through the U.S. mails. Divorces have skyrocketed, alcohol consumption climbs, and there is increasing narcotics use and addiction.

These failures are products of American schools, churches, and homes.

It is true that most Americans, like a majority of the American POW's in Korea, haven't done anything for which they can be criticized. They haven't done anything.

As one country after another has slipped, or been pushed behind the Iron Curtain, they have done nothing.

Their money is used to send foreign aid to the Communist enemy. They do nothing.

In their reactions, Americans are like a majority of the POW's in Korea. They do nothing to be criticized for. At least 98% of all Americans are opposed to communism. Yet, they watch elected and appointed officials give continual aid and comfort to the enemy—and they do nothing.

As Major Mayer pointed out, the Communist "brainwashing" in Korea wasn't designed to make Communists out of Americans. If it succeeded in making them "go along," it did its job. Similarly, Communists aren't interested in making all Americans, or any sizable segment of them, Communists. If Americans just "go along" and do nothing, communism will win without firing a shot.

What has transformed Americans who were once rugged individualists into a conforming, moldable, do-nothing mass?

FBI Chief, J. Edgar Hoover, who has so often decried the moral decay in our society, has also expressed concern about the failure of American prisoners in Korea. In 1959, in a speech to the National Strategy Seminar, Mr. Hoover said:

> The behavior of these prisoners of war was less an individual failure than it was an indictment of our entire society which had not prepared them adequately for their head-on collision with Communist indoctrination...We must not ignore this forceful example of the impact of Communist psychological pressures. Our continued survival may depend upon the action we take now

to insure that all citizens, not only military personnel, are fortified against the continuous Communist ideological assault.

The report of the Presidential Commission said pointedly:

The uninformed POW's were up against it. They couldn't answer arguments in favor of communism with arguments in favor of Americanism because they knew so little about America.

What the Chinese Communist intelligence chief in Korea had said about Americans is largely true. How has it happened?

A close look at the basic institutions of America, institutions which are almost universally respected by our citizens, would be in order. What are the goals and guiding principles of America's educators, churchmen, government leaders and officials? How have they failed in the job of inspiring young Americans to become useful citizens committed to preserving and extending freedom?

CHAPTER VI

EDUCATION

America is reaping the consequences of the destruction of traditional education by the Dewey-Kilpatrick experimentalist philosophy...Dewey's ideas have led to elimination of many academic subjects on the ground that they would not be useful in life...The student thus receives neither intellectual training nor the factual knowledge which will help him understand the world he lives in, or to make well-reasoned decisions in his private life or as a responsible citizen.

—*Admiral Hyman Rickover*[1]

WHO WAS THIS MAN, Dewey, who is so roundly criticized by the renowned Hyman Rickover, the "father" of the nuclear submarine?

John Dewey was an educational philosopher. His experimental philosophies of education were first tried in a model school at the University of Chicago before 1900. They were dismal failures. Children learned nothing. Undismayed, Dewey left Chicago in 1904 and went to Teachers College, Columbia University where he became the dominant figure and the most influential man in American education.

His influence can be measured by the realization that under Dewey's guidance fully 20% of *all* American school superintendents and 40% of *all* teacher college heads received advanced degrees at Columbia. They adopted Dewey's experimental theories, which came to be known as "progressive education," in the schools of the nation. Under the pretext of improving teaching *methods*, they changed *what* was taught to American children.

What did Dewey believe? In his writing and teaching, Dewey rejected fixed moral laws and eternal truths and principles. He adopted pragmatic, relativistic concepts as his guiding philosophy. Denying God, he held to the Marxist concept that man is without a soul or free will. Man is a biological organism completely molded by his environment. Dewey believed that because man's environment is constantly changing, man also changes constantly. Therefore, Dewey concluded, teaching children any of the absolutes of morals, government, or ethics was a waste of time.

On this amoral philosophy, he developed his teaching formulae, commonly labeled, *Progressive Education.*

Dewey published, *My Pedagogic Creed,* in 1897. In it he saw the destruction of a child's individualistic traits as the primary goal of education. Once this was accomplished the youngster would conform or adjust to whatever society in which he found himself. Ability to "get along with the group" became the prime measuring stick of a child's educational "progress."[2]

Taken to a logical conclusion, Dewey's theory would have the child who finds himself in the company of thieves become a thief also. The tendency to justify immoral or unethical conduct by rationalizing that "everybody does it" is rooted in Dewey's teaching. Dewey summarized his theories, saying:

> Education, therefore, is a process for living and not a preparation for future living.[3]

Dewey laid the foundation for the future "destruction of traditional education" decried by Admiral Rickover when he said:

> We violate the child's nature and render difficult the best ethical results by introducing the child too abruptly to a number of special studies, of reading, writing, geography, etc. out of relation to his social life...the true center of correlation of the school subjects is not science, nor literature, nor history, nor geography, but the child's own social activities.[4]

Strict acceptance of Dewey's theories would eliminate teaching world geography unless the child can take a trip around the world. History would be eliminated from the curriculum, because it is past and will not be relived by the student.

In practice, Dewey's theories, as modified by his disciples, have eliminated the teaching of strict rules of grammar. The student learns grammar by "living" (talking) with the "group," or by reading literature. Old fashioned drill in spelling, the ABC's, penmanship, multiplication tables, and other basics has been de-emphasized in favor of "learn by doing." Depending on the degree to which progressive education methods are carried, "learn by doing" can mean "learn not at all." Many parents have become dismayed to realize that children who have not memorized the ABC's through old-fashioned drill have difficulty in using a dictionary or telephone book without haphazardly paging through. They don't know that "M" comes after "L" and before "N," etc.

The *group* idea is the nucleus of the progressive system. No child is permitted to forge ahead of another. This would hurt the *group*. Promotions become automatic. Nobody is left behind because of poor work. This would disrupt the *group*. Grading and graded report cards are frowned upon. Grading promotes competition. Competition breeds rivalry and encourages students to excel and rise above the *group*. When competition is not permitted, children get the idea that personal excellence and trying to get ahead is not worthwhile.

Rosalie Gordon, author of the widely circulated, *What's Happened to Our Schools?*[5] said of progressive education:

> The progressive system has reached all the way down to the lowest grades to prepare the children of America for their role as the collectivists of the future...The group—not the individual child—is the quintessence of progressivism. The child must always be made to feel part of the group. He must indulge in group thinking, in group activity.[6]

She explains Dewey's obsession with the group and group activity by saying:

> You can't make socialists out of individualists.[7]

Dewey was a socialist.[8] At the climax of his career in 1950, he became honorary national chairman of the American counterpart of the British Fabian Society,[9] the League for Industrial Democracy.

A NEW SOCIAL ORDER

While at Columbia University, Dewey gathered about himself a group of young educationalists who called themselves, *Frontier Thinkers*. In the forefront of this group were Dr. George Counts, professor of education, and Dr. Harold Rugg. Known as the "hard" progressivists, they were to have a measurable and lasting effect on the nation's schools.

While Dewey's theories had been concerned chiefly with teaching methods, Counts and Rugg added the concept of using the schools as an instrument for "building a new social order."

Counts was the director of research for a 17-volume study of American education produced by the American Historical Association.[10] Financed by the Carnegie Corporation, the Counts-directed study was to serve as the authoritative guide for revamping the philosophy and concept of American education. The final volume, issued in 1934, contained the recommendations of the five year project, of which the following is typical:

> Cumulative evidence supports the conclusion that in the United States as in other countries, the age of individualism and laissez-faire [freedom and liberty] in economy and government is closing and a new age of *collectivism* is emerging.[11]

Of the Counts-directed study, the British socialist, Harold Laski, writing in *The New Republic*, said:

> At bottom, and stripped of its carefully neutral phrases, the report is an educational program for a socialist America.[12]

Laski is an authoritative commentator. He later became head of the British Fabian Society. Counts' hatred of free American economic and political traditions and his socialist goals were stated openly in a paper he presented to the Dewey-founded Progressive Education Association in Baltimore, Maryland, in February 1932. Counts said:

> Historic capitalism, with its deification of the principle of selfishness, its reliance upon the forces of competition, its placing of property above human rights,and its exaltation of the profit motive, will either have to be displaced altogether, or so radically

changed in form and spirit that its identity will be completely lost.[13]

Dr. Counts made clear that the changes he envisioned would result in:

... a coordinated, planned and socialized economy.[14]

Accomplishing such a drastic remaking of America would involve many changes, Counts admitted. He said:

Changes in our economic system will, of course, require changes in our ideals.[15]

Counts saw no wrong in abandoning even the traditional concepts of morality to achieve his goals. He pointed out in his book, *The Soviet Challenge To America* that even in Russia...

...new principles of right and wrong are being forged.[16]

Counts' obsession with achieving a socialized, planned economy and the methods he was apparently willing to accept to realize it were plain in the foreword he wrote for his translation from Russian into English of *New Russia's Primer* by M. Ilin, a communist textbook for junior high school students. Counts said:

A single glance at the contents of the book convinced me that here was a document of rare quality. Practically every page carried the work of genius.

It presents the major provision of the Five Year Plan (Russian) with extraordinary clarity and charm—but perhaps most important it reveals the temper of the revolutionary movement (communist) and the large human goals toward which it is consciously building.[17]

Counts' praise for the communist program could hardly have been more glowing. Very few of even the most dedicated apologists for the Soviet Union would publicly find the goals of the Soviet communist state to be "human." Counts continues:

Mr. Ilin has shown by example how textbooks might be written. In this competition, however, Mr. Ilin has certain clear ad-

vantages. The revolutionary struggle has placed in his hands some
very powerful aids. It has generated a great system of planning
organization through which society is endeavoring to shape its
own future...This translation is designed to acquaint adults,
teachers, and educators, with a phase of the Russian experiment
which in the long run may prove to be far more important than
those sensational aspects of the revolutionary struggle which are
emphasized in both the daily press and even the more serious
publications. I trust it will serve this purpose and at the same time
contribute to a better understanding of the American people of the
greatest social experiment of all time.[18]

The "sensational aspects of the revolutionary struggle"
which Counts found unimportant include the murder of millions of Russians who resisted state planning and control of
every aspect of their lives. Although not a communist, Counts'
tolerance of Soviet murder, was like that of most Fabian
socialists, a product of his admiration for state planning. This
"end" justified for Counts and many other advocates of planning the murderous "means" used in Russia to bring it about.
Twenty years later, Counts became disillusioned with Russian communism, although he has retained his socialist
views.

To achieve the "new social order," Counts, in 1932, called
for teachers of the nation to provide the impetus. In his
monograph, *Dare the School Build a New Social Order?*
Counts wrote:

> That the teachers should deliberately reach for power and then
> make the most of their conquest is my firm conviction. To the
> extent that they are permitted to fashion the curriculum and
> procedures of the school they will definitely and positively in-
> fluence the social attitudes, ideals and behavior of the coming
> generation.[19]

In "reaching for power" the *Frontier Thinkers* moved in two
directions. They rewrote the textbooks. They gained the prestige of the largest professional teachers organization by capturing the top jobs and control of the National Education
Association. At the 72nd annual meeting of the NEA in
Washington, D.C. in July 1934, Dr. Willard Givens, then a

California school superintendent, in a report entitled, *Education for a New America*, said:

> We are convinced that we stand today at the verge of a great culture...But to achieve these things many drastic changes must be made. A dying laissez-faire must be completely destroyed, and all of us, including the owners, must be subjected to a large degree of social control.[20]

A year after delivering this call for destruction of free enterprise and individual freedom (laissez-faire), Givens was named executive secretary of the NEA, a position he held for 17 years until his retirement in 1952.

TEXTBOOK REVISION

Meanwhile, another of the *Frontier Thinkers*, Dr. Harold Rugg, continued the job of indoctrinating teachers and preparing teaching materials designed to "influence the social attitudes, ideals, and behavior of coming generations." In his book, *The Great Technology*, written for teachers in 1933, Rugg said:

> A new public mind is to be created. How? Only by creating tens of millions of new individual minds and welding them into a new social mind. Old stereotypes must be broken up and new "climates of opinion" formed in the neighborhoods of America.[21]

What climate of opinion would Rugg create? On page 171 of his book, he said:

> We know, now, that a large and growing group of middle men and manipulators of sales, money, investment, and credit have interjected themselves into our economic system...Most of them, however, are exploiters. The postulate follows that the economic system can be operated efficiently and humanely only by elimination, re-education, and assignment to productive work of the parisitical members of this group of middlemen.

Clearly, Rugg was proposing the destruction of the small businessman and complete government control of every citizen's life and employment. Later in his book, he defined how the schools were to be used to transform American political and economic institutions and create the new "public mind" which would accept complete government control of the individual:

> ...through the schools of the world we shall disseminate a new conception of government—one that will embrace all of the collective activities of men; one that will postulate the need for scientific control and operation of economic activities in the interest of all people.[22]

Note that Rugg did not say "a new type of government" but a "new conception of government." Rugg proposed that this could be accomplished in three ways:

> *First and foremost*, the development of a new philosophy of life and education which will be fully appropriate to the new social order; *second*, the building of an adequate plan for the production of a new race of educational workers; *third*, the making of new activities and materials for the curriculum.[23]

It was in the area of new materials, textbooks, and teaching aids, that Rugg achieved greatest influence. The *Conclusions and Recommendations* of the American Historical Association's 17-volume report on education, of which Counts was research director, provided the opening. It proposed to consolidate the traditional subjects of history, geography, sociology, economics, political science, etc. into one composite course, called "social studies."

The idea was widely adopted. Completely new textbooks were needed. Rugg wrote them. All traditional presentations of subject matter was scrapped, and a variety of economic, political, historical, sociological, and geographical data was lumped into one textbook. With such a conglomeration of material in one book, the deletion or slanted presentation of key events, basic truths, facts and theories was not so evident.

Five million school children "learned" American political and economic history and structure in the 1930's from 14 social studies textbooks Rugg authored.[24] He also produced the corresponding teachers' guides, courses outlines, and student workbooks.

So blatant was the downgrading of American heroes and the U.S. Constitution, so pronounced was the anti-religious bias; so open was the propaganda for socialistic control of men's lives in Rugg's textbooks that the public rebelled.[25] Rugg, himself, told what happened in an open letter to President Roosevelt in 1942. He proposed to FDR that it would be a "thrilling experience" to sell the American people on the need for "social planning" through a massive program of government sponsored adult education. Rugg said:

> I know for I tried to do it during the great depression in my *Man and His Changing Society*—a series of books which was studied by some 5,000,000 young Americans until the patrioteers and the native Fascist press well-nigh destroyed it between 1939 and 1941.[26]

Rugg's textbooks went too far, too fast for complete public acceptance. They were replaced by those of other authors somewhat more skillful in the subtle promotion of socialism

In 1940, the National Education Association began promoting a set of "social studies" texts known as the *Building America* series.[27] They were replacements for the discredited Rugg series. They had been widely adopted when a few years later the Senate Investigating Committee on Education of the California legislature condemned the NEA-sponsored series for subtly playing up Marxism and destroying American traditions.[28] The Senate committee report...

> ...found among other things that 113 Communist-front organizations had to do with some of the material in the books and that 50 Communist-front authors were connected with it. Among the authors are Beatrice and Sidney Webb, identified with the Fabian Socialist movement in Great Britain.[29]

Seven years after these disclosures, the texts were still in use in the school systems of several states.[30]

Today, the typical text is cleverly done. Direct attacks on basic truths are avoided when possible. However, the destructive influence of Counts, Rugg, and the other socialistic *Frontier Thinkers* is clearly discernible.

CLASS HATRED

The presentation of American history as a *class struggle* by widely-used textbooks is a striking example of the continuing direct influence of Dr. George Counts on today's schools.

Once America was relatively free of class hatred.[31]

The progressivists realized that it would be impossible to pit one class against another for political gain, if such classes did not exist, or were without basic antagonism. Dr. George Counts proposed that the schools should disrupt this stabilizing influence in America. In the magazine, *The Social Frontier*, he wrote:

> In view of the absence of a class mentality among workers, it would be reasonable to assume that it is the problem of education to induce such a mentality rather than to take an existing mentality and base a course of action upon it.[32]

This cruel and cynical admonition to the educators of America to purposefully promote class strife and bitterness was an open acceptance of Lenin's strategy of "incite one against another." Twenty years later, most textbook authors were carefully following Counts' advice. Class hatred is induced in students by presenting American history as a prolonged class struggle. Read these examples:

Craven and Johnson in their textbook, *The United States: Experiment in Democracy*,[33] tell the student:

> The *upper class*, numerically weak, consisted of those who owned so much wealth that they did not have to engage in manual labor. They generally wore *finer clothes* to set themselves off from the *masses*.(pg. 60)

The class struggle theme continues through the book. In describing the American Revolution, the authors say:

> The rest of the *upper class* people joined in the American cause, but with the full intention of checking later the aspirations of the *average citizen* for a more democratic way of life. (pg. 103)

Todd and Curti, in writing their *America's History*,[34] laid the foundations for presenting American history as a class struggle in this way:

> They (the founding fathers) were determined to keep control of the government in the hands of the *well-to-do*, whom they con-

sidered more stable, more judicious, and more temperate than the *poorer*, and *less educated people*. (pg. 173)

This is the Marxist view of American history, first propagated early in this century by Charles Beard in *An Economic Interpretation of the Constitution*. It is followed blindly today by most textbook writers, even though Beard later repented and repudiated his interpretation as faulty.

Faulkner, Kepner and Merrill in *History of the American Way*,[35] use the same theme to describe the Constitutional Convention:

...the delegates were *conservative* or slow to change. And that is easy to understand. They were the *property holding class*... Two important groups were not well represented...First, the *common man* was not represented by any delegate who was a mechanic or a small farmer or the like. Secondly, most of the Revolutionary "radicals" were absent. (pg. 71)

The delegates were "conservative" in that they drew upon the accumulated wisdom and experience of the past in framing the Constitution of the new nation. To describe them as "slow to change" is absurd. They were largely the group which instigated, financed, and fought the American Revolution. Another deceit perpetrated by the authors is in failing to tell the student that at the time the Constitution was written over 90% of *all* Americans were *property holders*.

This handling of the U.S. Constitution by textbook writers demonstrates a commonly-used propaganda technique. Instead of directly attacking the provisions of the Constitution, they are ignored, and the motives of the men who wrote it are impugned.

F. A. Magruder in his *American Government* [36] uses a different technique. Instead of smearing the men who wrote the Constitution, he openly admits that important Constitutional safeguards are being by-passed today. The student is given the impression that such infringement on constitutional guarantees against an all-powerful government is "sophisticated and progressive." Magruder says:

The principle of checks and balances in government is not held in such esteem today as it was a century ago. The people no longer fear the officers whom they elect every few years. (pg. 73)

The people of Germany elected Hitler in 1933. Because they ignored the checks and balances of the German constitution, they never had an opportunity to vote him out. This, the student doesn't learn from Magruder.

The class struggle theme runs like a thread through most textbook presentations of U.S. History. Dumond, Dale and Wesley in *History of the United States*,[37] describe the period of great industrial growth in the late 19th Century this way:

> The real issue was whether the government would once again serve the needs of the *toiling masses* rather than the *interests of special groups*. (pg. 525)

ANTI-FREE ENTERPRISE

With the foundation for the class struggle firmly laid, business, free enterprise, and profits are painted as the source of all evil, just as Counts, Rugg, and other *Frontier Thinkers* recommended. Craven and Johnson, in their text say:

> Corporate industry represented a greater investment of capital and consequently a greater concentration of power in politics than the slaveholders had ever dreamed of possessing. (pg. 422)

If this subtle equating of business with slaveholding was not an adequate condemnation, the authors recite in an approving manner this quotation by Lincoln Steffens:

> Big business was, and still is, the current name of the devil, the root of all evil, political and economic. (pg. 516)

Steffens is quoted and praised in many texts. Students are not told that Steffens was a vocal supporter of the American Communist Party who said, "Communism can solve our problems."

Gavian and Hamm in *The American Story*[38] defame business and stir class hatred by quoting Mary Lease, an English socialist, who said:

> Wall Street owns the country. It is no longer a government of the people, by the people, and for the people, but a government of Wall Street, by Wall Street, and for Wall Street. The parties lie to

us...the people are at bay; let the bloodhounds of money who have dogged us thus far beware! (pg. 401)

Gavian and Hamm do not counter-balance this quotation by pointing out that nearly every American family has a stake in Wall Street. Over 25% of American families own stock in industry directly. Almost all others share in some way through private insurance policies, company pension plans, or union welfare programs whose assets are invested in Wall Street.

The class struggle theme is the vehicle used to openly advocate cradle-to-grave welfare care for all. Magruder equates opposition to the welfare state with selfishness of the few. In a section blatantly entitled, *Welfare of the People from the Cradle to the Grave*, Magruder says:

The United States has increasingly *curbed the selfish* and provided for the *welfare of the many*. The Government has established the Children's Bureau to look after the welfare of *every* child born in America. (pg. 15)

Magruder's text, *American Government*, is a study in propaganda techniques in itself. The class struggle idea is reinforced in this passage which uses a false premise to discourage thrift, saving, and family responsibility and justify welfare payments for all:

Because of sickness, accidents, and occasional unemployment it is *difficult or impossible* for a laborer who has reared a family to save from his meager wages (This is untrue-Author). And it is more just to place all the burden of supporting those who have been unfortunate, *or even shiftless*, upon everybody instead of upon some dutiful son or daughter who is not responsible for the condition. (pg. 339)

With the school children of America being educated in this philosophy, is it any wonder that total government expenditures for welfare have risen from under $5-billion annually during the depths of the depression to $ 35-billion in 1961, the most prosperous year the nation has ever experienced?

IN THE LOWER GRADES

Indoctrination in the availability and "rightness" of the "free" handout is not limited to high school students. The brainwashing starts today in the first grade. Recall the story, if you are old enough, in the first grade readers about the hard-working little squirrel who gathered and stored nuts for the winter. The story had a moral: Work hard and save wisely for uncertain days ahead.

For today's six-year old, that story has been rewritten. The new version is entitled, *Ask for It.*[39] In it, a little squirrel named, Bobby, ate nuts from a tree during the summer. Other squirrels suggested that Bobby put some nuts away for winter. As Bobby Squirrel didn't like to work, he ignored the advice.

Winter came and one morning Bobby awakened to find the world covered with snow—and all the nuts were gone from the tree. He got awfully hungry but remembered that a boy who lived in a *white house* had taken some of the nuts from *his* tree during the summer. Bobby went to the *white house* and gave a squirrel call. A door opened and a "fine brown nut" rolled out. Bobby Squirrel learned his lesson. The story concluded:

> "Well!" thought Bobby, "I know how to get my dinner. All I have to do is ask for it."[40]

This story is in the first grade reader, *Our New Friends*, published by the Scott, Foresman and Company in 1956. The authors are Gray, Monroe, Artley, and Arbuthnot. It is approved for use in most states.

Magruder's high school text, *American Government*, as mentioned earlier, uses nearly every classical propaganda trick to confuse students into accepting socialism. Consider this non-sequitur under the heading, *Medical Service Under Our System of Free Enterprise*:

> In a democracy we believe in evolutionary methods rather than the revolutionary methods of a dictatorship; and under our system of free enterprise, competition improves the standard of service and tends to reduce the cost. *Therefore, instead of jumping right*

into socialized medicine, why not have the Government support projects such as the following. (pg. 670)

If free enterprise medicine works so well, and Magruder acknowledges that it does, why consider socialized medicine at all, either immediately, or by the backdoor approach Magruder recommends. He advocates approaching socialized medicine *gradually* through such steps as federal aid for training doctors, federal funds for hospital construction, and government payment of hospital costs for lengthy illnesses.

INTERNATIONALISM

Since World War II, propaganda for World Government under the United Nations has been added to textbook agitation for the collectivist society envisioned by Counts and Rugg.

The drive, spearheaded in America by the National Education Association, is part of a world-wide movement by UNESCO (United Nations Educational, Scientific, and Cultural Organization). It received the official blessing of President Truman's Commission on Higher Education. The Commission's report, issued in 1947, had these recommendations:

> The role which education will play officially must be conditioned essentially by policies established in the State Department in this country, and by ministries of foreign affairs in other countries. Higher education must play a very important part in carrying out in this country the program developed by UNESCO...The United States Office of Education must be prepared to work with the State Department and with UNESCO.[41]

What was the UNESCO program which the Presidential Commission recommended that American schools should implement? Embodied in the nine-volume UNESCO study, *Towards World Understanding*, it is the blueprint for conditioning American children for the day when their first loyalty will be to a socialistic one-world government under the United Nations.

The work of Counts and Rugg laid the foundation for the first two steps—the destruction of the U.S. Constitution and free economy—so that America could be easily merged into a socialistic world federation.

UNESCO's Director General, under whom the plan was prepared, was Julian Huxley, an atheistic philosopher and member of the Colonial Bureau of the British Fabian Society.

The goal of UNESCO was stated plainly in the study's first volume. It recommended that children should be educated in...

> ...those qualities of citizenship which provide the foundation upon which international government must be based if it is to succeed.[42]

Under Huxley, UNESCO envisioned that destruction of children's love of country and patriotism was the first step towards education for world citizenship. The report said on the opening page of Volume V, *In the Classroom with Children Under Thirteen Years of Age*:

> Before the child enters school his mind has already been profoundly marked, and often injuriously, by earlier influences...first gained, however dimly, in the home.

The attack on home and parents continues. On page 9, the teacher is told:

> The kindergarten or infant school has a significant part to play in the child's education. Not only can it correct many of the errors of home training but it can also prepare the child for membership, at about age seven, in a group of his own age and habits—the first of many such social identifications that he must achieve on his way to membership in the world society.

After such guarded reference to the "injurious influence" of the family on the young child, the UNESCO study makes it plain that the errors of home training include parental encouragement of patriotism. On page 58, the guidebook for teachers says:

> As we have pointed out, it is frequently the family that infects the child with extreme nationalism. The school should therefore use the means described earlier to combat family attitudes.

Among the "means described earlier" are the suppression

of American history and geography which might enhance pro-American sentiments of the children. UNESCO gives specific suggestions in Volume V, page 11, on how this can be done:

> In our view, history and geography should be taught at this stage as universal history and geography. Of the two, only geography lends itself well to study during the years prescribed by the present survey (3-13 years). The study of history, on the other hand, raises problems of value which are better postponed until the pupil is freed from the nationalist prejudices which at present surround the teaching of history.

Translated, this means that if the grade school student is taught American history objectively he is very likely to realize that the American system of government, economics, and social values outstrip those found anywhere else in the world.

Three pages later, UNESCO admits that detailed study even of foreign countries will lead the student to the conclusion that America is a better place to live. This problem was solved by recommending that teachers obscure the truth from their pupils in this way:

> Certain delicate problems, however, will arise in these studies and explorations. Not everything in foreign ways of living can be presented to children in an attractive light. At this stage, though, the systematic examination of other countries and manners can be postponed, and the teacher need seek only to insure that his children appreciate, through abundant and judicious examples, that foreign countries, too, possess things of beauty, and that many of them resemble the beauty and interest of his own country. A child taught thus about the different countries of the world will gradually lose those habits of prejudice and contempt which are an impediment to world-mindedness.

Thus, UNESCO recommends the deliberate "under education" of children. The student who does not know or understand the accomplishments of America and the shortcomings of the rest of the world is more likely to accept a "world government." The student who knows nothing of the horrors of the communist system in Russia and the failures of socialism everywhere it has been tried might well agree to a communist-influenced socialistic one-world government.

Such deliberate "under education" is a theme which runs through the entire UNESCO program. Karl W. Bigelow, another professor of education at Columbia, and a UNESCO board member, directed a seminar on Volume II of the *Towards World Understanding* series. The UNESCO seminar report, *The Education and Training of Teachers*, recommended:

> Therefore, we regard it as a matter of first importance for social and international living that educators should be more concerned with the child, and the healthy development of his body and mind, than with content of the various subjects which go to make a school curriculum...Because of failure to adopt a wise approach to child growth and development, the primary school still tends to function as if it were an institution *for the abolition of illiteracy*.

Should the school's primary function be the teaching of reading, writing, and arithmetic (the abolition of illiteracy) or the "conditioning" of the child for "social and international living?" Bigelow's thesis, expressed in this UNESCO publication, is a simple restatement of John Dewey's original progressivist theories. The ultimate result can only be the "under education" of the child. The graduates produced by such "education" do not have the *basic* knowledge on which to make sound judgments. If they do not understand the source of America's strength, they cannot see the fallacies of a world collectivist order.

In short, UNESCO recommends that schools be converted into indoctrination centers for the production of emotionally-conditioned children who react like Pavlov's dogs rather than reason and think logically. The best selling book, Rudolf Flech's *Why Johnny Can't Read*,[43] exposes the results of such under-education in one curriculum area.

Teacher-training institutions, textbook writers, and professional education organizations picked up the theme of "education for world citizenship." Dr. Willard Givens, executive secretary of the National Education Association, joined the board of directors of the U.S. Commission for UNESCO.

Professional education journals and faculty members at Teachers College, Columbia University started agitating for mandatory revision of textbooks to conform to UNESCO standards, *even before the standards were publicly announced*. Writing in the *NEA Journal* in April 1946, Issac Leon Kandel of Teachers College, Columbia University, said:

> Nations that become members of UNESCO accordingly assume an obligation to revise textbooks used in their schools...unilateral efforts to revise the materials of instruction are futile. The poison of aggressive nationalism injected into children's minds is as dangerous for world stability as the manufacture of armaments. In one, as in the other, supervision by some kind of international agency is urgent.[44]

Textbook revision to obliterate national history and geography, downgrade patriotism and love of America, and build a tolerance for the communist enemy in Russia has been accomplished in line with UNESCO recommendations. A review of widely-used textbooks establishes this fact.

Patriotic impulses are generally belittled and equated with extremism, in line with UNESCO proposals for overcoming "injurious parental influences." In *The United States: Experiment in Democracy*, the authors, Craven and Johnson, say:

> In the 1920's many Americans were *excessively nationalistic and tolerantly patriotic*...The official (Ku Klux) Klan literature reflected the average middle class in its assertions of "100 per cent Americanism." (pg. 662)

Note the linking of the "middle class" and patriotism with the Ku Klux Klan. This is typical. Another text, *History of the American Way*, by Faulkner, Kepner, and Merill, says:

> ...there was an increase in the number of *so-called "100 per cent Americans"* whose behavior was quite un-American and undemocratic. The Ku Klux Klan for example...(pg. 650)

Gavian and Hamm in their high school text, *The American Story*, put it this way:

> National feeling was very strong, and it was often shown in undesirable ways. The strong nationalism of the years following

the war (WWI) was commonly expressed in such slogans as "America First" and "One Hundred Per Cent Americanism."

Decent Americans deplore fanaticism. However, with discussions of patriotism in textbooks limited to such slurring passages it is no wonder that love of country, one of man's most noble attributes, is in such disrepute; that today the citizen who is moved to express a patriotic remark feels impelled to preface it by saying, "I don't want to sound like a flag waver, but..."

Belittling references to patriotism in textbooks are not the only methods used for downgrading love of country. Display of the American flag in the classroom is neglected in many areas. The pledge of allegiance to the flag was once a standard exercise for opening the school day. This practice has been discarded to such a degree that in 1961 members of the California State Legislature felt compelled to pass a law requiring that the pledge of allegiance or the singing of the "Star Spangled Banner" be used daily. The bill passed—*but by only one vote*. A similar bill was passed in Illinois in 1963—but was vetoed by the governor.

The downgrading of American heroes contributes to national disillusionment. Todd and Curti in *America's History*, have this to say about George Washington:

> Outwardly Washington seemed to most people somewhat cold and overdignified. After his death *American patriots developed a myth of his godlike qualities*...(pg. 184)

After 15 or more years of such anti-patriotic propaganda in the schools, J. Edgar Hoover felt impelled to speak out. At Valley Forge on February 22, 1962, he said:

> Too often in recent years, patriotic symbols have been shunted aside. Our national heroes have been maligned, our history distorted. Has it become a disgrace to pledge allegiance to our flag—or to sign a loyalty oath, or pay tribute to our national anthemn? Is it shameful to encourage our children to memorize the stirring words of '76? Is it becoming opprobious to state "In God We Trust" when proclaiming our love of country?

What we desperately need today is patriotism founded on a real understanding of the American ideal—a dedicated belief in our principles of freedom and a determination to perpetuate America's heritage.[45]

Recall that UNESCO recommended that textbooks should be revised to play down those facts about foreign countries which are unattractive. Similarities rather than differences between countries were to be emphasized. In this way, UNESCO said, children "will gradually lose those habits of prejudice and contempt which are an impediment to world mindedness." Compare that UNESCO recommendation with the description of the communist government of Russia in F. A. Magruder's text, *American Government*. Magruder says that socialism in Russia is "an example of totalitarianism" but then proceeds to describe it this way:

> Under the Constitution of 1936 the Government is a federation. It is a Union of 16 Soviet Socialist Republics (USSR)...the powers are divided between the Union and the member republics *somewhat as those of our Union are divided between the United States and the States*. Suffrage (voting) is granted to men and women 18 years of age and over. The voters directly or indirectly elect the two houses comprising the Supreme Council. This body legislates and also chooses the Presidium, consisting of a chairman and 36 members which carries on the government. There are also Ministers *comparable to our Cabinet members*. (pg. 37-8)

At no point is the student told directly that the Soviet voter is given no choice, that the only candidates on the ballot are those selected by the Communist Party.

In describing Russian collective farms, Magruder says:

> The members of each collective have a sort of town meeting to determine policies and elect the manager. (pg. 38)

Magruder in line with UNESCO advice to "avoid the unattractive," does not mention that 10-million small Russian farmers were murdered before the remainder "accepted" the collective farm idea.

The summary of Magruder's discussion of the Russian communist government has the subtitle, *Swing from the Radical to the Conventional*. Under this heading, he says:

The Revolution of 1917 was fourfold: governmental, economic, religious and moral. An absolute monarchy was replaced by Soviets (Councils) dominated by a dictator, but the Constitution of 1936 granted direct suffrage (voting). (pg. 40)

From this passage, the student would assume that Russia no longer has a dictatorship. With such textbook descriptions of the Soviet Union, it is reasonable to believe that students might lose the "prejudice and contempt" for communism which UNESCO cites as " an impediment to world-mindedness."

In the treatment of American foreign policy, the origin and growth of world communism, and the influence communist agents have had in influencing U.S. foreign policy toward communist objectives, discernable textbook bias is the rule rather than the exception. Outright falsehoods are not uncommon.

Textbooks impart false information about the establishment of the communist state in Russia. Lenin and the Bolsheviks are given credit for overthrowing the tyrannical Czarist regime. The Czar was actually overthrown by Kerensy who established a constitutional republic, *which was subverted and seized by the communists*. But Dumond, Dale and Wesley, in *History of the United States*, say:

> At the end of World War I the source of greatest danger was thought to be Russia, where after centuries of oppression the masses revolted and established a communist regime...(pg. 698)

Harlow in *Story of America*[46] described the rise of the totalitarian state this way:

> In 1917 revolutionists in Russia overthrew the government of the Czar and established a communist nation. (pg. 557)

The cruel, harsh, inhumane methods used in the Russian communist state are ignored or deliberately distorted, while Soviet progress is praised. Mowrer and Cummings in *The United States and World Relations*[47] are guilty in this way:

> Notable progress has been made in many sections of the country

(Russia), particularly in those that are remote from Moscow, as shown by the really remarkable expansion in the Arctic. (pg. 157)

In accordance with the UNESCO instructions to disregard the "unattractive," students are not told that the "remarkable expansion in the Arctic" has been accomplished largely by the 20-million inmates of Soviet slave labor camps. The Mowrer and Cummings book points up the problem. On the surface it is anti-communist. But in the presentation of factual information it builds the attitude in the student that the Soviet system has its merits.

The pro-Soviet bias of textbooks becomes obvious when descriptions of Nazism are compared with passages on communism. Nazi methods, governmental structure, and plans for world conquest were similar to those of the communists. Not a handful of Nazis remain in the world. We are threatened by a world-wide communist conspiracy of 33-million fanatically-dedicated revolutionaries who have enslaved one-billion people. Yet, while textbook writers use justifiably vicious words to describe Nazism, the communists get a "neutral" appraisal. Harlow is typical. He writes of "brown-shirted Nazi gangsters" and "black-shirted Fascist plunderers" in describing the rise of totalitarianism in Germany and Italy. Of Communism, he writes:

Meanwhile, Russia had *organized* the Union of Soviet Socialist Republics and was ruled by a handful of Communist Party members led by Joseph Stalin. (pg. 606)

The bias becomes obvious in the treatments of the role of Russia and Germany in World War II. Of the early part of the war when Russia and Germany were still allies, Gavian and Hamm use these words to describe the joint destruction of Poland:

...While the *Nazis* quickly *overran* the western half of Poland, the Russians *occupied* the eastern half. (pg. 595)

Todd and Curti use almost exactly the same words, adding a few modifiers to describe the Nazis:

While the *Nazi storm troops quickly overran* the western part of the country (Poland), *Russian armies occupied* the eastern half. (pg. 757)

Note that German armies are described as Nazi storm troops while the Russian armies are not called *Communists* or the *Red Army*. Communism has rightly been described by J. Edgar Hoover as "Red Fascism." As such it deserves equally condemnatory textbook treatment with Nazism.

The Yalta Conference, one of the most sordid episodes in American diplomatic history, gets only passing mention in textbooks although agreements made there by Roosevelt, Stalin and Churchill resulted in the enslavement of 700-million people by the communists.[48] Here is how several textbook authors describe the agreement which resulted in communist domination of Poland, Yugoslavia, Hungary, Bulgaria, Rumania, China, and six other nations. Craven and Johnson say:

> In February 1945, Roosevelt met with Churchill and Stalin at Yalta to make plans for the final blows against Germany and Japan. (pg. 824)

Gavian and Hamm in *The American Story* say:

> At the Yalta Conference...Roosevelt, Churchill and Stalin outlined a plan for dividing both Germany and Austria. (pg. 670)

Faulkner, Kepner, and Merrill in their text go even further in distortion by omission. They say:

> At the Yalta Conference...Russia, Great Britain, and the United States agreed that the liberated peoples should "create governments of their own choice." (pg. 688)

Dumond, Dale and Wesley come closest to telling the student that there might be something in the Yalta story worth studying, They say:

> Some agreements between Russia, Great Britain, and the United States as to the postwar treatment of Germany were made at Yalta, though details still remain in dispute. (pg. 788)

Alger Hiss, a communist and adviser to Roosevelt at Yalta, is ignored as an influence on the Conference and the agreements made there. This is typical of the textbook "blackout" on high-level infiltration and subversion of the U.S. Government by communist agents.

Texts written in the 1950s ignore or belittle the influence of Hiss, Harry Dexter White, Owen Lattimore, and other high level agents. If their part in directing American policies toward communist objectives was thoroughly discussed, the student would likely gain an impression that communists were too treacherous to trust in any world government. If the continuous string of over 50 agreements broken by the communists since World War II were detailed, the student might rightly decide that negotiation of further agreements is unwise.

If the true story of U.S.-Soviet relations were told, students would never accept textbook propaganda for a United Nations world government and disarmament. Yet, these themes run through the textbooks from which students are supposed to learn about *American* government. Magruder, on the first page of his book says:

> We know that unity of our own states brought peace and strength to our country. We believe that similar cooperation will bring peace and good will to the nations of the world.

Magruder ignores the conditions which made unity possible in America, conditions which do not exist in today's world. They included a 500-year heritage of seeking freedom under English common law from 1215 when the Magna Charta was signed; common language, religious and racial heritage; agreement on an economic system; and true acceptance of a common goal of freedom.

Today, nearly one-third of the "new" nations of the world have no traditional concepts of law, some have not completely rejected cannibalism. Only a handful of United Nations members have concepts of private property and freedom similar to those which made America strong. Racial and religious differences further complicate the problem. Even if all these obstacles could be brushed away, the international communist conspiracy with its goal of world domination makes any form of unity, except eventual slavery for all, impossible.

Ignoring all these facts, Magruder repeats the same illogical reasoning on page 14 of his text:

> We have peace in the United States because we have agreed to federal laws and have an army to enforce them.

> When we have definite international laws and an army to enforce them, we shall have international peace. When atomic bombs are made only by a world government and used only by a world army, who could resist?

Who could resist? Certainly not the United States if the "neutralist" Afro-Asian block united, as usual, with the communist countries and voted *democratically* to place all Americans in slavery. Would it be wrong? Perhaps. But it would be democratic.

Yet throughout the book, the student is conditioned to accept world government, without discussing whether it would be good or bad. Finally, in the last two chapters, Magruder spells out in detail the specific steps which should be taken to prepare for world government. They include:

> Give the UN absolute power to regulate international trade and commerce. (pg. 715) Immigration control now handled by each country would be relinquished to the UN along with the power to arbitrarily remove people from one part of the world and settle them in a place a UN planner determines their skills, etc. are needed. (pg. 716)

> Place control of the Panama Canal under the United Nations. (pg. 716) Establish an international police force strong enough that no nation can resist its orders. (pg. 716-7) Give the UN power of taxation. (pg. 717) Place control of broadcast stations, press, speech, etc. under UN control to insure development of "cooperative" public opinion (brainwashing). (pg. 718)

As fantastic as many of these proposals sound, they were taught to the children of America as long as 12 years ago. Today, they are being discussed seriously as steps to be taken by the U.S. Government.

All those who support such programs are not communists. Those who write such textbooks, put them into school systems, and vehemently defend them when they are exposed are not communists, or even pro-communists. They are misguided socialist idealists consumed with the idea of solving world problems through a one-world socialist government. They believe that, if all human differences (economic, religious, political, etc.) can be eliminated, all mankind's problems will disappear as well. In striving for this idealistic goal, they emotionally banish all fact and reason. Past communist treachery, which would be an obstacle to world socialistic brotherhood, is pathologically ignored.

Under the protective cover offered by the misguided one-worlders, the communists have been able to operate in the schools of America.

As early as 1940, the Rapp-Coudert Investigating Committee of the New York State Legislature disclosed that the 11,000 member Teachers Union in New York City was under complete communist control. Over 1000 communists were teaching in New York City schools.[49]

In the committee's final report, it was stated:

> The communists and those under their influence in the Teachers Union comprised nearly one-fourth of all personnel in city colleges.[50]

After exposure by the Rapp-Coudert committee, communist influences in the schools lessened for a brief period. However, in 1952, the Senate Internal Security Subcommittee learned that no real cleanup had been accomplished. In a series of hearings on subversive influences in education the committee learned that 500 or more communists were still teaching in New York City. Administrative red tape, Supreme Court decisions, and opposition of teacher organizations have hampered efforts to utilize the information developed by the investigations.

Efforts to remove communist teachers from positions of influence have been strongly opposed by such influential organizations as the American Association of University Professors.[51]

Decisions of the U.S. Supreme Court have made nearly impossible the job of concerned school authorities in cleansing their own ranks. In the case of *Sweezy vs. New Hampshire*[52] the Warren Court reversed the New Hampshire Supreme Court and held that the Attorney General of New Hampshire exceeded his authority in questioning Professor Sweezy about suspected subversive activities. Questions which the Court said that Sweezy properly refused to answer included, "Did you advocate Marxism at that time?" and "Do you believe in communism?"

In the case of *Slochower vs. Board of Education of New York*[53] the Court reversed the decisions of three lower courts and held that it was unconstitutional to discharge a teacher because he took the Fifth Amendment when asked about communist activities. The court ordered Slochower, an identified communist, rehired in his position at Brooklyn College and granted him $40,000 in back pay.

Through the combined actions of the communists, and the disciples of Dewey, Counts, Rugg, and other *Frontier Thinkers*, many of our schools have become instruments for producing the "new social order." These criticisms do not apply equally to all 40,000 school systems in the United States.

Because of local control over the schools, alert parents, informed school board members, and patriotic school administrators and teachers in many areas have been able to unite to do an outstanding job in their schools.

For this reason, the "progressivist" thinkers are actively advocating a massive program of federal aid to education which would ultimately remove control of the schools from the local level and transfer it to Washington. The appointment of one "progressivist" thinker as head of the Office of Education would insure that the amoral, socialistic theories of Dewey, Counts, and Rugg could be permeated into those schoolhouses and textbooks which have thus far been immune.

Because control of the schools is at the local level, the job of insuring that they remain sound, or making them so if they are not, must be done locally. However, the parent, school administrator, or organized group which opposes, or even questions, the theories and methods of the progressivists is likely to bring down a storm of attacks, smears, and vilification.

The National Education Association's *National Commission for the Defense of Democracy Through Education*, can, and will, rush its trained propagandists to the scene. Charges of socialist bias in education is vehemently denied, or ridiculed. *The Pasadena Story*, an impressive publication issued by the NEA Defense Commission when parents in Pasadena, California, rebelled at the indoctrination of their children, is typical. Of the Pasadena parents, the report says:

> They apparently claim that this country has already moved into, or is rapidly moving toward, some form of socialism, collectivism, or statism. They contend that subversive elements have sifted into public education and that many teachers are seeking to change the American way of life. They charge that John Dewey's progressive education is an instrument designed to break down American standards and weaken the fabric of American society...They oppose certain educators who they assert are seeking to indoctrinate the youth of the country for a changed social and economic order.[54]

This report was issued in June 1951, by the National Education Association. The NEA executive secretary at the time was Willard Givens who himself had publicly stated:

> We are convinced that we stand today at the verge of a great culture...But to achieve these things, many drastic changes must be made. A dying laissez-faire must be completely destroyed, and all of us, including the owners must be subjected to a large degree of social control.[55]

Today, the NEA's Defense Commission, in Gestapo-like fashion, maintains a "blacklist" of individuals and organizations which publicly question or criticize the quality of education. The NEA Commission for "Defense of Democracy" in its 1961 annual report admitted:

> About 1000 requests for information concerning individuals or groups thought to be causing trouble for the schools or the profession were received during the year. Several new fact sheets and information bulletins concerning critics of education were prepared. The Commission has, probably, the most complete files of their kind of critics of education.[56]*

The *Tulsa Tribune*, after determining that a dossier on its editor was in the NEA files of "critics of education," asked editorially:

> What is the function of the National Education Association—to improve the education of America's children or to stifle criticism of present educational methods.[57]

---

*More current attacks on NEA critics are discussed in Chapters 23 and 25.

CHAPTER 7

SUBVERTING OUR RELIGIOUS
HERITAGE

*For, if the trumpet give an uncertain sound, who shall
prepare himself for the battle?*

—I Corinthians 14:8 (KJV)

THE WEAPONS OF HATE AND FEAR by which the collectivists have moved a generation of Americans to sell their freedom and integrity for security would never have worked had American roots in basic Judaic-Christian traditions not first been severed. God could not be replaced by Government as the source of all blessings until moral concepts were first blurred.

The collectivists, no respecters of institutions, no matter how sacred, planted their roots in the churches of America before the end of the 19th Century.

Dr. Walter Rauschenbusch and Dr. Harry F. Ward were probably most responsible for the "revolution in religion." They replaced the Bible-based belief that man was individually responsible to God for his own salvation with a concept of "social salvation." Rauschenbusch was a turn-of-the-century theologian and Ward was professor of Christian Ethics at New York's influential Union Theological Seminary for 25 years.

Analyzed, the "social salvation" which collectivist theologians teach is basically a restatement of the Marxian dogma of Economic Determinism—"change the economic environment and man will be transformed." A theology based on the message of Christ teaches that through true acceptance of Him and His teachings, man is changed, and can, in turn, change the world and correct its ills. Rauschenbusch spelled out his break with traditional Christianity clearly when he wrote:

> ...we differ from many Christian men and women who believe that if only men are personally converted wrong and injustice will gradually disappear from the construction of society. It does not appear such to us.[1]

Dr. Rauschenbusch graduated from Rochester Theological Seminary in 1885. He was a confirmed socialist even before making a trip to Europe in 1907 to visit with Beatrice and Sidney Webb, founders, with atheist George Bernard Shaw, of the British Fabian Society. Rauschenbusch was a shrewd practitioner of the Fabian methodology who realized that if he identified socialism as such in his preaching and teaching, many people in the church would be repelled. Therefore, in his new "theology" Rauschenbusch promised a "Kingdom of God on Earth."[2] As early as 1893, Rauschenbusch wrote:

> The only power that can make socialism succeed, if it is established, is religion. It cannot work in an irreligious country.[3]

Major Edgar Bundy, in his comprehensive and well-documented book, *Collectivism in the Churches*, said of Rauschenbusch, "Socialism, thus, was his first concern. Religion was only a means toward achieving socialism."[4]

What effect has Rauschenbusch had on the Church in America? Here are the words of Dr. A. W. Beaven, a former president of the Federal Council of Churches of Christ in America, written in 1937:

> It is clear, it seems to me, that the greatest single influence on the life and thought of the American Church in the last 50 years was exerted by Walter Rauschenbusch.[5]

Rauschenbusch and his "social gospel" provided the philosophy for the collectivist movement which has drained much of American Protestantism of its effect on man and his life. Dr. Harry F. Ward contributed the organizational and conspiratorial genius to the movement.

Ward is an identified Communist.[6] In 1908, he was the founder of the oldest, officially-cited Communist-front group in America, the Methodist Federation for Social Action.[7] A year later, he played a part in organizing the Federal Council of Churches, forerunner of the present day, National Council of Churches. He has been an organizer or promoter of nearly every important Communist-front activity in America since. In September 1961, while in his 80's, this durable old man was the keynote speaker at an officially-sponsored Communist rally in New York which protested the action of the Supreme Court in branding the Communist Party USA as a Communist-controlled organization.[8]

Identified under oath as a Communist by Benjamin Gitlow,[9] first head of the Communist Party USA; Manning Johnson, one-time leader of the Party's Negro Section;[10] and several others, Ward was branded as the "Red Dean" of the religious field before a committee of the U.S. Congress. Ward posed as a Methodist, but for 25 years he infected hundreds of young ministers of all denominations with his blasphemous ideas as a professor of Christian Ethics at Union Theological Seminary. He also served at Boston School of Theology at Boston University.

Ward recruited pupils, associates and disciples to his crusade[11] to produce, in his words:

...a changed attitude on the part of many church members concerning the purpose and function both of the Church and Christianity.[12]

Among his closest associates and most devoted pupils in the religious field were such conspirators as the Rev. Jack McMichael, Rev. Charles Webber, Rev. Alanson Smith, Dr. Willard Uphaus, and Rev. Lee Ball.[13] The controversial Methodist bishop, G. Bromley Oxnam, was Ward's pupil, secretary and one-time apologist.[14]

THEIR DISCIPLES

What effect have these Marxist conspirators, Fabian and Communist had on the Church, its people, its theology, and its teaching?

In 1960, a controversy developed over an official U.S. Air Force Reserve Training Manual which warned Air Force personnel that Communists, their dupes and sympathizers had infiltrated into churches. Church groups protested vehemently and Congress investigated. Richard Arens, staff director of the House Committee on Un-American Activities, testified during the hearings as to the evidence of Communist activity in the religious field. He said:

> Thus far of the leadership of the National Council of Churches of Christ in America, we have found over 100 persons in leadership capacity with either Communist-front records or records of service to Communist causes. The aggregate affiliations of the leadership, instead of being in the hundreds as first indicated, is now, according to the latest count, into the thousands, and we have yet to complete our check, which would certainly suggest, on the basis of authoritative sources of this committee, that the statement that there is infiltration of fellow travelers in churches and educational institutions is a complete understatement.[15]

Such consistent collaboration with Communists, knowingly or unknowingly, by the leadership of the largest church-related organization in America is a chilling revelation to most Americans. The Chairman of the House Committee on Un-American Activities, Congressman Francis Walter (D-Pa) stated when opening the hearings on the controversial Air Reserve Training Manual:

> This is not to say that these persons are necessarily consciously supporting Communist enterprises, but the net result is, for all practical purposes, the same.[16]

What is the net result? The National Council of Churches, its subordinate organizations, and the leaders of many of its affiliated denominations and their publications consistently parallel or follow the Communist Party line, as exposed by J. Edgar Hoover.[17] The collaboration is particularly evident on such issues as disarmament,[18] recognition of Red China and its admission to the United Nations,[19] opposition to the committees of Congress which investigate Communist infiltration, subversion, and agitation,[20] anti-anti-communism,[21] and in the promotion of visits to America by Communist "churchmen" from behind the Iron Curtain.[22]

How important are the churchmen, who, wittingly or unwittingly, support Communist fronts and causes? How many are there?

An independent group of Methodist clergy and laymen, Circuit Riders, Inc.,[23] have analyzed the influence achieved in the Church by the collectivists. From public records, newspaper ads sponsored by Communist fronts, the letterhead lists of sponsors of cited subversive groups, signers of Communist-circulated petitions, etc. Circuit Riders, Inc. has compiled and published names of over 7000 ministers and theological school professors who have supported Communist fronts and causes.

These 7000, some of whom have supported 100 or more Communist causes, and some of whom have been duped but once, comprise only a small segment of the more than 200,000 Protestant ministers in America. Are they important then?

An analysis of the "hierarchy" of the six denominations included in the Circuit Riders study, religious publications, and theological school faculties show that in typical Fabian and Communist fashion they hold positions of influence and control far out of proportion to their numbers.

For example, the Congressional hearings on the muchsmeared Air Reserve Training Manual cited the names of a few leading fellow-travelers in the ministry. They included: Walter Russell Bowie who has affiliated with 33 Communist fronts and causes, Henry J. Cadbury with nine, George Dahl with 18, Leroy Waterman with 20, and Fleming James with a verified total of 25 affiliations with Communist fronts and causes.[24]

These five men, and 25 others with records of support for Communist causes, served on the committee of 95 Bible scholars, translators, and theologians who produced the Revised Standard Version of the Holy Bible.[25] While less than three per cent of Protestant ministers have affiliated in any way with Communist fronts and causes, on this one important project nearly 30% of the participants have been so affiliated. In their translation ten years ago, these Church "liberals" laid the foundation for current attacks on the

validity of the Virgin Birth of Christ and the questioning of
the Deity of Christ which are currently the rage in "modernist" theological circles. In the translation of the Old Testament, these scholars changed the prophetic passage in Isaiah
7:14 which reads:

> Behold, a virgin shall conceive, and bear a son and shall call his
> name Immanuel.

In the "new" version, copyrighted by the National Council
of Churches, this beloved passage reads:

> Behold, a young woman shall conceive and bear a son and shall
> call his name Immanuel.[26]

Through control of religious organizations and magazines,
Sunday School literature, prominent seminaries and journals
of theological thought, they guide the thinking and paralyze
the action of thousands of other dedicated men of God—by
controlling the information they get.

CHURCH LITERATURE

Here is an example of the influence of these collectivist
thinkers. The *Christian Century* is perhaps the most widely
distributed and most influential publication for Protestant
clergymen. The magazine's editorial policy is viciously anti-
anti-Communist,[27] opposes Congressional investigation of
Communist subversion,[28] disseminated the line that Chinese
Communists were "agrarian reformers" and promotes the big
government concept that a central authority should do all
things for all men. The magazine was a stalwart supporter of
Fidel Castro. In fact, three months *after* Castro himself announced to the world on December 2, 1961, that he had been
dedicated to communism since his teens and that his revolution had been a Communist one, the *Christian Century* on
March 6, 1962, said:

> Fidel Castro's powerful position as the president of the Cuban
> Agricultural Reform Institute has been turned over to Cuban
> Communist Carlos Rodriguez...The question which now arises is
> whether Castro controls or is controlled by the new president of
> the C.A.R.I....Have the Communists now completely captured

Cuba and are they retaining Castro as a showpiece? It is possible that a man as vain and as courageous as Castro would turn over leadership without a struggle? Has there been such a struggle and has the Cuban Communist Party won it?[29]

That these thoughts should be voiced in an influential church paper three months after Castro *himself* announced that he was a Communist, and almost three years after his firing squads executed thousands of Cubans, is utterly fantastic. This complete refusal to face reality and facts is hardly a qualification for an influential church editor.

Not all propaganda which finds its way into church literature and publications is so obvious. The *Adult Student*, official Sunday School publication of the General Board of Education of the Methodist Church, in the September 1962 issue presented an "objective" study of Communism.[30] Through omission, distortion and clever use of adjectives, and outright attacks on those who are trying to *do* anything about the threat of communism many Methodists were misled or had their concern about communism dulled.

Admittedly, Communist theory was presented authentically. However, Communist theory has played only a minor role in the growth of world communism. Communist tactics of infiltration, subversion, bribery, lies, bluff, brutality, treason, and murder are played down or ignored as the force which has spread communism around the world. A certain tolerance of communism and its leaders is implied or stated. Here is an example:

First of all, we deceive ourselves if we visualize communism in stark black-and-white terms, as absolute evil opposed to our absolute good.[31]

Marx is pictured as a "humanitarian" and "devoted husband and father."[32] This whitewashing of Marx by a widely distributed church publication ignores the starvation death of three of his infant children and the unhappy suicides of two others while in their teens. Further, Marx is equated with Jesus as a revolutionary. Under the heading, "Two Revolutionaries," the *Adult Student* says:

Jesus and Marx each lived in a time of social crisis...each believed that a new order lay within the reach of man...Both recognized...the need for social and moral reform...Both revealed a messianic sense of destiny...both men drew on their heritage of Old Testament prophecy to denounce evils in the world...Thus Marx and Christ were revolutionary leaders.[33]

The article presents the outright Communist argument that we are no better than the Communists in this way:

How easily, in personal judgments or national policies, we too slip into the same moral relativism! We condemn a "Communist foothold" ninety miles from Florida, yet support a military outpost five miles from Red China.[34]

The writer conveniently ignores that Communist forces are in Cuba by virtue of a bloody military overthrow of an existing, elected government. Communist military forces in Cuba are threatening to aggressively spread slavery throughout Latin America. The Nationalist forces on Quemoy and Matsu are an outpost of the free world, a deterrent necessary only because of Chinese Communist threats to swallow up Formosa and the rest of Southeast Asia.

CORRUPTING CHRISTIAN DOCTRINE

The most tragic effect of the Harry F. Wards, and like thinkers, in the theological schools has been the warping of the basic precepts of Christian doctrine until it is no longer an effective force in man's life. The result is seen in our society. It was observed in Korea where hazy concepts of right and wrong were found in men who had no firmly held, fundamental religious convictions.

Redbook magazine, in its August 1961 issue, published an article which sparked more than a little discussion among Bible-believers, clergy and theologians. Based on interviews with 100 students at eight leading seminaries, the article found:

...that 56% of the young ministerial students do not believe in the virgin birth of Jesus Christ...that 11% said "No" when asked, "Do you believe in the divinity of Jesus?"...that many of the 89% who said "Yes" wanted to define divinity to suit themselves. Belief in the immortality of man ranked as a major belief of only 2% and only 1% were convinced there will be a Second Coming of Christ. While only 29% believe in a real heaven and hell, 46% believe that Jesus ascended physically into heaven as described in the Gospels of Mark and Luke. (This is a contradiction in itself as twice as many reported believing in the Ascension into heaven as believe in heaven).[35]

This disintegration of the basic tenets of Christianity is the outgrowth of "modernist" theologians who deny the divine inspiration of the Bible. With many Christians rejecting their intellectually bankrupt concepts, a new and even more insidious movement, the "neo-orthodox," has arisen. Admitting the divine inspiration of the Scriptures, the neo-orthodox theologian leaves each man free to "interpret" the Bible for himself. Such interpretation has led to the hazy concepts of right and wrong Army investigators found among American POW's who collaborated in Korea. It has contributed to the general breakdown of moral standards in our society which has resulted in a 100% increase in the rate of illegitimate births in 20 years and sexual promiscuity among young people. The Church, with its watered down "interpreted" doctrines, has failed to stem this tide.

An official publication of the General Board of Education of the Methodist Church, *Workers With Youth*, in the September 1961 issue, suggested that adult leaders use films at young people's meetings and social events. The teacher's guide advised:

> ...it would be unrealistic to demand that such dramas be immaculate before they can qualify for such viewing. For under guidance, we learn from the sordid and pathological.[36]

Today's young people are over-exposed to the "sordid and pathological" from every side without its being presented in church programs as well. The tone of the advice given Methodist youth leaders is further demonstrated by this excerpt from the same article:

> For many people, the church has become a symbol for repression, for restriction, for a desperate fear of wrong...Perhaps it is far

better for youth to risk moral stumbling than to shrivel into barren and empty spirits, alone with their regrets.[37]

The church should be the one last bulwark against decaying morals and the permissive, experimentalist attitude toward sex reflected in movies, literature, news media, and TV. The use of false alternatives: risk moral stumbling *or* shrivel into a barren, empty spirit is a typical collectivist weapon for destroying traditional truth. The decay of the church as a vital moral force would be serious even without the drift toward "neutrality" by church leaders in the battle between East and West. A moral vacuum is being created in which those dedicated to the destruction of our society can work unimpeded. Admiral Ben Morrell, decorated Navy veteran, founder of the World War II Seabees, and outspoken conservative philosopher, describes the dilemma in this way:

> We urge people to go back to church; but there they frequently find that the very forces which have impaired our traditional beliefs have also affected the source of those beliefs, the church itself. The contemporary religious scene is in a state of confusion. Many of our prominent and articulate churchmen and some of our most influential church bodies have favored socialization of our national life and have urged that more power be placed in the hands of government.[38]

Over the years, those who have attempted to question the "drift to the left" in the Church have been subjected to ridicule, persecution, and continual efforts to stifle such discussion. At the height of the smears against anti-communism in the press of the United States, *Look* magazine, in the April 24, 1962 issue, published an article, *The Rightist Crisis in Our Churches*, The author, the religious editor of the United Press, ridiculed charges of infiltration of church organizations and cited as his authority, William C. Sullivan, assistant director of the Federal Bureau of Investigation. The article quotes Sullivan as saying:

> It can be stated factually and without equivocation that any allegation is false which holds that there has been and is, on a national scale, any substantial Communist infiltration of the

American clergy...There can be no doubt as to the loyalty of the overwhelming majority of the clergy of our nation.[39]

Sullivan is, of course, correct. No responsible critic has charged that any *substantial* part of the clergy is Communist or pro-Communist. Even the largest estimates of the knowing or unknowing participation of clergymen in Communist fronts is under 5% and this is far from substantial. However, the remarks of the assistant director of the FBI are widely circulated to discredit those who are concerned that a small hard-core of clergymen who are serving something or someone other than God dominate church organizations, publications, etc. at the top. Sullivan's quoted words come from a 90-minute speech he delivered at the Highland Park Methodist Church in Dallas, Texas, on October 19, 1961.

The balance of Sullivan's speech is ignored by those who ridicule the threat of communism in the churches. Sullivan listed nine reasons why clergymen succumb to Communist appeals. They include:

Failing to recognize obvious Communist propaganda in petitions, open letters, clemency appeals, pamphlets, etc....mistaken notions that clergymen can work with Communists for peace, civil rights, ending racial discrimination, etc. without harming religion and strengthening communism.

Confusing the values of communism with those of Christianity...confusing the social doctrines of Karl Marx with those of Jesus Christ...a tendency to reject or drastically dilute the supernatural content of religion in favor of a naturalistic form of humanism which can make it hard to logically take a strong stand against communism.

Show a proneness to join organizations without questioning their real sponsorship, direction, policies, etc....Making statements and drawing conclusions relative to foreign policy, economics, and domestic politics which exceed their field of competence.[40]

A good example of the final point was the 400 laymen and 200 clergymen who participated in the Fifth World Order Study Conference in Cleveland, Ohio, Nov. 18-21, 1958. They unanimously passed a resolution in favor of diplomatic recognition of Red China by the U.S. and the seating of the Communist Chinese government in the United Nations. The Conference was dominated by officers, staff personnel and members of the General Board of the National Council of Churches. J. Edgar Hoover, in a series of articles in the fundamental church publication, *Christianity Today*, outlined the Communist strategy of deceit in their potent attack against the Churches. Mr. Hoover said:

"Look," the Communists are saying, "we are tolerant of religion, we do not want to attack your faith. Rather, let's work together on issues in which we are both interested—peace, civil liberties, economic justice. We Communists are believers in love, justice, and the brotherhood of man. Let's not fight but work together."

Here is the deadly "come along" of communism, directed today at the Christian pulpit. This enables the Party to move close to unsuspecting ministers and laymen who see only the exterior verbiage and not the concealed danger. How does the Party work here? In many ways: encouraging churchmen to endorse, support and even participate in Communist-front groups, Communist-sponsored petitions; *to neutralize clerical opposition to communism*. (If a minister can be influenced to keep silent about the dangers of communism, the Party has gained).[41]

How many churches today are effectively opposing communism? In his article Mr. Hoover asks the clergy who read the magazine:

Have you encouraged members of your church to read about communism and to learn of its evil nature? Have you urged formation of discussion groups to acquaint men and women with the challenge.[42]

Unfortunately, much of the clergy in America has not heeded this sound advice. It appears they have been largely neutralized in the fight, one of the Communist goals Mr. Hoover outlined. Patriotic clergymen have been misled into opposing anti-Communist programs of all sorts by the anti-anti-Communist propaganda in the religious press and a sincere desire to avoid "controversy"—and opposing communism can be controversial.

CHAPTER VIII

THE PRESS, RADIO AND TV

Our republic and its press will rise and fall together.
—Joseph Pulitzer

THE NEWSMEN OF AMERICA must share with the U. S. Department of State the responsibility for the fall of China, the butchering of Budapest, Castro's rise in Cuba, and the destruction of the anti-Communist forces in Indonesia, Laos, Algeria and the Congo.

If alert, conscientious reporters had rejected official State Department press "handouts" and "briefings" and dug out the known and documented backgrounds of Castro, Ben Bella, and Mao Tse-tung, these Communist dictators wouldn't be in power today in Cuba, Algeria, and China.

If the American press had consistently informed the American people about the repeated failures, mistakes, and stupidity of the State Department, the mess in Washington would have been cleaned up years ago. Communism would not be threatening America today from an armed stronghold just 90 miles from Florida.

Walter Trohan, distinguished chief of the *Chicago Tribune* bureau in Washington, charitably attributes press failures to the "system" in Washington. In an article entitled, *Decline of the Fourth Estate*,[1] first written in 1951 and republished ten years later, Trohan said:

> In Washington, where a thousand newspapermen ply their trade, there is mounting suspicion that members of the press have begun to grow weary of the exacting watch-dog role and have been attaching themselves to the First Estate, the ruling class.

> The simple truth is that the press has given up on fact-hunting for the less arduous and frequently more profitable role of interpreting

what has gone before and predicting what is to come, in conformity with the Administration's pattern.

Trohan described how the press is seduced with high living, first-name treatment by the "greats" of government, expense-paid press trips abroad, "tips," and "leaks" on important stories, and off-the-record "briefings" by high officials. Such invitations and access to news sources are not available to the conscientious newsman who asks embarrassing questions. Trohan continued:

> The temptations to abandon reporting in favor of revealing are many...it is far easier to run through the grist of official handouts than to grub for news...Once a reporter convinces himself that he can bring his readers great news from these handouts, he has little or no compunction in lengthening the stride of his dispatches to take in the propaganda.

> It is not difficult to convince a reporter that it isn't the news but the way he writes it that counts. Especially when he finds that those who hew the line most consistently are acclaimed as journalistic greats...and when he becomes aware that Pulitzer prizes go to reporters taking handouts from law firms defending loyalty suspects or from a foreign nation.

The sins of the press are not limited to printing what it is handed. Instead, the American press has ignored, and at times deliberately covered up, the disclosures of repeated stupidity, if not treason, in high places.

The press handling of the story of William Arthur Wieland, whose part in bringing Castro to power was detailed in Chapters I and III, is a clear-cut example.[2]

At the Presidential press conference on January 24, 1962, a woman reporter asked why William Wieland and another man had been appointed to key State Department positions. The *St. Louis Post-Dispatch* account of the incident was typical of press coverage of the incident. It was written by Anthony Lewis of the *New York Times* News Service. It said:

> President Kennedy vigorously defended two State Department employees yesterday against a newspaper woman's charges that they were security risks. He rebuked the reporter, Mrs. Sarah

McLendon, when she made the accusation at his press conference. He personally vouched for clearance of the two men and said he hoped they would continue to serve without detriment to their character by your question.[3]

The story quoted the President as saying that he and Dean Rusk had personally examined Wieland's record and found him suited for his assignment. The report continued:

Mrs. McLendon did not say what lay behind her charge that the two men were security risks.[4]

Such reporting might be excused if Lewis, the writer, was not aware of Wieland's record during 15 years in the State Department. That he had the information became obvious in the final paragraphs of the long article, which said:

The Senate Internal Security Subcommittee had made public accusations against Wieland. These were contained in testimony before the committee by three former ambassadors in Latin America, William D. Pawley, Robert C. Hill, and Earl E. T. Smith.[5]

The story used generalizations from the testimony about Wieland in this way:

Pawley charged that Wieland, while director of the State Department Office of Caribbean-Mexican Affairs between 1958 and 1960,had assisted the overthrow of Fulgencio Batista's government of Cuba by Fidel Castro.

Pawley said Wieland had done so by buying the idea of not selling arms to either side in the revolutionary conflict. He also said that Wieland had a "close association with Herbert Matthews of the *New York Times.*"

Hill attributed what he termed "wrong decisions" on Cuba to Wieland. He said Wieland was either "a damn fool or a Communist, and I don't think he was a Communist."

Smith mentioned Wieland's name in a long list of persons whom he criticized for helping in the overthrow of the Batista regime.[6]

If this was all the evidence against Wieland, Mrs. McLendon's charge that he was a security risk was irresponsible. In creating this impression, the writer of the *New York Times* article ignored all the damning evidence against Wieland in the Senate reports, which was detailed in Chapter III.[7]

In ignoring this evidence, it can only be concluded that the *New York Times* writer was deliberately covering up for President Kennedy, Wieland, and the failure of the State Department security system.

The Wieland case is not the only instance where the press has suppressed serious charges against Kennedy appointees.

The questionable record of Arthur Goldberg, Kennedy's first Secretary of Labor and Justice Felix Frankfurter's replacement on the U.S. Supreme Court have been ignored. *The Wanderer*, a St. Paul, Minn. Catholic newspaper, in its September 27, 1962 issue, published charges that Goldberg had served a number of Communist causes and fronts and had, as secretary of labor, appointed a Communist to a government position.[8] The article charged that Goldberg had been president of the Chicago Chapter of the National Lawyers Guild. The Guild has been officially cited by the House Committee on Un-American Activities as "the legal bulwark of the Communist Party."[9]

Goldberg, the article charged, served as a sponsor of the Conference on Constitutional Liberties in America, designated as a Communist front by the Attorney General.[10]

As Secretary of Labor, Goldberg appointed Walter Gellhorn of Columbia University as official arbitrator for the International Organization of Masters, Pilots, and Mates, a labor organization representing key men in the Merchant Marine. Gellhorn, the article said, was identified as a Communist by Louis Budenz before the House of Representatives Select House Committee to Investigate Tax-Exempt Foundations.[11]

Does the past record of Mr. Goldberg inspire confidence of the American people when he is appointed as a Supreme Court Justice? Hardly. Justice Goldberg has never denied these affiliations, and despite their wide circulation by conservative groups, the nation's press has ignored them.

A similar "blackout" has been imposed on more serious

charges against Adam Yarmolinsky, special assistant to Defense Secretary Robert McNamara.

During a 1962 Senate investigation, it was charged that Yarmolinsky had admitted to World War II Army security investigators that he had attended meetings of the Young Communist League. He denied joining the organization, but said, "They (the Young Communist League) believed and I was inclined to believe that a so-called Communist government was a desirable end."[12]

As an employee of the extreme left-wing Fund for the Republic, Yarmolinsky authored a vicious attack on Congressional committees which investigate communism and also security agencies such as the FBI which attempt to protect the nation from Communist subversion.[13]

Yarmolinsky's parents have long records of support for left-wing causes which they continued even after their son was appointed to the number two spot in the Department of Defense. Yarmolinsky's father, Avrahm, who was born in Russia,[14] and his mother, a writer who uses the name Babette Deutsch,[15] have been charged with being members of the John Reed club in 1930.[16] More recently they signed a public appeal to President Kennedy in 1961 for Christmas clemency for Carl Braden and Frank Wilkinson.[17]

During 1962, Babette Deutsch was listed by the *New York Times* on a committee seeking freedom for the Communist terrorist, David Siquieros, in Mexico.[18] She also had advocated abolition of the House Committee on Un-American Activities and its investigations of Communists.[19]

Herbert Romerstein, a former undercover agent in the Communist Party, in his book, *Communism and Your Child*, recited some of these facts and said:

> If a young GI in our armed forces had parents with records such as this, he would be the subject of an investigation to determine his loyalty.[20]

Press coverage of these aspects of the background of a top Defense Department official have been limited to ridicule of those who attempt to call attention to them.

Liberal or left-wing bias of the press is not a new development. The story of how the *Saturday Evening Post, Collier's,* and other influential publications dwelled on the shortcomings of Chiang Kai-shek's government while glorifying the Communists is told in detail in Chapter III. The *Saturday Evening Post* published over 60 articles which promoted the Communist line during this period.[21]

The "hatchet job" the *New York Times* did on Senator Joseph McCarthy discussed in Chapter III[22] was typical of the press coverage given the Wisconsin Senator's fight to expose Communist infiltration in government.

These are not isolated cases.

The *Indianapolis News* called attention to the double standard in an editorial on April 11, 1962. The News said:

> When the Columbia Broadcasting System staged its famous TV program called "Thunder On The Right" it devoted considerable attention to a house bombing in California.
>
> The network, it will be recalled, ran a longish interview with a minister who had been critical of "right wing extremists," and who had had a bomb thrown at his house. The episode was treated as an example of what right wing agitation could lead to.
>
> Not, of course, that anyone had identified the house bomber. But it was concluded, this was the kind of thing which happens in the emotional atmosphere created by the right-wing extremists. Even though it was unclear who executed the bombing, America's right wing revival was deemed ultimately responsible and judged accordingly.

The *Indianapolis News* editorial then called attention to the death by hanging of Newton Armstrong, Jr. Armstrong, 19, was the editor of a conservative student newspaper at San Diego State College in California. His father was a prominent member of the anti-Communist John Birch Society. Armstrong's hands, when he was found hanging in a bedroom in his home, *were bound behind his back*. His death was finally labeled a "suicide" by the authorities.

After recounting the details, the *Indianapolis News* said that if the nation's press would apply the same standards to the hanging as they had to the bombing of the minister's home, then Armstrong's hanging was clearly the responsibility of "liberal" extremists. The *News* challenged CBS-TV with these words:

> We think it would made a compelling documentary by CBS; but we won't hold our breath waiting for it.

The nation's press exhibited the same double standard shown by CBS. The home bombing made headlines across the nation. The minister and prominent screen stars were interviewed on network news broadcasts. Without proof, right wing "radicals" and anti-Communists were blamed. By contrast, the death of the Armstrong boy was ignored. Those who suggested foul play were ridiculed.

The news magazines have shown the same prejudice against anti-Communists.

In its September 1, 1961 issue, *Life* magazine depicted Dr. Fred Schwarz, head of the Christian Anti-Communism Crusade, as a money hungry cynic. After a storm of public criticism, *Life's* publisher, C. D. Jackson, personally appeared on the platform of Schwarz' anti-communism school in Hollywood Bowl on October 16, 1961, and apologized. Jackson said:

> I believe we were wrong and I am profoundly sorry. It's a great privilege to be here tonight and align *Life* with Senator Dodd, Representative Judd, Dr. Schwarz and the rest of these implacable fighters against communism.[23]

Although Jackson apologized before the 10,000 people in the audience, *Life* did not print a retraction to be read by the 6-million subscribers who had seen the original smear. In fact, just six weeks after Jackson made his public apology to Schwarz, *Life* in its December 1, 1961 editorial, *Crackpots: How They Help Communism*, took another swipe at Schwarz and his efforts, saying that Dr. Schwarz and his Christian Anti-Communism Crusade attract "people who are too superheated to teach or learn anything."

C. D. Jackson, Special Assistant to former President Eisenhower, led the militant anti-McCarthy forces in the

President's official family and eventually succeeded in masterminding the destruction of the Wisconsin Senator.[24]

Jackson's boss, Henry Luce, the owner of *Time*, *Life* and other publications is another Republican with an affinity for "liberal" causes. Luce served for a time as a trustee of the Institute of Pacific Relations[25] while Owen Lattimore and his associates were using the IPR to influence State Department far eastern policies.

Luce also conceived and financed the *Commission on Freedom of the Press*.[26] The commission spent $ 200,000 of Luce's money and in 1948 produced a five-volume report which was a blanket condemnation of the nation's press for its bias *in favor of big business, wealth and the status quo.*[27] Luce had selected the ultra-liberal Chancellor of the University of Chicago, Robert Hutchins, to head the commission. Ten of the 12 members had a total of 68 affiliations with Communist front organizations.[28]

Life's sister publications, *Time,* has shown a similar tendency to be in the vanguard of those attacking anti-Communists, while maintaining its reputation as an anti-Communist, Republican-leaning publication.

In its October 22, 1951 issue, for example, *Time* "exposed" Senator Joseph McCarthy and used as "evidence" of McCarthy's wrong-doing his persecution of Gustavo Duran. *Time* stated, "Duran, never a Red, was definitely and clearly anti-Communist," implying that McCarthy's charges were sheer fabrication. *Time* published this falsehood even though it had been furnished copies of the Military Intelligence Reports which showed that Duran, a State Department employee, had been a member of the Communist secret police in Spain in 1936-38 and had served the conspiracy in various European capitals during the 1930's.[29]

The editors of *Time* selected the March 10, 1961 issue, to launch an attach on the anti-Communist John Birch Society. The charges of Robert Welch, the society's founder, that Dwight Eisenhower was a tool or dupe of the Communists had first been published in Chicago and Milwaukee newspapers eight months before during the 1960 Republican

National Convention. Scattered left-wing organs repeated the "expose".

However, it was not until the charges against Welch and the John Birch Society were published in the February 25, 1961 issue, of *People's World*, the official west coast Communist newspaper, that *Time* and hundreds of other newspapers and magazines picked the story up.

Strangely, *Time*, even though its reporters had been supplied a full assortment of John Birch literature[30] made the *same* error as the Communist *People's World* in identifying John Birch, for whom the society was named, as a *Navy* rather than an *Army* captain. *Time* also identified only three of the 26 members of the Council of the John Birch Society— *three of the same four mentioned in the People's World article*. Significantly, *Time* included the name of Adolphe Menjou in its list of Council members, as did the *People's World*, even though the *Time* reporter was furnished an up to date list and had been advised that Menjou had resigned several months before.[31]

The press, after headlining the attacks of nearly every left-wing spokesman against the John Birch Society, ignored the objective or friendly evaluations of the organization which were made in the following two years. For example, Ezra Taft Benson, Secretary of Agriculture in President Eisenhower's cabinet, made an evaluation of the John Birch Society which directly contradicts the nearly unanimous condemnations and "exposes" of the press. In a formal statement in *Church News*, the official publication of the Mormon Church, of which he is an elder, Benson said:

> I have stated, as my personal opinion only, that the John Birch Society is the most effective non-church organization in our fight against creeping socialism and godless communism.[32]

Benson's statement was ignored, or was buried in back pages of newspapers, as was the report of the only official investigation and evaluation of the John Birch Society. In 1963, the Senate Fact-finding Subcommittee on Un-American Activities of the California Legislature completed a two-year investigation of the John Birch Society and its activities. The report made some criticisms of statements made by the founder of the society, Robert Welch, but concluded:

> There is no question, as *National Review* points out, that he has stirred the slumbering spirit of patriotism in thousands of Americans, roused them from lethargy, and changed their apathy into deep desire to first learn the facts about communism and then implement that knowledge with effective and responsible action.[33]

Of the society's membership, the California Senate report stated:

> We have found the average member to have been concerned about the advances of the world Communist movement and the advances of Communist subversion in this country. The John Birch Society has provided the only organization with a militant program of study and action through which the frustrations of these people can be released...The average member is firmly convinced that the real threat is not essentially abroad, but that since our foreign policies are evolved here, and as they are influenced here, and since our retreat from one European crisis after another has been engineered in Washington, then the problem must be faced in this country.[34]

In conclusion, the Senate report said of the John Birch Society:

> We have not found the society to be either secret or a fascist organization...there have been instances of imprudent activity and indefensible statements but such isolated occurrences are not typical of the organization as a whole...We believe that the reason the John Birch Society has attracted so many members is that it simply appeared to them to be the most effective, indeed the only organization through which they could join in a national movement to learn the truth about the Communist menace and then take some positive concerted action to prevent its spread.[35]

In contrast to headlines and front-page placement accorded every unsubstantiated charge against the John Birch Society since the Communists triggered the anti-Birch campaign in

1961, very little attention was given to this official "clearance" by a committee of the California Senate.

Volumes could and should be written on the press coverage of President Kennedy's assassination by a Communist killer. Even after Oswald was captured and his Marxist affiliations disclosed, TV and radio commentators have conducted a continual crusade of distortion and smear to direct the blame against right wing or conservative groups.

The bias in the press is not always intentional. It is not necessarily deliberate. It is, to a degree, the natural result of the basic education newsmen have received in American schools coupled with a change in the fundamental concepts of journalism. The net effect, however, is the same.

Traditionally, the job of the newsman was to report the five "W's"—the who, what, when, where and why. While following these age-old precepts of the newspaper field, the reporter covering a political speech, for example, told what the speaker said. Opinions and explanations were left to the editorial page.

About 20 years ago schools of journalism started teaching prospective newsmen the technique of "interpretive reporting" which had been popularized by the news magazine, *Time*, and other Henry Luce publications.

The interpretive reporter, rather than faithfully recording in an orderly way a speaker's words, instead explains the "meaning" and "overall importance" of what is said. Such interpretation is justified with the contention that the average reader might not understand the report otherwise, that the broadened latitude given the reporter permits him to bring in explanatory background material and use a writing style which is more lively and interesting.

The danger in such "interpretive reporting" is that the reporter may himself not fully understand the *meaning* of what the speaker says. When an ultra-liberal reporter covers the speech of a conservative speaker, or vice versa, the writer is in basic disagreement with the message presented. He would feel that the speaker was misleading his audience. The reporter would therefore feel it his duty, not to relate the speaker's words objectively, but to present the case in such a way so that the reader gets the "truth." The danger, of course, is that the reporter may not himself know the "truth" and the facts are never fully presented so that the reader may judge for himself.

The use and abuse of interpretive reporting was so widespread during the 1960 Presidential campaign that widespread criticism developed within the press itself in the months following the election. Four independent studies were made by news agencies or press related organizations of the campaign coverage.

Interpretive reporting by the Associated Press and United Press received detailed attention in an exhaustive study by Richard Pourade, editor Emeritus of the *San Diego Union*. Completed almost a year after the election, Pourade's report reproduced portions of 140 daily AP and UPI dispatches which showed bias in the coverage of both candidates in the last five weeks of the campaign. In his summary, Pourade said:

> One of the most surprising features of the Associated Press coverage was the extent to which the so-called interpretive column questioned the motives of the candidates, disparaged their remarks, and brought the doubt of the Associated Press on their integrity and character.

> Even if the benefit of the doubt were given to all wire service reporters covering the campaign, that they did their journalistic best to submerge their personal feelings, the fact remains that the editorial laxity granted them in their daily coverage resulted in emotional treatment too often keyed to the reporters' personal convictions.

> Wire service reporters set themselves up as a final judge of crowds, reactions, sincerity of statement, pertincy of the statements politically and ideologically, and passed judgments on the merits of the various proposals. Too often, what the candidate had to say was buried beneath how the reporter personally evaluated it in the context of the whole campaign, and what he thought was the crowd's reaction to it.[36]

Earl Johnson, editor of United Press International, in a letter defending UPI's coverage, included a statement which said that the attitudes and reactions of reporters covering the candidates was disgraceful.[37]

The "disgraceful" behavior of the press was described by Willard Edwards, Washington correspondent of the *Chicago Tribune*, in a comprehensive study he made of election coverage. Of the press corps assigned to Vice President Nixon's campaign, Edwards said:

> Ninety per cent of this press corps, which ranged between 50 and 100 at various periods in the campaign, were all-out supporters of Kennedy. They were not only opposed to Nixon, they were outspoken in their hatred and contempt of him...it was loud and open. When Nixon was making a speech, there was a constant murmur or ridicule from many in the press rows just beneath the platform.[38]

THE MEN OF THE PRESS

Walter Lippmann is often acclaimed as the "Dean of American Newspapermen." His syndicated column appears in over 300 newspapers. His name on a book makes it a best-seller. Yet, since 1940, his "scholarly" appraisals of world affairs, his soothing, nothing-to-worry about evaluations of Communist intentions have rarely been right.

Lippmann is a longtime leftist. As a student at Harvard, he joined the British Fabian Society in 1909.[39] He became president of the Harvard chapter of the Intercollegiate Socialist Society the same year and was a close associate of Felix Frankfurter.[40]

Today, Lippmann rather consistently opposes any action to free the captive peoples behind the Iron Curtain. When the Hungarian rebellion erupted in 1956, Lippmann was quick to caution against aid for the Freedom Fighters. In his October 26, 1956 column, he wrote:

> It is not in our own interests that the movement in Eastern Europe should go so far that no accommodation with Russia is possible...In the interest of peace and freedom...we must hope for a

time—not forever, but for a time—the uprising in the satellite orbit will be stabilized at Titoism.

In 1961, Lippmann, a long-time apologist for Castro, was shocked by the attempted invasion of Cuba at the Bay of Pigs and actually expressed relief when the try failed. In his May 2, 1961 column, Lippmann said:

> Bad as have been the consequences of failure, they are probably less bad than would have been the indecisive partial success which was the best that could conceivably have been received.

Thirty-eight years after Walter Lippmann helped start the Intercollegiate Socialist Society chapter at Harvard, other influential editors, columnists, and Washington correspondents helped to found another left-wing political group, the Americans for Democratic Action in 1947.

The ADA's political platform advocates Red China's admission to the United Nations, transfer of all national armaments to a UN peace force, elimination of barriers on trade with Communist countries, and a hands off policy towards Cuba.[41]

The domestic goals of the ADA include total state control of the economic life of the nation through application of the theories of the British Fabian economist, John Maynard Keynes. An end to loyalty checks for federal employees, elimination of loyalty oaths for students on government scholarships and a halt to Congressional investigations of Communist activities are other goals of the ADA.[42]

Among the founders of this left-wing group was Marquis Childs, Washington correspondent of the *St. Louis Post-Dispatch*.[43] Childs' writings are widely syndicated and he appears regularly as a panelist on the TV news interview show, "Meet the Press."

Other ADA founders included the Alsop brothers, Joseph and Stewart, whose columns are used by many newspapers.[44] They are also regular contributors to the *Saturday Evening Post*. Ken Crawford, now a featured columnist in *Newsweek* magazine, was an ADA founder, as was James Wechsler, editor of the *New York Post*.[45] Elmer Davis, influential newsman, author and head of the Communist-riddled Office of War Information, and other lesser known newsmen were also founders of the ADA.[46]

All newsmen are not liberals or socialists. However, as in so many other fields, the key jobs, acclaim as journalistic geniuses, opportunity to write syndicated columns, and guest spots as panelists on TV news shows go to the liberals.

THE BROADCASTERS

Edward R. Murrow, one-time vice-president of CBS, and now head of the United States Information Agency, Howard K. Smith of CBS and ABC, and Chet Huntley of NBC have, by their associations, writings, and actions, marked themselves as biased liberals.

Edward R. Murrow's service to leftist causes dates back to 1935 when he served on the board of the Institute of International Education, an organization which encouraged young American school teachers to take their summer training at the University of Moscow—and subsidized their trips there.[47]

As the nation's top producer of TV news "documentaries" Murrow pioneered the technique of "forgery by film." An ardent defender of Alger Hiss, Owen Lattimore, John Stewart Service and others discharged from government service for security reasons, Murrow's assistance earned him the praise of Owen Lattimore, who in 1950 in his book, *Ordeal by Slander*, said:

> Before I could speak for myself, Murrow kept the record straight by repeatedly drawing attention to the fact that nothing had been proved against me.[48]

Lattimore pointed out that Murrow consistently gave him "air time" to present his views. A year later, the Senate Internal Security Subcommittee found Lattimore to be "a conscious articulate agent of the Soviet conspiracy." Murrow's defense of Lattimore could possibly be excused as bending over backwards to be fair. However, when the subject of Murrow's broadcasts was the late Senator Joseph McCarthy, there was no fairness. The character assassination Murrow did in editing film to make McCarthy look like a giggling psychopath brought protests from even McCarthy's most bitter enemies.

The *Saturday Review's* Gilbert Seldes despised McCarthy but he was shaken by the viciousness of Murrow's "objective" film report. He said:

> The people who roared with delight should ask themselves quickly how they would have felt if the same technique had been applied to someone they liked—for example, to (Adlai) Stevenson.[49]

John Cogley, another vehement critic of McCarthy, writing in the liberal Catholic journal, *Commonweal*, pointed out...

> ...the Murrow show has set a potentially dangerous precedent which those who are now applauding may find good reason to regret in time to come.[50]

Murrow's filmed defense of another security risk, J. Robert Oppenheimer, drew criticism from even Dorothy Schiff, publisher of the ultra-ultra-liberal *New York Post*. Mrs. Schiff said that the Oppenheimer case did not seem to present a clear-cut issue on which liberals could make a fight. Yet, she said:

> ...Murrow asked Oppenheimer only questions that tended to put him in the best possible light. The impression left with the uninformed viewer was that of a hero and a martyr.[51]

Murrow's questioning of Oppenheimer avoided the fact that Oppenheimer's wife, brother, and mistress were Communists, that Oppenheimer had contributed sums of up to $1000 annually to the Communist Party, and that he had admitted lying under oath to government security agents when questioned during World War II when he headed the atom bomb project.[52]

Murrow carried his bias into government service. When the Communists broke the nuclear test ban in September 1961, Murrow's *Voice of America* broadcasts which supposedly send a message of freedom behind the Iron Curtain handled the announcement this way:

> Khrushchev, with aching heart, consented to test again.[53]

Howard K. Smith is another widely-heralded TV news commentator and producer of "documentaries."

Smith made headlines on November 11, 1962, when he brought Alger Hiss, convicted perjurer and one-time Communist espionage agent, out of obscurity. Hiss was invited to participate in the Smith-narrated, *Political Obituary of Richard M. Nixon*. Hiss discussed the character and personality of former Vice President Nixon, who as a young congressman in 1948, played a large part in exposing Hiss as a Communist agent.

Anyone familiar with Smith's views and writings would not have been surprised at his invitation to Alger Hiss. For instance, in his book, *The State of Europe*, published in 1949 when the cold war was four years old, Smith had this praise for the Communist satellites of Eastern Europe:

> Four years of "People's Democracy"—to sum up my conclusions—have probably yielded Eastern Europe a solid net gain. If the Communist regimes have been indistinguishable from their predecessors in political repression, they have been at least in the social and economic realms, an outstanding success.[54]

Smith exposed himself as a socialist in the same volume when he said:

> The maintenance of the system of private enterprise is not only becoming technically less possible; it is rapidly losing its last moral justifications.[55]

Smith explained his inability to oppose communism in this way:

> Whenever the merits and demerits of the Welfare State and its planned economy, the main point is that it is coming by one means or another. The only question is how long it will take and in what form it will come.

> It is the inherent inevitability of this great mutation that has made it impossible for me to take a clear anti-Soviet attitude. A good deal of the Soviet economic and social analysis is shrewder and more to the point than much of the thinking about what is going on in the west. For all their distorted vision, the Soviets have seen the clear fact that the survival of capitalism is impossible in

Europe. They have certainly brought to the common man of
Europe a richer life.[56]

In an earlier volume, *The Last Train from Berlin*, written
in 1942, Smith said:

Russia looked better the longer I stayed and the more I saw.[57]

Smith has held honored and responsible posts with both
CBS and ABC-TV networks. His views have been projected
into American homes as objective news analysis. He has won
the highest awards of the journalism and broadcast professions, the DuPont Award, the Overseas Press Club award for
best radio reporting from abroad, the Sigma Delta Chi award
for radio journalism, and a TV Emmy.[58]

Chet Huntley, ace commentator and news analyst for NBC-
TV, narrated an NBC "White Paper" on the controversy over
welfare reforms instituted in the small city of Newburgh, N.Y.
Entitled, "The Battle of Newburgh," it was broadcast on
January 28, 1962.

The day following the program, Joseph M. Mitchell, city
manager of Newburgh, issued an 18-point indictment of the
program. He made these charges:

Approximately 60,000 feet of film was taken of which 2,000
appeared on the show. Statements of the prominent city leaders
who *supported* the welfare reforms were edited out.

Biased witnesses, two former office holders and the husband of a
welfare department employee, criticized the reform program.
They were presented as typical Newburgh citizens without dis-
closing their personal involvements which caused them to oppose
the welfare reform.

NBC filmed the principal defense of the welfare reform program
in a bar which gave the impression that the only support for the
reform program came from those who sit around bars drinking.

False figures were used in presenting the Newburgh budget, the
entire city was pictured as a slum, and city officials were ridiculed
by editing which presented their remarks out of context.

The program was built for emotional appeal rather than a calm
examination of the facts. For example, the city manager was

pictured saying, "No truly needy person has suffered." This was followed by a filmed sequence of a crying man.[59]

Five months later, the crying man voluntarily confessed to city officials how the "documentary" had been staged. In a tape-recorded interview with the city council, Thomas H. Weygant, said he had been paid $50 by NBC for his part in the "news" film. He had been carefully rehearsed on what to say and how to say it. NBC employees, Weygant said, had deliberately undressed his children before they appeared on the show to make it appear that he could not afford to clothe them.[60] NBC denied the charges. The $50, they said, was a collection taken up by the cameramen to help the unfortunate, abused victim of the Newburgh welfare reform program.

Mitchell's most telling indictment of the NBC White Paper was the omission of any explanation of the 13 regulations which provoked the controversy.

Widely condemned by liberals as "cruel" and "inhumane" and praised by conservatives as long overdue, the Newburgh reforms included requirements that all able-bodied men on relief had to report for work in city maintenance departments; that those on relief who refused to accept offered employment would be denied further relief; that relief payments to any family could not exceed the take-home pay of the lowest paid city employee with the same number of children; and that relief be denied to mothers of illegitimate children who bear additional illegitimate children.[61] These provisions were not spelled out on the NBC "White Paper" so NBC viewers could not judge the reforms for themselves.

Chet Huntley, of course, was simply the commentator on the show. The words he spoke, the film he showed were the compilation of the producers, editors and writers of NBC news. The NBC "White Paper" series is a product of this team work. *The Battle of Newburgh* was the ninth NBC "White Paper"—and it was a typical production.

All newsmen are not biased. There are good publishers and conscientious reporters. Some of them are liberals—some are conservatives. However, they can't report the truth if they never get it. That's the spot many dedicated and responsible newsmen are in—without knowing it.

Rex Davis, veteran news director of the CBS-affiliate in St. Louis, KMOX, put the problem into words. He was interviewed by the *St. Louis Globe Democrat* when he completed 16 years on the air in St. Louis and said:

> How do you know what's the truth? You try like the devil but you are dependent on the news services (for national and international news) and if they goof, what do you do?[62]

Another newsman put it this way: "If you can't trust your news sources, what can you trust?"

This states the problem. Thousands of working newsmen across the country, being conscientious themselves, attribute these same characteristics to the men who reach top positions on the AP and UPI news services. They depend on AP and UPI for the news they report to their own readers and listeners. They base their own judgments of world happenings on these "facts."

How reliable are these sources?

Wire service coverage of the 1960 presidential campaign and the criticism of it within the press has already been discussed.[63]

There are other examples. When Whittaker Chambers died in 1961, the AP obituary used so many "hate words" in describing Chambers that a number of newspapers protested. The *Sentinel Star* of Orlando, Florida, published an editorial dissent and then lodged a formal protest with AP's general manager, Frank Starzel. The editorial said:

> The staid, powerful Associated Press handled the news of Whittaker Chambers in a peculiar way. Chambers, you may remember was a $30,000 a year senior editor of *Time* who, in 1948, put the finger on Alger Hiss, the State Department spy, and lost his job, his reputation, and his health. The only reason we can think of is patriotism. He made a clean breast of everything; he wanted to atone for his mistake by warning the US of its danger.

> The AP's handling tends to indict him for being loyal to the US. The AP calls him a "turncoat Communist." Turncoat is a despised

appellation and the inference is that anyone who turns from communism should be despised. The AP says Chambers "tattled." Telling the truth is honorable, but, from childhood, we are taught that tattling is unworthy. The AP says Chambers "recited" to a "Congressional spy-hunting committee." Here the inference is that he merely repeated a cooked-up story and that spy-hunting is not a serious matter.

Whereas the AP calls Hiss "brilliant," it kisses off Chambers as being "pudgy, short and fat" and says "he lived with a woman outside of marriage." This was before he married a woman to whom he was devoted for 30 years until his death.[64]

The *Sentinel Star* editorial concluded with this observation:

We are living in peculiar times, gentlemen of the Associated Press, when patriots are maligned.

We are indeed living in peculiar times. The maligning of patriots by the Associated Press and other segments of the communications industry is not limited to men like Whittaker Chambers. Even George Washington, the father of our country, is being downgraded.

On February 22, 1961, the Associated Press supplied its member newspapers with a feature story marking the birthday of our first president. It pictured George Washington as a gambling slavekeeper who was a sucker for con-man schemes.[65]

In September 1962, former General Edwin Walker went to Mississippi to observe the military forces which occupied Oxford to force the enrollment of James Meredith, a Negro, to the University of Mississippi. While in Oxford, Walker was arrested by military authorities and charged with inciting a riot, sedition against the United States, and other crimes.

The charges arose, in part, from Associated Press reports that Walker had incited students to riot against lawful authority and had led them in a charge against U.S. marshals. The AP account was written by a 21-year old AP reporter, Van Savell, who stated that Walker...

...took command of a group of students, climbed a Confederate statue, and told the crowd that Governor Ross Barnett had betrayed Mississippi.[66]

The story quoted Walker as saying, while perched on the statue:

> But don't let up now. You may lose this battle but you will have been heard. This is a dangerous situation. You must be prepared for possible death. If you are not, go home now.

The AP news story was the one that most newspapers and radio stations used. It was repeated and rephrased countless times. A completely different story was told by United Press International. In a dispatch received on the St. Louis UPI teletype at 11:23 PM CDT, September 30, 1962, the same incident was described in this way:

> During a lull in the rioting, General Edwin Walker mounted a Confederate statue on the campus and begged the students to cease their violence. He said: "This is not the proper route to Cuba." His pleas were greeted with one massive jeer.[67]

Almost four months later, after Walker's illegal confinement in a mental institution, a series of court appearances and hearings, the federal grand jury at Oxford, Mississippi, refused to indict him and all charges were dropped on January 21, 1963. Walker is suing Associated Press for $2-million, charging that he was libelled.

Walker's attorney, Clyde Watts of Tulsa, Oklahoma, has obtained a sworn statement from a deputy sheriff in Oxford, who was eating in the same restaurant as General Walker when news was received that students were rioting on the campus. Both Walker and the sheriff left the restaurant almost immediately. The sheriff's statement says that when he got into his car and turned the radio on he heard a news report that rioting students were being led by Walker—whom he had just seen leaving the restaurant.[68]

Another influence on working newsmen are the half dozen or so "prestige" newspapers which newsmen themselves rank as the "best" in the nation.

Of the ten newspapers which normally top the polls of journalism professors, newsmen and editors, only one, the

Chicago Tribune, presents a consistently conservative viewpoint on *both* national and international affairs. Three other papers are moderately conservative on economic matters but tend to blind internationalism in coverage of foreign news. The other six, the *New York Times, Washington Post, St. Louis Post-Dispatch, Atlanta Constitution, Louisville Courier Journal*, and *Milwaukee Journal* are ultra-liberal in their viewpoint.

The *New York Times*, consistently rated as the number one newspaper in America, is frequently regarded as the source of all truth by intellectuals, college professors, working newsmen, many advertisers, and even some conservatives. The untruths in the *New York Times* coverage of Senator Joseph McCarthy, its build-up of Castro, its omission of key facts against William Arthur Wieland, and the pro-Communist bias of its book review section during the tragic China period have already been noted.[69]

The *St. Louis Post Dispatch* is normally ranked as the top newspaper in the midwest and the third or fourth nationally, behind the *New York Times* and the *Washington Post*. It was read daily by President Kennedy. Adlai Stevenson and other top officials have appeared in ads publicly endorsing the paper.

An independent audit[70] of the 210 issues of the *St. Louis Post-Dispatch* published in the January 16-October 17, 1961 period showed that the paper published 28 editorials on disarmament and nuclear testing, 21 on Berlin, 15 on Red China, 10 on Cuba, 7 on Laos, and 7 on the Congo. There were 23 other editorials on the internal Communist threat.

An analysis of the position taken by the *St. Louis Post Dispatch* in these editorials[71] showed that the paper...

...urged maximum concessions to achieve agreements based largely on mutual trust with the Communists on disarmament and nuclear testing. The U.S. and Russia were blamed equally for the disarmament negotiations stalemate.

...advocated "accommodation" of Communist demands on Berlin and trading away American rights for agreements which the Communists might, or might not, keep.

...favored the admission of Red China to the United Nations.

...opposed any intervention in Cuba and condemned even feeble U.S. efforts to unseat Castro.

...spoke against U.S. aid to the anti-Communists in Laos and recommended that the anti-Communist government be forced to put Communists into key positions in a coalition cabinet.

... approved UN efforts to crush the anti-Communist forces of Moise Tshombe in Katanga and advocated a coalition government for the Congo with Communists in key spots.

On the domestic scene, the *Post-Dispatch*, during the same period published 23 editorials dealing with the activities of Communists in the United States, attempts by Congress to investigate subversion, and educational efforts by public and private figures to alert people to the menace of communism. The *Post-Dispatch* position...[72]

...suggested the need to abolish the House Committee on Un-American Activities and halt congressional investigations of communism.

...contradicted J. Edgar Hoover's statement that riots against the House Committee on Un-American Activities in San Francisco were Communist inspired.

...ridiculed a proclamation of Missouri's governor, John Dalton, declaring an anti-communism week in Missouri, claiming that the Communists were not a threat internally.

...condemned government rulings that the Communist Party, USA should register as an agent of a foreign power.

...linked all anti-Communist movements with Fascism and the Ku Klux Klan.

...praised Senator Fulbright's memorandum which said that "the American people have little if any need to be alerted to the menace of the cold war" because the principal problem of government leaders is to "restrain the desire of the people to hit the Communists with everything we've got" in Laos and Cuba.

The *Post-Dispatch* viewpoint differs little from those of

other top "thought molding" newspapers, the *New York Times, Washington Post, Milwaukee Journal, Louisville Courier Journal*, etc.

Whether the slanting, distortion, and control of news is done by Fabian socialists, misguided idealists, or actual Communists is not important. The result is the same.

Free, representative government is predicated on the assumption that the people, having the *facts*, will make the right decisions when they go to the polls. If the press abdicates its responsibility, the system will fail. Breaking through the "paper curtain" which screens most Americans from the truth is a primary challenge.

CHAPTER IX

MENTAL HEALTH

*The pretense is made that to do away with right and wrong
would produce uncivilized people, immorality, lawlessness,
and social chaos. The fact is that most psychiatrists and
psychologists and other respected people have escaped from
moral chains and are able to think freely.*

—Dr. G. Brock Chisholm, first head,
World Federation of Mental Health

FOR THE RARE CITIZEN who escapes indoctrination in
the "new social order" in progressive schools; for the Bible-
believing Christian who rejects "theologians" who teach that
socialism is the new "Kingdom of God on Earth;" for all the
sturdy souls who hold to age-old concepts of right and wrong,
and are vocal about it, the collectivists have one final, ultimate weapon. Declare them insane!

Fantastic? Not at all. Just as in the fields of education,
religion, press, radio and TV, the collectivists have succeeded
in infiltrating and twisting the honorable psychiatric and
psychological professions to their own ends.

The "new leaders" in the psychiatric field propose to re-edu-
cate the world's population using psychological procedures to
create a new breed of amoral men who will accept a one-world
socialistic government. They hold the weapon of commitment
to a mental institution over the heads of those "reactionaries"
who rebel at accepting the "new social order."

It sounds unbelievable? Listen to the words of Dr. G. Brock
Chisholm, first head of the World Federation of Mental
Health, and later head of the World Health Organization of
the United Nations. His address, sponsored by the William
Alanson White Psychiatric Foundation was delivered in October 1945, in Washington, D.C. to a large group of
psychiatrists and high government officials. Chisholm said:

What basic psychological distortion can be found in every civilization of which we know anything? The only psychological force capable of producing these perversions is morality—the concept of right and wrong. The re-interpretation and eventual eradication of the concept of right and wrong are the belated objectives of nearly all psychotherapy.

If the race is to be freed from its crippling burden of good and evil it must be psychiatrists who take the original responsibility.[2]

Chisholm has been obsessed for years with the idea that instilling concepts of right and wrong, love of country, and morality in children by their parents is the paramount evil. In another speech, he said:

The people who have been taught to believe whatever they were told by their parents or their teachers are the people who are the menace to the world.[3]

What besides concepts of morality and right and wrong does Dr. Chisholm consider to be a neurosis? He explains it in his speech:

Even self-defense may involve a neurotic reaction when it means defending one's own excessive wealth from others who are in need.[4]

Chisholm proposes that psychotherapy be used to eradicate such neuroses as a man wishing to defend his own private property in this way:

There must be an opportunity to live reasonably comfortable for all the people in the world on economic levels which do not vary too widely either geographically or by groups within a population. *This is a simple matter of redistribution of material wealth.*[5]

This is the basic Marxist concept that those who have, should have it taken away. How different are Chisholm's ideas from those of America's pioneers. Had they decided on some scheme of redistribution of the wealth, all would have stayed poor and hungry, because there was no wealth. Instead of redistributing what meager wealth was available, they conceived a system of government which safeguarded private property. Initiative was stimulated and people were encouraged to *produce*, and by producing, to *create* new wealth for themselves. In the process, all men benefited from more jobs, new products and services. In freedom, men have made more spiritual, moral, intellectual progress, and produced more material wealth for themselves and others than under any other system conceived by man.

The answer to the problem of poverty is not redistribution of wealth, or "cutting the pie" into smaller pieces. This is socialism. The true answer is stimulating people to create and produce more—making more and bigger "pies."

Chisholm and his "mental health" associates plan to achieve world-wide distribution of wealth. This means a world government in which all citizens can vote "democratically" to take away the wealth of every American and divide it up in little equal shares. All will then be poor.

Chisholm's ideas are not those of a single "crackpot." After expressing these views widely and frequently, he became head of the World Federation of Mental Health and the World Health Organization. Other psychiatrists and psychologists have similar views, officially expressed.

At the International Congress of Mental Health in London in 1948, prominent American "mental healthers" including Dr. George S. Stevenson, medical director of the National Association for Mental Health, Dr. Daniel T. Blain, and Dr. Harry Stack Sullivan served on the Preparatory Commission. Their goals were revealed in this declaration, published and distributed in the United States by the National Association for Mental Health:

> Principles of mental health cannot be successfully furthered in any society *unless there is progressive acceptance* of the concept of *world citizenship*. World citizenship can be widely extended among all peoples through applications of the principles of mental health...At a major turning point in world history there is an *obligation* on social scientists and psychiatrists to attempt this new formulation.[6]

Chisholm, in outlining his program for "enduring peace and social progress" said that psychiatry should meet this "obligation" by reaching people who matter with "clear thinking, talking, and writing." Who are the people who matter? Chisholm said:

> Teachers, the young mothers and fathers, the parent-teachers associations, youth groups, service clubs, schools and colleges, the churches and Sunday school... everyone who can be reached and given help toward intellectual freedom and honesty for themselves and for children whose future depends on them.[7]

Naturally, in speaking to such groups, the "mental health" advocate will seldom openly suggest abolishing right and wrong, private property, or loyalty to country. More likely, they talk of "adjusting to a changing world" and learning to "compromise." They may unfold the story of how one of nine Americans need psychiatric help. They cite the grievous need for increased funds for training "mental health" workers. How many times have you been exposed to the "mental health" pitch?

Chisholm's associates have achieved positions of great influence. He suggested working through PTA's. Professor Harry Overstreet, and his wife, Bonaro, have served as consultants to the National Congress of Parents and Teachers (PTA) and its magazine for many years. Here are excerpts from one of Overstreet's many books, *The Great Enterprise*, published in 1952:

> Through clinical experience, we have come to recognize one invariable characteristic of that sick condition of the mind we call neurosis: namely, Rigidity.[8]

> ...the rigidity is found in several areas. In each one of these we can predict that the individual will respond with trigger-quickness and in exactly the same way. Sometimes, it appears, such persons have constellations of prejudice areas. A man, for example, may be angrily against race equality, public housing, the TVA, financial and technical aid to backward countries, organized labor, and the preaching of social rather than salvational religion.

> Try as we may, we can scarcely open up a subject that does not tap their permeative, automatic "againstness." Such people may appear "normal" in the sense that they are able to hold a job and otherwise maintain their status as members of society, but they

are, we now recognize, *well along the road toward mental illness.*[9]

Using such criteria, the mental health experts estimate that one out of nine, or five out of ten, and some say, every American needs "mental health" care. Are you among them? Do you hold rigidly to "outmoded" concepts of right and wrong? Do you reject socialism? Do you oppose foreign aid waste? Do you object to letting African cannibals vote on how we should live under a world government? If so, you are by "definition" well along the road toward mental illness and in need of "treatment."

How do the experts hope to achieve control over you and the other 25-million or more Americans they say need "care"? Chisholm provided the answer:

> We may begin to speculate on the advisability that psychiatrists, once the necessary one, two, or three million are available should be trained as salesmen and be taught all the techniques of breaking down sales resistance.[10]

How successful have they been? Think for a moment of all the stars of TV, radio, the movies, writers, etc. (the people who matter) who look upon their sessions with a psychiatrist or analyst as a "status symbol."

How many of these public figures are in the forefront of "peace" movements? How many are vocal advocates of unilateral disarmament and nuclear test bans? Are they among the "comedians" who were staunch and consistent supporters of Castro as a humane "reformer"? Are they the comedians who regularly poke "fun" at patriotism and conservative political leaders, ridicule God, and downgrade traditional concepts of morality?

For those too stubborn to succumb to the psychiatrist's super-salesmanship, Chisholm proposed one final remedy when he asked:

> Should attempts be made by the profession to institute *compulsory treatment* for the neurosis as for other infectious diseases?[11]

Since Chisholm offered this idea 18 years ago, legal systems have been established in a majority of states for involuntary and *compulsory* hospitalization and treatment of neurosis. The state laws have been based on a prototype bill published originally by the Federal Security Agency of the Public Health Service, now a part of the Department of Health, Education and Welfare.

Entitled, a *Draft Act Governing Hospitalization of the Mentally Ill*, it is, in fact, a skeleton bill designed for adoption uniformly by federal, state, and territorial governments to radically alter commitment procedures. The preface to the *Draft Act*, which has come to be known as the "model mental health law" was written by Dr. George Stevenson, participant in the London Conference.[12]

Few legislators who passed the "model mental health laws" realized that Chisholm, Stevenson and their associates define "mental illnesses" as a "sense of loyalty to a particular nation, a sense of loyalty to a moral code, strict adherance to concepts of right and wrong, opposition to foreign aid or communism."

Yet, today, if *you* hold these beliefs, two *examiners* who may or may not have psychiatric training or be doctors, can certify *you are mentally ill*.[13] If you won't consent to voluntary treatment, a police officer can arrest you. You can be subjected to three to five days of treatment of the psychiatrist's choosing *before you even get a hearing to protect your rights* in most states. Treatment can include electric shock treatments, chemotherapy, hypnosis, or conceivably, a frontal lobotomy. The procedures under which the *patient's* rights are "protected" are open to serious question. When the hearing is held to determine whether permanent commitment and further treatment is necessary, the patient need not be notified of the proceedings and may not be present if the psychiatrists "believe" such attendance would be injurious to the patient.[14] The court conducting the hearing need not be bound by the normal rules of evidence.[15] Basically, all that is necessary to "revoke" all the constitutional rights of any citizen is to accuse him of being "mentally ill."

"Loopholes" in the same laws permit the commitment of

innocent, sane people by a greedy relative, a bored husband, or an "interested" friend. They were exposed by the *Reader's Digest* recently in an article, *The Tragedy of Sane People Who Get "Put Away."*[16] It said:

> Under faulty "reform" laws, thousands of normal men and women are being railroaded into mental hospitals every year.[17]

POLITICAL WEAPON

The threat of discrediting a conservative political leader by branding him as mentally ill, or committing an anti-Communist to a mental institution has been used sparingly, but frequently enough to establish a frightening pattern.

Attempts were made to discredit Whittaker Chambers testimony when he unmasked the high State Department official, Alger Hiss, as a Communist traitor. A psychiatrist *who had never examined Chambers* took the witness stand and under oath branded him as a psychopath.[18] Such charges do not have to be made formally to be effective. The late Eleanor Roosevelt in her column *My Day* for August 4, 1948, branded the testimony of Elizabeth Bentley in exposing high government officials as Communists as "the fantastic story of this evidently neurotic lady."

In 1957, an obscure Californian was committed to a mental institution because of public utterances against the United Nations. The examining psychiatrist testified at the sanity hearing that the man *did not come to conclusions of the community*.[19] Do you always agree with the majority?

To protect Hungarian Freedom Fighters who testified before the UN Committee on Hungary from possible Communist reprisals, Povl Bang-Jensen, a Danish diplomat and assistant secretary of the committee, refused to divulge their names. In addition, he charged, and documented, that errors were being written into the draft of the Committee's report which would make the document a laughing stock rather than a sharp indictment of Communist terror in Hungary.[20]

To discredit and silence him, UN medical authorities circulated a report intimating that Bang-Jensen was "mentally ill." He was dismissed by Secretary General Dag Hammarskjold. Meanwhile, he had assembled evidence, from two Russians wishing to defect, that the Communists had achieved working control of the highest policy-making levels in the UN Secretariat.[21]

Two years later, after his sanity had been established by a reputable psychiatrist,[22] and a long fight to get official recognition of his story, Bang-Jensen was found, shot to death near his New York home. Police quickly labeled the death a suicide.

The United States Senate Internal Security Sub-committee after an 18-month study of the case said:

> It is the opinion of this report, however, that the finding of suicide was based on incomplete evidence. There are too many solid arguments against suicide, too many unanswered questions, too many serious reasons for suspecting Soviet motivation and the possibility of Soviet implication.[23]

Note the pattern. First, an attempt to discredit the Dane with unfounded charges of "mental illness" and later a probable phony suicide, at which the Communists are past masters.

On April 25, 1962, Mary Kimbrough Jones, a secretary in the Department of Agriculture was sitting on a powder keg. Her boss had just been transferred and denied access to the office where the files contained information implicating top government officials in the $200-million Billie Sol Estes farm storage scandals. Already, one government official who had possibly stumbled onto such evidence had committed "suicide" by shooting himself *five times* with a cumbersome bolt action rifle!

Shortly before noon on April 25, police arrived in Mary Jones' office. They seized Miss Jones and transferred her to a mental hospital. Two days later, two government psychiatrists certified that she was mentally ill.[24] News reports were circulated that her own doctor had agreed with the findings. He denied these statements as false.

After a public clamor, and 12 days in isolation in a psychiatric ward, Mary Jones was certified as sane and released by the District of Columbia Mental Health Commission. Even so, ten days after her release as sane, the two psychiatrists, *without any further observation of the woman,* once again announced to the press that she was mentally ill. This was a blatant attempt to impugn her possible testimony in the Estes case.[25]

THE WALKER CASE

Major General Edwin A. Walker, a decorated war hero and outspoken anti-Communist, was arrested leaving Oxford, Mississippi, on October 1, 1962, on orders of Attorney General Robert Kennedy who was in Washington. Walker was charged with seditious conspiracy and insurrection, despite conflicting newspaper accounts of his actions. United Press said that Walker cautioned the crowds against violence. The Associated Press said he advocated rioting.[26]

A government psychiatrist in Washington, D.C. *who had never seen or examined Walker,* adjudged him "mentally ill" on the basis of newspaper stories.[27] Even before getting this long distance "diagnosis," the government spirited Walker out of Mississippi in a Border Patrol plane. He did not get to raise bail or obtain a lawyer. He was committed to the Federal Prison Medical Center at Springfield, Missouri, for psychiatric examination, estimated to take 60 to 90 days.[28]

Even ultra-liberal groups were shocked at the crude violation of Walker's civil rights, and after eight days as a political prisoner, he was released. The case became too *hot* for the government to handle.

After release, Walker voluntarily submitted to a psychiatric examination and was pronounced "mentally sound" and "operating on a superior level of intelligence" by the head of one of the Southwest's largest psychiatric centers.[29] His final vindication came when a federal grand jury refused to indict him and the sedition and insurrection charges were dropped.

Walker's treatment, while outrageous, was legal under the provisions of the United States Code, Sections 4244, 4245, 4246, 4247, and 4248. Undoubtedly, they would be found unconstitutional if tested in the Courts. However, they are presently the law. Any citizen's rights could be denied just as Walker's were.

All psychiatrists do not accept the amoral, socialistic theories of Brock Chisholm and Harry Overstreet. Reputable psychiatrists learn whether psychological disturbances result from actual organic difficulties in the central nervous system for which rather specific therapy is available.[30] If not, attempts are made through counseling to reinforce the concepts of good and evil, right and wrong in the patient. With such help, the weight of current psychiatric evidence is that nature will itself be the best healing agent.[31]

The Chisholms faced by a patient overcome with guilt because of extra-marital relations, homosexual practices, or other anti-social tendencies will devote their efforts to convincing the patient that such actions are perfectly normal, that no guilt should be experienced.

This is an outgrowth of the materialistic, psycho-dynamic approach to understanding human behavior. This school holds that when an individual feels a drive (desires to do something) that the drive must be satisfied (regardless of moral principles) or resulting tensions will produce insanity.

Accepting this largely discredited theory, the psychiatrist's job is to destroy the stabilizing concepts of right and wrong and man's conscience which cause guilt when anti-social, immoral impulses are satisfied. Such treatment, like Dewey's theories of education, will ultimately produce a breed of amoral, Pavlovian men with minds conditioned to respond to physical stimuli (bread and circuses) of a "master psychologist" or master politician. Not relying on free will, morals, or conscience for guidance, such amoral, criminal minds are typical of the man Marx envisioned. Is it any wonder that Dr. G. Brock Chisholm's appointment as head of the World Health Organization was warmly sponsored by his friend, Alger Hiss?[32]

Within the psychiatric profession itself criticism has been mounting against the psycho-dynamic approach to human behavior. Dr. Dalbir Bindra, president of the Canadian Psychological Association, summed up the repudiations, saying:

All that can be said now is simply that so far there exists no proof of the value of the psychodynamics approach. Thus, I believe that this approach has turned out to be a wrong lead and that any further research along these lines would be a waste of time.[33]

Even though thoroughly repudiated, ideas of the Chisholms and the Overstreets have achieved deep-rooted influence in schools, churches, PTA's as Chisholm advocated.

CHURCH ACCEPTANCE

For example, *Coronet* magazine, in a shocking article, *Religion and Sex: A Changing Church View*,[34] outlined the new, more permissive attitude of many liberal churchmen towards sex, pre-marital relations, adultery, etc. The article states:

These thinkers have been influenced not only by recent Biblical scholarship, *but also by the findings of psychiatry*—especially the revelation of psychic damage that may be done by sexual repression.[35]

The article quotes a minister who was visited by a married man, troubled by guilt over an affair he was having with another woman. Adultery is a very serious Christian offense, the article points out. However, because the man's wife was a bedridden invalid, the minister with the "new" church view said:

There were no easy platitudes that applied here. The only function I could serve was to relieve the man's feeling of guilt.[36]

IN-SCHOOL PSYCHOLOGICAL TESTING

The inroads made by the "mental healthers" in the field of education was spotlighted in *Life* magazine. An article, *The New Tests in Our Schools—The Three R's and a P (For Psyche)*, in the September 21, 1962 issue, said:

In the first few weeks of the new school year several million pupils from the first grade through senior high school will open examination booklets that pose some surprisingly personal questions.[37]

Among the questions mentioned by *Life* were:

Are you too nervous? Most of the time I wish I was dead. I hear strange things when I am alone. I am afraid I am losing my mind.

Life pointed out that while State Education laws often prevent even a licensed physician from giving a child an aspirin tablet without parental permission, school testers can administer highly personal tests. Children's records can be marked "maladjusted" or "potential schizophrenic" without the parents ever being notified. Most parents, *Life* said, are amazed to learn that their child's "personality" is recorded in black and white in locked files outside the principal's office.

Psychological testing and counseling and guidance in the schools received a big boost as a result of the National Defense Education Act of 1958. This bill provided money for trained counselors and testing programs to assist students in selecting higher education opportunities.

That the program has fallen into the wrong hands was made clear by Congressman John Ashbrook (R-Ohio) on October 10, 1962, when he introduced HR 10508 which would ban psychological testing of students, without advance permission from parents. Ashbrook said:

> I believe there is an urgent need for this legislation so that proper guidance and counseling will not be confused with brainpicking and interference.[38]

To support the need for legislation, Ashbrook cited examples of widely-used tests which include "difficult or impossible to answer questions—tests which pit loyalties of religion, home, and parents against each other." He cited these specific examples of loyalty-splitting questions from one "moral value" exam.[39]

> Which is worse: (1) spitting on the Bible; (2) spitting on the American flag?

> Which is more important: (1) taking the oath of allegiance to the United States; (2) joining a church?

> Which is worse: (1) denying the existence of God; (2) laughing while the Star Spangled Banner is played?

Consider the conflict for normal youngsters forced to make these differentiations. Note the implied suggestions that it is "less bad" to spit on either the Flag or the Bible.

Often containing 300 or more questions, personality tests are depressingly negative in approach. A typical test is the Science Research Associates *Youth Inventory*. Form A of this test includes 30 to 40 questions which tend to destroy respect for and authority of parents and teachers. Students answer "yes" or "no" to these questions:

> I can't discuss personal things with my parents. I feel there's a barrier between me and my parents. My father is a tyrant. I am ashamed of my parents' dress and manners. I hate school. I wish I could quit school now. My teachers play favorites. My teachers are too strict. Class periods are not well organized.

Sex questions with an abnormal slant are asked of sub-teen age children in the same test:

> I wonder if I am normal in my sexual development. I think of sex a good deal of the time. I wonder if high school students should pet and make love. I want to know more about venereal disease.

Traditional religious beliefs and concepts of right and wrong are dulled or shaken in this way:

> I'm bothered by thoughts of Heaven and Hell. I'm losing faith in religion. Is it wrong to deny the existence of God? Does it really pay to be honest? How does one set standards of "right" and "wrong?"

The Board of Educational Research, Ohio State University has developed a psychological test used widely in many states. Called *The Wishing Well*, it plants doubts about God and free enterprise in the *fourth grade students* to whom it is administered and stimulates fear of economic security, with questions like this:

> I wish I could be sure that my father would always have a steady job. I wish I could know how you can believe that God is always right and at the same time believe that you should think for yourself. I wish I knew how you can make lots of money and still be a very good citizen.

Those concerned about the serious rise of juvenile delinquency and teen-age violence often ask, "Where do children get these ideas?"

Some ideas may come from a seven-part, 344 question test developed at the University of Kansas with a grant from U.S. Public Health Service. It is administered to normal junior high school students. A section entitled, *Rules We All Break*, implies by the title that the listed actions are normal, expected behavior for teen-agers. Typical *Rules We All Break* according to this test are:

Damage or disfigure furniture in schools. Steal goods from warehouses or storage houses. Puncture or cut automobile tires, bike tires. Tied up person with rope, string, or wire to a tree or similar object and then left them that way. Damage cemetery property. Become so angry that you threw things at or hit a teacher or principal or other school official. Taken part in fights where knives or switchblades were used. Injured or hurt someone not in your family, but arranged matters so that someone else got the blame.

There are 78 such *rules we all break* in the test. The normal, decent child might well get an inferiority complex through answering "no" to all of them. Congressman Ashbrook in introducing his bill to require parental consent before administering such tests said:

A parent could well ask what all of this has to do with educational process. Suggestions often plant seeds of doubt. Children who are normal may begin to think they are not normal. To read all the questions (in a test) tends to give anyone an inferiority complex.[40]

Many competent school guidance counselors reject as "more harmful than helpful" such testing, which has its genesis in largely discredited psycho-dynamic, Freudian approaches to psychology. School psychologists in Denver, Colorado, protested their use and dropped them.[41] Dr. Henry S. Dyer of the Educational Testing Service, Princeton, N.J. says:

I take a dim view of current personality tests and I think the general public is being much too frequently taken in by the mumbo jumbo that goes with them.[42]

Yet, millions of school-age children are subjected to these brainpicking, psychiatric tests which implant doubts about God and religion, break down parental authority; downgrade

American traditions and generally create a mood of sordidness, depression and cloudy thinking about right and wrong. These are exactly the goals set by Dr. G. Brock Chisholm as a goal for mental health programs.

So through the schools, churches, PTA's, changes in mental health legislation, and indiscriminate branding of patriotic Americans as mentally ill, these warped practioners work to create the "amoral" man, the criminal mind which will accept a one-world socialistic government, as envisioned by Chisholm.

CHAPTER X

THE ORGANIZED LABOR MOVEMENT

*It is necessary to be able to withstand all of this, to agree to
any and every sacrifice, and even—if need be —to resort to
all sorts of devices, maneuvers, and illegal methods, to
evasion, and subterfuge, in order to penetrate into the trade
unions, to remain in them, and to carry on Communist work
in them at all costs.*[1]

—*Nicolai Lenin*

ON JANUARY 20, 1934, Walter and Victor Reuther wrote
a letter from Russia where they were working and studying
the Soviet labor movement. Written to Melvin Bishop, a close
friend in Detroit who later became CIO educational director,
the letter said in part:

...the daily inspiration that is ours as we work side by side with
our Russian comrades in our factory, the thought that we are
actually helping to build a society that will forever end the
exploitation of man by man, the thought that what we are building
will be for the benefit and enjoyment of the working class, not
only of Russia, but for the entire world is the compensation we
receive for our temporary absence from the struggle in the United
States.[2]

After further praise for Russian thinking and methods, and
vilification of American business leaders, the letter, which
was signed, "Vic and Wal," concluded:

Carry on the fight for a Soviet America.[3]

What Reuther believes today cannot be known. For years
after his return to America his close cooperation with and
sometimes leadership of the "Communist" faction in the
United Auto Workers Union has been exposed in numerous
Congressional hearings.[4]

In the late 1930's, Communists controlled 21 of the international unions affiliated with the CIO. Nearly one-half of the members of the executive board of the CIO, its governing body, were Communists.[5] Lee Pressman, general counsel of the CIO was a party member.[6] He has since broken with the Party and remains in this high post. Despite exposure of the Communist control of the CIO by congressional investigations in 1938-39, the Communists remained in open control for at least seven more years.[7]

After World War II, when public feeling against Communists and communism reached a peak, Walter Reuther publicly identified himself with the movement which expelled known Communists from union posts. However, officers and members of union locals who tried to enlist Reuther's aid in breaking the Communist hold in some UAW branches testified before Congressional committees that their requests to him were ignored.[8]

When Reuther's speeches are analyzed and the programs supported by his union are checked carefully, there can be no doubt that Reuther is, today, at least a dedicated promoter of class hatred and the socialist movement to control every aspect of American life. He is rarely found in the ranks of those who speak out vigorously against the Communist menace.

In fact, just the opposite is true. At the United Auto Workers Convention in Atlantic City, N.J., May 10, 1962, Reuther and the executive committee of the Union passed a series of resolutions. They advocated measures which would so hamper attempts to control internal subversion that even the Communist Party, U.S.A. in its official publication, *The Worker*, expressed elation.[9]

The resolutions which Reuther rammed through the closely-controlled executive committee (without permitting delegates representing UAW members across the country to vote on them) included:[10]

A request for clemency for the convicted Communist, Julius Scales.

A call for abolition of the House Committee on Un-American Activities.

An expression of opposition to official government finding that the Mine, Mill & Smelter Workers Union is Communist-dominated.

A demand that government action to deport aliens found to have been members of the Communist Party be halted.

A condemnation of Congressional efforts to stop the importation of Communist propaganda into the United States.

Two weeks after Reuther's UAW passed the resolutions, the United Packinghouse, Food and Allied Workers (AFL-CIO) convention passed essentially the same measures.

Contrast Reuther's record and actions with these remarks of George Meany, president of the AFL-CIO:

> The conflict between communism and freedom is the problem of our times. It overshadows all other problems. This conflict mirrors our age, its toils, its tensions, its troubles, and its tasks. On the outcome of this conflict depends the future of mankind.[11]

Basic differences between Meany and Reuther are reported to be the source of conflict between them, and the basis for recurrent reports that Reuther will, when strong enough, move to challenge Meany for the top spot in the AFL-CIO.

Reuther's concept of the function of organized labor differs sharply also with that of Samuel Gompers, founder of the American Federation of Labor, and champion of the rights of the working man as a self-reliant citizen. Contrast Reuther's anguished pleas for placing medical care for the aged under social security, a measure which has lead to socialized medicine in every country where it has been adopted, with this Gompers' statement:

> Compulsory social insurance is in its essence undemocratic and it cannot prevent or remove poverty. The workers of America adhere to voluntary institutions in preference to compulsory systems, which are held to be not only impractical, but a menace to their rights, welfare, and their liberty. Compulsory sickness insurance for workers is based on the theory that they are unable to

look after their own interests and the state must use its authority and wisdom and assume the relation of parent and guardian.[12]

Contrast Reuther's background as President of the Intercollegiate Socialist Society at Wayne University in Detroit[13] and his ardent championing of Keynesian and Fabian economics as a backdoor, "respectable" approach to socialism with another of Gompers' statements:

> I want to tell you socialists that I have studied your philosophy...I have heard your orators...I have kept close watch upon your doctrines for 30 years and know how you think and what you propose. I know too what you have up your sleeve. Economically, you are unsound; socially, you are wrong; industrially, you are an impossibility.[14]

Gompers, in his wisdom, had the true interests of American workers and their progress at heart.

He knew that socialists "had up their sleeve" only schemes for *control* of the workers of the world. This became sharply clear in an article Arthur Schlesinger, Jr., assistant to President Kennedy, wrote which set forth the plan for achieving socialism in America. Proposing a continuing series of "New Deals" as a backdoor approach to socialism,[15] Schlesinger, a "darling" of Reuther's CIO, said of labor:

> The trade union is as clearly indigenous to the capitalist system as the corporation itself, and it has no particular meaning apart from that system. In a socialist society its functions are radically transformed: it becomes, not a free labor movement, but a labor front. Even in England as Sir Walter Citrine remarked on joining the coal board, strikes can no longer be trade union instruments in a nationalized industry. Unions inevitably become organs for disciplining the workers, not for representing them.[16]

This state is rapidly approaching in America. The Administration's action in August 1963, which banned strikes in the railroad industry is a step in this direction. In a modern socialist state, labor terms are dictated by government officials—not negotiated at a bargaining table between labor and management.

POLITICAL ACTION

Before the 1930's, labor unions restricted their activities principally to the legitimate function of representing their members at the bargaining table and expressing union views when labor legislation was before Congress or state legislatures. Walter Reuther's mentor, the late Sidney Hillman, took the labor movement strongly into the political field. Hillman formed the broadly-based, labor-financed, National Citizens Political Action Committee (PAC).

Investigations by the Special House Committee on Un-American Activities in 1944 disclosed that 117 of the 141 members of the PAC national advisory board were leaders in other officially-cited Communist fronts. The PAC was designated by the House Committee as a Communist-front.[17]

After the PAC was discredited as a Communist-front, the CIO formed the forerunner of today's *Committee on Political Education (COPE)*. Through COPE, millions of dollars are collected from union members who believe in the free enterprise system. This money is used to finance and propagandize measures that will replace American traditions of economic and political freedom with socialist state control. The methods used have been described by President Kennedy's special assistant, Arthur Schlesinger, Jr.[18] Through COPE, Walter Reuther, who in the '30's advised his followers to "work for a Soviet America" is possibly the most powerful political figure in America.

He can mobilize a disciplined core of over 100,000 paid union organizers and business agents for political action. They win their political battles, not by convincing 51% of the population that they are right, but through effective use of the time-tested methods developed years ago by the old-fashioned "ward heelers" and political bosses.

COPE's skilled organizers and their well-paid precinct workers determine on a block-by-block basis in advance of elections which voters will vote "right." They insure they are properly registered. On election day, all "friendly" voters are taken to the polls.[19]

In many elections, when half or less of those eligible actually vote, COPE can control the outcome by finding that 25% of the population which will vote, either blindly for a party label, or knowingly in favor of socialism—*and getting them to the polls*.

Applying these principles, in recent years COPE has elected sufficient Senators in normally conservative states to control the U.S. Senate. They have gained control of state legislatures and elected governors. Candidates pledged to the Reuther-COPE program have unseated conservative Congressmen in many parts of the nation.

COPE's activities are concentrated principally in areas where they can have the greatest success such as highly industrialized areas, Negro and minority sections in large cities and lower income suburbs. Frequently, they can pile up 3, 4, 5, 8, or 10 to 1 margins for their candidates in these areas, and overcome conservative majorities in other areas.

While he can be politically non-partisan when it means defeat of an advocate of sound economics and limited self-government, Reuther is conceded to hold veto power over the Democratic nomination for President.

At the 1960 Democratic convention in Los Angeles, for example, TV news analysts made it clear that over one-third of the delegates were COPE-controlled. With over 25% of the delegates to any Democratic convention from the more conservative southern states, Reuther holds the balance of power in the controlling northern section of the Democratic Party.

Reuther's political stranglehold on the Democratic Party is not the only dangerous influence in the labor movement. Despite the well-publicized "cleanup" of the AFL and CIO in the 1940's when known Communists were driven out, Communists still control the unions in certain strategic areas of the economy.

The Communist-control of the American Communications Association, whose members service many of Western Union's telegraph lines and the communications circuits from the Pentagon to key defense installations around the world was documented in an earlier chapter.[20]

Harry Bridges, the Australian-born Communist leader of

the International Longshoremen's and Warehousemen's Union, has successfully fought government attempts to deport him and strip him of his power. With a word, Bridges can tie up all shipping of defense supplies, military equipment, etc. through the West Coast ports. His Communist associates in Hawaii have organized the dock workers, government employees, and sugar and pineapple plantation workers.[21] They hold a virtual political and economic stranglehold on the life of our 49th State.[22] Bridges' union was expelled from the CIO in 1950 as Communist-dominated.[23]

Eleven other strategically-placed labor organizations were expelled at the same time, including the Mine, Mill and Smelter Workers, United Public Workers of America, United Farm Equipment and Metal Workers of America, and the United Office and Professional Workers of America.[24]

Russell Nixon, a top-ranking Communist[25] has since 1941 been a top-rank official of the United Electrical, Radio and Machine Workers Union, except for periods when he has served in the government. Nixon's union, kicked out of the CIO in 1950, also represents workers in the key electronics, electrical and missile producing fields.[26]

Communists became entrenched in the labor field in the 1930's when Nathan Witt, a Communist, became Secretary of the National Labor Relations Board, and Edwin S. Smith, another Communist, gained a seat on the five-member board.[27] During this period rules were established which regulate labor-management relations even today. Witt hired and supervised hundreds of people to staff the regional offices of the growing NLRB. His influence is felt even today, years after he was publicly exposed.

American working men and union members are as loyal and dedicated to the United States as any group in the nation, and probably more so, on a percentage basis, than university graduates. Yet, their money, the prestige of their organizations, and their votes are frequently committed to the destruction of America. In a number of industries, sound thinking working men and dedicated union leaders have performed meritorious service in the difficult battle against Communist infiltration. In other industries, the job still needs to be done.

CHAPTER 11

THE TAX-EXEMPT FOUNDATIONS

We all know that foundation aid can increase measurably the pace of any social tendency, but we don't seem to know when this artificial acceleration ceases to be desirable.

—*F. P. Keppel, President, The Carnegie Corporation*

FROM WHERE HAS THE MONEY COME to build and finance the vast collectivist underground which reaches its tentacles into education, the churches, labor and the press?

Amazingly, the fortunes of America's most successful tycoons, dedicated by them to the good of mankind, have been re-directed to finance the socialization of the nation.

Two special Congressional committees exposed the extent to which tax-exempt foundations are using their resources for un-American and subversive activity. Yet, apparently nothing has been done to check this flow of millions of dollars annually into the hands of conspirators. In 1952, the investigation was started by a Special Committee of the House of Representatives headed by Congressman E. E. Cox (D-Ga).[1] It continued in the 83rd Congress under the direction of Congressman Carrol Reece (R-TN).[2]

Both efforts were hampered by lack of staff to do the monumental research job necessary to unravel the complex multi-billion dollar dealings of the foundations and their interlocked agencies. Gross lack of cooperation from governmental agencies under President Eisenhower and the foundations themselves slowed the studies.[3]

Even so, the investigations proved incontrovertibly that money of American capitalists—Ford, Rockefeller, Carnegie, Guggenheim, etc.—has largely financed those working for the establishment of a "new world order."

The Reece Committee acknowledged the magnificent service rendered by the foundations in medicine, public health, and science. However, large sums have been wrongly committed to "changing society." A handful of foundation executives reluctantly acknowledge the misdirection.

Raymond B. Fosdick, in *The Story of the Rockefeller Foundations*, quoted the Rev. Frederick T. Gates, long-time adviser to the Foundation and John D. Rockefeller, Sr., as follows:

> If I have any regret, it is that the charter of the Rockefeller Foundation did not confine its work strictly to national and international medicine, health, and its appointments. Insofar as the disbursements of the Rockefeller incorporated philanthropies have been rigidly confined to these two fields (medicine and public health) they have been almost universally commended at home and abroad. Where they have inadvertently transgressed these limits, they have been widely, and in some particulars not unfairly condemned.[4]

What have been the transgressions for which foundations "have been widely and not unfairly condemned?" The Reece Committee found that grants in the social sciences and international affairs were almost totally committed to "liberals" who advocate the socialization of America and world government. Direct grants have been made to Communists and socialists. Foundation executives have exhibited a naivete about communism which has already contributed directly to one tragedy, the loss of China to the Communists.[5]

Frederick P. Keppel, President of the Carnegie Corporation, admits that foundation funds can "change" America. In his book, *The Foundation, It's Place in American Life*, he wrote:

> We all know that foundation aid can increase measurably the pace of any social tendency, but we don't know when this artificial acceleration ceases to become desirable.[6]

How have foundation grants been used to "accelerate" social tendencies? Here are some of the ways uncovered by the Reece Committee:

> Aggregate contribution of over $4-million were made by six American foundations to the London School of Economics.

Beatrice and Sidney Webb founded the school as the international "headquarters" and intellectual center of the Fabian socialist movement.[7]

Foundations grants made possible the writing and publication of anti-American, anti-free enterprise books and texts:

The Carnegie Corporation financed the writing and publication of *The Proper Study Of Mankind*. Written by Stuart Chase, the book praised the Communist agents, Harry Dexter White and Lauchlin Currie, and outlined an "ideal" society in which the individual is suppressed. Over 50,000 copies of the book were distributed by the Carnegie Foundation to libraries and scholars. One of Chase's earlier books recommended that profit-making be punished by firing squads.[8]

When advised of these facts and of Chase's record of support for more than 20 Communist fronts and causes, Dr. Charles Dollard, president of Carnegie Corporation, defended the selection of Chase to author the book. In a statement filed with the Reece Committee, Dollard said that Chase was "an extremely able writer."[9]

The Carnegie Corporation made continuing grants to the Communist-fronting Professor Robert A. Brady,[10] to finance study and ultimately a book, *Business as a System of Power*. The book's theme, as stated in the foreword, was:

... capitalistic economic power constitutes a direct, continuous and fundamental threat to the whole structure of democratic authority everywhere and always.[11]

The movement to socialize America via education discussed earlier was largely financed by foundation funds. The Reece Committee found:

The Rockefeller and Carnegie funds provided the financing for the radical movement in education lead by Counts, Dewey, Kilpatrick and Rugg. Direct grants were made to the National Education Association, Progressive Education Association, American Historical Association, and to the center of the revolutionary movement, Teachers College, Columbia University.[12]

The 17-volume study on American education directed by Dr.

George Counts, termed later by British Fabian leader Harold Laski as "an educational program for a socialist America," was financed by a $340,000 grant from Carnegie.[13]

Foundation grants have financed the gigantic program of revising textbooks to serve socialist ends. For example:

> The Rockefeller Foundation provided over $50,000 to finance the *Building America* textbooks series. The California Senate's Investigating Committee on Education condemned these texts for playing up Marxism and destroying traditional concepts of American government.[14]

The California Senate committee determined that 113 Communist front organizations contributed material to the Rockefeller-financed *Building America* texts. Works of over 50 Communist-front authors were included. Beatrice and Sidney Webb, founders with George Bernard Shaw of the British Fabian Society, were among the authors. One of the writers renounced his American citizenship to become ambassador to the United Nations from Communist Poland. Broadly promoted for years by the National Education Association, the textbook series was still in use in a number of states in 1954.[15]

In its final report, the Reece Committee observed:

> It would be interesting to aggregate the total funds poured by the foundations into the dissemination of leftist propaganda and compare it with the trickle which flowed into the exposition of the fallacies and frailties of collectivism.[16]

INTERNATIONAL RELATIONS

The role of the foundations in "Changing America" has been massive. Their impact on the international scene has been, if possible, even more tragic.

The Rockefeller Foundation in its 1946 Annual Report stated this goal:

> The challenge of the future is to make this world one world—a world truly free to engage in common and constructive intellectual efforts that will serve the welfare of mankind everywhere.[17]

There was only one pitfall in the high-sounding program.

Foundation executives, like other advocates of "one-world government" and "world peace through world law," choose to ignore the nature of world communism whenever it would be a roadblock to realization of their one-world dream. They have tried to make the world "one world" in line with their goal while it is not yet "truly free." Looking upon world government as the answer to the Communist threat, they can't or won't see that the only world government the Communists will embrace is one in which communism can eventually triumph.

On May 2, 1945, Raymond Fosdick, president of the Rockefeller Foundation, addressed the Woman's Action Committee for Victory and Lasting Peace in New York and voiced the sentiment on which foundation decisions and grants have been based since. He said:

> The growing mistrust of Russia menaces the future of world peace.[18]

A more realistic observation is that if more Americans in high places, including those in foundations, had a *greater* mistrust of Russia, over 800-million human beings would not be in Communist slavery today. Yet, Fosdick's naive attitude toward communism persists in foundation circles even today, as will be seen.

In some instances, the aid and assistance which foundations have given to world communism cannot be excused as naivete. The 1947 Yearbook of the Carnegie Endowment For International Peace opens with *Recommendations of the President to the Trustees*. The program spelled out is in line with the goals of the Rockefeller Foundation's 1946 annual report. It is typical of the goals and efforts of most foundations in the international field. The recommendations included:

> ...that the Endowment work for the establishment of United Nations headquarters in New York...that the Endowment construct its programs primarily for support of the United Nations...that the endowments program should be broadly educational in order to encourage public understanding and support of the United Nations at home and abroad...that Endowment supported organizations such as International Relations Clubs in

colleges, the Foreign Policy Association, the Institute of Pacific Relations, the Council on Foreign Relations, and local community groups be utilized to achieve these goals of achieving broader understanding and support for the United Nations.[19]

This program, recommended and backed with foundation billions, throws some insight into the "halo" constructed around the United Nations in the 17 years following World War II. Was it done in good faith, with a belief that the United Nations was truly man's great hope for world peace? That program and those recommendations were written by the President of the Carnegie Endowment for World Peace, the infamous Communist agent, Alger Hiss.[20]

They were a logical sequel to his State Department activities only 18 months before. Hiss' role as Roosevelt adviser at Yalta was thoroughly aired in the month's following his exposure as a Communist agent. His part in the formation of the United Nations was largely ignored. The probable influence he exerted in creating the framework of the UN Charter in sessions with the Communists at Yalta received no headlines. His assignment as Secretary General of the organizing conference of the United Nations at San Francisco in April 1945, was carefully kept in the background after his exposure.[21]

The Reece Committee found that foundations, headed by Communists like Alger Hiss, and by innocents like Raymond Fosdick (against whom only bad judgment can be proved) contributed significantly to the spread of world communism. For example:

The Rockefeller and Carnegie foundations contributed over $3-million to the Institute of Pacific Relations,[22] branded by the Senate Internal Security Subcommittee as a transmission belt for Communist and pro-Communist propaganda. The IPR also served as a "base" for Owen Lattimore, a "conscious articulate instrument of the Soviet conspiracy." Lattimore and his fellow agents, with foundation supplied funds, influenced American far-eastern policy against Chiang Kai-shek. Their actions, along with their foundation-financed propaganda efforts convinced the American people and press that the Chinese Communists were simple "agrarian reformers." China was lost to communism, and the enslavement of 600-million Chinese followed. The foundations paid the bill. Years later, they were still justifying the "change" in China as "progress."[23] The Reece committee in its report stated:

> ...the loss of China to the Communists may have been the most tragic event in our history, and one to which the foundation-supported Institute of Pacific Relations contributed heavily.[24]

The Carnegie Endowment for International Peace financed the Foreign Policy Association and underwrote distribution of its literature.[25] Research director of the FPA for over 20 years until her retirement in 1961 was the notorious, Russian-born, Communist-fronter, Vera Michaels Dean. The FPA's dissemination of the works of pro-Communist authors under the guise of objectivity through affiliated organizations across America has been thoroughly documented by a Fulton County, Georgia grand jury. Its report, with hundreds of exhibits, has been republished by the American Legion.[26]

With the almost total commitment of foundation funds in the international field to leftist causes, dozens of other examples can be cited.

Because of their widespread activities and the high esteem in which foundations are regarded, they became a logical source of "experts" to staff military government organizations in Germany, Japan, and Italy at the conclusion of World War II. Efforts to sabotage the rebuilding of German and Japanese economies became evident. Doors were opened wide for Communists to assume leading positions in postwar Germany and Japan. These actions became apparent to top military personnel and the plot was uncovered. Foundation executives had loaded their lists of recommended "expert" personnel with Communists and fellow travelers.[27]

Propaganda efforts financed by the Foundations and actual pro-Communist bias in materials prepared by Foundation staffs have played a leading role in the confusion and misguidance of the public and the intellectual community. The

Foundation, because of its charitable "halo", connotes an air of "objectivity" and has great, if undeserved, influence. The Ford Foundation Annual Report for 1951 is a prime example. It stated:

> Our policy in Asia has failed to lead us to the real objectives of the American people because its preoccupation with strategy and ideology has prevented our giving sufficient weight to the economic, social and political realities of Asia. There, as elsewhere, we have tended to label as Communistic any movement that sought a radical change in the established order...It is surprising that we have not been able to understand the situation in Asia, because Americans should be peculiarly able to comprehend the meaning of revolution. Our own independence was achieved through a revolution, and we have traditionally sympathized with the determined efforts of other peoples to win national independence and higher standards of living. The current revolution in Asia is a similar movement, whatever its present association with Soviet Communism.[28]

Are the officers of a foundation who compare the Russian-armed and financed coup in China with our Revolutionary War qualified to spend millions of tax-free money to influence public and governmental opinion in the field of foreign affairs—or any field? This report was issued after Chinese Communists had been killing American boys in Korea for 18 months! It was released three years after the Communists completed their conquest of China and started on their well-publicized murder of 40-million Chinese.

The affinity of the tax-exempt, charitable foundations for left-wing causes continues today. The Rockefeller Brothers Fund financed and published a study entitled, *Prospects for America*. It reflects the personal work and participation of the Rockefeller Brothers and a sizable group of leftist-oriented public figures, many of whom hold top spots in the Kennedy and Johnson Administrations.[29] Of communism, the report says:

> It has been necessary to drum up support for United States foreign policy by stressing imminent threats and crises and *by harping on the less attractive features of communism.*[30]

What features of communism do the Rockefeller Brothers and their panel of "distinguished" Americans find attractive?

Without saying, "We must recognize Red China," the Rockefeller Brothers Panel Report tears down or ignores all arguments against recognition and presents the "reasons" for recognizing Red China.[31]

The Fund for the Republic, an off-shoot of the Ford Foundation, has become notorious for financing vicious and distorted attacks on the internal security program of the U.S. government, Congressional committees which investigate communism and the FBI.[32]

The Reece Committee expressed the opinion that the Fund for the Republic had been founded for the specific purpose of attacking government security programs and anti-Communists.[33] Paul Hoffman, first president of the Fund, denied the allegation. However, attacks by Fund officials on the FBI, Congressional investigating committees, and government security measures have continued.

W.H. Ferry, a vice president of the Fund for the Republic, for example, delivered a typical attack of ridicule and smear against J. Edgar Hoover and the FBI at a meeting of western Democrats in Seattle, Washington, on August 6, 1962. Ferry described the FBI's attempts to fight communism as "ineffective spy swatting."[34]

The Ford Foundation has supplied continual grants, totaling over $1-million to the American Friends Service Committee to encourage pacifism, resistance to military service, conscientious objectors, and opposition to military preparedness.[35] The Friends Service Committee sponsored the World Youth Conference, a Communist front and sent delegates to the Communist-sponsored youth conferences behind the Iron Curtain.[36] The Friends Service Committee chairman, Henry J. Cadbury, and the executive secretary, Clarence Pickett, have lengthy records of affiliation with Communist fronts and causes.[37] Yet, the Ford Foundation in its 1951 Annual Report justified its grants because the Friends Service Committee "had demonstrated over a long period its capacity to deal effectively with many of the economic, social, and educational conditions that lead to international tensions."[38]

The Reece Committee, in its evaluation of the impact of the tax-exempt foundations on education, public opinion, and foreign relations in the United States, charged in its final report:

> It is the conclusion of this committee that the trustees of some of the major foundations have on numerous occasions been beguiled by truly subversive forces. Without many of the trustees having the remotest idea of what has happened, these foundations have frequently been put substantially to uses which have adversely affected the best interests of the United States...used to undermine many of our most precious institutions and to promote radical changes in the form of our government and our society.

> It is difficult to realize that great funds established by such conservative individuals as Rockefeller, Carnegie, and Ford have turned strongly to the left. It appears to have happened largely through a process of administrative infiltration and through the influence of academic consultants of leftish tendencies. The trustees of these foundations with a few possible exceptions could not have intended this result. It seems to us that it must have happened through their lack of understanding or through negligence.[39]

In retrospect, viewing the reactions of most foundation executives to the Reece Committee's thorough study, it is difficult to accept the charitable attitude shown toward Foundation trustees by the Reece Committee. The committee efforts were met with ridicule, abuse, and scorn by the majority of trustees and executives of Foundations. Their leftist orientation continues today.

CHAPTER XII

ECONOMICS AND GOVERNMENT

*A people may want a free government, but if, from insolence,
or carelessness, or cowardice, or want of public spirit, they
are unequal to the exertions necessary for preserving it; if
they will not fight for it when it is directly attacked; if they
can be deluded by the artifices used to cheat them out of it; if
by momentary discouragement or temporary panic, or a fit of
enthusiasm for an individual they can be induced to lay their
liberties at the feet of even a great man, or trust him with
powers which enable him to subvert their institutions; in all
these cases they are more or less unfit for liberty; and though
it may be for their good to have had it even for a short time,
they are unlikely long to enjoy it.*

—John Stuart Mill[1]

GOVERNMENT CONTROL has been the ultimate goal of
the collectivist thinkers who have been infiltrating every
segment of American life for 60 years. In government, as in
every other field, the collectivists have first infiltrated quietly, and then grabbed for control.

The seeds of Fabian socialism had already been sown in
Washington, in the multitude of government bureaus when
passage of the 16th Amendment in 1913 gave the federal
government and its managers unrestricted access to the
wealth of the American citizen.

Since then, bureaus have been piled on top of bureaus. Two
World Wars, the depression of the 1930's, a police action in
Korea and the Cold War have been used as excuses for
creating new offices and departments. Each one usurped, or
was given by Congress, some right or power once reserved to
the people, the states, or the peoples' representatives.

The offices were staffed, first with a trickle, then with a

flood of Fabian-indoctrinated theorists and professors from college campuses.

Seymour Harris of the Harvard Economics Department and a member of President Kennedy's "task force on the economy" in an article in the September 18, 1961, issue of *New Republic* revealed their influence. He said:

> Economics is one thing; politics is another. No one has criticized the President for lack of political acumen. I have seen no evidence that Congress is prepared to go along with large deficits except for security reasons...But no administration has advanced as far as the Kennedy Administration in accepting Keynesian economics.[2]

What is Keynesian economics?

As collectivists have grabbed for control of the federal government they have skillfully used the "economic" theories of John Maynard Keynes, a British Fabian economist, as the vehicle for *buying* the votes and support of the masses with *their own money*.

Today's advocates of Keynes and his theories present him respectably as the "last hope for saving free enterprises,"[3] in the typical Fabian fashion of "never calling socialism by its true label."[4] However, no less an authority than Norman Thomas, six-time Socialist candidate for President of the United States, writing in *A Socialist's Faith*, said:

> ...Keynes has had a great influence and his work is especially important in any re-appraisal of socialist theory. He represents a decisive break with laissez-faire capitalism.[5]

Keynes, with foresight, had himself predicted the use to which his theories might be put. Before publishing his major work, *The General Theory of Employment, Interest, and Money*, Keynes wrote these words to Fabian founder, George Bernard Shaw:

> To understand my state of mind, however, you have to know that I believe myself to be writing a book on economic theory which will largely revolutionize—not I suppose at once, but in the course of the next ten years—the way the world thinks about economic problems. When my new theory has been duly assimilated and

mixed with politics and feelings and passions I can't predict what the upshot will be in its effect on action and affairs.[6]

As Keynes foresaw, his theories have been skillfully blended with propaganda of hate and fear to stir "feelings and passions" between rich and poor, white and negro, labor and management, Catholic and Protestant, Christian and Jew in Lenin's technique of "divide and conquer." Fear, insecurity and class hatred have dominated presidential campaigns and congressional elections in America for 30 years.

The Keynes brand of socialism differs from the Marxist variety in that it advocates strict *control* of the means of production and the supply of credit and money rather than government *ownership*. On the theory that when control is possible, ownership is not required, the Keynesian theories are particularly suited to the Fabian goal of "change everything except the outward appearance." The national socialist movements headed by Hitler and Mussolini recognized the beauties of control rather than ownership and adopted Keynes theories in Germany and Italy.[7]

John Strachey, a one-time Communist who entered the British Fabian Society in 1943 and became War Minister in the Labor Government of Great Britain in 1950, explains Keynes theories this way:

> The positive part of Keynes' work was a demand that capitalism should now be regulated and controlled by a central authority...The principal instruments of its policy should be variations in the rate of interest, budgetary deficits and surpluses, public works and a redistribution of personal incomes in equalitarian direction. This positive side of Keynes' work requires an authority to do the regulating, and that authority can be, in contemporary conditions, nothing else but the government of a nation state.[8]

Strachey hints to his socialist followers the ultimate possibilities in Keynes' theories. He says:

> Was it not apparent that Keynesism had only to be pushed a little further and a state of things might emerge in which the nominal owners of the means of production, although left in full possession

of the legal title to their property, would in reality be working not for themselves, but for whatever hands grasped the central levers of social control? For Keynes had rashly shown that those levers had only to be pulled and pushed this way and that, in order to manipulate the system at will. And, in a democracy, would not those hands in the end almost certainly be those of the representatives of the wage-earning majority of the population? Might not the end of the story be that once proud possessors of the means of the production would find themselves in effect but agents and managers on behalf of the community?[9]

Strachey cold-bloodedly admits the falsity of the "saving capitalism" mantle wrapped around Keynesian theories:

...the capitalists have really good reasons for their reluctance to be saved by Keynesian policies.[10]

The vanguard of the Fabians who were to ultimately impose Keynes theories on the economy of the United States was led by Felix Frankfurter and Walter Lippman during World War I. Both came to government from Harvard University where they had been active in the Intercollegiate Socialist Society. As special assistants to the Secretary of the Navy, these two Fabians were to meet and develop a lasting, and world-shaping friendship with the young Assistant Secretary of the Navy, Franklin Delano Roosevelt.[11]

When the first war ended, Frankfurter went back to his Harvard teaching post. At least 300 of Frankfurter's students, including two very special pets, Alger Hiss and Dean Acheson, have found their way into strategic government posts. For 30 years, Frankfurter's disciples in government have hired, promoted, and covered up for each other and like-minded collectivists. A number of them were Communists. Frankfurter, 25 years later as a Supreme Court Justice, appeared as a "character witness" at the perjury trial of his former pupil, Alger Hiss.[12]

The 1929 depression, the "temporary panic" John Stuart Mill warned about years before, gave the collectivists their opportunity. Franklin D. Roosevelt was the "great man" at the feet of whom the American people would lay their liberties, as Mill had also predicted.

In 1930, Franklin Roosevelt, as governor of New York, expressed the American tradition when he said:

> ...the Constitution does not empower the Congress to deal with a great number of vital problems of government such as the conduct of public utilities, of banks, of insurance, of business, of agriculture, of education, of social welfare and a dozen other important features... and Washington must not be encouraged to interfere in these areas.[13]

Just two years later, however, the widely-heralded "liberal" brain trust presented the newly-elected FDR with a catchy slogan and the blueprint of the program through which in succeeding years they have nearly accomplished the collectivization of America. Roosevelt accepted the program, deserting the principles he enunciated so clearly two years before and the Democratic platform on which he was elected.

Stuart Chase, a longtime Fabian, in his book, *A New Deal*, written in 1931, outlined the ideal government. He said:

> Best of all, the new regime would have the clearest idea of what an economic system was for. The sixteen methods of becoming wealthy would be proscribed (punished)—by firing squad if necessary—ceasing to plague and disrupt the orderly processes of production and distribution. The whole vicious pecuniary complex would collapse as it has in Russia. Money-making as a career would no more occur to a respectable young man than burglary, forgery or embezzlement.[14]

One year later, FDR used Chase's title as the rallying cry for his Administration. He named Chase to the National Resources Commission where he is credited with authoring FDR's order banning ownership of gold by U.S. citizens, the first step in the destruction of the citizen's independence and U.S. financial strength. Fabians, like Chase, advocate firing squads only when their gradual methods fail.

Chase moved steadily upward in the New Deal hierarchy. He served successively on the Securities and Exchange Commission, the Tennessee Valley Authority, and finally settled in UNESCO, the United Nations agency charged with the re-education of the United States to accept a one-world socialistic state.[15]

Thousands of others like Chase swarmed in to Washington to join holdovers strategically placed during World War I and the ensuing ten years. They played the ego of FDR and the economic plight of the nation like the strings on a violin. Congress was induced and coerced to transfer its Constitutional powers to the new bureaus, agencies, boards, and commissions which sprung up almost overnight. George N. Peek, appointed by FDR as the first head of the Agricultural Adjustment Administration, described it this way:

> A plague of young lawyers settled on Washington—in the legal division were formed the plans which eventually turned the AAA from a device to aid the farmers to a device to introduce the collectivist system of agriculture into this country.[16]

The "young lawyers" eventually drove Peek to resign from his position. He opposed their collectivist schemes for agriculture, the New Deal's first farm program, the successors to which still plague America today. Among the "young lawyers" were Alger Hiss, Adlai Stevenson, John Abt, Nathan Witt, Nathaniel Weyl, and Charles Kramer. All of them, except Stevenson, were to be identified 15 years later as secret Communist agents.[17] Before they were exposed, they completed their dirty work in the Agriculture Department and spread out to capture other branches of government.

In 1952, the Senate Internal Security Subcommittee published results of hearings which showed the Communist net of control, which started with this group in the Agriculture Department, had extended over the Labor, Treasury, State and Commerce Departments, the independent agencies and cabinet offices concerned with national defense, and later, the Central Intelligence Agency and United Nations agencies.[18]

This Communist penetration and control of the United States government was the result of activities of two exposed Communist cells. Two others known to have operated in the government at the same time have never been uncovered.[19]

Few in Congress, and even fewer Americans at the time, or

even now realize, or will admit, what was happening. One lone voice spoke out and was quickly smashed, as nearly every vocal opponent of communism has been since. Dr. William Wirt, the superintendent of schools from Gary, Indiana, was invited to dinner at the home of a government employee while in Washington to attend a school administrators meeting in September 1933.

After dinner, the hostess, Alice Barrows, an employee of the Department of Education, and other guests disclosed that Communists had infiltrated and taken control of the New Deal. Four of the dinner guests were government employees. The fifth was the Washington representative of *Tass*, the Soviet news agency.[20]

Wirt summarized what was said at the meeting and when government officials brushed him off, he mailed a statement to about 100 conservative leaders and newspapers across the United States. This provoked a Congressional investigation of his charges.

Wirt's statement was read into the record as the basis on which he would be interrogated. Because it deserves deep and detailed study much of it is reproduced here. The techniques Wirt was told would be used to discredit business, to entice labor, management, school officials, and farmers to "go along" are frighteningly similar to those *which have been used* in the ensuing years. Wirt stated:

> "Brain Trusters" insist that the America of Washington, Jefferson, and Lincoln must first be destroyed so that on the ruins they will be able to construct an America after their own pattern. They do not know that the America of Washington, Jefferson, and Lincoln was the real New Deal for the common man. They wish to put the common man back into the feudal society of the Dark Ages.[21]

Wirt's statement as read into the record of the public hearing continued:

> I was told they believe that by thwarting our then evident economic recovery they would be able to prolong the country's destitution until they had demonstrated to the American people that the Government must operate business and commerce. By propaganda they would destroy institutions making long-time

capital loans—and then push Uncle Sam into making these loans. Once Uncle Sam becomes our financier he must also follow his money with control and management.[22]

Today, the Federal Government is very much in the business of making long term capital loans through the Area Redevelopment Administration, Small Business Administration, the Rural Electrification Administration, Export-Import Bank, Federal Land Banks, the various housing agencies, and dozens of other departments large and small.

Wirt stated that the "Brain Trusters" said, "We believe we have Roosevelt in the middle of a swift stream and that the current is so strong he cannot turn back or escape from it. We believe we can keep Mr. Roosevelt there until we are ready to supplant him with a Stalin. We all think Mr. Roosevelt is only the Kerensky of the Revolution."[23] Asked why the President would not see through the scheme, they replied:

> We are on the inside, we control the avenues of influence. We can make the President believe he is making the decisions for himself...soon he will feel a superhuman flow of power from the flow of decisions themselves, good or bad.[24]

Wirt was told that most Americans under-estimate the power of propaganda, that since World War I propaganda had been developed into science. They said further:

> ...That they could make newspapers and magazines beg for mercy by threatening to take away much of their advertising by a measure to compel only the unvarnished truth in advertising.[25]

This is, of course, just exactly the power exercised over newspapers, magazines, radio and TV and their advertisers today by the Federal Trade Commission. Wirt went on to say in his statement before the Congressional committee:

> They were sure that they could depend on the psychology of empty stomachs and they would keep them empty. The masses would soon agree that anything should be done rather than nothing. Any escape from present miseries would be welcomed even though it should turn out to be another misery.[26]

Wirt was told that leaders of business and labor would be

silenced by offers of government contracts for materials and services, provided they were subservient; that colleges and schools would be kept in line by promises of Federal Aid, until the many "new dealers" in the schools and colleges gained control of them; they believed the farmers could be brought into line by letting them "get their hands in the public trough for once in the history of the country." To any opposition that developed, they would ask, "Well, what is your plan?"[27]

Wirt testified that the meeting at which he learned of these plans was held following a dinner party on September 1, 1933, at the home of Alice Barrows, an employee of the Department of Education. The home was located in a Virginia suburb of Washington. In attendance were:

> Robert Breuere, a member of the New Deal Textile Code Advisory Board and a World War I supporter of the revolutionary IWW (International Workers of the World) movement; David Cushman Coyle, an employee of the Public Works Administration (PWA); Laurence Todd, Washington representative of the Soviet news agency, *TASS*, and a former official of the American Civil Liberties Union; Hildegarde Kneeland, an employee of the Department of Agriculture, member of the ACLU, and the person Dr. Wirt claimed did most of the talking about the Communist plans to take over the New Deal; and Mary Taylor, also an employee of the Department of Agriculture.[28]

Wirt reported that the group indicated they looked for leadership to Dr. Rexford Guy Tugwell, a radical, who was assistant to Henry Wallace, and to Wallace himself. At the time, Henry Wallace was Secretary of Agriculture. He became vice president of the United States in Roosevelt's third term.

Of the six persons Wirt reported in attendance at the dinner, all testified. They admitted the dinner had been held, but denied Wirt's report of the after-dinner conversation. However, before the hearings began, A.A. Berle, Jr., a New Deal official, had been quoted by the Associated Press as admitting the conversations had taken place but that the government employees were just pulling Wirt's leg.[29]

During the hearing, to substantiate the charges that the

economic recovery was being held down, Dr. Wirt cited figures
to show that in the period April 19, 1933-August 1, 1933, that
the country was recovering from the depression at a pace
three times faster than ever before experienced in America.
Business had reached 82% of normal, before the recovery
mysteriously stopped. Wirt cited articles from *Collier's*
magazine which said, "The farmer is whistling over the
bettering times." At the same time the Department of
Agriculture was saying, "This is an illusion, we must have
controls." Controls were imposed and the recovery stopped.[30]

Republican members of the committee and Wirt's counsel,
Senator James A. Reed (D-Mo) wanted the investigation
continued, but the Democratic majority refused. Wirt's efforts
were to no avail. He was ridiculed by *Time* magazine, the *New
York Times*, and the far-left press. Wirt was "silenced" and
within two years *he died in a mental institution*.

Eighteen years later in 1952, the Senate Internal Security
Subcommittee in another investigation was to reveal that
Alice Barrows, at whose home the meeting was held, had been
a Communist agent from the time she was employed in the
U.S. Office of Education in 1919![31]

Even so, Wirt was not "cleared". The "trail" was "covered"
in the Cumulative Summary Index 1918-1956, Congressional
Investigations of Communism and Subversive Activities.[32] In
this reference volume which lists all hearings into Communist activities conducted by governmental agencies and all
witnesses who have testified down through the years, Alice
Barrows is listed in the cross reference for her first appearance in 1934 as "Alice P. Barrows" and as "Alice P.
Borrows" on her second appearance in 1952.[33] This "mistake," in this official reference makes it unlikely that many
students would encounter the second appearance which
"proves" Wirt's case.

Wirt's charge that the "brain trusters" of the New Deal
deliberately sabotaged the economic recovery which was well
underway in the fourth and final year of the Hoover Administration is not without substantiation. Said the
Democratic-oriented *New York Times* on June 16, 1934:

The change for the better in the last half of 1932 is beyond dispute. That this evident revival of confidence was suddenly reversed in February 1933, is equally true.

Wilbur and Hyde, in their book, *The Hoover Policies*, said:

In the months of August, September and October 1932, bank failures had almost ceased while banks reopened were more than suspensions. The great flow of gold the months previous to July reversed itself into an enormous inflow. The whole banking structure greatly strengthened. Wholesale commodity prices advanced during July, August and September. Cotton and wheat advanced over 20 per cent. U.S. cotton manufacturing advanced from 51.5 per cent of mill capacity in July to 97 per cent in October. Domestic wool consumption advanced from 16,500,000 pounds in May to 46,100,000 in September. The Federal Reserve Board's index of industrial production swept upward from 56 in July to 68 for both September and October.[34]

After the election of November 1932, President Hoover, the press, spokesmen for economic bodies all pleaded with Roosevelt to do a simple thing: merely assure the country that he intended to abide by his campaign promises.[35]

Roosevelt remained silent.

Rumors ran rampant that despite FDR's conservative campaign promises that the country was heading for alarming monetary, economic and social experiments.

Panic resulted.

Banks later found to be completely sound were stampeded into closing their doors. The recovery, well-advanced under Hoover, ground to a halt, and Roosevelt's supporters on the "far-left" were quoted as saying, "The worse the better."[36]

The senior editor of *The Reader's Digest*, Eugene Lyons, in his book, *The Herbert Hoover Story*, quotes Charles Michelson, chief of the Democratic Party Publicity Staff during the 1932 campaign as saying:

The President-elect (FDR) told me on one occasion that the bank crisis was due to culminate just about inauguration day...Naturally he did not care to have the dramatic effect of his intended proposals spoiled by a premature discussion of them in advance of their delivery.[37]

Lyons says that if Roosevelt and his brain trust had planned to push the country over the brink in order to take over at the lowest possible point in history they would have behaved no differently. They did not merely refrain from doing or saying anything that would bolster confidence; they did and said precisely those things which shook confidence and confirmed fears.[38]

Press agentry built Roosevelt and the New Deal as saviors. Good hard statistics reveal that unemployment during the Hoover Administration averaged 6.2-million annually, or just slightly higher than it has reached several times in the post-war era. In the first two Roosevelt Administrations, average annual unemployment was 9.9-million.[39] In other words, despite appropriation of billions for relief purposes, other billions for make-work schemes, and the transfer to the federal government of almost complete control over the nation's economy, things got worse, and not better, under Roosevelt. The advent of World War II, and not the New Deal and government intervention, ended the Depression.

By 1938, Garet Garrett, distinguished newspaperman, author and editorial writer for the *Saturday Evening Post*, published an essay, "The Revolution Was." In the opening paragraph, he said:

> There are those who still think they are holding the pass against a revolution that may be coming up the road. But they are gazing in the wrong direction. The revolution is behind them. It went by in the Night of Depression, singing songs to freedom.[40]

Garrett went on to show that every problem faced by the New Deal was solved in a way which transformed the traditional concept of limited self government into a system that could not fail to:[41]

> Ramify the authority and power of executive government—its power, that is, to rule by decrees and rules and regulations of its own making.

> Strengthen its hold on the economic life of the nation.

> Extend its power over the individual.

Degrade Congress and the parliamentary principle.

Impair the great American tradition of an independent Constitutional judicial power.

Weaken all other powers—private enterprise, private finance, and the power of state and local government.

In no instance was any action taken which did not contribute to the process which Garrett points out moved unerringly toward a redesign of the governmental structure into totalitarian *form*. With thousands of individual actions, decrees, and rules all meshing to accomplish this end, Garrett concluded that it was all according to a great master plan.

Checks and balances placed in the Constitution to prevent such centralization of power worked for a time. The Supreme Court declared early New Deal measures unconstitutional.

Roosevelt's heavily Democratic Congress facing the crisis of the Depression gave the President and the bureaucrats nearly everything they asked for. In rapid succession, the National Recovery Act (NRA), the Agricultural Adjustment Act (drafted by Hiss and fellow Communists), and the Bituminous Coal Act were all passed, giving the federal bureaucracy unprecedented power, and control of every phase of American life.

Citizens were subjected to varying degrees of federal harassment and red tape, all justified as being in the "public interest." A New York poultry dealer was arrested for letting a customer pick and buy a particular chicken from a cage, a violation of the NRA code.[42] Under the code, the customer was required to say, "I want a chicken," and take "potluck" on which one he got. The operator of a little tailor shop was jailed for charging 35 cents for pressing a pair of men's trousers.[43] This was five cents *below* the NRA minimum.

The Supreme Court found the NRA and its companion measures in violation of the Constitution—and every concept of American freedom.[44] Roosevelt, infuriated, retaliated with schemes to by-pass or replace the "Nine Old Men." All were rejected by even the New Deal controlled Congress.

However, several justices soon bowed to mounting pressure

and several New Deal measures were upheld by 5 to 4 decisions of the high court.[45] Then, within two years of the defeat of the court-packing plans, deaths and retirement gave FDR his chance to control the Supreme Court. He appointed four new justices, Hugo Black, Felix Frankfurter, Stanley Reed, and William O. Douglas. None of the four had judicial experience prior to being named to the highest court in the land.[46]

In succeeding years, the four were to lead the Court in reversing dozens of previous Supreme Court decisions, making a mockery of American jurisprudence. Some actions stretched both the law and reality to the point of tragedy.

The Constitution, as written, distributed power between the three separate, but equal, branches of the federal government—the executive, legislative and judiciary. Authority was divided to prevent a concentration of power in any one part of the government, thus preventing the possibility of a dictatorship in the future.

A further safeguard was provided by spelling out specifically those areas in which the federal government could, *and could not*, function. These restrictions on government power were embodied in the Bill of Rights, the first ten amendments to the Constitution. The Ninth and Tenth Amendments reserved for the states and the people *all* powers not specifically given to the federal government.

One of the powers the federal government was logically given was the function of regulating *interstate* commerce, trade and businesses which operated across state lines. Regulation of *intrastate* commerce, business or trade conducted wholly within one state was left to the states. Thus, most of the owner-operated retail, commercial, and service business in the nation were free from interference in any way by the federal government.

In 1942, the Supreme Court, with Felix Frankfurter in the lead, changed this 150 year old concept. Without precedent in law or fact, the Court voted that because one of the tenants that rented space in a building in New Jersey sold its products in other states, that the building itself was in interstate commerce and thus subject to federal regulations.[47] Even more fantastic, the Court decided that the elevator operator who spent his days running the elevator up and down was also in interstate commerce.

Through such legal twisting and turning, the bureaucrats evaded constitutional limitations on their power and achieved control over nearly every segment of American business, large and small, *and their employees*.

In the same year, similar nimble "legal" footwork by the Supreme Court affirmed the federal government's complete control over American farmers. A farmer named Filburn planted 12 acres of wheat for which he did not have a federal allotment. He fed the wheat to animals raised on his own farm and slaughtered as food for his own family.

The government fined Filburn, who appealed the case to the Supreme Court. He argued that the government had no right to control his actions in producing food for the sole use of his own family. He claimed that under no conceivable stretch of the law could his actions be interpreted as "interstate commerce." "Oh, yes," the Court said. If you had not used your own wheat for feed, you *might* have bought wheat from someone else, and that *might* have affected the price of other wheat which was transported in interstate commerce.[48] Therefore, the Court ruled, the federal government is perfectly justified under the interstate commerce clause of the Constitution in applying these controls.

The Supreme Court's role in the socialist-Communist plan to transform the United States into part of a one-world socialistic society has been the subject of Congressional inquiries,[49] and several lengthy books.[50]

Criticism of the Supreme Court, which started early in the New Deal period, reached a peak on June 25, 1962, when the Court, by a 6 to 1 decision, denied New York school children the privilege of opening the school day with a non-sectarian prayer.[51] The same day, the Court decided that pornographic literature designed to appeal to homosexuals was not obscene and indecent and therefore could not be barred from the U.S. Mails.[52]

Twenty-five years after FDR appointed Justice Black to the Supreme Court in 1938, the leftist trio in black robes, Douglas, Frankfurter and Black still held sway. They contributed to the destruction of the rights of the separate states, permitted federal intervention into every phase of business and private life; and led the movement to destroy the security laws of the nation.

Justice Black, in his first 25 years on the bench, participated in 102 cases in which subversion and Communists were involved. He compiled the astounding record of *reaching a decision favorable to the Communists in all 102 cases.*[53] Justice Douglas participated in 100 such cases and *favored the Communist position 97 times.*[54] Frankfurter, third man in the trio, went along with Douglas and Black until his final three years on the bench when he switched and rather consistently opposed the Communist position.[55]

In recent years, as recounted in Chapter III, Roosevelt's appointees have been joined by those of President Eisenhower, Earl Warren and William Brennan. Practically all legal restraints against Communist subversion of our society have been destroyed by Court Action. The Communist infiltration of the New Deal was opposed at the time the Supreme Court controversies started, but to no avail. The Democratic Party's nominee for President in 1928, Alfred E. Smith, was one of those who spoke out. Al Smith watched the transformation of our government in silence until January 25, 1936, when in Washington, D.C. he said:

> It is not easy for me to stand up here tonight and talk to the American people against the Democratic Administration. This is not easy. It hurts me. But I can call upon innumerable witnesses to testify to the fact that during my whole public life I put patriotism above partisanship. And when I see danger...it is difficult for me to refrain from speaking out.[56]

Smith did speak out clearly and distinctly, but few listened. He said:

> What are these dangers I see? The first is the arraignment of class against class. It has been freely predicted that if we were ever to have civil strife again in this country it would come from the

appeal to passion and prejudices that comes from demagogues that would incite one class of our people against another.

In my time I have met some good and bad industrialists; I have met some good and bad financiers, but I have also met some good and bad laborers, and this I know, that permanent prosperity is dependent on capital and labor alike.[57]

After announcing that he had only one choice, his withdrawal of support from the New Deal, Smith concluded:

Now in conclusion, let me give this solemn warning. There can only be one Capital, Washington or Moscow! There can be only one atmosphere of government, the clear, pure fresh air of free America, or the foul breath of Communistic Russia.

There can be only one flag, the Stars and Stripes, or the Red Flag of the Godless Union of the Soviet.[58]

Al Smith was not the only Democrat to rebel. Former Congressman Martin Dies, head of the Special House Committee on Un-American Activities in the 1930's recalled later in a speech that his committee "compiled lists of thousands of Communists, agents, stooges, and sympathizers on the government payroll.[59] He took the information to President Roosevelt personally. Roosevelt said, furiously:

I have never seen a man who had such exaggerated ideas about this thing. I do not believe in communism anymore than you do but there is nothing wrong with the Communists in this country; several of the best friends I've got are Communists.[60]

Dies continued his fight against Communist infiltration until 1944 when facing a "purge" by FDR he withdrew from the 1944 Democratic primary in Texas. Some of the actual Communists and agents Dies tried to expose were rooted out of the government years later. Many escaped exposure and even today, FBI files are reported to contain evidence reflecting on the loyalty of between 2000 and 3000 federal employees, according to a statement entered in the *Congressional Record* by Congressman Paul Kitchin (D-NC) in 1962.[61]

For over 20 years, warning after warning has been ignored.

In 1946, for example, President Harry Truman promoted Harry Dexter White, the assistant secretary of the Treasury, to a high post on the International Monetary Fund, *after J. Edgar Hoover personally had White's complete record as a long-time Communist agent delivered to the White House.*[62]

MODERN REPUBLICANISM

The collectivist-conceived bureaucratic empire grew and thrived and was threatened only once—by the possible selection of Robert A. Taft as the Republican Presidential candidate in 1952.

The Fabians and internationalists in the Republican Party, assisted by transfers from the normally Democratic-oriented political arm of the Fabian movement, the Americans for Democratic Action (ADA), succeeded in nominating Dwight Eisenhower as the Republican standard bearer.

Just four years before, in 1948, Eisenhower and the open ultra-liberal Supreme Court Justice William O. Douglas had been the ADA's choices for the Democratic nomination.[63] The late Philip Graham, publisher of the ultra-left-wing *Washington Post* was among the many "liberals" who moved into the Republican Party briefly to stop Taft and nominate Eisenhower. Arthur Hays Sulsberger of the *New York Times* was another.[64]

Eisenhower talked like an *economic conservative* but was supported by liberals, avowed internationalists like Thomas Dewey, and the "practical politicians." Their slogan was, "I like Taft, but he can't win."

Taft was beaten in a convention where disputed delegations, charges of fraud, and whispers of huge sums changing hands marred the proceedings.[65]

During Eisenhower's eight years in office, he *talked* about balanced budgets and fiscal responsibility. His actions and programs increased the national debt by $25-billion.[66]

Republicans in Congress, who with a few conservative Democrats had blocked the most radical New Deal programs, bowed to party discipline and acceded to Eisenhower's requests. The establishment of the Health, Education and Welfare Department is an example.

Proposed and rejected regularly during the Truman Administration, the Health, Education and Welfare Department was established by Eisenhower in 1953 with a first year budget of less than a billion dollars. By 1960, HEW gathered in state and local programs and initiated its own new ones to control the powerful political weapon of disbursements to the states and people of over $15-billion annually[67]—this growth took place during an administration which publicly was "economy conscious."

Much of the increase financed Eisenhower's "matching grants-in-aid" which were supposed to "help" states meet "responsibilities" (as defined by the federal bureaucracy).

State legislatures accepted federal "guidance" and control of their unemployment compensation, highway construction, scientific education, and welfare programs to get the "free federal money" which had been collected in the states.

Over 400 cities accepted federal "guidance" on building codes, zoning laws, planning commissions, and land use plans to become "eligible" for federal urban renewal and public housing funds. At the same time, a direct line of authority was established between Washington and local governments, by-passing the state governments.[68]

The budget, the size of the federal government, and federal influence zoomed. For example, spending for purely *domestic* programs averaged $17.7-billion annually in Truman's last five years. In Eisenhower's last five years, it averaged $33.6-billion, an increase of 89%.[69]

It was this betrayal of the principles on which the Republican Party was elected in 1952 that prompted Senator Barry Goldwater (R-Ari) to rise in the Senate on April 8, 1957, to deliver the following speech, thus, breaking with the Eisenhower Administration:

> It is, of course, with deepest sorrow that I must pass judgment upon my own party...Until quite recently I was personally satisfied that this administration was providing the reliable and realistic leadership so vital to the maintenance of a strong domestic economy, which, in turn, is a vital factor in maintaining world peace.

It is true that after 20 years of New Deal-Fair Deal experiments in socialism, Americans have been considerably softened to the doctrine of federal paternalism but what degree of slavish economic indigence has resulted should be treated with lessons in free enterprise and States Rights, not as the President recently suggested in a speech in Washington by educating people—to accept federal moneys for a project which they ought to be paying for themselves, directly through their State and local governments.

It is equally disillusioning to see the Republican Party plunging headlong into the same dismal state experienced by traditional Democrat principles of Jefferson and Jackson during the days of the New Deal and Fair Deal. As a result of those economic and political misadventures, that great party has lost its soul of freedom; its spokesmen are peddlers of the philosophy that the Constitution is outmoded, that States Rights are void, and that the only hope for the future of these United States is for our people to be federally clothed, federally supported in their occupations, and to be buried in a federal box in a federal cemetery.

In the Republican Party there are also vociferous exponents of this incredible philosophy. It may be, in fact, that they are among the "Modern Republicans" about whom there has been so much discussion in recent months. Certainly, the faulty tenets of Modern Republicans do not refute this big government concept.[70]

The next year, in 1958, the Eisenhower Administration ran up the biggest peace-time deficit in American history, a $12.5-billion endorsement of the Keynesian concept of "spend yourself to prosperity."[71] Goldwater won re-election to the U.S. Senate that year by a record majority—while Republicans in general were losing 12 seats in the U.S. Senate and about 40 seats in the lower House.

THE NEW FRONTIER

Fabian control of the Washington bureaucracy is now more openly acknowledged. Fewer Americans seem repelled by socialism. The attitudes of many have softened toward communism. Shocked and shaken by the subversion cases 15 years ago, Americans have become apathetic about high government officials with Communist front records. Those who expose them are right-wing radicals.

Even John Kennedy was affected. In 1953, as a Senator, Kennedy said:

> I'm not a liberal at all. I never joined the Americans for Democratic Action. I'm not comfortable with those people.[72]

Not many Americans are comfortable with the ideas of the political arm of the Fabian Society. But as president, John Kennedy appointed 40 members of this political under-world to high government posts.

For example, Arthur M. Schlesinger, Jr., a Harvard professor and ADA-founder, is Kennedy's special assistant. In 1947, Schlesinger wrote:

> If socialism (i.e., ownership by the state of all significant means of production) is to preserve democracy it must be brought about step by step in a way which will not disrupt the fabric of custom, law and mutual confidence upon which personal rights depend.
>
> That is, the transition must be piecemeal; it must be parliamentary; it must respect civil liberties and due process of law. Socialism by such means used to seem fantastic to the hard-eyed melodramatists of the Leninist persuasion; but even Stalin is reported to have told Harold Laski recently that it might be possible... There seems no inherent obstacle to the gradual advance of socialism in the United States through a series of New Deals.
>
> Socialism, then, appears quite practical within this frame of reference, as a long-time proposition. It's gradual advance might well preserve order and law...The active agents in effecting the transition will probably be, not the working classes, but some combination of lawyers, business and labor managers, politicians and intellectuals, in the manner of the first New Deal.[73]

In these three short paragraphs, Schlesinger confirms vividly what good Americans are called right-wing extremists for saying: That the Fabians (gradualists) are socialists; that Keynesian economic policy is the path to socialism; that goals of communism and socialism are essentially the same; that New Deal welfare state proposals whether enacted by

Democrats or Republicans are socialistic; that establishment of socialism will result in a curtailment of freedom; that socialism and communism appeal, not to the working class or the poverty stricken masses, but to the "liberal" intellectual, the college professor, and the turncoat businessman.

CHAPTER XIII
INTERNATIONALISM

A real internationalist is one who brings his sympathy and recognition up to a point of practical and maximal help to the USSR in support and defense of the USSR by every means and in every possible form.

—Andrei Vyshinsky

FOR OVER 100 YEARS American Presidents and diplomats faithfully followed the advice left with them by George Washington when, in his farewell address, he said:

> The great rule of conduct for us, in regard to foreign nations, is in extending our commercial relations, to have as little *political* connections as possible... 'Tis our true policy to steer clear of permanent alliances, with any nation of the world.[1]

Since World War II, America has become so entangled in a web of treaties, executive agreements, and secret pacts that we have lost control of our political decisions, monetary system, and military forces. In 1954, a Congressional committee found that...

> ...there is a definite tendency to sacrifice the national interest of our country in dealing with foreign affairs.[2]

By 1961, the sacrifice of the national interest became the rule rather than the exception. For example, the U.S. Army's crack 24th division was alerted in Germany in the spring of 1961. Part of it prepared to resist possible attacks from East Germany while other units stood by to be airlifted to the Congo to protect the Communist-dominated Central Congolese government by fighting the pro-Western, anti-Communist forces of Moise Tshombe.[3] Major General Edwin A. Walker, who commanded the 24th at the time, told a Congressional committee...

> ...under our national policy and by our own command, American

sons were alerted in readiness to go to the Congo to fight the anti-Communists and also to go to the East-West Zone to fight Communists. Those two boys, in my opinion, without any doubt are fighting each other.[4]

In 1963, the military forces of the United States were unleashed in the Caribbean area, not to protect Latin America from Communist subversives spreading out from Cuba—but to protect Castro, Cuba, and Communism from attacks by liberty-loving Cubans. Meanwhile, halfway around the world, Americans were being killed in the guerrilla warfare in South Viet Nam—by Communists.

Traditional U.S. foreign policy was based on the concept that the primary function of American military forces and diplomats should be the protection of American lives, rights and property. This traditional concept has been replaced by a foreign policy which sacrifices national interest—and common sense—to something called "world opinion."

To fully understand how the transformation has been effected, it is necessary to examine several facets of national policy, including relations with the United Nations, the foreign aid program, the effect of treaties on the basic rights of Americans and the growth of the group which has engineered the basic changes in U.S. foreign policy.

THE UNITED NATIONS

In the 1930's, with each breach of the peace, in Manchuria in 1931, Ethiopia in 1935, China in 1936, Spain in 1937, and when Europe exploded in 1939, Americans were told that somehow it might not have happened if the U.S. Senate and "isolation- minded" Americans had not rejected the League of Nations in 1919.A national guilt complex was induced in America through reiteration of this theme in the press, textbooks, and through church publications and programs and government and other opinion-molding agencies.

After this preconditioning, when World War II ended the United Nations treaty was ratified by the U.S. Senate with only two dissenting votes.[5] A majority of Americans grasped the UN as the "best hope for world peace."

The Communist Party, USA wholeheartedly supported the newly-forming organization. *Political Affairs*, the party's official theoretical journal, in the April 1945, issue gave Communists this order:

> Great popular support and enthusiasm for the United Nations policies should be built up, well organized and fully articulate. But it is also necessary to do more than that. The opposition must be rendered so impotent that it will be unable to gather any significant support in the Senate against the U.N. Charter and the treaties which will follow.

The few voices in America which urged caution were rendered impotent, just as the Communists planned. The opposition was assured that the UN could never act against American interests because the United States would have veto power. That other countries large enough to disrupt the peace also had the veto was ignored.

The Communist leadership realized it. They knew in advance that the structure of the UN could be used to prevent it from ever acting against the Communists. They knew what few Americans realize even today...

> ...that Alger Hiss was the principal American representative in discussions of plans for the UN and its Charter at the Yalta and Dumbarton Oaks conferences; that Hiss was to be the Secretary General of the United Nations Organizing Conference in San Francisco when the Charter was written and adopted; that in his dual role as Secretary General and top State Department official for UN affairs he could channel his choices into key positions in the newly forming UN Secretariat.[6]

In 1948, when Alger Hiss was exposed as a Communist agent, the web of protective propaganda which guards the UN prevented most Americans from learning that he had been the UN's chief architect.

Disciplined members of the world-wide Communist conspiracy were informed almost immediately that the UN was planned as the agency "which will smash the anti-Soviet intrigues of imperialist reactionaries." The entire Red scheme for the UN was revealed in a Communist pamphlet, *The*

United Nations, published in English in September 1945, by the People's Publishing House, Bombay, India.

According to this official Communist pamphlet, the Soviet Union planned to...

> ...automatically veto any UN measure restrictive to or harmful to world communism while using the UN to promote friction between non-Communist nations and frustrate their foreign policy.

> ...use the UN trusteeship council and the UN special agencies to detach all dependent and semi-dependent areas from any foreign influence except that of the Soviet Union—eventually bringing about a one-world Soviet system.[7]

In the ensuing years, the Communists have followed the plan, using the veto 100 times. The U.S. has never used it.

As a result, the United Nations, established to prevent or stop wars, has watched ineffectively, or aided the aggressors, while wars have been waged in China, Malaya, Indo-China, Tibet, Laos, Hungary, Korea, the Middle East, Cuba, Indonesia, Algeria, the Congo, Goa, Angola, and on the Indian-Chinese border. The anti-Western forces have won, or are winning them all.

There has been no major war, not because the UN has prevented it—but because the Communists are winning the world without one. The plan "to detach all dependent and semi-dependent areas from any foreign influence except that of the Soviet Union," is being fulfilled as dozens of former colonies become "independent" and adopt the "neutralist" pro-Communist position in the world struggle.

Despite 17 years of continual failures, in 1962 nearly 85% of the American people still placed faith and trust in the UN as the best hope for peace.[8] They fail to see the truth because emotion-provoking slogans have been substituted for factual, accurate information about the UN's founding, its structure, and its operation. UN failures in Hungary, Korea, and the Congo are frequently called victories.

Few Americans know that the UN Secretariat has become a haven for the Communists and security risks who had been officials of the U.S. government in the 1940's. In 1952, the

Senate Internal Security Subcommittee spent two months studying the activities of U.S. citizens employed by the UN.[9] Its report stated:

American Communists who had been officials of the United States Government penetrated the Secretariat of the United Nations after the United States Government had been apprised of security information regarding their conspiratorial activities.

In all, 21 Americans employed in key UN administrative posts took the Fifth Amendment during the SISS hearings when asked about their participation in the Communist conspiracy. UN Secretary General Trygve Lie studied the Senate report and discharged the Fifth Amendment cases.

Lie's action was appealed and the UN Administrative Tribunal ruled that Lie had no right to fire employees who had permanent UN civil service status. Reinstatements with back pay and "damages" of up to $40,000 per employee were awarded.[10]

Dr. Robert Morris, who was chief counsel of the Senate committee which investigated the security risks in the UN, commented on the reinstatement of the Fifth Amendment cases and the large cash grants they received. In his book *No Wonder We Are Losing*, he said:

Here was a Communist victory accomplished with the sanction of free delegations. The decision established, in effect, that even if UN authorities discovered secret Kremlin agents in their employ, they could do nothing about it. Let it be remembered that these were not Soviet-appointed officials, but part of the U.S. quota.[11]

Dr. Morris' comment points up a dilemma. Even if it were possible to eliminate all Americans of doubtful loyalty from the UN Administrative staff, many Communists would still hold key UN positions. Under a quota system, each member nation, including the Communist ones, names its own citizens to fill an allocated percentage of clerical, technical, and administrative jobs in the UN Secretariat. In theory, those appointed should function as unbiased "international

280 None Dare Call It Treason---25 YEARS LATER

civil servants" working for the best interests of the UN as a whole.

How it actually works in practice was described in the report of the Senate committee which studied the case of Povl Bang-Jensen in 1961. Bang-Jensen, a Danish civil servant, was fired in 1958 by Dag Hammarskjold for refusing to reveal the names of refugees who testified in the UN Hungarian inquiry to a high UN official from a Communist country. Bang-Jensen feared Communist reprisals against the relatives of the witnesses who were still in Hungary. As was discussed in Chapter IX, Bang-Jensen continued his fight to correct the serious lack of security in the UN Secretariat until his death by "suicide" two years after he was fired.

Quoting a study made by the International League for the Rights of Man, the Senate report on the Bang-Jensen case said:

> If the Secretary General retains on his staff Soviet nationals there is prima facie a possibility of leaks of information to the Soviet Union. Only those persons of extraordinary naivete would fail to recognize that, as between loyalty to the international civil service and the Soviet Union, the Soviet citizen is under extreme pressure to conform to the wishes of his government.[12]

The report cited cases of Soviet employees of the UN Secretariat caught while engaging in espionage activities against the U.S. and concluded:

> So long as Soviet nationals are members of the Secretary General's staff or serve directly under him, there is always a risk that confidential information in the office of the Secretary General which is desired by the Soviet government will find its way into their hands.[13]

The risk is not limited to information leaks. With some of the UN's highest staff offices held by Communists, the manipulation of UN programs to benefit world communism is a distinct threat.

As an example, under a secret agreement made in 1945 by U.S. Secretary of State Edward Stettinius, a Communist has always filled the second most important UN post, that of

Under or Assistant Secretary for Political and Security Council Affairs. This committee implements Security Council police actions, oversees disarmament enforcement, etc. Under the terms of the secret agreement, the nine men who have held the post since the UN was organized in 1945 have all been from Iron Curtain countries.[14]

During the Korean War, for example, the chain of command from the UN Security Council to General MacArthur, was through the Under-Secretary for Political and Security Council affairs, Constantine Zinchenko, a Communist.[15] Is it any wonder that General George Stratemeyer, the Air Force commander in Korea, returned to tell a Senate committee:

> We were required to lose the Korean War.[16]

The threat continues today. If U.S. proposals for arms control and disarmament are accepted, U.S. military forces will be transferred to the UN peace force, which is directed by the Under-Secretary for Political and Security Council Affairs, who has always been a Communist.

There is still another danger in blind faith, trust, and respect in the UN. With Communists filling administrative and technical positions in the Secretariat, the reports they write, the decisions they make carry the prestige of the United Nations. Unsuspecting Americans have no indication that the UN pamphlet they receive may have been written by an open Communist.

The 1963 UNESCO bulletin on Colonialism is an example. Under the UN seal it said:

> The unequal treatment of nationalistic colonialist oppression and discrimination on grounds of race or nationality, which still characterizes a number of capitalist countries today, are to be explained by the political and social systems prevailing in those countries.[17]

The UNESCO report completely ignored "oppression and discrimination" in the Soviet "colonies" of Hungary, Poland, Tibet, etc. and praised the Soviet Union for...

> ...successful establishment of full equality of rights between races and nationalities in the USSR.[18]

The United States pays 31% of the cost for the Soviet propaganda which is distributed into the under-developed nations of the world under the respectability of the United Nations emblem.

How many Americans look behind the blue UN "seal of approval" on the UNESCO literature and materials used in American schools to build "attitudes" for "world under-standing" and "world citizenship" in their sons and daughters?

How secure would they feel in accepting this "seal of approval" if they knew that this program was directed for years by Mrs. A. Jegalova, chief of the UNESCO division of Secondary Education. Before becoming an "international civil servant" Mrs. Jegalova was chief inspector of the Ukrainian Branch of the Soviet Ministry of Education. Being a Communist, Mrs. Jegalova is unlikely to approve any program originating in her department which is detrimental to world communism. If she did, the Kremlin would quickly call her home.

The UN Special Agencies, of which UNESCO is typical, have from their founding aided and assisted the world Communist movement. For example, UNRRA, the United Nations Relief and Rehabilitation Agency, distributed billions of dollars in American aid following World War II.[19] In Yugoslavia, Poland, and China, where Communist and anti-Communist forces were maneuvering for control, UNRRA channeled its aid, 72% of which was supplied by the U.S., through Communist groups.

Arthur Bliss Lane, American ambassador to Poland following the war, described in his book, *I Saw Poland Betrayed*, how UNRRA funds were used to solidify Communist control of the country. He told how, in advance of the elections, official approval was given to the Communist-dominated coalition government, and then:

> Over my personal protest...the agreement concluded in Warsaw provided that the Polish Government, and not UNRRA, should have complete jurisdiction over the distribution of UNRRA supplies in Poland...I learned of attempts to force the populace to join

the two principal parties, the Workers (Communist) and the Socialist. Those who joined were given preference ration cards entitling them to receive choice UNRRA supplies...as the agreement with the Polish government gave UNRRA no control over distribution of goods imported by UNRRA, Drury (local administrator-Auth.) could not prevent supplies being used for political purposes.[20]

The Polish people supported the Communists or they didn't eat. The story was the same in Yugoslavia and much of China.

How was such a faulty agreement made? David Weintraub, identified as a Communist by Whittaker Chambers, left the U.S. government in 1944 to become chief adviser to UNRRA Governor General, Herbert Lehman. Later, he became chief of UNRRA supplies.[21] When UNRRA disbanded, Weintraub transferred into the UN Secretariat as Director of the Economic Stability and Development Division.

Similar records have been established by the UN Special Fund, the World Health Organization, and UNICEF. All have channeled American aid to Communist countries. In 1961-62, for example, the UN Special Fund, as discussed earlier, gave Castro $1.6-million.[22]

By 1963, the UN was headed by avowed Marxists. Following his election as Secretary General, U Thant was interviewed by *Newsweek*. He said:

I believe in the philosophy of thesis, antithesis, and synthesis. From its present antithesis, I believe the world is moving towards a new synthesis.[23]

Newsweek did not tell its readers, but Thant's "philosophy" is a simple restatement of Hegel's dialectic, the basis or root of Karl Marx's dialectical materialism. Thant has also adopted another Marxist idea to finance the "synthesis" toward which he sees the world moving—the one-world socialistic government financed by the United States. Thant says:

The concept of taxing the rich according to their capacity to pay, in order to cater to the poor according to their needs, is now well established as a simple canon of social justice in all democratic countries. It requires only a little imagination to lift this concept to a higher plane, namely the international plane, and to extend its scope from the country to the universe.[24]

How much of your income would the UN representative of Gabon, Algeria, Cuba or the Soviet Union vote to take away as simple "social justice?" The United States has no veto in the General Assembly.

In the maneuvering which followed the death of Dag Hammarskjold, the Soviet Union first demanded that UN administration be handled by a troika [three persons sharing power]. This demand was withdrawn, *provided* that Ralph Bunche, American delegate to the UN, and a Soviet delegate, George P. Arkadyev, be named as under-secretaries to "neutralist" U Thant.[25] This was done.

Did Russia get its troika? Thant's views have been examined. Arkadyev was a Russian Communist. The record of Bunche, who supposedly represents America, was examined in detail on the floor of Congress in two speeches by Congressman James Utt (R-Cal). Utt said:

> Russia now has its troika: one an avowed Marxist, the second a dedicated Communist; and the third with a pro-Communist bias.[26]

Utt detailed Bunche's record as contributing editor of the openly Communist magazine, *Science and Society*, in the 1930s; as founder of the National Negro Congress, cited as subversive by the Attorney General; as a high official of the Institute of Pacific Relations; and as an advocate of UN employment for a notorious Communist agent.[27] Utt concluded his remarks, saying:

> It is my considered judgment that Dr. Bunche must be considered a security risk for our country. The "troika" arrangement engineered by the Communists is frightening and devastating when you consider that the United States of America has no foreign policy of its own except the United Nations.[28]

The implications of the Soviet use of the veto to block any effective anti-Communist action; the use of UN headquarters as a base for Soviet espionage and propaganda activity within the United States; the UN's long record of aid to the world

Communist movement; the UN action in the Congo which destroyed the pro-Western anti-Communist government of Moise Tshombe, have impelled several distinguished world figures to speak out. Lord Beaverbrook, the noted British newspaper publisher, said:

> Here in New York City, you Americans have the biggest fifth column in the world—The United Nations.[29]

Before his death in 1953, the late Senator Robert A. Taft issued this warning:

> The UN has become a trap. Let's go it alone.[30]

In a speech at his birthplace in Iowa during the summer of 1962, former President Herbert A. Hoover, once a supporter of the United Nations, reluctantly announced:

> Unless the UN is completely reorganized without the Communist nations in it, we should get out of it.[31]

What force keeps the United States in the United Nations despite its consistent record of failures, financial bankruptcy, and pro-Communist bias?

Why do so few Americans know of Alger Hiss's role as chief architect of the world organization; of the UN's refusal to fire American Communists uncovered in key positions; of the Senate investigations which show that the UN is a base for Soviet espionage and propaganda activities in the United States; that official UN studies and records are actually the work of Communists on the UN staff?

How can the murder of children, machine gunning of hospital invalids, rape, plunder and pillage committed by the UN Peace Force in Katanga be described as "peace-keeping operations" without the American people rebelling.

In 1954, a prominent U.S. Senator delivered a cryptic speech which might provide some answers. Senator William Jenner (R-Ind) said that there was a force operating to merge the United States into a one-world socialist system. He describes it this way:

> We have a well-organized political action group in this country, determined to destroy our Constitution, and establish a one-party

state. This political action group has its own local political support organizations, its own pressure groups, its own vested interest, its foothold within our Government, and its own propaganda apparatus.

The important thing to remember about this group is not its ideology but its organization. It is a dynamic, aggressive, elite corps forcing its way through every opening to make a breach for a collectivist one-party state...It cares nothing for party changes directed by the sovereign people...It has a strategy which is not derived from anything known to the two parties... Outwardly we have a constitutional government. We have operating within our Government and political system, another body representing another form of government, a bureaucratic elite, which believes our Constitution is out moded and is sure it is on the winning side.[32]

What is this force? How does it operate? What are its goals? Is it the force which provides the protective web of propaganda and emotion-provoking slogans which safeguard the United Nations from rational evaluation?

THE ORGANIZED INTERNATIONALISTS

In May 1919, a group of young intellectuals who had helped draft the League of Nations Charter during World War I met at the Majestic Hotel in Paris. They were bitterly disappointed. The U.S. Senate and the American people had rejected the concept of a world governing body. In their discussions they conceived an organization which might study and promote a better "understanding" of international affairs.

The group included Christian Herter and the brothers, John Foster and Allen Dulles. They came home from Paris and incorporated the *Council on Foreign Relations*.

The influence achieved by Herter and John Foster Dulles 25 years later as Secretaries of States under Dwight Eisenhower, and Allen Dulles, as head of the powerful and controversial Central Intelligence Agency, is one indication of the power obtained by the group. This tells only part of the story.

Extremely selective in its membership, the Council has never been a "mass" organization. However, according to the CFR's 1960 membership roster,[33] its 1400 members control the U.S. State Department, many top cabinet posts, the major newspapers, magazines, and radio and TV networks, most of the large tax-exempt foundations, a host of other opinion molding groups and organizations, and the nation's largest companies including U.S. Steel, AT&T, General Motors, du Pont, IBM and others.

Despite its influence, the CFR is relatively unknown. It has been the subject of one official, although brief, pronouncement by Congress. In 1954, the Special House Committee to Investigate Tax-Exempt Foundations headed by Congressman Reece said that the CFR's "productions are not objective but are directed over-whelmingly at promoting the globalistic concept."[34] The committee's final report expressed concern that the CFR had become...

...in essence an agency of the United States Government...carrying its internationalist bias with it.[35]

How the Council on Foreign Relations functions as "an agency of government" became clear in an eight-part examination of the organization published in 1961. The author, Dan Smoot, a former FBI man and Administrative Assistant to J. Edgar Hoover, found that...

...since 1944, all candidates for President, both Republican and Democrat, have been CFR members, except Truman who became President by "accident." Every Secretary of State since Cordell Hull (except James Byrnes) has been a CFR member. Over 40 CFR members comprised the American delegation to the UN Organizing Conference in San Francisco including Alger Hiss, Nelson Rockefeller, Adlai Stevenson, Ralph Bunche, John Foster Dulles, and the Secretary of State Edward Stettinius. CFR affiliates have controlled an unusual number of cabinet posts and top Presidential advisory positions.[36]

The influence is so great that Smoot labeled the group, *The Invisible Government*, and published a book by that name on its membership, activities, and philosophy.

CFR members continue in key government posts under both Democratic and Republican Administrations. The Dulles Brothers, Herter, Arthur Dean, Douglas Dillion, Charles Bohlen, John McCloy, John McCone, Henry Cabot Lodge, and Ralph Bunche hold high positions no matter which party is in power. Except for Bohlen, and possibly Bunche, all are regarded as Republicans.

The Kennedy-Johnson Administrations appear to be totally controlled by CFR members and former members. They include:

President John F. Kennedy, Secretary of State Dean Rusk, Secretary of Treasury Douglas Dillon, Secretary of Labor and Supreme Court Justice Arthur Goldberg, UN Ambassador Adlai Stevenson, Presidential assistants Arthur Schlesinger, Jr. and McGeorge Bundy, State Department Adviser Dean Acheson, Federal Reserve chairman William McC. Martin, Assistant and Under-Secretaries of State Chester Bowles, Averell Harriman, George McGhee, George Ball, Harlan Cleveland, and Brooks Hays, Assistant Secretaries of Defense Roswell Gilpatric and Paul Nitze, State Department Policy Planner Walt Whitman Rostow, Presidential Disarmament Adviser John McCloy, Chief Disarmament Negotiator Arthur Dean, Presidential Assistant for Science and Technology Jerome Wiesner, and USIA Director Edward R. Murrow.[37]

These are just a few of the more than 60 CFR members who have held top advisory posts, ambassadorial appointments, etc. in the Kennedy-Johnson Administration—a remarkable achievement for a group with only 1400 members.

Even when CFR members retired or are replaced, another CFR man gets the job. When General L.L. Lemnitzer (CFR) retired as Chairman of the Joint Chiefs of Staff, he was replaced by General Maxwell Taylor (CFR). When Allen Dulles (CFR) became a center of public controversy over the failure of his CIA-directed Cuban invasion, he was replaced by John McCone (CFR).

How can so much power be concentrated in the membership of such a small organization without public attention? As

Senator Jenner pointed out, this group has its own propaganda apparatus. Among the 1400 CFR members are:

Henry Luce, editor-in-chief of *Time, Life* and *Fortune*; David Lawrence, *U.S. News & World Report*; the late Philip Graham, publisher of *Newsweek* and the *Washington Post*; Gardner and John Cowles, who publish *Look* and own several influential newspapers and broadcasting companies; Arthur Hays Sulzberger, chairman of the board, *New York Times*; Mark Ethridge, publisher, *Louisville Courier Journal*; syndicated columnists Marquis Childs, James Reston, Ernest K. Lindley, Walter Lippmann and Hanson Baldwin; plus dozens of other lesser known writers, editors and publishers.

Other key editors and publishers belong to local affiliated CFR "chapters" in 30 key cities in the United States. Other CFR members who hold important posts in other opinion-making media are:

William S. Paley, chairman of the board, CBS; David Sarnoff, chairman of the board, Radio Corporation of America (operators of NBC); broadcasters Edward R. Murrow, Charles Collingwood, William L. Shirer, and Irving R. Levine; Harry Scherman, founder and board chairman of the Book-of-the-Month Club; Joseph Barnes, editor-in-chief, Simon & Schuster, John Gunther, best-selling author of the "Inside" series; public opinion pollsters George Gallup and Elmo Roper and others.

CFR member William Benton is a principal owner of the *Encyclopedia Brittanica,* which may account for the omission of Alger Hiss' role in the founding of the United Nations in this standard reference work.[38]

Senator Jenner described a "political action group" with its own pressure groups, political support organizations, etc. CFR members hold controlling influence in the American Association for the United Nations, The Foreign Policy Association, World Affairs Council, U.S. Committee for the United Nations, United World Federalists, Atlantic Union, NATO Citizens Council, and other one-world propaganda organizations. The Council for Economic Development, Business Advisory Council, and the Advertising Council are similarly controlled.[39]

ACCORDING TO PLAN

What are the goals of this small organization whose members exert such influence on the United States and the World?

Since 1945, CFR members have largely controlled the United States government and its foreign policy. In that time, world communism has increased the number of its slaves by 520% to over one-billion. Communism has received no serious setback in its drive toward world domination, despite military and foreign aid expenditures of over $500-billion by the U.S. government to "fight" communism. That record, in itself, is an indictment.

The writings and speeches of CFR members reveal that the failures of the West have not been accidents. Events since World War II have developed largely according to plan.

Arthur Schlesinger, Jr., member of the CFR and now special assistant to President Kennedy and Johnson, spelled out the "no-win" policy which the CFR-dominated State Department has been following since 1945. Writing in the May-June 1947 issue of *Partisan Review*, Schlesinger said:

> Reduced to its fundamentals, the American problem is to arrange the equilibrium of forces in the world so that, at every given moment of decision, the Soviet General Staff will decide against aggressions that might provoke a general war on the ground that they present too great a risk. At the same time, the U.S. must not succumb to demands for an anti-Soviet crusade nor permit reactionaries in the buffer states to precipitate conflicts in defense of their own obsolete perogatives.[40]

The United States, according to Schlesinger, should *not* try to "win" over communism, free the captive peoples, *or even permit them to free themselves*. The "obsolete perogatives" which Schlesinger would deny to the Eastern Europeans, Tibetans, Loatians, Koreans and others in the satellites are national sovereignty, and freedom—the right to choose their own governments. Is this one man's view? Schlesinger said:

Can the United States conceive and initiate so subtle a policy?

Though the secret has been kept pretty much from the readers of the liberal press, the State Department has been proceeding for some time along these lines. Both Byrnes and Marshall have perceived the essential need to be firm without being rancorous, to check Soviet expansion without making unlimited commitments to the anti-Soviet crusade, to invoke power to counter power without engaging in senseless intimidation, to encourage the growth of the democratic left. The performance has often fallen below the conception, but the direction has been correct. Men like Ben Cohen, Dean Acheson, and Charles Bohlen (all CFR members-Auth.) have tried to work out the details and whip up support for this admittedly risky program.[41]

The "risky" policy of containment-rather-than-victory which Schlesinger outlined, and which the State Department still follows, has resulted in nearly 800-million people going behind the Iron and Bamboo Curtains. The leaders of the "democratic left" which the policy was to encourage—Mao Tse-tung, Ben Bella, Sukarno, Nkrumah, Adoula, Lumumba, Fidel Castro, Juan Bosch, Romulo Betancourt, and Cheddi Jagan—inevitably turn out to be Communists, or complete tools of the world Communist movement.

John Foster Dulles was perhaps the most successful practitioner of the "admittedly risky program" which Schlesinger outlined. A founder of the CFR, Dulles served in the State Department as an assistant and adviser to Dean Acheson and later as Secretary of State under President Eisenhower. Dulles was widely acclaimed for slowing down the Soviet offensive from the pace it maintained under Acheson. Few realized, however, that he promoted no aggressive steps to topple their empire.

Under his direction, the State Department initiated aid to Communist countries and cultural exchanges, agreed to permanent partitions of Korea and Viet Nam, tolerated and encouraged the rise of "neutralism" and implemented the rule laid down eight years before by Schlesinger in denying the Hungarians their right to win their revolt.

To understand Dulles' actions, it is necessary to ignore his vigorous anti-Communist statements and well-publicized policy of "brinkmanship" and learn his true beliefs and goals from his early writings.

In 1942, Dulles was chairman of the Federal Council of Churches Commission to Study the Bases of a Just and Durable Peace. The report he prepared recommended:

> ...a world government, strong immediate limitation on national sovereignty, international control of all armies and navies, a universal system of money, world-wide freedom of immigration, progressive elimination of all tariff and quota restrictions on world trade and a democratically-controlled world bank.[42]

The report also called for world-wide redistribution of wealth. It held that a "new order of economic life is both imminent and imperative." It accepted Marxian concepts by denouncing various defects in the profit system as being responsible for breeding war, demagogues, and dictators.

Four years later, Dulles authored another statement for the Federal Council of Churches. Entitled, *Soviet-American Relations*, it was published in the Council's 1946 Biennial Report. It is one of the earliest published speculations that "changes" in both Russia and the United States will make possible a merger of the two systems into a world government. Dulles said:

> Moreover, Communism as an economic program for social reconstruction has points of contact with the social message of Christianity as in its avowed concern for the underprivileged and its insistence on racial equality...neither state socialism nor free enterprise provides a perfect economic system; each can learn from the experience of the other...the free enterprise system has yet to prove it can assure steady production and employment...Soviet socialism has changed much particularly in placing greater dependence upon the incentive of personal gain.[43]

In finding similarities between Communism and Christianity, Dulles chose to ignore the mass murder of 20-million human beings in the first 25 years of Communist control of Russia and the 15-million persons in Soviet slave labor camps as he spoke. In the 17 years after Dulles saw signs of "mellowing" the Communists have exterminated another 40-million people in Russia, China, Hungary, Cuba, Poland, Tibet and Korea.

When Methodist Bishop G. Bromley Oxnam revealed in testimony before the House Committee on Un-American Activities in 1953 that Dulles was the author of the statement, the *Chicago Tribune* suggested editorially that Scott McLeod, State Department Security Chief, might do some checking on his boss.[44]

The thesis that communism is mellowing, first stated by Dulles in 1946, is the underlying theme of most CFR-influenced projects. It is the basis for the overall State Department policy plan prepared by Walt Whitman Rostow (CFR) which was discussed in Chapter IV.[45]

In accepting the theory that communism is "mellowing," these CFR members reject the concept that communism is total evil. Dulles' comparison of communism with the "social message of Christianity" is indicative of this view-point. There are other examples. Arthur Schlesinger, Jr., in the article previously quoted, "condemned" communism in this way:

> The crime of the USSR against the world is its determination to make experiments in libertarian socialism impossible.[46]

Was not the extermination of millions of human beings a crime, Mr. Schlesinger? A similar attitude was expressed by a panel assembled by the Rockefeller Brothers in 1956 to study the major problems facing the world. Of the 14 citizens serving on the Foreign Policy panel, nine were CFR members, including Philip Moseley, director of studies for the CFR, John Nason, president of the CFR "subsidiary," the Foreign Policy Association, Dean Rusk, and Adolf Berle,Jr. About communism and the Soviet threat and U.S. reactions to it, their final resort states:

> It has been necessary to drum up support for United States policy by stressing the imminent threats and crisis and *by harping on the less attractive features of communism*, including the brutalities of the regime and the persistent exploitation of its own and other peoples.[47]

What features of communism does this CFR-dominated panel find attractive? Perhaps, they share the attitude expressed by Arthur Schlesinger, Jr. who on his return from the Soviet Union stated:

> The answer to the Soviet success is as plain as day. It lies in the power of the Soviet Union to focus its national energies. The visitor to Soviet Russia finds it frightening to see what energy a great nation can generate when it allocates its talent and resources according to an intelligent system of priorities.[48]

If this Communist dictatorship is the success that Schlesinger envies, why was it necessary for the United States to ship the Soviet Union $11-billion in lend-lease aid during World War II? Why can't the Soviets produce sufficient food for their people? Why must the United States pump billions of dollars in aid into the Soviet satellites and supply Russia itself with machine tools, industrial plants, and technical know-how?

WHY?

As Americans awaken to examine the U.S. State Department's long and consistent record of aid and comfort to the Communist enemy, and read the statements of those who formulate the policies, they logically ask, "Are these people Communists or Communist sympathizers?" If they aren't Communists why do they protect communism at every opportunity, send aid to Communist countries, help install Castro in power knowing that he was a Communist and now protect him from anti- Communist harassment?

The answer was provided by another CFR-member, Dr. Lincoln P. Bloomfield, in an official study entitled, *A World Effectively Controlled by the United Nations*. It was prepared on a contract with the State and Defense Departments in 1962. In it, Dr. Bloomfield discloses, perhaps unwittingly, why U.S. planners consistently aid world communism. He says:

> ...if the Communist dynamic was greatly abated, the West might lose whatever incentive it has for world government.[49]

That is the answer. *If American aid were stopped, the Communist empire would likely collapse.* The internationalists would lose their principal arguments for turning American weapons over to a UN peace force, instituting world-wide redistribution of American wealth, and the socialization of America, all of which are advocated as necessary to meet the "threat of communism."

Of course, the Communists are working for world government also. That is why Alger Hiss, Harry Dexter White, Lauchlin Currie and other Communists, and their agents, sympathizers, and dupes have worked within the CFR. The Communists need a world government to achieve world domination. They are confident that once a world governing body is established in coalition with American socialists, internationalists, and idealists that they, the Communists, can control it, just as they have controlled every other coalition government into which they have entered.

Naturally, all 1400 members of the Council on Foreign Relations do not advocate a socialized economy and one world government. They do, however, support individual "pieces" of the overall program. Senator Jenner, in the speech quoted earlier, explained with a story how patriotic Americans help the movement bent on destroying America without comprehending the ultimate results of their actions. He said:

> Under the Nazi regime in Germany, a man worked making baby carriages. His wife was going to have a baby, but the Nazi government would not let anybody buy a baby carriage. The man decided he would secretly collect one part from each department and assemble the carriage himself.

> When the time came he and his wife gathered up the pieces and assembled them. When they finished they did not have a baby carriage. They had a machine gun.[50]

That story, Senator Jenner said, explains what has been happening to our form of government. He continued:

> Someone, somewhere, conceived the brilliant strategy of revolution by assembly line. The pattern for total revolution was divided into separate parts, each of them as innocent, safe and familiar

looking as possible. But...when the parts of a design are carefully cut to exact size, to fit other parts with a perfect fit, in final assembly, the parts must be made according to a blueprint drawn up in exact detail.

The men who make the blueprints know exactly what the final product is to be...This assembly line revolution is like a time-bomb...It is ready to go off, but is not going to be set off until the time is ripe, until a switch is pulled. The switch is not to be pulled until the American people are conditioned, or convinced that resistance is hopeless.[51]

Thus loyal Americans—businessmen, editors, Congressman, civic leaders—are entrapped into producing the pieces and supporting the programs which when assembled can destroy the United States.

What are these pieces? Some of them have been discussed separately: Disarmament, foreign aid, and assistance to keep the Communist empire from disintegrating, the socialization of the American economy to permit easy merger into a one-world socialist system, the power treaties have to override or supersede the Constitution. How do they all fit together?

Each year, as protests against foreign aid spending develop, Americans are told that because they are the richest people on earth they must help the poorer countries to keep them from going Communist.

DEFICITS FROM FOREIGN AID

As a result, in the years 1945-63, the United States added $106-billion to its national debt,[52] borrowing this money to give $107-billion in foreign aid to 80 countries.[53] The recipients of this American aid have a combined national debt substantially less than that of the "rich" United States.

By 1963, the drain on the American economy and credit had reached a point where national bankruptcy was entirely possible. American gold reserves available to meet foreign obligations dropped to below $4-billion while the U.S. owed other countries $22-billion, payable in gold.[54] If these creditors demanded payment, bankruptcy would result.

This risk might be worth taking if the slogan a Missouri

senator uses to justify his foreign aid votes were valid. He regularly tells constituents, "I'd rather vote dollars to fight communism than send American boys to die."

No one can dispute the sentiment, but unfortunately, most American foreign aid dollars *help* rather than *harm* communism.

As has been discussed, since the early foreign aid grants which helped Europe to rebuild after World War II, manipulation of U.S. aid has been a key factor in the communization of Poland, Yugoslavia, China, Laos, Indonesia, British Guiana, Ghana, and Algeria. Over $6-billion has been given directly to the Communist enemy.

Foreign aid has been used to socialize the economies of once friendly nations. Established patterns of life have been disrupted. The turmoil and chaos necessary for eventual communization has been created with foreign aid money. For example:

> Multi-million dollar public housing developments were built on the outskirts of five Lebanese cities. Natives of mountain villages were enticed to occupy the housing projects. When these villagers left their farms, they lost their livelihood, and the drop in food production caused a national crisis.[55]

Bolivia is a prime example of how U.S. foreign aid has been used, not to raise living standards of the poor, but to socialize an economy:

> In 1952, a new revolutionary government seized Bolivia's tin mines, the country's principal industry. The railroads were also nationalized. Under government operation, the number of miners has doubled, even though tin output has dropped by 50%. The mines and the railroads, once operated at a profit, have been losing $20-million a year, subsidized by annual American foreign aid grants of this amount. The aid has simply paid for the bureaucratic inefficiency which socialism always produces—while inflation and higher taxes have actually lowered the living standard of the people.[56]

Most Americans, in believing that foreign aid stops communism, do not realize that Joseph Stalin was one of the earliest proponents of American aid to under-developed nations. In 1944, in his book, *Marxism and the National Colonial Question*, Stalin said:

> It is essential that the advanced countries should render aid—real and prolonged aid—to the backward countries in their cultural and economic development. Otherwise, it will be impossible to bring about peaceful coexistence of the various nations and peoples—within a single economic system, which is so essential for the final triumph of socialism.[57]

That Stalin advocated foreign aid is not, in itself, a condemnation. However, the results of over $100-billion grants given by the U.S. speak for themselves. Nations have been socialized, friends have been antagonized and destroyed, and the drain on the U.S. economy, public and private, could bring an economic collapse and the socialization of America "which is so essential for the final triumph of Socialism." If foreign aid were limited to small grants for technical assistance to show people how to help themselves, it might do a good job. That was not the role Stalin foresaw for foreign aid—and that is not how it has been administered by American "planners."

GOLD OUTFLOW AND INFLATION

Between 1950 and 1963, the gold bullion owned by the U.S. Treasury which was available to meet foreign obligations dropped by 75%. The overall stock of gold dropped from $24-billion to $15.8- billion.[58]

Theoretically, loss of gold results when foreign nations sell more in America than we sell overseas. The difference, or balance of payment, is settled in gold. Actually, American exports have regularly exceeded imports—but not by enough to cover the cost of foreign aid grants overseas, the sale of agricultural products for "soft" currencies which are not redeemable in gold, and the cost of maintaining our military bases and personnel in foreign lands. The problem has been accentuated because foreign banks and investors are no longer willing to accept U.S. currency in payment. For years, the American dollar was "as good as gold" but inflation produced by unbalanced budgets in 27 of the last 33 years has eroded the value of the dollar. Payments in gold rather than dollars are demanded.

Our gold stock has dwindled steadily. Of the $15.8-billion remaining, almost $12-billion must, by law, be reserved as "backing" for the paper money in circulation. Therefore,by 1963, just under $4-billion was available to meet foreign obligations, *which totaled over $22-billion.*[59] At anytime, the investors, bankers and governments of Western Europe could force America into bankruptcy by demanding payment of American debts in gold—which is not available.

Treasury Secretary Dillion (CFR), economists and bankers like David Rockefeller (CFR) have recommended repeal of the requirement that gold backing equal to 25% of the paper money in circulation be maintained. Such a bill was introduced in the 87th Congress.[60] It would free $12-billion in gold to meet foreign obligations, postponing the crisis *temporarily*.

Without the restraint imposed on the issuance of paper money by the gold reserve requirement, future national deficits could be financed with printing-press dollars. Printing-press inflation, as contrasted with the gradual, long-term debasement of currency, could reduce the value of the dollar to 10 cents or even one cent within months.

Such runaway inflation would destroy confidence in free enterprise and representative government. The insurance and savings of millions of individuals, rich and poor, would be wiped out.

The resulting "national emergency" could be used as justification for abolishing the constitutional processes and establishing a totalitarian, socialistic government. The Americans who might be expected to oppose such a takeover would have no resources to finance opposition. Their savings would have been confiscated by runaway inflation.

Fantastic? Part of a plan? Do the pieces fit the "blueprint" Senator Jenner discussed? Whether part of a plan or not, the events are developing, the trend is established. It has happened in several nations. Reporting on his experience in Hungary in 1946, *Saturday Evening Post* writer Demaree Bess said:

...the Russians had unleashed the wildest currency inflation on record...that wild inflation was aimed at certain groups of Hungarians as deliberately as guns aimed in battles. It wiped out the savings of the country's most solid citizens, the thrifty, and hard-working middle class.[61]

In the same article, Demaree Bess described how inflation was a key weapon in the communization of China. He said:

When Red Armies entered Shanghai, they were openly greeted by the Shanghai American Chamber of Commerce in the belief that they could not possibly be more dangerous to business interests than Chiang's inflation had been. Those Americans, like their Chinese counterparts, soon discovered how wrong they were. But then it was too late.[62]

The inflation which discredited Chiang Kai-shek's government was planned in Washington by Assistant Secretary of the Treasury Harry Dexter White (CFR) and implemented in China by the Treasury Department's representative, Solomon Adler, who was also a Communist agent.[63]

A similar pattern was established in Bolivia. When the revolutionary MNR group seized power in 1952, a systematic program of runaway inflation was implemented. The free market rate of exchange on the Bolivian peso for the dollar stood at 190 on the day of the revolution. Four years later, the exchange rate was 15,000 pesos for one dollar.[64] The Bolivian citizen who had pesos worth $10,000 on the day of the revolution had buying power of only $124 four years later. The Minister of Foreign Affairs of the revolutionary MNR government as much as admitted that the inflation was planned to destroy political opposition. In commenting on the failure of other revolutions, he said:

Liberalism liquidated conservatism politically but not economically...It let the conservatives keep economic power in their hands. This was a great mistake: those who retain economic power will one day recover political power.[65]

The lesson of Bolivia should stand as a warning. It could happen here. It will happen here unless more Americans awaken to reverse the trend which has taken the nation to the brink of fiscal disaster.

TREATIES VS. THE CONSTITUTION

A key "piece" in the blueprint for revolution described by Senator Jenner is an interpretation of the U.S. Constitution which permits the Constitution to be changed—*or even abolished*—by a treaty. Article VI provides:

> This Constitution, and the Laws of the United States which shall be made in Pursuance thereof; and all Treaties made, or which shall be made, under the Authority of the United States, shall be the supreme Law of the Land; and the Judges in every State shall be bound thereby, anything in the Constitution or Laws of any State to the Contrary, notwithstanding.[66]

As interpreted by the U.S. Supreme Court, this means that treaties supersede the Constitution. American rights of freedom of speech, religion, press, assembly, etc. can be changed or abolished by a treaty.

The first such Supreme Court ruling was in the case, *Ware vs. Hylton*,[67] in 1796. The taking of Hylton's property to fulfill a treaty with Great Britain, in violation of the "due process" clause of the Fifth Amendment, was upheld.

In a more recent case, *Missouri vs. Holland*,[68] the Supreme Court decided in 1920 that powers reserved to the States by the Tenth Amendment to the Constitution could be given to the national government by a treaty.

In 1942, the doctrine that treaties supersede or override the Constitution was extended to apply to executive agreements negotiated by the President, or in the name of the President by members of the bureaucracy. In this case, *United States vs. Pink*,[69] the Court held that a personal agreement between President Roosevelt and the Russian Foreign Minister, Litvinov, nullified provisions of the laws of New York state, and of the American Constitution, which forbid confiscation of private property.

The implications are frightening. The founding fathers envisioned that the Constitution could be changed only with the approval of three-fourths of the states. Today, an executive agreement, perhaps made in secret without Congress and the States being aware of it, much less approving, can at some future date be judged to have changed the Constitution.

In 1954, during debate on a Constitutional Amendment which would have corrected this "loophole" in the Constitution, Senator William Jenner reviewed the situation. He said:

> Since 1920, we have had the most insidious development of this new principle by one little extension after another. The doctrine that treaties were outside the limits of the Constitution meant that they were above the laws of the States. The doctrine that treaties were above the Constitution was soon extended to executive agreements.
>
> If we note that today executive agreements mean personal arrangements, like that between Roosevelt and Litvinov, or administrative decisions by a minor foreign policy official like John Stewart Service; if we add that these agreements on foreign affairs now spread into areas formerly considered purely domestic, we come closer to the full measure of our danger.[70]

The danger is great. Over 10,000 executive agreements have been negotiated with reference to the North Atlantic Treaty Organization alone.[71] Many of these are secret, yet, all have the power to override the Constitution. The tragic Yalta Pact, part of which has never been revealed, has the power to supersede the Constitution.

Other agreements and treaties are proposed or made nearly every day. Any one of them could have the power to destroy the United States, the Constitution, and the rights of American citizens. For example:

> A proposed United Nations Treaty Against Genocide provides penalties for causing "mental harm" to a member of a minority group. Such an offender, under the terms of the treaty, could be arrested, transported abroad, and tried without a jury and punished by the proposed International Criminal Court.[72]

Refusing to give a Negro, Catholic, or Jew a job for any reason, or describing such minorities in derogatory terms could be construed by the International Court as causing "mental harm." Even though these actions are deplorable, the "remedies" proposed by the Treaty would violate an American citizen's rights of freedom of speech, to trial by jury, and to trial in the State and District where the crime is alleged to have been committed.[73] The Congress would be prevented by Article I and Amendments IX and X of the Constitution from defining such actions as crimes—but a treaty would do so. Even so, the Treaty was endorsed by the State Department. It is, however, still awaiting the action by the Senate which would make it the law of the land. Other UN Treaties on human rights, against discrimination in education, etc. have similar rights-destroying "hooks."

During debate on the Bricker Amendment which would have closed this Constitutional loophole, Senator Pat McCarran (D-Nev) showed that obligations assumed by the United States in Articles 55 and 56 of the UN Charter gives Congress absolute powers prohibited to it by the Constitution. He said:

> The Congress of the United States today, because of power granted to it by treaty, could enact laws...taking over all private and parochial schools, destroying all local school boards...and substituting a federal system. If Congress should find that international cultural cooperation required international control of all radio communications...Congress could by law provide for censoring all radio programs...it could provide for censoring of all press telegrams.

> Congress could utilize this power to put into effect a complete system of socialized medicine, from cradle to grave...Congress could even legislate *compulsory* labor, if it found that the (UN Charter's) goal of full employment required such legislation or would be served by it.[74]

The Bricker Amendment would have safeguarded American rights and the Constitution from destruction by treaties. It would have prevented world government through a "backdoor approach." It provided:

> A provision of a treaty or other international agreement which conflicts with this Constitution, or which is not made in pursuance

thereof, shall not be the supreme law of the land nor be of any force or effect.[75]

The Bricker Amendment received a favorable 60-31 majority in the U.S. Senate, but was one vote shy of the two-thirds majority needed for passage. President Eisenhower and Secretary of State John Foster Dulles used the full prestige of their offices to defeat the measure. Both claimed the amendment would hamper the President in conducting American foreign policy.

Concerned Americans might ask how the Bricker Amendment would have hampered the conduct of *legitimate* American foreign policy. Were those who opposed it planning treaties and agreements which would conflict with the Constitution? Were they protecting such agreements already in existence?

An agreement which could be enforced to limit the right of Americans to speak out against communism or advocate the defense of Laos, Berlin or Cuba or even the United States, may already be in effect.

When Soviet Foreign Minister Andrei Gromyko proposed an agreement to outlaw "war propaganda" at the Geneva disarmament talks early in 1962, American Secretary of State Dean Rusk rightly termed such a ban "impossible." Rusk said that enforcement would infringe on the Constitutional rights of private citizens and the press to criticize Communists or advocate firm action against communism.

Yet, six weeks later on May 25, 1962, the United States and the Soviet Union agreed on a *Joint Declaration Against War Propaganda.*[76] Under its terms...

...an American who suggests blockade or invasion of Cuba, or engages in other "war propaganda" activities may be risking "condemnations" or "punishment by appropriate practical measures, including measures in legislative form."[77]

Decoded, the legal double-talk means that offenders maybe jailed or have other punitive action taken against them.

The Communists withdrew their approval of the joint declaration within four days, so whether it is still binding on the United States is not clear.

It could be a "ticking timebomb" waiting for some nation to ask the International Court of Justice (World Court) to order the United States to enforce a "gag" on its citizens and press.

In such an event, the U.S. citizen would have one protection, if the U.S. State Department used it. Before ratifying the United Nations Charter in 1945, the U.S. Senate amended the agreement on the International Court of Justice Statute to bar the Court from jurisdiction over matters which were essentially domestic "as determined by the United States."

Without that six-word reservation authored by Senator Tom Connally (D-Tex) the World Court might interfere in American internal affairs on the pretext that our tariffs, immigration policies, racial conflicts, or school curriculums affect U.S. relations with other countries and are therefore "foreign" and not "domestic."

Advocates of repealing the Connally Reservation and removing this safeguard for the American people include Presidents Eisenhower and Kennedy and leading members of Congress. They attack the reservations as a "roadblock" to achieving "world peace through world law." This is an idealistic slogan which is, unfortunately, meaningless. There is no significant body of international law except maritime regulations. The Statute of the Court specifically prohibits building up an acceptable body of international law by forbidding the use of prior decisions as precedents in future cases. Article 59 of the Statute provides:

> The decision of the Court has no binding force except between
> the parties and in respect of that particular case.[78]

Therefore, the judges can make a decision favoring a Communist nation using one set of standards and refuse to grant the United States the same consideration under the same circumstances. This places the judges in the unique position of deciding what the "law" shall be for each case they hear. There is no appeal from their decisions, no matter how unjust,[79] and the decisions can be enforced with the military power of the United Nations "peace force."[80]

THE UN PEACE FORCE

As has been discussed, what is widely labeled as "disarmament" is in reality a transfer of the weapons of the world—and therefore the power to rule the world—to the United Nations. If this should be accomplished, and the official policy of the U.S. Government is to work for this end, then a decision of the Court could be enforced on the United States. If, for example, the Court should decide that the wealth of America is a source of irritation to less well-to-do nations, it could order that America's wealth be redistributed throughout the world.

The UN Peace Force would be charged with enforcing that edict. If all American weapons had already been transferred to the UN, the U.S. could not resist the Court order. Such a set of circumstances seem fantastic—but they follow exactly the reasoning and justification given by the UN for using armed force to prohibit self-determination for the people of Katanga in Africa.[81]

IS THERE A PLAN?

Is there a conspiratorial plan to destroy the United States into which foreign aid, planned inflation, distortion of treaty-making powers and disarmament all fit?

This question divides many knowledgeable and dedicated conservatives. They waste time and effort and split their ranks with senseless debate. It doesn't really matter whether the "parts" have been planned for an "assembly line revolution" as Senator Jenner charged, or if they are the work of well-meaning but misguided idealists.

The fact is that the "pieces" exist. They fit the pattern whether they were planned by the Communists or some other secret and mysterious revolutionary group or not. They can be used by the Communists or other power seekers.

To some, the implications of foreign aid, the gold outflow situation, the aid and comfort to Communists by elected and appointed officials, the abuse of treaty-making, etc. are overpowering. A key factor in the plan is to make the "trend" look "inevitable"—to convince Americans that resistance is hopeless.

Those who have constructed the "pieces" are few in number, but they exert fantastic control in government, financial circles, the press, unions, schools, etc.

The power of an informed people can be greater. People still have the right to vote, the freedom to educate and alert. These are difficult, time-consuming, costly, and often discouraging jobs. They can be done. They must be done. There is still time to reverse the trend in 1964 by putting patriots in Washington, in state capitals, and in county court houses and on city councils and school boards.

Senator Jenner sounded the call in 1954—but he was not heard. His message must be taken across our nation if America is to survive. He said:

> The American people may be confused about minor issues. They may accept for a time so-called remedies for very real difficulties, which eat away at the foundation of their liberties. But once they recognize any act of government or party or faction as a threat to their Constitution they will rise up in determined anger....

> In times of danger to the Constitution there can be no partisan differences between the historic political parties which work under the Constitution....The line of division today is between real Democrats and real Republicans on one side in defense of the Constitution, and on the other the secret revolutionaries and those they have brainwashed in their ruthless pursuit of power.

That is the task—to educate and alert the great mass of apathetic Americans to the danger and to show them what to do.

CHAPTER XIV

WHAT CAN YOU DO?

It is natural to man to indulge in the illusions of hope. We are apt to shut our eyes against a painful truth... Is this the part of wise men, engaged in a great and arduous struggle for liberty? Are we disposed to be of the number of those who, having eyes, see not, and having ears, hear not, the things which so nearly concern their temporal salvation? For my part, what- ever anguish of spirit it may cost, I am willing to know the whole truth; to know the worst and to provide for it.

—Patrick Henry[1]

DO WE FACE A HOPELESS BATTLE? Has time run out for America? The answer is up to *you.*

The end will not come when the commissars finally haul 60-million hopelessly diseased, capitalistic "animals" off to liquidation centers or when Communist Party Chief, Gus Hall, gets his wish to see the "last Congressman strangled to death with the guts of the last preachers."

If the battle is lost, the real end will come long before. It will come when those who oppose collectivism have been so discredited by smears, discouraged by disasters, or divided by dissenters that they can no longer continue to fight.

The end will come when businessmen accept "You can't fight city hall" as their philosophy and settle down to "exist" within the framework of a completely-controlled, federally-dominated economy. When fear of a lost government contract, an income tax audit, or the disfavor of a vocal customer is more important for most Americans than standing up for principle, the fight will be over.

The battle will be lost, not when freedom of speech is finally taken away, but when Americans become so "adjusted" or "conditioned" to "getting along with the group" that when they finally see the threat, they say, "I can't afford to be controversial." Time will run out for free men, when individuals read facts like those in this book, shrug their shoulders, and say, "What can one person do? It's too big to fight."

How far down that path are we? Look around and see for yourself. We are losing rapidly. A cold analysis of the world situation and of the degree of control exercised by the collectivists can only produce the realization that the odds against our survival are great.

The communists are extremely close to total victory. But it is not inevitable. Their one fear is that Americans will awake in time to the danger and do something about it.

That is our hope and our challenge.

What should you do?

INFORM YOURSELF

Before his death, the late Congressman Francis Walter (D-Pa) who served for eight years as Chairman of the House Committee on Un-American Activities gave Americans a brief, but concise guide to follow. His statement, *How To Fight Communism*, said:

Get the facts...get the help of others...organize...act.[2]

The words of J. Edgar Hoover quoted in the first chapter of this book tell how to get the facts. Mr. Hoover said of communism and its threat:

The way to fight it is to study it, understand it, and discover what can be done about it. This cannot be accomplished by dawdling at the spring of knowledge; it can only be achieved by dipping deeply into thoughtful, reliable, authoritative sources of information.[3]

Two years earlier, Mr. Hoover issued a similar statement, and added:

This program must encompass, not only a penetrating study of Communism, but also a thorough grounding in the basic principles of our individual freedom under law.[4]

Within those two statements can be found the basic

guidelines for intelligent action against communism. Congressman Walter gave more detailed advice, saying:

> Get the facts. Study communism. You can't fight an enemy you don't know. This is a fundamental rule of warfare. Learn communism's basic doctrines, its strategy, its tactics; its line on current national and international affairs; the names of major communist fronts and leading communists and fellow travelers. This is minimum knowledge required for effective anti- communism.[5]

ENLIST OTHERS

Once you have informed yourself, the next most important job is awakening others. Congressman Walter gave this advice:

> Get the help of others. Two heads are better than one —and ten men are more powerful than two.[6]

Before you can convince others you must gain their attention and build respect for your knowledge. The communists recognize this fact. In the official communist *Manual on Organization*, party members are given these instructions:

> In order to win the confidence of the workers, the unit must be able to give a correct answer to every question which bothers the workers. The units must follow very carefully every step that is taken by the capitalist class in the city and county councils, state legislatures, and Congress and expose all their moves.[7]

Can you do less? Communists use "facts" slanted to tell the communist story. They present them in person or in the propaganda they spread through the communications media they control. You can only combat the false propaganda with the truth.

To stay informed, once you get a basic knowledge, try to read at least two daily newspapers with opposite editorial viewpoints. In addition, subscribe to at least one weekly newspaper or magazine which specializes in in-depth coverage of conservative activities. There are many of varying format, quality, price, etc. [*Of the general publications listed in 1964, the Washington news weekly, HUMAN EVENTS, has* *presented a consistent conservative view from the nation's capital for over 40 years. Its address is 410 First Street SE, Washington DC 20003. The 1989 subscription price is $35 per year.]*

TAKE ACTION

Once you are informed—and have started to inform others—you must start acting. Knowledge without action produces demoralization. Congressman Walter gave this admonition:

> Knowledge that is not put to use is wasted. No matter how much you learn about communism, you will contribute nothing to the fight against it unless you...translate your learning into deeds that weaken communism.

Uncoordinated action has little effect. Too many concerned people jump from project to project, never completing any. Congressman Walter warned:

> Organize your helpers and plan your action. Mere numbers are not enough. Any project you undertake should have at least as much planning and organization as the communists normally put into their schemes. And that's plenty.

It is not necessary to form your own organization. Thousands have already been formed by concerned Americans, including this author. Many have been ineffective because of lack of resources, inability of part-time leadership to plan and supervise activities, and lack of coordinated effort between small groups.

There are a number of well-established national organizations. Some, like the American Legion and the Daughters of the American Revolution oppose communism as part of their overall program. Others, like the John Birch Society, are primarily anti-communist organizations. Still others are formed for a single purpose, such as opposing Red China's admission to the UN. Well-established, national conservative anti-communist groups likely to have a local branch near you [with 1989 addresses] include: The John Birch Society, P.O. Box 8040, Appleton WI 54913; The Cardinal Mindszenty

Foundation, P.O. Box 321, St. Louis MO 63105; and the Christian Anti-Communism Crusade, P.O. Box 890, Long Beach CA 90801

The John Birch Society is a non-sectarian organization directed by a full-time staff which coordinates the group's program of education and action against communism including a monthly bulletin and *The New American*, a biweekly news and opinion journal. The Cardinal Mindszenty Foundation is a Catholic-oriented group directed by a council of bishops and priests who have suffered under communism. It offers a study program on communism and distributes radio programs and newspaper columns on communism nationally. The Christian Anti-Communism Crusade has an evangelical Protestant orientation. It conducts anti-communism schools and seminars in the U.S. and supports an extensive Christian missionary and education program overseas. All three groups are supported by persons of all religious faiths.

MISCELLANEOUS GROUPS

Those specialized groups listed in 1964 which have survived (with areas of concentration) include the Twentieth Century Reformation Hour, Collingswood, NJ 08108, a fundamental Christian organization which sponsors Bible-based anti-communist radio and TV broadcasts; America's Future, 542 Main St., New Rochelle, NY 10801 (schools); Young Americans for Freedom, 300 I Street NE, Washington DC 20002 (conservative action and education); The Foundation for Economic Education, Irvington-on-the-Hudson NY 10533 (economics education); plus many, many others.

Concerned Americans should carefully investigate the goals, programs, policy, personnel, and leadership of these or other anti-communism organizations to decide for themselves how effective they are. Rather than judge solely on word of mouth or the sometimes slanted newspaper accounts, write to any or all for their literature.

GET INTO POLITICS

A program for victory over communism cannot be achieved until Americans elect a President and a Congress with the will to win *and* the courage to "cleanse" the policy-making agencies of government of those who, for one reason or another, have aided the communists down through the years. To accomplish this, conservative Americans must make their voices heard in the political parties.

The Communist Party General Secretary, Gus Hall, sees this danger to communism and is working to prevent it. In June 1963, he ordered communists to join with the "non-communist left" within the Democratic Party to elect candidates of the "people's political movements" (i.e., Red favored movement) and to...

...single out for defeat such individuals as Keating and Dodd, as well as a number of others.[8]

Hall specifically called for the purging from the Republican Party of the ultra-right (anti-communist) forces. Hall admitted that while "moderates" of the Eisenhower-Kuechel wing of the Republican Party had not lost out completely...

...as can be seen from the speech of Senator Keuchel of California...the alliance of the ultra-right and Conservative aggressive imperialist elements has pushed the Republican Party to the right.[9]

Within two weeks after Hall's demand for defeat of the ultra-right in the Republican Party, a massive smear campaign was launched in major news media, with a lengthy article, *Rampant Right Invades the GOP*, in *Look* magazine's July 16, 1963 issue. Nelson Rockefeller called upon Senator Barry Goldwater to repudiate his ultra-right support.[10] Drew Pearson and other prominent columnists, wittingly or unwittingly fell into line with the Gus Hall directive. Pearson accused Young Republicans of "fascist tactics" in electing a Goldwater supporter as their national chairman.[11]

Within six weeks after Gus Hall issued his order against the ultra-right the "purge" reached all the way down to the local level as "modern Republican" officials fired conservative precinct captains and workers.

Whether the American people, in general, and rank-and-file Republicans, in particular, will fall for the communist-led attack to drive the anti-communists out of key positions in

the Republican Party will probably be a major factor in
determining whether the battle against communism is won
or lost. If the communists and the "liberal internationalists"
control the presidential nominations in both parties in 1964,
as they have for 30 years, the hope for victory over communism will receive a massive setback. Work in the party
organizations by informed conservatives can prevent this.

Cries of "We are being sold out to the communists" or
decrying the strength and success of the AFL-CIO machine
will not win the 1964 elections. COPE has devised no secret
formula for winning elections. It puts into practice the instructions an obscure county chairman of the Whig Party
gave his workers in 1840. His name was Abraham Lincoln,
and he said:

> ...the following is the plan of organization...divide (your) county
> into small districts, and...appoint in each a subcommittee, whose
> duty it shall be to make a perfect list of all the voters in their
> respective districts, and to ascertain with certainty for whom they
> will vote...keep a constant watch on the doubtful voters, and from
> time to time have them talked to by those in whom they shall have
> the most confidence... on election days see that every Whig is
> brought to the polls.[12]

Lincoln knew that elections are not necessarily won by the
party or candidate which is right—but by the organization
which gets its voters to the polls. Issues and beliefs of a
candidate are important—but they cannot win unless they
are backed by a functioning organization geared to locate
friendly voters, register them, and get them to the polls on
election day...then, keep the election honest.

Issues, properly used, can motivate average, apathetic
citizens to become doorbell ringers for candidates with principles. Several thousand informed, motivated workers in a
congressional district of several hundred thousand voters can
turn the tide, *if they are properly trained, organized and
directed.*

In 1962, for example, 29-year old William Brock of Lookout
Mountain, Tennessee, ran for Congress in a district where
Democrats outnumbered Republicans 8 to 1. Brock was a

Republican, yet he was elected to Congress because his presentation of the issues attracted workers who put Lincoln's plan into action.

Half of the American people cannot be educated about communism overnight. However, if one out of every hundred citizens is alerted, educated and mobilized into a functioning political organization, they can nominate and elect good Americans.

A SPIRITUAL COMMITMENT

Conservatives can win the political battles necessary to insure America's survival—and still lose the long term war against communism.

J. Edgar Hoover gave the ultimate answer in accepting an award from the Freedom Foundation at Valley Forge on February 22, 1962. He said:

> The basic answer to communism is moral. The fight is economic, social, psychological, diplomatic, strategic—but above all it is spiritual.

Another anonymous writer said the same thing in a slightly different way. His advice:

> Pray to God with the knowledge that everything depends on him—and work as if everything depended on you.

Without God, man can accomplish nothing. Yet, today, unfortunately, millions of Americans attend churches which are "man-centered" rather than "God-centered." Millions of persons who call themselves Christians attend church regularly and have never heard the Bible message of personal and individual salvation.

The answer to man's problems, the solution to the peril facing America is found in the Holy Scriptures. In II Chronicles 7:14, God tells us:

> If my people, which are called by my name, shall humble themselves and pray and seek my face, and turn from their wicked ways; then will I hear from heaven, and will forgive their sin, and will heal their land.

CONCLUSION

There is much to be done if America is to block communist domination of the world. Much of the work is up to *you*.

First, you must educate yourself. Determine that the facts in this book are true. Then, alert and educate others. Stay informed—and start to act. Join with others who are already well-organized for the battle against communism.

Recognize that those who refuse to work politically to protect their freedom may someday face a choice between fighting with guns or becoming slaves. Avoid being sidetracked into ineffective, defensive actions. Most of all, avoid demoralization. Examine your own personal religious beliefs. Is God a meaningful, consuming force in your life?

The books, literature and other aids you'll need all cost money. Political activity, even on the precinct level, involves expenses. Political campaigns, anti-communist organizations all need financial support. As you evaluate costs, remember that if rampant inflation comes to America your savings will be worthless. If Communism comes to America you will lose not only your money, but your freedom, your children, your home, and possibly your life.

EXPECT TO BE ATTACKED

The costs cannot be measured in money alone. Educating and alerting others will not make you popular. Many dedicated Americans have already suffered smears, economic sanctions, and personal attacks for standing up for what they knew was right. J. Edgar Hoover commented on this tragic fact in a speech to the Daughters of the American Revolution in 1954. Mr. Hoover said:

In taking a stand for preservation of the American way of life, your organization became the target of vile and vicious attacks. So have all other patriotic organizations and, for that matter, every other person who has dared to raise his voice against communism. It is an established fact that whenever one has dared to expose the communist threat he had invited upon himself the adroit and skilled talents of experts of character assassination. The Federal

Bureau of Investigation has stood year after year as taunts, insults and destructive criticism have been thrown its way.

To me, one of the most unbelievable and unexplainable phenomena in the fight on Communism is the manner in which otherwise respectable, seemingly intelligent persons, perhaps unknowingly, aid the communist cause more effectively than the Communists themselves. The pseudo liberal can be more destructive than the known communist because of the esteem which his cloak of respectability invites.[13]

Six years later, Mr. Hoover repeated much the same message, when in a letter to law enforcement officials, he said:

It is indeed appalling that some members of our society continue to deplore and criticize those who stress the communist danger. What these "misguided" authorities fail to realize is that the Communist Party, USA, is an integral part of international communism. As the world-wide menace becomes more powerful, the various Communist parties assume a more dangerous and sinister role in the countries in which they are entrenched. Public indifference to this threat is tantamount to national suicide.

Lethargy leads only to disaster...Only the intelligent efforts of all Americans can prevent the decay of public apathy from laying open our Nation to the Red Menace.[14]

Because the repeated warnings of J. Edgar Hoover and other great Americans have been suppressed, ignored, and ridiculed, only great sacrifices in time, energy and money will turn the tide.

The choice is yours. You can throw out your chest with pride and say, "It can't happen here." But nearly every one of the 800-million people captured by the communists since 1945 doubtless said the same thing.

The alternative is to begin immediately to educate yourself; to embark on a program of action. If you delay, your motivation will pass, your concern will recede, but the danger will increase.

The choice you must make was enunciated by Winston Churchill when he told the people of England:

If you will not fight for right when you can easily win without bloodshed; if you will not fight when your victory will be sure and not too costly; you may come to the moment when you will have to fight with all the odds against you and only a precarious chance of survival.

Because we have ignored warning after warning, we are now at that place in history. Unless you do your part now, you will face a further choice, also described by Mr. Churchill. He said:

There may be even a worse case. You may have to fight when there is no hope of victory, because it is better to perish than live as slaves.

What will you do?

CHAPTER 15

IN THE 25 YEARS SINCE...

*Is there anything whereof it may be said, See this is new? it
hath been already of old time, which was before us...there is
no new thing under the sun.*

— *King Solomon, Ecclesiastes 1:9-10* [1]

TWENTY-FIVE YEARS HAVE PASSED since *None Dare
Call It Treason's* challenge was published originally in 1964.
It was read by 7-million Americans.

The book and its warnings didn't elect Barry Goldwater to
the presidency in 1964. But it did have an impact on people—
and through them on the nation.

Millions were awakened to the threat of communism. They
became an important addition to the conservative revolution
which elected Ronald Reagan and a Republican Senate six-
teen years later. The 90-year old former congressman and
spell-binding keynote speaker at the 1960 Republican National Convention, Dr. Walter Judd, recently wrote:

> Your book has been a powerful influence in so many lives and on
> so many actions—up to the highest levels.

Even so, twenty additional countries went into the Marxist
camp. (They were listed in the preface of this book.) Millions
of people were slaughtered by their Communist "liberators."
Over 3-million were murdered in Cambodia. Other millions
starved to death when communism came to Ethiopia. Students wanting to institute some basic reforms in the Communist system in China were massacred in Tiananmen
Square as the world watched on TV in June 1989.

Multiplied millions of others who were free in 1964 now live
in poverty and bondage—in Soviet puppet states or single-
party "socialist" regimes which are sufficiently Marxist so

that they are no longer targets of Communist aggression. Israel, South Africa, South Korea, the Philippines and El Salvador were top Red targets as the 1990s began.

The chapters which follow in this new edition show that the pattern of continual and consistent American "mistakes" which pushed dozens of countries into the Communist orbit before 1964 have continued largely unchecked since. "Mistakes" which "none have dared to call treason" include:

Over 50,000 Americans died in Vietnam—fighting a war against communism they were not permitted to win. As they fought and died, their government and businessmen at home provided the technology and tools to build up the Soviet industrial machine which produced 85% of the guns and bullets used against them in Vietnam.[2]

When the United States stopped using its veto power in the United Nations the Communists were given China's seat. The anti-Communist Chinese from Taiwan were expelled. Shortly thereafter, U.S. diplomatic recognition was granted to the Red Chinese and withdrawn from the friendly, anti-Communist free Chinese government in Taiwan.

By one-vote over the constitutionally-required two-thirds majority, the United States Senate approved President Jimmy Carter's Panama Canal treaty by a 68-32 vote. The treaty gives the strategically-important American canal in Panama to the left-leaning, drug-dealing Panamanian government. *Panama was paid $400-million to agree to take it![3]*

The ABM, SALT I and II and INF arms control and disarmament treaties were negotiated with the Communists (even though the Reds have broken every promise they have ever made when breaking them advances the cause of communism). "Fine print provisions" in the disarmament agreements protect Soviet superiority in strategic weapons. At the same time *they prevent the United States from catching up or even building a defense which would protect America if the Soviets should cheat and launch a sneak nuclear attack.*[4]

During these same years, the internal security system which should have been checking to see if these actions and decisions were Communist-influenced was dismantled. Internal security investigations and surveillances by the FBI were practically eliminated. The Congressional committees which once investigated Communist infiltration and subversion in America were abolished.[5]

Those like Oliver North, former UN ambassador Jeane Kirkpatrick, former POW Jeremiah Denton and other lesser-known heroes in the battle against communism find themselves either dropped from government, defeated for reelection or prosecuted for their efforts to stop the Red advance.[6]

The tragedies continue because millions of sound-thinking Americans, including many of those awakened by reading *None Dare Call It Treason* fail for at least five basic reasons. The reasons include:

1. Most sound-minded Americans trust leaders elected on basically conservative, anti-communist platforms to carry on the fight. They have not made them accountable when they fail to do so—and have often not even noticed the failures.

2. Too many conservatives still expect officials in Washington and leaders of conservative groups to solve the problems. They fail to personally seek responsible positions in church congregations and denominations, their labor unions, Chambers of Commerce, Rotary and Kiwanis clubs, senior citizens groups, political parties, local school boards, city councils and state legislatures. These are the arenas where crucial decisions are influenced or made—and from which future Congressmen and Senators come.

3. Even most conservatives do not fully understand the true nature of the battles being fought on the local level or in the world-wide conflict.

4. Conservative activists get caught up in the very necessary "finger-in-the dike" efforts of opposing Communist advances around the world and Communist-humanist influences in their local communities and organizations—but they frequently do not realize that being "anti" is not enough. Defensive action, no matter how effective, can never win—in football, in business or in the struggle for freedom and liberty in America and the world. A vision for victory and a program to achieve it is essential.

5. Most conservatives have not learned how to be effective in the struggle for freedom. Personal leadership and communications skills must be developed—along with the ability to recognize and utilize the channels of influence in the community which must be activated for the cause of freedom and liberty.

In the chapters which follow, the on-going failures will be examined. Of greater importance, readers will be given a "vision for victory." Tremendous opportunities are opening for freedom-loving people world wide as the last decade of the 20th century begins. These opportunities must not be lost by ignorance nor neglect!

CHAPTER 16

SOVIET MIGHT—AMERICAN MADE

Shouldest thou help the ungodly, and love them that hate the Lord? therefore is wrath upon thee from before the Lord.
                                                    —II Chronicles 19:2[1]

COMMUNISTS CONTROL more of the world's people and more of the earth's land mass than any other would-be world conqueror in history.

They have enslaved 2-billion of the world's people and control one quarter of the earth's surface even though their system and all of their great plans are dismal failures. During the 70 years since Lenin and his Bolsheviks brought communism to Russia, no Communist country has ever been able to feed its people.

Under the Czars, the Ukraine was the breadbasket of Europe—supplying the wheat for all of Russia and most of Europe. For 70 years—on the same ground—in the same area—with the same climate—the Soviets have had consistent and regular crop failures. When the fields do produce, up to half of the crops rot in the fields or through mismanagement on the way to the consumer. Wherever communism takes over, food is rationed.[2]

Slaves do not produce—socialism won't work without a gun at the back of the worker and the threat of Siberia to keep them in line. Wherever communism takes over, walls and fences must be erected to keep the slaves from fleeing. The tragic pattern has been repeated in China. Cuba, Nicaragua, Ethiopia and Southeast Asia—wherever communism seizes power. Vietnam was once the Rice Bowl of the Orient. Today it imports food. Czechoslovakia once had 1.2% of the world's trade. After 30 years of Communist rule, its share dropped to .15%—a ten-fold decline. Communism fails to meet the basic needs of people wherever it is tried.

How has a system which has failed so miserably wherever it has been tried succeeded in capturing one-third of the earth's people and one quarter of the earth's land mass in just 70 years?

A careful look at history reveals that the world Communist system has been built on regular and consistent American aid and assistance. Developments in the Soviet Union, as the decade of the 1980s ended, substantiate the charge.

Intelligence evaluations made by the Central Intelligence Agency (CIA) and the Defense Intelligence Agency (DIA) in late 1987 indicated that the Soviet economy was in such shambles that even Moscow's military might was threatened.[3] The intelligence agency reports concluded that the Soviet Union could not survive as a global power into the 21st Century unless drastic changes were made.

The ruin that communism wreaks touched every area of Soviet society. Here are examples:

Even though the Soviet Union has a larger population than the United States and two and a half times as much territory, the U. S. has one and a half times as much railroad track and seven times more paved roads.[4]

The United States also has six times as many telephones, 13 times the number of mainframe computers and more than 50 times as many personal computers as the Soviets.[5]

On the average an American farm worker outproduces his Soviet counterpart by ten times....Soviet farms must plant three times as much seed per acre as in the U.S. to get a comparable harvest....Because of lack of proper grain storage, poor roads and bad transportation, up to 30% of the yearly Soviet wheat crop is lost and spoilage rates for vegetables and fruits are over 60%.[6]

Soviet hospitals reuse hypodermic needles hundreds of times...teeth are extracted without anesthesia....Infant mortality rates are three times higher than those in the U.S.[7]

Soviet families spend up to four hours a day waiting in lines for food and other necessities[8] (Families of the more privileged whose wives do not have to work live better because their wives can spend their days in the lines waiting to buy food, etc.)

Gorbachev acknowledged the seriousness of the economic failures in announcing the perestroika program in November 1987. His April 25, 1989 speech to a closed- door meeting of the Party's Central Committee put the crisis in down-to-earth terms. Gorbachev told Kremlin leaders that shortages of housing, food and consumer goods were growing despite his reforms. He cited shortages of everything from syringes to laundry detergent and said:

> The food problem is far from solved. The housing problem is acute. There is a dearth of consumer goods in the shops. The list of shortages is growing. The state's financial state is grave.[9]

The United States reaction to the impending collapse of the Soviet economy was anticipated by syndicated columnist and former White House aide, Patrick Buchanan. The headline on his December 27, 1987 column[10] asked:

> Will we bailout the deadbeat enemy?

Buchanan's question stemmed from his knowledge of the history of American-Soviet relations. He wrote:

> Aware of this deepening crisis Mr. Gorbachev will be seeking here what Leonid Brezhnev sought and achieved, a $100-billion Western bailout of the Communist bloc.

> Three times since Lenin's coup—during the New Economic policy of the '20s; during World War II with Lend Lease; during the detente decade of the '70s—the West has rescued communism from the economic consequences of failed ideology.

Against the background of that history, Buchanan said:

> Today, Western businessmen, bankers, grain dealers and manufacturers, supported by the usual complement of "useful idiots" are prepared to come to Moscow's rescue once again. This time they must be stopped.

They weren't. Withholding aid would have increased the pressure from disgruntled consumers on the faltering Communist system and its despot leaders. Instead, hundreds of American businessmen at the urging of top government officials flocked to Moscow to "sell the rope" which Lenin

predicted Communists would use to hang the greedy
capitalists. A flood of 1988 headlines tells the sordid story:

> 500 American businessmen to talk trade with Moscow....Joint
> ventures with Soviets expected to multiply....Dozens of Western
> firms signing up for Soviet ventures....7 U.S. Firms Join In Soviet
> Trade....4 major firms to build Soviet petrochemical com-
> plex....More Grain Sold To Soviets....[11]

Economic commitments President George Bush made at
the December 1989 Malta summit gave the Soviets access to
additional Western credit for such projects and opened
Western markets to the output of the ventures.[12]

Gorbachev needed the free world goods to keep consumer
discontent from toppling his shaky regime. Under the headline, "Soviets Put U.S. Goods On Shelves," a *New York Times*
news service story from Moscow said:

> The Soviet government has begun buying Western consumer
> goods—from razor blades to pantyhose—to pacify consumers
> distressed by perpetual shortages.

HIGH-TECH TRANSFERS TO REDS

The rush to shore up Moscow's collapsing economy was not
limited to the $8-billion in consumer goods the Reds pur-
chased. High technology items essential to the Soviet military
and space programs were included. Again, newspaper headlines tell the story:

> Arms profits lure firms into doing business with the
> Soviets....Soviets to work with U.S. firm in space....Classified
> process sold to Soviets....Computer export to Moscow probed.[13]

Despite Pentagon opposition and controls on export of high-
tech equipment which would aid the Soviet military buildup,
the U.S. Commerce Department has regularly licensed such
shipments. The Department annually publishes a report
listing commodities licensed for export to the USSR, its
Eastern European Communist satellites and Communist
China. The 1981 report, for example, listed hundreds of
millions of dollars worth of such high-tech items as electronic
computing equipment and software, lasers and laser equip-

ment, equipment and processes for semiconductor design and production and oil field drilling equipment and petroleum refinery equipment.[14]

In addition to actual equipment shipped, the United States sold or gave the Communist bloc nations over 120 categories of technical data and assistance including data for jet engine part manufacture, gyrocompass production (for guidance systems), technical data for helicopter manufacturing, semiconductor manufacturing processes, etc. etc. etc.[15]

In 1987 hard-liners in the Congress and the government became concerned over the transfer of extremely sensitive classified processes by American and Japanese firms to the Soviet Union. Among the items were technology and equipment for producing quieter Soviet nuclear attack submarines,[16] top-of-the-line computers used by military planners to gauge the impact of nuclear explosions and help determine optimal targets for nuclear missiles,[17] and an advanced, heat-resistant material that can significantly improve the accuracy of nuclear warheads.[18]

Sale of the heat-resistant carbon-carbon material for making nuclear warheads more deadly was estimated to save the Soviets a minimum of five years development time.

When the U.S. Senate voted 92-5 to impose sanctions on companies selling classified processes and equipment to the Communists, the State Department reacted. The news article carried the headline, "State Department opposes punishing firms that sold technology to Soviets," and said:

> The State Department expressed concern that a Senate plan to punish foreign companies for selling secret technology to help Soviet submarines evade detection could spark retaliation against U.S. businesses....E. Allan Wendt, the State Department's senior representative for strategic technology policy, acknowledged on Tuesday that the sales have resulted in substantial security damage. But he urged Congress not to "limit presidential discretion and flexibility in conduct of foreign policy."[19]

Giving the Soviets what they need to build their economy and their military efforts world-wide was not something new in the 1980's. In 1973 a Republican Congressman from Ohio,

John Ashbrook, spoke for 60 minutes in the House of Representatives on the subject, "Soviet Military Might: Western Made."[20] Ashbrook said:

> Soviet space shots, Soviet missiles, Soviet invasions, and Soviet aid to other aggressive countries have all depended on their ability to produce weapons of war—depended on their technology. But that is not quite true either. In a few words there is no such thing as Soviet technology.

> Perhaps as much as 90 to 95 percent of Soviet technology came directly or indirectly from the United States and its allies. Now this may sound incredible, but the facts substantiate this claim. Soviet aggression is dependent upon American-made and Western-made technology.

Ashbrook quoted a statement made by Soviet dictator Joseph Stalin to the one-time United States Ambassador to the Soviet Union, Averell Harriman. Stalin told the American ambassador:

> About two-thirds of all the large industrial enterprises in the Soviet Union have been built with United States help or technical assistance.

Ashbrook summed up the fallacies of building the Soviet industrial machine with these words:

> Fifty years of dealing with the Soviets has been an economic success for the U.S.S.R. and a political and economic disaster for the United States. It has not stopped war, it has not given us peace. It has given the Soviets increased industrial and military power and the ability to accomplish its never ceasing goal of world domination.

> The United States is spending billions of dollars a year on defense. A defense that is made necessary by the threat and aggression of the Soviet Union and other Communist countries. While we are spending billions on defense, we still help build that enemy we are defending against.

DURING WAR AND PEACE

The American buildup of the Soviet industrial machine goes on during war and peace. During the Vietnam war the Soviet

Union was the biggest supplier of weapons and economic aid to the Viet Cong who killed 58,000 Americans and wounded multiplied thousands of others. The Soviets, Red China and the Eastern European satellites supplied upwards of 85% of all the guns, bullets, surface-to-air missiles, MIG airplanes, etc. used to kill 58,000 Americans in Vietnam—and wound multiplied thousands of others.[21]

As 100 American boys were being killed in Vietnam each week with Soviet-supplied weapons during the first half of 1966, U.S. trade with Iron Curtain countries jumped 44%.[22] The Associated Press spotlighted the Red trade buildup and pointed to an even further expansion of trade with the Communists, saying:

> In mid-October, the Johnson Administration moved to increase exports to Russia and her satellites by easing controls on about 400 non-strategic items.

All trade is strategic if it strengthens a country's economy. The Johnson administration appeared to recognize this on one hand while ignoring it on the other. Three weeks after moving to ease the ban on exports to the Soviets, it ordered an 80% cut in trade with a friendly nation, Rhodesia. Fines of up to $10,000 and jail terms of ten years were imposed on businessmen who continued trading with Rhodesia.[23]

The Rhodesian export ban was announced because Rhodesia denied some of its citizens some of their rights. Meanwhile, of course, Johnson moved to expand trade with the Soviet Union which denied all of its citizens all of their rights—and was supplying the guns and bullets which were killing Americans in Vietnam at the rate of 100 a week.

Richard Nixon became President in early 1969. Within months he proposed legislation to further expand trade with Red nations even though the war in Vietnam was still raging.[24] By September 1969, the Associated Press reported:

> The United States and 14 allied countries are lowering their barriers on exports of strategic products to the Soviet bloc....the previously banned items which the Soviet bloc now will be able to buy include certain types of computers, rare metals and their

alloys, chemical and petroleum equipment, a wide range of industrial, electrical and transport goods, and certain categories of electronic and precision instruments.[25]

Without continual supplies of military equipment from the Soviet bloc the North Vietnamese Communists could not have continued their war of aggression against South Vietnam and the United States troops there.

BIG TRUCK PLANT FOR SOVIETS

The transfer of America's high-tech know-how and equipment has continued whether Democrats or Republicans are in the White House. In the closing days of the Carter Administration, the prestigious trade magazine, *Industrial Research & Development* reported:

> U.S. government efforts to influence the actions of Communist nations by giving away or selling "peaceful" technology have failed—in the very least. At worst, they may have been the prelude to tragedy.

> For more than a decade the U.S. government has encouraged manufacturers and R&D firms to export, transfer, and even give away technology to the Soviet Union and East European countries....Recently, however, officials have begun to admit a growing worry that this strategy not only has failed, it may well have backfired.

> When Soviet ground troops invaded Afghanistan at the end of last year, they did so in trucks, tanks, armored personnel carriers. Many of these, the Pentagon says, had been built at Russian facilities originally constructed with U.S. and Western- supplied equipment and technology.[26]

The vehicles used in the Afghan invasion were produced in the Kama River truck plant in the Soviet Union. It was built in the early 1970s almost entirely with $500-million worth of Western-supplied equipment, technology and know-how. Much of it came from such U.S. companies as Honeywell, Swindell-Dressler, IBM, and Ingersoll-Rand. No guarantees were even requested from the Soviets that vehicles produced would not be used for the Soviet military.[27]

Communists appear to regularly use American-made transportation equipment to move troops. The Chinese troops which carried out the brutal massacre of up to 3000 students in Beijing's Tiananmen Square in June 1989 were ferried to Beijing in a variety of aircraft. A State Department official acknowledged that about 60 of the transports were of U.S. origin.[28]

Even so, within four weeks...

...the Bush Administration waived military sanctions it imposed on Beijing after the crackdown [massacre], clearing the way for the Boeing Co. to deliver to China four new 757-200 jets—whose sophisticated navigation systems, manufactured by Honeywell, are on the State Department's munitions list of items whose export is strictly controlled.[29]

An administration official defended the action, saying, "This is essentially a commercial sale." That the "commercial" aircraft sold to the Red Chinese earlier had been used to transport the murderous troops "doesn't change our mind," he said.

A Boeing official when asked about Chinese use of other Boeing aircraft as troop transports said:

We haven't heard anything like that at all. I don't know if we have any means of keeping track of what a customer does with an airplane once it's delivered.[30]

That's exactly why aircraft, machine tools, electronic equipment, etc., etc., etc. should not be sold to Communist countries.

Because of the continual transfer of American technology to the Communist countries, Navy Secretary John Lehman told the 1983 graduates of the U.S. Naval Academy at Annapolis:

Within weeks many of you will be looking across just hundreds of feet of water at some of the most modern technology ever invented in America. Unfortunately, it is on Soviet ships.[31]

RED CHINA GETS HELP

Increased trade with the Soviet Union was frequently justified in the 1960s and early '70s as being necessary to enlist their friendship because of the threat from the "bad" Communists in China. Then, however, President Nixon led the way in resuming relations with the Communists on the Chinese mainland and paved the way for their admission to the United Nations. This opened the door for high-tech economic aid as well—first a dribble and then a flood. Soon Americans were reading headlines which said:

> U.S. Confirms Computer Sales To Russia, China.....U.S. Lifts Restrictions On Exports To China....McDonnell Douglas In Milestone China Pact—Workers in Shanghai To Build 25 Jetliners For U.S. Aerospace Firm....U.S. and Peking Agree To Establish Panels To Speed Up Technology Sales To China.[32]

The export policies, ordered or expanded by President Reagan, removed curbs on about 75% of China's requests for high-technology goods from the United States. China was able to purchase U.S. mainframe computers, microprocessors, digital computers, semiconductors and a wide list of other strategic goods.[33] Protests such as those raised by an official of the Energy Research and Development Administration said the agency opposed sales of Control Data Corporation computers because they had military potential were brushed aside.[34]

The transfer of technology to the Chinese was supposed to cement improving U.S. relations with the Communist giant. However, the Red Chinese government repaid American help by breaking its word and selling high-tech Silkworm missiles to Iran[35] and lending the Communist government of Nicaragua $20-million.[36]

ALL ON CREDIT

Attempts might be made to justify trade with the Communists on the basis that it is good for business—good for the balance of payments—and that it reduces trade deficits. However, most of the trade with the Soviet Union and its satellites is paid for with money borrowed from the West—from U.S. and Western European banks. By 1989, loans to Soviet-bloc Communist nations from the United States,

Japan and Western Europe totaled $130-billion and were increasing by $2-billion monthly. Most are low interest and unsecured loans with no strings attached.[37]

Two stories on the front page of the July 27, 1973 *Los Angeles Herald Examiner* point up the foolish and near treasonous nature of loans to the Communists. The big banner front page headline read:

RECORD PRIME RATE
New York Bank Goes To 8-3/4%

The interest rate major banks charged their best customers reached a record (for then) 8-3/4%. A second story on the front page carried the headline, "U.S. Food Credit For Communist Countries." The United Press story said:

> Congressional conferees Thursday tentatively agreed to authorize low interest, long term credit sales of food to Russia, China, Cuba and other Communist countries....Repayment under such deals can extend 30 years *with interest rates as low as 2 percent.*

American businessmen had to pay interest rates four times as high as those offered to Communists—and the Communists were given up to 30 years to pay. Even so, they frequently do not meet agreed to repayment schedules.

For example, on May 20, 1981 President Ronald Reagan signed the following loan authorization for Communist Rumania:

> Pursuant to Section 2(b)(2) of the Export-Import Bank Act of 1945, as amended, I determine that it is in the national interest of the United States to extend a credit in the amount of $120,742,500 to the Socialist Republic of Rumania in connection with its purchase of two nuclear steam generators and related services and spare parts.[38]

No payments were required for eight years. The interest rate was 7-3/4 per cent. To make the loan to the Communists, the United States borrowed the money at interest rates which were about 40 per cent higher. The American taxpayer footed the bill for the difference. The Rumanians, besides being one of the most repressive of the Eastern European Communist regimes, were not a good risk. Within two years, the *Wall*

Street Journal reported that Rumania was asking banks to "reschedule" 70% of the repayments due in 1983 on loans made earlier.[39] They had already "rescheduled" payments on $1.7-billion of debt which had come due in 1981 and 1982. (Even as President Reagan authorized the $120-million loan the Rumanians were already in default on past borrowing.)

The day before the *Wall Street Journal* announced the Rumanian "rescheduling" Yugoslavia arranged "rescheduling" of a big chunk of its debt. Payments due on the Yugoslavian debt were postponed 90 days until new loans of $1.3-billion were received from its creditors.[40] In effect, banks loan new money to customers who are broke so they can make their payments. In this way the loan does not show up on the bank's books as being "non-performing" or in default. If this subterfuge was not widespread, particularly on loans to Third World and Communist countries, many major New York and Chicago banks would be insolvent and subject to closing by bank regulators. In fact, a banker who regularly practiced the "rescheduling" of loan payments in this way for domestic consumer or business customers could face possible jail sentence for phony bookkeeping.

Not only are many of the loans to Communist governments bad risks, they violate other sound banking practices as well. In August 1987, Congressmen Jack Kemp (R-NY) and Toby Roth (R-WI) introduced legislation to restrict "untied" loans to the Soviet Union.[41]

Untied loans are not made to finance specific projects or products which is the usual banking practice. Normally when a customer seeks a loan from a lending institution the banker wants to know how the money will be used. For an individual the loan may be tied directly to the purchase of a new car, home modernization, college tuition, etc. A business might be granted a loan to build or modernize a plant, finance inventory, etc. The proceeds of the loan would be made available as the construction proceeds, inventory is received, etc. This is normal banking procedure.

Such procedures are not followed by the banking community, according to Congressmen Kemp and Roth, when making loans to Communists. During 1986, Western banks provided $6-billion in loans to the Soviet Union of which $4-billion were "untied"—not granted for a specific purpose or project.[42] Kemp explained:

> The Soviet bloc now receives low-interest rate loans for non-specific projects or trade transactions at a rate lower than a small businessman in America would pay. These loans can be used for any purpose, including financing military aggression abroad and oppression at home.[43]

The co-sponsor of the bill to ban untied loans to the Soviet bloc, Toby Roth, added to Kemp's explanation, saying:

> These are not rubles we are lending. It's hard currency dollars which the Soviets can use to pay for anything ranging from their financial obligations to Cuba to acquiring illegal, sophisticated Western high-technology.

BACK-DOOR FINANCING FOR CASTRO

It may be no coincidence that the $4-billion in "untied loans" Moscow received from Western bankers in 1986 was the exact subsidy Gorbachev gave Cuba to keep Fidel Castro's Communist nation from collapsing economically. A high-ranking Cuban who defected testified that Cuba was near economic collapse and "in a desperate situation" when the Soviet Union provided a massive hard-currency loan to bail them out.[44]

The Kemp-Roth bill would have restricted the untied loans which give the Soviets cash to finance Castro and other revolutions around the world. News reports said the proposal...

> ....faces stiff resistance from Mr. Reagan and from the State Department. The State Department reacted in a "totally disdainful manner" to his proposal, Mr. Kemp said.[45]

The State Department reaction was typical of the bureaucracy's response to any proposal which would hurt the Communists over a 40 year period—whether limitation on loans, punishing firms or countries which supply strategic technology to the Communists or attempts to uncover Communist sympathizers or security risks from the government.

SUBSIDIZED WHEAT SALES

The United States, its businessmen and its banks consistently give the Communist bloc nations what they need to avoid economic disaster. The Reds are permitted to pay for what they get with low interest, unsecured loans. In addition, the sales are frequently made at subsidized prices with American taxpayers paying the bill. Wheat sales are an example. During the 12 months ending in April 1988, private U.S. exporters sold 10.8-million tons of wheat to the Soviet Union.[46] The Communists paid an average of 59 cents a bushel ($21.95 per ton) less for the wheat than the bakers pay who bake bread for Americans. American taxpayers paid more for their bread—and then paid again to supply the $237-million subsidy the government gave to the private exporters who sold grain to the Soviet Union during late 1987 and early 1988.[47]

The program continues under the Bush Administration. President George Bush who had initially argued for eliminating subsidies approved their resumption in early 1989. The shipments of subsidized wheat to the Communists resumed in May 1989.[48]

FEEDING THE RED OCTOPUS

Ronald Reagan took some of the firmest actions against the Communists of any president in 50 years. He battled Congressional opposition and bureaucratic foot dragging to support anti-Communist freedom fighters in Nicaragua, Angola and Afghanistan. Grenada's Communist government was replaced and American medical students on the little island were rescued in a boldly-executed invasion in November 1983.

However, an octopus will never be defeated by slapping at its tentacles while feeding its head. Mr. Reagan's Administration not only continued but expanded the feeding of the Russian octopus which has been a feature of the foreign policy of America's government and business community since 1917. Were it not for the continual transfer of food, technology and equipment paid for by untied, unsecured, low-interest loans, the Soviet octopus would not have the resources to finance revolutions and shore up faltering client states around the world.

William Safire, the Pulitzer Prize winning *New York Times* syndicated columnist, took issue with President Reagan's remarks to a conservative group when he claimed as a major achievement, "We have significantly slowed the transfer of valuable free world technology to the Soviet Union." Safire commented that perhaps the President was referring to blocking certain illegal shipments of high-tech supplies and computers, and then added:

> But when it comes to "the transfer of valuable free world technology" that will strategically benefit the Soviet Union, it was during the Reagan administration that the floodgates were opened.[49]

Safire's article carried the headline, "Reagan's Selling The Soviets Enough Rope To Hang The U.S." Safire detailed the multi-billion dollar expansion of Soviet oil and gas projects for which the United States supplied key technology and equipment and said that under Mr. Reagan's administration...

> ...Not only do we aid the Russians militarily, we strengthen them economically and strategically.
>
> Perhaps Reagan thinks he can truthfully boast of keeping his campaign promise of slowing the transfer of technology to the nation that invests its profits in our demise. Some conservatives who heard him last week were aware that Ronald Reagan was incredibly misinformed.[50]

APPOINTMENTS THE KEY

How could a president be so misinformed about something which he was supposedly so committed to? Presidents are elected. They are dependent on the people they appoint to carry out their views. Many of Mr. Reagan appointees were not people who held to his publicly-announced views. A good example was C. William Verity, Jr. Verity was appointed to replace Malcolm Baldrige as commerce secretary in 1987. The Commerce Department issues licenses for exports to

Communist countries. It is charged with keeping strategic goods from going to the Reds. The guidelines were seriously eroded under Baldridge. Verity opened the floodgates and used the full prestige of his cabinet position to expand trade with the Communists. His actions were no surprise. Verity was a retired steel executive and a longtime chairman of the U.S.-U.S.S.R. Trade and Economic Council, the principal, longtime lobbying group for expanded trade with the Soviets.[51] For over 15 years Verity had established himself as a principal advocate of aid and trade with and to the Communist empire.

Howard Phillips, chairman of *The Conservative Caucus* testified against Senate confirmation of Verity's appointment to the President's Cabinet. He said:

> If William Verity is confirmed as Secretary of Commerce, Mikhail Gorbachev will have a voice at the Cabinet table and representation will have been denied to those of us who believe that communism should be opposed, not subsidized...[52]

Verity's appointment won overwhelming approval in the U.S. Senate. He used the influence of his office to host receptions for Gorbachev with American businessmen,[53] sent 500 American business executives to the Soviet Union[54] and oversaw a flood of new joint ventures which will help produce what the Communists need to keep their economy from collapsing.[55]

Keeping the needed aid and credits coming from the West is a key goal of Gorbachev's glasnost and perestroika programs—and it is working.

If America is to survive and freedom is to be extended around the world, the United States must stop feeding the head of the Red octopus which has its tentacles reaching out into Asia, Africa and Central and South America.

If the United States, its government and its bankers would stop feeding the Red octopus, neither Moscow nor Peking would have the resources to foment revolution and rebellion all over the world. The West wouldn't have to worry about a nuclear showdown. The Red nations would face such economic stagnation and consumer discontent that they would soon wither and die.

If U.S. allies saw a real and consistent commitment on the part of the United States to starve the Communist economy they could be encouraged to join the boycott effort. The United States is more valuable as a trading partner for Japan, England, West Germany and every other free world country than any Communist nation.

CHAPTER 17

THE TREATY TRAPS

The chief aim of the foreign policy of the Communist Party of the Soviet Union is to ensure peaceful conditions for the building of a Communist society in the USSR and the development of a world system of socialism.

—Draft Program of CPSU, 1961

AMERICAN AID to the Communists has not been limited to economic assistance. The Reds' greatest victories have come at the diplomatic conference table. Treaties and agreements have ensnared more countries into the Red orbit and enslaved more people than any other weapon or combination of weapons in the Communist arsenal.

Earlier chapters examined (1) results of promises the Soviets made in 1933 to gain diplomatic recognition from the United States, (2) those they made at Yalta to gain control of Eastern Europe and (3) at Potsdam concerning access to Berlin, etc. All produced disasters for the West and for freedom.

Communists teach, "Promises are like pie crusts—made to be broken." They make treaties—and then they break them. A 136-page staff study issued by the Senate Internal Security Subcommittee in 1964 showed that the Soviet Union broke every agreement made during the 1917-64 period when it was to their advantage to do so. The study was titled, *Soviet Political Agreements And Results.*[1]

Since then, the Reds broke the promises they made in Geneva and Paris to end the Vietnam War. South Vietnam, Cambodia and Laos quickly went into Communist hands and millions were slaughtered. Even so, the United States has gone back to the bargaining table again and again to make agreements with the Communists on which the future of freedom in Nicaragua, Angola, Afghanistan and other nations depend.

Continuing attempts to resolve international tensions and insure peace through negotiations fail for at least five reasons. They include:

1. Communists always break their agreements whenever it is to their advantage to do so.

2. When Communist violations are proven, the United States does nothing (except to negotiate more treaties and agreements).

3. Treaties are presented as being equal for both sides but the "fine print" written into many agreements give unfair advantages to the Communists.

4. Legislators who attempt to make U.S. ratification or financing of agreements conditional on the Communists fulfilling their commitments are attacked and ridiculed.

5. Those who expose Communist treaty violations are attacked by the U.S. State Department as being "irritants" in U.S./U.S.S.R. relations.

Specific examples from both human rights and arms control treaties negotiated with the Soviets during the 1970s and 1980s substantiate those charges.

HELSINKI HUMAN RIGHTS ACCORDS

The 1975 Helsinki agreement, for example, was widely heralded as a great breakthrough in the area of human rights. It was signed by 35 nations including the Soviet Union and eight other Communist countries of Eastern Europe. All the signatories agreed to cooperation in a wide variety of areas. The agreement broadly and specifically committed participating states to respecting....

> ...freedom of thought, conscience, religion or belief, for all without distinction as to race, sex, language or religion....the right of the individual to know and act upon his rights and duties in this field.... [and] the rights of peoples to self determination.[2]

The Helsinki agreement neglected any commitment to freedom of speech, press or assembly which are vital for those seeking to exercise their right of self-determination. In addition, the Communist nations were exempted from all the high-sounding commitments to freedom in Articles VII and VIII of the treaty by the innocuous sounding provisions of Articles I through VI. In Article I, for example, the 35 signing nations agreed that each participating *state* would respect the rights of all other *states* to...

...choose and develop its political, social, economic and cultural system, as well as its right to determine its laws and regulations.[3]

These rights were guaranteed to each *state* and not to the people of the country. Therefore, each Communist country was guaranteed its right to be Communist and to institute whatever laws and measures were necessary to guarantee that it would remain Communist. Other provisions in Articles I through VI gave further protection to the Communist nations as the signing nations agreed to...

...respect each others sovereign equality and individuality as well as all the rights inherent in and encompassed by its sovereignty

....refrain from any intervention, direct or indirect, individual or collective, in the internal or external affairs falling within the domestic jurisdiction of another participating state....[and] refrain from direct or indirect assistance to terrorist activities or to subversive or other activities directed towards the violent overthrow of the regime of another participating State.[4]

Read through Western eyes the provisions of the first six articles appear to place strong restrictions on many traditional aggressive actions of the Soviet Union. In actuality, they accept and legitimatize Communist control of the Eastern European Soviet satellites. They release the Soviet Union from its Yalta agreements to guarantee free elections in Eastern Europe. They ban any free world support for those in Communist countries who would attempt to replace Communist regimes with truly democratic ones.

That the Soviets interpret the Helsinki accords in this manner was confirmed within two years after the agreement was signed.

In early 1977 the United States lodged official protests over specific Soviet human rights violations including....

> The Soviets arrested five prominent human rights activists in the Soviet Union....restricted Andrey Sakharov's contacts with Western newsmen....used Moscow police to disperse people assembled in Pushkin Square to express a silent protest against disparities between the theory and practice of Soviet constitutional law....convicted 90 dissidents...and sentenced a Belgian citizen to five years imprisonment for distributing political pamphlets to Soviet students.[5]

United States protests and expression of concern over the human rights violations were rejected. In a nationally-televised speech Soviet leader Leonid Brezhnev referred to the Soviet dissidents as "renegades" and warned:

> We will not tolerate interference *in our internal affairs* by anyone under any pretext.[6]

When the United States expressed support for Andrey Sakharov, the Soviet press charged that...

> ...the State Department pronouncement constitutes an unprecedented act of interference *in the internal affairs* of another country.[7]

The Soviets were within their rights. Under the Helsinki accords which American diplomats helped draft, the United States was prohibited from "interfering in the internal affairs of the Soviet Union" even to protest Soviet suppression of the rights of its citizens. The Helsinki accords formalize the status quo in the Communist countries of Eastern Europe—while being heralded in the West as a great breakthrough for human rights.

ARMS CONTROL AGREEMENTS

Citizens of the Soviet Union and the Eastern European satellites are locked into living under Communist control by a so-called "Human Rights" accord. The future freedom and safety of generations of Americans could depend on the arms control and disarmament agreements the United States has made with the Soviet Union. They are also deeply flawed. Several will be examined.

MUTUAL ASSURED DESTRUCTION

Arms control efforts must be evaluated and understood in the context of American defense strategy and policy. Since the early 1960s, United States defense against a Soviet nuclear attack has been based on a policy of *Mutual Assured Destruction*. The theory is that if both nations have the capability to absorb a major nuclear first strike and still launch a massive retaliation then neither side would risk striking first.

When the policy was first conceived in the days of President Kennedy's Defense Secretary Robert Strange McNamara, the United States had nuclear superiority over the Soviets. In implementing the policy of *Mutual Assured Destruction* (called MAD for short) the Soviets were to be allowed to achieve either nuclear parity—or even a slight superiority—so they wouldn't feel threatened.

ANTI-BALLISTIC MISSILE DEFENSE TREATY

The theorists who devised the Mutual Assured Destruction (MAD) concept soon became concerned. If one side or the other developed a defensive system which could destroy incoming nuclear weapons before they hit their targets it would destabilize MAD. They feared that a nation with an operational defense against missiles could launch its own first strike confident that it could stop the enemy's retaliation.

To combat the possibility that an anti-missile defense system would destabilize Mutual Assured Destruction, the U.S. and the U.S.S.R. signed an Anti-Ballistic Missile (ABM) Treaty in 1972.[8] Both parties agreed not to test, construct or operate an anti-missile defense system. The treaty was one of a series of "equal but not equal" agreements between the United States and the Soviets.

Proponents of the ABM treaty focussed on the need to prevent either side from protecting itself from retaliation if it should launch a first strike against the other. They ignored the need of the United States to protect its cities and its people in the event the Soviets cheated (as they always do) and launched its own first strike. The danger was particularly great as evidence piled up that the Soviets were developing super missiles with a first strike capability of destroying America's retaliatory capacity. In 1972, as the Senate was considering ratification of the ABM treaty, Senator Henry Jackson (D-WA) pointed out that the SALT I treaty...

> ...confers on the Soviet Union the authority to retain or deploy a number of weapons based on land and sea that exceeds our own in every category, and by a 50% margin. Is this parity?...The agreement gives the Soviets more of everything: more light ICBM's, more heavy ICBM's, more submarine launched missiles, more submarines, more payload, even more ABM radars. In no area of the SALT I agreements is the U.S. permitted to maintain parity with the Soviet Union.[9]

The one equalizer was the know-how of American space scientists who succeeded in landing men on the moon with pinpoint accuracy. They were hard at work developing an anti-missile defense (ABM) system which would defend America's cities and retaliatory forces if the Soviets used their treaty-permitted 2-to-1 superiority to launch a first strike.

The pressing need for a defense against a pre-emptive Soviet first strike was emphasized by the Blue Ribbon Department of Defense panel. Its report to President Richard Nixon pointed up the dangers in the shifting balance of military power. The report warned that there was...

> ...convincing evidence that the Soviet Union seeks a pre-emptive first strike capability...there is no longer any certainty that our nuclear deterent will remain credible...the weakness of the U.S.— of its military capability and will—could be the gravest threat to the peace of the world [and the survival of the United States].[10]

With growing prospects of an American defense against the threat of a Soviet first strike, the arms control enthusiasts in both countries went to work again and the Anti-Ballistic Missile Treaty was negotiated, signed and ratified in 1972.

Senator Jackson's facts, the blue ribbon panel's report and

history demonstrate how an "equal" ABM treaty may not be "equal." History demonstrates that the United States and the Soviet Union do not pose an equal threat to use first strike capabilities against the other.

Look at the record: Following World War II, the United States had an absolute monopoly on operational nuclear weapons for ten years. They were not used except to end World War II which saved the one or two million Japanese and Americans who would have been lost in an invasion and battle for Japan (which was set free and rebuilt).

The United States did not then use its ten-year nuclear monopoly and its additional ten years of nuclear superiority to capture other nations or crush the Communists. Nothing could have prevented an American conquest of the world. During these same years the Communists imposed their police state system on a dozen countries and more than 1.5-billion people—and regularly dedicated themselves to the conquest of the United States and the world.

So the Soviets did not (and do not) need a missile defense system to guard against a sneak American attack. However, the U.S. did need such a system once the Soviets were permitted to gain nuclear superiority. America needed the system for protection in the event the Soviets cheated as history shows they have always done—or if they should try nuclear blackmail by threatening an attack. So the treaty which applied "equally" to both nations was not in fact "equal" because of the differing needs and threats faced by the two nations.

All treaty imbalances are not the result of language written into the treaty documents. Frequently, the United States is placed at a serious disadvantage by actions of the Congress or the treaty interpretations of the entrenched Foreign Service bureaucracy.

The ABM treaty, for example, did not outlaw all anti-missile defense systems. Both nations were permitted to select one area to protect.[11] The Soviets chose to protect their capital and main population center, Moscow. Instead of defending Washington DC or New York, the United States chose to defend Grand Forks, North Dakota, site of a few missile silos.

The Soviets moved ahead full steam with their Moscow ABM system which was soon operational and is regularly upgraded. By 1976 the United States Congress, under the leadership of Senator Ted Kennedy (D-MA), killed the appropriation for even the Grand Forks ABM complex. As a result all of America is totally defenseless against a sneak Soviet missile attack.***

The U.S. has adhered to its obligations under the ABM treaty, restricting some aspects of the development and testing of President Reagan's Strategic Defense Initiative announced in 1983. At the same time, the Soviets construction of the giant battle-management, phased-array radar complex at Krasnoyarsk is a major and flagrant violation of the ABM treaty.[12]

The Reds break their promises and we do nothing. The Soviet violation gave the U.S. a basis for withdrawing from the treaty. Congress passed a resolution declaring the Soviet complex a substantive violation of the ABM treaty. The Reagan State Department refused to follow up. Withdrawal from the ABM treaty would have allowed United States to move "full speed ahead" on development, testing *and* deployment of the SDI defense system. Steps which would protect American citizens and industry against a sneak Soviet missile attack were not taken.

Relying on the ability of each side to totally annihilate a hundred million or more of the citizens of the other country is an immoral approach to defense—particularly when the technology is available to protect the citizens of both sides from a deliberate attack or an accidental nuclear launch.

***The author participated in a day-long briefing at the Pentagon in April 1987. A top military official was asked what defenses America had if the Soviets should cheat and launch a sneak missile attack. The general paused for what seemed like an eternity and finally said, "If an enemy were to launch a missile attack today or in the foreseeable future, we have but one defense: Prayer." By 1992, there was no change.

President Reagan promised to make SDI technology available to the Soviet Union so they too could be free from the fear of a surprise attack. They rejected his offer as a propaganda ploy and ridicule the system as unworkable. If SDI doesn't work, some ask, "Why then have the Communists, their scientists and their agents and dupes in the United States and worldwide been waging an all-out campaign to stop U.S. development of the SDI system?"

SDI will not stop 100 per cent of an enemy's missiles. No defense system has ever been or ever will be 100 per cent effective. However, a deployed system which is even 50 per cent effective can insure survival of sufficient retaliatory forces to deter an aggressor from making a first strike attempt in the hopes of totally crippling its victim.

Breakthroughs in non-nuclear SDI technology in 1988 and 1989 (the Brilliant Pebbles concept, for example, described in some detail in the September 1989 *Reader's Digest*) hold the promise of a cost-effective shield within five years. SDI would therefore eliminate the need for costly mobile missile systems, etc. now seen as necessary to insure survivability of America's retaliatory missile forces if the Soviets should launch a first strike.

To achieve deployment within the five year time frame, a full commitment of resources is needed quickly. Such commitment is opposed by the Communists, the peace and arms control lobbies and a significant number of powerful figures in the military and Congress. As a result, further cuts were made in research funds and people in the budget Congress approved in the summer of 1989.[13]

STRATEGIC ARMS LIMITATION (SALT I & II)

During the 1970s, the United States and the Soviet Union negotiated two Strategic Arms Limitation treaties. Known as SALT I and SALT II, the treaties were presented to the American public as a way of reducing the numbers of missiles, warheads and other mass destruction weapons while still basing defense policy on the theory of Mutual Assured Destruction.

Both treaties, billed as equal, legitimized Soviet superiority in missiles and super bombs and limited U.S. ability to catch up. Other advantages were built in for the Soviets as well. The imbalance was put into focus for members of the Senate Armed Services Committee considering the SALT II treaty by Dr. Richard Pipes. Pipes is a Harvard University faculty member and expert on Soviet history, government, etc. He was asked by Senator James Exon (D-NE) whether it was possible to expect that the Soviet Union could become a responsible member of the world community and keep its treaty obligations. Pipes replied:

> You can make agreements with people who do not respect you—and if it is in their interest, they will adhere to them. This treaty in particular, I think, is so advantageous to the U.S.R.R. that its leaders will have no reason to violate it.[14]

The SALT II treaty merits special examination because of both its clearly "unequal" provisions and the "equal but not equal" requirements which give the Communists such an advantage. Three glaring "unequal" provisions are:

> Both sides are limited to an equal number of nuclear weapon delivery systems including heavy bombers, missile silos, nuclear submarines and cruise missile launching platforms. However, the U.S. knowingly accepted a false Soviet claim that its several hundred Backfire bombers did not have intercontinental range and therefore should not count against its launcher quota. At the same time, U.S. negotiators agreed to have some U.S. B-52 bombers in Arizona junkyards count against the American quota.[15]

> Similarly, the U.S. acquiesced to Soviet insistence that their SS-17 and SS-19 were "light" rather than "heavy" ICBM's even though the Soviet missiles have three times the throw weight of the U.S. Minuteman which is counted as a heavy missile.[16]

> During the negotiations the Carter administration accepted provisions which permit the Soviets to keep 308 "heavy" SS-18 missiles armed with multiple warheads while preventing the United States, which has no comparable missile, from building any. The 308 Soviet SS-18's can deliver 3080 1-megaton warheads—a destructive force exceeding all U.S. land-based and submarine-based ballistic missiles.[17]

These "unequal" provisions of the SALT II treaty give the Communists a definite advantage. They get additional advantages from several "equal but unequal" provisions including:

The treaty does not limit missiles or warheads but "launchers."[18] This is a critical mistake because of differences in the U.S. and Soviet launch methods. As many as fifty percent of Soviet missiles use a *cold* launch system. A cold launched missile is propelled out of the silo or launcher by compressed air or other mechanical means and is fired once it is in the air. *The launcher can then be reloaded.*[19] The United States uses a *hot* launch method. The missile is fired in the silo. The blast-off effectively destroys the launcher and prevents reloading.

SALT II therefore permits the Soviets to maintain a 3 or 4 to 1 superiority in potential missile firings even though they adhere to the treaty terms specifying an equal number of launchers. It is hard to conceive that the American "experts" who negotiated the treaty did not recognize the "equal but unequal" provisions they allowed to be built into the treaty. There is another:

At Soviet insistence, each party to the treaty agreed not to deploy cruise missiles with a range in excess of 600 kilometers (370 miles) on sea-based launchers (primarily submarines).[20]

The provision applies equally to both the United States and the Soviet Union—but a look at a world map or globe shows that it is not equal. Soviet nuclear submarines patrol the east and west coasts of the United States and the Gulf of Mexico continually. Almost 80% of America's population and most of our industry is within the 370 mile range permitted for Soviet cruise missiles launched with nuclear warheads from their subs.

Contrast the threat which Soviet sub-launched cruise missiles tipped with nuclear warheads pose to most of America's cities and people with the very minimal threat to Soviet cities and population. American subs cannot get within a 370 mile range of any part of the Soviet Union except the Arctic regions and Siberia where few people live and little industry is located. SALT II was "equal but unequal."

SALT II was never ratified by the Senate of the United States—but not because SALT II was a bad treaty. Rather, at a critical time in the ratification process, the Soviets invaded Afghanistan. Even many peaceniks drew back from formalizing another agreement on which America's future safety and freedom depends with an adversary which had showed itself openly to be so untrustworthy.

That's the good news. The bad news, however, is that the United States under both Presidents Carter and Reagan has unilaterally adhered to all the provisions and limitations of the badly flawed, "equal but unequal" treaty.

After the United States had voluntarily stayed within the limits of the unratified treaty for years, Communist Party head Gus Hall in December 1986 called for Senate ratification of SALT II. Liberals in Congress devised a way to by-pass the Constitution which requires that two-thirds of the senators present and voting must approve a treaty. In October 1987, the Congress, *by majority vote*, attached amendments to the Defense Appropriations bill which forbid spending the appropriated money in any way which would violate the unratified SALT II treaty. Gus Hall's goal was accomplished. The Associated Press reported:

> The Senate kept alive on Thursday a proposal ordering President Ronald Reagan to observe SALT II, the unratified nuclear arms pact. The action came in a Senate deeply divided along party lines as it struggled to write a Pentagon budget bill.
>
> The vote was 55-44. The action rejected a move to table, and thus kill, the Democratic-backed SALT II amendment.
>
> The treaty was never ratified by the Senate and although Reagan termed it "fatally flawed" during his 1980 presidential campaign, he lived up to its restrictions during his first six years in the White House.... while charging that the Soviets have continually violated the pact.[21]

THE INF TREATY

In 1979, William Van Cleve, a longtime arms control expert

and negotiator, opposed the ratification of SALT II in testimony before the Senate Armed Service Committee. Dr. Van Cleve pinpointed many technical and strategic shortcomings in the badly flawed treaty and added:

> The treaty contains too many ambiguities and loopholes that the Soviets can exploit and that are certain to cause future problems. It is a lawyer's nightmare as well as a strategist's.[22]

The Intermediate Nuclear Forces (INF) treaty signed by Ronald Reagan and Mikhail Gorbachev on Pearl Harbor Day in 1987 has even more loopholes. They will not be examined here because the treaty contained one provision which alone would have overridden every safeguard in even a well-drafted document.

President Reagan made headlines before and during the meeting with Gorbachev with his slogan, "Trust But Verify," which he voiced in both Russian and English. His seeming pledge to the American people was made meaningless by Article XI, Paragraph 3 of the treaty. It said:

> Beginning 30 days after entry into force of this Treaty, each Party shall have the right to conduct inspections at all missile operating bases and missile support facilities *specified in the Memorandum of Understanding.*[23] (Emphasis added)

The six italicized words effectively wiped out President Reagan's widely publicized "Trust But Verify" pledge. American inspectors have no right to conduct short-notice, on-site inspections at suspect sites other than those that the Soviets have chosen in advance to make subject to inspection. If the Soviets should cheat, would they be likely to do it at a site subject to inspection—or in one of the off-limits areas?

Despite the Soviet "veto" over effective on-site inspections and all the other loopholes and ambiguities, the Senate ratified the treaty by an overwhelming 92-5 vote.

Prior to ratification, a *New York Times* editorial brushed aside solid evidence of Soviet cheating on past treaties and on the INF treaty's disclosure documents. The editorial was headlined:

Some Arms Cheating Doesn't Matter[24]

Senator Steve Symms (R-ID) proposed five amendments to bar the treaty from taking effect until President Reagan certified that the Soviets were in full compliance with five previous arms limitation treaties including SALT I & II, the 1972 ABM treaty, a 1963 pact banning open-air nuclear tests, and a 1925 Geneva protocol banning chemical weapons.[25]

Senate Republican leader Bob Dole of Kansas called the Symms proposal a "killer amendment." Other Senators denounced it as "nonsense", "extraneous" and "an obvious attempt to slow Senate approval of the pact." The Reagan Administration opposed each of the proposed amendments and they were defeated by votes ranging from 89-8 to 82-15.[26]

By their votes the 80-plus senators told the Communists, "It doesn't matter whether you fulfill your past promises or not, we'll give you the new treaty you want right now."

WHAT HAPPENED TO REAGAN'S PROMISES?

Ronald Reagan's campaign for the Presidency in 1980 included a pledge of no more treaties with the Communists until all past agreements were fulfilled. Early in his presidency he labeled the Communist system "an evil empire" and there were no new treaties with the Reds for six years. Then things changed. What happened?

People determine policy. In the aftermath of the Iran-Contra disclosures in November 1986, significant personnel changes produced dramatic changes in Reagan Administration words, policies and actions. The headlines told of the firing of John Poindexter and Oliver North. The changes which started at the top quickly rippled down through policy-making and policy-implementing levels of the Executive Branch.

Frank Carlucci's appointment to replace John Poindexter as National Security Adviser had a far reaching effect in transforming U.S. attitudes and actions toward the Soviet Union.

Within 90 days, much of the knowledgeable, hard-line anti-Communist, pro-American cadre assembled at the National Security Council in the early Reagan years was gone. They were the unnamed "heroes" who planned and fought for and oversaw the rescue of American students in Grenada, the capture of the *Achille Lauro* killers, the battle for aiding the freedom fighting anti-Communist contras in Nicaragua and the raid on Quaddaffi's Libya which told the Marxist madman that no more terrorism would be tolerated.

Their briefings reinforced President Reagan's basic anti-Communist inclinations in the ongoing struggle with State Department bureaucrats over control of U.S. foreign policy. In his Iran-Contra hearing testimony Secretary of State George Schulz testified that "there was a guerrilla war going on at the White House."[27] The battle was between those who supported Mr. Reagan's basically anti-Communist position and the traditional, compromising State Department approach.

United Nations Ambassador Jeane Kirkpatrick and William Clark, the President's longtime California friend and adviser and the individual who assembled the strongly pro-American NSC cadre, were early casualties in the "war" to control the President and the direction of U.S. foreign policy.[28]

Naming the courageous Mrs. Kirkpatrick as UN ambassador was one of the few appointments Mr. Reagan reportedly made personally as president. She gave some insight into the ongoing battle in the foreign policy area in a syndicated column in 1988.[29] Mrs. Kirkpatrick related a surprising encounter and conversation she had with Presidential adviser and Nancy Reagan friend, Mike Deaver, during an intermission at the Gridiron Dinner in 1983. Deaver said:

I may as well tell you this, you'll have to find out sometime," Deaver began. "This President may have an opportunity to make peace for our times."

"That would be wonderful," I responded.

But after praising me on my role as a top presidential adviser, Deaver then said, "When the time comes that the President has the opportunity to make peace we can't have you and Bill Clark around raising questions."

"Wait a minute, Mike," I said, "I'm for peace too. I would never stand in the way of an agreement that met the President's standards."

"We just can't have you and Bill Clark around raising questions," Deaver reiterated and turned away. The conversation was finished.

Mrs. Kirkpatrick was stunned. She wrote, "Even in retrospect I find it incredible that this Presidential aide with no known role in foreign affairs had decided that two senior officials had to be moved out to prevent them from 'raising questions' when the time came for negotiations with the Soviets." She continued her personal reminiscence in the column writing:

> I did not know what to make of this extraordinary conversation. I still don't. [But there were] rumors circulating in Washington at the time that Deaver was working with Armand Hammer, the multimillionaire pal of Soviet rulers, to change Ronald Reagan's views about the Soviet Union and to bring about a new, expanded detente between the U.S. and the U.S.S.R. The principal obstacles to the plan were said to be Reagan's own deep-felt anti-Soviet convictions and the advisers who shared these views.

Mrs. Kirkpatrick added, "In the intervening years I have wondered from time to time what questions Deaver and his associates didn't want us to raise."

Within three months after Carlucci became National Security Adviser the others on the National Security Council staff who shared the President's deep-felt anti-Soviet convictions were gone. The lower-level voices which might have raised Kirkpatrick- like questions had been silenced also.

Without the close support of the hard-liners, President Reagan's long held convictions about the Soviets, their evil system and the need for iron-clad verification and inspection provisions in any treaty, showed signs of wavering. Negotiations on the INF treaty moved into high gear in the spring of 1987. By late August, a *St. Louis Post-Dispatch* headline said, "Reagan To Back Away From Arms Inspections." The story read:

> President Reagan's administration, retreating from a key tenet of

its arms control policy, will propose sharp limits for on-site inspections under a U.S.-Soviet treaty eliminating medium and short-range missiles, U.S. officials said Monday.

The proposal was approved by Reagan over the weekend and sent to U.S. negotiators....The proposal would retract previous demands by the U.S. for continuous on-site inspections of Soviet missile production, assembly and maintenance plants, the officials said.

It would also sharply limit the right of either side to send a team of inspectors on short notice to a site in the other's territory where a treaty violation was suspected—a procedure the administration has long demanded in response to allegations of Soviet violations of previous arms treaties.[30]

By the time the Reagan-Gorbachev Summit convened three months later, Mr. Reagan withdrew his charge that the Soviets had "an evil empire."[31] He also told the nation that he was sure that the Communists had abandoned their goals of world conquest.[32]

By the time Reagan and Gorbachev signed the INF treaty on Pearl Harbor Day, Frank Carlucci had moved from his White House assignment as National Security Adviser to the Pentagon to be Secretary of Defense. An immediate ousting of hard-line anti-Communists followed. Within hours after Carlucci's appointment was approved by the Senate the axe started to fall. The press reported:

Incoming Defense Secretary Frank Carlucci has ousted Frank Gaffney, a hard-liner distrustful of the Soviet Union, as the Pentagon's top adviser on arms control policy, administration officials said:

"Gaffney was crosswise with Carlucci and the administration on arms control," said one official, insisting on anonymity. "He is a real hard-liner and his views are not popular."

Gaffney believed that the Soviets could not be trusted and that the United States must have a strong nuclear defense. Before leaving office Gaffney told reporters he was worried about verification provisions in the proposed treaty eliminating medium and short-range missiles.[33]

Gaffney wasn't the only anti-Communist to feel Carlucci's axe at the Pentagon. The press reported:

> Army Lt. Gen. William E. Odom, director of the National Security Agency, is expected to resign soon as the top official at the super-secret electronic spy agency, according to Reagan administration officials.
>
> ...some U.S. intelligence sources said the three-star general was passed over for promotion to four-star rank as a result of differences with Defense Secretary Frank Carlucci and was being forced to resign.
>
> A conservative stalwart...he privately has criticized the administration's intermediate-range nuclear forces [INF] treaty because of its strategic impact on European security and because of problems with verifying the pact.[34]

With all of the outspoken critics out of the way, the treaty was signed by Reagan and Gorbachev and ratified by the U.S. Senate with few dissenting votes. As shown earlier, the treaty permits no on-site inspection of suspected violations except at those sites the Soviets had listed before the treaty was signed.

People are policy. When the wrong people are appointed policy goes wrong. Who is Frank Carlucci? Who is this man who completed the removal of NSC and Pentagon hardliners—the process which started when Mike Deaver told Jeane Kirkpatrick she and Bill Clark would have to go when "the President gets the opportunity to make peace?"

Carlucci was a longtime bureaucrat. Repeatedly given assignments in some of the world's most crucial trouble spots, Carlucci was on-the scene again and again when freedom forces were crushed and international communism gained great victories.

Carlucci was the State Department's political officer in the Congo from 1960 to 1964 when the U.S. and the U.N. cooperated in crushing the pro-Western, free enterprise, Christian leadership of Moise Tshombe in the Katanga province.[35] The sordid five-page description of the ruthless, brutal and almost unbelievable action is in Chapter IV. With the pro-freedom forces crushed, much of the region went into the Marxist orbit with State Department help during Carlucci's tour.

After domestic assignments in the Office of Economic Opportunity and the Department of Health, Education and Welfare in the Nixon Administration, Carlucci was assigned to another key area of conflict. He was the United States ambassador to Portugal from 1975-78 during the time when the United States pressured Portugal to free its Angolan colony in Africa.[36] The Communist MPLA forces grabbed control with Fidel Castro's support. The war between the Communists and the freedom fighting UNITA forces of Jonas Savimbi continues today.

Carlucci "accomplishments" in Portugal earned him another step up the ladder. President Carter named him Deputy Director of the Central Intelligence Agency in 1978.[37] During his four-year tour as the CIA's #2 man, America's longterm friends and allies in Iran and Nicaragua were pressured to share power with dissident elements in their nations and were finally toppled. The madman Khomeini came to power in Iran and the Ortega brothers and the Sandinista Communists siezed control in Nicaragua. Both initially had United States support. U.S. intelligence forces had goofed again—and Carlucci was the #2 man in the CIA.

After these fiascos, Carlucci spent five profitable years in the private sector. Then in 1987, the man who had been Jimmy Carter's Deputy CIA Director returned to government as President Reagan's National Security adviser. The purging of hardline anti-Communists from Carlucci's areas of responsibility at the National Security Council and later at the Defense Department have been recorded. During the same months President Reagan's realistic, hardline attitude toward the Communists changed dramatically.

The dramatic shift in attitudes and policy showed clearly that "people are policy."

In the world of Washington, competent pro-freedom individuals (the Jeane Kirkpatricks) too often find themselves on the outside looking in. Others like Frank Carlucci climb the ladder to power leaving behind a consistent record of wrong judgments, tragic failures and Communist victories.

As a result, in 1978 the Chief of the Soviet General Staff, Marshal Ogarkov, told Congressman Breckenridge that...

> ...Today the Soviet Union has military superiority over the United States, and henceforth the U.S. will be threatened. You had better get used to it.[38]

In 1959, a former Secretary of State, Dean Acheson, told why. He said:

> In the present century the Soviet state has perfected the use of negotiation, including negotiation by mass conference, as a method of warfare.[39]

Tragically, the secretaries of state since then have not taken to heart the words of this man who learned too late that Communists come to the conference table with a different objective than the west. They regard negotiations, not as a means for resolving differences but as another realm in which war is waged. The Draft Program of the Communist Party of the Soviet Union for 1961 said:

> The chief aim of the foreign policy of the Communist Party of the Soviet Union is to ensure peaceful conditions for the building of a Communist society in the USSR *and the development of a world system of socialism.*

Americans, meanwhile, go to the conference table with the hope that differences can be resolved and arms reduction will ease world tensions. They fail to understand that the arms race does not produce tensions—but are a symptom that they exist.

What can be done to put a halt to the almost pathological belief that world tensions can be eased by another agreement or treaty with the Communists whether or not they ever keep them?

If America is to survive, informed Americans must work to awaken others to the folly of making further agreements with an enemy which has never kept past agreements when it was to their advantage to break them. Once a sizeable segment of the American people is awakened, elected officials (and appointed bureaucrats) who make, approve or do not actively oppose such agreements must be replaced.

Asking carefully phrased questions at every opportunity is the way to start. Because most Americans are still distrustful of the Communists, intelligent use of questions is effective. At every opportunity, ask, "Would you be willing to base your future freedom and safety on Communist promises.?" About 80% of the American people say "No." Then ask, "Why then do our leaders go on making such agreements?"

CHAPTER 18

MILITARY AID TO COMMUNISTS—
THE TRAGIC STORY OF VIETNAM

*...abnormal and unprecedented political restrictions on the
use of air power in the Vietnam war...unnecessarily cost
American lives, aircraft and the chances of permanent success in the war.*

—*Senator Stuart Symington (D-MO)*

THE PATTERN OF GIVING regular and consistent
economic and diplomatic aid to the Communists manifests
itself in the military area as well. The unbelievable restrictions on the use of available military power to achieve victory
in Korea was discussed earlier. The tragic pattern was
repeated and expanded in Vietnam.

The first major commitment of U.S. troops to Vietnam was
made in mid-summer 1965. A study released twenty months
later by the U.S. Senate Preparedness Subcommittee recognized that the Reds were working to destroy the will of
Americans to resist Communist efforts to conquer the world.

The Senate committee report stated that the Johnson Administration, by "overly restricting" military efforts to win
the war in Vietnam, might be falling into the Communist
trap. The report said that...

> ...The enemy strategy is to engage us in a protracted war of
> attrition which will tax the patience and undermine the determina-
> tion of the American people to resist, once the true cost in precious
> blood and treasure is fully realized.[1]

The Senate study was prophetic. American involvement
dragged on for another seven years. Over 50,000 Americans
lost their lives. American boys won every battle they fought—
but they were not permitted to win the war. Disillusionment

mounted. Finally the United States accepted a phony peace program based on Communist promises and pulled out. The Communists quickly broke their promises. South Vietnam, Cambodia and Laos were soon solidly in the Marxist orbit and millions died.

The North Vietnamese military received regular and consistent aid from the United States all through the war. The Reds received major aid from the restrictions placed on American fighting units which kept them from winning. Sometimes the aid took the form of official notification to the North Vietnamese about what we would and wouldn't do. A member of the Preparedness Committee, Senator Stuart Symington (D-MO) spent several weeks in Southeast Asia. He returned to tell the Senate that the Johnson Administration was placing...

> ...abnormal and unprecedented political restrictions on the use of air power in the Vietnam war.[2]

Symington charged that the restrictions "unnecessarily cost American lives, aircraft, and the chances of permanent success in the war." Statements made to him by American airmen support the charges.

One pilot told Senator Symington of flying over barges loaded with trucks, ammunition, and oil which had been unloaded from Soviet ships. He was forbidden to attack this barge or the Soviet ship in the harbor. Later, he said, he would be required to risk his life and his airplane trying to destroy the trucks one at a time after they had been unloaded from the barge and were traveling down the Ho Chi Minh Trail. The pilot asked Senator Symington:

> Is not a North Vietnamese barge loaded with weapons and ammunition a legitimate military target?[3]

Another pilot told the Senator that he was forbidden to attack and destroy Russian-built MIG-21 fighter planes when they were vulnerable on the ground at their base near Hanoi. However, he was allowed to fight back when the MIG's took to the air and attacked him from the rear. Senator Symington said:

American military men and civilians in Vietnam are baffled by their orders from Washington.[4]

Is it any wonder that American military men were "baffled"—that many returned bitter and with mental and emotional turmoil? They were sent to Vietnam to fight and die against the Communist enemy—but they were denied the right to protect themselves or harm the enemy, except under certain mysterious "no-win" guidelines established in Washington.

Washington kept American military men from hitting the enemy with all they had. The Pentagon also kept the Communists informed officially on which targets would be hit—and which were safe from American attack. In September 1967, for example, American fighter bombers attacked a Communist facility near the port of Haiphong. Some newspapers interpreted the attack to mean that Defense Secretary McNamara's long-time ban on bombing of the port itself had been overruled.[5] Two days later Washington notified the North Vietnamese officially that this was not the case. The port of Haiphong was to be safe from attack. The Associated Press reported from Washington:

> The Pentagon, in its eagerness to show that Secretary of Defense Robert S. McNamara was not overruled in recent war decisions, has given North Vietnam official word that port facilities of Haiphong are safe from attack at present.[6]

Because the Communists got official word from Washington on which targets would be attacked—and which would be safe—they were able to concentrate their air defenses at the vulnerable sites. As a result air losses from ground fire in Vietnam were extraordinarily high. Good men died. Others spent years in brutal North Vietnamese torture camps after being shot down. Good evidence exists that some of the POW's from Vietnam, like those in Korea, have never been returned.

When American pilots intentionally or by accident overstepped the bounds placed on them, the United States *apologized to the Communist enemy!* On June 20, 1967, for example, the U.S. apologized because a Soviet ship was damaged in an American air attack. It was hit while delivering a cargo to the North Vietnamese port of Cam Pha. The Associated Press reported the incident on June 29 saying that...

> ...After initially denying an attack on the Soviet vessel, the State Department acknowledged June 20 that 20-mm cannon fire directed against a North Vietnamese antiaircraft position at Cam Pha might have struck the [Soviet ship] *Turkistan. Regrets were expressed for the death of the crew member and damage to the ship, and assurances were given that every effort would be made to ensure that such incidents do not occur in the future.*[7] (Emphasis added)

Is it any wonder that thousands of career officers and enlisted men—the backbone of U.S. military forces—left the services in protest against high level orders which aided the enemy?

The dead too cried out—even if most Americans didn't.

When Lieutenant J.D. Hunter of Arlington, Virginia was killed in Vietnam, President Johnson sent the boy's parents the usual letter of condolences. The father answered the President saying that his son had been proud to serve in the U.S. Army but had complained that he and his men were required to fight a "no-win" war. Mr. Hunter asked the President to give our fighting men an opportunity to win. The grieving father concluded:

> Anything short of a real victory will only mean to Mrs. Hunter and myself and to thousands of other fathers, mothers, wives, brothers and sisters that their loved ones are being sacrificed on an altar of political intrigue.[8]

The President didn't answer. Instead, Mr. Hunter's heartfelt plea to the President was shuffled to Assistant Secretary of Defense Phil Golding, who wrote:

> We are engaged in a limited war for limited objectives. Our military actions must be weighed against those limited objectives. Our bombing operations in the North are conducted within certain constraints because they are tied to our limited political objectives

in the South...*we are not seeking to destroy the Government of North Vietnam.*[9] (Emphasis added)

After receiving this official, top-level acknowledgement that victory was not the goal in Vietnam, the anguished father wrote a final letter to the Defense Department. He said:

> My son often told me that he and his men were being called upon to fight a "no-win" war. How right he was! The inference in your letter is clear that, because of our "limited political objectives" in Vietnam, our soldiers will be allowed to fight only a "no-win" war with one hand tied behind their backs. What a miserable way to fight a war! You say we are not seeking to destroy the Government of North Vietnam. If the North Vietnam government and its stooges are not our real enemy in South Vietnam, pray tell me, who is?[10]

No-win complaints from Army and Marine ground troops stemmed from official policies. Ground was taken from the enemy again and again at great cost—and then the troops were withdrawn without being allowed to hold the position. For example, during Operation "Hickory One" between May 18-28, 1967, two divisions moved into an area south of the Demilitarized Zone which separated North and South Vietnam and totally cleared it of invading North Vietnamese. When the operation ended on May 28, rather than being allowed to keep the ground they had won, the Marine and Vietnamese divisions were ordered to march back to their original positions. John Randolph of the *Los Angeles Times* reported:

> At that time, Marine infantrymen, dubious about 119 Marine dead and 817 wounded, grumbled, "Those bastards will be back in here the minute we leave."[11]

They were correct. On July 2, a battalion of Marines sent into the same area were ambushed. Before the fighting was over, 93 more Marines were killed and 309 were wounded. Again the Marines were withdrawn. Three weeks later, another battalion was sent into the same area and had 23 men killed and 191 wounded. The *Los Angeles Times* said:

It is this constant fighting and taking casualties for ground that is never held that lies behind the growing criticism of the official strategy.[12]

The stalemated war dragged on for almost eight years—longer if the involvement of the U.S. military advisers before 1965 is considered. At the peak of the fighting, the death toll of American boys totaled between 50 and 100 per week. The restrictions on using available military force to win the victory or even to protect American lives continued year after year.

The honor roll of those who in frustration hit an off-limits enemy and were disciplined grew—including top level commanders.

In 1972, Major General John D. Lavelle, commander of the 7th Air Force, was fired by Air Force Chief of Staff John D. Ryan. Lavelle's crime? He was relieved of his command and returned to the United States for ordering 28 air strikes against North Vietnam involving 147 planes. The Air Force chief of staff said the air strikes Lavelle ordered against North Vietnamese airfields, missiles and artillery violated rules prohibiting all but "protective reaction" strikes into North Vietnam in line with the 1968 bombing halt.[13]

Lavelle said he ordered the strikes...

...after his pilots saw and photographed a five-month buildup of Soviet-built MIG jet fighters at three airfields just across the demilitarized zone, along with SAM missile sites, heavy 133-mm artillery guns, antiaircraft guns and tanks.[14]

Lavelle said he requested permission for the air strikes but never received authorization from Washington to hit the enemy. He said that he could understand that from Washington's viewpoint he exceeded his authority. Then he added:

At that time as a commander on the spot concerned with the safety of my men and at the same time trying to stop the buildup that was being made for Hanoi's invasion of the South, I felt that these were justifiable actions.[15]

Called to testify by a subcommittee of the House Armed Services Committee, Lavelle said:

If I had it to do over I would do the same thing again.

Lavelle was permitted to retire and leave the service.

Disenchantment with the no-win strategy caused many patriotic Americans to say "let's pull out—let's end the stalemate."

Others added to the clamor for less patriotic reasons. Pro-Hanoi anti-war protesters on college campuses were egged on by the traitorous actions and words of celebrities like "Hanoi Jane" Fonda and peacenik senators and some actual Communist agitators. The national media which consistently finds reasons for opposing action against communism beat the drums for troop withdrawal and ending the war.

Richard Nixon was elected President in 1968. On the campaign trail he told the American people he had a plan for ending the war in Vietnam. (Americans apparently didn't notice that he promised *not victory* but an end to the war.)

As the ensuing five years unfolded it became apparent that Nixon's plan was basically one of continuing the stalemate until the American people became so disillusioned that they would accept an American withdrawal based on Communist promises to be good. Columnist Stewart Alsop spelled out what was happening. Four months after Nixon took office, Alsop's back-of-the-book feature in the May 5, 1969 *Newsweek* ran under the headline, "Is The War Lost?" Alsop discussed the role of Henry Cabot Lodge, Nixon's negotiator in the Paris peace talks and said:

Lodge's mission is to attempt to negotiate with Hanoi and the NLF [National Liberation Front] an "honorable" political settlement in Vietnam, based on mutual withdrawal of North Vietnamese and American troops. But the Communist side knows...that the Nixon Administration is so anxious to "de-Americanize" the war that a unilateral American withdrawal is inevitable anyway. Under the circumstances, why in the name of Marx and Lenin should the Communists agree to a mutual withdrawal.

The war dragged on for four more years before the agreement was finally negotiated by Henry Kissinger. There were a few exceptions to the seeming stalemate. The 1970 probe into Cambodia was one. The Cambodian action stirred mass campus protests across America (and at Kent State). Soon they grew into an orchestrated chorus for American withdrawal.

The Paris peace accords were followed by strict congressional bans against any further U.S. involvement even if the Communists violated their promises. Repeating the tragic pattern followed earlier in China and Cuba and later in Rhodesia, Nicaragua and Iran, Congress cut off most military aid to the South Vietnamese army at a critical time. The door was open and the Communists moved 17 divisions south for a coordinated attack against South Vietnam.

Over 500,000 refugees fled before the advancing Red armies. They doubled the size of Da Nang in a few days.[16] The refugees hoped for American help in escaping the oncoming Reds but American LST's were able to evacuate only a few thousand.

The world was stirred briefly by a UPI photo of a South Vietnamese soldier clinging to the landing gear of a Boeing 727 airliner taking off from Da Nang airport.[17] It was the last plane out with refugees. As the plane gained altitude, the South Vietnamese soldier lost his grip on the landing gear and fell to his death. A few weeks later the TV evening news pictured helicopters evacuating the last Americans from the roof of the embassy in Saigon as that city fell to the Reds.

Bitterness swept Saigon with many believing that the United States had betrayed them. The *New York Times* News Service reported that South Vietnamese anger centered on three arguments:

(1) That Americans encouraged the fight against the North Vietnamese, trained the army and then failed in large measure to supply the South Vietnamese military when it faced its gravest crisis.

(2) That Secretary of State Henry Kissinger pressured the Saigon government into signing the Paris Peace agreement with the Communists, thus insuring the withdrawal of American troops,

and then failed to assist South Viet Nam in the face of Communist attacks.

(3) That shrinking American aid levels and American disinterest, played a key role in the North Vietnamese strategy to launch their offensive.[18]

The Nicaraguan freedom fighters (contras) experienced similar reactions when Congress cutoff the aid for their battle against communism ten years later in Central America.

South Vietnam fell to the Communists and then quickly, like dominoes, Cambodia and Laos fell before advancing Red forces. Millions died.

As the millions were dying, Henry Winston, national chairman of the Communist Party, USA visited Hanoi for the celebration of the Communist victory over U.S. imperialism. Winston met with Le Duan, first secretary of the Vietnamese Communist Party. Le Duan told Winston:

> We are thankful for the great movement of peace in the U.S., uniting many currents opposed to U.S. aggression. We are grateful for the integral and leading role of the CPUSA in this struggle to end U.S. imperialist aggression in Vietnam.[19]

Le Duan added that he appreciated the Communist Party USA's statement that "the [Communist] victory in Vietnam is our victory."

Earlier, Nguen Huu Tho, head of the Communist Revolutionary South Vietnamese Republic visited Moscow. In commenting on the Communist triumph, he said:

> Victories were won in the first place by the resolute and energetic struggle of our own people determined on freedom and sovereignty, by the effective aid of the socialist countries, *and by the efforts of the world's progressive and peaceful people including those in the United States.*[20] (Emphasis added)

The Red leader gave particular thanks for the Communist victory to the newspapers and journalists...

> ...including those in the United States who have given moral and political aid to our just struggles.[21]

The tragic fall of millions into Communist slavery, starvation and death was not necessary. The Communist triumphs in Southeast Asia were not the result of an inevitable unfolding of a tide of history—the process of historical determinism Karl Marx theorized about. The Communist victories were produced by "dovish", peace-at-any-price congressmen and senators in Washington, by the Red-agitated mobs on college campuses and by the "talking heads" on the evening news shows with their distorted words and news clips from the war front.

NEWS MEDIA AID RED CAUSE

The Moscow statement of the leader of the Vietnamese National Liberation Front expressing "thanks" to the news media and journalists in the United States for their "moral and political aid" had basis in fact.

Journalist Allan Brownfield in a special report, "How Media Bias Distorts Our View of the World"[22] after reviewing media blindness to Communist revolutionaries in China and Cuba years earlier [discussed in Chapters III and VIII], said:

> The mindset of many journalists not only led to the victory of Communists such as Mao and Castro—because they were portrayed in benevolent and false terms—but has made it increasingly difficult for the United States to resist Communist aggression.

> The Vietnam war, many believe, was lost not on the battlefield but on the homefront. The Viet Cong was portrayed in the media not as a Communist army supported and controlled by Ho Chi Minh and the North Vietnamese but as "nationalists" who only wanted a better life and independence...Now, of course, a ruthless tyranny has been inflicted upon Vietnam, hundreds of thousands have fled, and the media is seen to have been completely wrong [again].

Brownfield's charges were supported by the "confession" of one avowedly anti-Vietnam war journalist. William Shawcross spoke at a "Vietnam Reconsidered" conference at the University of Southern California in February 1983. A published report said that Shawcross delivered...

> ...a moving and eloquent confession of the miscalculations that

he and others like him had made about what would happen to Vietnam, Laos, and Cambodia after the Communists took over. He said they never dreamed that Vietnam would maintain the fourth largest army in the world, that it would invade neighboring Cambodia with nearly 200,000 troops, that it would create such harsh conditions that hundreds of thousands of Vietnamese would risk their lives and flee their homeland on small boats.

He didn't anticipate that two or three million gentle Cambodians would perish as a result of the cruel, inhuman rule of the Khmer Rouge, and he recalled how the correspondents in Cambodia had mocked those in the American Embassy who warned them that a Communist victory would produce a horrible bloodbath. They didn't know that North Vietnam would overrun the South, unceremoniously dump the Vietcong leadership, and send tens of thousands to prison and to concentration camps.[23]

The Media Elite by Robert Lichter and Stanley Rothman is a 1986 book which examined the beliefs of those who transformed the American media from reporting the 5W's (who, what, when, where, etc.) to advocacy journalism. Advocacy journalism presents "facts" which advance a particular philosophy or viewpoint. The authors said:

> The current era of more adversarial media-government relations probably dates from 1965, the year American advisors were replaced by regular forces in Vietnam.[24]

CBS Correspondent Morley Safer's report on a Marine unit's 1965 search-and-destroy mission in the village of Cam Ne (an area with heavy Vietcong operations) was cited as an example of the "new journalism." The authors said:

> Safer sent back a dramatic report showing the Marines using their cigarette lighters to ignite the huts of villagers. His story stressed the futility of the operation and the Marine's apparent cruelty. In his "closer" he asserted, "to a Vietnamese peasant whose home means a lifetime of back-breaking labor, it will take more than Presidential promises to convince him we are on his side."[25]

Safer's 1965 report became typical of TV's coverage of the Vietnam war. Such "news" became a major force molding American public attitudes concerning the war and the

American men and boys who were doing the fighting. Lichter
and Rothman quoted David Halberstam in his book, *The
Powers That Be* as saying that Safer's Cam Ne story showed
that...

> ...one correspondent with one cameraman [can] become as impor-
> tant as... twenty senators.[26]

There is also a flood of evidence that news media reporting
of the Communists 1968 TET offensive turned a major
American military victory into a disaster for America and a
propaganda victory for the Reds. (TET was a major holiday-
launched, often suicide-like offensive by over one-million
Communist troops in January and February 1968.) In a 1982
New York Review of Books article, the Vietcong's former
Communist Minister of Justice, Truong Nhu Tang, said:

> TET proved catastrophic to our plans. It cost us half of our forces.
> Our propaganda transformed the military debacle into a brilliant
> victory.[27]

Al Santoli, in his book, *To Bear Any Burden* quoted Truong
Nhu Tang as saying that the Vietcong worked with the
American media and groups opposed to the war...

> ...to weaken the resolve of the American government...the
> American media is open to suggestion and false information given
> by Communist agents. The society is completely hypnotized by
> the media.

Arnaud De Borchgrave, a senior editor of *Newsweek*, gave
important insight on how it was done. De Borchgrave was
assigned to Saigon at the time of the TET offensive in 1968.
In a White House meeting in February 1986, he told how his
reports from Saigon were handled by *Newsweek*. His comments were reported in an account of the meeting published
by Accuracy in Media. De Borchgrave said that...

> ...he had reported to *Newsweek* from Saigon that the Vietcong
> TET offensive had been an unmitigated disaster for them. He said
> that Osborn Elliot, then the editor-in-chief of *Newsweek*, engaged
> in a bit of advocacy journalism and declared that it was the
> consensus of the senior editors of *Newsweek* that we had lost the

war and that we should get out. De Borchgrave said: "My file from Saigon reported just the opposite, and not one word of what I filed got in [to *Newsweek*]. He added that even though he was a senior editor, he had not been consulted and was obviously not part of the alleged consensus of senior editors.[28]

CBS anchorman Walter Cronkite added to the "America was defeated" propaganda with an on-air call for peace negotiations. This plea by the "most trusted and respected" CBS commentator continued the propaganda war which changed the American military victory into a defeat in the minds of people.[29]

In his book, *Why We Were In Vietnam*, Norman Podhoretz adds further insight into the totally slanted and inaccurate picture the American public was given by the TV. He wrote:

In 1968, Jack Fern, a field producer for NBC, suggested to Robert J. Northshield a three-part series showing that TET had indeed been a decisive military victory for America...The idea was rejected because, Northshield said later, TET was already "established in the public's mind as a defeat, and therefore it was an American defeat." From then on the networks to all intent and purposes, had joined the major newspapers and magazine as members of the anti-war movement.[30]

Peter Braestrup was in Saigon at the time as a reporter for the very liberal, very anti-war *Washington Post*. In his 1977 book, *Big Story*, he documented how the American media turned the massive military defeat suffered by the Communists into a political defeat for the United States. He then commented:

Rarely has contemporary-crisis journalism turned out, in retrospect, to have veered so widely from reality. Essentially, the dominant themes of the words and film from Vietnam...added up to a portrait of defeat for the allies. Historians, on the contrary, have concluded that the TET Offensive resulted in a severe military setback for Hanoi in the South. To have portrayed such a setback for one side as a defeat for the other—in a major crisis abroad—cannot be counted as a triumph for American journalism.[31]

The media distortions and the anti-U.S., anti-war mindset of so many journalists was no accident. Arnaud De Borchgrave, then a senior editor of *Newsweek* who later became the editor-in-chief of *The Washington Times*, cited three examples to show the degree of influence the Communists achieved with the American media. He said:

> Throughout the 1960's the North Vietnamese and their Vietcong puppets convinced most of the non-Communist world [through their media] that the South Vietnamese National Liberation Front was an autonomous, independent front that was even hostile to Hanoi at time and that we should be cutting a deal with them.[32]

To support that charge, De Borchgrave quoted the "confession" of French journalist, Jean Lacouture, who said:

> During my trips to Hanoi, during the war, I conducted myself more as a militant than as a journalist, and I deliberately concealed from my readers the Stalinist aspects of that regime of which I was well aware.[33]

De Borchgrave said that Lacouture's admission was significant in that he was a "trailblazer" for such American journalists as *New York Times* writers Anthony Lewis, Harrison Salisbury and Tom Wicker. De Borchgrave then cited the case of Pham Xuan An, who was listed in *Time* magazine's masthead as a "staff correspondent." *After the war he surfaced as a colonel in North Vietnamese intelligence and by 1986 was in the Communist Vietnamese mission to the United Nations.*

The very realistic film, *Hanoi Hilton*, portrayed the years of torture and brutality the North Vietnamese Communists inflicted on American POW's. One scene showed the North Vietnamese officer taunting an American POW with the words:

> What we don't win on the battlefield, your journalists will win for us on your doorstep.[34]

Those in the news media did the job. They created a climate in America which the Communists then exploited to build anti-war sentiment in churches, on the campuses and in Congress. The Vietnamese Communist Party head's words of gratitude quoted earlier "for the integral and leading role of the CPUSA in the struggle to end U.S. imperialist aggression in Vietnam" were not idle chatter. Throughout the war, the CPUSA and its allies and dupes fanned anti-war sentiments and protests. Nearly 100 ROTC buildings on college campuses were bombed or burned. An armed mob took over at Cornell University. The armed revolutionaries who seized control at Cornell were featured on the cover of *Newsweek's* May 5, 1969 *issue*. The headline screamed, *Universities Under The Gun*. The Red-fanned pressures continued to mount. The turning point in public attitude toward Vietnam came with the Kent State tragedy in May 1970.

THE KENT STATE TRAGEDY

Kent State University in north Central Ohio was the site of a major demonstration in May 1970 against the Vietnam War. A group of students were stirred to demonstrate and riot. The Ohio National Guard was called in to keep order. As the culmination of a series of growing confrontations a group of students charged the Guardsmen. Shots were fired and several of the students were killed and others were wounded.

The tragedy and the resultant reactions marked the turning point in the Vietnam War. Within months, President Nixon began the troop withdrawals which ultimately resulted in a complete American withdrawal and the Communist conquest of South Vietnam. Stewart Alsop set the pattern in his *Newsweek* column quoted earlier. Alsop had written:

> President Nixon may...have no choice but to begin withdrawing troops. For the basic weakness in Cabot Lodge's bargaining position here lies in the simple fact that the American people have lost stomach for the war in Vietnam, and the Communists know it. People who have lost stomach for a war in the end generally lose the war. If that happens it will be interesting if perhaps a bit frightening to see how the American people react to their first lost war.[35]

ONE RED PROFESSOR

One college professor played a key role in developing the

pressure which resulted in the tragedy at Kent State. In a real way he was responsible for the Kent State tragedy which robbed America of the victory in Vietnam that 58,000 American boys died trying to win.

The professor's name was Dr. Sidney Jackson. He was a professor of library science at Kent State. He was also the first faculty adviser of the "Kent Committee To End The War In Vietnam." That was the organization which laid the foundation for the protests which ended in the deaths of a number of them—and produced the martyrs the Communists needed to spark nationwide disillusionment with the Vietnam war effort.

Had you called Sidney Jackson a Communist in 1970 you might have been sued—but his Communist Party membership and his role in the Kent State tragedy were made public by the Communists themselves after his death. He died in May 1979. His obituary was published in the *Daily World*, the official Communist newspaper. It said:

> KENT,Ohio, May 15 - Over 350 faculty members, students, unionists and townspeople attended services here for Dr. Sidney L. Jackson, senior professor of library sciences at Kent State University. Dr. Jackson died in his sleep May 7. He was 64 years old. He had been a member of the Communist Party since 1936.[36]

While they are alive and working to gain influential positions in organizations, etc. Communists hide their party membership. Once they die, however, the Party brags about their party affiliation and their activities. Jackson's importance to the Communist Party is pointed up by the top Communist leaders who attended his funeral. The article says:

> Among the speakers were Henry Winston, chairman and Gus Hall, general secretary of the Communist Party USA, and Jim West, Ohio chairman of the CPUSA.[37]

Communists are activists and gain positions of influence in whatever organizations they join because they are willing to accept responsibilities, as the next paragraph shows. The obituary quotes Ohio Communist Party Chairman Jim West as saying that...

> ...Jackson authored many books and over 1000 articles and reviews; had helped organize a faculty union, edited a number of publications and held leading responsibilities in state and national library associations...He was vice president of the Kent State Chapter of the NAACP...[and] *served as the first faculty adviser of the Kent Committee To End The War in Vietnam.*[38] [Emphasis added]

The appearance of America's two top Communists, Hall and Winston, at Jackson's funeral indicates his importance. They were honoring their hero.

Top officials of the college participated in the funeral service with the Communist leaders. Those who joined Gus Hall and other top Communist leaders in paying tribute to the professor whose activities resulted in the deaths of six students included:

> Dr. Herbert Goldsmith, Dean of the KSU University School; Dean A. Robert Rogers, KSU School of Library Science; Dr. Kenneth Calkins, KSU Dept. of History and president of the United Faculty Professional Association; Dr. Dennis Carey, KSU Center for Peaceful Change; Anita Bixsdenstine, KSU Honors and Experimental College; Alvin Jones, Kent NAACP; William Arthrell, student, Kent Committee Against the War in Vietnam; and Greg Rambo, student, May 4th Task Force.[39]

Jackson's work and influence goes on even after his death. A note in the obituary says:

> Miriam R. Jackson, daughter of Dr. Jackson and a peace activist student, had been welcomed home by her father just before he died on her return last Sunday from the Washington demonstration.

The "Washington demonstration" was the May 4, 1979 peace demonstration held in the nation's capital. Professor Jackson had been an adviser to the group which planned the meeting.

Those who refuse to face the Communist danger often point to the relative handful of dues-paying members of the Com-

munist Party in the United States—ten to twenty thousand—
as evidence that the Communists are weak and ineffective.
The record of Dr. Sidney Jackson shows the tremendous and
tragic impact just one Communist has had and can have
through stirring and agitating others to do the Communists
work. At his funeral, Ohio state Communist party chief Jim
West said:

> We in the Communist Party are proud of his membership and his
> life's work.[40]

The official program for the memorial service showed that
West's eulogy of Professor Jackson was followed by the playing of *The Internationale*, the anthem of the world Communist movement.[41]

Jackson's obituary was also published by the Kent, Ohio
Record-Courier, the college's *Daily Kent Stater*, the *Cleveland
Plain Dealer*, and the *Akron Beacon Journal*. None of them
mentioned Jackson's Communist Party membership nor the
participation of top Communists in the small town funeral.[42]

However, the Communists and the news media have made
the results of Jackson's work at Kent State as much a part of
the American vocabulary as *McCarthyism*, the word the
Communists placed in our language to label any form of
anti-communism.** The tragedy at Kent State and the news
media use of it was the turning point in the public's attitude
toward the Vietnam war. The specter of "Kent State" continues to be the banner raised against any proposed efforts
to stop Communist aggression anywhere in the world.

The United States could have ended the war in Southeast
Asia within 30 days at any time during the unfolding of the
eight year struggle. Bombing the dredges which kept the
Haiphong harbor open for Soviet shipping would have ended
the war. Several million lives—both American and Asian—

** The success of the communist effort was demonstrated in June 1989 when
the author conducted a three-day orientation for 160 Alabama high school
students going to the Soviet Union on a summer echange program. Even
though all the students had been born since the May 1970 tragedy, 90%
of them indicated that they were acquainted with the event.

would have been spared. A few well-placed bombs on dikes in North Vietnam would have flooded key areas through which supplies and men were channeled. These targets and most other strategic sites were off-limits for American bombers through most of the war.

The Red plan to destroy the American "will to resist" Communist aggression was exposed six years earlier by the U.S. Senate Preparedness Subcommittee. The committee had warned that the Johnson Administration by "overly restricting" military efforts to win the war in Vietnam could fall into the Communist trap. Recall the words of the committee report which said:

> The enemy strategy is to engage us in a protracted war of attrition which will tax the patience and undermine the determination of the American people to resist...[43]

The warning wasn't heeded. The no-win policies continued and the Communist plan succeeded. Millions died and other millions live in Communist tyranny today.

CHAPTER 19

NO INTERNAL SECURITY

*For among my people are found wicked men: they lay wait,
as he that setteth snares; they set a trap, they catch men.*
                                                        —*Jeremiah 5:26*

NO ONE AWAKENS to the communist threat and the consistent failures of American policy without asking, "Who or what is behind it all?"

Could some of those who make the tragic decisions and implement the wrong programs consistently be communists? Could decision makers be influenced by key advisers who are communists or communist sympathizers? Have high levels of government and positions of public influence and trust been infiltrated again as they were in the 1930's and 1940's?

The answer to those vitally important questions is: We don't know and we can't know. We can't know because the internal security system which once gave the United States a semblance of a defense against communist infiltration and influence has been totally dismantled.

Ralph De Toledano is a syndicated columnist and longtime student of Communist activity in America. His book, *Seeds of Treason*, was the definitive study of the Alger Hiss case. In a July 1986 syndicated column, De Toledano wrote:

> It will come as a shock to most Americans that the United States has no domestic intelligence or security agency.

> The FBI is barred from gathering information on a terrorist group or subversive apparatus until there is what lawyers call a "criminal nexus." In simple English, this means that the FBI cannot investigate or infiltrate a suspected terrorist organization until an act of violence has been committed.[1]

Another syndicated columnist, M. Stanton Evans, supplied

the statistical evidence which put De Toledano's charge into concrete, factual form. In a column titled, "How U.S. Internal Security Was Destroyed," Evans reported:

> The number of domestic security cases under FBI investigation dropped from 24,414 in 1973 to 51 in 1983.[2]

The 24,000 communists and other subversives the FBI was investigating in 1973 did not all get religion, leave the Communist Party or emigrate to Russia by 1983. The FBI was simply forbidden to conduct surveillance or maintain files on their activities unless they had actual proof that a crime had been committed.

The FBI had been effectively hogtied and prevented from fulfilling its longtime mission of safeguarding the internal security of the United States. How did it happen? De Toledano told the readers of his column:

> This situation has existed since 1976, when the late Democratic Senator Frank Church held hearings that pilloried the FBI, CIA and other security agencies. Their crime, in his eyes, was that they were attempting to ferret out terrorist activity before the bombs exploded.
>
> The Church Committee, assisted by the national media, put the kibosh on further information gathering by the FBI, which Mr. Church considered nefarious, ungentlemanly, and unconstitutional. This left the country without a domestic security agency to protect it.[3]

In response to the Church Committee hearings, the so-called "Levi guidelines" (named for President Gerald Ford's attorney general) were issued. The FBI was restricted from conducting surveillance of individuals or groups until a crime had been, or was about to be, committed. Columnist Stan Evans commented:

> Since the point of surveillance is quite often to determine if crimes are *going* to be committed, this, in essence, meant the Bureau had to know the results of an investigation before it could start one.[4]

Evans explained that the situation became so bad, according to official testimony, that the FBI could not maintain a file on a self-professed Communist organization, prone to violence, that had openly published its intention of infiltrating the U.S. military. Since such infiltration would not be a crime in and of itself, it fell outside the Levi guidelines and the FBI had to ignore it. Evans quoted then FBI Director William Webster as saying:

We're practically out of the domestic security field.

Extremely narrow application of the so-called Levi guidelines has also placed serious restrictions on the ability of the FBI to protect U.S. citizens from the actions of international terrorist groups.

Three FBI officials were suspended without pay and three others censured for conducting an "unnecessarily broad" investigation of the Committee in Solidarity with the People of El Salvador (CISPES).[5]

According to independent research studies and State Department documents, CISPES was formed in October 1978 as a result of meetings between...

...representatives of the Marxist Salvadoran rebels, officials of the Communist Party USA, the United States Peace Council (the U.S. affiliate of the Soviet-controlled World Peace Council) and the Cuban Mission to the United Nations.[6]

A year later the FBI investigated allegations that CISPES was supplying money and material to the communist rebels in El Salvador, a violation of domestic security laws. By March 1983 the FBI, in attempting to determine whether CISPES was a front group for international terrorists, started checking activities of 180 local chapters of CISPES. The investigations included surveillance, undercover attendance at CISPES meetings and peace rallies, interviews with organization members and law enforcement agency record checks. Nine groups and 169 individuals were checked before the investigations were stopped by protests from Congress, the ACLU and the media.[7] The FBI officials who attempted to learn the degree to which CISPES was a front group for international terrorists were suspended or censured.

The six FBI officials were disciplined, FBI Director William Sessions, said because...

> ...there was no reason to believe that *all* (Emphasis added) CISPES members nationwide knew of or had any involvement in support of El Salvadoran terrorists.[8]

Consider the long range impact of the suspensions on future decisions of dedicated FBI agents. How the Levi guidelines might be applied or interpreted in the future will hang over every future investigation of possible Communist terrorist activity. A wise agent or supervisor might decide to play it safe and suspend a borderline investigation rather than risk his job. That could result in tragedy in a real terrorist situation.

Sessions went even farther in limiting FBI effectiveness. CISPES sued to force removal of the names of all persons and organizations collected during the investigation from FBI files.. A federal judge dismissed the suit but Sessions then agreed to...

> ...transfer records of the bureau's investigation of the Coalition in Solidarity with the People of El Salvador (CISPES) to the National Archives and Records Administration.[9]

The decision put the records off limits to investigators into the 21st century. Three weeks earlier, the FBI made a similar decision to seal all records collected between 1940 and 1975 in investigations of the National Lawyers Guild.[10] The National Lawyers Guild was described in the Congressional *Guide To Subversive Organizations and Publications* as a Communist front and...

> ...the foremost legal bulwark of the Communist Party, its front organizations, and controlled unions...[which] since its inception has never failed to rally to the legal defense of the Communist Party and individual members thereof, including known espionage agents.[11]

The *Handbook for Americans* published by the U.S. Senate Internal Security Subcommittee said of the National Lawyers Guild:

To defend the cases of Communist lawbreakers, fronts have been devised...Among these organizations are...the National Lawyers Guild. When the Communist Party itself is under fire these offer a bulwark of protection.[12]

In his book, *Covert Cadre,* S. Steven Powell said of the National Lawyers Guild:

Since the 1960s the National Lawyers Guild (NLG) has grown from an association of some five hundred "old Left" lawyers to an organization claiming some five thousand law students, paralegals, and lawyers as active members. Despite the influx of new blood, the policy position remains basically unchanged from the 1950s, when the NLG was cited as a communist front. NLG's International Committee remains aligned with Cuba and Vietnam, and the International Association for Democratic Lawyers, a Soviet front.

At the close of an NLG convention in Austin, Texas in the 1970s delegates sang the "Internationale," [the Communist world revolutionary anthem] which includes: "'Tis the final conflict, let each stand his place. The International Soviet shall be the Human Race!"[13]

There had been no FBI surveillance of the National Lawyers Guild since 1975. It was stopped by the restrictions of the Levi guidelines. The agreement made in 1989 turned even all the old records of the pre-Levi investigations over to the National Archives where they will be sealed until the year 2025. Michael Krinsky, a National Lawyers Guild attorney described the agreement as a victory for the Guild in that it...

...makes sure that the information that the Government had collected for all those years can never be used against it.[14]

The agreements with CISPES and the National Lawyers Guild had an important and questionable precedent. In 1974, the Institute For Policy Studies (IPS), a leftist Washington "think-tank" filed a civil suit against FBI Director Clarence Kelly, Attorney General John Mitchell and a number of other administration officials and FBI agents. The out-of-court settlement agreed to by the Carter Administration five years later was unbelievably broad. It provided immunity from any prosecution resulting from information gathered in any present or past FBI monitoring of IPS activities and a blanket prohibition of any future intelligence gathering on the IPS by the FBI or by any other government agency.

Steven Powell in his authoritative book on the IPS, *Covert Cadre*, said:

> In effect, IPS was given carte blanche to support domestic and foreign parties, movements and governments hostile to the United States. The institute's activities to socialize American society, divide and weaken American alliances, and generally frustrate U.S. foreign policy efforts to contain communism would not be disturbed.[75]

Powell's carefully researched 469-page book, *Covert Cadre*, shows conclusively that this is the IPS agenda. The IPS was incorporated in 1963 by Richard Barnet and Marcus Raskin with grants from leftist sources including the Stern Family Fund and the Samuel Rubin Foundation. Steven Powell's *Covert Cadre* indicates that the Rubin Foundation provided major funding for the IPS.

Rubin, a Russian emigre was a member of the Communist Party. He made his fortune as the founder of the Faberge cosmetic firm which he founded in 1936. He sold the business for $25-million in 1963, the year the IPS was founded.[16] Other funding has come from the Stern Fund, headed by IPS trustee Philip Stern. Stern is a nephew of Alfred Stern who fled to Czechoslovakia in 1958 after being indicted on three counts of spying for the Soviet Union. IPS funding has also come from the Rabinowitz Foundation headed by Victor Rabinowitz. Rabinowitz is a member of the law firm which has represented the Castro government since 1960 and which also defended accused Soviet spies, Judith Coplon and Alger Hiss.[17]

Longtime leaders of the IPS include Sam Rubin's daughter, Cora Rubin Weiss, and her husband, Peter Weiss, chairman of the IPS board of trustees and Saul Landau.

David Horowitz was a leader of the "New Left" radicals in the 1960s. Having since moved away from his earlier leftist commitment, he wrote the introduction for the *Covert Cadre*. He said:

> I was born in 1939 into the same "progressive" generation as the architects of IPS, and in particular, Saul Landau and Cora Weiss, two of its guiding influences who typify the links between the radical generations. My parents (like those of Landau and Weiss) were members of the Communist Party, together with all of our family friends.[18]

Of Landau, who is frequently billed in the media as an IPS Fellow and "expert" on Central America, Horowitz said:

> Saul Landau had begun his political life in the Communist movement and for nearly thirty years has been a collaborator and a supporter of the totalitarian regime in Communist Cuba.[19]

Horowitz said, "The IPS style has aspects that are flexible and disarming...But its substance is defined by the covert agendas that shape its attitudes of unrelenting hostility toward the United States, and solidarity with Soviet-backed regimes."

Powell said that the IPS and its "fellows" and "associates"...

> ...applaud Soviet foreign policy to the extent that it helps Marxist revolutionary movements in Central America, Africa, and the Middle East. In the area of third-world development and modernization IPS is enthusiastic about socialist "solutions" despite socialism's record of perpetuating poverty and underdevelopment in every third-world country where it has been adopted.[20]

> IPS lauds Fidel Castro, and helps raise funds for the Sandinista Communists to consolidate their power in Nicaragua, while, at the same time attacking Central American allies of the United States for their imperfect human rights record.[21]

> ...IPS provides training for radical activists. Many of its fellows have become leaders in other organizations...the disarmament network associated with IPS wages a major campaign against the Strategic Defense Initiative (SDI), which it prefers to call Star Wars.[22]

IPS hopes to "move the Democratic Party's debate internally to the left by creating an invisible presence in the party" to which end Director Borosage praised the 1984 Jesse Jackson presidential campaign.[23]

During the Vietnam War the IPS made an unceasing effort to undermine U.S. policy. Powell wrote:

>...a number of its fellows and associates worked in the league with the communist regime in Hanoi, even as American soldiers were dying in rice paddies and jungles.[24]

Cora Weiss went to North Vietnam at the invitation of the Communist Hanoi government. On her return she reported that American POW's were well treated and housed in "immaculate" facilities. A few weeks later at the request of the North Vietnamese she formed the Committee of Liaison with Families of Servicemen Detained in North Vietnam (COL). The North Vietnamese government made Cora Weiss the channel for mail and messages between POWs and their families. The U.S. House of Representatives Committee on Internal Security [since abolished] declared that COL was...

>...a propaganda tool of the North Vietnamese government, and appeared to be acting as an agent for a foreign power.[25]

The IPS bills itself as a scholarly think tank. But IPS leaders advocate violence. IPS Fellow Karl Hess said that he saw...

>...no alternative but to use violent tactics to destroy the U.S. Government.[26]

Robert Burlingham, an IPS associate fellow, agreed saying, "I do not believe that an equitable, just, free, democratic world order can be achieved any other way but through violence." Powell quoted others with similar views.

Despite its radical background and agenda, the *Washington Post* described IPS as "the first respectable offspring of the New Left." IPS tentacles and influence reach deeply into the membership and staff of the House and Senate. Approximately 80 members of the House of Representatives rarely deviate from IPS positions on legislation. IPS and its associates and trainees have spawned an entire network of organizations which work to influence foreign policy, economics, peace and disarmament, restrict intelligence operations, the media, churches, etc. Powell's book, *Covert Cadre*, does a masterful job of tracing the lines and people of influence who tie the network together and link up with other established organizations such as the National and World Councils of Churches, CISPES, the National Lawyers Guild, etc.

From the record it is understandable why the FBI maintained an interest in developing information about the IPS and its activities and influence. However, with the advent of the Levi guidelines and the out-of-court settlement agreed to by the administration of President Jimmie Carter...

> ...the Federal Bureau of Investigation shall not collect, gather, index, file, maintain, store or disseminate any information regarding the plaintiffs [IPS], their associations, speech or activities...[27]

A whole series of other security-destroying decisions and actions were taken in quick succession during the 1970's. They included:

> Civil Service authorities decided that membership in the Communist party was not a bar to federal employment, even in sensitive positions. The FBI which was supposed to do checks to see if such individuals were connected to revolutionary groups acknowledged in 1979 that it was out of this business also.[28]

> The committees of the House and Senate which investigated communist activity in America were abolished in the mid-1970's.[29] They once had the three-fold responsibility of (1) investigating possible communist influence in areas of public trust, (2) proposing legislation to protect against forces seeking to overthrow the United States and (3) checking on how effectively the executive branch was enforcing statutes against espionage, terrorism or subversion. No Congressional committee functions in these vital areas today.

> The Subversive Activities Control Board was also abolished[30]....the Attorney General stopped compiling and publishing the official list of organizations found to be controlled by Communists and other subversives[31]...and intelligence files maintained by local police agencies were destroyed rather than

give subversives access to them under court decisions and the Freedom of Information Act passed during the period.[32]

Even the CIA was restricted in its efforts to protect itself against infiltration by its Soviet counterparts in the intelligence field. James Jesus Angelton developed and later ran the CIA's counterintelligence section between 1954 and 1973, at a time when counterintelligence—detecting and manipulating enemy spies and agents—played a major role in U.S. intelligence.

Angelton clashed with President Nixon's CIA Director William Colby over policies and programs for safeguarding the CIA against Soviet spies within its ranks. He left the agency in 1974. Within a year after his departure the counterintelligence staff he built was reduced from 300 to 80—during the period when all other government security forces and programs were being slashed or abolished also.[33]

Executive department actions and Supreme Court decisions in the 1950s and 1960s crippled U.S. internal security programs. The actions in the 1970s effectively eliminated them. By October 1987, President Ronald Reagan suggested in a newspaper interview that Communist influence was growing in Congress and the press—and pointed to the absence of any agency to combat the Red menace. The President said:

> Remember there was once a Congress in which they had a committee that would investigate even one of its own members if it was believed that the person had communist involvement or communist leanings. Well, they've done away with those committees. That shows the success of what the Soviets were able to do in this country with making it unfashionable to be anti-communist.[34]

The following day the presidential spokesman, Marlin Fitzwater amplified the President's remarks. Fitzwater told newsmen that Reagan...

> ...believes that the communists, through various disinformation techniques and plans and programs, have influence on the Congress, on the public, on the press, and on everybody.[35]

Even so, Fitzwater said that Reagan was not calling for any new Communist-hunting organizations. If the threat is as widespread as the President indicated why doesn't he and others lead the fight to reestablish the domestic security responsibilities of Congressional Committees, the FBI, and the Justice Department?

Congressional leadership similarly refuses to face the problem. In his column quoted earlier, Ralph De Toledano showed how U.S. internal security was destroyed in the mid-1970s and said:

> What is even more shocking is that Congress, which seems to be more suspicious of our own government than it is of its enemies, is fully aware of this but does nothing.

Those who do attempt to do something are attacked as McCarthyites. A few months before President Reagan turned the spotlight on communist influence in Congress and the media, a coalition of conservative organizations and congressmen protested House Speaker Jim Wright's appointment of Congressman George Crockett as chairman of the House Subcommittee on Western Hemisphere Affairs.

Crockett, a three-term congressman from Michigan, has made no secret of his leftist views. David Horowitz and Peter Collier summarized Crockett's views in a syndicated column.[36] (The two were themselves leaders of the radical "new left" in the 1960's. They now take a firm pro-America, anti-communist position.) Their column said that Crockett....

> ...believes that the Sandinistas are architects of a brave new world in Managua...has consistently supported groups of U.S. radicals sending money to Marxist guerrillas in El Salvador and elsewhere in the region.

> Crockett defended the "peoples' democracies" in Eastern Europe in 1947 when President Truman was establishing a plan to contain Soviet communism...[and] attacked U.S. "imperialism" during the Vietnam War and defended Fidel Castro throughout the 1960s.

> In 1983, when the Soviets shot down Korean Airlines Flight 007 and the House voted 416-0 to condemn the act, Crockett

abstained. In 1985, when U.S. Army Major Arthur Nicholson was shot down in Germany and was denied medical attention for 45 minutes while he bled to death, Crockett defended the Soviet actions on the floor of Congress.[37]

Syndicated columnist Joseph Sobran reported other background on Crockett which the concerned conservatives had revealed at their news conference. Sobran reported that Crockett...

...had sponsored several officially designated Communist-front organizations and had been vice president of the National Lawyers Guild, described by Congressional investigators in the 1950s as "the foremost legal bulwark of the Communist Party." The lawyers guild president under whom Crockett served was an overt communist.

In 1949 Crockett represented 11 Communist Party leaders charged with conspiring to overthrow the U.S. government by force. In his closing charge to the jury Crocket said, "For the record, the Communist Party is, in truth and in fact, the conscience of America." Crockett's Communist clients were convicted and Crockett himself served four months in prison for contempt of court.[38]

Crockett's background was cited by conservatives at a news conference as their basis for opposing Jim Wright's appointment of Crockett to a crucial foreign policy chairmanship. (In the post, Crockett would be overseeing U.S. actions to stop the spread of communism in the Western Hemisphere—one of the positions to which Oliver North was required by Congress to report his activities.)

When the spokesman for the conservative coalition finished summarizing Crockett's long record of support for communist causes, the questions from the press had nothing to do with Crockett's record. Rather they challenged the right to raise the issues of Crockett's background at all. Horowitz and Collier in their column[40] reported the facts and commented:

A reporter from *Newsweek* spoke for his colleagues when he said, "Isn't this McCarthyism?" The mention of the word, *McCarthyism*, meant the discussion was over.

It was a symptomatic episode that suggests the degree to which the issues of divided loyalties and political subversion, once central concerns of this country's politics, have become taboo....using terms like "communist" or "fellow traveler" are considered bad form these days. Some people may be friendly to communist totalitarianism; but to raise the issue is to commit an even worse offense. It is to be guilty of *McCarthyism*.

McCarthyism has become an aggressive term used to stifle discussion and establish left-wing orthodoxy. A "McCarthyite" is no longer narrowly defined as someone engaged in character assassination and reckless disregard for due process. It is usually someone who is an anti-communist....A charge of "McCarthyism" is thus a way of invoking cloture on what should be an important debate; a way of ruling a critical subject [whether an individual has Communist affiliations or sympathies] off limits.

Congressman Crockett's long record of support for Communist causes (although not pertinent or usable by today's liberal standards) was collected by various security agencies. These agencies have either been abolished or are no longer permitted to collect such information in the domestic security field. Therefore official information on the backgrounds and activities of individuals, under perhaps age 40, which would point to Communist sympathies or affiliations are no longer available.

So it is impossible to answer the important question, "Could the long record of disastrous decisions and actions by the U.S. government in relations with the Soviet Union result from the influence of actual Communist or other security risks?"

If America, her people and her leaders are to be protected from the influence of the Communist Party and its agents several steps are needed:

The FBI must again be given authority to maintain surveillance of Communist and other subversive or terrorist organizations which threaten the internal security of the United States and to report to the President, the Congress and the people on their activties.

Both houses of Congress must re-establish committees with

adequate staff and financing to (1) hold hearings and collect information on the activties of organizations which advocate the overthrow of the government of the United States, (2) determine if the Executive branch is enforcing existing security laws and programs properly and (3) recommend any additional legislation needed to meet the threats posed to the security of the United States by subversive organizations.

Effective measures must be instituted to prevent employment of those who by reason of personal habits, attitudes, actions or associations could pose a threat to the security of the United States.

The Freedom of Information measures instituted by Congress and the courts in the mid-1970s which opened raw files on security matters to communists, the media and others must be reevaluated to guarantee the integrity of the security system.

Before such a rebuilding of America's domestic security system can be undertaken the philosophic makeup of Congress must be changed by the voters of the nation.

CHAPTER 20

WHY DO OUR LEADERS BETRAY US?

...for the wisdom of their wise men shall perish, and the understanding of their prudent men shall be hid.

—Isaiah 29:14b

FOR OVER 40 YEARS nearly all decisions made by the United States concerning Communist nations and all the actions taken against the Communist threat have resulted in Communist victories.

The dismal record prompts the question: Why? Why have America's leaders consistently fought communism with one hand while aiding it economically, diplomatically, psychologically and militarily with the other?

Enough Americans were asking that question in the early 1960s that Dean Rusk, Secretary of State under Presidents Kennedy and Johnson, tried to give an answer. His explanation is the key to understanding American foreign policy for the last forty years. In a speech entitled, "Why We Treat Different Communist Countries Differently,"[1] Rusk said:

> We are asked how we can object to other free countries selling goods to Cuba when we are willing to sell wheat to the Soviet Union. We are asked why we refuse to recognize Peiping when we recognize the Soviet Union....We are asked why we enter into cultural exchange agreements, or a test ban treaty, with a government whose leader has continued to boast that he will "bury" us.
>
> If Communists as a group have as their aim the destruction of our way of life, how is it that we can treat one Communist country differently from another? And why do we enter into an agreement or understanding with a Communist government over one matter, while accepting the hard necessity of continued hostility and conflict over other matters?

In other words, "Why do we fight them with one hand and aid them with the other?" Rusk's 4000-word answer is summed up in a few sentences from this key speech:

> Within the Soviet bloc the Stalinist terror has been radically changed. And within the Soviet Union, as well as most of the smaller Communist nations, there are signs, small but varied and persistent signs, of yearnings for freedom...it is our policy to do what we can to encourage *evolution* [Emphasis added] in the Communist world toward national independence and open societies...to promote trends within the Communist world which lead away from imperialism, away from dictatorships—and toward independence and open societies with freely chosen governments, with which we can live in enduring friendship.

The hope, as expressed by Rusk, was that communism would "evolve" and "mellow" if not threatened by the west. This was the theory upon which Franklin Roosevelt was induced to give Stalin's armies occupation rights and therefore working control over a dozen Eastern European countries following the Yalta conference.

Stalin, of course, did not mellow nor grant the promised elections to Eastern Europe. Instead, the yoke of Communist dictatorship was placed on them. Even so, the theory that communism would eventually "evolve" and "mellow" into some sort of open society with which America could live peaceably became the basis for American foreign policy in 1946. It remained so in 1964 as Dean Rusk speech shows—and it was still the basis of American foreign policy as the decade of the 1980's ended.

The detailed examination of the history and philosophy of the "mellowing theory" which follows is essential to comprehending the consistent failures of American foreign policy since World War II—and the Reagan-Bush pronouncements in the late 1980s that communism had changed and was no longer "an evil empire."

Arthur Schlesinger, Jr., historian and special assistant to Presidents Kennedy and Johnson, was perhaps the first liberal spokesman to write about the "mellowing" theory for public consumption. Portions of his article from the May-June

1947 issue of *Partisan Review* were quoted in Chapters IV, X, XII, and XIII. In addition, Schlesinger said:

> The United States must maintain a precarious balance between a complete readiness to repel Soviet aggression *beyond a certain limit* and complete determination to demonstrate within this limit no aggressive intentions toward the USSR...*At the same time, the U.S. must not succumb to demands for an anti-Soviet crusade nor permit reactionaries in the buffer states to precipitate conflicts in defense of their own obsolete prerogatives.* (Emphasis added)

> ...Given sufficient time, the Soviet internal tempo will slow down. The ruling class will become less risk-minded, more security-minded. Greater vested interests will develop in the existing order. Russia itself will begin to fear the revolutionary tendencies which modern war trails in its wake....At the same time, U.S. backing to the parties of the [Socialist] non-Communist left and U.S. support for vast programs of economic reconstruction may go far toward removing the conditions of want, hunger and economic security which are constant invitations to Soviet expansion.[2]

Schlesinger was here advancing the theory on which American foreign policy has been based since. The dream has been that if communism were to be "contained" within its borders long enough it would eventually "mellow" and "evolve" and give up the goal of world domination—particularly if the Communists see that the rest of the world is achieving Marx's goal of world socialism through peaceable means. Schlesinger words from Chapter XIII also bear repeating. He said:

> Can the United States conceive and initiate so subtle a policy? Though the secret has been kept pretty much from the readers of the liberal press, the State Department has been proceeding for some time somewhat along these lines. Both Brynes and Marshall have perceived the need to be firm without making unlimited commitments to an anti-Soviet crusade, to invoke power to counter power without engaging in senseless intimidation, to encourage the growth of the democratic left. The performance has often fallen below its conception but the direction has been correct. Men like Ben Cohen, Dean Acheson, and Charles Bohlen

have tried to work out the details and whip up support for this admittedly risky policy.[3]

During the 40 years that this "admittedly risky program" of *containment rather than victory* had been the basis for American foreign policy, nearly 1.8-billion people have gone behind the Iron and Bamboo curtains. Nearly 40 countries have been swallowed up. Over 100,000 Americans died in Korea and Vietnam trying to "contain" communism while being forbidden to defeat it. The State Department has continued to cling to the theory and blind hope that communism will "evolve" and "mellow" down through the years in spite of the millions of deaths and other tragic failures.

In 1989 President George Bush became the first American president to acknowledge openly that containment rather than victory over communism had been and continued to be was the goal of American foreign policy. In his May 12, 1989 speech at Texas A & M University Mr. Bush said:

Wise men—Truman and Eisenhower, Vandenberg and Rayburn—Marshall, Acheson and Kennan—crafted the strategy of containment. They believed that the Soviet Union, denied the easy course of expansion, would turn inward and address the contradictions of its inefficient, repressive and inhumane system. And they were right...Containment worked...and now, it is time to move beyond containment to a new policy for the 1990s.

...the United States now has as its goal much more than simply containing Soviet expansionism. We seek the integration of the Soviet Union into the community of nations...our objective is to welcome the Soviet Union back into the world order.

We hope to move beyond containment...Western policies must encourage the *evolution* [Emphasis added] of the Soviet Union toward an open society...and achieve a lasting political pluralism and respect for human rights.[4]

The President closed his speech by promising to work with Congress to grant the Soviet Union a "Most Favored Nation Trade Status." A few days later he gave a similar message at the Coast Guard Academy graduation. He said:

The grand strategy of the West during the post-war period has been based on the concept of containment: checking the Soviet's expansionist aims, in the hope that the Soviet system itself would one day be forced to confront its internal contradictions. The ferment in the Soviet Union today affirms the wisdom of this strategy. And now we have a precious opportunity to move beyond containment...Our goal—integrating the Soviet Union into the community of nations—is every bit as ambitious as containment was at its time.

Mr. Bush's hopes were based on his evaluation of the world scene. He told the Coast Guard Academy graduates:

We live in a time when we are witnessing the end of an idea—the final chapter of the communist experiment. Communism is now recognized—even by many within the Communist world itself— as a failed system—one that promised economic prosperity but failed to deliver the goods, a system that built a wall between the people and their political aspirations...and even as we speak today, the world is transfixed by the dramatic events in Tiananmen Square. Everywhere those voices are speaking the language of democracy and freedom, and we hear them and the world hears them, and America will do all it can to encourage them.

Within two weeks after the President recited communism's obituary in this speech, the Chinese Communists crushed the freedom seekers in Tinanamen Square. As many as three to five thousand students were murdered. The United States issued some words of protest which were followed by business as usual with the Red murderers.

President Bush's repeated pronouncements in May 1989 that "containment has worked" were typical of the judgment of most foreign policy "experts" for 40 years. In fact, the man who claimed to have been the architect of the policy of containing communism until it mellowed has said repeatedly that his dreams have been realized.

George Kennan, who has served as a U.S. ambassador in various Communist capitals, testified before the Senate Foreign Relations Committee on January 20, 1967. Kennan reviewed his 40 years of experience as a professional diplomat dealing with communism. He recalled his role as architect of the "containment policy" after World War II and said the program was based on...

> ...a confidence that the Soviet Union would undergo changes that would permit easier relations with Moscow.[5]

Kennan claimed that the early hopes for a "mellowing" in the Soviet Union had been realized. He said...

> ...these changes have come. They are, in my earnest opinion, of such a nature to give us, for the first time since perhaps 1917, real and hopeful possibilities for the adjustment by peaceful means of our relations with certain of these Communist countries, particularly the Soviet Union.[6]

As Kennan was giving his testimony in 1967, Soviet-supplied missiles, jet airplanes, machine guns, etc. were killing and wounding Americans at a rate of nearly 1000 per week in Vietnam!

Two weeks before Kennan testified, President Johnson told Congress the same story. In the 1967 state of the Union message, Johnson said:

> As the first postwar generation gives way to the second, we are in the midst of a great transition from narrow nationalism to international partnership; from the harsh spirit of the cold war to the hopeful spirit of common humanity on a troubled and threatened planet...

> We are shaping a new future of enlarged partnership in nuclear affairs, in economic and technological cooperation, in political consultation, and in working together with the governments and people of Eastern Europe and the Soviet Union.[7]

American leaders had been issuing such hopeful statements about "meaningful changes" in the Soviet Union for nearly 20 years when Johnson spoke, but the Communists were still holding boldly to their goals of world domination. Their role in Vietnam said so. Their words said so. But America's leaders never seemed to notice. On June 25, 1967 President Johnson and Soviet Premier Alexi N. Kosygin met at Glassboro, N.J. for "peace talks." At the conclusion of their meeting President Johnson told the press and people of the world...

> ...it is fair to say the summit has made the world a little less dangerous...he [Kosygin] and I agreed we wanted a world of peace for our grandchildren.[8]

Both men were telling the truth—but they were each using their own definition of the world peace. Johnson's concept of peace was a world in which nations could live together in cooperation. Kosygin also had a sincere desire for his grandchildren to live in a world of peace. Kosygin's peace, however, was the "peace" defined in the Communist dictionary. For a Communist the word "peace" means "an absence of all opposition to communism."

That this was Kosygin's definition and desire can be demonstrated. While the Soviet leader and President Johnson were meeting in New Jersey, the Communist Party of the Soviet Union was releasing its proclamation in Moscow commemorating the 50th anniversary of the Russian Revolution. It said:

> The experience of the 50 post revolution years has borne out the conclusion of revolutionary theory that capitalism is doomed...

> Imperialism, notably U.S. imperialism, was and continues to be the main enemy of the National Liberation movements.

> The successes of socialism have consistently demonstrated that the working classes ultimate aims can be achieved only through a radical reorganization of society. At the same time history has proved the futility of the reformist way.[9]

In this statement the Communists announced to the world that (1) they were still planning to destroy capitalism and enslave mankind, (2) that the United States was the main obstacle between them and world domination, and (3) that communism must be established by radical revolutionary means rather than through gradual reforms.

The tactic of quickly following a smiling propaganda appeal to the world with a hardline "we haven't changed and we're not going to" statement to party members is a consistent

Communist practice. It is a strategy for (1) mocking the west's leaders and media, while (2) insuring that Party members are not misled by the smiling propaganda campaigns.

Gorbachev's widely-heralded book, *Perestroika*, has three prime examples of the technique in action. The first two examples were discussed in the introductory chapter of this book. They include (1) the release of *Perestroika* editions which had greatly differing introductions in the west and behind the Iron Curtain and (2) the wealth of statements in the body of the book reassuring the Communist reader that "...Perestroika is closely connected with socialism [communism] as a system...and those in the West who expect us to give up socialism [communism] will be disappointed."

The Communist reader of *Perestroika* understands that Gorbachev, by such statements, is recommitting himself and the Red system to world conquest. Under Marxist-Leninist doctrine it is impossible to even conceive of achieving full socialism and the eventual Communist state until every influence of the diseased bourgeoisie class is eliminated from the world.

For the Communist reader, Gorbachev's book contradicted in a very significant and important way the reassuring message drawn from the book by Western leaders and media.

There is a third and even more significant way in which Gorbachev insures that Communist readers will not misinterpret "perestroika." In his book Gorbachev traces the beginnings of "perestroika" and "glasnost" to actions of the March and April 1985 Plenary meetings of the Central Committee of the Communist Party of the Soviet Union. He then emphasizes that *the perestroika concept was ratified by the 27th Congress of the Communist Party of the Soviet Union held in Moscow February 25- March 6, 1986.*[10]

This is *very* significant in that the same Party congress which ratified perestroika *also issued strongly worded, vicious denunciations of the United States as an imperialist aggressor destined for defeat.* Careful examination of the CPSU Congress pronouncements dash hopes for perestroika and give important insights into Communist dialectical thinking. The CPSU Congress statements condemning the United States filled 11 pages in *International Affairs,* an official Communist journal. The Party statement said that...

> ...the U. S. imperialist bourgeoisie is bent on blocking humanity's progressive development...is a growing threat to the very existence of mankind...is relying more and more on openly terrorist and tyrannical regimes...[and] methods of strategy and violence which were characteristic of Nazi Germany...State terrorism is the practical reflection of the USA's misanthropic policy and ideology on the international scene.[11]

The Communist reader would understand the charge that U.S. imperialists are "blocking humanity's progressive development" to mean that the U.S. stands in the way of what Communists believe is the inevitable, *historically determined* "progress" of the world toward communism. The Congress condemned the United States for attempting "to resolve in favour of imperialism the historical dispute with socialism worldwide." It then proclaimed:

> A reality of our time is the existence of two opposite social and political systems—the socialist and the capitalist, with the future belonging to the former and the latter being outdated and condemned by history itself...imperialism, US imperialism primarily, tries to slow down humanity's advance as if giving all peoples and states an ultimatum: either submit to foreign diktat or be plunged into a nuclear holocaust.[12]

These statements are all made within the framework and context of traditional Marxist-Leninist teaching. They expound the socialist dialectical "truth" that the world is divided into two warring classes with the victory assured to the socialist camp by the inevitable progress of history. That is a foundational premise of Marxism-Leninism. The Congress reiterates the teachings of Marx and Lenin that "progress" to socialism and communism will be resisted by the bourgeoisie and its dying capitalism. The CPSU Congress statements ridiculed U.S. opposition to the advancement of socialism worldwide as futile, saying:

What can be said about this behaviour on the part of the US

imperialist bourgeoisie? First of all, no one can render invalid the laws of social development discovered by the founders of scientific communism; they have been operating independent of people's will and desire, whatever Washington may think...[13]

The destiny of peace and progress and the destiny of humanity are now closely bound up within world socialism...[U.S.] imperialism is parasitical, decaying, and moribund capitalism...As a system of exploitation and oppression, capitalism is doomed, but it does not follow from this that it will sink into oblivion without fierce resistance, using all means fair and foul, including the latest weapons.[14]

Socialism has become a powerful force blocking the way of imperialist reaction, which it opposes not only with peaceloving Leninist policy but also with its real military and political might.[15]

The statement of the 27th Party Congress statement couples the "peaceloving Leninist policy" with "real [Communist] military and political might."

The "peaceloving Leninist policy" which socialism uses to counter free world resistance to Communist advances includes the formation of peace fronts worldwide. The Communists and their sympathizers and dupes agitate and work for "peace" which the Communists understand to be the end of all opposition to communism. Soviet military power becomes more and more threatening and deadly as the West under pressure from the "peace" forces disarms or limits its arms buildup.

Tragically, America's leaders seem deaf to repeated official Soviet reaffirmations of their dedication to the cause of world revolution—just as they also seem blind to every evidence whether in Vietnam, Nicaragua, Angola, Afghanistan, Southern Africa, China, etc. that communism has neither been "contained" or "mellowed". Instead, for 40 years they have regularly insisted that "communism isn't all bad"—or if it was "all bad" that it is now "changing."

For example, when world leaders gathered for the funeral of India's Premier Shastri in early 1966, Vice President Hubert Humphrey had a 90-minute conference with Kosygin,

who had just come to power in the Soviet Union. On his return
to the U.S. Humphrey gave the nation a TV report on the
conference. He described the Soviet leader as...

...frank, candid, polite, and reasonable.[16]

Humphrey said that he was convinced on the basis of his
talk with the Soviet leader that in the years to come...

...contacts between ourselves and the Soviet Union will expand
and improve because of our mutual interests.

Two days before Humphrey gave this reassuring report to
the American people on the *Face The Nation* TV program,
Kosygin's government in Moscow announced stepped up shipments of arms and aid to Vietnam to repel the "American
aggressors."[17]

One week later, Averill Harriman finished a 22-day, 12-na-
tion peace tour for President Johnson. TV newsmen asked
him how Soviet leaders felt about the war in Vietnam. Harriman, supposedly the State Department's top expert on the
Kremlin, replied that the Russians were...

...embarrassed by that war. They don't like it and they would like
to see it stopped.[18]

If Soviet leaders really wanted the war ended, why didn't
they stop shipping the guns, ammunition, missiles and MIG's
to North Vietnam which kept the war going?

SIMILAR CONGRESSIONAL BLINDNESS

Leaders of Congress have consistently demonstrated the
same blind refusal to see the Communists as enemies. On
July 1, 1965, at the end of 10-day state visit to Moscow, the
Yugoslav dictator, Tito, joined with Soviet President Anastas
I. Mikoyan in pledging "all necessary aid to North Vietnam."[19] Tito had also accused the U.S. with conducting a
campaign of "mass murder" against civilians in Vietnam.[20]
He regularly denounced America even though he had been
given over $3-billion in American aid since the end of World
War II. Even so, America's leaders refused to recognize Tito's
allegiance to the world Communist movement.

Three weeks after Tito lined up openly with the Viet Cong in their fight against America, Senator William Fulbright, then chairman of the Senate Foreign Relations Committee, made a major speech in which he announced that Yugoslavia was...

> ...a nation which is for most important purposes friendly, and certainly not hostile, toward the United States...

> On the whole their policies neither harm their neighbors nor threaten American interests...it [Yugoslavia] has proven itself a reliable and stalwart associate in the advancement of certain interests on which our interests coincide.[21]

Tito might have been "neutral" in the cold war in Senator Fulbright's eye—but three weeks earlier in Moscow he made it plain that he was on the Communist side in the hot war in Vietnam.

Senator Fulbright's judgment of Communists and communism hasn't changed or improved as the years have passed. After Chinese Communist leader Deng Xiaoping approved the brutal killing of several thousand student protesters in the massacre in Beijing's Tiananmen Square in June 1989 Fulbright said of Deng:

> He is a good man. He just lost his patience.[22]

Fulbright has never seemed able to find anything bad to say about a Communist. Henry Kissinger, Nixon's Secretary of State and perennial "expert" for the media during every foreign policy crisis, displayed an almost unbelievable callousness toward those who died in the China massacre. ABC's Peter Jennings looked to Kissinger for comments when the student demonstrators were crushed in June 1989. Jennings asked, "What should America do? Should the U.S. impose military sanctions—cut off military aid? Kissinger replied, "I wouldn't do any sanctions," and stressed the importance of maintaining an unchanged relationship between the U.S. and the Chinese. A month later Kissinger's column for the *Los Angeles Times* praised the Chinese leader Deng Xiaoping for his economic reforms and added:

No government in the world would have tolerated having the main square of its capital occupied for eight weeks.

The *Wall Street Journal* in its September 15, 1989 issue reported Kissinger's attitudes and words over the several month period and then revealed:

Most TV viewers and readers of his column probably don't know that Mr. Kissinger has unique business ties to the Deng regime—connections that had him on the verge of earnings hundreds of thousands of dollars from a limited partnership set up to engage in joint business dealings with a ministry of the Chinese government. The arrangement is legal and, in itself, proper. Nonetheless, it has elicited criticism.

The *Wall Street Journal* quoted Kissinger as saying that he finds the controversy over his activities and views "painful" and "outrageous."

The "blindness" with which Senator Fulbright was and is afflicted and the callousness Kissinger displays towards Red murderers has permeated the bureaucracy in Washington for decades. Within six months after Tito, the Communist dictator of Yugoslavia, lined up publicly with the Communists in the Vietnam war, the Johnson Administration...

...sold Tito 700,000 tons of American wheat, 92,000 bales of cotton, and 25,000 tons of food oil——all on a ten-year easy credit payment plan.[23]

...loaned the Yugoslav dictator $175-million to shore up his economy and finance purchase of $40-million worth of industrial machinery and equipment including the Communist nation's third nuclear reactor.[24]

...described U.S.-Yugoslav relations as the best in five years.[25]

REPUBLICAN BLINDNESS ALSO

Republicans show a similar blindness. After Dwight Eisenhower concluded his eight years in the White House, he was interviewed by the magazine, *U.S. News & World Report*. Eisenhower was asked his impressions of Nikita Khrushchev. The former president replied...

...Khrushchev is not another Hitler. Hitler was all black; Khrushchev is not. The Russian has a sense of humor and gives all evidence of being a family man. He likes children and has a faculty for making them like him.[26]

Hitler was charged with killing 6-million people. Khrushchev, whether he liked children or not, was responsible for the deaths of over 10-million human beings. He was Stalin's chief hangman in the purge trials in 1936. He butchered Budapest in 1956.[27]

Why, then, couldn't Eisenhower see that Khrushchev was every bit as evil as Hitler? Why did President Johnson talk of a "new partnership" and "economic and political cooperation with the Soviet Union" even as they stepped up shipments of the arms used to kill Americans in Vietnam? How could an experienced diplomat, George Kennan, tell Congress that communism was "contained" and that it had "mellowed" during the years when the Reds were enslaving 1.8-billion people and killing millions of others?

How could Kennan as an "experienced diplomat" fail to learn from experience. In 1989 Kennan, in receiving a $25,000 award from the *Encyclopedia Britannica*, said that...

...U. S. misinterpretation of Soviet policy had led to decades of fighting "imaginary wars against an imaginary adversary." Kennan added that if the United States "had not over- militarized, the whole concept of our relationship with the Soviet Union—what has happened in the last three or four years—might well have happened 20 or 30 years ago."[28]

A few months later, President George Bush honored George Kennan by presenting him with the coveted *Medal of Freedom* in a White House ceremony. Why?

Why did President Reagan conclude that the Soviets were no longer "an evil empire?" He made that pronouncement to the nation and proclaimed that the Reds had given up their goal of world communism within 30 days after Gorbachev told the Supreme Soviet:

We are moving towards a new world, the world of communism. We shall never turn off that road![29]

How can supposedly intelligent men—presidents, leaders

of Congress and the media—all seem so blind? Why do they look at the smiles of Communist leaders and ignore the Reds officially published words *and actions* which consistently contradict the smiling propaganda?

Why have America's leaders, clinging to the blind hope that communism had "evolved" and "mellowed," continued to fight communism with one hand while aiding it economically, diplomatically, psychologically and militarily with the other?

Could some of those who make the tragic decisions and implement the wrong programs consistently be Communists? Or are the decision makers influenced by key advisers who are Communists or Communist sympathizers? Have high levels of government and positions of public influence and trust been infiltrated again as they were in the 1930s and 1940s?

The answer to that vitally important question as shown in the previous chapter is: We don't know and we can't know. We can't know because the internal security system which once gave the United States a semblance of a defense against Communist infiltration and influence has been totally dismantled.[30]

However, no one awakens to the Communist threat and the consistent failures of American policy without asking, "Who or what is behind it all?" Some ask, "Could it all be the result of some gigantic conspiracy?" One scholar in examining that question looked to the words of Thomas Jefferson. Our third president once said:

> Single acts of tyranny may be ascribed to the accidental opinion of a day; but a series of oppressions, begun at a distinguished period, and pursued unalterably through every change of ministers, too plainly prove a deliberate systematical plan of reducing us to slavery.[31]

The existence of conspiracies and other forces which shape, influence or control world events to some degree cannot be denied. Among these forces, which overlap and interlock, are several discussed earlier including the Communists, the international socialists (Fabians), and the Council on Foreign Relations (CFR). CFR influence in the Eisenhower and Kennedy Administrations discussed earlier continued to grow through the Nixon, Ford and Carter presidencies and reached a new high during the Reagan and Bush administrations.[32]

After his 1980 election, Reagan's transition team—the group that selected the key personnel for his administration—had 28 CFR men. From their recommendations, Reagan appointed 80 CFR members to key posts.

By June 1987, the CFR claimed that 318 of its members were serving as U.S. government officials.[33] Heading the list was Secretary of State George Pratt Schultz, a director of the CFR and a member of the Pratt family (Standard Oil fortune) which donated Pratt House, the New York headquarters of the CFR.[34]

George Bush continued the pattern. Shortly after the election, he named Brent Scowcroft, a retired Air Force general as his national security adviser. The news story on the appointment said:

> Scowcroft is known for his pragmatism and moderation rather than as an ideologue. He has long been Bush's friend, and the two worked closely together when Scowcroft was national security adviser to President Gerald R. Ford and Bush was director of the Central Intelligence Agency.[35]

Appointment of CFR member Scowcroft (a moderate pragmatist and no ideologue) caused deep concern among informed anti-Communist observers. Arnold Beichman is a Hoover Institute research fellow and nationally-syndicated columnist. He revealed that Scowcroft along with Henry Kissinger stopped President Ford from receiving the Russian author and anti-Communist hero Alexander Solzhenitsyn at the White House or even attending a dinner honoring Solzhenitsyn sponsored by George Meany, then the president of the AFL-CIO.[36] The Kissinger-Scowcroft memorandum which dissuaded President Ford from honoring the anti-Communist survivor of a Soviet slave labor camp said:

> The Soviets would probably take White House participation in this affair as either a deliberate negative signal or a sign of administration weakness in the face of domestic anti-Soviet pres-

sures. We recommend that the invitation to the president be declined and that no White House officials participate...

During Solzhenitsyn's Washington visit another problem may arise: Pressure may be generated by Meany, members of Congress or others for the president to receive Solzhenitsyn in the White House. He is a Nobel prize winner, he is widely admired in the United States and the Senate has passed a resolution granting him honorary United States citizenship (if the House follows suit he would be the only person except Churchill so honored)...The arguments against such a meeting are as compelling as those against accepting the banquet invitation, but more difficult to defend publicly.[37]

Beichman published what he described as additional "sickening sentences" from the memorandum. The "sickening" Kissinger-Scowcroft words were:

Solzhenitsyn is a notable writer; but his political views are an embarrassment even to his fellow dissidents. Not only would a meeting with the president offend the Soviets but...such a meeting would lend weight to his political views as opposed to his literary talents.[38]

What Solzhenitsyn political views embarrassed his fellow dissidents? What Solzhenitsyn political views did Kissinger and Scowcroft want President Ford to avoid endorsing?

Solzhenitsyn believes in God and is unalterably opposed to communism *as a system*. His "fellow dissidents" like Andre Sakharov, for example, continue to be atheists and Communists. Their "dissent" is not against communism as a system but rather against practices by Soviet leaders which corrupt the "good" system and give it a bad name.

The Kissinger-Scowcroft memorandum reveals and confirms in a "sickening" way that the Kennan policies which Arthur Schlesinger revealed in 1947 have continued to be the controlling philosophy in U.S. foreign policy. Whoever has been President, CFR advisers have insured that...

The United States must maintain a precarious balance between a complete readiness of repel Soviet aggression *beyond a certain limit* and complete determination to demonstrate within this limit no aggressive intentions toward the USSR...*At the same time, the U.S. must not succumb to demands for an anti-Soviet crusade nor permit reactionaries in the buffer states to precipitate conflicts in defense of their own obsolete prerogatives.*[39] (Emphasis added)

Acting on the Kissinger-Scowcroft (CFR) reasoning, the House Judiciary Committee killed the resolution granting honorary citizenship to Solzhenitsyn. He was never invited to the White House by Ford, Carter or Reagan. Scowcroft used similar reasoning in convincing President George Bush to veto a bill which granted extended stays or asylum in the United States for students from Red China. The students would be in danger if they returned to China because they were openly involved in the protests in support of the Tiananmen Square demonstrations. Scowcroft argued that if Bush signed the measure it would offend the Chinese government.[40] [For a more detailed look at the CFR/Trilaterialist influence in the Carter/Reagan/Bush administrations, see *The Shadows of Power* by James Perloff.]

Other "conspiracies" or forces influencing world events include David Rockefeller's Trilateral Commission, the Bilderbergers, the international banking interests, the working coalition of the world's liberal religionists (the World and National Council of Churches, Vatican II Catholics, theologically-liberal Jewish groups, etc.), the amalgamation of world crime forces, the New Age coalitions and possibly a world network of homosexuals which exerts tremendous influence in government, the media, entertainment, etc.

Generally these forces share goals for some type of one-world government and economic system. A degree of cooperation exists between the forces and each is probably certain that its people will gain ultimate control.

Individually and collectively the Communists, the CFR, the Trilateralists and the other forces are real and powerful. However, it is unrealistic to believe that all the presidents, cabinet officers, business leaders and media people with influence or "final say" over the tragically flawed trade policies, treaties or no-win restrictions on military actions could be knowing collaborators in a gigantic conspiracy to merge the United States into a one-world socialist system.

That being true, why then have America's leaders consistently fought communism with one hand while aiding it economically, diplomatically and militarily with the other hand for over seventy years?

Why do so many American leaders, diplomats, legislators, educators, clergy and media people cling to the "evolving" and "mellowing" theories when the Communists own words and actions disprove their validity? Why do so many Americans have a "will to disbelieve the horrible" which former UN Ambassador Jeane Kirkpatrick says can destroy America?

It is the result of a gigantic "conspiracy"—but it is a "conspiracy of shared values." The seeming inability or unwillingness of so many to face the unpleasant truth about the Communists and the tragic sequence of world events stems from their philosophic foundations. The dominant philosophic precepts of higher education for half a century have produced a people who share a "faith" that enables them to believe that communism will "evolve" and act responsibly. The key to understanding the blindness is seeing that government leaders, the press, educators, etc. appear to be functioning as part of a gigantic conspiracy not because they are all under a centralized discipline or control but because they share the same foundational philosophy and beliefs.

The author's training at Penn State in the years after World War II was probably somewhat typical of that received by millions of Americans who are part of the "conspiracy of shared values." Penn State was not the most liberal school in the land at the time, but...

...philosophy classes exposed students to logic which denied God or questioned His existence. In most other classes God was not denied, He was just ignored.

The existence of absolutes of right and wrong was denied or questioned. All things were seen as relative. Life's big issues were not black or white but shades of gray which varied with circumstances.

There being no all-powerful Creator, science and sociology taught that man was the most advanced product of evolution. Man, through coping with his varying physical environment, was continually evolving into an ever higher and better form of life. Psychology classes taught similarly that man's behavior was primarily determined by his emotional and educational environment. *This being "true," changing an individual's environment would change his behaviour.*

The one required history course for engineering students was *The Economic History of the United States*. The thesis was that...

...the people and events of history are *economically determined* by the prevailing economic system. The history class laid the foundation for the economics instructor's teaching that "The Great Depression" from which the nation had just recovered demonstrated that capitalism had failed. Therefore, the nation needed some means of government control to protect the nation and the little guy from the abuses and the wide swings which unfettered capitalism produces.

The foundational concepts from which these teachings stemmed permeated American universities from early in this Century. Millions of Americans were exposed to the teachings. The concepts were formalized into *The Humanist Manifesto* in 1933. Its 15 affirmations or principles were produced by liberal intellectuals led by John Dewey, father of modern American education. They were amplified and expanded in *Humanist Manifesto II* in 1973. Basic tenets of *Humanist Manifesto I* and *Humanist Manifesto II*[41] are:

Rejecting God, humanists regard the universe as self-existing and not created—that man gradually evolved by chance from lower forms of life—that man is the product of his natural environment, his social heritage and the culture into which he is born.

...there are no absolutes, everything is relative and man as the highest form of being is his own ultimate authority making decisions determined by situational circumstances—that individual freedom of choice exists in life and should be increased, permitting individuals to express their sexual proclivities and pursue the life styles as they desire.

...free enterprise and private ownership of property should be replaced by a socialized and cooperative economic order with government insuring an equitable distribution of the means of life—that national independence and self determination should be replaced by a one-world government.

Humanist Manifesto II denies unequivocally that man is eternal, saying:

There is no credible evidence that life survives the death of the body and promises of immortal salvation or fear of eternal damnation are both illusory and harmful. No deity will save us.[42]

Paul Kurtz, editor of *The Humanist* and moving figure in the formulation of *Humanist Manifesto II* emphasized that concept in the preface for a volume which published both manifestos. He said:

What more pressing need than to recognize in this critical age of modern science and technology that, if no deity will save us, we must save ourselves.[43]

The Kennedy-Johnson assistant, Arthur Schlesinger, Jr. was presenting pure humanist doctrine in the statement quoted in Chapter IV. It bears repeating here. Schlesinger said that liberalism...

...dispensed with the absurd Christian myths of sin and damnation and believed that what shortcomings man might have were to be redeemed, not by Jesus on the cross, but by the benevolent unfolding of history. Tolerance, free inquiry, and technology, operating in the framework of human perfectibility, would in the end create a heaven on earth, a goal accounted much more sensible and wholesome than a heaven in heaven.

Hundreds of the world's most influential intellectuals, professors and activists signed *Humanist Manifesto II*. They included:

Harvard psychology professor B.F. Skinner, Swedish socialist professor and author Gunnar Myrdal, former UNESCO head Sir Julian Huxley, Planned Parenthood President Alan Guttmacher,

N.O.W. founder Betty Friedan, civil rights leader A. Philip Randolph, the dissident-Communist Ardre Sakharov, a leader of an officially designated Communist front organization, and Vice President Mondale's brother, Lester.[44]

The concepts they formalized in the two Humanist manifestos had become the philosophical foundation of American higher education during the first half of this century. Ultimately they have filtered down into the primary and secondary school systems as well.*

A two-year study sponsored by the U.S. Department of Education's National Institute of Education found that textbooks generally reflect a secular humanist and liberal bias. The study by Dr. Paul Vitz, a psychology professor at New York University determined that 60 representative grade and high school textbooks excluded (1) the contribution of religion to America's development, (2) traditional family values and (3) conservative political and economic positions. The Vitz report to the U.S. Department of Education was expanded and published under the title, *Censorship: The Evidence of Bias In Our Children's Textbooks*, in 1986.[45]

Studies done on the prevailing views, attitudes and philosophies of those working in the media show similar patterns. S. Robert Lichter and Stanley Rothman made an exhaustive study of the attitudes of American journalists. Sponsored by the Research Institute on International Change at Columbia University, the study based on their research and that of others was published by the two men as a book under the title, *The Media Elite*.[46] They showed that:

> In 1964, media people supported Lyndon Johnson over Barry Goldwater by a 15 to 1 margin. In 1968, when Richard Nixon won the Presidency, media people supported Hubert Humphrey by a 7 to 1 margin. The media supported McGovern over Nixon and Carter over Ford by 4 to 1 margins in 1972 and 1976.

---

*For examples of how the tenets of the *Humanist Manifestos* are promoted in textbooks, see *Humanism/Moral Relativism In Textbooks*, 1988, The Mel Gablers, P.O. Box 7518, Longview, TX 75607, $1.50.

The authors commented:

These presidential choices are consistent with the media elite's liberal views on a wide range of social and political issues. They show a strong preference for welfare capitalism...income redistribution and guaranteed employment.

The authors found that 90% of the "media elite" favor abortion or are "pro-choice." Only 1 in 4 believes strongly that homosexuality is wrong, one out of six thinks adultery is wrong and only one out of 30 believes that homosexuals should not be permitted to teach in public schools. Fewer than one out of ten attends church regularly.

Allan Brownfield in a study *How Media Bias Distorts Our View of the World*[47] quoted extensively from a 1982 survey on the attitudes and values of students at the Columbia University School of Journalism. It found that the future journalists...

...were overwhelmingly non-religious. Over 80 percent said they seldom or never attended church or synagogue, and only eight percent said they attend religious services regularly. Politically, 85 percent of the students described themselves as liberals and only 11 percent called themselves conservative.[48]

The students attitudes showed a hostility to free enterprise and the American political system. In rating prominent men and women, Brownfield said that the students...

...rated Fidel Castro more positively than Ronald Reagan. The Sandinista Communists of Nicaragua were rated in a more favorable manner than Prime Minister Margaret Thatcher of Great Britain or former U.S. Ambassador to the United Nations Jeane Kirkpatrick. Forty-one percent of the students approved the San-dinista-Marxist regime and only 26 disapproved.[49]

Four specific teachings of the humanist manifestos have produced the philosophic foundations which are manifested in the schools and media and undergird America's leaders belief that communism will "evolve" and "mellow." They are:

The teaching and resultant belief (1) in the continuing evolution of the species (2) in the basic goodness and eventual perfectibility of man, (3) in the "fact" that man and his behavior is the product of his environment, and (4) in denying the certainty of life after death.

Consider how those four foundational beliefs produce an irrational clinging to the failed foreign policies of the last 40 years:

If evolution is true and a continuing process then it is logical to believe that communism will "evolve" and "mellow" if given enough time.

If man who is by nature basically good (or totally a product of his environment) does bad things it must be some influence in his environment which causes him to do it. If the bad influence can be determined and changed, then man's basic goodness will manifest itself.

If there is no life after death, then it would be better to crawl to Moscow and even live as a slave rather than risking one's life in the struggle for freedom.

That these are and have been the motivations of many who have influenced American policies can be shown from their statements which have already been examined. For example:

The numerous statements, already quoted, of Dean Rusk, Arthur Schlesinger, Jr. and George Bush demonstrate that they base their hopes for changes within the Communist system on the theory of evolution—that communism will "evolve" and mellow if given enough time.

Former Senator William Fulbright rationalized the Communist massacre of the Chinese students as the action of "a good man (Deng) who lost his patience." Deng, as Fulbright said, was pushed by factors in his environment (the protesting students). George Kennan's February 1989 statement blames the environment—"that the U.S. has over militarized"—for the fact that basically good Communists have not "evolved" faster.

Paul Nitze's essay from the late 1950's (quoted in Chapter IV) advanced the theory that continuing negotiations with the Communists are vital to survival. Having accepted this viewpoint, Nitze said, the only logical corollary is that "if we cannot get them to agree to our viewpoint, we must accept theirs if we are to survive."

Nitze's position is valid if the humanist view of no life after death is accepted. Nitze's "far out" view was an issue when he was appointed as Secretary of the Navy by John Kennedy. It was not mentioned when he served as principal disarmament negotiator during much of Ronald Reagan's presidency.

Operating from such a philosophical base, millions have become a part of the "conspiracy of shared values." They include the young journalism student in his first media job—the young appointee to the foreign service—the graduate assistant in a prestigious university. They are open to the teaching of the "scholar" who perpetuates the "evolving" and "mellowing" theories. As they learn their lessons they climb the ladders to positions of influence and prominence where they perpetuate the "hopeful" concept to the next generation.

Because of their humanist philosophic foundation they are open to influence or manipulation by Soviet disinformation agents—domestic or foreign. When efforts have been made to expose an actual Communist infiltrator in government, the press, the church, etc. participants in the *conspiracy of shared values* rush to the defense. "He couldn't be a Communist," they reason, "he thinks just like me." It happened when Alger Hiss, Harry Dexter White, Owen Lattimore, etc. were exposed in the 1940s and 1950s. It doesn't happen anymore because the agencies which once exposed Communist infiltrators are no longer permitted to do so.

Once the philosophic foundation of those in the *conspiracy of shared values* is recognized and understood, their blindness makes sense—to a degree and for a time. But why don't they at some point awaken to the reality that Communist philosophy, words and actions show that they are still dedicated to the establishment of world communism? Why do America's leaders continue down the 40-year path of betraying us and the hopes of mankind worldwide for freedom? Why do they remain so blind?

Man's answers to those questions are inadequate. However, God has an answer. In the Bible, God, speaking through the prophet Isaiah, warned His people of a time when He would take away the "wisdom of your wise men and the understanding of your prudent men." God said:

> Forasmuch as this people draw near me with their mouth, and with their lips do honour me, but have removed their heart far from me, and their fear toward me is taught by the precept of men: Therefore, behold, I will proceed to do a marvellous work among this people, even a marvellous work and a wonder: for the wisdom of their wise men shall perish, and the understanding of their prudent men shall be hid. (Isaiah 29:13- 14)

God blinded the eyes of Israel's rulers. They had tried to buy allies. They engaged in programs of aid to their enemies. They made pacts or alliances with the enemy (See Isaiah 30:1-7 and Hosea 8:10 & 12:1). They failed in most of the ways America's leaders have failed for the last 40 years. Their folly eventually took the nation into captivity. God took away the wisdom and understanding of Israel's wise men because the people honoured Him with words, rituals, tithes, sacrifices, legalistic observances of the sabbath, etc.—but kept their hearts far from Him.

America is paying similar lip service to God. Our money carries the national motto, "In God We Trust" but the Supreme Court banned prayer and Bible reading from America's schools. In the Pledge of Allegiance, Americans still say we are, "One nation under God." Rising crime, increasing rates of divorce, drug addiction, births to unmarried teenagers, X and R-rated movies, etc. make the words an empty slogan—lip service—rather than reality.

One very positive aspect of Ronald Reagan's presidency was his practice of closing radio and TV addresses by asking God's blessing on his hearers. Mentioning God became acceptable in public life again. This was an important accomplishment of Mr. Reagan's presidency. However, disclosure of the Reagans' longtime practice of looking to astrologers before scheduling treaty signings, important conferences, etc.[50] was one indication of the spiritual "split personality" which God condemned in Isaiah 29. At least in this area of their lives, the Reagans appeared to be honoring God with their lips while their hearts were far from Him.

In this regard, the Reagans were typical of many of those who elected them. Too many Americans decry the Supreme Court decisions banning prayer and Bible reading from public schools but fail to gather their families to start each day with prayer and Bible reading. Are they guilty of paying lip service to God?

God dealt with Israel for such sin 2500 years ago. Would He deal with America today in the same way? Could these remote verses of Old Testament scripture still apply? God anticipated that question. After speaking His warning, He told Isaiah:

> Now, go, and write it before them in a table, and note it in a book, that it may be for the time to come forever and ever. (Isaiah 30:8)

Why are America's leaders betraying us? Why do they seem unable to face the Communist threat? Why do they fight communism one place in the world while aiding it everywhere else? God's Word has the only reasonable and responsible answer. Because a nation which has been so blessed of God now honors Him with their lips while keeping their hearts far from Him...

> ...the wisdom of their wise men shall perish, and the understanding of their prudent men shall be hid.

The Jews, to whom God directed this warning, paid lip service to the Messiah and King who was to come but when He came they rejected Him. The Scriptures say:

> He came unto his own, and his own received him not. But as many as received Him, to them gave he power to become the sons of God, even to them that believe on his name: which were born, not of blood, nor of the will of the flesh, nor of the will of man, but of God. (John 1:11-13)

Many in America pay lip service to God today just as the Jews did 2000 years ago. They join a church. They've been baptized and confirmed. They send their children to Sunday school. They may be leaders in a congregation, may lead moral lives—but their hearts are far from God. They are professing Christians—but practicing humanists. They give Jesus the title of "Lord" but retain final authority over how they will use their time, spend their money, or fulfill the marriage vow of "till death do us part."

They pay lip service to the Saviour who came 2000 years ago. They call themselves Christians but they've never let the Risen Christ come into their hearts to redeem them *personally* from their sins and give them a new nature.

Men and women have religion today—but it is a religion of lip service. God commanded:

> Thou shalt love the Lord thy God with all thine heart, and with all thy soul, and with all thy might. (Deuteronomy 6:5)

God wants to be at the center of every individual's life. He can't be until He has been received into an individual's heart to live and rule. Man, by nature, is in rebellion against God. Adam and Eve rebelled against God in the Paradise He created for them in the Garden of Eden. The Jews rebelled against God in the Promised Land into which He lead them. Man today, in a nation so blessed by God, is in rebellion against God's rule. That's why man needs a new nature and a new birth. To provide it, God sent His Son, Jesus Christ, to suffer the full penalty that every man's rebellion and sin deserves. After dying for the sins of the world, Jesus arose from the dead to be the new life of all those who will believe upon Him and receive Him as Saviour, Lord and Master. Anything less is lip service.

Why are America's leaders seemingly so blind to the threat of communism—so unable to learn from the tragedies of the past? God said:

> Forasmuch as this people draw near me with their mouth, and with their lips do honour me, but have removed their heart far from me...the wisdom of their wise men shall perish, and the understanding of their prudent men shall be hid.

God said it. Do you believe Him?

CHAPTER 21

THE COMMUNIST PARTY USA—HOW IT MANIPULATES THE U.S. CONGRESS

...we can play on the ambition of thousands of politicians of all sizes, who have come from the bourgeoisie...men who are unable to reach their goals because their abilities are not in accord with their ambitions.

> —*Chinese Communist theorist, Li Li Siang*

TO UNDERSTAND the importance of the Communist Party USA and the influence it wields in America it is vital to see the CPUSA's place in the world Communist structure. For over 70 years Communists have been using a three-pronged attack in their drive to capture the world.

At the Third Congress of the Comintern which opened in Moscow on June 22, 1921, Lenin charted the course for the international Communist movement and described...

> ...the world revolution as a single process of the interaction of the three forces (the country of the victorious proletariat, *the working class movement of the capitalist countries* and the national libera-tion movement).[1]

Lenin's organizational blueprint has been followed ever since. The three "prongs" function in unison as a monolithic world-wide network. The Communist parties in the capitalist countries and the national liberation forces in colonial states are in submission to and receive support from the "country of the victorious proletariat," the Soviet Union.

Reporting on a 1969 Moscow meeting of the International Communist and Workers' Parties which reiterated Lenin's blueprint, Gus Hall, General Secretary of the Communist Party USA, said:

What has irreversibly and fundamentally changed the world scene is *the rise of the three currents making up the world revolutionary process.* The powerful world socialist system of states—in the first place, the Soviet Union—the world-wide national liberation movements—and the working class movements in the capitalist world—these are the main movers of history.[2] [Emphasis added]

The Communist parties in capitalist countries are duty bound to support the Soviet program world-wide, the national liberation movements in each of the world's hot spots and also to work to have the masses in each nation support the world wide revolutionary struggle. After hearings in 1982 on *Soviet Active Measures in the United States* the House of Representatives Select Committee on Intelligence reported:

Throughout its history, the CPUSA has been one of the most loyal, pro-Soviet Communist parties in the world and has unfalteringly accepted Soviet policy guidance and has implemented Soviet policy directives. (Pg. 223)

Gus Hall's own words prove that charge. In a 1969 speech in Moscow at the height of the Vietnam war, Hall said:

For an effective struggle in any arena, one must know one's enemy...U.S. imperialism remains the most aggressive war-like force in the world. It is a powerful and dangerous foe.

Permit us to again express our deep sense of warm comradeship and oneness with the fighters against US imperialism the world over. We feel especially indebted to the valiant people of Vietnam, who by unparalleled heroism and sacrifice, are administering US imperialism a historic defeat.

To these fighters the world over, we can only promise to heighten our efforts to match their great contributions in the struggle against imperialism.[3]

As Hall was speaking, the North Vietnamese were killing and wounding nearly 1000 American boys every week. Article III, Section 3 of the Constitution defines treason as levying war against the United States "or in adhering to their enemies, giving them aid and comfort." Hall's words make him a traitor.

How much influence does the Hall-led, Moscow-loyal Communist Party USA exert in American life and society? Anyone who tries to answer that important question is sure to be called a McCarthyite—but the question remains: How much influence do the traitorous Communists have in America? What do they contribute to the world-wide struggle directed from Moscow?

An important measure of Communist influence and effectiveness is their ability to announce specific legislative goals and then see them enacted by the U.S. Congress. Several such Communist successes will be cited and the methods the Reds used to achieve their goals will be examined.

In December 1986, Gus Hall, general secretary of the Communist Party, U.S.A. addressed the party's Central Committee. His speech was printed in the January issue of *Political Affairs*, the party's theoretical journal.[4] Hall rejoiced over the election "victories" in November 1986 which gave left-wing Democrats control of the U.S. Senate. Hall called for party members to use their positions and their influence in civil rights groups, peace organizations, trade unions, the feminist movement and other leftist pressure groups to build support for Communist goals in the Congress during 1987. He said the four goals[5] were:

(1) End all nuclear testing

(2) Stop Star Wars (SDI)

(3) Stop all aid to the contras

(4) Ratify Salt II

Knowledgeable individuals will recognize that the four-point Communist legislative agenda for 1987 was also the agenda of a majority or near majority of the Congress of the United States and about 90% of the major newspapers in America. Therefore, most of the Communists' 1987 legislative agenda was implemented either by a vote of Congress—or executive action.

The Communists were jubilant. The headline on James Steele's Christmas Eve column in the *People's Daily World*[6] read:

1987 was a very good year; 1988 can be even better

Steele is secretary of the Legislative and Political Commission of the Communist Party. His column detailed ten events that made 1987 "the year that was" for Communists. They included:

* The make-up of the 100th Congress which tilted in an anti-Reaganite direction

* The reelection of Mayor Harold Washington in Chicago

* The Iran-Contra inquiry which resulted in many hard line anti-Communists leaving the administration and put the brakes on much of the administration's anti-Communist activity

* The launching of the Central American Arias peace offensive

* Senate rejection of Robert Bork's nomination to the Supreme Court

* Jesse Jackson's front runner status for the Democrat presidential nomination

* Senate and House Democrats holding firm on requiring the administration to narrowly interpret the ABM and SALT II treaties

* The signing of the Reagan-Gorbachev treaty banning short-range nuclear missiles from Europe

Steele's article described each of these events as Communist "victories" and said:

Well, one could go on and on, but the above examples give a good account as to why 1987 has been a vintage year [for the Communists].

Steele then set two goals for making 1988 "even better." He said:

Winning Senate ratification of the INF treaty and denying further aid to the contras emerge as immediate tasks.

Both of these Communist goals were soon enacted by the Congress.

How do the Communists achieve such influence? Is the near

total adoption of the Communists' four principal legislative goals for 1987 and all their other victories just a coincidence? Or do they have real power and influence in Congress—in the news media—and in the Democrat and Republican parties? How many Communists are there?

In December 1988, the *New York Times* asked Gus Hall, "How many Americans consider themselves Communists and support the party?" Hall replied...

> Half a million. What J. Edgar Hoover would have called hardcore, card-carrying Communists, about 20,000. The party is more influential now than at anytime in our history. I think we have been a factor in changing the atmosphere from anti-Communist to a more leisurely, down-to-earth policy toward our party and to the idea that the Soviet Union is not an enemy or a military threat.

> We're a minority party, but the truth is I know more world leaders on a first-name basis than any other American.[7]

Hall's estimates on the Party's numbers which he has also given during appearances on the Donahue show, etc. are probably accurate. The *People's Daily World* prints 60,000 copies daily, of which 10,000 are individual mail subscriptions[8]. (In the August 1989 *Political Affairs* the party's national organizational secretary, Judith LeBlanc indicated that only 20% of the party's membership functions openly with the other 80% working underground.)

In the *New York Times* interview Hall claimed the support of half a million people in addition to actual Party members. The Reds obtained just about that many signatures on nominating petitions to put the party on the ballot in 23 states in 1984. Hall added that Gorbachev's visits to America would increase the party's popularity and acceptance even further.

The relative handful of almost universally-scorned Reds succeeded in getting Congress to adopt its four legislative goals *over the opposition of the President of the United States.* Understanding how they do it requires a knowledge of how they work.

Communists have never won a majority to openly and

knowingly support communism in any nation. Rather communism has been imposed on nation after nation by building a dedicated, disciplined cadre which in turn becomes expert at manipulating others to do their work. Lenin taught:

> One of the biggest and most dangerous mistakes made by Communists is the idea that a revolution can be made by revolutionaries alone. Without an alliance with non-Communists in the most diverse spheres of activity there can be no question of any successful Communist construction.[9]

Lenin was reinforcing the teaching of Karl Marx who said:

> ...the Party cannot make the revolution alone. The concept of the united front is absolutely essential.[10]

For several decades the CPUSA started front groups. The Reds would enlist an array of knowing sympathizers, willing dupes and unsuspecting clergy and celebrity do-gooders into organizations to work for the Communist cause of the moment. Hundreds of such peace organizations, civil rights and civil liberties fronts, etc. were organized and controlled by Party members. The Attorney General regularly published a list of such organizations officially found to be Communist controlled.

In the early 1980's, while continuing to operate such officially designated fronts as the National Alliance Against Racial and Political Oppression, the National Lawyers Guild, etc, the Party's emphasis shifted. The new approach emphasized building influence in mass organizations which could be manipulated to support Communist goals rather than seeking outright control.

The shift began in June 1981 when the Communists issued a call for an extraordinary conference in Milwaukee to form a "united front." They called for Communists and their sympathizers and fellow travelers to work within the groups in which they had influence to bring them together in an *All People's Front. Political Affairs*, the theoretical journal of the Communist Party USA gave the background six years later in its July 1987 issue.

Opposition to Ronald Reagan's domestic and foreign

policies was the rallying point to draw trade unionists, peace groups, the feminists, farm activists, senior citizens and civil rights organizations into the *All People's Front.* Gus Hall's report to the Party's Central Committee in December 1981 gave the effort a major push. He said:

> Our task is to build an all-people's front...with special emphasis on mobilization of the working class and the trade union movement on all levels, but especially the grass roots.

> This front must include Americans who are racially oppressed and discriminated against because of their nationality, the professionals, intellectuals, farmers, youth, women, senior citizens, small and medium-size business people...a mass wave that will mainly express itself through the Democratic Party and *especially during primary campaigns.*[11] [Emphasis added]

As the *All People's Front* took shape during the 1980s the operation has had significant impact in expanding Communist influence and pressure on Congress and national policy.

The importance and emphasis the Party placed on building the *All-Peoples Front* is shown by the amount of continuing space given to the concept in the party press. During the decade of the 1980s the Communist press ran hundreds and hundreds of articles directing Party members effort in building the *All-People's Front.*

To appreciate the significance of the attention given the *All-People's Front* in the Party's publications, it is necessary to understand the role of the Communist press. Louis Francis Budenz was probably the highest ranking American Communist who ever became disillusioned and left the Party. He was a key member of the Party's Central Committee. When he left the Party after World War II, he was editor of their official newspaper, *The Daily Worker.*

In his book, *The Techniques of Communism,*[12] Budenz provided the most authoritative look free men have ever been given into the functioning of the Communist Party and its members. In the book, Budenz said that the Communist press is distinctly different from all other forms of journalism. In the chapter on "The Role of the Communist Press" he stated:

> The *Daily Worker* is the most powerful publication in the United States today and has been for a number of years...The power of the *Daily Worker* cannot be measured by its subscription lists...it is not a normal newspaper but a telegraph agency for the conspiracy.[13]

Budenz goes on to tell how the Communists use their papers:

> ...Every morning the Communist leader in each part of the country picks up his *Daily Worker* to learn from its editorials and articles what he should order to be done immediately...Thereupon, he calls in the functionaries of the District Bureau, who are in charge of the various areas to be penetrated and gives them instructions...The functionaries of the District bureau then get in touch with the representatives of the cells planted in newspapers, religious groups, cultural organizations, and labor unions—transmitting to them the orders which have come from above. Many of these persons also read the *Daily Worker* and are prepared for the orders they receive.[14]

Budenz explained that to properly understand the Communist press it is necessary to evaluate what they say *and how often they say it.* He wrote:

> There is one practice of the Communist press which must be known if we are to properly appraise what it is up to. It is the accumulation of articles around a given subject. Communist designs are clarified and made definite by articles which follow up on the same topic. The Communist functionary has this constantly in mind, and of course reads all Communist material as a whole.[15]

The accumulation of articles on a given subject gives Communists insight into the importance of the topic or project. In view of what Budenz wrote, the importance of the *All People's Front* can be sensed from the constant 10-year stream of instructions Communists have been given in their publications on building the *All People's Front*.

Political efforts of the All-People's Front are channeled

principally through the liberal wing of the Democratic Party, a study of the Communist press shows.

Gus Hall issued a booklet titled, *A Lame Duck In Turbulent Waters,* after Richard Nixon's reelection in 1972. In it Gus Hall revealed Communist involvement in and use of the Democrat party. He wrote:

> Our electoral policy has for some 25 years been expressed in the phrase "the three legs of a stool"...The stool was constructed at a time when the Party was under sharp attack...the concept was built on the idea that when the two legs, namely, the Communist Party and "the forces of political independence", get strong enough, then and only then would the stool sit on three legs. But until that day comes the one operating leg would be the liberal wing of the Democrat Party.[16]

Hall then asked his Communist readers: "Is that not how it has in fact operated?" Hall added...

> ...in practice the only operational electoral leg [of the Communist political effort] was the movement around the liberal Democratic Party candidates...the blueprints called for the united front and the people's front policies to be carried out through the Democratic Party.[17]

The "three-legged stool" concept was implemented as Communists became active in the regular Democrat Party—but more often as they formed rump groups (organizations using the name "Democrat" even though they were not part of the regular party structure). These rump groups pressured the regular Democrat organizations and achieved great success in moving the Democrat Party to the left.

Hall mentioned such activity by Communists in the Reform Democratic Clubs in New York and the California Democratic Clubs (CDC).[18] In Minnesota, Hall said that Communists provided the lead in liquidating the old Farmer-Labor Party (which was formed with strong Communist influence and leadership in the 1920s and became a major force in Minnesota politics for many years.) Actually the process of "liquidation" was largely one of moving into the Democrat Party which began operating as the DFL (Democrat-Farm-Labor) coalition.[19]

The California Democrat Club movement, the CDC, which Hall mentioned as a place for political activity by some Party members was the political base from which Alan Cranston came to the United States Senate. The DFL coalition in Minnesota started Hubert Humphrey on his way to becoming a Vice President of the United States by electing him mayor of Minneapolis and later as a United States senator. (Neither Cranston nor Hubert Humphrey have been accused or identified as Communists although they, like most liberal politicians, have many goals in common with the Communists.)

The Reform Democrat clubs Gus Hall cited in New York were influential in electing Percy Sutton as Manhattan Borough President, a post in which he served twelve years. Sutton's leanings were revealed at the memorial service for Henry Winston, chairman of the Communist Party USA in early 1987. Sutton joined Gus Hall and other Communist leaders in praising Winston. The *People's Daily World* said Sutton "spoke passionately of the impact that [the Communist Party chief] Winston had on his life."[20] This man—with such admiration for the Communist leader—was president of the Manhattan Borough Council in New York for twelve years. His successor, David Dinkins, had strong Red support as the Democrat candidate for mayor of New York in 1989.[21]

In the early 1960s, the struggle to wrest control of Democrat ward organizations in Chicago from the forces of long-time Mayor Richard Daley got detailed coverage in the party's theoretical journal, *Political Affairs*. These "reform" democrat organizations in Chicago sent Harold Washington to Congress and later elected him Mayor of the city. They also elected a long-time Communist functionary and union leader, Charles Hayes, to replace Washington in Congress.[22]

Although Hayes has been identified as a party member, most of the liberal Democrat politicians who benefit from

Communist support are not. Georgi Dimitrov, General Secretary of the Communist International, told why. He said:

> As Soviet power grows, there will be a greater aversion to Communist Parties everywhere. So we must practice the techniques of withdrawal. Never appear in the foreground: let our friends do the work. We must always remember that one sympathizer is generally worth more than a dozen militant Communists. A university professor, who without being a party member lends himself to the interests of the Soviet Union, is worth more than a hundred men with Party cards...the writer who without being a Party member, defends the Soviet Union, the union leader who is outside our ranks but defends Soviet international policy, is worth more than a thousand Party members...[23]

During 1988 Gus Hall claimed in a *New York Times* interview that the Communists in America have 20 close sympathizers for every actual party member.[24]

The Chinese Communist theorist, Li Li Siang, revealed the scorn Communists have for politicians they use. He said:

> ...we can play on the ambition of thousands of politicians of all sizes, who have come from the bourgeoisie...men who are unable to reach their goals because their abilities are not in accord with their ambitions.[25]

The former Speaker of the House of Representatives Jim Wright is an example of the type of ambitious politician the Marxists promote and use. In his early years in Congress Wright was an anti-Communist. He represented a conservative Texas district. He apparently learned, however, that support of the 50 to 70 hard-core leftists in the House is essential for advancing to a leadership position in the House of Representatives. By the early 1980s he joined them.

Wright was one of ten Congressmen who wrote the "Dear Commandante" letter to Nicarguan Communist dictator, Daniel Ortega at a critical time in March 1984. The letter undercut the official position of the President (charged constitutionally with conducting the foreign policy of the United States). Filled with glowing praise for Ortega, Wright and his comrades, commended Ortega for...

...taking steps to open up the political process in your country [by establishing a one-party Communist state???].[26]

The ten influential Democrats then pledged to oppose support for the Nicaraguan anti-Communist freedom fighters (contras) and urged Ortega to "behave" in a way which would...

...significantly stregthen the hands of those in our country who desire better relations.[27]

Once Jim Wright deserted his earlier anti-communism he was on the way to becoming Speaker of the House. He paid his bill to his Marxist supporters by providing the leadership which killed the anti-Communist freedom fighters in Nicaragua. That was the charge made by a fellow Democrat, Senator Fritz Hollings of South Carolina, in the United States Senate the day after Wright used his leadership position to kill further aid to the anti-Communist contras in Nicaragua. Hollings' remarkable charges can be found on page S-565 of the February 4, 1988 *Congressional Record.*

The Chinese Communist theorist Li Li Siang told how the Marxists use the politicians whose "ambitions are greater than their abilities." He said:

If we Communists, with the large or small forces at our disposal, offer our support to these politicians, they will come to our camp—not as registered members of our party, which would not suit them or us, but as servants. Servants of expediency. It will be to their advantage to serve us.[28]

The opportunists are not all Democrats. Dr. Bella Dodd was a member of the Central Committee of the Communist Party. She was in charge of legislative activities for the party in New York state. After she left the Party in the early 1950s she testified before the Senate Internal Security Subcommittee. She said that Jacob Javits had come to her after World War II to get instructions on where he should settle and whether he should pursue a political career as a Democrat or a Republican.[29]

Javits was subsequently elected to Congress as a Republican. Later New Yorkers elected him as their attorney

general and U.S. Senator. He became one of the most powerful men in Washington.

The Senate committee received testimony from other witnesses which supported that of Bella Dodd—in addition to
supplying a wealth of information about Javits association
with important Communists on both the west coast and in
New York.[30]

Javits was serving as Attorney General of New York at the
time. He asked for an opportunity to "answer" the accusations. However, on the witness stand he did not deny the
accusations—he just couldn't remember any of the many
incidents.[31]

Gus Hall put Red use of liberals (and his scorn for them)
into perspective in his 1972 explanation of the "three legged
stool approach." He said that Communists...

> ...can make use of liberals only if they have no illusions about
> their basically wavering and vacillating nature...Liberals will
> continue to be liberals. They can be allies but they cannot be the
> base.[32]

Communists work with liberals (Democrats and
Republicans) to achieve their intermediate goals. In the book,
*Leninism and the World Revolutionary Working Class Move-
ment*, published in Moscow, Gus Hall explained:

> The idea of intermediate goals is that we walk with, talk with and
> unitedly fight jointly with the masses for an objective that we have
> to reach anyway before we reach our goal of socialism. We do so
> with people who are not ready to start the march to socialism
> [communism]. In fact most of them are convinced that they will
> part company with us when the halfway goals are reached.[33]

Liberals who think they can use the Communists are those
whom Lenin termed, "...useful idiots."

The Communists "three-legged stool" approach of working
through the liberal wing of the Democrat party has produced
successes for the Communists. Even so, Gus Hall made it
plain in 1972 and Party literature regularly teaches that it
can not be the ultimate goal. The Reds' longterm goal is a new
party through which the Communists and the independent

forces (those who while not Party members are sympathetic to and supportive of most Communist goals) can achieve their full goals. Until that time, however, Communists are instructed to work to unify "the independent political forces" working within the Democrat Party.[34]

The term "forces of political independence" deserves definition because of the importance Communists give to it. A study of Communist literature shows that the "forces of political independence" are those people and movements whose loyalty to some goal or cause is stronger than their commitment to either the Republican or Democrat Party.

Such forces or causes would include civil rights, the feminists, peace activists, the pro-choice [pro-abortion] forces, and trade unionists. These people may be nominal Democrats or Republicans but they will work through any channel to achieve their goals. In the years since 1972, farm activists and senior citizens movements have become part of the "forces of political independence."

[The pro-life, anti-abortion forces in America would be a "force of political independence." The pro-lifers may be Republicans or Democrats but their commitment to the pro-life position is stronger than their Democrat or Republican affiliations. The pro-lifers are not generally a force the Communists would look to merge into the united front they are building and leading. However, some efforts are made to enlist pro-lifers into the peace movement and anti-capital punishment fronts on the basis that to be consistently pro-life it is necessary to oppose nuclear arms and capital punishment.]

The operation to unite "the forces of political independence" and mobilize them to work through the Democrat Party moved into high gear after Ronald Reagan's inauguration in 1981 with the formation of the *All-People's Front*. By December 1981, Hall told the Party's Central Committee that the *All-People's Front* was to become...

...the mass wave that will mainly express itself through the Democratic Party *and especially during the primary campaigns*.[35] (Emphasis added)

As Hall had envisioned in his 1972 "Lame Duck" booklet, the "united front"—the forces of political independence—was to work through the Democratic Party. Concentrating their efforts in primary campaigns when only a small segment of the electorate votes multiplies the weight of each vote generated by the APF forces. In Hall's 1982 election instructions to Party members he discussed the growing influence of the forces of political independence and how they had produced up to 25,000 votes for Communists running in ward races. He said:

> There are literally dozens of such new formations sprouting in every part of the country. [The *All-people's Front* had formed eight months earlier.]

> Most of the independent coalitions tend to crystallize into what can be called "umbrella" formations. They bring together people who *continue to work through the Democratic Party,* as well as those who carry out electoral work through independent channels. They are independent, but they work with *and pick candidates who run through the most effective electoral channel available.*[36]

As evidence of the success of the pragmatic approach, Hall pointed to the victory of a Communist in a Washington D.C. ward election and the 25,000 votes a Communist received in a Minneapolis school election. He then cautioned:

> In the 1982 elections we must keep in mind the over-all challenge of the moment. Therefore we must consider when and where Communists should run even more carefully than we have in the past . We must be careful not to appear to be in any way dividing, rather than uniting, those who are against the Reagan forces.[37]

The *All-People's Front* and the Communist's electoral efforts got a major boost from—and contributed to—Jesse Jackson's campaign for the Presidency. The lead editorial in the November 4, 1983 *Daily World* said:

> Jackson's candidacy represents a crucial component of the emerging independent political front.[38]

A week later Gus Hall opened the 23rd Annual Communist Party national convention. In his speech, he said, "Jesse

Jackson's candidacy also adds a new dimension to *political independence.*[39]

On March 10, 1984, James Jackson (no relation to Jesse), the Secretary of the Central Committee and member of the Polit Bureau of the CPUSA, published an article in the *People's Daily World.* It had the headline:

Jesse Jackson, a vital force in the anti-Reagan front

In the glowing full page article, the Communist leader commended Jackson's candidacy saying:

Jesse Jackson's Rainbow Coalition program and alliance concept which would gather into a common front the broadest spectrum of categories of the popular forces...already is expressing itself as a new progressive influx into the liberal wing of the Democratic party.[40]

At the Democrat convention itself Jackson used the Communists' language when he said that "because of the presence of *independent forces*" the convention devoted an entire day to debating issues of peace, affirmative action, etc. and helped "write the planks of the Democratic platform." After the convention, the *Daily World* for July 21, 1984 commented:

Jackson made not only a mighty contribution to the Democratic Party, but also to progress in U.S. political life. His campaign, views and activities are objectively playing a role in building the *All People's Front.*[41]

Jackson's campaign, with the full support of the Communists, never deviated from the foreign policy and domestic positions of the Communist Party U.S.A. and the Soviet Union. He has continued this support. For example, Jackson spoke to a May 5, 1985 commemoration of the 10th anniversary "of the liberation of Vietnam."[42] Among the 75 groups which organized the meeting were the National Lawyers Guild (designated as the foremost legal bulwark of the CPUSA), the U.S. Peace Council (American affiliate of the Soviet-controlled World Peace Council) and the Communist

Party USA. The rally, attended by 1000 celebrated "the heroic victory of the people of Vietnam."[43]

Even though Jackson's 1988 campaign had similar support in the Communist press, the Communists never expected Jackson to get the Democrat nomination or win the presidency. However, his sizable block of votes gave the "independent political forces" a major impact on the platform and major concessions from the candidate who was nominated—and the struggle added new faces to the *All People's Front.*

A long-range Communist goal will be advanced also. Historically, Communists have had very little success recruiting American blacks. Since Jackson was dumped by the Democrats, however, the Communists can go to blacks with the argument that they have no future within the mainstream of America—that working with the Communists to restructure our society is their only hope.

Jackson continues to contribute to the Communist cause. In February 1989 he visited Moscow and proclaimed, "Coexistence is the only path to progress." The two key words in his statement—"coexistence" and "progress"—have special significance for Communists. Jackson's statement ran as the banner headline on the front page of the Communist *People's Daily World* for February 3.[44]

The emphasis Communists place on "coexistence" is demonstrated by a full book they have published on Lenin's teachings on the use of coexistence. The preface said:

> Peaceful coexistence promotes the development of the revolutionary movement of the working class in the capitalist countries and creates conditions for successful struggle by oppressed nations against colonialism...The peaceful coexistence of states with different social systems is a specific form of the class struggle in the international arena.

> This, in rough outline, is the policy that has been consistently pursued by the Soviet people and their government for more than fifty years.

> The policy of peaceful coexistence was first proclaimed and fully substantiated by Lenin.[45]

Jackson, like so many American leaders, regularly falls into the trap of advancing Communist programs and causes by using their words which have a completely different connotation for American hearers.

By 1986, the Communist Party was still building its own coalition with the "independent political forces" while working through the Democrat Party to stop Ronald Reagan's anti-Communist efforts and carry out its own agenda.

A look at the 1986 elections shows how effective these forces have become. James Steele is Secretary of the Legislative and Political Action Department of the Communist Party, U.S.A. In the March 1986 *Political Affairs* he set the political goals for Party members for the year. In his article he said:

> The task of the Communist Party is to help develop united legislative and electoral action to inflict a net loss of four Republican senators, wiping out their senate majority.

> Ending Republican control of the Senate would change the political equation not only in Congress, but in the entire country...The pressure on President Reagan to negotiate and make concessions would increase. The *leverage* of the "people's forces" would increase.[46]

Steele explained the strategy—and proved to be a remarkably astute political prophet. He said:

> While the number of Reaganites who must be defeated to change the balance in Congress is small, to defeat them will require a tremendous level of mobilization. The very process of struggling for such united action will strengthen the capacity of the "people's forces."...If past patterns hold, relatively few votes in strategic districts can tip the overall balance.

Steele's instructions to the comrades targeted thirteen races to concentrate on. The Democrats won eight of them—and control of the United States Senate. Steele's analysis that "relatively few votes in strategic districts can tip the overall balance" proved to be too true. Switching just 50,000 votes in six states out of 40-million cast nationwide would have kept the control of the U.S. Senate in somewhat more conservative, anti-Communist hands.

Party Secretary Gus Hall rejoiced over the election "victories" and said:

> The growth of the role of *the forces of political independence* is the difference in the results of the 1984 and the 1986 elections. Their influence and ability to mobilize continues to develop at a rapid pace.[47]

Hall called for...

> ...an "all-people's electoral unity" geared to an all-out, coordinated effort in 1988 to defeat as many ultra-Right Republicans as possible, and some Democrats...and to cut the number of Republicans in state legislatures.[48]

Hall said that the "forces of political independence" would continue to work and grow through the "medium of the Democratic party in both the presidential and congressional elections."

By 1989 the Communists were claiming another triumph in their effort to gain influence in the Democrat Party. Their official newspaper, the *People's Daily World* announced Ron Brown's election as Democrat national chairman saying:

> Brown's election is part of a process in which people's unified forces for progress have been utilizing the Democratic Party as one of their vehicles.[49]

The phrase "people's unified forces for progress" is an Aesopian term the Communists use to describe the forces which are moving a country in the direction of communism.

The Communists and their *All People's Front* did not succeed in defeating Ronald Reagan in 1984 nor George Bush in 1988. However, in their evaluation of the seven- year effort of the *All People's Front* they correctly concluded...

> The all-people's front against Reagan must be seen as the primary force that prevented the Reagan victory from becoming a victory for Reaganism.

That was a very astute observation. Reagan was reelected in 1984 despite strong Communist opposition. However, he never succeeded in implementing his campaign promises or much of the 1984 Republican platform. The *All-People's Front* and its influence in Congress blocked one Reagan effort after another.

Front page headlines in February 4, 1988 newspapers across America told of two major defeats for Ronald Reagan in Congress. Grass roots opposition stirred by the *All People's Front* had an impact on wavering congressmen. The big banner headline across the top of the *St. Louis Post-Dispatch* front page told the story:

CONTRA AID REJECTED BY 8 VOTES

The other headline on the same front page said:

Kennedy Confirmed For Court

Congress acted to stop aid for the Nicaraguan freedom fighters and confirmed Judge Anthony Kennedy's appointment to the Supreme Court seat for which Judge Robert Bork had been nominated originally. Both actions were major victories for the Communists and the *All-People's Front.* Here's why:

Contra aid was defeated by eight votes on February 3, 1988. The vote did not occur in a vacuum. Congress had adjourned six weeks before—two days before Christmas. The Christmas Eve *People's Daily World* had the headline:

Congress Recesses, But
Lawmakers Face Lobbies
At Home vs. Contra Aid

Where were those lobbies to come from? While most Americans were thinking about their families and Christmas trees, Communists were gearing up for the six week battle against further aid for the anti-Communist freedom fighters in Nicaragua. Page 3 of the Christmas Eve *People's Daily World* highlighted the instructions:

> Block Contra Aid! Visit your representatives at home. Lobby the senators and representatives over the holiday recess in their home districts. Demand a firm commitment for "No" vote.[50]

Another story indicated that the "Days of Decision" peace group had contacted "peace activists" in 180 congressional districts. They organized emergency phone campaigns against contra aid. The story indicated that Speaker Jim

Wright had instructed his staff to keep a running tally on the calls.[51]

On January 2, the *People's Daily World* carried this front page headline:

Contra Aid Foes
Launch Campaign
To Sway Feb. Vote

Inside, the comrades were informed that an "up or down" vote on contra aid would be scheduled by the Congress for either February 3 or 4. It was a full three weeks later when the leading conservative newspaper, *Human Events*, headlined the February 3rd or 4th vote. Red readers of the *People's Daily World* had already been at work for over a month stirring the grass roots. When the February vote was tallied, aid for the Nicaraguan freedom fighters was defeated by eight votes.

The Communist's biggest, most highly coordinated and successful effort through the *All People's Front*—the anti-Bork drive—culminated in victory the same day contra aid was defeated. The campaign started on June 27, 1987, the day after Justice Lewis Powell resigned. The *Peoples Daily World* for June 27, 1987 filled the top half of the front page with the big headline:

POWELL RESIGNS; WAS SWING VOTE ON SUPREME
COURT

Hall Says: Senate should block any ultra-right nominee.

The *People's Daily World* speculated that either Judge Robert Bork or Senator Orin Hatch would be nominated for the spot. Strategy to use against each was outlined along with organizations which should be targeted for mobilization.

As the campaign unfolded, daily updates were given on the success in enlisting feminist groups, civil rights organizations, the pro-abortionists, the National Education Association, trade unions, etc. Hundreds of articles in the *People's Daily World* and *Political Affairs* orchestrated the activities of Party members in moving great numbers of non-Communists to do their bidding.

Collected clippings from the four-month Communist press

barrage weighed over three pounds! [Remember what Louis Budenz said about the Communist press being a telegraph agency. Recall what he said about the accumulation of articles demonstrating the importance of a subject for the Communist reader.]

The anti-Bork crescendo grew. Over 300 organizations were mobilized against the man described by former Chief Justice Warren Burger as the most highly-qualified court appointee in over 50 years. Bork was defeated. The Communists were jubilant. *Political Affairs* for December 1987 carried the headline:[52]

THE BORK REJECTION A VICTORY
FOR ALL-PEOPLE'S UNITY

The article rejoiced that Bork was defeated and in the acceptance and respectability Communists gained through the campaign. A cartoon pictured Bork as a pig and said:

> Communists participated in statewide and local anti-Bork committees with an unprecedented acceptance. In some areas, the Party and YCL were recognized openly as valued allies. Even where local circumstances thrust them into anonymity Communists were welcomed into leadership and full participation.

> In one dramatic instance, Angela Davis, Communist leader, was one of five people elected to present thousands of anti-Bork petitions to Senator Pete Wilson.[53]

The same issue of *Political Affairs* stated that when Bork was nominated Senator Teddy Kennedy and Joe Biden were resigned to his eventual confirmation. (Both had voted to confirm Bork's appointment to the U.S. Court of Appeals three years earlier). It was not, *Political Affairs* said, until the grass roots had been stirred by the *All-People's Front* that Kennedy and Biden got the vision for actually defeating Bork.[54]

How do they do it? How can even 20,000 Communists and perhaps 100,000 fellow travelers achieve such power? Are these Communist "victories" just a coincidence—or are they the result of actual Communist influence and activity? That important question will be answered in the next chapter.

CHAPTER 22

COMMUNIST INFLUENCE—
HOW DO THEY GET IT?

Communism becomes the dominant thing in the life of a Communist. It becomes something to which he gives himself completely.

—Former Communist Douglas Hyde[1]

THE VOTES OF INDIVIDUAL COMMUNISTS and their knowing sympathizers and supporters comprise less than one tenth of one percent of those who vote in America—perhaps fewer than one out of a thousand people. That being so, consider this question:

> How can a force of fewer than 100,000 individuals—Communists and their fellow travelers and sympathizers—exert the influence on the American political process which was examined in the last chapter.

The survival of freedom in America could depend on getting the correct answer to that question.

The Communists' secret is not in their numbers but in dedication to their cause and the leadership abilities they develop. They multiply their power by becoming active members of trade unions, peace lobbies, civil rights groups, feminist organizations, senior citizens clubs and tenants rights and a variety of other organizations. By volunteering their time and talents, they become influential. Through the positions they achieve they agitate and organize the "masses" to support Communist goals and objectives. Gus Hall spelled out the tactic in a speech to the 24th Convention of the Communist Party in August 1987. Hall said:

> Communists should display maximum initiative in all organizations they belong to, have contact with, or help lead—trade

unions; civil rights, civil liberties and senior citizens' organizations; the youth and student movement; community coalitions.
We should strive to be the driving force for *all-people's unity.*[2]

That's their key. It's in line with the teaching of Karl Marx
which was quoted earlier. Marx wrote:

...the Party cannot make the revolution alone. The concept of
united front is absolutely essential.

In his book, *The Riot Makers,* the senior editor of *The
Readers' Digest,* Eugene Methevin, tells how the Communists
operate once they take their place in a non-Communist organization. Methevin says:

Here, in capsule, is the Grand Strategy of radical mass manipulation. The Communist sees himself as the orchestrator of all the
discontent that exists in society. Each spark, each friction, he must
see and seize, promote and fan until it grows into an ever rising
flame. Constantly scanning society, he must locate each new
"pressure point," nurture each new grievance, sandpaper each
complaint. As the crescendo rises, he assumes the role of conduc-
tor, waving his baton as the grand "vanguard of the vanguard,"
the general staff of the [orchestrated] revolution...[3]

Communists move societies because they are dedicated and
they understand *the principle of leverage*. Levers are used in
the physical world to multiply and concentrate force on an
object to be moved. Someone once said, "If I had a lever that
was long enough and somewhere to place it, I could move the
world."

The Communist knows that as an individual he can only
apply so much pressure to a public official, newspaper editor,
TV executive, etc. But if he uses the principle of leverage and
applies his pressure through a group, his efforts will be
multiplied by the number of members in the group. Communists use this principle to get others to move the world for
them. That was their goal in forming the *All People's Front*.

To understand how they succeed in getting non-Communists to do their dirty work, look at the approach they
might use in a senior citizen's group, for example. (In March
1986, senior citizens were targeted in *Political Affairs* as a

group the Communists could use. The article said: "The senior citizen's movement, for instance, *representing the most consistently active bloc of voters*, has greatly increased its organization and mobilization.")[4]

The older Communist who is active in a senior citizen's organization would promote Communist goals or programs subtly but continually. However, when the time comes to mobilize senior citizens to oppose contra aid he might not use Marxist foreign policy arguments. Instead, he would raise the cry, "Why should Reagan be allowed to send $100-million to a bunch of cut-throats down there in Central America while the deductible we senior citizens pay on our Medicare is being raised by $225 a year? We gotta tell our congressman right now to keep this money at home." *Communists appeal to people's own interests—and it works.*

ONE RED CAN MAKE A DIFFERENCE

Kent State Professor Sidney Jackson's role in robbing American boys of the victory they won on the battlefields of Vietnam was discussed in Chapter XVIII. That was not the only impact of his 40 years as a Communist.

Communists are activists. They join and then gain positions of influence in organizations because they are willing to accept responsibilities. In most organizations responsibilities go begging, so a Communist's climb to a position of influence is easy. At Jackson's funeral Ohio Communist Party Chairman Jim West said that...

> ...Jackson authored many books and over 1000 articles and *reviews*; had helped organize a faculty union, edited a number of publications and held leading responsibilities in state and national library associations...He was vice president of the Kent State Chapter of the NAACP...[and] served as the first faculty adviser of the Kent Committee To End The War in Vietnam.[5]

Jackson helped organize the faculty union, he was a prolific writer who promoted the Marxist viewpoint, he was active in his professional organizations and played an active role in the civil rights movement. Jackson was a staunch supporter of the National Alliance Against Racist and Political Repression (an officially cited Communist front organization), and had actively campaigned for the release of the Rev. Ben Chavis and the Wilmington 10, Angela Davis and many others. Jackson had been an adviser to the group which planned the massive peace demonstration held in the nation's capital just before his own death. Communists are activists!

Jackson used his leadership positions in the state and national library associations to promote use of libraries for advancing the Communist cause. He actively promoted American publication and use of such Red works as "Tasks of Libraries in the Cultural Revolution" by his friend, the Czech Communist library expert, Jaroslav Drtina. According to Jackson's synopsis, the Drtina article...

> ...expanded on the twin theme that the cultural revolution was very much a part of political revolution and that any disciple of Lenin's would grant a leading role in the cultural revolution to books and libraries.[6]

Jackson's work in the field of library science confirms former Communist leader Louis Budenz's charge that...

> ...For twenty years, the Communists have had the advantage of penetrating our libraries, with cells in many of the important ones, and with influence in the library world and the book review world.[7]

Early in his career Jackson worked as a cataloger in the Brooklyn Public Library, as a Red Cross historian, and in the Buffalo office of the Anti-Defamation League. During World War II he was a captain in the Army Signal Corps. He was a Communist Party member through it all.[8]

Those who refuse to face the Communist danger often point to the relative handful of dues paying members of the Communist Party in the United States—ten to twenty thousand—as evidence that the Communists are weak and ineffective. The record of Dr. Sidney Jackson shows the tremendous and tragic impact just one Communist has had and can have through stirring and agitating others to do the Communists work. His obituary did not record how many students Jackson influenced or recruited into the Party during his 21 years on the faculty at Kent State. At his funeral, Ohio state Communist party chief Jim West said:

> We in the Communist Party are proud of his membership and his life's work.[9]

Jackson's life and activity illustrates that Communists live the life Gus Hall called for when he said:

> Communists should display maximum initiative in all organizations they belong to, have contact with, or help lead—trade unions; civil rights, civil liberties and senior citizens' organizations; the youth and student movement; community coalitions. We should drive to be the driving force for *all-people's unity*.

How do the Communists get men and women like Jackson to give their lives so completely to the task Gus Hall outlined? Douglas Hyde was a top leader of the Communist Party of Great Britain for 20 years. After he left the Party he wrote a book, *Dedication and Leadership*, in which he attempted to answer the question...

> ...why are Communists so dedicated and successful as leaders whilst others so often are not?

Hyde's book-length answer to that question is summarized in the closing chapter of this book. For now, three sentences from that answer will give the non-Communist a glimpse into the total commitment Communists make to their cause. Hyde said:

> ...Communists know there is a battle going on all over the world which in the final analysis is a struggle for men's hearts, minds and souls....Their aim is a Communist World...Communism becomes the dominant thing in the life of the Communist. It becomes something to which he gives himself completely.[10]

Sidney Jackson was not the only Communist professor in the United States. In its January 25, 1982 edition, *U.S. News & World Report* carried a full feature on "Marxism In U.S. Classrooms." The magazine reported:

> Clusters of radical scholars are influencing students—and outraging critics—at such institutions as the University of Massachusetts, Rutgers, Boston University, Stanford, the University

of Chicago, NYU and American University. A host of radical organizations has emerged, publishing a rising number of academic journals and claiming a combined membership of more than 12,000. (pages 42-45)

The draft-card burning, bomb-throwing, building-burning, run-to-Canada radical students of the 1960's and early '70s were the college professors of the 1980s.

Each year, three-to-ten day Marxist scholars conferences attended by professors from all over America are held on major campuses. Top functionaries of the Communist Party participate. University of Minnesota, University of Chicago, University of South Florida at Tampa, University of California at Berkeley, University of Washington-Seattle, Duke, University of Northern Iowa, University of Louisville and others have hosted such conferences since 1985. "Marxist Scholars Conferences" have been conducted at the University of Minnesota as part of the Marxist Summer Institute since 1976.[11] Sidney Jackson actively recruited participants.[12] In 1985 another Kent State University speaker was featured at the ten day Marxist Scholars Conference at the University of Minnesota.[13] Herbert Aptheker, top theoretician of the CPUSA spoke on "Imperialism and Latin America." In a classic example of Marxist "scholarship" he told the assembled scholars, college professors, etc.:

> We have to develop a mass movement in opposition to intervention in Latin America and Nicaragua of the dimensions of the mass movement in the case of Vietnam...What I would project is *that* kind of method: imaginative civil disobedience, illegal action, mass action, picketing, demonstration, demonstrating, marching, sitting down, interfering with the armed forces, interfering with maneuvers—doing everything possible...Can it be done? Oh yes. We have to have *that* kind of a tactic and strategy that, by God, almost immobilized this country. And if we can get anything approaching that, it will play a very great part in decisions of the American ruling class not to invade [Nicaragua]...this is the kind of work the left has to do.[14]

Two years later when President Reagan sent 3000 troops to Honduras pickets surrounded federal installations in

major cities within hours. The demonstrations did not grow
when it became obvious that the troop movement was a
gesture and not a serious effort to move against the Reds in
Nicaragua.

THE WAR IN THE STREETS

Kent State was not the first demonstration of the
Communists' ability or willingness to stir people to violence.
Riots stemming from conflicts between the races killed nearly
150 persons and injured thousands of others between 1964
and 1967. Looting, sniper attacks on police and massive civil
disobedience destroyed the centers of almost 100 American
cities. Over $1-billion worth of property was destroyed.[15]

As Americans started to ask, "Why?" evidence mounted that
the upheaval was not purely the result of "spontaneous com-
bustion." They were part of the Communist program for
destroying America's ability to resist. In February 1967, FBI
Chief J. Edgar Hoover told a committee of the U.S. Congress:

> Communists and other subversives and extremists strive and labor
> ceaselessly to precipitate racial trouble and take advantage of
> racial discord in this country. Such elements were active in
> exploiting and aggravating the riots, for example, in Harlem, .
> Watts, Cleveland and Chicago.[16]

Other law enforcement agencies and judicial commissions
have issued similar warnings. On the fourth day of the
Harlem riots in 1964, acting New York city mayor Paul
Screvane stated that "known Communists" had been involved in the inflammatory rallies and meetings which
preceded the riots and that Communist money had probably
financed some of the demonstrations.[17]

Former Communist Philip Abbot Luce later confirmed
Screvane's charges. In his book, *Road To Revolution*, written
after he left the conspiracy, Luce told how he and other
Communists were "in the center of these riots and did everything possible to expand and extend the riot condition." He
said:

> All of us, as good Communists, were responsible for some work

in the riots and each of us longed for the possibility that Harlem would herald the beginning of a nationwide guerrilla war."[18]

The Cuyahoga County Special Grand Jury which investigated the 1966 summer riots in Cleveland reported:

> This jury finds that the outbreak of lawlessness and disorder was both organized, precipitated, and exploited by a relatively small group of trained and disciplined professionals at this business. They were aided and abetted, willingly or otherwise, by misguided people of all ages and colors, many of whom were avowed believers in violence and extremism, and some of whom are either members or officers of the Communist Party.[19]

Police officials from Cincinnati, Ohio, Nashville, Tennessee and other cities told the Senate Judicial Committee that racial harmony existed in their cities *until* outside agitators moved in. Cincinnati Police Chief Jacob W. Schott charged that four months of firebombing and guerrilla-type violence followed an April 29 speech in which agitator Stokely Carmichael urged Negroes [as they were described then] to "fight the police and burn the city."[20]

Nashville Police Captain John Sorace testified than an April 8, 1967 riot in his city followed a week of agitation by Stokely Carmichael, H. Rap Brown and other leaders of the Student Non-Violent Coordinating Committee (SNCC).[21]

An outbreak of violence in Dayton, Ohio followed a speech by H. Rap Brown who succeeded Carmichael as head of SNCC.[22] Brown spoke in East St. Louis, Illinois on September 10, 1967. Four days later the *St. Louis Post Dispatch* summed up what happened saying:

> In the four days since Brown's appearance at Lincoln Senior High School there have been almost 80 fires, most of them minor, 13 injuries, one death, and 49 arrests. Arson is suspected in many of the fires. No damage estimates have been made.[23]

Brown was also blamed for a riot in Cambridge, Maryland on July 24. Cambridge Police Chief Brice Kinnamon told Congress that a "highly inflammatory speech" by Brown was "the sole reason for our riot." Kinnamon said:

The street was full of guns seconds after the speech. It was a well organized and well planned affair.[24]

The speech received national press coverage at the time. Brown told the Cambridge, Maryland crowd:

...get a gun. I don't care if it's a BB gun with poisoned BB's. America has got to come around or black people are going to burn it down.[25]

As these police officers testified of the role agitators such as Carmichael and Brown played in sparking riots, Carmichael himself visited Castro's Cuba and said that America's Negroes would wage a guerrilla "fight to the death." In Havana for a meeting of Latin American Communist revolutionary leaders, Carmichael said:

In Newark we applied the war tactics of the guerrillas. We are preparing groups of urban guerrillas for our defense in the cities. The price of these rebellions is a high price one must pay. This fight is not going to be a simple street meeting. It is going to be a fight to the death.[26]

After Carmichael's speech in Cuba, the national headquarters of the Student Non-Violent Coordinating Committee in New York announced that "our representative, Mr. Stokely Carmichael," was going to Hanoi, North Vietnam, to...

...see for himself the savage aggression being carried out against that country by the United States.[27]

The testimony of the police chiefs and the boasts of Stokely Carmichael are collaborated by a detailed study of the 1967 Detroit riot done by a militant Negro civil rights activist. Louis Lomax, then one of America's leading Negro authors, had his eyes opened by the activities of trained revolutionaries in Detroit. Lomax reported that the Detroit riot occurred because...

...an organized group, largely from outside the Detroit area, had been operating in the city more than a month...this group had an assignment: burn and destroy.[28]

Lomax said the group was highly organized and well trained—"not thieves and arsonists in the ordinary sense of the words." They are instead, he said...

...revolutionaries committed to the conclusion that the power structure does not have the moral fiber to repent for its socioeconomic sins; that the only truly corrective measures is to leave the nation in ashes.

The principal U.S. cities have been chosen as the battleground simply because they afford the kind of cooperation by the innocent and the uninformed that such revolution needs.[29]

In his series of five articles,[30] Lomax told how these revolutionary agitators, posing as magazine salesmen, worked through the Negro neighborhoods of Detroit, spreading hate and poison. They laid a foundation of hate—and then—waited until an incident occurred between a Negro and the police which was used to spark the riot. Lomax told what happened once the trouble started. He said:

Methodically breaking store windows, the revolutionaries urged the milling Negro people to loot and steal. But—and at least a dozen observers confirmed this—the professionals did no looting on their own. They are not thieves. They are men at war, revolutionaries bent on reducing the nation to ashes.

The looters unknowingly cooperated by having a happy time. The streets teemed with whites and colored who stole with abandon and glee. People came in cars from miles away and hauled off freezers, sofas, television sets and clothing.

Lomax concluded that much of the rioting, burning and looting was carried out by unknowing citizens who "joined the fun" once the riots started. On the other hand, he said...

...the hard core of sniper activity was highly organized. The link between the dedicated revolutionaries and the organized sniper is more philosophical than organizational. The snipers, on the whole, were Detroit's own sons who are trained in guerrilla warfare.

How do riots start? The testimony of J. Edgar Hoover, police officials and concerned black citizens clearly indicate that

subversive agitators provided the sparks which started the
flames burning in America's cities in the mid-1960s. Congressman E.E. Willis (D-La) said a report by staff investigators of the House Committee on Un-American Activities...

> ...clearly indicates that certain subversive elements have been
> involved in some of these riots and in creation of racial unrest
> generally.[31]

That Communists work to exploit and aggravate racial
tensions and rioting and terrorism in America's cities is no
surprise to any student of Communist theory and tactics.
Communists seek to exploit any differences—between black
and white, rich and poor, labor and management, Catholic
and Protestant, or Democrat and Republican. In 1902, Lenin
wrote this guide for future Communists:

> We must go among all classes of people as theoreticians, as
> propagandists, as agitators, and as organizers...The principal
> thing. of course, is propaganda and agitation among all strata of
> people.[32]

As early as 1925, the Communist Party USA instructed its
members:

> The aim of our party in our work among the Negro masses is to
> create a powerful proletarian movement which will fight and lead
> the struggle of the Negro race against exploitation and oppression
> in every form and which will be a militant part of the revolutionary
> struggles of national minorities and colonial peoples of all the
> world and thereby further the cause of the world revolution and
> dictatorship of the proletariat.[33]

J. Edgar Hoover outlined the goals for Communists working
among blacks. He said:

> Communists seek to advance the cause of communism by inject-
> ing themselves into racial situations and in exploiting them (1) to
> intensify the frictions between Negroes and whites to "prove" that
> discrimination against minorities is an inherent defect of the
> capitalist system, (2) to foster domestic disunity by dividing
> Negroes and whites into antagonistic warring factions, (3) to
> undermine and destroy established authority, (4) to incite Negro
> hostility toward law and order, (5) to encourage and foment racial

strife and riotous activity, and (6) to portray the Communist movement as the "champion" of social protest and the only force capable of ameliorating the conditions of the Negro and the oppressed.[34]

How do Communists achieve these goals among Negroes? J. Edgar Hoover answered this question in an earlier appearance before the House Appropriations Subcommittee. Mr. Hoover said that the Communist Party...

...strives only to exploit what are often legitimate Negro complaints and grievances for the advancement of Communist objectives. Controversial or potentially controversial racial issues are deliberately and avidly seized upon by the Communists for the fullest possible exploitation. Racial incidents are magnified and dramatized by the Communists in an effort to generate racial tensions. As a result, such campaigns are actually utilized as a stepping stone to extend Communist influence among the Negroes.[35]

Mr. Hoover summarized the results of Communist efforts to exploit the Negro with these words:

The cumulative effect of almost 50 years of Communist Party activity in the United States cannot be minimized, for it has contributed to disrupting race relations in this country and has exerted an insidious influence on the life and times of our nation...the net result of agitation and propaganda by Communist and other subversive and extremist elements has been to create a climate of conflict between the races in this country and to poison the atmosphere.[36]

The FBI and Congressional investigating committees can no longer expose the agitators who exploit racial tensions. The outbreaks of violence continue with some regularly. Tensions between Blacks and Hispanics have produced four major outbreaks of rioting, burning, looting and violence in Miami since 1980. The January 1989 outbreak followed the shooting of a black man by a Hispanic policeman. Fires lit the Miami sky. Twenty buildings were burned and others were looted. Police were targeted by gun fire and rock throwers.[37]

As in nearly all the riots, immediate charges of police brutality were raised and the Miami City Commission appointed a panel to investigate police use of deadly force.

Later in 1989 racially-stirred rioting, violence and looting erupted in the east coast resort city of Virginia Beach, Virginia over the Labor Day weekend.[38] Approximately 25,000 students converged on the city from predominately black colleges for a "Greekfest" celebration. Because a similar celebration a year earlier got out of hand, the City had prepared to control the activity. A press account said:

> Students were greeted Friday with the sight of police on every street corner and strict rules at resort hotels to prevent a recurrence of shoplifting and rowdiness that hit the town last year.

On Saturday night rioting, violence and looting erupted which continued sporadically for two days. The press accounts said:

> After several small clashes between police and revelers, the crowd, estimated at about 100,000 people, went on a rampage down the main thoroughfare, looting stores, pelting police, shooting guns and setting fires.

Over 100 stores were destroyed and looted. Thirty police officers were injured by rocks and bottles thrown by the crowds. Thirteen demonstrators were injured in scuffles with police. The *Washington Times* reported:

> For two nights this normally tranquil family resort area looked more like a combat zone. Mayor Meyera E. Oberndorf estimated damage to be "in the millions."

Order wasn't restored until the Virginia governor ordered the National Guard to assist city and state police. NAACP officials quickly charged the state and local police and National Guard with "over reacting" and "police brutality."

How do such disturbances occur? Are they a spontaneous reaction to overcrowding, police wrong-doing, etc. or are they deliberately agitated. Could someone be practicing techniques for producing civil turmoil?

In the 1960 riots Black writer Louis Lomax and other

observers and police regularly reported "outside agitators" provoked the violence and the looting. Similar reports were heard in Virginia Beach. Radio and press reports quoted students as charging that problems had been minor until outside agitators triggered the violence. A typical report came from a sophomore from the University of the District of Columbia who said:

> ...some guys from New York are starting the stuff—it's not the students.

In his September 26 column in the *San Francisco Chronicle* Richard Reeves quoted Brenda Adams, publisher of a Virginia Beach area black-oriented newspaper, as saying:

> We're seeing a recurrence of the kind of hatred and bigotry that we saw in the '60s...It's not going to be the Martin Luther King response...Unless there are changes—like increased opportunity in employment, education and housing—we're going to see some pain.

Tragically, much of the work of agitating and organizing the revolution has been financed with taxpayer's dollars. It started in the 1960s.

Rather than directly facing the problem of Communist agitation of racial disorders in America's cities, President Johnson asked Congress for billions of dollars to bolster the war on poverty. Such spending was supposed to help eliminate the conditions in the slums which the Communists (which supposedly didn't exist) would exploit. Any merit such an approach might have had was canceled out when Communists and other agitators *were among those selected to administer the programs.* In effect, arsonists were hired to help fireproof the buildings they planned to burn! In 1964, for example, America's largest circulation newspaper, the *New York Daily News,* revealed that...

> ...Mobilization For Youth, a war on poverty organization with millions of tax dollars to spend, had three dozen employees with current or past connections with the Communist Party and other subversive organizations, including a member of the Communist Party's State Committee in New York. With Communists helping

to call the shots tax dollars were spent to promote rent strikes (organized by a Communist), school boycotts, and to train 300 young hoodlums in the use of rifles.[39]

Even the then ultra-liberal *New York Post* spoke out. It charged that the Mobilization For Youth Director, Carl Brager, had turned...

...fulltime paid agitators and organizers of extremist groups loose on the community to create disorder, disharmony, and violence— the very conditions MFY was created to combat.[40]

In March 1966, 50 New York policemen raided the head-quarters of the Black Arts Repertory Theater which had received more than $100,000 in federal antipoverty funds. In the building, police discovered a rifle range and a well-stocked arsenal of deadly weapons. The head of the project, playwright LeRoi Jones, said, "I don't see anything wrong with hating white people." Federal funds were used at the "theater" for an eight-week summer school where 400 black children were instructed in hard-core black nationalism.[41]

Poverty war director, Sargent Shriver (a Kennedy brother-in-law) conceded that the program was "crude and racist in character." Even so, LeRoi Jones was back on the payroll of one of Shriver's Office of Economic Opportunity organizations a year later. In 1967, poverty fighter Jones was convicted for illegal possession of weapons during the riot in Newark. Charles McCray, chief accountant for Newark's anti-poverty office, was convicted with Jones on the same charge.[42]

A "liberation school" where 10 and 11 year old black children were taught to hate whites was operated in Nashville, Tennessee with federal financing. Nashville Police Chief John Sorace told a Senate committee that the "school" operated on anti-poverty money with...

...Fred H. Brooks as director. Fred Brooks is driving a station wagon leased with OEO funds. He started driving it right after the grant was made. Not only is he a member of SNCC (Student Non-Violent Coordinating Committee) but so are half the student aids. It is almost common knowledge in our community that

SNCC members have received the funds to operate these "hate white" programs.[43]

Poverty officials first denied, then confirmed Sorace's charge that federal grants had been made for the program. When contacted by the press for comment, poverty fighter Brooks said that the federal government...

...can keep their funds—we're going to continue operating. I think Sorace is a racist. He should be killed. He no longer serves a function in society.[44]

FBI Director J. Edgar Hoover had said that Communists work to "undermine and destroy established authority and to incite Negro hostility toward law and order." This Communist program has been implemented with federal tax money.

The then widely-read labor columnist Victor Riesel charged that poverty war offices were riddled with revolutionaries. In a column published in August 1967, Riesel said:

...the Office of Economic Opportunity (OEO) and thousands of its tiny—sometimes store front—headquarters are loaded with literature and promoters of street action. Some of the later are of the New Left, the independent Maoists, the Trotskyites, the pro-Peking Progressive Labor Party "youth" and even Muscovite Communist Party activists...these young revolutionaries...run the poverty program.[45]

Two weeks after Riesel made this charge, police in Kentucky charged three anti-poverty workers with sedition. They had been distributing *The Communist Manifesto* by Karl Marx and Lenin's *The Task of the Proletariat In Our Revolution*. Supplies of such subversive literature were seized in the raid in which poverty war workers were arrested.[46]

Commonwealth Attorney Thomas Ratliff said he would protest against the assignment of Appalachia Volunteers, VISTA workers, and workers from other anti-poverty groups in the area who...

...use federal funds to support subversive activities in Appalachia.

The U.S. Supreme Court ordered Kentucky officials to free

the poverty workers, ruling that the state had no authority to prosecute sedition cases. Bail for the three poverty workers had been posted by Carl Braden, a longtime Communist activist.[47]

Communists and those with close connections with Communists held high positions in poverty war organizations. For example:

> West End Community Council of Louisville, Kentucky of which Braden's wife was an incorporator, received $28,000 in federal funds. The incorporation papers listed the Braden home as headquarters for the group.[48]

> Deputy Director Hal Witt of the United Planning Organization, the principal Washington, D.C. anti-poverty group, was a son of longtime Communist Nathan Witt. Witt's $21,000 a year salary [comparable to $60,000 in 1989 dollars] was paid with federal funds.[49]

The Congressman who exposed Witt's background said that while Witt had never been charged with being a Party member himself, he had a long record of support for left-wing causes and fronts. The situation in New York was even more fantastic:

> Robert Schrank, an identified Communist, was director of the Neighborhood Youth Corps in New York City. An assistant to the New York mayor, John Lindsay, explained that Schrank had dropped his party membership to take the anti-poverty job.[50]

After Schrank's background was exposed, New York Mayor John Lindsay described him as a "distinguished public servant." Schrank was then promoted to the No. 2 spot in New York's anti-poverty structure. Mayor Lindsay later served as a member of the Presidential Commission which couldn't find any evidence of Communist influence behind the 1960s riots.

Communist use of federal funds to further the revolution was all *according to plan*! When Communist Party spokesman Henry Winston returned from a Moscow consultation, he was quoted by *U.S. News & World Report* as saying:

> Today the Economic Opportunity Act has already become the basis for organizing the slums and the ghetto communities and it

offers the point of departure for helping to rally the rank and file millions to a mass movement.[51]

The same issue of *U.S. News & World Report* quoted young revolutionaries as planning to...

> ...latch onto the poverty war funds and use the money to stir trouble.

Are federal funds still being used "to stir trouble?" Have Communist agitators used federal funds to build the *All People's Front* in the 1980s? Are the "politics of discontent" still being financed with taxpayers money? Pinpointing specific Communists who are financed with public money is much more difficult in 1989 than it was in the 1960's. The intelligence agencies which gathered evidence of Red activity in the anti-poverty field in the 1960s have been disbanded or forbidden to collect such information.

However, massive amounts of federal money flow into the coalition of organizations of the types which form the *All People's Front*. In 1981, for example, an Urban Institute study documented the dependence of not-for-profit groups on federal financing.[52] The study showed that...

> ...in 1980 nonprofits such as hospitals, universities, *special interest groups*, and research centers received $40-billion—35% of their budgets from the federal government. *Social and community development groups received $9.6-billion (almost 50% of their operating funds) from taxpayer funds.*

Some of these may be deserving organizations. However, those with a leftist slant such as the League of Women Voters Education Fund, Planned Parenthood Affiliates, the Urban Institute, Welfare Research, Inc., the Legal Services Corporation and a multitude of others have received major funding from the federal government. Among the "social and community development groups" which received nearly $10-billion of taxpayer money are the successors to the "community action groups" which fomented the riots in the 1960s.

The funds come from a variety of sources in the federal budget. In 1989, Senator Jesse Helms (R-NC) and other Congressional critics focussed attention on the National Endowment For The Arts (NEA). The endowment makes grants of about $175-million annually to artists, writers and art and literary projects. (There is absolutely no constitutional basis, of course, for giving any federal money to support artists, etc. but this is no longer an issue.) The 1989 controversy was provoked by grants which financed a perverted and vulgar collection of unbelievable homosexual photos and "artwork" in which the "artist" displayed a crucifix in a jar filled with his own urine. The work was titled "Piss Christ". The two "artists" received $45,000 in federal money for their projects.

The Congress gave the NEA a slap on the wrist by reducing its $170-million appropriation for 1990 by $45,000. Senator Helms' very specific amendment banning use of federal funds to subsidize any blasphemous or perverted or obscene artwork was voted down in both the House and Senate. An innocuous resolution instructing the NEA staff to refrain from subsidizing art projects believed to be obscene was passed instead.[53]

In addition to paying for filthy art, the National Endowment for the Arts has provided on-going financing for leftist projects managed by those with close connections to the Communist Party USA. The Fall 1984 Midwest Distributors Catalog carried an introduction which said:

Since 1978, our organization has distributed small press literature across the middle of our country, *supported by grants from the National Endowment for the Arts. We also mail books to libraries, bookstores and individuals nationwide.*[54]

The catalog carries the notation, *Catalog printed under a grant from the National Endowment for the Arts, a federal agency.* Books listed include those issued by Communist and other militant publishing houses and Communist authors. Midwest Distributors catalogs and literature have carried endorsements by such identified Communists as Angela Davis and Pete Seeger. The catalog lists Fred Whitehead as "Director." Whitehead has frequent by-lined articles in the Communist theoretical journal, *Political Affairs* and the *People's Daily World.*[55] The financing continued for at least eight years. The 1986-87 catalog indicated that NEA funding had stopped because Midwest Distributors was "a service organization rather than a business." Midwest Distributors catalog and literature distribution activity continued with private financing. The 1986 edition indicated that similar "distributors on the Coasts" were continuing "to receive large amounts" from the National Endowment for the Arts.

Taxpayers dollars finance the enemy internationally and internally. The financing comes directly through grants from the federal budget plus other hundreds of millions (or billions) of dollars in grants from tax-exempt foundations.

WHERE AND HOW DO THEY WORK?

Communists recruit, motivate and work with people by appealing to them on the basis of their own interests. They continually challenge their people to be reaching out to others. In December 1974, *Political Affairs*, the party's theoretical journal, taught...

> The Central Committee of the Party has clearly noted that young people because of their aspirations as youth, that women because of their aspirations as women, that Christians because of their aspirations as Christians, that intellectuals because of their aspirations as intellectuals can be led in greater numbers and ever more firmly into the union [with Communists].

A single Communist in an organization or on a campus or union can have a tremendous impact—as the story of Dr. Sidney Jackson at Kent State shows. Communists work to have input into every area of society. They have been particularly successful in reaching into the four groups cited in the 1974 Central Committee statement: youth, women, Christians and intellectuals.

REDS INFLUENCE YOUNG PEOPLE

Communists stirred several thousand San Francisco area college students to riot against the House Committee on Un-American Activities in May 1960. The HCUA was attempting to hold hearings on Communist influence in the Bay Area. FBI Director J. Edgar Hoover issued a special report on the riot titled, *Communist Target: Youth*. In it Hoover said:

The successful Communist exploitation and manipulation of youth and students groups throughout the world today are a major challenge which free world forces must meet and defeat. Recent world events clearly reveal that world communism has launched a massive campaign to capture and maneuver youth and students groups.

In the relentless struggle for world domination being waged by them, Communists are dedicated to the Leninist principle that "youth will decide the issue of the entire struggle—both the student youth, and, still more, the working-class youth."

The Communists demonstrated in San Francisco just how powerful a weapon Communist infiltration is. They revealed how it is possible for only a few Communist agitators, using mob psychology, to turn peaceful demonstrations into riots. Their success there must serve as a warning that their infiltration efforts aimed not only at youth and student groups, but also at our labor unions, churches, professional groups, artists, newspapers, government and the like, can create chaos and shatter our internal security.[56]

Congressman Francis Walter (D-PA), Chairman of the House Committee on Un-American Activities at the time, issued a similar warning. He said:

Although the overwhelming majority of the young people of this nation are of unquestioned patriotism, this must not beguile us into feeling that because Communist infiltrators among our youth are numerically in a minority, their threat is necessarily insignificant.

The strength of the Communist movement bears little relationship to the number of its members; that instead, its strength and effectiveness are in direct ratio to the intensity of the efforts of the few who are trained and disciplined agents. It was with only a relative few that Lenin seized control of the government of Russia. Only a few—some 3 or 4 percent—in Soviet Russia today are Communists.

The Communist conspiracy operating on American soil—let it be emphasized and reemphasized—is part and parcel of the world conspiracy and the thousands of Communists in the United States

are for all intents and purposes foreign agents on American soil
who are dedicated to our destruction.[57]

Stirring warnings like those are no longer given to the
American people. The longtime Communist goal of abolishing
the House Committee on Un-American Activities was accomplished in the mid-1970s. Today's FBI no longer is permitted to investigate and educate to keep the American
public informed as they once did.

Meanwhile the Communist efforts to ensnare and use
America's youth has continued. During the 1960s and 1970s
the Communists demonstrated their ability to agitate young
people to do the Reds bidding. Multitudes burned their draft
cards or went to Canada to escape Vietnam war service.
ROTC buildings on nearly 100 campuses were bombed or
burned during protests against the war. An armed mob of
militants seized control of Cornell University at gunpoint.
Pictures of the grubby terrorists with their guns and ban-
doliers of ammunition slung over their shoulders ran in
newspapers across America and on the front cover of the May
4, 1969 *Newsweek*. (Even though New York had the strictest
gun laws in the nation at the time and the heavily armed
terrorists could be easily identified in the photos, none of
them was prosecuted.) The mounting pressures and lawlessness continued to mount and culminated in the Kent State
tragedy in May 1970.

Red successes in reaching young people continued in the
decade of the 1980s. Over 200 student leaders from dozens of
campuses participated in a Young Communist League meeting held in April 1989 meeting at Brown University in
Providence, Rhode Island. The president of the United States
Student Association, Fred Azcarte was a special guest
speaker.[58] He told the Communist conference:

> It is important to work together everywhere we can...Unity is the
> key. That's our future: working together.

In a full-page interview in the *People's Daily World* Azcarte
said, "We're going to be a thousand voices of dissent."[59] The
United States Student Association he heads is the largest and

oldest student organization in the country. It has chapters on 250 campuses which have over 2-million students.[60]

A leader of the Young Communist League, Jason Rabinowitz, was elected co-president of the student body at the University of Massachusetts-Amherst in 1988.[61] (Communists triumph when good men do nothing. The Red won when only 2000 out of 25,000 students bothered to vote in the election.)

RED INFLUENCE AMONG WOMEN

The Communist Party USA has strongly supported the feminist movement in the Unites States since its inception. Both groups share a similar agenda—abortion, ERA, gay rights, etc. (Communist support for the equal rights movement for women in the United States is hypocritical in that as of early 1989 no woman served on any of the top councils of the Soviet Union.)

Continued close cooperation between the Communists and the feminists was assured with Molly Yard's election in late 1987 as president of the National Organization of Women. The *St. Louis Post-Dispatch* story[62] announcing her election carried a headline which said:

New President of NOW
Attacks Bork and Pope

Molly Yard is a longtime leftist. The news story said that her activism dates back to the Socialist Presidential campaigns of Norman Thomas in the 1930s. She received an early challenge to political activism from Eleanor Roosevelt. She is definitely not a mainstream American.

Nearly 40 years ago, according to the *Post-Dispatch* story, Yard was accused by a Republican city chairman of being a Communist. She was involved at the time in an effort to dislodge an entrenched city political machine. She sued the Republican chairman for libel and won a $1000 out-of-court settlement for dropping the suit. He had assumed she was a Red because of her leftist activities and views.

With Molly Yard in charge, NOW maintained its leftward orientation—its program effectively meshing with the agenda of the *All People's Front*. Gus Hall noticed and *was pleased*.

Following the 1989 NOW convention in Cincinnati, Hall, in his weekly cassette tape message[63] *to CPUSA members and fellow travelers, said:*

> The convention of NOW—the National Organization of Women—reflects a new militancy on all questions. NOW is a multi-racial, multi-national organization *and it cuts across class lines*...it's clear from many of the speeches *that they more clearly now see the struggle for the equality of women as related to the class struggle.* That is a very important step in the political arena.

> The most important result of the convention is that NOW will pursue a policy of building alliances and move towards organizing a new political party. When you put the two together—the move toward building alliances and the need for a new political party...it brings political independence to a new level.

> Women are the advance force [of the revolution] in the present day period...Since the decision on abortion and the affirmative action decisions of the Supreme Court the membership of NOW has increased ten fold—they can't keep up with the applications.

As the Communist Central Committee report said, "We will appeal to women on the basis of their aspirations as women."

RED INFLUENCE IN RELIGION

The 1986-87 report of the FBI on *Soviet Active Measures in the United States* was published in the December 9, 1987 *Congressional Record.*[64] (The FBI, though banned from investigating domestic Communist activity is still charged with maintaining surveillance of Soviet agents operating within the U.S.) The detailed and exhaustive FBI report spotlights Soviet efforts to attack SDI, manipulate the peace movement, influence religious organizations and use the United Nations in New York as a base for espionage activity.

In a section titled "The Soviet Campaign To Influence Religious Organizations", the FBI report said:

> It is clear...that the Soviet Union is increasingly interested in influencing and/or manipulating American churches, religious organizations, and their leaders within the United States...The apparent Soviet objective is to generate a bloc of opposition

against U.S. military spending for new weapons systems, specifically SDI, and to influence religious opinions against U.S. defense
policies.[65]

The FBI said that the new campaign "has targeted the
members and leaders of a broad range of religious organizations within the United States" and uses several channels for
its campaign of disinformation. They include:

The Moscow Patriarchate of the Russian Orthodox Church
(ROC). The ROC apparatus is carefully monitored and controlled
through the Council for Religious Affairs of the USSR. Therefore
only politically loyal and obedient church leaders reach positions
of authority and are allowed to have contact with foreigners.

The All-Union Council of Evangelical Christian-Baptists
(AUCECB) is officially recognized by the Soviet government and
is registered with the State Committee for Religious Affairs. It is
composed of Baptist and Pentecostal congregations which col-
laborate with Soviet authorities on both the national and local
level *and should not be confused with "unregistered" dissident
Baptists and other Christians who are persecuted by the same
Soviet authorities.* (Emphasis added)

The Foreign Relations Department of the Moscow Patriarchate is
responsible for ROC relations with the Soviet Committee for the
Defense of Peace, the Christian Peace Conference and other
Soviet front organizations. It also coordinates activities with the
U.S. Peace Council's Religious Circles Committee, the World
Council of Churches, the U.S. National Council of Churches and
other religious organizations outside the Soviet Union.[66]

The FBI report states that Soviet church and government
officials have utilized statements obtained from visiting
"prominent, conservative Christian leaders" concerning the
growth of religious freedom "to encourage the development of
a more favorable attitude toward the Soviet government."
The FBI ended the religious section of its report on Soviet
active measures in the United States with this statement:

Many individuals with sincere desires for disarmament, human
rights protection, and religious freedom in the Soviet Union are
purposely being misinformed by the powerful Soviet organiza-

tions that control the activities and actions of all state-sponsored organizations in the Soviet Union.[67]

The leftist influences in the National and World Councils of Churches have been well documented by committees of Congress, by the *Reader's Digest* and can be proven convincingly from their own literature.

A *Reader's Digest* article, "Do You Know Where Your Church Offerings Go?" in January 1983 sparked major controversy. The Digest said...

> In the last decade the National Council [of Churches] has become increasingly politicized. Critics charge that it supports Marxist-Leninist governments in the Third World and that it has become obsessed with the alleged injustices of America.[68]

The charges were supported by a study done by David Jessup, a Methodist layman (he worked for the AFL-CIO's Committee on Political Education at the time). Jessup discovered and documented that during a two year period $442,000 in American churchgoers money had been channeled to political organizations...

> ...supporting the Palestine Liberation Organization, the Communist governments of Cuba and Vietnam, the pro-Soviet totalitarian movements of Latin America, Asia and Africa and several violence-prone fringe groups in the United States.

> The Domestic Hunger Network, coordinated by the NCC, raised $650,000 in 1980 with appeals showing pictures of needy children. Some money from the hunger appeals went for emergency help (the agency could not say how much, but a significant portion funds political activists.)

> The World Council of Churches Church World Service arm provided nearly half a million dollars for Communist Vietnam's "New Economic Zones" which major newspapers described as little better than "concentration camps for political undesirables."[69]

In commenting on the obsession of church leaders to finance causes that contradict the basic beliefs of most churchgoers, David Jessup said:

People just can't believe that their church, the church they've loved all their lives, can be financing all these Marxist-Leninist projects. The very idea seems preposterous, an affront to common sense.

The *Reader's Digest* article contrasted NCC statements condemning capitalism, and alleged injustices in the United States and other friendly anti-Communist nations with highly favorable reports on conditions in Communist countries like Cuba and Vietnam.

Methodist evangelist Edmund Robb heads the Institute on Religion and Democracy. The *Reader's Digest* articles quoted him as saying that church support for Marxist-Leninist causes stems from...

...the secularization of the church. The NCC has substituted revolution for religion.[70]

That has happened because "mainline" denominations which comprise the NCC have largely turned away from the Bible and the supernatural. Having lost faith in the power of God to change men's hearts and lives, they have largely accepted the Humanist-Marxist concept that changing man's environment will change his heart. They now offer a humanistic mixture of man's wisdom and Marxism. That judgment is supported by a statement of a World Council of Churches leader. Dr. Nina Koshy is director of international affairs for the World Council of Churches. In a 1989 statement distributed by the Ecumenical Press Service, she stated:

To a large number of Christians in all parts of the world, the social and political message of Marxism has been a challenge and even inspiration...This has also led to active collaboration between Christians and Marxists in liberation movements, in struggles for peace and justice in revolutionary situations and in building socialism together.[71]

The "collaboration" was formalized by the 1988 visit of Konstantin Kharchev to the World Council of Churches headquarters in Switzerland. Kharchev was chairman of the State Council for Religious Affairs in the Council of Ministers of the

USSR. He met with the general secretaries and top staff of the World Council of Churches, World Alliance of Reformed Churches and the Lutheran World Federation.[72]

Kharchev as the top religious official in the Soviet Union told the assembled church leaders that while he disagrees with the belief that God exists, "I respect and must respect the other point of view."

After giving a glowing report about new freedoms for religion under "perestroika," Kharchev then noted that...

> ...the arrival of "full communism" will mean an end to religion, but such a day is far off. For now and the foreseeable future, Communists and religious believers need to live in mutual respect and build a good life for people together on earth.[73]

The World Council of Churches response to this official reaffirmation that communism will eventually abolish all religion was to go to Moscow for its July 1989 Central Committee meeting.[74]

CATHOLIC INVOLVEMENT

Since Vatican II, the Catholic Church which had long taken a strong position against communism and socialism has moved to the left and opened itself to influence by Communists. In Gus Hall's post-1984 election recap he reported on Communist inroads in many areas including an important one in the Catholic Church. Gus Hall's analysis of the 1984 elections mentioned the success the Party had in influencing the Catholic Bishop's Pastoral Letter on the Economy. Hall said:

> On the Bishop's Pastoral letter on the economy: I wish they had released it before the elections but the release date was a compromise. As far as it goes it is a good draft, a sharp condemnation of the inequalities in the [economic] system, but not a condemnation of the system itself. It is very careful not to do that. However, I was surprised at how sharp the wording is in exposing and condemning the extent of unemployment, hunger, poverty, and unequal distribution of wealth. We shall see if and how it is watered down under the influence of the more conservative bishops and the pressures of the Reagan administration.[75]

Hall then instructed the comrades on the potential for using the Bishops' letter as a door opener for Communist activity among Catholic groups. He said:

> The document has possibilities of being an effective educational, agitational and even mobilizational instrument for reform.

This is a typical Communist tactic and goal. They work to have some of their concepts or views inserted into a non-Communist organizational statement or position paper which is then used as an opening with the group's membership or followers. Why or how did the Catholic Bishops turn out a left-leaning report on the American economy which Communists can use to agitate and mobilize Catholics to support Communist causes? Hall told the Party faithful:

> You should know, we had some input into the best aspects of this letter. The bishop's drafting committee studied the material we provided.

THE RED WORK AMONG EDUCATORS

Communists say that "intellectuals because of their aspirations as intellectuals can be led into ever closer union with Communists." A story from the July 25, 1981 *Daily World*, the official Communist newspaper uses the Communist Aesopian language to tell of growing Red influence in the teacher's union. One paragraph in the article points up Communist success in influencing the NEA. It states:

> Nowhere in the basic documents of the NEA, in their resolutions or new business items, are there any anti-Soviet or anti-socialist positions. This is susceptible to change, of course, if progressive forces are not vigilant.[76]

Careful study of the resolutions passed by NEA conventions in the eight years since fails to show any anti-Soviet or anti-socialist resolutions. Communist publications regularly feature favorable articles on the NEA, interviews with NEA leaders such as Mary Hatwood Futrell, etc.[77]

The NEA has become one of the most powerful lobbying organizations in Washington and state capitals across

America. Its clout is built on the people power and the big warchests it can turn lose on election day.

The NEA move into political activism was announced by the NEA executive secretary, Sam Lambert, in the *NEA JOURNAL* in December 1967. Lambert said:

> NEA will become a political power second to no other special interest group....NEA will organize this profession from top to bottom into logical operational units that can move swiftly and effectively with power unmatched by any other organized group in the nation.[78]

That political clout has developed. In the January-February 1974 *Today's Education* NEA President Helen Wise told the teachers:

> Teachers are 2-million strong, and any politician who can count knows how much power an active, determined group of that size can generate.[79]

The leftist ideological commitment of the NEA's leadership was demonstrated in 1980. The board of directors endorsed the Carter-Mondale presidential ticket over Reagan-Bush *by a vote of 118 to 4.* The leadership's leftist leanings do not represent the views of most of the NEA's 1.5-million teacher members.[80]

In 1988, NEA President Mary Hatwood Futrell told delegates to the NEA Convention in New Orleans on July 4...

> ...I have decided that the most electable and desirable candidate is Michael Dukakis...Our job is to turn out every one of our 1.9-million members...Fortunately, we have an effective weapon...That weapon is our political power...We have succeeded in building one of the most powerful political networks in the nation. There are literally thousands of organized and motivated NEA members in each congressional district in America.[81]

> Starting today, we are going to completely mobilize that network, and we are not going to rest until midnight, November 8, 1988.

The highly effective NEA political machine didn't elect Dukakis but its efforts helped keep control of Congress in leftist hands. The NEA political machine promotes an updated version of the Dewey/Rugg/Counts/Givens "progressivist" agenda outlined in Chapter VI and the Communists love it. On June 25, 1987, for example, the *People's Daily World* ran a glowing two-page tribute to "A Fighting Teachers Union." The Red paper applauded NEA resolutions supporting...

> ...the Equal Rights Amendment, affirmative action, nuclear disarmament and ratification of SALT II; its opposition to apartheid and U.S. aid to the anti-Communist Nicaraguan contras; and its support for such Communist-originated demonstrations as the massive 1981 Solidarity Day effort.

The Communist paper concluded its tribute to the NEA saying:

> The union's progressive policies and united actions indicate that the 1987 convention will continue to provide leadership for its membership and set an example for the labor movement as a whole.(Page 15A)

The 1987 NEA Convention, which the Communists were anticipating, passed a host of resolutions which supported...

> ...abortion and ERA...gay, lesbian and AIDS infected teachers...sex education and access to birth control methods without parental consent ...AIDS education including the prevention option of "medically accepted protective devices"...a nuclear freeze...absolute teacher control over curricula, books, etc. without accountability...and education emphasizing "global citizenship." (For the actual text of the resolutions, send $1 for the October 1987 *Phyllis Schlafly Report*, Box 618, Alton, Illinois 62002.)

The NEA, as evidenced by the leftist orientation of the resolutions passed at its conventions and absence of any anti-Soviet or anti-Communist positions, lines up comfortably with the agenda of the Communist-mobilized *All People's Front*.

In addition to pushing a leftist agenda, NEA resources are also committed to fighting the leaders and activities of groups which oppose their leftist, anti-morality agenda—and those who support   pro-American, pro-family, anti-Communist positions.

NEA targets include groups favoring school prayer, gun owners' rights, free enterprise, a strong military defense and traditional American religious and family values. Opposing abortion, homosexuality, school sex education, communism, etc. also gets individuals and groups on the NEA "enemy" list.

The Western States Regional Staff of the NEA developed a 50-page training manual for teachers and NEA leaders titled "Combatting The New Right." It targeted as enemies the leaders and activities of just about every conservative, pro-God, pro-America political and educational organization in America. Phyllis Schlafly, Rev. Jerry Falwell, Pat Robertson, the Heritage Foundation, black conservative economist Thomas Sowell and Senators Jesse Helms, Bob Dole and Paul Laxalt were among the many effective conservative leaders spotlighted as part of the dangerous "new right."

NEA executive board member, Jim Lewis spoke to over 200 groups. In his appearance before the Kansas NEA Assembly on April 27, 1985 he listed most of those targeted in the NEA "Combatting The New Right" manual and added the *Readers' Digest* and its senior editor, Eugene Methevin. He denied that these people were conservatives and labeled them as dangerous "radical rightists." Lewis then said:

> Now we've had radical right movements throughout history, and you can't have a radical right movement if they don't have a scapegoat enemy. For instance, for the Nazis it was the Jews. For the Romans, it was the Christians. For the Catholic church it was the heretics. For the Protestants it was the witches. For the know-nothings, it was Catholics, Jews and Blacks. For McCarthy, it was the Communists. But for the New Right, the enemies are public education and secular humanism. Radical right groups always polarize and emotionalize their issues.(Page 3-4)

Lewis would probably abhor what he would have labeled Joe McCarthy's "guilt by association" tactics but this speech showed him to be a rather skilled practitioner.

As the NEA has developed its left-leaning political machine, the education of American children suffered a tragic decline.

Headlines told that scores on the SAT and ACT college entrance exams were dropping. Functional illiteracy in cities reached epidemic levels. The crisis in education steadily worsened. Then in April 1983, President Reagan's *National Commission on Excellence in Education* issued its historic report, "A Nation At Risk." It said:

> The educational foundations of our society are presently being eroded by a rising tide of mediocrity which threatens our very future as a nation and as a people...If an unfriendly foreign power had attempted to impose on America the mediocre educational performance that exists today, we might well have viewed it as an act of war.[82]

The NEA responded with proposals for giving the NEA-dominated education establishment more money and more control while resisting teacher accountability measures. Their proposals were among the "reforms" passed by legislatures in the Excellence in Education acts in the mid-1980's.

The "band-aid" patchup of education didn't work. By 1989, the *Chicago Tribune's* September 12th front-page headline screamed:

College Entrance Test Scores Show Further Decline

RED INFLUENCE IN UNIONS

Organized labor has, of course, always been a target for Communist infiltrators. For years the leadership of the old American Federation of Labor (AFL) exercised vigilance to combat Communist efforts to influence and control the unions. The battles were sometimes vicious.[83] As some of the older union leaders who had gone through battles with the Reds retired or died, the Communists sought—and gained—new influence in the trade union movement.

The 1986-87 report of the FBI on *Soviet Active Measures in the United States* had a major section on Soviet efforts to influence U.S. labor organizations and trade unions.[84] Much of the Red's labor-directed subversion is channeled through the World Federation of Trade Unions. Headquartered in Czechoslovakia, this pro-Soviet trade union organization claims 300-million members 90% of which are in Communist-controlled countries. The FBI report says:

> The Labor Research Association (LRA) which was founded by the CPUSA in 1927 is the U.S. component of the WFTU. Its self-stated goals are to provide publications, research materials, and educational programs for U.S. labor and trade unions.[85]

The FBI report states that the LRA receives its direction from the Labor Department of the CPUSA and has an advisory board of 13 individuals who are nearly all CPUSA members. The FBI said:

> LRA espouses the official line of the CPUSA and during 1986 was actively involved in the peace and disarmament movement as it affects the labor movement in the United States.

LRA's influence in the American labor movement can be seen from the support unions and their leadership give to the Communist-controlled LRA's annual fund raising events. In recent years important governmental and labor leaders have participated. These include: NEA president Mary Hatwood Futrell, Kenneth Blaylock, the head of the 700,000 member American Federation of Government Employees, Machinist Union head William Winpisinger, TV mogul and one-time Screen Actors Guild head Ed Asner, Manhattan Boro President David Dinkins (a candidate for mayor of New York in 1989), and the Congressional Black Caucus.[86]

As many as 600 heads of powerful unions have attended the annual LRA fundraising luncheons in recent years—pouring huge sums of money from the dues of American workers into the coffers of the Communist organization. Co-sponsor lists for the Communist-controlled LRA fund raisers read like a "Who's Who" of American labor leaders. Names of co-sponsors listed in the Communist *Daily World*, have included:

> Douglas Fraser, president of the United Auto Workers; Lloyd McBride, president, United Steel Workers of America; Henry Nicholas, president, National Union of Hospital and Health Employees; John Sweeney, president, Service Employees International Union; Moe Biller, general president, American Postal

Workers Union; Boris Block, general secretary treasurer, United
Electrical Workers;

Shannon Wall, president, National Maritime Union; Murray Fin-
ley, president, Amalgamated Clothing Workers; Thomas
Gleason, president, International Longshoreman's Association;
Robert Goss, president, Oil, Chemical and Atomic Workers;
Barbara Hutchinson, vice president, American Federation of
Government Employees; R.I. Kilroy, president, Brotherhood of
Railway and Airline Clerks; Henry Foner, president, Joint Fur-
riers Board plus officers of many union locals.[87]

That high-powered list of labor leaders has participated in
and/or sponsored a fund-raiser for an officially designed Communist-controlled organization.

William Winpisinger, the head of the mammoth International Association of Machinists, is a real favorite of the
Marxists. Winpisinger is a longtime socialist. He has regularly promoted the Communist goal of a breakaway labor-con-
trolled third party in America.[88] Winpisinger's Machinists
Union represents many of the workers in America's aerospace
and defense industries. Even so, he regularly advances the
Communist line on disarmament—which would abolish the
jobs of his members. In March 1981, for example, Winpisinger
addressed a peace conference in Cleveland. He told the crowd
that...

The Reagan budget and the arms race are madness...We should
start looking at things from Russia's perspective.[89]

How many of Winpisinger's IAM members know that their
dues payments finance his speeches and lobbying in
Washington to stop the military buildup which would weaken
America and *eliminate their jobs*?

That points up the problem. The leadership of many organizations does not represent the real needs of members. In
1988, the author used the Winpisinger example in a
Rochester, N.Y. church on a Sunday evening. The 150 people
in the congregation were asked, "How many of you are union
members?" Twenty-nine people raised their hands—twenty
seven men and two women. They were asked, "How many of

you attend your union meetings?" There were only two. As the English political philosopher Edmund Burke said 200 years ago:

Evil triumphs when good men do nothing.

Good Americans who fail to participate in the organizations which "represent" them give the Reds an opportunity to take over. Leftists gain influence and power and then use the dues money and the prestige of their numbers to promote causes which are not in the best interest of the Union, its members or America.

In the May 1987 *Political Affairs*, the theoretical journal of the Communist Party USA, Communists were instructed to target state legislatures and told how to gain new influence in trade unions.

An article headlined, "State Capitals: A Vital Venue For People's Politics,"[90] laid out the strategy. Rap Lewis, the author, in a 3-page article repeatedly pointed Party members toward influencing state legislatures. He said:

I believe the importance of work in the state legislatures is under-estimated by the Party....Congress is the decisive arena of legislative struggle. But state legislatures are a much more accessible area. It is there that workers can be most readily involved and educated in the legislative side of the class struggle....In all struggles at the state legislative level, we should consciously work to relate the issues to the national level.

In the 18 months after Lewis called for more focus on national issues, an increasing number of resolutions on foreign policy, disarmament, etc. were introduced into state legislatures.

Three months after Lewis kicked off the campaign to intensify Communist efforts in state capitols, Gus Hall picked up the baton. In a major presentation at the Communist Party's 24th Annual convention, Hall said:

The struggle to defeat the Reaganites in the presidential election, to further shift the political balance in Congress, to elect more trade unionists, women, Afro-Americans, Mexican-Americans, Puerto Ricans, Asian-Pacific Americans, American Indians *and*

> *to cut the number of Republicans in state legislatures,* will help
> lay the basis for the trade union and people's movements to go
> over to the offensive.[91]

In the 1988 elections, observers were surprised by the
defeat of veteran Republican legislators and some conservative Democrats in a number of states. The Party gives the
directives—its members then stir the *All People's Front* to do
the work.

In his May 1987 *Political Affairs* article Rap Lewis instructed the comrades to use trade union political action
committees to accomplish their goals. Lewis said:

> Each district [of the Communist Party] should find a way to
> initiate or become involved in existing AFL-CIO action commit-
> tees in the congressional districts. Reports on their work should
> be funneled to the National Legislative Department [of the Com-
> munist Party].

On the next page, Lewis emphasized the importance of the
earlier order. He said:

> I believe that the AFL-CIO's recently-inaugurated "legislative
> action committees" (LAC's) offer a supreme opportunity to
> bridge the gap between local union memberships and congres-
> sional struggles. Each LAC is based in a congressional district
> and is open to participation by the rank and file.

The words "open to participation by the rank and file" would
be understood by the Communist reader to be a command to
get involved. The term "rank and file" is Communist jargon
for their workers. Lewis made the point even more clearly
saying:

> Clearly, it is possible to make each LAC into a mass form and a
> vehicle for worker education in effective legislative action.

In the Aesopian language Communists use, "mass form"
means an organization controlled or manipulated by the
Communists and used to educate workers to support the
Communist legislative program.

The Communists instructed their members to get involved
in and work to take control of the AFL-CIO Legislative Action

Committees. Could Communists do it? Would union officials permit it? The door had already been opened for the Communist infiltrator. The Missouri State Labor Council's official newsletter, *View Points* is published monthly and mailed to Missouri union members. In the January 1987 issue, Daniel J. (Duke) McVey, the MSLC President issued a call for help. He wrote:

> Among the State Labor Council's highest priorities for 1987 is a formal attempt to organize your voices so that grassroots labor opinion is more evident to Missouri's congressional delegation and members of the Missouri House and Senate.

> The national AFL-CIO began a Legislative Action Committee network in 1981, and the program now operates in 40 congressional districts. The network has posted notable successes.[92]

McVey's article confirmed the existence of the LAC network the Communists ordered its members to infiltrate and use for Communist goals. In the next paragraph, McVey unwittingly opened the door for Communist participation. He wrote:

> The state council this month will solicit volunteers in selected congressional, Missouri Senate and Missouri House districts to establish such a network on the state level. In launching such a program we know that we must concentrate our limited resources in areas where legislators are newly elected or considered "swing" votes on critical labor issues.[93] Those who volunteer must be workers in the true sense of the word. The Legislative Action Network will require time and effort.

There it is—the open door. In any organization, very few members will volunteer for any job. But Communists look for any opportunity—any open door—where they can gain influence and respectability for the red cause. Were there Communists in Missouri who could walk through the open door?

In recent years, the CPUSA has raised $500,000 annually to expand the circulation of the *People's Daily World*. Goals are established for each of the Party's 34 districts. In 1989, as in several previous years, the Missouri-Kansas District was among the first five to seven districts to over subscribe its quota.[94]

Communists use leverage—multiplying their individual strength and power by working to gain positions of influence in all sorts of non-Communist organizations. They play upon the fears, the greed, and the guilt of individuals manipulating them to do the Communists bidding—or at least not to oppose Communist programs.

Communists work like the leaven the Bible warns us about when it says:

A little leaven leaveneth the whole lump.[95]

When leaven (like yeast) is introduced into a ball of dough, its effect permeates the whole lump of dough. The Bible uses the effects of leaven to demonstrate the effect of sin. A little sin, not dealt with, will take over and poison an entire life. So too, the poison which Communists introduce into an organization or group or society. The Communist "leaven" because it appeals to man's greedy, self-seeking, rebellious nature—a nature which often does not want to face and solve real problems—will spread through the entire group or organization.

That's the problem. What can be done to expose and oppose the Red efforts? In the Sermon on the Mount, the Lord calls His people to be the "salt of the earth." In Bible times salt had many uses, one of the most important of which was in curing meat. When salt permeated a piece of meat it retarded spoilage—*held back the corruption*. That's what the Lord envisioned that His people would do in society when He said:

Ye are the salt of the earth: but if the salt have lost his savour, wherewith shall it be salted? It is thenceforth good for nothing but to be cast out, and to be trodden under foot of men. (Matthew 5:13)

That is what is happening today. America is being trodden under foot of wicked men. God's people are not permeating society and functioning as the "salt" which should hold back the Communist/humanist/hedonist "leaven."

The Lord described the Christian's function in another way

which gives further understanding of the answer to the Communist "leaven" in society. He said:

Ye are the light of the world. (Matthew 5:14)

Light drives away darkness so that man can see. God's people should be able to show forth the light of truth in society so others will not be blinded by the darkness.

Putting these two challenges together gives the answer to the Communist leaven in society's organizations. God's people must be the "salt" which holds back corruption and wickedness and the "light" which exposes error and gives understanding to the issues groups and organizations face.

Communists are effective because they know and understand issues and can present them from the Communist viewpoint. When they do so in a meeting many may feel that something is not quite right. However, when the Communist appears to have facts and is skillful at presenting them, others will be reluctant to speak up, fearing that they will be made to look foolish.

However, if just one or two people who recognize the error speak up, others will follow. These same informed individuals can provide leadership in a sound direction.

It can work—it will work. In I Chronicles 12:32, the Bible says:

And of the children of Issachar, which were men that had understanding of the times, to know what Israel ought to do; the heads of them were two hundred; *and all their brethren were at their commandment.*

That is our challenge—that is our hope—that we might be a people with an *understanding of the times*—a people who know what our nation ought to do. Once we have this knowledge and understanding, we must develop the same degree of dedication and leadership and communications skills the Communists exhibit. Then we can go out into society's groups and organizations to be the "salt and light" which holds back the wickedness and corruption and leads our society in the direction of truth and liberty. Will you accept the challenge? Your future may depend on it!

CHAPTER 23

THE COMMUNIST BLUEPRINT
FOR CONQUEST WITHOUT WAR

As long as capitalism and socialism exist we cannot live in peace; in the end one or the other will triumph—a funeral dirge will be sung over either the Soviet Republics or over world capitalism.

—V.I. Lenin

FOLLOWING LENIN'S PLAN, the Communists have succeeded in capturing one-third of the earth's people and 25% of the earth's land mass—more people and more of the earth's surface than any other would be world conqueror in history.

Every communist leader and theoretician since Karl Marx has believed and taught that the worldwide triumph of communism is inevitable. The United States is the last major obstacle between communists and world control—and they plan to conquer America without a war.

Violent revolution was once thought to be the only pathway to socialism. However, in 1948 a relative handful of Czech communists successfully pressured the Czech's national legislative body to accept a "peaceful" transition to socialism. The Red success in Czechoslovakia has become the pattern for the conquest of more advanced industrialized countries, including the United States.

Jan Kozak, historian of the Czech Communist Party, wrote a detailed account of how a small minority of communists manipulated the nation into "peacefully" accepting a Red takeover. His report was titled, "How Parliament Can Play A Revolutionary Part In The Transition To Socialism" and "The Role Of The Popular Masses."

RED PLAN OBTAINED

A copy of Kozak's report fell into Western hands. It was reprinted and released to the public in December 1961 by the House of Representatives Committee on Un-American Activities.[1] The Committee's introduction said:

From behind the Iron Curtain has come one of the most amazing Communist documents of our time.

Brazen, boastful and amazingly frank, it is a detailed account of treachery and intrigue employed by the Reds during the three years preceding their 1948 conquest of Czechoslovakia. The document offers the case history of Czechoslovakia as a Communist blueprint for subversion and coercion in all free world nations.

It places special emphasis on the use of parliaments in bringing about Communist revolutions...Whereas destruction was formerly the Communist plan for a national legislative institution, it is now their policy to convert it into an "active revolutionary assembly."[2]

The HCUA introduction to Kozak's history of the Red takeover of Czechoslovakia said that it shows that...

...bold and deceitful Communist tactics can overcome strategical and numerical disadvantages when the non-Communist opposition fails to comprehend a threat to its existence until it is too late.

Kozak himself emphasized that the Czech experience was a milestone in the development of communist strategy. He wrote:

Our experience provides notable and practical proof that it is possible to transform parliament from an instrument of the bourgeoisie into an instrument of the revolutionary will of the people [i.e., a Communist dictatorship] and into an instrument of power for the peaceful development of the socialist revolution.[3]

In January 1961, the Soviet dictator Nikita Khrushchev acknowledged that the tactics developed in Czechoslovakia had been adopted by the world communist movement. He said:

We proceed from the premise that wars are not necessary for the victory of socialism....The transition to socialism in countries with developed parliamentary traditions may be effected by utilizing Parliament and in other countries by utilizing institutions conforming to their national traditions [i.e. Congress in the U.S.].[4]

Later the same year, Petr Zenkl, who was vice premier of Czechoslovakia and a member of its Parliament at the time of the Red takeover, confirmed that the Communists used his country as a "dress rehearsal" for new "techniques to undermine free governments without the use of military force". In an article in *This Week* magazine[5] he ranked Kozak's document along with Lenin's *State and Revolution* and Hitler's *Mein Kampf* for the insights it provided into communist plans for imposing a totalitarian system on a free and unsuspecting country.

In the two years from 1946 to 1948 the communists successfully eroded what Kozak himself described as strong mass support for the bourgeoisie [anti-communist] majority in the Czech parliament to a place where...

...for all practical purposes, parliamentary resistance to the communist takeover had ended....In 1948 when the decisive fight between the workers' class and the bourgeoisie drew closer, the bourgeoisie had only a shade of the power and influence it had in 1945.[6]

In a 1963 book, *The Strategy of Deception*, Jeane Kirkpatrick, later the courageous U.S. Ambassador to the United Nations, wrote:

The example of Czechoslovakia is important to students of Communism because the "peaceful takeover" provides an instructive lesson in the methods by which an advanced country may succumb to Communism without electoral success or violent revolution.[7]

Mrs. Kirkpatrick added an insight which should provide a solemn warning to Americans and their leaders. She said that the most important ingredient of the Communist success in Czechoslovakia was...

...failure on the part of democratic political leaders to comprehend fully the character of the force which challenged them and Czech democracy.[8]

An examination of the Kozak record of the tactics and strategy the Reds used in conquering Czechoslovakia follows. Bracketed comments [ ] will relate the Czech blueprint to certain developments in the United States which fit the pattern. These include formation of the *All People's Front*, communist efforts to work within the Democratic Party, etc. discussed in the last two chapters.

HOW THE REDS DID IT

It took less than three years for the Reds to "peacefully transform a newly freed Czech republic into a Communist police state." Key to the Czech communist success was their refined usage of two forces envisaged by Lenin as the key to successful revolution—*pressure from above* and *pressure from below*. The 1961 Congressional analysis of the Czech communist strategy as revealed by the Kozak report explained the use of *pressure from above* and *pressure from below*. It said:

> From the outset, the plan followed was one of creating "pressure from below" (the organized masses) and combining it with "pressure from above" (Reds in key government posts and parliament) to clamp the non-communist opposition in the jaws of a pincer.[9]

In practice, the Reds and their close allies in Parliament and the government bureaucracy generated the *pressure from above* by advocating "reform" measures which would appeal to the masses. The reform proposals (1) excited mass support for (2) measures which moved the nation in the direction of an all-powerful socialist state.

Communists in the towns and rural areas worked to organize people into the mass organizations which became the *pressure from below*. As the *pressure from below* grew it was focussed on wavering legislators who then joined those creating the *pressure from above* and the process accelerated. [Exactly the same pattern has been followed in the United States as the Reds and their allies in Congress, the media, etc. create *pressure from above* to block contra aid, reject

Judge Bork's Supreme Court nomination, impose sanctions on South Africa, cut defense spending, etc. The Reds then stir the people and organizations in the *All-People's Front* to create the *pressure from below* on other members of Congress, etc.]

For example, in September 1986, President Reagan vetoed legislation which imposed economic sanctions on South Africa and American companies doing business there. The bill was sponsored initially by Congressional leftists (pressure from above) and was passed by a Congress which was feeling the massive *pressure from below* generated by groups in the All-People's Front coalition.

The author, who was in Washington on other business, visited the office of Senator John Danforth just before the Senate was to consider overriding the President's veto. He presented the view that economic sanctions and requiring withdrawal of American companies (who had been a major influence in breaking down apartheid barriers) would do much more harm to blacks than to the South African government, white business owners, etc. The resulting black unemployment, economic hardship, and discontent would add fuel to the fires of revolution being sparked by the Communist African National Congress and groups it was agitating.

A knowledgeable Danforth aid, who had served in State Department posts in Southern Africa, agreed with the scenario. Then he added, "Even so, Senator Danforth must vote to override the President's veto. The vote on the veto is being perceived as a litmus test on how senators stand on apartheid. He cannot afford to be viewed as favoring apartheid."

The perception that the vote on the veto override was the "litmus test" on apartheid had been skillfully created by *pressure from above* and *pressure from below*. The president's veto was overridden and economic sanctions were imposed on black and white South Africans.

The *pressure from below* is crucial. Kozak told the role of the Czech Communist Party in its creation. He wrote that the "broad *National Front...*

...consisted not only of the political parties *but also broad united national mass organizations,* [the *All People's Front* in the United States] the establishment of which the CPCS achieved with the help of the revolutionary activity of the masses.

These organizations comprised broader masses than the political parties [Gus Hall's "forces of political independence"]; they fortified the unity of the people and, at the same time, considerably reinforced the positions of the workers' class and the positions of left progressive democratic forces in the other parties of the National Front [primarily within the Democratic Party in the U.S.].

The united mass organizations, [*All People's Front*] *which were led and influenced to a large extent by the Communists,* represented, in this way, *virtually the direct reserves of the Party.* Through them the strong influence of the policy of the Communists also penetrated into the other political parties, and thus the unity of the National Front was strengthened from below over the heads of the leaders.[10]

Kozak emphasized that the unity of the National Front and the resultant *pressure from below* enabled the Communists to achieve...

...effective cooperation with the leadership of other socialist parties. This tactic, which the Communists employed during the transition from national and democratic revolution to socialist revolution, led to strengthening the left wing of the Social Democratic Party and to its successive shift to positions of true revolutionary Marxism and ideological harmony with the Communists. [The last chapter showed Communists working to move the Democratic Party to the left in the U. S. using their influence in organized labor, the *All People's Front*, etc.]

It (the Communist effort in other Czech political parties) prepared conditions for the left wing of the Social Democratic Party to expel right-wing representatives from the party at the moment when the right reformist wing prepared for an open crossing to the side of the bourgeoisie in the February crisis in 1948.[11]

All the Communists asked of Czech President Benes and the Parliament initially was a socialist economic system and placement of a few Communists in the coalition government. One of the cabinet posts was, of course, the Department of Interior which controlled the police forces.

As the orchestrated political crisis developed in February 1948, opposition to a communist takeover wilted under the pincer of *pressure from above* and *pressure from below*. Parliament gave the communists working control of the government. Before the people awakened to the danger, the Reds moved quickly to enact measures which would block a counter-revolution. Anti-communist leadership and personnel were purged from the military. While moving to eliminate and/or disarm the potential opposition to the open Red takeover, Kozak reported that the communists also had to face...

> ...the necessity of arming the most mature part of the workers' class for repulsing the counter-revolutionary machinations of the bourgeoisie and for ensuring the undisturbed building of socialism.[12]

The Reds also moved quickly to reorganize the police forces and to insure that safeguards written into the Czech constitutional structure could not be used to overthrow the revolution. Kozak said:

> Within less than three months...the Parliament approved a new constitution which safeguarded all the progress made so far and ensured the sovereignty of the working people in the state, the popularization of the state apparatus and the liquidation of the remnants of the bureaucratic police state apparatus; anchored nationalization as a firm economic basis of the people's democratic state and, in its totality, strengthened and ensured the transition of the country to socialism.[13]

The Kozak words are a classic example of Red use of Aesopian language. The new constitution "which safeguarded all the progress made so far" was the means for "legitimatizing" Czechoslovakia's new communist dictatorship. Ensuring "the sovereignty of the working people" was Kozak's way of saying "the dictatorship of the proletariat through the Communist Party." The phrase saying the new constitution "anchored nationalization as a firm economic basis of the people's democratic state" in practice meant that total state control of all property and means of production was guaranteed.

Soon President Benes and legendary leader Jan Masyrak, who had cooperated with the Communists, and countless other Czechs, who resisted, were put to death or committed suicide. An Associated Press foreign affairs editor wrote the story. He said:

> Jan Masyrak, although deeply devoted to democracy, thought he could do business with Communism. His suicide is a monument to his recognition, and a warning to the world, that no such cooperation with Communism is possible.[14]

In a preface to its reprint of the Kozak report, the House Committee on Un-American Activities said:

> The Kozak document provides a unique insight into the techniques employed by the Communists in their takeover of Czechoslovakia.

> By the same token, the committee believes that it serves as a clear warning of how Communists in this country will attempt to subvert Congress, as well as state and local legislatures [The previous chapter showed that this is the current program of the Communist Party USA.], if unwary voters present them with the opportunity to do so.

> The history of the fall of Czechoslovakia should strongly impress upon the American people why a thorough understanding of the strategy, tactics and objectives of the Communist conspiracy is vital—if we are to make true the expression, "It can't happen here.."[15]

THE REFINED PLAN

The Kozak report was a Communist "look back" on their successful takeover of Czechoslovakia. In 1974, Alexander Sobolev, head of Moscow's Institute of Marxism-Leninism, organized Kozak's "look back" into a forward looking, precise blueprint for *effecting the revolutionary transformation of society by peaceful means.* Published in the February 1974 issue of *World Marxist Review* it said:

> The aggregate experience of the world proletariat helps to specify certain key conditions and prerequisites for the peaceful revolutionary process in various countries.[16]

While emphasizing the "peaceful revolutionary process" Sobolev added the caution that Communists do not rule out the use of violence when needed to bring about the transition to socialism. He said:

> The experience of the international proletariat's class struggle suggests that to recognize the possibility of peaceful transition from capitalism to socialism *does not mean making an absolute of it, let alone rejecting all social-political violence.*[17] (Emphasis added)

After keeping the door open to the use of violence, Sobolev's 10-page article outlined the prerequisites for successfully organizing a peaceful transition to socialism. He summarized the blueprint saying:

> First of all, the decisive prerequisites for a peaceful transition to socialism are (1) a nationwide political crisis, (2) a unity of the working-class movement, (3) a solid alliance of the working class with all working people, (4) the winning of the middle strata of town and country for the cause of freedom and socialism, and (5) the adoption of effective measures to neutralize wavering social strata.

> Secondly, the working class and its allies must have a mass political organization capable of taking and holding power in both the provinces and the capital, no matter what turn developments may take.

> Thirdly, to hold and extend their gains, the revolutionary action must be strong enough politically to defeat every attempt at armed violence against the people by countering it with revolutionary violence.

> Fourthly, in the struggle, there is a limit to constitutional opportunities. At a certain stage, the Party has to fight for a change in

the constitution itself...reorganization of the old machinery of state to uphold the people's interests is imperative.[18]

Sobolev's outline appears to be a general blueprint. However, it becomes extremely comprehensive when the communist terminology used is interpreted and integrated with the Czech experience *and present day conditions in America.*

THE COMING ECONOMIC CRISIS

The Communist Party USA is implementing the Sobolev blueprint step-by-step. "The coming national crisis"— Sobolev's first prerequisite is a recurring theme in literature of the CPUSA. The Reds plan to exploit a coming economic crisis to produce the political crisis. Following the October 1987 stock market crash, Communist Party chief, Gus Hall, opened the Party's next Central Committee saying:

> There is no question the stock market crash will move the date of the cyclical economic crisis up...Monopoly capital created the crisis. Let them pay the cost.[19]

The Central Committee's report on the meeting amplified the theme. It said:

> The crash will shake people's already shaky confidence in capitalism even more. People will be open to new and more radical solutions. There will be political fallout from the crisis.[20]

The report emphasized the importance of Communists being ready for a quick and determined response to the coming economic crisis. It said:

> Historically, Communist and working class revolutionary parties become mass parties on the basis of how they react in periods of crisis. It is always the parties that respond fastest, with the clearest most popular explanations and best working class solutions that become mass parties.[21]

The statement was drawing upon the Czechoslovakian experience. The Czech Communist Party gained 237,384 new members in the first ten months of 1947 as the Czech crisis intensified.[22]

The importance of using a national crisis is restated

regularly in communist literature. In the June 1989 *Political Affairs,* for example, Jack Kurzweil in discussing "Crises and Mass Struggle" wrote:

> A fundamental proposition of Leninism, as I understand it, is that a cumulative crisis of the system generates divisions in the ruling class which, together with intensified mass struggle, create the opening for fundamental social change [i.e.,Revolution].[23]

Kurzweil added another significant facet to the concept of the coming crisis. He anticipated that struggles over AIDS, drugs and abortion will produce a "social crisis." Kurzweil, a professor of electrical engineering at California's San Jose State University, was a key leader of the 1987 Marxists Scholars Conference at the University of California at Berkeley. Kurzweil anticipates that the "social crisis" will intensify the economic and political crisis the Communists are preparing to manipulate.

The use of crisis, as proposed by Sobolev and continually emphasized by the CPUSA, follows the clear teachings of Lenin, who said:

> A revolution is simply impossible without an overall national crisis.[24]

Gray L. Dorsey, professor of international law at Washington University in St. Louis, explained the vital relationship between crisis and revolution. He wrote:

> Governments collapse when they cannot handle a crisis....the first ingredient of the takeover and transformation of a Nation State therefore, is a crisis. If a crisis does not exist, it must be created. Revolution is a mass movement, and mass support will not be forthcoming if, for most people, things are going well, not even if things are bad but not hopeless.

> The revolutionary Marxist-Leninist Party must make the situation hopeless. When this is not possible, the Communist Party must bide its time and try to get the confidence of the masses by working together with other political parties and movements for reforms within the framework of Nation State institutions—meanwhile indignantly denying that when the opportunity arises it will betray the confidence it has won and turn to destruction and revolution.[25]

This was the exact process followed by the Czech communists until the *pressure from above* and the *pressure from below* wilted the opposition, producing the collapse of the government and the subsequent revolution.

The crisis is the key. The CPUSA anticipates using the next "cyclical economic crisis" to precipitate conditions favorable for the "peaceful transition to socialism." The "coming crisis" is an on-going theme in Red literature. They anticipate, perhaps correctly, that the next cyclical recession will be a deep and drastic one. Judith Leblanc, the Party's organizational secretary, in a speech at Harvard University in November 1988 said:

> The Reaganite debt crisis has yet to hit home; of course, when it does, it will hit hard. The vote for George Bush was built on the illusion of economic stability, charged to an overdrawn account.[26]

SKYROCKETING DEFICITS AND DEBT

As the 1980s ended the nation had enjoyed the longest period of economic expansion in modern history. However, the income tax cuts of the early 1980s which sparked the recovery were not matched by reduced governmental spending. Ronald Reagan had promised a balanced budget by 1984. But when Congressional Democrats gave him the first big deficit budgets he failed to use his veto pen. Government size and costs ballooned. One columnist pointed out:

> When the President came to power in 1981, the federal government employed 4,966,000 people. By the beginning of fiscal 1986 [five years later], it employed 5,210,000—an increase of 244,000 on the federal payroll.
>
> In 1981, federal outlays totaled $590.9-billion. By fiscal 1986, they were $979.9-billion, a two-thirds increase.[27]

Deficits skyrocketed and the national debt more than tripled during the decade of the 1980s. To finance the deficits, the federal government borrowed twice as much money during the 1980s as had been borrowed during all of America's first 200 years! Interest on the debt reached the $200-billion level annually. *The interest payments alone were twice as high as the total national budget during John Kennedy's presidency 25 years before.*

During the same period imports from abroad skyrocketed while sales of American goods to other countries fell. A balance of payment deficit resulted. Americans were looking to Germany, Japan and other Far Eastern countries for automobiles, TV's, VCR's, stereos, cameras and steel and to the Arabs for oil. Deficits in the annual balance of payments for trade approached the level of the federal deficit.

Normally, big deficits in the federal budget and the balance of trade would trigger big increases in both interest rates and inflation. However, it didn't happen immediately. Four factors held interest rates and inflation down and delayed the day of reckoning. They were:

(1) Cuts in the top American income tax rates gave some Americans capital to invest in industry and federal debt securities. (Although massive increases in Social Security taxes raised the overall tax burden on most taxpayers.)

(2) IRA's encouraged millions of Americans to save up to $60-billion annually which helped finance the federal debt.

(3) As America's dollar weakened foreign interests (the English, the Dutch, the Japanese and the Arabs) invested billions in U.S. government debt securities.

(4) The same interests invested other billions buying stock (ownership) in U.S. corporations. These investments sparked the longterm uptrend of the stock market. They also bought almost half of the prime real estate in New York, Los Angeles and San Francisco. Big apartment complexes, many of the shopping centers in major metropolitan areas and much good farm land changed hands during the 1980s. Managed by big city real estate interests, no one appears to know for sure who the real owners are.[28]

In short, significant portions of the ballooning federal debt and the massive balance of trade deficits of the 1980s were financed by mortgaging or selling the best of America piece by piece to foreign investors. When America has little or nothing left to sell, the communists (and other more conservative observers) are expecting a massive economic readjustment in the United States. It may be called a recession—or it could be labeled a depression.

Whatever it is called it could make the skyrocketing inflation and interest rates of the Carter years look like "the good old days." The misery would compound. Loan defaults by Communist and Third world nations can trigger bank failures and multiply the burden of paying for the $250-billion bailout of the Savings and Loan industry several times.

UNIFYING THE MASSES

While watching and waiting for the "cyclical economic crisis," Communists work to increase their influence and leverage among the masses who will feel the pain of the economic readjustments. They seek to achieve Sobolev's prerequisite of the "solid alliance of the working class [communists] with all working class people." Building such alliances was a key goal in the formation of the *All People's Front*.

Growing unity of the left resulted from the anti-Bork drive in the fall of 1987. At the December 1987 meeting of the Central Committee of the CPUSA...

> ...members of the Party's leading body reported on the work and activities of anti-Bork coalitions in their respective states, and the role of Communist Party members in them. The report showed that in almost every case, the committees had become truly mass movements...[with] a high level of Communist participation, in most cases as part of the official leadership, and in many cases as initiators of the activities.

> Examining the impact of the anti-Bork struggle the meeting concluded that...through this struggle the people's forces have come closer together.[29]

Other Red efforts to unify the left have intensified also. A November 1988 conference at Harvard University on the dangers of anti-communism helped. Over 1200 participants—professors, students and leftist activists—paid $75 each to register for the three-day meeting.[30] Conference organizer William Schaap was quoted as saying that...

...new Soviet glasnost policies have created an "opening" for the left to attack and discredit anti-Communism. We hope this conference...will lay important groundwork for a vocal public opposition to knee jerk anti-communism during the next administration.

Scheduled speakers included university professors, top journalists, the deputy foreign minister of Cuba, Communist Party chief Gus Hall, Jesse Jackson's key aid Jack O'Dell and President Kennedy's economic adviser John Kenneth Galbraith—an honor roll of the left.[31] The theme? ANTI-COMMUNISM IS DANGEROUS because it keeps liberals and other leftists from openly unifying with communists to work for common goals. Gus Hall told the conference:

As long as the false specter of anti-communism can frighten people, it will be used in the struggle against democracy...anti-communism remains an obstacle to unity among progressive forces.[32]

Judith Leblanc, organizational secretary of the CPUSA, presented the same theme. She said:

The bottom line on anti-communism is that it has always been used to derail *unity in the people's movements,* disarm their militancy, and undermine the struggle against capitalism.[33]

Sponsored by the Institute of Media Analysis the funding for the conference on the dangers of anti-communism was provided by eight foundations and 26 individuals including Abby Rockefeller.[34]

Participants were offered audio and videotape cassettes of the conference plus an organizer's kit for use in producing followup conferences on campuses, etc. across America. IMA announced development of a high school curriculum on anti-communism in association with *Educators for Social Responsibility*.

WINNING THE MIDDLE CLASS

The Harvard conference will help achieve unity of the working class, an important Sobolev "prerequisite for revolution." His next prerequisite was "the winning of the middle strata of town and country for the cause of freedom and socialism." [Communists only acknowledge existence of two classes in society—the proletariat and the bourgeoisie. Therefore they must use the term "middle strata" rather than "middle class."]

The "social crisis" produced by the abortion, drug and AIDS struggles discussed earlier will help the Reds draw middle and upper class abortion supporters, homosexuals, etc. into the coalition. The coalition will elect liberal legislators who will go along with most other Red goals.

"Winning the middle strata" will come largely, however, as a result of the economic crisis. Consider these facts: In the 1988 elections George Bush defeated Michael Dukakis by a margin of just 54-46% even though the lines were rather clearly drawn over economic prosperity, patriotism, national defense, gun control, etc.

How deeply would the economy have to dip to change one out of twenty votes cast in that election? Those who were hurting economically—or feared they would be hurt—would respond to the "pressure from above" which promised government [socialist] remedies for the economic ills. The balance of power would shift. A significant segment of "the middle strata of town and country" would join the masses creating *pressure from below*. Another of Sobolev's "prerequisites for the peaceful transition to socialism" would be solidified. If it should develop this way in America it would fit not only Sobolev's theories but also the tragic Czech experience. Kozak wrote:

> While prior to the elections of 1946 the bourgeoisie had a relatively strong mass basis, the short time of less than two years of people's democratic development had been sufficient for the disintegration of the political army upon which it could formerly count.

> The broad masses of the people, especially working peasants, lost their illusions as regards the bourgeoisie and went over to the side of the workers' class...In 1948 when the decisive fight between the workers' class and the bourgeoisie grew closer, the bourgeoisie had only a shade of the power and influence that it used to have in 1945.[35]

NEUTRALIZING THE OPPOSITION

Not only must portions of the "middle strata" be enlisted into the masses who produce the *pressure from below* but those who would oppose any aspect of the transition to socialism must be neutralized or destroyed. Sobolev taught that Red "adoption of effective measures to neutralize wavering social strata" was essential.

At least five tactics are employed. Perhaps most important is the removal or destruction of leaders who would themselves block Red progress and/or rally those elements of society which would be natural opponents of a socialist takeover. Kozak described how forces manifesting the *pressure from above* and the *pressure from below* had a direct effect on...

> ...limiting the influence and positions of waverers and enemies standing in the path of further progress of revolution.[36]

During the Reagan years the true-Reaganites with influence and/or a potential national following had their "influence or positions limited." Among them were:

> UN Ambassador Jeane Kirkpatrick and National Security Adviser Bill Clark (their removal was discussed earlier), Interior Secretary James Watt, Labor Secretary Ray Donovan, Attorney General Ed Meese, Supreme Court nominee Robert Bork and Oliver North. There was a host of others who were lesser known. (Senator Gary Hart, a Democrat who was no favorite of the Reds, was also a target.)

POLITICAL EXPOSURE

Some like Kirkpatrick and Clark were removed or shunted aside by those operating from shadowy positions of power. Others were victims of the technique of "political exposure." In his 1905 book, *What Is To Be Done*, Lenin advocated such exposure, saying that...

> ...political exposures in themselves serve as a powerful instrument for *disintegrating* the system we oppose, as a means for diverting from the enemy his casual or temporary allies, as a means for spreading hostility and distrust among the permanent partners of the autocracy.

In our time only a party that will organize really nationwide exposures can become the vanguard of the revolutionary forces...We Social-Democrats [the name Lenin's Bolsheviks operated under before they came to power] will organize these nationwide exposures...uniting into one inseparable whole the assault on the government...a comprehensive political education through the medium of political agitation and political exposures.

Political exposures are as much a declaration of war against the *government* as economic exposures are a declaration of war against factory owners...And is it not clear that precisely for this work we need "allies in the ranks of the liberals and intellectuals" who are prepared to join us in the exposure..."[37]

An election year statement of Communist Party chief Gus Hall confirms that Lenin's teaching on political exposure continues to guide the CPUSA. Hall Said:

We shall expose in order to defeat.[38]

Various forms of exposure may be used. When George Bush named black Republican William Lucas to head the Justice Department's Civil Rights Division Lucas seemed to be an ideal choice—but the left went to work. Consider his background:

Raised in Harlem and orphaned at the age of 12, Lucas worked his way through college and Fordham Law School while serving as a fulltime officer in the New York City Police Department. He became one of the first black FBI agents. After four terms as sheriff of Wayne County, Michigan which surrounds Detroit, he was elected as chief executive of Wayne County which then had a population greater than some 20 states.

Lucas and his wife of 42 years reared five children—three are doctors, one is in medical training and the fifth is following his father's footsteps and serves as a policeman in Detroit.

In 1988, Lucas after life-long allegiance to the Democrat Party became a Republican and the GOP candidate for governor of Michigan.[39]

With this shining record, the Washington political weekly, *Human Events* said that Lucas should have been "the toast

of the civil rights establishment, a perfect candidate for a high
Justice Department post, and an example to be held aloft so
that minority children facing obstacles similar to those once
faced by the young Lucas will know that they, too, can
overcome." Instead, the newspaper reported...

> ...the same crowd that ambushed the Bork nomination to the
> Supreme Court—including Ralph Neas' Leadership Conference
> on Civil Rights, the Norman Lear-founded People for the
> American Way, and the NAACP—are doing the same number on
> Lucas. No innuendo or smear is out of bounds if it will keep Lucas
> from becoming Assistant Attorney General for Civil Rights.[40]

The attack worked. With mounting *pressure from below*
from the *All People's Front* egged on by the *pressure from
above* from Senators Kennedy, Biden and Metzenbaum, a 7-7
tie vote of the Senate Judiciary Committee killed the Lucas
nomination.[41] *Human Events* asked:

> After sifting through 80,000 pages of documents concerning
> every conceivable aspect of his personal and political life in a
> search for dirt, what did the Democrats come up with?

The intensive search of his background revealed that early
in his career he did not report failing the District of Columbia
bar examination on a New York application. That he passed
it later was ignored. [Even more serious failings in the background and legal education of Teddy Kennedy and Joe Biden
were ignored. Both men voted against Lucas pointing up the
double standards used when the left implements a program
of political exposure.]

The other disclosure which made headlines was a family
failure to list $4000 in purchases on a custom declaration
form when returning from a Far Eastern trip. The committee
"exposed" the lapse even though the "evidence" included a
statement signed at the time by Lucas' daughter attesting
that her father was not told of the undeclared purchases and
that the family thought they were duty-free because they
were bought in duty-free stores.[42]

The purveyors of *pressure from above* proclaimed that
Lucas was unqualified and discredited. *Pressure from below*

mounted and a 7-7 tie vote in the Senate Judiciary Committee killed the Lucas nomination. Lucas' real crime was the absence of a background as a civil rights radical, his switch from the Democrat to the Republican party and his refusal to condemn several Supreme Court decisions liberals didn't like. The lynch mob that got Judge Bork [for disagreeing with Supreme Court decisions the liberals did like] had another victory. *Human Events* said:

> In his rabble-rousing heyday, George Wallace had a slogan, "Send 'em a message," that sent chills down many a black spine. Last week...some good ol' boys on the Senate Judiciary Committee named Kennedy, Biden and Metzenbaum sent their own chilling message to black Americans: Remember your place—with liberal Democrats—and we'll see that you are fed and comfortable. But you start thinking independently (read conservative or Republican), and we'll cut you off at the knees.

Gus Hall said, "We shall expose in order to defeat." The tactic, used by the Reds and used by the liberals, has worked—again and again.

One of Bush's earliest appointments was the naming of former Texas Senator John Tower as Secretary of Defense. The yapping mobs went to work. The media headlined charges that Tower was a womanizer who sometimes drank too much. His close ties with defense contractors brought further headlines. The Senate killed his appointment. One commentator observed that if being a boozing womanizer disqualified one from holding a responsible position then Ted Kennedy and many of the other Senators who voted to block Tower's appointment should be sent home. Tower's crime was not his drinking and womanizing but his conservative philosophy and longtime record of advocating a strong defense for the United States.

Some conservative Reagan Administration officials were also forced from office or had their reputations damaged by smears.

Interior Secretary James Watt was hounded from office by *pressure from above* generated by Congressional figures and the media. His crime? He poked fun at the ridiculous "tokenism" some liberals go to in achieving affirmative action "balance." Watt expressed the tongue-in-cheek hope that a new committee he had named would pass the test because it was comprised of "a black, two women, a Jew and a Hispanic cripple."

Labor Secretary Ray Donovan spent several years and over $1-million fighting charges of labor racketeering before courts found him "Not Guilty." When he left the courtroom, he asked, "Now who is going to give me my reputation back." It took former Presidential assistant Lynn Nofziger years before the courts cleared his record.

Dan Quayle had a distinguished record as a United States senator. He was an acknowledged expert and leader on arms control measures—and was co-sponsor with Teddy Kennedy of landmark legislation in the area of job training for workers displaced by the technological revolution, foreign imports, etc. When George Bush chose Quayle, an outspoken conservative, to be his running mate at the 1988 Republican National Convention, the political exposure experts went to work. Quayle's Vietnam war service in the Indiana National Guard was made an issue—and Quayle name became a joke among many. (He hadn't run to Canada to evade military service as many of his liberal critics did.)

The exposure of Gary Hart's extra-marital escapes when he was leading the race for the 1988 Democrat presidential nomination puzzled many. "Why Hart?" many asked. "Since when did the media start exposing liberals?" The questions had a valid basis. Many other liberal politicians have strayed from the "straight and narrow" without being followed by newsmen and having their infidelity headlined day after day. However, Hart's unusual treatment may have resulted from his having committed, from the Communist viewpoint, the unpardonable sin.

During his 1984 race for the Democrat nomination, Hart attacked Walter Mondale as a captive of "special interests." Hart was referring to Mondale's having sewed up the endorsements of organized labor and its big block of delegates (and money) early in the campaign. Attacking labor is unforgivable from the Communist viewpoint. Hart, even though he was a far-out liberal and supported the Communist position on issues about 98% of the time, became the target of Red attacks. Ultimately he became the victim of a massive political exposure effort.

Long before Hart's extra-marital escapades made the headlines, he was being regularly attacked by Gus Hall in the Communist press. The first attack came in July 1984. Hall charged:

> From the very beginning of his campaign Gary Hart made his so-called "special interests" charge into a major election issue, including calling on the Department of Justice to take criminal action against the labor PACS...to this day, Hart continues his anti-labor harangue.[43]

Hart was charged by the Reds with anti-working class sentiments and with using the "corrupt language of the Right." These are unforgivable sins. In 1987 in his book, *Working Class USA: The Power and the Movement*, Hall continued the attack on Hart and explained why Hart's "sin" was so grievous. Hall wrote first of the trade union movement:

> The U.S. trade union movement has taken the lead in the struggle against the reactionary policies of Reaganism. *It has become the strongest and best organized politically independent force in the electoral arena.* (Emphasis added) It has become the most consistent anti-monopoly, anti-ultra-Right, anti-fascist and anti-racist force.

> We must not even inadvertently undermine, underrate or attack trade unions. We must at all times take their point of view into consideration, defend them and refuse to be critical in any way that is destructive.

> Not seeing the significance of the new—the independent role of labor in the presidential elections—has already led some to draw wrong conclusions from the 1984 elections. Because they did not see the new independent role of labor they did not see the damage done by Gary Hart's anti-union "special interests groups" campaign.[44]

In his main report to the 24th National Convention of the

Communist Party USA, Gus Hall continued the attack on Hart, who by then was the runaway leader in the race for the 1988 Democrat presidential nomination. Hall said:

All, including those with an anti-labor past, actively seek trade union support, and implicitly reject Gary Hart's divisive 1984 "special interest" charge.

Hart was a consistent target of Gus Hall and the Reds. A few months later Hart, the big liberal, was exposed and lost his front-runner status in the Democrat presidential race. He was finally forced to withdraw.

Political exposure has a dual purpose: removing those who oppose Red plans from their positions and/or destroying the public image of those who might rally the opposition.

Discrediting potential leaders also serves to "neutralize" that part of society which those leaders might someday awaken to the danger of communism. It's all in accordance with Sobolev's prerequisites for "the peaceful transition to communism."

Liberal churches and their leaders are also used to "neutralize the wavering social strata." Denominational resolutions, Sunday School literature and pulpit messages combine to make it "not respectable" or "unchristian" to oppose or question disarmament treaties and other peace moves, liberal social programs which multiply the size and power of government, etc. In this way, church people who potentially should be the strongest base of opposition to communism are effectively neutralized.

INTIMIDATE THE OPPOSITION

Another Red technique for "neutralizing the wavering social strata" is the use of *pressure from above* to intimidate potential opponents of the "peaceful transition to socialism." For example, a small businessman might be subjected to OHSA and EPA harassment, IRS audits, etc.

The technique was used in Czechoslovakia. Kozak told how *pressure from above* was applied by the Ministry of the Interior [Justice Department] and State Security forces for a "systematic fight against enemies, traitors and collaborators" and "the direct suppression and destruction of the counter-revolutionary machinations of the bourgeoisie." Kozak added:

> Other organs of the state also served for the direct suppression of bourgeoisie sabotage and obstructionism [actions which would hinder the communist takeover]. For instance, the Ministry of Agriculture quickly completed, by means of "roving commissions" the confiscation of the land of enemies and traitors...the Ministry of Internal Trade, controlled by Communists...liquidated, for all practical purposes, the private capitalist textile wholesale business by the setting up of state textile distribution centers.

> The organs holding power and the components controlled by Communists, in this way, became unusually effective levers for the defense of the revolutionary achievements of the people and for the further advancement of the revolution.

> They made it possible to suppress directly bourgeois counter-revolutionary elements (to render harmless their sabotage and subversion). They made an outstanding contribution to the isolation of the bourgeoisie.[45]

The potential for such abuse exists in the United States. In 1971, for example, the Federal Communications Commission used alleged fairness doctrine violations to revoke the operating license of Radio Station WXUR in Media, Pennsylvania. It overruled the findings and recommendations of its own hearing examiner in doing so.[46] The station, owned by Faith Theological Seminary, was viewed as the originating station of Dr. Carl McIntire's *Twentieth Century Reformation Hour*. The daily half hour program was broadcast on a network of over 600 independent stations coast-to-coast.

McIntire combined "no-holds barred" preaching of the Word of God with exposure of (1) governmental weakness in the face of the communist threat and (2) the anti-Biblical and pro-Communist positions of the National and World Councils of Churches and their affiliated denominations.

Liberal and leftist religious and other pressure groups were mobilized to apply *pressure from below* on the FCC from the moment McIntire acquired the station in 1965.[47] The federal agency finally bowed to the *pressure from below* and revoked WXUR's operating license in 1971. Other radio station owners quickly got the message. A flood of cancellations from worried radio station owners cut hundreds of stations from McIntire's network which was awakening many to heresy in liberal churches and the threat of communism. The eight year legal battle cost McIntire and his supporters about a million dollars in legal fees.

U.S. Senator Sam Ervin (D-N.C.), a constitutional authority, delivered an hour-long speech on the Senate floor on the abuse of federal power in the WXUR case. He said:

> I wish to bring to the attention of the Senate and the public an exercise of governmental power which I believe has transgressed the limits of constitutional propriety required by the first amendment. I am referring to the closing down by the Federal Communications Commission of radio station WXUR in Media, Pa.

> To my knowledge, this represents the first time that the FCC has successfully invoked its so-called fairness doctrine to deny the renewal of a broadcasting license...the consequence is that a unique voice on radio was stilled because of an arbitrary and unique application of FCC rules.

> Of all the thousands of radio and TV licenses that have come before the FCC since the "fairness doctrine" was enunciated, this is the only station which lost its license for violating the rule. When we recall the extremely controversial nature of Reverend McIntire's opinions and the fact that the criticism the FCC received came from those who vehemently opposed his views, the real reason for the termination is clear.[48]

Senator Ervin told how bureaucratic power was exercised to stop exposure of governmental weakness in opposing communism and pro-Communist activities of liberal religious groups. Ervin explained:

> The station was forced by the FCC to make commitments. These, the FCC would argue, were voluntary—it always denies that it ever presumes to dictate programing. That, of course, would violate the first amendment—which the FCC likes to assure us it never would do. Having forced these promises, the FCC then

denies the [license] renewal on the grounds that the station failed to keep promises that it was not legally required to make in the first place.

Ervin then got to the heart of the matter. McIntire's strong opposition to Communism brought leftist *pressure from below* on the FCC to stifle the anti-communist, pro-Bible voice. Ervin said:

> When all the legal mumbo-jumbo is cleared away, the fact remains that the FCC chose to apply highly technical rules to this single station, *having been forced by outside political pressure to do so.*

RICO ACT PROSECUTIONS

The awesome powers given to governmental agencies in the last 50 years are used as *pressure from above* to intimidate and stifle opposition to the on-going pressures for a communist revolution. A weapon Congress enacted to fight drug trafficking which is being applied increasingly in other areas has such potential. Under the 1970 Racketeering and Corrupt Organizations Act (RICO) someone simply *charged* with a violation can have all their assets frozen until the issues are resolved by the courts *which can take years.*

The law was used in August 1989 in a federal crackdown on corruption and racketeering at the Chicago Board of Trade and the Chicago Mercantile Exchange. News accounts of the grand jury indictments said:

> Sixteen of the traders were charged with violating the federal Racketeer Influenced and Corrupt Organizations Act *which empowers the government to freeze defendants' assets before a trial for seizure upon conviction.*

> The government increasingly has been using the law—enacted to fight organized crime such as drug trafficking—to crack down on securities crime and other white collar corruption.[49]

Such laws were enacted to combat admittedly very serious problems. They have given the government awesome power to tie up the assets of those charged with but not yet convicted of violations. That power could be used at some future date to freeze the assets of those opposing measures leading to a socialist takeover. Not too many small businessmen, political figures, etc. would have to become targets of such action before others would think twice before speaking out. The WXUR case, the potential for using IRS audits, OHSA and EPA harassment and the Anti-Racketeering procedures all fit the Czech blueprint.

COURTROOM TERRORISM

A RICO act provision permits private individuals who claim to have been damaged to file suits against those they charge with "racketeering." The technique has been used by leftist groups in an attempt to intimidate and bankrupt aggressive anti-communists. Such use of the RICO act has been labeled "courtroom terrorism" by those who have been its targets.

In May 1986, the little known *Christic Institute* filed a massive $23.8-million lawsuit against retired Maj. Gen. John Singlaub, Nicaraguan Contra leader Adolfo Calero and about 25 others in the U.S. District Court in Miami. All were involved in various ways with the anti-communist freedom fighters in Nicaragua. They were charged with being part of a "secret team" which had participated in a 25-year pattern of "racketeering activity" including "acts or threats of murder, kidnaping, bribery, and the felonious manufacture, importation, selling and otherwise dealing in cocaine and proscribed drugs."[50]

After two years of costly courtroom maneuvering, the Federal District Court Chief Judge James Lawrence King dismissed the charges, ruling that the plaintiffs had...

> ...failed to produce any admissible evidence regarding causation [and that] the Christic Institute's allegations...were based on unsubstantiated rumor and speculation from unidentified sources with no first hand knowledge.[51]

In an unusual action, the judge issued a more than $1-million judgment against the leftist Institute and its lawyers for "bringing a frivolous or fanciful suit." The award was appealed by the Institute.[52] General Singlaub and his co-defendants had "won" a big victory—but even in winning they lost. In addition to much of two years spent preparing their defense (which limited their anti-communist activity), Singlaub and his co-defendants had to raise and spend almost $1.1-million for legal expenses to defend themselves.

LAWSUITS AGAINST CHRISTIAN ACTIVISTS

The left started a flood of such lawsuits in 1989—lawsuits which could serve to intimidate conservatives and slow their activities. Some of the well-known names and causes attacked in the courts included:

A RICO-type lawsuit was filed against Dr. Jerry Falwell and the Moral Majority by a Florida chapter of the National Organization of Women. The suit charged Falwell with conspiracy for his support of Operation Rescue in its anti-abortion clinic demonstrations.

Madelyn Murray O'Hair and her atheist organization sued Beverly LaHaye and the Concerned Women for America for $4-million. Mrs. LaHaye said the suit stemmed from her distribution of a *USA Today* article which revealed Mrs. O'Hair was trying to stop use of the national motto, "In God We Trust," on money.

The Florida Chapter of the American Family Association was sued, charged with racketeering and extortion because of its efforts to suppress the sale of adult magazines. *Playboy* magazine and Waldenbooks were among those who filed the RICO suit against the anti-porn group.

CHIEF JUSTICE SPEAKS OUT

Supreme Court Justice William Rehnquist said that such civil RICO suits were being used "in ways Congress never intended." Rehnquist said that RICO-type claims were being filed in divorce, trespass and accounting malpractice situations and even in inheritance squabbles among family members. The chief justice spoke out—but the RICO threat remains in the law books and is being used as a weapon against conservative, pro-family, pro-God groups.[53]

LABEL ANTI-COMMUNISTS AS FASCISTS

Red literature shows that Communists and their allies are taught to label knowledgeable, aggressive anti-communists as "fascists." Gus Hall used the label to describe the 1984 Republican convention as...

> ...a coordinated network of fully mobilized, disciplined, sophisticated and well-financed ultra-Right and fascist forces. This new ultra-Right [fascist] coalition also took over the Republican Party.[54]

The Gus Hall statement was used in a *Political Affairs* article by Jim West. West was instructing Party members on identifying and labeling the conservative, anti-communist enemy. He said:

> Beginning in the early '60s, the Rightists initiated their drive for power under cover of misleading, demagogic fronts—patriotic, democratic and religious in appearance—financed in the hundreds of millions. Gradually, the various pieces were put into place. It amounted to a kind of night-crawling, inchoate fascism.

West listed most of the active conservative organizations in America as part of what he labeled "this reactionary *fascist-tinged* conglomeration" including...

> ...the Heritage Foundation, American Security Council, Committee for a Free Congress, Coalition for Peace Through Strength, the Conservative Caucus, Young Americans for Freedom, the Moral Majority, the Christian Anti-Communist Crusade, the Religious Roundtable, Christian Voice, the Coors Foundation, etc.

The broad brush West used linked such conservative and anti-communist leaders as Paul Weyrich, Howard Phillips, Lt. Gen. Dan Graham, Jerry Falwell, Oral Roberts, Robert Schuller, Dr. Fred Schwarz, Senator Jesse Helms (R-NC), Congressmen Phil Crane (R-IL) and Mickey Edwards (R-OK) to the "fascist network." (A year later the National Education Association's *Combatting The New Right* training manual just about duplicated the people and organizations the Reds targeted.)

The *Political Affairs* article said that the incipient U.S. fascism wraps itself in morality and religion and portrays itself as defender of home, family and peace and...

...does not, *at this stage,* parade armed bands of storm troopers through the streets to terrorize and intimidate, to hound and beat people...It is more sophisticated, skillful and clever at hiding its true identify.[55]

The article challenges Party members with the words of Gus Hall who said:

> ...just as war is not inevitable, fascism is not imminent nor inevitable...Vigilance against the ultra-Right will be necessary no matter what the outcome of the elections...Reaganism must be driven from the White House and the halls of Congress.

The article closed with a challenge by one-time Comintern head, Georgi Dimitrov. As Dimitrov's challenge is read, remember that the entire *Political Affairs* article equated love of country, fundamental religious beliefs, anti-communism and conservatism with fascism. In that light, Dimitrov said that the working class and democratic forces...

> ...must not allow fascism [anti-communism] to take it unawares, it must not surrender the initiative to fascism [anti-communism], but must inflict decisive blows on it before it can gather its forces; it must not allow fascism [anti-communism] to consolidate its position; it must repel fascism [anti-communism] wherever and whenever it rears its head; it must not allow fascism [anti-communism] to gain new positions.[56]

The label "fascist" brings to mind Hitler and Nazism. Applying the term to legitimate, pro-American, pro-God, anti-communist efforts causes decent Americans to draw back from involvement. The tactic "neutralizes" sizable segments of the "wavering social strata"—those who would aggressively oppose the Reds "peaceful transition to socialism." (Fascists, like Communists, work for total government power and control. Conservative, pro-God, free enterprise, anti-communist people cannot be "fascists." They strongly support limited government. The ultra or extreme right position would not be fascism—total government—but anarchy or no government.)

A MASS POLITICAL ORGANIZATION

The Communist Party USA's 25-year effort to achieve influence within the Democratic Party and its longrange goal of a new labor-based political party fit Sobolev's prerequisites exactly. Sobolev wrote:

> The working class and its allies must have a mass political organization capable of holding power in both the provinces and the capital, no matter what turn developments may take.

The CPUSA's efforts to use the political efforts of party members and the "forces of political independence" to achieve influence in the Democratic Party were detailed in the previous chapter. Using *pressure from below* is a key tactic. In an August 1987 report to the Central Committee of the Communist Party, Gus Hall gave his instructions concerning the 1988 elections. The report was titled, "1988 Elections: Unity—The Only Way." Hall said:

> The broadly liberal-to-progressive direction of most of the Democratic candidates on many issues reflects the massive *pressure from below*, from the grassroots and the rank and file around the country. [Emphasis added.]

> The consensus reflects *the tremendous pressure* the forces of political independence are putting on the Democratic Party.[57]

Following the 1988 Democratic National Convention, James Steele, political and legislative director of the CPUSA reported in *Political Affairs* on the successful use of "pressure from above and below" at the convention. The report said:

> Jackson intensified the *pressure* [from above] for inclusion of his constituency and their issues in the platform and in the campaign....the combination of *independent pressure* [from below] and Jackson's reaching out for "common ground" resulted in concessions to the Jackson forces on nine of twelve platform planks.

> One of the chief lessons of the Democratic convention is that Dukakis and Bentsen are susceptible to *mass pressure*.[58]

Despite their success at achieving influence within the

Democrat Party, the *Political Affairs* article reemphasized the longrange Party goal. It said:

A third party, that is, a progressive people's electoral alternative is a desirable objective, indeed. The fact is, its creation is inevitable.[59]

In the meantime, Steele's article advised:

In the absence of a mass-based third party, it is possible and necessary for the people's movement to make use of the Democratic Party in the struggle for reforms...

For the last fifty years the Democratic Party has housed a broad mix of class and social forces that are often in conflict with each other. This has given sharp rise to a sometimes subtle, sometimes sharp struggle over direction. *The status and intensity of this struggle depend on the level and strength of the political independence of the labor movement and other people's forces operating inside the party.*

The emergence of a Democratic Party progressive wing with a powerful independent mass base is likely to extend efforts to use the Democratic Party...Developments in 1988 make clear that achieving gains through the Democratic Party has not been exhausted... *The effort to consolidate a progressive wing has already intensified the struggle over direction of the Democratic Party.*[60]

This portion of Steele's article confirms that the Reds are following the Czech blueprint in their work within the Democratic Party. Compare Steele's words with Kozak who said:

The united mass organizations which were led and influenced to a large extent by the Communists...penetrated into the other political parties...strengthening the left wing of the Social Democratic Party and to its successive shift to positions of true revolutionary Marxism and ideological harmony with the Communists.[61]

The Communist Party USA is following the same blueprint in working within the Democratic Party.

The Party also moved quickly to apply "mass pressure" on

President George Bush and the Republican Party within days after Bush took office. *People's Daily World* headlined a January 31, 1989 report on its national committee meeting with the bold words: "Hall says *mass action* can influence Bush." The article said:

> NEW YORK - The Bush Administration "will be a conservative, big business, big oil administration," that will come under increasing *pressure* to pull away from the more fanatical Reaganite policies, said Gus Hall, national chairman of the CPUSA.

> Hall addressed the CPUSA's National Committee over the past weekend, eight days after George Bush's inauguration. He said *mass pressure*, "if used by the people's forces, can influence the administration in a positive direction. But it will take action— united actions. It will take unity—broad people's unity, left unity, working-class unity, Black-white unity."

Hall was not just speculating on what could happen but was clearly calling for unified *pressure from below* on Bush and the Republicans from the forces of the *All People's Front*.

DISARMING THE OPPOSITION

Kozak emphasized the vital importance of blocking counter-revolutionary efforts by (1) purging the military of anti-communist officers and personnel and (2) arming "the most mature part of the workers' class." Sobolev said that to protect the revolution the Reds must prepare...

> ...to defeat every attempt at armed violence against the people by countering it with revolutionary violence.

Both Sobolev and Kozak were implementing the teaching of Lenin. He said repeatedly...

> ...one of the basic conditions for the victory of socialism is the arming of the workers and the disarming of the bourgeoisie....Only the Soviets can effectively arm the proletariat and disarm the bourgeoisie. Unless this is done, the victory of socialism is impossible....make mass searches and hold executions for found firearms.[62]

Stalin's teaching was the same. He said:

If the opposition disarms, well and good. If it refuses to disarm, we shall disarm it ourselves.[63]

That is still Soviet policy. Ethnic "unrest" developed in the Soviet Republic of Georgia in the spring of 1989. The Associated Press reported that police immediately seized tens of thousands of guns which rural Georgians used in hunting wild game for meat.[64] (Under the Soviet system they were all registered and so were easy to locate and confiscate.)

Growing pressure in the United States for gun control is so prevalent that examples are unnecessary. The purging of aggressive anti-communists from military fits the pattern also.

Since 1951 a consistent pattern of relieving anti-communist military officers from commands, muzzling their speeches, denying them promotions, etc. has developed.

General Douglas MacArthur was recalled and replaced for wanting to win the Korean War...General Edwin Walker's efforts to give his troops anti-communist training resulted in his leaving the service... Military officers efforts to speak out against the communist danger were censored in the early 1960's. Those cases were all discussed in Chapter III, VIII, and IX.

An Air Force commander in Vietnam, Maj. Gen. John Lavell was replaced for bombing communist targets which Washington had not approved...Maj. Gen. John Singlaub, the American commander in Korea, was returned home and permitted to retire after disagreeing publicly with President Carter's announcement that American troops would no longer be needed in Korea because of the diminished Communist threat...Lt. Gen. William Odom was denied promotion to full general and permitted to retire when he raised objections to the INF treaty with the Soviets.[65]

Marine Lt. Col. Oliver North's conviction and Admiral John Poindexter's prosecution for circumventing the efforts of Congress leftists who wanted to end aid to the anti-communist freedom fighters in Nicaragua are well known.

At least two other officers involved in aiding the contras were denied promotions. In October 1988, the Senate Armed Services Committee removed the name of Col. James Steele from the list of officers being promoted from colonel to general. Steele had commanded the American military advisers in El Salvador and helped supply contras from bases in El Salvador. Committee chairman Sam Nunn scratched Steele's name from the promotion list after Senator Tom Harkin (D-IA), a leftist supporter of the Nicaraguan communist regime, protested the promotion. Steele was the only officer on the list denied the promotion to general.[66]

Six months earlier, the Senate Armed Services Committee also removed just one name from the list of Marine officers being promoted to colonel. He was Marine Lt. Col. Robert Earl who had served an 11-month tour as North's deputy in the White House. Committee Chairman Nunn said that he was troubled that the Marine Corps apparently had not considered Col. Earl's activities at the White House when it recommended his promotion.[67]

The Marines got the message. When Earl came up for promotion again in 1989, his name was not on the list the Marines sent to Congress.

The message should be plain to military officers. The military careers of those who take a tough stand against the Communists will suffer.

CHANGING THE CONSTITUTION

In Sobolev's guide for achieving the "peaceful transition to socialism," he admits that existing constitutions limit how far existing legislative bodies can move the revolution. He said:

> In the struggle, there is a limit to constitutional opportunities. At a certain stage, the Party has to fight for a change in the constitution itself....reorganization of the old machinery of state to uphold the people's interests is imperative.

Kozak said that within three months after the Communist takeover in February 1948...

> ...the Parliament of the Czechoslovak Republic approved a new constitution which safeguarded all the progress made so far.[68]

Influential forces in America are advocating drastic constitutional changes. Conservatives who support a constitutional convention to get a balanced budget amendment may be falling into their trap.

James MacGregor Burns is a political historian and a Pulitzer Prize winner. He wrote definitive biographies of Franklin Roosevelt and John Kennedy and is a leading advocate of a "New World Order." In his 1984 book, *The Power To Lead*, Burns discusses the difficulties of changing the U.S. Constitution so the United States can fit into the new world order in the 21st Century. He wrote:

> Let us face reality. The framers [of the Constitution] have simply been too shrewd for us. They have outwitted us. They designed separated institutions that cannot be unified by mechanical linkages, frail bridges, tinkering. If we are to "turn the founders upside down" we must directly confront the constitutional structure they erected.

> Others might press for major constitutional restructuring but I doubt that Americans under normal conditions could agree on the package of radical and "alien" constitutional changes that would be required. *They would do so, I think, only during and following a stupendous national crisis and political failure.*[69] [Emphasis added]

Of course, a crisis is exactly the condition the communists anticipate will enable them to make the constitutional changes needed to solidify the "peaceful transition to socialism."

Burns spelled out some of the "radical and alien constitutional changes" he proposes in speeches commemorating the Constitution's 200th birthday. In a 1989 appearance at Southwest Missouri State University in Springfield, Missouri,[70] Burns advocated adoption of the European parliamentary system. He said:

> Give the party that wins an election control of the government—as is done in England.

Democrats could be induced to support the change. Under a parliamentary system Democrat control of the House of Representatives would have given them the presidency for most of the last 57 years. It would have eliminated the Republican presidencies of Richard Nixon, Gerald Ford,

Ronald Reagan and George Bush—and one of Dwight Eisenhower's two terms.

It's perhaps not surprising, therefore, that former Democrat Senator Tom Eagleton of Missouri has stated that if he were a new founding father for the United States he would argue for a parliamentary system.[71] [Eagleton would be a prime candidate to represent Missouri at any future Constitutional Convention.]

Eagleton spoke at a "Jefferson Meeting," commemorating the 200th anniversary of the Constitution. The "Jefferson Meetings" were held throughout the country discussing the question, "Should a constitutional convention be held to amend the Constitution?" Eagleton told the group that the current system which allows a president of one party to be elected while Congress is dominated by a majority of a different party was not as effective as it could be. He said:

> A divided government on the one hand is checks and balances. On the other hand it is a gridlock.

The "gridlock" which developed when the U.S. Senate refused to confirm the nominations of Robert Bork to serve on the Supreme Court and John Tower as Secretary of Defense added to arguments for ending the stalemates through adopting the parliamentary system. Syndicated Columnist David Broder in a column headed, "The Contra Deal Shows The Weakness of Coalition Government" added further fuel by quoting a "thoughtful scholar" who said:

> ...when the ticket splitting minority of voters (about one-quarter of the electorate) give Republicans the presidency but put Congress back into Democratic control, as they have done with increasing frequency in recent decades, the result is often costly to good policy and good government.[72]

Surprisingly, with the obvious advantage to the Democrats, two of President Bush's cabinet members have joined James MacGregor Burns and other longtime leftists to advocate constitutional restructuring. Treasury Secretary Nicholas Brady (Bush's college roommate) and Attorney General Richard Thornburg are among 51 prominent Americans on the board of the Committee on the Constitutional System.[73] Nationally syndicated columnist Phyllis Schlafly said the group is known among its own members as...

> ...the "parliamentary government group" because they are unhappy with our American separation-of-powers and want to change it to a European-style parliamentary process.

> CCS members aggressively seek large-scale reforms in our constitutional structure and hope that a depression in the near future will create a favorable climate for these changes. They want to be ready to apply "radical reform" if the opportunity arises through a major economic crisis.[74]

In seeking to capitalize on a coming economic crisis to transform America's government, the CCS closely parallels the Communist Party. If a parliamentary system is adopted and the traditional two-party system is splintered, the Communists through the *All-People's Front* will have the leverage to gain real power in a coalition government of the European [or Czech] variety.

In addition to Bush cabinet members Thornburg and Brady, the CCS group includes U.S. Senators Ernest Hollings, Daniel Patrick Moynihan and Nancy Kassebaum; West Virginia Senator John D. Rockefeller's wife; former leftist Senators William Fulbright and Charles Mathias and President John Kennedy's Secretaries of Defense and Treasury, Robert Strange McNamara and C. Douglas Dillon.

The group wants constitutional restructuring to...

> ... adopt a "more efficient" parliamentary system by eliminating the "checks and balances" and separation of powers in the present constitution.

> ...change the terms of office of all elected federal officials so that the President, senators and congressmen will be elected at the same time for concurrent terms of four years each—adopt tax payer financing of congressional campaigns—repeal two term constitutional limitation for presidents—limit congress to five terms and abolish the electoral college.

...include procedures for forcing a President to resign and Congress to dissolve when there is "a loss of public confidence."

...eliminate the two-thirds vote required in the Senate for ratification of treaties to make it easier for future presidents to make agreements with foreign powers.[75] [To see the extreme danger in this proposal, reread the "Treaties vs. The Constitution" section in Chapter XIII.]

The CCS blueprint appears to put many of the pieces in place for merging the United States into an all-powerful world government—or achieving Sobolev's "peaceful transition to communism" on the Czech blueprint.

Schlafly's column charged that CCS members believe that Americans will never adopt the changes one-by-one and think it would be "better" to call a new constitutional convention. By 1989, the machinery was near to being in place.

Richard Thornburg, before becoming George Bush's attorney general, disclosed that a constitutional convention to consider a balanced budget amendment was the key to revamping the federal government. On October 22, 1986 he testified before the State Government Committee of the New Jersey General Assembly. Speaking in support of a constitutional convention to consider a balanced budget amendment to the constitution, he said:

> The Executive and Legislative branches at the federal level are, in truth, caught up in a system badly in need of structural adjustment. The balanced budget amendment is the key element in such an adjustment.

As of early 1989, 32 states had passed resolutions calling for a convention to consider a balanced budget amendment. If two more states should pass resolutions, Congress must call such a convention—although the issue was clouded as legislatures in five states, seeing the danger, rescinded their earlier calls.

Phyllis Schlafly in a speech at the American Bar Association's 1987 Convention listed the perils of a constitutional convention.[76] She said:

> Article V of the U.S. Constitution...says that Congress "*shall* call

a convention for proposing Amendments" whenever requests are received from two-thirds of the states. Note that the word "amendments" is used in the plural. These are the only instructions we have about a Constitutional Convention. *There are no other rules or guidelines.*

We don't know how a Constitutional Convention would be apportioned, or how the delegates would be elected. We don't know what rules the Convention would operate under. We don't know whether amendments could be proposed by a simple majority. We don't know if the agenda could be limited or would be wide open to any proposal.

Mrs. Schlafly warned that precedent should be considered in evaluating the dangers of a "runaway" Constitutional Convention. She told the ABA:

The Constitutional Convention of 1787 was called for the exclusive purpose of amending the Articles of Confederation and wrote an entirely new Constitution, and even changed the ratification procedure so they could get it adopted more easily. The 1787 Convention is the only precedent we have for a national Constitutional Convention.

After citing those and other perils, Mrs. Schlafly quoted the "father" of the U.S. Constitution, James Madison. He said:

Having witnessed the difficulties and the dangers experienced by the first Convention, which assembled under every propitious circumstance, I should tremble for the result of a second.

In recent years amendments have been proposed to remedy a variety of abuses of the present Constitution by the Supreme Court, the Congress and the Executive Branch. The continuing refusal of Congress and the President to balance the budget is just one example. The answer is neither "band-aid" amendments to the present document nor a new Constitution. Instead an aroused and informed people must vote true statesmen into office who will interpret and apply the Constitution as it was written by the founding fathers. The prospect of such a man serving on the U.S. Supreme Court provoked the frenzied opposition from politicians and pressure groups in 1987 which defeated Robert Bork.

It all fits into the Sobolev blueprint for "the peaceful transition to socialism."

RED PLAN SUMMARIZED

A 25-year student of the Communist conspiracy's literature has prepared a 10-point summary of their longrange program and goals for America. He wrote:

Penetration of political parties, chiefly the Democratic Party.

Penetration and assumption of key positions in "mass" organizations.

Development of independent political forms, i.e., the forces of political independence.

Bring together the forces of political independence into the All-People's Front, Unity Coalition and Progressive Coalition which will work mainly through the Democratic Party using the politics of discontent.

Elimination of internal security agencies and emasculation of the FBI.

Aggressive use of "political exposure" to isolate and discredit enemies of the revolution.

Achieve respectability and acceptance of Communists and the Communist Party.

After exhausting use of the Democratic Party as a transitional vehicle for gaining acceptance for radical views, form a new political party by pulling together all the elements of the coalition of independent forces.

Further splintering of the traditional two-party political structure by conservatives when Republican leaders, under *pressure from below*, move to the left.

Coalition politics to achieve key positions in Congress which under a multi-party parliamentary system will form the government after electing a malleable president.

If not thwarted, these longrange goals of the CPUSA and their witting or unwitting allies will have all the pieces in place to effect "the peaceable transition to socialism [communism]" when the crisis comes.

WHAT CAN BE DONE?

In 1954, Senator William Jenner (D-IN) issued a perceptive warning about "a force operating to merge the United States into a one-world socialist system." His warning was published in Chapter 13. A portion of that warning bears repeating here. Jenner said:

> We have a well-organized political action group in this country, determined to destroy our Constitution, and establish a one-party state. This political action group has its own local political support organizations, its own pressure groups, its own vested interests, its foothold within our Government, and its own propaganda apparatus.

> Outwardly we have a constitutional government. We have operating within our Government and political system, another body representing another form of government, a bureaucratic elite, which believes our Constitution is outmoded and is sure it is on the winning side.

Jenner told the story of the factory in Nazi Germany which made baby carriage parts which when assembled became a machine gun. He said:

> Someone, somewhere, conceived the brilliant strategy of revolution by assembly line. The pattern for total revolution was divided into separate parts, each of them as innocent, safe and familiar looking as possible. But...when the parts of a design are carefully cut to exact size, to fit other parts with a perfect fit in the final assembly, the parts must be made according to a blueprint drawn up in exact detail.

> The men who make the blueprints know exactly what the final product is to be...this assembly line revolution is like a time-bomb...It is ready to go off, but it is not going to be set off until the time is ripe, until a switch is pulled. The switch is not to be pulled until the American people are conditioned, or convinced that resistance is hopeless.

The economic crisis which both the communists and those

who are working to fit the United States into a "new world order" expect to use can bring an uninformed people to support a "restructuring" as the answer to their problems.

Jenner sounded his warning in 1954—but he was not heard. In 1964 *None Dare Call It Treason* said "His message must be taken across our nation if America is to survive." The book awakened many but the piece-by-piece assembling of the revolution continues. Jenner laid out the answer in 1954. It is still the only solution. Jenner said:

> The American people...may accept for a time so-called remedies for very real difficulties which eat away at the foundation of their liberties. But...in times of danger to the Constitution there can be no partisan differences between the historic parties which work under the Constitution...the line of division today is between real Democrats and real Republicans on one side in defense of the Constitution, and on the other the secret revolutionaries and those they have brainwashed in their ruthless pursuit of power.

By 1989, how many Americans, Democrat or Republican, really understand how the Declaration of Independence is the foundation for America's Constitution and the freedoms it protects? Without that foundational knowledge how can attacks be recognized and defenses rallied? Rebuilding an understanding of America's exciting uniqueness and greatness is a task to which readers will be called in the final chapter.

CHAPTER 24

WHY DOES COMMUNISM KILL?

Political power grows out of the barrel of a gun.
        —Mao Tse-tung, quoted by TIME Magazine[1]

COMMUNIST TANKS AND SOLDIERS crushed the student democracy movement in China in June 1989. Thousands were machine-gunned or run down by tanks. When the government radio announced that over 1000 had died, the station's personnel were quickly removed.[2] Soon the government was denying that anyone had died but a shocked Chinese journalist said:

> It was a sheer massacre.

In the days that followed those accused of leading the pro-democracy movement were tracked down, quickly convicted and then executed with bullets into the backs of their heads. Military officers who refused to order their troops to participate in the massacre met the same fate.[3]

The world was shocked. It shouldn't have been. Communism was proceeding as it always has—worldwide. Three weeks after the Tiananmen Square massacre the Communist New People's Army (NPA) in the Philippines slaughtered Sunday school teachers, pastors and women and children. This massacre got little attention from the world's media but Bryan Johnson of the *Toronto Globe and Mail* reported:

> In all, 39 villagers died in the June 25 assault on tiny Barrio Binaton, 660 miles southeast of Manila and 13 miles outside this sleepy capital of Davao del Sur province.

> Only five of the victims were adult men, two of them Protestant lay ministers who were beheaded by the rampaging communist guerrillas. The other 34 included pregnant women, year-old babies and cowering youngsters.

"They just kept shooting at us for more than an hour," said 14-year old Randy Mancol, who escaped death only because several bodies fell on top of him. "They would fire and reload, fire and come in to see if any of us were still alive. Then they went outside and fired into the hut again...the NPA knew we were just women and children because the kids were all screaming and crying and the women tried to wave handkerchiefs at them when they stopped to reload their guns."[4]

The news account indicated that the beheadings and mass slaughter were the Communist response to activities of local religious groups and the anti-communist movement fostered by the local military. Another account reported that after beheading the church's pastor and youth leader, they surrounded the building where the women and children had taken refuge. Before opening fire, they chanted:

...where is your God...your God will not protect you now.

If communism or some other form of renamed Red tyranny under the guise of world government comes to America what would it mean for you and your family?

Congressional committees provided answers to that question before they were abolished in the mid-1970s. Congress documented and exposed the mass liquidation of millions of Chinese, Russians, Poles,Hungarians, Latvians, Cubans, etc. Planned starvation, the firing squad, and the slow agonizing death of the slave labor camps are among the execution methods the Reds have used.

Rev. Shih-ping Wang, East Asia director of the Baptist Evangelization Society, told the House Committee on Un-American Activities what happened to the individual in the early 1950s when communism took China. Rev. Wang testified:

The family unit is broken up. Husbands and wives are separated in different barracks. The children are taken away from the parents and placed in government-run nurseries. Husbands and wives meet only once a week for two hours—they have no other contact....The parents may see their children once a week and when they see them they can show no affection toward their children. Names are taken away from children and they are given numbers. There is no individual identity.[5]

In China, 40-million people were liquidated during the first five years of Communist rule. Rev. Wang told how some of them died:

> All the elderly people 60 years of age and above who cannot work are put in the old people's "Happy Home." After they are placed in the homes they are given shots. They are told that these shots are for their health. But after the shots are taken they die within two weeks. After they die the corpses are placed in vats. When the bodies decay and maggots set in, the maggots are used to feed the chickens. The remainder of the body is used for fertilizer.[6]

A young journalist, Kyung Rai Kim, who later edited a leading Seoul, Korea newspaper, told the congressional committees about persecution and murder of thousands of Christians when communism came to Korea. Mr. Kim said:

> An evangelist friend of mine, Lee Chang Whan, was killed...He was killed by the Communists because he was trying to publish the Bible in secret...The Red police stripped him naked, bound him, and put him in an empty water pool. It was 17 degrees below zero that day. They filled the pool. My friend froze to death in 30 minutes. Then the police exhibited his body to the people.[7]

The Communists do not simply execute enemies of the state. They practice planned, deliberate terror on the individual and then display the results to intimidate others. Mr. Kim continued:

> A lady evangelist, Kim Keum Sun, was tied between two horses. Then the horses were sent running in different directions. This happened in 1951...She was guilty of not letting a portrait of the chief of Northern Korea be placed in her church.

> In January 1951, 250 pastors were killed by the Communists on the same day in the same place at Hong Jai Dong, Seoul, Korea. The Red police made holes through the pastors' hands with an ax and bound them with wire rope, and then they shot them. In February 1951, at Wong Dang church, Red soldiers burned 83 Christians to death with gasoline.[8]

As the decade of the 1980s ended 80% of the Korean population had grown up since the war and the Communist atrocities. Without personal first-hand knowledge of Communist treachery many Koreans were at least open to reunification with the Communist north.

Atrocities, designed to discourage man's worship of God, similar to those by the Reds in Korea and the Communist guerrilla armies in the Philippines, are reported wherever communism works to take over. Dr. Thomas Dooley, the young American doctor who gave his life in the early 1960s while establishing hospitals to help the people of Vietnam, wrote three books. They include detailed descriptions of atrocities carried out by the Viet Cong against the people they said they were trying to liberate and help. One such incident shows what happens when communists gain control in an area. Dr. Dooley wrote:

> Having set up their controls in the village of Haiduong Communists visited the village schoolhouse and took seven children out of class and into the courtyard. All were ordered to sit on the ground, and their hands were tied behind their backs. Then they brought out one of the young teachers, with hands also tied. Now the new classes began.[9]

The children were charged with treason. An informer had reported to police that these children had been attending secret classes conducted by their teacher at night. The subject of the classes was *religion*. As a punishment, the seven children were to be deprived of their hearing. Dr. Dooley described how it was done:

> Two Viet Minh (communist) guards went to each child and one of them firmly grasped the head between his hands. The other then rammed a wooden chopstick into each ear. He jammed it in with full force. The stick split the ear canal wide open and tore the ear drum. The shrieking of the children was heard all over the village.

> Both ears were stabbed in this fashion. The children screamed and wrestled and suffered horribly. Since their hands were tied behind them, they could not pull the wood out of their ears. They shook their heads and squirmed about, trying to make the sticks fall out.

Finally they were able to dislodge them by scraping their heads against the ground.[10]

To prevent the teacher from teaching again—and as a warning to others teaching children about Jesus Christ—the Communist guards pulled the teacher's tongue out with a pair of pliers and cut it off. He was left to drown in his own blood. These victims were brought to Dr. Dooley's hospital from the Communist-controlled areas for treatment. Recounting dozens of such incidents, he wrote:

> The purpose of this book is not to sicken anyone or to dwell upon horror...but I do want to show what has come upon these people of the Delta. And justice demands that some of the atrocities we learned of in Haiphong be put on record...

> Early in my Haiphong stay I was puzzled not only by the growing number but by the character of Communist atrocities. So many seemed to have religious significance. More and more I was learning that these punishments were linked to man's belief in God.[11]

The terror has been repeated wherever the Communists are working to take power. In South Africa, the Communist-controlled African National Congress liberation front developed the "necklacing" technique for terror. Blacks who were accused of cooperating with the white South African government in any way (or their relatives) would be seized, a rubber tire filled with gasoline or other flammable liquid would be placed around their neck and set afire. Onlookers would watch terrified during the 20 to 30 minutes it took the victim to die.

This is not the picture of communism the TV networks present. This is not the picture of communism presented to the world when a smiling American president goes to the summit with a hand-waving Soviet leader. This is communism in action. It is the fulfillment of the words of Lenin who said:

> We have never rejected terror on principle, nor can we do so. Terror is a form of military operation that may be usefully applied.[12]

The terror does not cease even when communism is firmly established. Dr. Jurgen Dennert, a correspondent for a German news magazine, was in Peiping (now called Beijing) in 1966 when the Red Guards were unleashed on the people. His shocked eye-witness account was reported in America by the liberal editor and columnist Ralph McGill who quoted Dennert as saying:

> I have never seen such brutality and cruelty. The attacks seemed directed mostly at older persons...I saw several persons beaten to death and others so savagely treated by the failing of heavy sticks of steel or wood that many of them must have surely died.

> One of the sights I shall never forget was the treatment of two old persons. Their belongings had been brought from their rooms and piled on the street and set afire. Red guards then took the old man and woman by the neck and thrust their bodies into the smoke and so near the flames they were seared.. There were many instances of old couples having their belongings pulled out of their rooms and destroyed. The two tortured by fire were more unlucky.[13]

That wave of terror swept China in 1966 and 1967, seventeen years after communism came to China. Five years later, the United States lead the way in welcoming the Chinese Communist terrorists back into "the family of nations." They were given U.S. diplomatic recognition and the United Nations seat of the free Chinese who were expelled. Tiananmen Square and its massacre in 1989 showed that communism had not changed.

Why does communism kill and mutilate and torture?

Before coming to power Communists use terror to intimidate those they are seeking to liberate into supporting the revolution. Once they come to power the killings are necessary to "purify" society.

Marx taught that society was composed of two warring classes—the bourgeoisie (the property owners) and the proletariat (the workers). Marx taught that there could be no real "peace" and a perfect society could not develop until private property and free enterprise were eliminated. Along with the elimination of property and profit, the property owners—the bourgeoisie "animals" who had become "diseased" through contact with their capitalist environment—had to be eliminated. In the *Communist Manifesto*, Marx wrote:

> You must, therefore, confess that by "individual" you mean no other person than the bourgeois, than the middle-class owner of property. This person must, indeed, be swept out of the way, and made impossible.[14]

When Communism kills it is by definition a good act. The killings purify society's environment of its diseased animals.

Even the smiling, handshaking advocate of perestroika and glasnost, Mikhail Gorbachev, approves of killing property owners. In his three hour *Perestroika: The Revolution Continues* speech to the Supreme Soviet on the 70th anniversary of the Revolution in November 1987, Gorbachev reviewed Communist history. He discussed the "excesses" in the period in the early 1920s when 9-million kulaks—small farmers—were systematically exterminated through planned starvation, mass deportation to Siberia or a bullet in the back of the head. A careful reading of Gorbachev's words, however, shows that the 9-million deaths were not the "excesses" he deplored. Gorbachev said:

> ...if there had been a consistent line to promote the alliance with the middle peasant against the kulak [property-owning small farmers], then there would not have been all those excesses that occurred in carrying out collectivisation.

> Today it is clear...the basically correct policy of fighting the kulaks was often interpreted so broadly that it swept in a considerable part of the middle peasantry too. Such is the reality of history.[15]

Gorbachev was not objecting to the elimination of millions of "capitalist" kulaks but rather to "excesses" of bureaucrats who eliminated many working peasants as well.

When Pol Pot and his Khmer Rouge Communists seized control of Cambodia in April 1975 they killed over 2-million of Cambodia's 7-million people within a year. *The Reader's*

Digest told the sordid and tragic story in February 1977 in a condensation of the book, *Murder of a Gentle Land,* by John Barron and Anthony Paul. *The Reader's Digest* introduction said:

> Since the Communists took over the country in April 1975, a pitiless terror has emptied the cities and turned the villages, fields and jungles into charnel houses where unburied corpses lie putrefying in the sun. The numbers of dead are staggering. Yet no protest is made; indeed, the world knows almost nothing of what has happened.[16]

Within six days after "peace" came to the capital city Phnom Penh, a city of 3-million people was empty. *The Reader's Digest* account said:

> Phnom Penh had been transformed into a wasteland occupied only by corpses, stray dogs, pigs, ducks and chickens and Angka patrols standing guard to insure that human life did not return. By April 23 the Communists had begun to empty the other principal cities of Cambodia...On the highways, roads and trails, the 3.5 million people driven from the cities wandered toward an unknown future.

The founder of the Christian Anti-Communism Crusade, Dr. Fred Schwarz, published the 16-page booklet, *Why Communism Kills.*[17] He used the Cambodian experience to illustrate his thesis that communist killing stems from communism's basic philosophy. He said:

> The leaders of the Cambodian Communist Party were convinced Marxists. They set out to be the best Marxists the world had ever seen. They conducted the programs demanded by their Marxist doctrines with an amazing consistency and ruthlessness. These doctrines taught them that the environment generates character; that the capitalist environment generates an evil character; that the cities are the headquarters of capitalism; that the bourgeoisie must be liquidated and the residual people removed from the capitalist environment of the cities; that physical labor is regenerative.

> Translating these doctrines into deeds, they ordered the evacuation of the cities of Cambodia. Everyone had to go. No one was exempt for humanitarian reasons. These people were animals and

could be treated like animals. Three million people who were crowded into Phnom Penh, were ordered to leave the city in one day. Everyone had to leave as they were. Children in schools were not permitted to go home and join their parents but were driven out of the city like cattle. Hospitals were emptied of doctors, nurses and patients.

Multitudes died on the roads from exhaustion or starvation or from thirst in the 100-degree sun. Others were systematically executed. Barron and Paul described typical killing scenes in *Murder of a Gentle Land.* They wrote of ten civil servants and their families rounded up in Banteay Village:

> Weeping, sobbing, pleading for their lives, the prisoners were formed into a ragged line, the terrified wives and children clustering around each head of family. One at a time, each official was thrust forward and forced to kneel between two soldiers armed with bayonet-tipped AK-47 rifles. The soldiers then stabbed the victim simultaneously, one through the front and the other through the back. Family by family, the Communists proceeded methodically down the line. As each man lay dying, his wife and children were dragged up to his body. The women, forced to kneel, also received the simultaneous bayonet thrusts, then the children and babies...By refusing to bury the slain, the Communists advertised their deeds...to intimidate the populace.[18]

What kind of monsters could order the brutal mass slaughter of a million human beings? Amazingly, they were well educated economists, lawyers and teachers—but they were *Communist economists, lawyers and teachers.* Barron and Paul reported that the Cambodian Communists were largely controlled by eight people with similar backgrounds:

> All were in their mid-40s; they had studied in France during the 1950s, and all ardently embraced communism. They were educated as economists, lawyers or teachers, and in the context of their values and beliefs, all apparently were principled, honest and courageous.[19]

One of them, their foreign minister Ieng Sary, flew to New York to attend a special session of the United Nations. He left behind a nation without universities, commerce, art, music, literature, science or any semblance of culture. Upon his arrival in New York, he boasted, "The towns have been cleaned." He was not troubled by the dead. He said:

> As long as we have one million left, that will be enough to make the new [communist] man.[20]

Why do Communists kill? They kill because communism requires that they kill to be good Communists. Communism is an idea which came out of a twisted mind. Communist killings demonstrate that ideas do have consequences.

If communism should ever come to America, Americans will be added to the lists of those killed in every part of the world.

Many years ago, a dedicated anti-Communist showed a film which documented the awfulness of the Communist threat. In his closing remarks, he left the audience with this challenge. He said:

> If communism should come to America—God forbid—will you be able to look your children in the eye and say, "I did all I could to prevent it from happening?"

CHAPTER 25

KNOW YOUR ENEMY—AND
THE BASIS OF THE CONFLICT

The basis of victory in war is to know your enemy and the
basis of the conflict.

—Sun Tzu, ancient Chinese general

THE STRUGGLE FOR POLITICAL CONTROL of a group
of people, a nation or a strategic geopolitical point in the world
is not where the real battles are being fought with the
Communists and the forces of evil. They are just skirmishes
in the real war. Tragically, most freedom fighters battle
symptoms and never see where the real battles are being
fought—and too often lost. The ancient Chinese general and
tactician Sun Tzu said:

> The basis of victory in war is to know your enemy and the basis
> of the conflict.[1]

The hearts and minds and souls of men have been the
target of an on-going war ever since Satan beguiled Eve in
the Garden of Eden six thousand years ago. That battle
continues today worldwide—in schools, churches, and the
media.

THE BATTLE OF THE TWO BOOKS

For the last 140 years the battle has largely stemmed from
a conflict between the two most widely distributed books of
all history. One was completed 1900 years ago. The other is
140 years old. The on-going, world-wide, age-old battle for the
hearts and minds and souls of men stems today from the
conflict between *The Holy Bible*—the Word of God—and Karl
Marx's *Communist Manifesto*.

The two books have amazing similarities in their focus on

the world and its problems—and yet propose solutions which are in total opposition. The contrasts and conflicts include:

In the Bible, God reveals that He IS. The Communists in their manifesto deny God's existence.

In the Bible God reveals that He created the world and everything in it, including man. Karl Marx believed that an infinite series of random accidents caused moving molecular matter to evolve and produce life and everything else in the universe.

In the Bible God reveals that He carries out His work in the world through three basic institutions—the family, the church, and the state. In the manifesto, Karl Marx calls for the abolition of the family, church and state.

In the Bible God establishes a system for protection of man and his property. Karl Marx in the Communist manifesto calls for the abolition of private property AND the property owner.

Both books see that man and his world are evil and need transformation—but set forth totally different sources for the evil and completely different methods for changing man and his world.

Both books—the Bible and the Communist's manifesto—issue calls for winning the world—but again they are in total conflict—one based on proclaiming the Gospel of God's love and the other a call to revolution.

ABOLISH THE FAMILY

The conflicts between the two books and the proposals of the Communists are startling and amazing. To correctly understand the extent of the conflict, they must be examined in detail. In his manifesto, Marx acknowledged that his goals were so unbelievable that even the most radical would choke on them. He said:

Abolition of the family! Even the most radical flare up at this infamous proposal of the Communists.[2]

The family was to be destroyed! Society-controlled public schools were to be the primary channel through which Marx envisioned the family could be destroyed. The last of Marx's ten prerequisites for bringing about the Revolution was...

...free education for all children in public schools.[3]

ELIMINATE PRIVATE EDUCATION

In calling for free, compulsory education for *all* children Marx wasn't interested in seeing that all children were educated. He was instead advocating abolishing all Catholic schools, Lutheran schools, Baptist Schools, private schools, parent-operated schools, etc.

Marx saw replacing church schools—Christian schools—with public schools was essential to weakening the family and its traditions. He acknowledged that this was his goal in advocating public school education for *all* children when he wrote:

> But you will say, we destroy the most hallowed of relations when we replace home education with social.[4]

Marx labeled talk "about the family and education, about the hallowed co-relation of parent and child" as "bourgeois clap-trap" which he said "becomes all the more disgusting."

Marx saw that the way to destroy the family was to take away the family's right and responsibility for the education of its children. His words, "But you will say, we destroy the most hallowed of relations when we replace home education with social," jump off the page in the context of nationwide attacks on parents who claimed the right to determine how their children would be educated in the decade of the 1980s.

Families in Nebraska—in Idaho—in Iowa went to jail. Others in Maryland, Missouri, Michigan, etc. were threatened with the loss of their children. Their crime? They were resisting the efforts of the state to take the basic responsibility for education away from families—replacing as Marx said, "...home education with social" education controlled by the state.

His goal for the "new" education for *all* children was contained in the words:

> The Communists have not invented the intervention of society in education; *they merely seek to alter the character of that intervention, and to rescue education from the influence of the ruling class.*[5] (Emphasis added)

Marx saw the schools as the agency through which society's traditional values could either be maintained or destroyed. Marx chose the path of destruction. He wrote:

> The Communists disdain to conceal their views and aims. They openly declare that their ends can be attained only by the forcible overthrow of all existing social conditions.

The history of the takeover of the public schools in the 1930s by the progessivists planning to transform society was examined in an earlier chapter. To comprehend even more fully why parents risked jail in the 1980s to remove their children from public schools, one particular curriculum area deserves attention. Parents began discovering that curriculum materials had been undermining the family and good parent-child relationships for over 25 years. That charge is so amazing that it demands concrete examples.

TEACHING MATERIALS ATTACK FAMILIES

In 1962 a young congressman from Ohio, John Ashbrook, became concerned that personality tests being administered in America's schools might actually be shaping attitudes of students rather than measuring them. He introduced HR 10508 to give parents access to such tests and control over whether their children would be required to take them.

To support the need for the legislation, Ashbrook placed half a dozen tests, or excerpts from them, into the *Congressional Record*[6]. One of them, The Science Research Associates *Youth Inventory*, was used throughout the nation. This test asked high school students 298 questions about their attitudes about themselves, their school, the future, boy-girl relationships, health, etc. There were 53 questions about the relationship of the students with their parents. Here are examples:

> There is constant bickering and quarreling in my home...I feel there is a barrier between me and my parents...I can't discuss personal things with my parents...I don't feel I belong in the family...my parents interfere with the spending of the money I earn...My parents are too strict about my dating...My parents won't let me make my own decisions...I feel like leaving

home...My parents hate to admit that I'm sometimes right...etc., etc. etc.

There were 53 such questions—all conveying a negative view of the parent-child relationship. Congressman Ashbrook believed that such tests were designed not so much to measure attitudes as to implant them in students' minds. Repetition is the key to learning.

One such test, of course, would not weaken or destroy a good parent-child relationship but the emphasis is reinforced throughout the school curriculum. Scott Foresman Company's *Guide To Modern English*[7] is an excellent seventh-grade English text. It has unusually good emphasis on developing writing skills. However, page after page of examples and exercises in the text emphasize that which is negative in life and in the home. Here are some sample phrases from the chapter on writing paragraphs:

Little brothers can be big problems...Uncle Dave's bellowing on the phone...His yelling at Ted...Uncle Dave's annoyance at Ted for sleeping so late...Mother's saying that Ted was one of the laziest of the relatives...Chris's being bitten by at least five dogs when little...Dad's story about being punished when a dog ripped his cuff off.

My father's parents were unbelievably stern with him when he was a child...I guess my main problem is that Mother and Dad just don't realize I'm growing up...I'm sorry I argued about TV though, because Dad got awfully sore....That was probably because Denny and Lois and I had argued so hard earlier in the day about whether to watch cartoons or the two hour movie.[8]

These are scattered but representative statements from exercises students are asked to read, analyze, classify and rewrite—a lot of repetition. And again, the focus is on the negative—on family problems.

FOCUSSING ON FAMILY PROBLEMS

The family living course for eighth grade students in another school used *The Family You Belong To* workbook from the Turner-Livingston Reading Series. The book

presented 225/250 word stories about family problems. Then
the students work three or four exercises which help them
relate personally to the family problems in the stories. One
chapter was titled "Marry Again." After reading the story,
students were given 20 questions under the headline, "Have
you ever wanted..." and told to place a check mark beside any
of the changes they ever wished would take place in their
families. The 20 choices included:

> ...to have no brothers or sisters?...to have a different family?...to
> have a different father?...to have a different mother?...to live in
> another place?...to have your mother get married again?...to have
> your father get married again?...to have a happier family?...to have
> a richer family?...to have your mother and father get divorced?...to
> be an adopted child?...etc., etc., etc.[9]

Every choice had negative implications. Students were
given no opportunity to express contentment with the family
God had given them. The next chapter was titled, "Explosion." The story dealt with family arguments. The accom-
panying exercise listed 25 reasons for arguments and told the
students, "Put a check mark beside any of the topics you and
your family argue about *sometimes.* Put a double check mark
beside any of the topics you and your family argue about *all
of the time!*[10] One irate mother commented, "It's not the
school's business what we argue about at home." It is also not
the school's business to focus children's attention on the
sometimes difficult aspects of family living.

Another exercise was titled, "Old-Fashioned." The story
concluded:

> Roxanne felt that everything in her home looked old-fashioned.
> Teenagers often feel this way about things in their homes. They
> often feel that some of the ideas their parents have are old-
> fashioned too.
>
> In a way, teenagers are right because parents are and always will
> be, *a generation older.* And, from generation to generation,
> fashions and ideas and things are bound to change.
>
> Now in the spaces at the right, list things in your home, or ideas
> your parents have, that you feel are *old-fashioned.*[11]

The student was then given six blanks in which to list old fashioned things in their homes AND six more blanks for listing "old-fashioned ideas your parents have." When the school provides six blanks students are likely to conclude that there must be six appropriate answers. Such an exercise causes students to scrutinize and question the parents' standards and values and decide some are outmoded.

Textbooks frequently present the Marxist view of the family. In the manifesto, Karl Marx asked: "On what foundation is the present family, the bourgeois family, based?" He answered:

> On capital, on private gain...the exploitation of children by their parents.[12]

Marx continued his attack on the family and particularly on the father as the head of the home saying:

> The bourgeois sees in his wife a mere instrument of production. He hears that the instruments of production are to be exploited in common, and, naturally can come to no other conclusion than that the lot of being common to all will likewise fall to women.[13]

This Marxist view of the family is found frequently in history books. In *Land of the Free*, a high school American history text, a section headed "The Family" says:

> The family was the most important social unit...With labor so much needed, a wife and children were important to any young man who wanted to get ahead...In the family, the man was the dominant figure...the colonial woman could rarely expect to have a career outside the home.

> Children were under the complete control of their father until they were grown. If a father wanted to send a child away to learn a trade, the child was expected to go. If he stayed at home, he would have to work as his father ordered, and he would be punished for any disobedience.[14]

The same Marxist view that economic motivations moved men to have families was presented in *Our Nation From Its Creation*. Of the colonial period the text said:

> A large family seemed desirable since making a decent living

depended to a large extent upon the size of the family...Land was cheap but labor was expensive...Children were treated as little adults. They worked far more than they played...they were sometimes apprenticed to a craftsman at as young an age as ten.[15]

ATTACKS START IN FIRST GRADE

Alone, none of these examples would undermine a good parent-child relationship. Repeated continually (and reinforced by the TV, etc.) they make their impact. The attacks on the family start in first grade.

A number of years ago an Ohio mother gave her six-year-old a pencil and a 3 x 5 card with which to amuse herself while the pastor was preaching on Sunday morning. Part way through the sermon the mother was shocked to see that her daughter had written, "Sam is a filthy...mom is a filthy rat....dad is a filthy rat..." Below the writing, the little girl had drawn a picture of a women's body with a rat's head. She had labeled the picture, "Mom."

Almost in panic, the mother asked, "Brenda—where did you learn anything like that?" The little girl replied, "In school, Mommy." When the girl persisted in her story the mother went to school. She found a collection of papers her little first grader had written. They said:

Mom is a nut...Pop is a nut...Pat is a nut...Tim is filthy...Tom is filthy...mom is filthy...dad is filthy...Pop is a pest...Mom is a pest...Mommy is filthy....Tommy is filthy...Daddy is filthy...

The teacher had marked several of the papers, "Good!"

Investigation determined that neither the daughter nor the teacher were perverted. It was all the result of a new method for teaching reading called, *Words in Color*. Developed in Ethiopia by UNESCO (United Nations Education, Scientific and Cultural Organization) Words in Color had been introduced into America and was being distributed by the educational materials division of a large encyclopedia publisher. It was listed among new and innovative approaches to teaching reading in the January 1970 issue of *Today's Education*, the official journal of the National Education Association.[16]

To help students differentiate between long and short

sounds, etc., words with different vowel sounds were printed in different colors. Some reading teachers applauded the method. Unfortunately, they like many unsuspecting teachers only looked at the skills being taught and not at the ideas transmitted by the materials. In their workbooks students were told, "Write down more sentences using words you now know." If the student word list only includes words like "pest, dirty, filthy, rat, mom, dad," and the first-graders are given an "is" and told to make sentences using the words they now know, they are limited in the thoughts they can express.

A further check of the workbook showed that much of the material carried dismal, negative connotations. The workbook was filled with phrases like, "Cherries have pits....Roses have thorns..."

NO MORE HEROES

A first-grade social studies curriculum guide developed and used in the schools of California's Contra Costa County told the teachers:

> No longer can history, geography, and civics taught separately as in the recent past, be considered adequate preparation for effective citizenship.[17]

Someone asked, "Why not?" However, starting from that premise the first-grade "social studies" guide ignored George Washington and the heroes and events of the past. Instead the course focussed on family living, human ecology, personality and socialization processes, etc. One theme teachers were to develop through the year emphasized that parents didn't spend enough time with their children. Teachers were told to emphasize that:

> Families carry on many work/play activities together...Parents who commute to work have little time to spend with children in the evening...Fathers who travel have time with their children on certain days...[18]

As the year progressed teachers were told, "Set up some role playing situations...such as:"

a. Dick's father works at night and sleeps in the morning. Dick started to play on his new drum, but his big brother said......

b. Jimmy's father drives so far to work everyday that he is very tired when he gets home. Jimmy always wanted to wrestle with his father but......

c. Donald's father always reads the newspaper as soon as he comes home. One night Donald said....

In this section,[19] first-graders are taught a "cute" little poem called, "Newspaper," by Aileen Fisher. The poem reads:

I always hope Father is going to play,
with the paper in front of his face that way.
I think he might look from the edge and wink
or peakaboo me, but what do you think:
He reads all the pages from A to Z
and never once thinks of being Daddy to me.

Once that sad but catchy poem is etched into the child's memory, each time daddy picks up his newspaper (as he should do to stay informed) the child gets the message, "Daddy doesn't really love me." This is diabolical. Maintaining a good parent-child relationship is the key to success all through life. God's Word says:

Children obey your parents in the Lord: for this is right. Honour thy father and mother; which is the first commandment with promise; that it may be well with thee, and thou mayest live long on the earth. (Ephesians 6:1-4)

God promises that honoring parents is the key to a long life *and blessing and success in every area of life*. Those who erode and undermine good parent-child relationships are condemning children to conflict and failure in every area and shortened lives. The child who is not rightly related to his parents cannot have a right relationship with his teachers, his employer or to his mate in marriage.

Curriculum materials from the schools of the 1960s were used intentionally to show how long the family has been under attack in school curriculum materials. Students exposed to these constant attacks on the family in the 1960s were the generation who turned to drugs, sex and revolution. They are contributing to the 60% increase in divorce rates since 1960. Their children are among the multiplying numbers of functional illiterates educators were trying to help in the 1980s.

ACCORDING TO PLAN

Is there any real relationship between Karl Marx's call to use the schools to destroy the family and the anti-family influences in the schools 100 years later—or is it all coincidence? A book published by Harper & Row and distributed widely to high school guidance counselors, etc. in 1967-68 as the monthly selection of a leading behavioral science book club shows a direct connection.

MIND MANIPULATORS TO REMAKE SOCIETY

In the book, *The Triumph of the Therapeutic—Uses of Faith After Freud*,[20] author Philip Rieff sets forth the concept that the "therapeutics,"—the psychiatrists, sociologists, counselors, etc.—can use their skills and theories to remake and control society. Rieff has impressive credentials. He has taught sociology at the University of Chicago, Brandeis, Harvard, the University of California at Berkeley and the University of Pennsylvania. From 1961 to 1964 he served as the chief consultant to the Planning Department of the National Council of Churches. He has been at all the right—or "wrong" places. In the introduction to his book, Rieff highlights a statement from Bronislaw Malinowski's *Culture as a Determinant Behavior* which said:

> That we are passing through a cultural crisis of unprecedented magnitude and of a definitely putrid quality nobody doubts...I can see only one way out...the establishment of a scientific control of human affairs.

This is a Marxist view and premise—the remaking of man through the application of "science" (falsely so-called). Rieff shows his own orientation and prejudice in this area and his dream for reorganizing society using therapeutic principles when in his foreword he wrote:

The long period of deconversion...by which Christian culture has been displaced...which first broke the surface of political history at the time of the French Revolution appears all but ended. The central symbolism of personal and corporate experience seems to me well on its way to being differently organized with several systems of belief competing for primacy in the task of organizing personality in the West.

I intend drawing certain implications for the reorganization of Western culture and personality from the divergence between Freud and those of his most powerful successor-critics studied in this book—C.G. Jung, Wilhelm Reich, and D.H. Lawrence.[21]

Wilhelm Reich was a psychiatrist *and a Communist*. Rieff says Reich left the Bolshevik Communist movement reluctantly. He believed that by failing to convert Lenin's political revolution into the first moral revolution fought on scientific principles, the Marxists defeated themselves.

Reich in his teachings followed Marx and Engels in their attacks on the family but said they didn't go far enough. Rieff summarizes Reich's beliefs this way:

The chief institutional instrument of repressive authority is the family. As a political revolution must overthrow the power of the state, moral revolution must overthrow the power of the family— all families. Reich makes the standard point: the family, being the training ground of morality, is authoritarian by definition. It is the "factory of reactionary ideology and structure"... A revolution must sweep out the family and its ruler, the father, no less cleanly than the old political gangs and their leaders. However radical the revolution, so long as the family persists, authority will creep back.[22]

Having so summarized the theories and teachings of the Bolshevik Communist, Rieff then added:

The destruction, then, of the ancient mystique of fatherhood defines the revolutionary task. For this eminently theoretical reason, Reich became a fierce feminist...Because "political reaction favors the patriarchal theory," Reich supposed that matriarchy must be the "natural" and free form of social organization...The patriarchal family became the main device for suppressing freedom...A triumphant father supposedly ended the primitive utopia of freedom.[23]

SEX EDUCATION THE WEAPON

What remedy did Philip Rieff see for reorganizing society? He again drew on Wilhelm Reich. He said:

> Set into the context of Reich's attack on the family as the nucleus of all authoritative institutions, his repeated calls for a do-it-yourself adolescent sex education acquires political significance. Sex education becomes the main weapon in an ideological war against the family; its aim was to divest the parents of their moral authority.[24]

This is an amazing admission. It confirms the concerns of many who have battled schoolroom sex education since the middle 1960s. Rieff concludes:

> There is something adolescent about the Reichian theory; for him all hope rests with the possibility of creating revolutionary children...Because Marx theorized in terms of an adult world, he could not possibly be subversive enough. With John Dewey [father of modern public education], Wilhelm Reich is one of the great theorists of the child as the agent of social change...though publicly labeled an eccentric, Reich was anything but a fool.[25]

Reich's book, *The Mass Psychology of Fascism*, which proposed adolescent do-it-yourself sex education as a weapon in the war against the family was published in 1946. Rieff's book, promoting Reich's theories, was widely available to high school guidance counselors in 1967-68. Those who read it could have known the far-reaching anti-family implications of the sex education programs even while they were being introduced into American schools in the 1960s.

CHURCHES JOIN THE ATTACK

Philip Rieff's influence reached into the churches also. From 1961 to 1964 he was chief consultant to the Planning Commission of the National Council of Churches (NCC). It was during this period that the church council started issuing materials which opened the door for the sexual revolution—

and the Sunday school literature of some NCC member denominations joined the anti-family attack.

Called to Responsible Freedom: The Meaning of Sex in the Christian Life was published in 1961 by the United Christian Youth Movement of the National Council of Churches. The booklet discussed society's "arbitrary" rules for sexual behavior and said:

> Both Jesus and Paul were seeking to set men free from this sort of legalistic bondage...For the Christian there are no laws, no rules, no regulations....Life is a series of grays and not pure blacks and whites.[26]

The message of the booklet, in effect, told young people in church youth groups that if they loved each other anything was OK. It said:

> The difficulty with Western society's legitimate regulation of sexual conduct is that it has been far too negative and too monolithic...Our culture declares that all sexual activity within marriage is legal, proper, and good, while any such activity outside marriage is illicit, sinful and wrong. This is to ignore the personal dimension in life, to seek to force everyone under one massive legal umbrella.

> You and I know perfectly well that there are many marriages that are simply matters of convenience, that such sex as goes on within them that is selfish, exploitative, and evil. We know further that there is sexual contact between unmarried couples that is motivated by love and which is pure and on occasions beautiful.

> From the perspective of the personal dimension then, the crucial question to be asked about any sexual contact—from holding hands to complete intercourse—is not so much what is done but what is meant...What justifies and sanctifies sexuality is not the external marital status of the people before the law but rather what they feel toward each other in their hearts.[27]

With that "standard" being promoted by the National Council of Churches, is it any wonder that the nation experienced a sexual revolution in the 1960s?

SUNDAY SCHOOL LITERATURE

The NCC set the standard. Individual denominations went even farther. *YOUTH* magazine was published for high school young people of the United Church of Christ, the Episcopal Church, the Anglican Church of Canada. A special Horizons edition was issued for young people of the Church of the Brethren.

The January 14, 1968 issue featured an article by Larry Beggs, director of Huckleberry House, a youth "ministry" in San Francisco's Haight-Ashbury district. Begg's article blatantly attacked the authority of the family and its values and Biblical sexual standards. It presented a not-so-subtle encouragement for teenagers to runaway from home and join the leftist causes and revolution of the late 1960s. Beggs said:

> The hundreds of teenagers I have met in the Haight-Ashbury have come for many reasons. Some come because they have been kicked out of the house—simply unwanted. We call them "push-aways." Many come because they have accumulated hurts from years of family living.
>
> A significant number come because of value differences. The teenager is exploring and validating values which may be different than those held by his parents...He [the runaway] knows that some values endure and that most are dated...Far from being a juvenile delinquent, the runaway in our eyes is often the most responsible member of the family.[28]

Beggs attacks the authority of the home and family, picturing as dictatorial and unreasonable parents who fulfill their Biblical responsibilities to train and discipline their children. Beggs writes:

> It is shocking and sad to me to meet some parents who regard their runaway child as having no more freedom than a domestic animal. This is expressed in the familiar remark, "As long as Bob is in my house, eating my food, he will obey my rules of dress and deportment..." The legal machinery of this culture supports this point of view.[29]

Beggs then advocates a change. He states:

I think it is so crucial to look at the denial of [basic human] rights to teenagers in almost every area of their lives. The self-determination of so many teenagers is put on ice until they are 21. This means that their decision-making humanity is thwarted and the nation loses an invaluable natural resource...At its best the adult world is an enlightened colonial power...Adam and Eve became human when they realized and actualized their power of decision.[30]

PROMOTE THE "PILL"

The Sunday School article then listed eight ways in which it said that the self-determination of teenagers was denied by their parents and the "adult colonial powers". The list included juvenile courts which teenagers are not permitted to run, compulsory school attendance laws, the military draft for service in the "illegal" undeclared war in Vietnam, restrictions on the reading material young people can obtain, bans on smoking and sexual activity. Author Larry Beggs was at the time a United Church of Christ minister. Under the heading *The pill and responsible freedom,* he said:

The colonial powers whose majority is declining have set the very arbitrary time of from five to eight years after sexual maturation as the time when young Americans can enjoy sexual relations. A girl under 18 cannot get birth control pills without her parents' approval [the article is 21 years old]...Young people as sexual beings have sexual rights...If the pill were allowed, young people could assume this responsibility! We immediately hear the colonials roar, "Promiscuity, promiscuity, promiscuity!"

The freedom to use your God-given body to express your affection toward another person cannot be labeled promiscuous merely because the persons involved are not ready for marriage and parenting.

In all these areas, the self-determination of young people has been duly and arbitrarily postponed. If the Christian gospel is one of liberating the captives it should certainly apply here.[31]

This is blasphemy in liberal church Sunday school literature. Anti-family poison has also found its way into the literature of even more evangelical groups. The Southern

Baptist Sunday school quarterly, *Bible Study for Young People* in its May 11, 1969 lesson pictured one young man and his family this way:

> Allen is a member of the "dropout" generation. He ran away from a beautiful suburban home and parents who are slaves to someone else's business [they work for a living?], monthly payments [they pay their bills?], status and whose lives have turned into gray waste and meaningless.

The youth director of an independent Bible-believing church prepared a questionnaire for young people which asked the same "focus on the negative" questions as the local school district was asking in its family living curriculum. Questions included:

> With whom do you have more arguments and conflicts in your family?...How often do you have a "major argument" with someone in your house?...What are most of the arguments with your family about?

The questionnaire listed 12 "faults" of parents and asked young people to "Check the faults you believe your parents have." Clearly, Marx's dream of using public schools as a tool in his campaign to destroy the family has been expanded to include the churches as well.

The Communist call for abolishing the family was not a one-time, off-the-cuff proposal in *The Communist Manifesto* but rather the start of a longtime, on-going war. Thirty-five years after the Manifesto was published, Marx's co-author, Friedrich Engels laid out an eight point program for destroying the family.[32] Allan Carlson of the prestigious Rockford Institute summarized Engels proposals as calling for...

> ...the return of women to the factories, free and easy divorce, the elimination of sex roles, the transformation of housekeeping into a social industry, the communalization of child care, the elimination of the concept of "illegitimacy," an open definition of "family," and unrestrained sexual activity.[33]

DIVORCE RATES SKYROCKET

Within 100 years after Engels issued his treatise on the

family most of his eight proposals had been or were being implemented in the United States. The impact on the family had been tragic. In 1900, 15 years after Engels proposals were first published, one out of 100 American marriages ended in divorce. By 1960, the divorce rate had climbed to 3 out of 10 and by the late 1980s half of all marriages were ending in court. Then the rate leveled off not because there were fewer divorces but because so many young couples had not married before starting to live together. Their separations, therefore, did show up in the divorce statistics.

Without strong families, society will crumble—which is the Communist goal. They plan to rebuild out of the ashes.

ABOLISH THE CHURCH ALSO

Marx not only wanted to replace the family, he also wanted to replace God and the church as the source of truth, guidance, and morality in society. Marx said:

> Communism abolishes all eternal truths, it abolishes all religion, and all morality, instead of constituting them on a new basis; it therefore acts in contradiction to all past historical experience.[34]

In the introduction to his book, *The Myth of Separation*, David Barton listed the flood of court decisions which since 1947 has banned or restricted religious activity. Among those he cited were decisions of the U.S. Supreme Court and other federal and state courts which ruled:

> A verbal prayer offered in school is unconstitutional, even if it is both denominationally neutral and voluntarily participated in... Freedom of speech and press is guaranteed to students unless the topic is religious, at which time such speech becomes unconstitutional... If a student prays over his lunch, it is unconstitutional for him to pray aloud...

> It is unconstitutional for kindergarten students to recite: "We thank you for the flowers so sweet; We thank you for the food we eat; We thank you for the birds that sing; We thank you for everything." Even though the word "God" is not contained in it, someone might think it is a prayer.

> It is unconstitutional for the Ten Commandments to hang on the

walls of a classroom since it might lead the students to read them, meditate upon them, respect them, or obey them.

It is unconstitutional for students to arrive at school early to hear a student volunteer read prayers which had been offered by chaplains in the chambers of the U.S. House of Representatives and Senate, even though those prayers are contained in the *Congressional Record* published by the U.S. government.[35]

Each of these activities and actions were practiced constitutionally during America's first 150 years—but the courts now say they are unconstitutional. Contrast those modern decisions with typical court rulings from America's early history which said:

No free government now exists in the world unless where Christianity is acknowledged, and is the religion of the country...it is the purest system of morality, the firmest auxiliary, and only stable support of all human laws...Christianity is part of the common law..."

The purest principles of morality are to be taught [in schools]. Where are they found? Whosoever searches for them must go to the source from which a Christian man derives his faith—the Bible.[36]

A CHRISTIAN NATION

The 1892 Supreme Court decision in the case of the Church of the Holy Trinity vs. United States was typical of many earlier court rulings. The court reviewed the religious references in America's founding documents, the early Supreme Court decisions and the references to God in the Constitutions of 44 of the 45 states then in existence and said:

These and many other matters which might be noticed, add a volume of unofficial declarations to the mass of organic utterances that this is a Christian nation..[37]

As late as 1931, the U.S. Supreme Court, ruling in the case of the United States v. MacIntosh, said:

We are a Christian people, according to one another the equal right of religious freedom, and acknowledging with reverence the duty of obedience to the will of God.[38]

The first Chief Justice of the U.S. Supreme Court, John Jay, said:

> Providence has given to our people the choice of their rulers, and it is the duty, as well as the privilege and interest, of a Christian nation to select and prefer Christians for their rulers.[39]

America was founded as "a nation under God." That is the secret of America's strength and greatness and prosperity. Psalm 33:12 says:

> Blessed is the nation whose God is the Lord; and the people whom he hath chosen for his own inheritance.

That concept is under attack today. The United States because it was founded as a Christian nation and has been so blessed of God is the particular target of the Communists, the humanists and other leftist anti-God groups. The American Civil Liberties Union (ACLU), a humanist group which had Communists among its founders, is working to totally secularize American society. (The founding board of directors included William Z. Foster and Elizabeth Gurley Flynn, both of whom later headed the Communist Party USA.[40]) Roger Baldwin was the founder and executive director for 30 years. Twelve years after forming the ACLU Baldwin wrote of his goals and beliefs. He said:

> I am for socialism, disarmament, and ultimately for abolishing the State itself as an instrument for violence and compulsion. I seek the social ownership of property, the abolition of the propertied class and sole control of those who produce wealth. Communism is the goal.[41]

In recent years lawsuits and legislation proposed or instigated by "civil liberties" groups have included:

> Elimination of tax exempt status for churches and their schools and other ministries...Elimination of military and prison chaplains... Elimination of nativity scenes and other religious symbols from public property...Repeal of laws upholding the observance of the Lord's Day...Elimination of "Under God" from the pledge of allegiance to the flag and "In God We Trust" from U.S. coins and paper money.

These and other ACLU efforts to remove God from American society knowingly or unknowingly fit into Karl Marx's goal of "abolishing all eternal truth." Along with direct attacks on public religious expressions or acknowledgements of America's Biblical heritage, the American Civil Liberties Union also fights legislation and actions which would uphold the Bible-based standards of decency and morality in society. ACLU positions which made Democratic presidential candidate Michael Dukakis's membership an issue in the 1988 election included:

> Legalization of drugs...abolishing the death penalty...elimination of laws restraining obscenity and pornography...ending legal restraints against homosexual practices...legalization of "gay" marriages... legalization of prostitution...gun registration...abortion... and more.

LAW GROUP JOINS THE ATTACK

By 1989, the American Bar Association joined the attack. The ABA hosted a seminar in San Francisco to train lawyers in techniques to use in suing churches, clergy, deacons, etc. A workshop session on "Tort Law As An Ideological Weapon" taught the lawyers how to build suits against churches for brainwashing, guilt manipulation, and causing emotional stress. (Evangelism—attempting to get people to face their sin and hell as its consequence and turn to Jesus Christ for life-changing salvation—is increasingly classified as brainwashing, guilt manipulation, and causing emotional stress by "expert" witnesses who are psychiatrists.) The seminar also discussed techniques for making an entire organization and the members of the group liable for damages when there is sexual misconduct by a clergyman or other staff member in their employment.[42]

Legal actions against churches are mounting. During the 1970s there were several hundred active cases nationwide. By the mid-80s the number of open files in organizations which assist churches in protecting their religious liberty jumped from a few hundred to over 10,000. Karl Marx said, "...abolish all religion." The courts are helping.

PRIVATE PROPERTY ATTACKED

The Bible recognizes man's right to property in many ways. One is the Eighth Commandment. When He says, "Thou Shalt Not Steal" He is acknowledging the existence of individual ownership of property and the need to protect it from covetous eyes and hands. When God tells man to give He is also acknowledging private ownership of property and the need to use it properly.

Marx takes a directly conflicting view. He wrote:

> ...the theory of the Communists may be summed up in a single phrase "Abolition of private property"...you reproach us with intending to do away with your property. Precisely so; that is just what we intend.

CHANGING MAN—WHOSE WAY?

The conflict between the two books—between God's Holy Bible and the Communist's manifesto goes even further. Both books see that the world and man need changing.

In the Bible God says that all of the evil in the world—and the evil that men do comes from man's heart. Jesus said:

> For from within, out of the heart of men, proceed evil thoughts, adulteries, fornications, murders, thefts, covetousness, wickedness, deceit, lasciviousness, an evil eye, blasphemy, pride, foolishness; all these evil things come from within, and defile the man. (Mark 7:21-23)

Jesus said, therefore, that man needs to be "born again"—that man needs to get a new heart. The Bible teaches that after the Lord Jesus died to take away man's sin He arose from the dead to be the new life of those who would believe and receive Him. These changed men—men with new hearts—could then work to change the world.

Karl Marx envisioned a completely different source for the world's problems and the evil which men do. Marx taught that man was the product of his environment—that any evil seen in man and done by man was simply a reflection of the evil economic system which comprised man's environment. In the manifesto he wrote:

Your very ideas are but the outgrowth of the conditions of your bourgeois production and bourgeois property, just as your jurisprudence is but the will of your class made into a law for all, *a will, whose essential character and direction are determined by the economical conditions of existence of your class.*[43]

A few pages later Marx repeats his contention that human nature is a reflection of man's economic environment. He said:

Does it require deep intuition to comprehend that man's ideas, views and conceptions, in one word, man's consciousness, changes with every change in the conditions of his material existence, in his social relations and in his social life.[44]

Marx believed that man was not a responsible moral creature but rather a "reflector" of his evil capitalistic economic environment. He taught therefore that once Communists got control of the entire world and abolished private property and free enterprise and eliminated the bourgeoisie that man would be dramatically transformed by the socialist environment. A perfect world would result.

With the bourgeoisie eliminated as a class, the age old class struggle between the bourgeoisie and the proletariat would be no more. It was in this context that Marx and Engels taught that...

The state is the product and the manifestation of the *irreconcilability* of class antagonisms...the state is an organ of class domination, an organ of oppression of one class by another...with an end to all class differences and class antagonisms, it puts an end to the state also as the state.

Formerly society, moving in class antagonisms, had need of the state, that is, an organization of the exploiting class...for the holding down of the exploited class in conditions of oppression...

As soon as there is no longer any class of society to be held in subjection...the interference of state power in social relations becomes superfluous in one sphere after another, and then becomes dormant itself...The state is not "abolished," *it withers away.*[45]

This is, of course, another major conflict with God's Word which teaches that governments are given their power by God. God instituted human government as the means of maintaining order and preventing wicked men from infringing upon the God-given lives, rights and property of others. The Bible says:

> Let every soul be subject unto the higher powers. for there is no power but of God: the powers that be are ordained of God. Whosoever therefore resisteth the power resisteth the ordinance of God: and they that resist shall receive to themselves damnation. For rulers are not a terror to good works, but to the evil. (Romans 13:1-3)

Tragically some important churchmen and many mainline church denominations have departed from the Bible and have adopted Marx's view that man's basic nature can be changed through a change in his environment. The World Council of Churches Central Committee met in Moscow in July 1989. The WCC's top official, General Secretary Emilio Castro, gave the response to the speech of the Soviet Prime Minister Ryzhkov. The World Council spokesman said:

> I might be tempted to quote some of the most beautiful pages of Karl Marx, dreaming of the New Man, the new creature. He was dreaming out of the same biblical traditional from which we come. In that common dream, we hope that between us we will have many steps to take in common.[46]

Castro's words from a supposed Christian leader were blasphemy. Marx's "New Man" was to result from the new socialist environment created by brutally eliminating all the diseased bourgeois "animals" and the private property they controlled. In contrast the Bible says of the new man:

> Therefore if any man be in Christ, he is a new creature: old things are passed away; behold, all things are become new. And all things are of God who hath reconciled us to himself by Jesus Christ. (II Corinthians 5:17-18a)

WINNING THE WORLD—TWO WAYS

The contrasts between the two books do not stop with their

diametrically opposed views of how man was to be changed.
Each book has its own plan for reaching the world. At the end
of each of the four Gospels, the Lord Jesus gave the Great
Commission to his disciples. He said:

> Go ye into all the world, and preach the gospel to every creature.
> He that believeth and is baptized shall be saved; but he that
> believeth not shall be damned. (Mark 16:15-16)

In Matthew 28:19-20, He said:

> Go ye therefore, and teach all nations, baptizing them in the name
> of the Father, and of the Son, and of the Holy Ghost: Teaching
> them to observe all things whatsoever I have commanded you:
> and, lo, I am with you alway, even unto the end of the world.
> Amen.

Jesus envisioned transforming man through the preaching
of the Gospel. The transformed men and women would function as "the salt of the earth" and "the light of the world." They
would resist and hold back the world's corruption and wickedness and make the world a better place for everyone. Marx
had a different plan. He closed the manifesto with the call to
revolution. He said:

> The Communists disdain to conceal their views and aims. They
> openly declare that their ends can be attained only by the forcible
> overthrow of all existing social conditions. Let the ruling classes
> tremble at a Communist revolution. The proletarians have nothing
> to lose but their chains. They have a world to win. Working men
> of all countries, unite!

The Bible—God's Word—and Marx's manifesto are two
books in conflict—two books with completely different approaches and commands for winning the world.

THE RESULT

What has been the result? The Lord Jesus gave his command to reach all the world's people with the Gospel almost
2000 years ago. After 2000 years of effort, about 900-million
people have been reached by the disciples of Christ world-
wide. The 900- million are not all "Christians" in the true
Bible sense of the word but include anyone and every group

that in any way looks to the Bible and claims the name of Christ.

How are the Communists doing? They have not been working for 2000 years but for just 140. After 140 years, the followers of Marx and the disciples of Lenin now control almost 2-billion of the world's people and 30% of the earth's land mass. They control more land and more people than any other would-be world conqueror in history. And they exert unmeasured influence over most of the rest of the world.

They've done it by recruiting a relative handful of people, inspiring them to unbelievable dedication and then training them to be leaders. These trained and dedicated people are winning the world by faithfully working a plan—Lenin's plan for world conquest. Summarized and paraphrased again, the plan states:

> First, we will take Eastern Europe, then the masses of Asia. Then we will encircle the United States, which will be the last bastion of capitalism. We will not have to attack. It will become so rotten from within that it will fall like an overripe fruit into our hands.

They are working on the last stages of that plan now—they are consolidating their influence and power in Asia—in Africa and in Central America. In the last thirty years, America, founded as a nation under God, has lived through a Revolution. The nation which says, "In God We Trust" on its money has been transformed into a sex-crazy, drug-dependent, violence-torn, sick society. America is becoming more and more like the "overripe fruit" which Lenin said would one day fall into Communist hands.

THE SECRET OF THEIR SUCCESS

Why and how have the Communists been so successful? Douglas Hyde was a member of the Communist Party of Great Britain for twenty years. Before becoming disillusioned and leaving the Red Conspiracy in 1948 he served on the Central Committee of the Party and was the editor of *The Daily Worker*, the party's official newspaper. In his book, *Dedication and Leadership*,[47] he asked:

Why are Communists so dedicated and successful as leaders whilst others so often are not? (pg. 5)

He said that after he left the Party he saw that Communists were right in certain important respects. Communists are right he said when they say...

...there is a great battle going on all over the world which in the final analysis is a struggle for men's hearts, minds and souls (pg. 10).

How many Christians live with that kind of realization of the battle which is being waged world-wide. Hyde showed that Communists not only recognize the battle they are in but that they are working for a clear-cut goal. He said:

Their aim is a Communist world...and in the past half century they have achieved one-third of that aim. So it is probably true to say of the Communists that never in man's history has a small group of people set out to win a world and achieved more in less time (pg. 11).

Hyde states that many find in communism what they had hoped, without success, to find among the Christians. Communists get their recruits by appealing to the idealism of the young. They appeal to idealism—and then train the young idealists to lie, cheat, steal or murder to achieve the "idealistic" goals they hold out. Hyde says:

Communism becomes the dominant thing in the life of the Communists. It becomes something to which he gives himself completely (pg. 18).

Of how many Christians could that be said—that Christ is the dominant force or power or *person* in their lives? How many Christians can be seen giving themselves totally and completely to the Lord Jesus and His great commission? That's why Communists have enslaved twice as many of the world's people as Christ's followers have reached. And the Communists have done it in a fraction of the time.

PRODUCING DEDICATION

How do the Communists obtain this commitment? Hyde says:

> Like attracts like. Those who are attracted by the dedication they see within a movement will themselves be possessed of a latent idealism, a capacity for dedication—thus dedication perpetuates itself.

> If the majority of members of an organization are half-hearted and largely inactive, then it is not surprising if others who join it soon conform to the general pattern.

> If, on the other hand, the majority of members, from the leaders down, are characterized by their single-minded devotion to the cause, then those who consider joining will assume that this is what will be expected of them (pg. 27).

Hyde continues:

> The Communists make far bigger demands upon their people than the average Christian organization would ever dare to make...Communists say that if you make mean little demands on people, you will get a mean little response which is all you deserve, but, if you make big demands on them, you will get a heroic response (pg. 18.)

Hyde illustrates how the Party's demands are greater than any Christian organization makes—and how Communists respond. God's Word commands Christians to tithe—to give ten percent of their income to God's work. Hyde described "payday" when he was a staff member and then editor of the British Communist Party's newspaper. He said:

> We got our pay packets, opened them and immediately gave eight fourteenths [57%] of their contents to the Party and the paper— before it burned our fingers...it just went direct to the cause. And so it continues to this day.(pg. 19)

Hyde wrote his book 20 years ago but Communist giving continues to this day. Because Communists give they can publish their official daily newspaper, *The People's Daily World* and mail it to any home in America every day *for just $15 a year!* Party members' gifts and money from Moscow has subsidized the distribution. In recent years, the Communists have published the paper simultaneously in New York, Chicago and San Francisco using technology similar to that of *USA Today* or *The Wall Street Journal*. Meanwhile Christian and conservative newspapers and magazines struggle to exist.

Hyde points up the contradiction. Speaking of the potential recruits to the Communist Party among those who have been exposed to Christianity, Hyde says:

> ... although Christianity has taught him that total dedication is something to be admired and something one should aspire to in one's own life, a Communist may be the first totally dedicated person he has met...the Communist may be the first dedicated person he has met who is not wrapped up in his own salvation but is devoting himself to the transformation of society and reaching the world (pg. 37).

How do the Communists produce this sort of dedication in their recruits? Hyde says:

> Individual members of the Communist Party are brought to believe that together they and others like them can change the world...When you have succeeded in making men believe that change is necessary and possible and that they are the ones who can achieve it; when you have convinced them that they and the small minority of whom they are a part can transform the world in their lifetime, you have achieved something very considerable indeed (pg. 31).

That's what the Lord Jesus did. The Lord gave His eleven disciples the message that would change men's lives and hearts. He convinced them that they could take that message to the whole world because He would work with them where ever they would go until the end of the age. Church history indicates that those eleven and those they won did reach the then known world in their lifetimes. God's people today need a fresh new vision for reaching their own nations and then the world.

A careful study of Hyde's book brings the realization that the Communists are succeeding by taking the principles and methods God gave to the church and to His people—and using them for their own evil ends. God's methods work. The Communists use them while so often God's people do not.

Communist training of new party members, for example, covers exactly the same subjects that a good training program for new Christians or the members of a newly- formed political movement should cover. The new Communist party member is given four basic lessons from the Communist perspective. They are:

(1) The kind of world we live in...(2) How that world can be changed...(3) The force that can change it...and (4) The Communist Party, the body through which that force is channeled (pg. 51).

A training class for Christians, using that very outline (substituting the church for the Communist Party), would provide a Biblical world view and a cause and a goal to live for. A similar study for political activists would cause them to examine what they believe and what they really want to achieve.

ACTION-ORIENTED TRAINING

Communist classes are NEVER just theoretical. Every class ends with the question...

What are the comrades going to do about what they learned today? (pg. 56)

The first item on the agenda for the next class session is...

How did you comrades apply what you learned last week?

The party member is convinced through the training he receives that he is fighting against monstrously evil things...that he is on the side of good and involved in a struggle against evil. How many of God's people live with such a realization burning in their hearts and minds?

Communists are taught continually to do their best where ever they are—in whatever they are engaged in. They are constantly challenged ...

...you are more likely to be effective if you are respected...if you are going to be really effective in your place of work, you must set out to be the best man at your job [or in your union or your neighborhood]. (pg. 98)

This is another Christian concept they have stolen. In John 13:20, the Lord Jesus told His disciples:

> Verily, verily, I say unto you, He that receiveth whomsoever I send receiveth me; and he that receiveth me receiveth him that sent me.

Whether in political action, a Christian endeavor or business those who are most successful learn quickly that winning others to themselves is the first step in reaching them for a cause or a sale. Jesus taught it. The Communists practice it. God's people need to learn it.

DISCOURAGEMENT

Other challenging lessons can be learned from Hyde's book. For example: After Hyde left Great Britain's Communist Party he became a Catholic. He soon faced great discouragement and disillusionment with what he encountered. He said:

> ...one thing I had not bargained for was the many people I met who told me that the Catholic community in Britain suffered from something they described as a minority complex. I had not expected this, because I was coming from an organization which at the time had some 45,000 members to one which was numerically 100 times as strong and which represented some 10 percent of Britain's population.
>
> As Communists we firmly believed that, relatively few though we were, we had a world to win and were going to win it....it astounded me that [in my new church] there should be people with such numbers at their disposal and with the truth on their side, going around weighed down by the thought that they were a small beleaguered minority carrying on some sort of an impossible fight against a big majority (pg. 33).

Hyde's words could be used to describe the attitudes of many Bible-believers—many concerned conservatives. How many have the attitude, "We're just a minority—the other side controls the media—we can expect to be persecuted—we can't expect to accomplish a whole lot." Some Bible-believers add, "After all we are living in the last days."

Contrast those attitudes with the Bible—God's Word—which still says...

> I can do all things through Christ which strengtheneth me...with God all things are possible...one of you shall chase a thousand—and two shall put ten thousand to flight...Occupy till I come.

Those promises and commands are true. But how many live in the reality of them? Those who are God's people need to shift their eyes off the circumstances and put them onto Jesus and His promises and get about the work He has given us to do. And it must be done God's way using the methods He has given His people.

A careful study of the Communist's tactics and methods shows that they are successful because they have stolen the principles and methods God has given His people. The Reds use them for their evil Satanic ends. God's methods work for whoever uses them. Hyde's book shows that the Communists are using them to win the world. Hyde's book, *Dedication and Leadership*, should be must reading for every preacher—for every Christian—for every concerned American.

WHAT MUST BE DONE?

Recognizing that most of the differences between people and much of the strife in the world stems from the fundamental and irresolvable conflicts between God's Bible and Karl Marx's manifesto, every individual must:

1. Make an inventory to determine whether he or she is standing as firmly with Christ and true Bible Christianity as the Communists have shown themselves to be committed to Marxism-Leninism and the Communist/humanist alternatives to God's way.

2. Recognize that the Bible is truth and the source of all truth, faith and strength and make a commitment to read the scriptures daily, growing thereby in an understanding of God's way.

3. Stand against all error and for what is right, decent, kind, wise, proper and loving in every situation and circumstance.

4. The family being the focal point of the Communist/humanist attack, individuals should assess their own family relationships and work to strengthen them.

5. Determine to develop the leadership and communication skills needed to be as effective as Communists are.

6. Seek circles of influence in which to be effective for Christ, liberty and freedom.

7. Read and study Douglas Hyde's book, *Dedication and Leadership*, to learn the methods God's people should be using to be effective in the world-wide struggle for "the hearts and minds and souls of men."

CHAPTER 26

KNOW YOUR STRENGTHS—AND

THE BASIS OF VICTORY

When the enemy shall come in like a flood, the Spirit of the
Lord shall lift up a standard against him.

—Isaiah 59:19b (KJV)

IS THERE ANY HOPE for America? Can the Communist/Humanist/Hedonist forces be thwarted? Can their ability to influence and manipulate America's churches, schools, press, labor unions, business organizations, Congress and the bureaucracy be countered? Are there any real prospects for preserving freedom and liberty in America—*and extending it world-wide?*

America's hope, humanly speaking, rests in a body of concerned, informed Americans developing and implementing the "cadre concept." This is the Communists' greatest fear. The Communist concern was demonstrated by an attack they launched against the author and a project he initiated in 1987.

In early 1987, the author started developing a videotaped *Understanding The Times* curriculum for use in Christian high schools and colleges. The program was built around 32 classroom-length videotapes featuring some of the nation's best-informed pro-American, pro-family, pro-God, anti-Communist speakers. The year-long course teaches young people the dangers from communism and its influence in America and gives them an understanding of the contrasting world views of communism, humanism and Christianity. Classroom work integrates the videotaped lectures with training in leadership and communications skills and practical assignments in political action. Students are taught how to write letters to editors, use radio call-in show opportunities and be effective in presenting truth in community organizations, etc. Adult Sunday schools and neighborhood home study groups also use the program.

COMMUNISTS ATTACK

The Communists learned of the project and called for a counter-attack. Herbert Aptheker, a leading Communist theoretician and member of the Party's Central Committee, devoted his full column in the *People's Daily World* to an attack on *Understanding The Times*.

His column was headlined:

Ultra-Right Fanatics Set For Comeback.

Aptheker said that the *Understanding The Times* curriculum is...

> ...a fascistic one; it is an effort by a desperate ultra-right to harness its forces for a comeback *and to train cadre for the long haul.* It should be met by...a concerted popular counterattack in the press and all other media.[1]

The term *cadre* on which Aptheker focuses is a military one. The cadre concept is the key to Communist efforts and success. It is also the means through which a relative handful of dedicated Americans can reverse the Red tide—and provide leadership to other Americans, the vast majority of whom are still right-thinking although uninformed and unorganized. They are, in the words of the title of a bestseller of 25 years ago, *A Nation of Sheep*. Sheep wait to be led. Some "cadre" will provide the leadership—for good or evil—into safety or danger.

A dictionary definition of *cadre* is "a framework—particularly the key group of military officers and enlisted men necessary to establish and train a new military unit."

Before World War II, the United States never maintained a large standing military force. The Army, Navy and Marines had a peacetime complement which totaled less than 300,000 men. They were well-trained and their two-fold mission was to (1) resist an initial attack by an enemy and (2) provide the "framework" or skeleton force into which draftees could be integrated and trained in a time of emergency. They were the "cadre" upon which the massive military forces of World War II were built when the war came.

Communists see their hard-core dedicated membership as the *cadre* of the revolution. The Communist cadre reaches out into all areas of society. It agitates and stirs the masses to create the *pressure from below* examined in Chapters 21, 22 and 23. When the pre-revolutionary crisis comes, the cadre will provide the framework into which the discontented masses will be integrated and through which they will be led. The Communists are masters of the "cadre concept." Using it they extend their tentacles and influence into society's mass organizations, manipulating and influencing them to do the Reds work. It has been the secret of their success world-wide. A relative handful of Communists—the cadre—first brought the revolution to Russia in 1917 and to country after country since then.

STEPS TO TAKE

If concerned Americans have any hope of turning back the revolution the Communists are working to bring to America, they must also get a vision for the "cadre concept." To become an effective cadre which can implement the *What Can You Do?* program outlined in Chapter 14 individuals must:

(1) Become informed personally and then work to stay informed.

(2) Develop (a) long-range goals for stopping Communist advances and extending freedom around the world and (b) have a short-range agenda for moving toward the long-range goals.

(3) Develop circles of influence in neighborhoods, churches, schools, business organizations, labor unions, political organizations, etc. through which they can exert *leverage* and multiply their outreach and effectiveness.

(4) Work continually to improve personal leadership and communications skills, and...

(5) Specialize and become expert in some area of the battle while standing ready to assist others who are concentrating on other aspects of the overall struggle.

(6) Develop and maintain contacts and communication with other concerned citizens with a goal of building a network of informed people which reaches into every type of community organization and avenue of influence.

(7) Recognize that the battle will be a life-long one from which "there is no discharge."

Reading the former Communist Douglas Hyde's outstanding book, *Dedication and Leadership* could be an individual's first step in developing and implementing the "cadre concept." Hyde's book should be must reading for every preacher—for every Christian—and for every concerned American.

THE GOALS

The first goals of those who start forming the cadre must be...

... to understand, expose and oppose the programs and philosophies which aid communism's advance in the United States and around the world.

All forms of economic, diplomatic, military and psychological aid to communism must be opposed and stopped.

Communist/Humanist/Hedonist influences and philosophy in America's basic institutions must be recognized and opposed and those who promote them must be rooted out of their positions of influence.

America's internal security system must be rebuilt. Congressional committees with responsibility for investigating Communist influence and activity in America must be re-established. The FBI must be again authorized to maintain surveillance on the Communist Party and its front organizations.

Work to recruit, train and elect knowledgeable, dedicated pro-God, pro-American, pro-free enterprise candidates to school boards, city councils, state legislatures and the U.S. Congress.

Assist and encourage those who are elected in implementing sound, pro-freedom, anti-Communist legislation—*and make them accountable and answerable for their actions and their votes.*

Pray for those in authority (and their families) that they will seek and have God's wisdom and protection and have the strength to do right even when it may not be popular at the moment. (See I Timothy 2:1-5)

DEFENSE ALONE CAN'T WIN

As essential as these actions are, they will not bring victory. Being "anti" is not enough. Defensive actions, no matter how effective and necessary, will not bring victory in football, business or the worldwide ideological struggle for men's hearts and minds and souls. Even though a football team plays the best defense, it will never win unless it also gets the ball and takes it across the opponent's goal line.

As the decade of the 1990s begins, there are tremendous opportunities for going on the offensive. People are seeking freedom all over the world. Most of them will not succeed because they are asking or demanding freedom from their governments. They will fail because governments never give freedom. Governments restrict and restrain man's free exercise of his freedom and use of his property.

SHARE THE AMERICAN SECRET

The world's freedom seekers must be given a vision for what made America great. America and Americans have enjoyed more freedom and used their freedom to achieve more prosperity for themselves and others than any other nation or people in the history of the world. Here's why: America was established on a concept that was and is different from that of any other nation on earth.

Our founding fathers didn't give us our rights and our freedoms. We did not get them through our Bill of Rights or our Constitution. Many nations have had—and lost— freedoms granted by a ruler or a constitution. What makes America different is that our founding fathers discovered and set forth the truth that the rights of the individual come, not from a king, a government, a Constitution or a Bill of Rights, but from God. Our governmental documents acknowledge this truth and restrict government from interfering with man's God-given rights. The *Declaration of Independence* affirms:

> We hold these truths to be self-evident, that all men are created equal, *that they are endowed by their Creator with certain unalienable rights*, that among these are Life, Liberty and the pursuit of Happiness.—That to secure these rights, Governments are instituted among Men, deriving their just powers from the consent of the governed. [Emphasis added]

IS THE DECLARATION BIBLICAL?

Were the founding fathers correct? Is it a Biblical concept that rights come from God? Certainly life does. Genesis 2:7 says:

> And the Lord God formed man of the dust of the ground, and breathed into his nostrils the breath of *life*; and man became a living soul.

Liberty also is a gift of God. True liberty results from the presence of God's Spirit in our lives. II Corinthians 3:17 says:

> Now the Lord is that Spirit and where the Spirit of the Lord is, there is liberty.

In Ecclesiastes 3:13, God's Word says, "And also that every man should eat and drink, and *enjoy* the good of all his labour, it is the gift of God." In John 13:17 the Lord Jesus makes the gift of happiness dependent on serving others. He told his disciples to serve one another and then promised:

> If ye know these things, happy are ye if ye do them.

So the concept that life, liberty and the pursuit of happiness come from God is Biblical. But what about freedom of speech, assembly and religion—the freedom to keep and bear arms, etc.? Where are they in the Bible? They are not spelled out—but the founding fathers didn't say they were. They said they were *self-evident*. The Lord Jesus told His disciples:

> Go ye into all the world, and preach the Gospel to every creature. He that believeth and is baptized shall be saved; but he that believeth not shall be damned.

It was obvious—or *self-evident*—that the Lord meant for
His people to have the freedom of speech to fulfill his Great
Commission (although it must be obeyed even where the
freedom is denied). Likewise, the Bible commands Christians
to meet together...

> ...not forsaking the assembling of ourselves together, as the man-
> ner of some is; but exhorting one another: and so much the more,
> as ye see the day [of his return] approaching.

So the freedom of assembly is also a Biblical concept. What
about freedom of religion? Does God actually give men the
freedom to choose whatever religion they might want? In
Joshua 24:15, God's leader Joshua told the people:

> And if it seem evil to you to serve the Lord, choose ye this day
> whom ye will serve.

In I Kings 18:21, the prophet Elijah, speaking for God,
challenged the people saying:

> How long halt ye between two opinions? If the Lord be God,

God has made us free—even in the area of religion. However, He has shown us His way, through faith in Jesus Christ.
We will all sometime have to answer to Him for how we used
the "freedom of religion" He gives us. One final example:
What about the freedom to keep and bear arms? Is that a
self-evident Biblical right with which our Creator has endowed us? In Luke 22:35-36, just before He went to the Cross,
the Lord Jesus spoke with his disciples and said:

> When I sent you without purse, and scrip, and shoes, lacked ye
> any thing? And they said, Nothing. Then he said unto them, But
> now, he that hath a purse, let him take it, and likewise his scrip:
> and he that hath no sword, let him sell his garment, and buy one.

So God means for man to have the right to keep and bear
arms. The concept the founding fathers spelled out that our
rights were "endowed by our Creator" is Biblical.

THE DECLARATION IS FOR ALL PEOPLE

The *Declaration of Independence* is usually regarded as an
American document—and it is. However, if the concept that

man's rights come from God is true—and it is—*then all men everywhere are born with the same God-given rights Americans enjoy.* The *Declaration of Independence* proclaims God's truth and it applies to all men because God is no respecter of persons.

Congressman Jack Kemp enunciated this truth as a candidate for the Republican nomination for the presidency in 1988. He added, "For this reason I support the freedom fighters all over the world—the Contras in Nicaragua, Jonas Savimbi in Angola, the mujahadeen in Afghanistan."

God endows everyone born into the world with the same basic rights every American enjoys and often takes for granted. Few people, however, have ever lived in real freedom. Why? Men can only enjoy and exercise their God-given rights to the extent that the nation in which they live in is "a nation under God." Freedom-seeking people around the world need to hear this message. It has power and a dynamic which no "anti" message possesses. The author had an opportunity to outline this truth to a meeting of 1500 preachers from all over the world—men from India, South Africa, Pakistan, Indonesia, Central and South America, South Korea, free China, and half a dozen struggling African states.

They had been guests in America for two weeks. They had seen and tasted of the unbelievable (for them) blessings and material prosperity Americans enjoy (and take for granted.) In the message they heard the truth that Americans enjoyed their tremendous blessings and freedom not because they were smarter or worked harder or had a better Constitution than others in the world—but because America had been founded as "a nation under God." America enjoys the fruits of God's word which promises the blessings, saying:

> Blessed is the nation whose God is the Lord; and the people whom
> he hath chosen for his own inheritance. (Psalm 33:12)

The 1500 preachers from all over the world heard the basis upon which America was established. They caught the vision that they too had been endowed by their Creator with the same rights and freedoms Americans had exercised to achieve such abundance and prosperity. They exploded with excitement. Many dedicated themselves to returning home to work to see their nations become "a nation under God" also.

When exchange students in America from Communist China got involved in the student protests which resulted in the Tiananmen Square massacre, a similar opportunity developed. Some of them, long-schooled in Communist-atheistic philosophy, understood the message and got the vision for the freedoms they had already been given *by God*.

The message has power—but before Americans can take it to the world, it must be relearned in the United States. No public school history or government textbook published in over 50 years has told young Americans the true source of their rights. (To acknowledge God in the history or government classroom would violate "the separation of church and state" and would create conflicts with the science department which teaches that we all evolved from green slime.)

OPPORTUNITIES BUT LITTLE HOPE

There are tremendous opportunities developing as the decade of the 1990s begins. Informed and dedicated individuals who understand the "cadre concept," can have a great impact.

However, any realistic appraisal of (1) the influence of the left, (2) the threat of an economic crisis produced by a ballooning national debt, and (3) the moral decay and decadence which pervades every area of American life shows that, logically and from a human viewpoint, there is little reason for hope. The forces of evil are too deeply entrenched and have been in control too long to be dislodged by mere human effort.

GOD'S PROMISE

But as dim as the prospects are for reversing the Red tide through human effort alone, there is another resource—another source for hope. God's Word, the Bible, has a promise. In Isaiah 59:19, God promises:

> ...When the enemy shall come in like a flood, the Spirit of the Lord *shall* lift up a standard against him.

The enemy, as the preceding chapters show, has "come in like a flood" on America—a country founded as "one nation, under God." God has promised that He will raise up a standard against the evil. His promise is unconditional—but He does not work in a vacuum. He works through people.

In every generation men have believed that the problems they faced were unique—that they were more threatened and closer to disaster than any others who ever lived down through history. However, man doesn't change and his problems change very little.

America has been living through a revolution which touches every area of society—but there have been revolutionary ages before. England—and all of Europe—were in turmoil in the late 17th and early 18th centuries. Of England during this period, a one- hundred-year-old history records:

> Corruption and mismanagement in high places were the rule...Bribery among all classes was open, unblushing, and profuse...adultery, fornication, gambling, swearing, Sabbath breaking and drunkenness were hardly regarded as vices at all. They were the fashionable practices of the people in the highest ranks of society...such was England in the 18th Century.[2]

Revolutionary societies and conspiratorial groups which were forerunners of communism placed their members in high places in government.[3] Seats in Parliament were sold for $20,000. Distribution of pornographic literature was a serious problem. There was even a "God is dead" movement. A noted church historian looked at the decay and corruption and said:

> Christianity seemed to lie as one dead, inasmuch that you might have said, "She is dead."[4]

The clergy of the day, witnessing the collapse of morality, decency, and order in society and the seeming inability of the church to reach the masses with the age-old message, quit trying. They dropped what bare skeleton of the Christian doctrine remained in their formal services and liturgy and attempted to "restate Christianity in a formula which all could accept." By stripping Christianity of what was regarded as its "superstitious elements" they hoped to "make the natural rather than the supernatural the basis of belief." They were the forerunners of the 20th Century Humanists— those who have done the same thing to America's mainline denominations in this century.

A collection of letters by John Newton, the 18th Century English preacher who wrote the hymn, *Amazing Grace*, gives a concise account of the progressive deterioration which followed the "humanizing" of the church. The introduction to the *Letters of John Newton* said...

> ...England was in a state of religious and moral decay. For many years the land had been sinking into darkness and paganism. Intemperance and immorality, crime and cruelty were increasingly becoming the characteristics of the age.[5]

This could be a description of the crime, violence and moral decay in America today. The report continued:

> The National Church was in such dead condition that instead of being the salt, preserving the nation from corruption, she was only adding to the immorality by weakening the restraints which Christianity imposes on the lusts of men...

The National Council of Churches and the other humanist influences in America have similarly "weakened the restraints" Christianity is supposed to impose on men. Young people are told that "for the Christian there are no laws, no rules, no regulations..." Denominational leaders condone homosexuality "if both parties really love each other." Sodomites are ordained to the ministry. Truly, as King Solomon said, "there is nothing new under the sun."

WHAT SAVED ENGLAND?

After reviewing the seriousness of the situation, the introduction to John Newton's letters concluded:

> If the nation was to be saved, the Church would first have to be revived. And that is what took place. What the arm of the flesh could not do, the arm of omnipotence accomplished. God was pleased to send a mighty revival which in the course of 50 years transformed the religious and moral life of the land.

Many would look to politics and politicians to solve America's problems, but J.C. Ryle, the bishop of Liverpool, England, said of the transformation of England in the 1700s:

> The government of the country can lay no claim to credit for the change. Morality cannot be called into being by penal enactments and statutes. People were never yet made religious by Acts of Parliament...Nor yet did the change come from the Church of England, as a body. The leaders of that venerable body were unequal to the times.[6]

What were the forces which held back the revolutionary tide in the 18th century? God raised up a few preachers—John Wesley, George Whitefield and a handful of others—*and a host of awakened lay people to follow them*. They taught that there was an inseparable connection between true faith and personal holiness. They taught that when a person really believed that he became "a new creature in Christ" and that the change was manifested in every area of life.

Even though less than two-and-one-half percent of the population was converted during Wesley's 50 years of ministry, the face of England was changed.[7] His followers attacked decay and decadence in government, business and the church. As that handful became the "salt of the earth" the slave trade was stopped. Four out of five taverns closed for lack of business. Prison and penal reforms were instituted. The dangerous conditions under which children worked in factories were improved—and corruption in government declined.

Professor Elie Halevy in his multi-volume *History of the English People* said the spiritual awakening provided the...

> ...moral cement which restrained the plutocrats who had newly arisen from the masses from vulgar ostentation and debauchery, and placed over the proletariat a select body of workman, enamored of virtue and capable of self-restraint. Evangelicalism...restored in England the balance momentarily destroyed by the explosion of revolutionary forces.[8]

GOD'S WAY—OR MAN'S?

The same revolutionary forces which ate at the heart of

England in the early 18th century troubled France and most of the continent also. England turned to Jesus Christ and laid the foundations for the political freedom which Britain and America have enjoyed for 200 years. The French instead rebelled against the corrupt and decadent church—and against God as well. Their revolution degenerated into a total rejection of the established economic, social and moral order. France has never recovered. Every generation of Frenchmen since has seen its land overrun by a foreign conqueror—or ruled by a domestic despot. The revolution came later to Germany, Italy and Spain. Without reformation or a revival of true Biblical Christianity, each has suffered similarly from almost continual political and economic turmoil.

The dramatically different way in which the revolutionary forces which troubled France and England developed demonstrate the truth of General Douglas MacArthur's words:

> History fails to record a single precedent in which nations subject to moral decay have not passed into political and economic decline. There has been either a spiritual awakening to overcome the moral lapse, or a progressive deterioration leading to ultimate national disaster.

In 1922, the British Prime Minister David Lloyd George stated that Great Britain...

> ...owed more to the movement of which Wesley was the inspirer and leader, than to any other movement in the whole of its history...It civilized the people...There was a complete revolution effected in the whole country...it has given a different outlook to the British and American people from the outlook of the Continentals.[9]

Lord Baldwin, during his term as prime minister, said that historians...

> ...cannot explain nineteenth century England until they can explain Wesley. And I believe that it is equally true to say that you cannot understand [early] twentieth century America, unless you understand Wesley.[10]

IN AMERICA TOO

As the words of the British prime ministers indicated, the revival spread to America. The 30th President of the United States, Calvin Coolidge, said:

> America was born in a revival or religion. Back of that revival were John Wesley, George Whitefield, and Francis Asbury.[11]

In his autobiography, Ben Franklin, provided an eyewitness account of the supernatural way God worked to change men's hearts and the whole face of America during that revival. Although the 31-year old Franklin did not become a part of the revival he was enthralled by the results and impact of it on individual lives and cities. He wrote:

> It was wonderful to see the change soon made in the manners of our inhabitants. From being thoughtless or indifferent about religion, it seemed as if all the world were growing religious, so that one could not walk thro' the town in an evening without hearing psalms sung in different families of every street.[12]

This was Franklin's description of the effects of the revival on Boston. *Even Harvard University was affected.* Before George Whitefield preached in Boston, the president of Harvard wrote to a friend complaining of the moral decay in the college. He said:

> Whence is there such a prevalency of so many immoralities amongst the professors? Why so little success of the gospel?[13]

Later, describing the revival which came to the Harvard campus, President Willard wrote:

> That which forbodes the most lasting advantage is the new state of the college. Gentlemen's sons that were sent here only for a mere polite education, are now so full of zeal for the cause of Christ and the love of souls as to devote themselves absolutely to the study of divinity. The college is entirely changed; the students are full of God—and will I hope come out blessings to this and succeeding generations.[14]

Some of our founding fathers were among the Harvard students who heard Whitefield preach in 1739. Others attended churches whose pulpits were filled by men converted under Whitefield's ministry—pulpits which were "aflame with righteousness." A similar transformation occurred at Princeton University, where John Witherspoon took charge and trained young men who joined him later in signing the Declaration of Independence.

THE WARNINGS

A French political philosopher visited our shores when America was a new young nation. Alexis de Tocqueville came to learn what magic quality enabled a handful of people to defeat the mighty British Empire twice in 35 years. He looked for the greatness of America in her harbors and rivers, her fertile fields and boundless forests, mines and other natural resources. He studied America's schools, her Congress and her matchless Constitution without comprehending America's power. Not, he said, until he went into the churches of America and heard pulpits "aflame with righteousness" did he understand the secret of America's genius and strength. De Tocqueville returned to France and wrote his classic two-volume study, *Democracy in America.* In it he said:

America is great because America is good, and if America ever ceases to be good, America will cease to be great.[15]

America was born in a period of spiritual revival. It has been living since on the spiritual and political foundations laid by those men who believed and obeyed God's command to...

...render unto Caesar the things which are Caesar's, and to God the things that are God's. (Mark 12:17)

Americans of this generation have made a mockery of fulfilling both responsibilities. America is therefore in danger because as Alexis de Tocqueville warned...

...if America ever ceases to be good, America will cease to be great.

The author of the *Declaration of Independence*, Thomas Jefferson left a similar warning for Americans. He said:

Yes, we did produce a near perfect Republic. But will they keep it, or will they, in the enjoyment of plenty, lose the memory of freedom? Material abundance without character is the surest way to destruction.

Much of America has ceased to be good. Will she cease to be great? Will America turn back to God and His blessings as England and colonial America did—or must she take the path of the French Revolution? The anti-God revolution in France and those that followed on the continent were led by the spiritual and philosophic "fathers" of the Communist societies of the 19th Century which produced Marx, Engels and Lenin and the tragedies and terrorism of the last 140 years. Must America take the path of France's 1789 revolution which culminated...

...in the Reign of Terror when Paris gutters ran red with human blood; when a prostitute was crowned Goddess of Reason; and when each new champion of freedom, crying "Liberty, Equality, and Fraternity," rushed his fellow champions to the guillotine, lest they rush him there first. So ended the first French Republic, denying all spiritual values and mocking God.[16]

GOD'S PROMISE

America doesn't have to follow this awful path. As strong as the Communist/Humanist/Hedonistic forces are which are pushing America toward a revolution, God has promised:

When the enemy shall come in like a flood, the Spirit of the Lord *shall* lift up a standard against him.

God has fulfilled that promise in the past. The Lord will again "lift up a standard" against the enemy and exert His supernatural power against him *to the degree and extent that God's people yield themselves to Him.* He will then make them part of the "standard" which *shall* be lifted up.

What is the standard? As seen in the last chapter, God works in the world through the family, the church and the state. The "standard" God has promised to lift up "when the enemy has come in like a flood" is a triune, three-in-one standard. *Godly homes* and *power-endued churches* will work together to establish *righteous government.* The standard is *triune*—or three-in-one—because one part of the standard cannot exist or function without the other two. There can be no righteous government in a nation apart from Godly homes and power-endued churches—and Godly homes and power-endued churches are so completely interdependent that one cannot exist or function without the other.

As individuals recognize God the Holy Spirit for whom He really is and what He wants to do and be in their lives, He will again do His supernatural work in and through them. That is God's part. It must start with the individual and spread to others. Are you willing to let God use you in the three-part "Godly families—Power-endued Churches—Righteous Government" standard He wants to raise up? If you do, tell Him so now.

CAN IT HAPPEN AGAIN?

If you and others like you can awaken to the danger and seek to understand it, you can help provide the leadership needed in our families, our schools, our churches and in our entire society. Leadership is essential to developing resistance to communism, protecting America and extending freedom around the world. The Bible says so. In the Old Testament scriptures—in I Chronicles 12:32—the Word of God commends one of the twelves tribes of Israel for providing leadership to their nation. The Bible says:

> And of the children of Issachar, which were men that had understanding of the times, to know what Israel ought to do; the heads of them were two hundred; and all their brethren were at their commandment.

God says that people who have an *understanding of the times* will know what their nation ought to do. Because of this knowledge, they can provide leadership to others. That's what America needs today—that's what the world needs today: People who first *know* the times—*know* what is happening—and then *understand the times* from a Biblical perspective. They will know what their nation ought to do and can provide leadership to others.

Even if there were no Communist plan for world conquest,

America and the world is becoming like an overripe fruit. Moral decay and corruption will enslave and destroy us even if communism should disappear world-wide. But there is good news.

In Matthew 5:13, the Lord Jesus gave his people a responsibility and a warning. He said:

> Ye are the salt of the earth: but if the salt have lost his savour, wherewith shall it be salted? It is thenceforth good for nothing but to be cast out, and to be trodden under foot of men.

God's people can awaken to the rottenness which is developing world-wide and start being the salt which will hold back the corruption. They can do this whether the Communists have a plan or not. Unless those who are God's people start fulfilling this preserving function in society, we will be cast out and trodden under foot—by the Communists or one of the devil's other forces. Are you willing to face the threat? Are you ready to be what God will have you to be? Are you willing to make the effort to become one of those people who "understand the times"—who know what your nation needs to do? These are the people who can awaken sleeping Americans and give them the leadership they need to preserve freedom and extend liberty throughout the world.

EPILOGUE

...MAKING IT PERSONAL

*Truly in vain is salvation hoped for from the hills, and from
the multitude of mountains: truly in the Lord our God is the
salvation of Israel.*

—Jeremiah 3:3

WHEN THE BOOK *None Dare Call It Treason* was published in 1964, its last chapter closed with a call for a "spiritual
commitment." J. Edgar Hoover was quoted as saying that
while the fight against communism was being fought on
economic, psychological, diplomatic, and military fronts, that
the battle, at its heart, was a spiritual one.

As the author, I admonished each reader to "examine your
own personal religious beliefs," and asked the question, "Is
God a meaningful, consuming force in your life?"

Although I was sincere in asking that question, God was
not "a meaningful, consuming force to me" because I had
never personally accepted His gift of salvation. I thought I
was a Christian. From my childhood, I had been active in the
work of my church. I edited a church paper for a time. As a
layman, I had spoken from the pulpits of a number of good
Bible-believing churches—yet I had never really become a
Christian *in the Bible sense of that word*.

On February 19, 1965, I came to see that in spite of my
"good" life and church affiliations I was a sinner who deserved
to go to hell. At that point, the words, "Christ died for our
sins," which I had always believed *in my head* became very
real—and very important—to me. About 2:30 a.m. the next
morning I asked God to forgive my sins *on the basis that I
believed that Jesus Christ—God in the flesh—had already
taken all of my punishment*. Although I wasn't consciously
making a "spiritual decision" that night, the Lord Jesus

Christ came into my heart and became my Saviour. It was almost a week before I realized what had happened to me.

Since that time, God has made me a new person, doing things in my life I was never able to do for myself. The Bible started making sense. It came alive and I wanted to read it. Prayer became, not a duty, but a time of talking to my Heavenly Father—the God of this entire universe. Suddenly, I looked forward to going to church to hear God's Word preached. I was filled with love for other Christians—and most important, He gave me a desire to tell others what the Lord Jesus had done for me. In short, He fulfilled in these and a thousand other ways the words of St. Paul who wrote...

...if any man be in Christ, he is a new creature: old things are passed away: behold all things are become new. And all things are of God. (II Corinthians 5:17-18a)

Because of what God has done during these last 25 years (and continues to do) I know that He can do anything. I know that our nation's very serious problems will be solved only if our country returns to the place where it is truly "one nation under God" again. This book, *None Dare Call It Treason...25 YEARS LATER*, reflects this knowledge.

Are you willing to have the spiritual awakening which can save America start in your heart? If you have never definitely accepted God's gift of salvation and eternal life, now is the time to seriously consider that decision. Read the simple prayer printed below. If you believe it *without reservation* and want Jesus Christ to come into your heart and be your Saviour and give you a new life, use these words *or your own* to tell the Lord.

I know that I am a sinner who deserves to go to Hell. I know that I cannot save myself. I believe that Jesus Christ, who is God, came to earth, lived as a man, and then suffered and died as my substitute on the cross of Calvary, shedding His blood to pay for my sin. I am now asking for, and by faith receiving, forgiveness for all my sins. I believe that Jesus rose from the dead and I want Him to come into my heart right now to give me a new life and be my Lord and Saviour.

Once you have trusted Jesus Christ, Satan will try to make you doubt. Your own feelings will change from day-to-day, particularly when you sin. God's Word, however, never changes. He promises:

> Whosoever shall call on the name of the Lord shall be saved...him that cometh to me I will in no wise cast out. (Romans 10:13, John 6:37)

Once you have accepted God's gift of salvation, you need to tell others, and then daily read your Bible, pray, and confess your sins (specifically naming them) realizing that He already died for them. Find a good Bible-believing, Bible-preaching church to help you grow in your new life. If you write to me—John Stormer, Box 32, Florissant MO 63032—I'll rejoice with you and send you a note of encouragement and a little booklet to help you start living your new life in Christ.

REFERENCES

INTRODUCTION
Did Communism Really Die?

1 St. Louis Post-Dispatch, Aug. 30, 1991

2 Washington Times, Sep. 17, 1991

3 USA Today, Dec. 9, 1991

4 St. Louis Post-Dispatch, Dec. 22, 1991

5 Ibid., Dec. 23, 1991; Washington Times, Jan. 8-9, 1992

6 Washington Times, Dec. 18, 1991; Dec. 21, 1991, Dec. 28, 1991; St. Louis Post-Dispatch, Dec. 28, 1991

7 Washington Times, Dec. 16, 1991

8 Ibid., Dec. 31, 1991; St. Louis Post-Dispatch, Oct. 31, 1991, Dec. 22, 1991

9 Ibid., Sep. 12, 1991

10 Washington Times, Sep. 11, 1991

11 Ibid., Aug. 26, 1991

12 Ibid., Sep. 17, 1991

13 National Policy Watch, Vol. 6, No. 2 - National Center for Public Policy Research, Washington DC; Washington Times, Jul. 19, 1990, Nov. 15, 1991; St. Louis Post-Dispatch, Dec. 22, 1990

14 ABN Correspondence, New York, May-June 1991; St. Louis Post-Dispatch, Dec. 23, 1991; Washington Times, Jan. 2, 1992, Jan. 8, 1992, Jan. 9, 1992

15 Sen. Jesse Helms, Cong. Record, Aug. 3, 1990, pg. S12320-24; S12329-34; Issues & Strategy Bulletin, Vienna VA, Aug. 5, 1991

16 Washington Times, Sep. 9, 1991

17 St. Louis Post-Dispatch, Sep. 28, 1991

18 Washington Times, Dec. 29, 1991

19 Patterns of Communist Espionage, Report, House Committee on Un-American Activities, Jan. 1959, Pg. 1

20 Public Affairs Guidance Bulletin, Hq. USAF, May 18, 1990, Pg. 4

21 Dodd, Mead and Company, New York, 1984

22 William Buckley, St. Louis Post-Dispatch, Aug. 15, 1991

23 Summary, The Strategy of Perestroika Exposed, 31 pages, 1990

24 Washington Times, Aug. 22, 1991, Sep. 6, 1991; St. Louis Post-Dispatch, Sep. 6, 1991

25 Washington Times, Jan. 2, 1992; St. Louis Post Dispatch, Jan. 3, 1992

26 Ibid., Sep. 8, 1991

27 Schwarz, You Can Trust The Communists to be Communists, Prentice Hall, Inc. 1960, pg. 153

28 Gorbachev, Perestroika: The Revolution Continues, Nov. 2, 1987, Northern Neighbors edition, pg. 13-14

29 Washington Times, Sep. 15, 1989, pg. A6

30 Ibid.

31 Harper & Row Publishers, New York, 1987

32 Gorbachev, Perestroika, pg. 52 footnote

33 Gorbachev, Perestroika: The Revolution Continues, November 2, 1987, Northern Neighbors edition, pg. 55

34 World Marxist Review, August 1972, pg. 137

35 Dailey & Parker, Editors, Lexington: Hoover Institution Press, 1987

36 Summary, Nightwatch, SIS, 2800 Shirlington Road, Suite 405, Arlington, VA 22206, pg. 20

37 Evans, How U.S. Security Was Destroyed, Human Events, Aug. 5, 1985, pg. 7

38 St. Louis Post-Dispatch, Sep. 23, 1987, pg. 1A

39 Ibid., Sep. 18, 1987, pg. 11A; St. Louis Post-Dispatch, Nov. 3, 1989, pg. 1

40 Ibid., Oct. 2, 1987, pg. 11A

41 People's Daily World, Dec. 24, 1987, pg. 9A

42 Denton, When Hell Was In Session, Traditional Press, 1982, pg.183

43 Ibid., pg. 181

44 Barton, America To Pray Or Not To Pray, Wall Builder Press, 1988, pg. iv

45 Ibid., pg. 9-35

46 Ibid. pg. 33-49

47 Ibid., pg. 49-107

48 St. Louis Globe-Democrat, Apr. 10, 1975, pg. 1

49 Ibid., pg. 107-142; Chicago Daily News, Sep. 3, 1976, pg. 9

50 Johnstown, Pa. Tribune-Democrat, Aug. 17, 1973, pg. 3

51 St. Louis Globe Democrat, Dec. 11, 1975, pg. 1

52 Ibid., Dec. 24, 1975, pg. 11B

53 Ibid., Jan. 26, 1978, pg. 1

54 Notice of Cooperative Agreement Award, Grant # U62/CCU2001065-01, Dept. of Health Education and Welfare, Public Health Service, Centers For Disease Control, May 1, 1986

55 Chicago Tribune, Jul. 27, 1989, pg 6; Washington Times, Sep. 29, 1989, pg. A6; Oct. 9, 1989, pg. A6

56 Chicago Tribune, Jul. 27, 1989, pg. 6

57 Washington Times, Sep. 14, 1989, pg. 1

58 St. Louis Sun, Nov. 22, 1989, pg. 16

59 Kramer, The Normal Heart, Samuel French, Inc., 1985

60 Springfield, Mo. News-Leader, Nov. 1, 1989, pg. 1

61 St. Louis Post Dispatch, Nov. 17, 1989, pg. 11A

62 The News-Leader, Nov. 14, 1989, pg. 4A

CHAPTER 1
Have We Gone Crazy?

1 Lenin, Selected Works, Vol. VII, pg. 298

2 Report, U.S. Foreign Assistance, U.S. Agency for Int. Dev., Mar. 21, 1962

3 Dallas Morning News, Oct. 13, 1961

4 Cong. R.H. Poff, Human Events, Jul. 14, 1961, pg. 443; Nov. 10, 1961, pg. 748; Cong. Pelly, Cong. Record, Aug. 14, 1961

5 N.Y. Times News Service, Dallas Morning News, Jul. 13, 1961

6 Cong. D.L. Latta, Human Events, Aug. 4, 1961, pg. 506

7 Letter, SF/131/1 Cuba, Jun. 8, 1961, Paul Hoffman, Managing Director, United Nations Special Fund

8 Sen. Thomas Dodd, Southern Calif. School of Anti-Communism, Los Angeles, Aug. 28, 1961

9 Ibid.

10 Ibid.

11 Arens, Dangers To U.S. Internal Security, National Education Program, Jun. 22, 1959, pg. 6

12 Ibid.

13 Ibid.

14 House Document 227, 85th Congress, 1st Session, Vol. II, pg. 892

15 Hearings,Communist Threat To The U.S.Through The Caribbean, Senate Internal Security Subcommmittee, 86th-87th Congress, Parts 1-12

16 Ibid., pg. 798

17 Ibid., pg. 799

18 National Review, Jan 16, 1962

19 Report, American Bar Association Committee on Communist Strategy and Tactics, Congressional Record, Aug. 22, 1958

20 Hearings, Communist Threat To The U.S., SISS, pg. 726

21 Senate Report 2050, 82nd Congress, 2nd Session, pg. 224

22 Human Events, Jul, 14, 1961, pg. 437

23 Report, Interlocking Subversion In Government Departments, SISS, 83rd Congress, 1st Session, pg. 6, 8-10

24 Ibid., pg. 29-32

25 Ibid., pg. 5, 40-43

26 Ibid., pg. 5

27 Ibid., pg. 5

28 Ibid., pg. 2

29 Ibid., pg. 1 fn.

30 Donovan, Eisenhower, The Inside Story, pg. 253-4; Adams, First Hand Report, pg. 142-3

31 Hoover, FBI Law Enforcement Bulletin, Apr. 1, 1961

CHAPTER 2
The Origin of World Communism

1 Weyl, Red Star Over Cuba, pg. 104-05

2 Skousen, The Naked Communist, pg. 103-04

3 Dodd, Freedom and Foreign Policy, pg. 197-200

4 Burnham, Web Of Subversion, pg. 80

5 The Communist Party, USA, What It Is, How It Works: A Handbook For Americans, Senate Document No. 117, 84th Congress, pg. 43

6 Ibid., pg. 45

7 Ibid., pg. 8

8 Hearing, Communist Espionage in the U.S., Testimony of Frantisek Tisler, HCUA, May 10, 1960, pg. 1726

9 Report, The Communist Mind, HCUA, 85th Congress, May 29, 1957

10 Ibid.

11 Lenin, Selected Works, Vol. IX, pg. 475-8

12 Report, The Communist Mind, HCUA, May 29, 1957

13 Ibid.

14 Ibid.

15 Ibid.

16 St. Louis Globe Democrat, May 12, 1963

17 Skousen, The Naked Communist, pg. 7-30

18 A Manifesto, Fabian Tract No. 2, 1884, quoted: Shaw, Man Of The Century

19 Henderson, George Bernard Shaw, Man Of The Century, An Authorized Biography, pg. 343

20 Ibid., pg. 219

21 Ibid., pg. 240

22 Shaw, Intelligent Woman's Guide To Socialism, pg. 470

23 Webb, Socialism In England, pg. 27, quoted: Keynes At Harvard, pg. 19

24 Henderson, GBS, Man of the Century, pg. 284

25 Keynes At Harvard, pg. 33

26 Hubbard, Political and Economic Structures, pg. 111

27 Ibid., pg. 112

28 Lenin, Selected Works, Vol. II, pg. 155

29 Ibid., Vol. X, pg. 140

30 Lenin, Left-wing Communism, An Infantile Disorder, pg. 38

31 Lenin, Selected Works, Vol. VIII, pg. 284

32 Quoted by J. Edgar Hoover, Struggle On A New Plane, House Doc. 227 pg. 4

33 Hoover, Communist Target Youth, HCUA, Jul. 1960

34 Declaration of 81 Communist Parties, Moscow, Dec. 5, 1960

35 Report, New Drive Against The Anti-Communist Program, SISS, Jul. 11, 1961

36 Moorhead, The Russian Revolution, pg. 81

37 Lansbury, My Life, quoted: Keynes At Harvard, pg. 22

38 Henderson, GBS,Man of the Century, pg. 316

39 Ibid., pg. 310

CHAPTER 3
The Growth of World Communism

1 Congressional Record, Sep. 22, 1950, pg. A6832

2 Syndicated Column, Ralph McGill, Miami News, Dec. 5, 1962

3 See page 44

4 World Communist Movement, Selective Chronology, HCUA, 1960, pg. 18

5 Lyons, The Herbert Hoover Story, pg. 190-1

6 Hearing, Export of Strategic Material To USSR, SISS, Oct. 23, 1961, Pt. 1, pg. 5

7 Wittmer, The Yalta Betrayal, pg. 14

8 Report, Interlocking Subversion In Government Dept., SISS, Jul. 30, 1952

9 Skousen, The Naked Communist, pg. 164-5

10 Hearings, Shipment of Atomic Material to USSR, HCUA, 81st Cong., pg. 1156

11 Report, Interlocking Subversion In Gov. Dept., SISS, Jul. 30, 1952, pg. 29

12 Hearings, Occupation Currency Transactions, Senate Appropriations, Armed Services and Banking Committees, 1947, pg. 8, 27, 175-9

13 Sherwood, Roosevelt and Hopkins, pg. 590
14 Foreign Relations of the U.S., Diplomatic Papers, The Conferences at Cairo and Teheran, 1943, Dept. of State, 1961
15 Protocol of Proceedings, The Crimea (Yalta) Conference, Feb. 11, 1945, Sec. III, VII, VIII, X, XI
16 Ibid., Agreement Regarding Japan, Sec. 1, 3
17 Welles, Seven Decisions That Shaped History, pg. 217
18 Hearings, Institute of Pacific Relations, SISS, 82nd Congress, p. 81
19 Senate Report No. 2050, 82nd Congress, 2nd Session
20 Report, Interlocking Subversion In Gov. Depts., SISS Jul. 30, 1952, pg. 32
21 Senate Report 2050, 82nd Congress, 2nd Session, pg. 225
22 Ibid., pg. 224
23 Flynn, While You Slept, Chapter 9

24 Ibid., Chapter 10-11
25 Speech, Acheson, National Press Club, Washington, D.C., Jan 12, 1950
26 Higgins, Korea and the Fall of MacArthur, pg. 48
27 Ibid., pg. 53, 68
28 Ibid., pg. 91
29 Ibid., pg. 112
30 Hearings, Interlocking Subversion in Gov. Depts., SISS, 1954, pg. 1653-1708; 1711-33; 2019-46; Committee on Armed Forces, Military Situation In The Far East, 1951, pg. 3-320
31 Adams, First Hand Report, The Story of the Eisenhower Administration, pg. 28
32 Donovan, Eisenhower, The Inside Story, pg. 126
33 Ibid.
34 Ibid., pg. 125-6
35 Ibid., pg. 126
36 Ibid., pg. 247
37 Ibid., pg. 249
38 Adams, First Hand Report, pg. 381-93 39 Donovan, Eisenhower, The Inside Story, pg. 400
40 Report, U.S. Foreign Assistance, Jul. 1, 1945-Jun. 30, 1961, Revised,

Statistics and Reports Div., U.S. Agency for Int.   Dev., Mar. 21, 1962, pg. 25
41 Speeches, Tito, Jun. 7-12, 1956
42 Yugoslav Communism, A Critical Study, SISS, Oct. 18, 1961, pg. 258-9, 282
43 Ibid., pg. 283
44 Ibid.
45 Ibid., pg. 266
46 Ibid., pg. 257
47 Morris, No Wonder We Are Losing, pg. 207
48 Report, U.S. Foreign Assistance, Agency For International Dev., Mar. 21, 1961, pg. 33
49 Ibid., pg. 89
50 Judd, Speech, The Basic Themes of Survival, Reserve Officers Association of the United States, Part IV
51 Ibid.
52 Consultations: Soviet Justice; Showplaces Prisons vs. Real Slave Labor Camps, HCUA, Apr. 4, 1960; How The Chinese Reds Hoodwink Visiting Foreigners, HCUA, Apr. 21, 1960
53 Charts, Congressional Record, May 2, 1962, pg. 7028-31
54 Ibid.
55 Ibid.
56 Pennsylvania vs. Nelson, 350 US 497 (1956)
57 Cole vs. Young 351 US 536 (1956)
58 Slochower vs. Board of Education of New York 350 US 551 (1956)
59 Watkins vs. United States 354 US 178 (1957)
60 Consul General For Yugoslavia vs. Artukovic
61 Service vs. Dulles 354 US 363 (1957)
62 Report, Committee on Federal-State Relationships, The Conference of Chief Justices, August 1958
63 Congressional Record, Aug. 22, 1958
64 Hearings On Dept. of Justice, House Appropriations Comm., Jan. 16, 1958, pg. 173-4
65 News Record Of 1957, Information Please Almanac, 1958, pg.11

66 Donovan, Eisenhower, The Inside Story, pg. 253-54

67 Adams, First Hand Report, pg. 142-43

68 Hearings, Institute of Of Pacific Relations, SISS, pg. 4777-8

69 Ibid., pg. 4776

70 Report, Interlocking Subversion In Gov. Depts., SISS, Jul. 30, 1953, pg. 43-4

71 Hearings Scope of Soviet Activity In The U.S., SISS, Part 49, Nov. 21, 1956

72 Donovan, Eisenhower, The Inside Story, pg. 246

73 Hearings, Army Personnel Actions Relating To Irving Peress, Senate Comm. on Gov. Operations, Part 3, Mar. 17, 1955, pg. 189; Part 5, Mar. 23, 1955, pg. 389, 424

74 Congressional Record, Nov. 15, 1954, pg. 16039

75 Hearings, Communist Infiltration In The Army, Senate Committee on Gov. Operations, Part 3, Feb. 18, 1954, pg. 152-3

76 Lokos, Who Promoted Peress?, pg. 37

77 For a detailed study of the conflicting Zwicker testimony and Senate correspondence with the Justice Department over perjury action, see Who Promoted Peress?, pg. 44-58

78 See Lokos, Who Promoted Peress?, Chap. VI, pg. 148-56

79 Hearings, Doctor Draft Amendments, Sen. Armed Serv. Comm. Apr. 1, 1954, pg. 12

80 Pg. 247

81 Adams, First-Hand Report, pg. 137, 141, 148, 151

82 Congressional Record, Mar. 30, 1950, pg. 4402

83 Senate Report 2050, 82nd Congress, pg. 225

84 Hearings, Institute of Pacific Relations, SISS, pg. 122-3, 85 Ibid., pg. 4938

86 Ibid.

87 Ibid., pg. 122-3; Report, pg. 147-8

88 Congressional Record, Jun 2, 1950, pg. 8000; Hearings, IPR, SISS, pg. 81

89 Congressional Record, Mar. 30, 1950, pg. 4403-4

90 Hearings, State Dept. Employee Loyalty Investigation, Senate Foreign Relations Comm., pg. 226, 263, 269-70

91 Ibid., pg. 267

92 Ibid., pg. 247

93 Ibid., Report, pg. 43

94 Buckley, McCarthy and His Enemies, pg. 97

95 Christopher News Notes, No. 119, April 1962

96 Congressional Record, Aug. 31, 1960, pg. 17407

97 Dodd, Freedom and Foreign Policy, pg. 39

98 Ibid.

99 Crimes Of Khrushchev, HCUA, Part I, pg. 3

100 Ibid., Part II, pg. 2

101 Ibid., Part I, pg. 7

102 Ibid., pg. 1

103 Ibid.

104 Illinois State Journal, Springfield, Illinois, Sep. 29, 1959

105 Cushing, Questions and Answers About Communism, 4th Edition, pg. 230

106 Page numbers refer to Hearings, Communist Threat To The U.S. Through The Caribbean, SISS, 1960-61, 12 Parts

107 Hearings, Communist Threat To The U.S., SISS, pg. 761

108 Ibid., Part 10

109 Time, Jul. 27, 1959

110 Dubois, Fidel Castro, pg. 145

111 Weyl, Red Star Over Cuba, pg. 195

112 Ibid., pg. 17

113 Ibid.

114 Hearings, Communist Threat To The U.S. Through The Caribbean, SISS, pg. 737

CHAPTER 4
Words vs. Actions

1 Ware, The Sayings of Confucius, pg. 26

2 New York Times, Jan. 25, 1962

3 Kennedy, Foreword, To Turn The Tide, pg. xiv

4 Dallas Times Herald, Mar. 26, 1961

5 The New York Times, Jan. 3, 1962

6 Dallas Morning News, Mar. 5, 1962

7 Human Events, Jun. 23, 1962, pg. 455

8 The New York Times, Jun. 14, 1962

9 The Baltimore Sun, Jun. 18, 1962

10 Reprinted, Congressional Record, Aug. 23, 1961, pg. A6656

11 St. Louis Globe Democrat, Feb. 16, 1961

12 Report, Special Committee to Investigate Tax-Exempt Foundations, 83rd Congress, Dec. 16, 1954, pg. 180-1

13 Rusk, Speech, World Affairs Council, Univ. Of Pa., Jun. 14, 1951

14 Baltimore Sun, Jun. 18, 1962

15 New York Daily News, May 15, 1962

16 Human Events, Dec. 6, 1961, pg. 826

17 Ibid., Jul. 21, 1962, pg. 544

18 Hearings, Communist Threat To U.S. Through Caribbean, SISS, Part 13, pg. 873-9

19 Columnist Edith Roosevelt, Speech, St. Louis, Mo. May 22, 1963

20 Edith Roosevelt, Column, Shreveport Journal, Sep. 15, 1962

21 St. Louis Post-Dispatch, Apr. 22, 1961

22 Rickenbacker, National Review, Aug. 13, 1963, pg. 106

23 Hearings, Communist Threat To U.S. Through Caribbean, SISS, Part 13

24 Ibid., pg. 874-5

25 Ibid., pg. 875-8

26 Ibid., pg. 877-8

27 Letter to Gen. Delmar T. Spivey, USA (Ret) as quoted on The Manion Forum broadcast, No. 353, Jul. 2, 1961

28 Letter, SF/131/1 Cuba, Jun. 8, 1961, Paul Hoffman, Managing Director, United Nations Special Fund

29 Congressional Record, May 11, 1961

30 Ibid., Aug. 18, 1961

31 Human Events, Sep. 15, 1962, pg. 691

32 Ibid.

33 Dallas Times Herald, Oct. 6, 1962

34 St. Louis Globe Democrat, Oct. 23, 1962

35 The New York Times, Oct. 6, 1962

36 News & Courier, Charleston, S.C., Dec. 10, 1962; St. Louis Globe Democrat, Dec. 13, 1962; St. Louis Post-Dispatch, Apr. 3, 1963

37 St. Louis Globe Democrat, Jul. 27, 1963

38 Bulletin, Cuban Information Service, Dec. 1, 1962

39 St. Louis Globe Democrat, Jul. 27, 1963

40 St. Louis Post-Dispatch, Mar. 28, 1963

41 Russell, Interview WSB-TV, Atlanta, Ga., St. Louis Globe Democrat, Dec. 12, 1962

42 Kennedy, TV Report To Nation, Jun. 5, 1961, To Turn The Tide, pg. 170-2

43 Ibid., Jul. 25, 1961, To Turn The Tide, pg. 184

44 Ibid., pg. 183

45 Human Events, Aug. 11, 1961, pg. 510

46 Cong. Thomas Pelly, Human Events, Aug. 25, 1961, pg. 550

47 Dallas Morning News, Jul. 13, 1961

48 Report, Visa Procedures, The Struelens Case, SISS, Aug. 6, 1962, pg. 1

49 Ibid., pg. 1-2; Dodd, Cong. Record., Aug. 3, 1962, pg. 14528-46; Schuyler, Who Killed The Congo?, Human Events, Aug. 4, 1962, pg. 579; Barron's Tragedy In The Congo, Human Events, Dec. 22, 1961, pg. 877

50 Report, Visa Procedures, The Struelens Case, SISS, pg. 2

51 New York Times, Sep. 6, 1961

52 Dodd, Congressional Record, Sep. 8, 1961

53 Human Events, Sep. 22, 1961, pg. 622-3

54 Dodd, Congressional Record, Aug. 3, 1962

55 Report, Visa Procedures, The Struelens Case, SISS, pg. 28

56 Dodd, Congressional Record, Sep. 8, 1961

57 Bruce, Congressional Record, Sep.12, 1961

58 New York Times, Dec. 14, 1961

59 Dr. E. Van den Haag, Report, War

In Katanga, American Comm. To Aid Katanga Freedom Fighters

60 Dodd, Congressional Record, Jan. 25, 1962

61 St. Louis Post-Dispatch, Dec. 31, 1962

62 Ibid., Dec. 19, 1961

63 Ibid., Apr. 18, 1963

64 Report, The Struelens Case, SISS, 87th Congress, Aug. 6,1962

65 Ibid., pg. 69-70

66 Ibid., pg. 71

67 Ibid., pg. 50-2

68 Ibid., pg. 48-50

69 Ibid., pg. 65-9

70 Ibid., pg. 69

71 Ibid.

72 Human Events, Sep. 15, 1961, pg. 608

73 St. Louis Post-Dispatch, Oct. 16, 1962

74 Kennedy, Inaugural Address, Jan. 20, 1961

75 Johnson, Message to Congress, Nov. 27, 1963

76 Human Events, May 12, 1961, pg. 290

77 Ibid., Jun. 30, 1961, pg. 405-6

78 Ibid., Dec. 1, 1961, pg. 806

79 St. Louis Globe Democrat, Nov. 6-19, 1963

80 Ibid., June 30, 1961, pg. 405

81 Ibid., Apr. 7, 1961, pg. 210

82 Ibid., Mar. 31, 1961, pg. 195

83 Chicago Tribune, as reprinted, Human Events, Sep. 15, 1961, pg. 619

84 Ibid.

85 St. Louis Globe Democrat, Jul. 4, 1963

86 Ibid.

87 Ibid.

88 Editorial, St. Louis Post-Dispatch, Aug. 25, 1961

89 St. Louis Post-Dispatch, Oct. 7, 1962

90 Human Events, Mar. 24, 1961, pg. 180

91 Report, Proposed Shipment of Ball Bearing Machines, To USSR SISS, Feb. 28, 1961; Hearings Export of Strategic Materials, SISS, Part 1, pg. 26-9

92 Letter, Luther Hodges to Cong. John Moss, Jun. 28, 1961

93 Statement, Gen. Counsel, P.O.Dept. Concerning Foreign Propaganda, Undated

94 Congressional Record, Mar. 1, 1962, pg. 2828

95 Human Events, Oct. 13, 1961,pg. 671

96 Hearings on SR 191, Senate Armed Services Committee, 1961

97 Ibid.

98 Ibid.

99 Human Events, Aug. 11, 1961, pg. 510

100 Ibid.

101 Ibid.

102 Report, Military Cold War Education and Speech Review Policies, Sen. Armed Services Comm., Oct. 19, 1962, 203 pages

103 Ibid., Part VII

104 Hearings on SR 191, Sen. Armed Services Comm., 1961, pg. 53, 123

105 National Review, Nov. 18, 1961

106 NBC News, Three Star Extra, Sep. 14, 1961, 6:45 PM EDT

107 Letter, J. Herbert Stone, Regional Forester to Forest Supervisor, Okanogan National Forest, Jul. 12, 1961

108 Letter, Leo D. Caron, Forester, to J. Herbert Stone, Regional Forester, Jul. 26, 1961

109 Kennedy, State of the Union message, Jan. 29, 1961

110 Report, New Drive Against The Anti-Communist Program, SISS, Jul. 11, 1961, pg. 3

111 Ibid., pg. 32

112 The Worker, Jul. 14, 1961

113 Hearings, New Drive Against The Anti-Communist Program, SISS, pg. 44-5

114 Ibid., pg. 33-7, 38-44, 51-6, 63, 65-7, 69-70

115 Ibid., pg. 75

116 New York Times, Nov 19, 1961

117 Hoover, Speech, The Faith To Be Free, NBC-TV, Dec. 7, 1961

118 Document 7277, U.S. Department of State, Sep. 1961, pg.5-8

119 Ibid., pg. 19

120 Sports Afield, August 1963

121 Tower, Congressional Record, Jan. 29, 1962

122 Ibid.

123 Clark, Congressional Record, Mar. 1, 1962, pg. 2936

124 1962 Annual Report, Arms Control & Disarmament Agency, pg. 57-83

125 Ibid.

126 Arms Control and Disarmament Act, Sep. 26, 1961, Sec. 2a, b, c, d

127 1962 Annual Report, Arms Control & Disarmament Agency, pg. 46-8

128 St. Louis Globe Democrat, Mar. 27, 1963

129 1962 Annual Report, Arms Control & Disarmament Agency, pg. 58

130 St. Louis Post-Dispatch, Mar. 2, 1963

131 St. Louis Globe Democrat, Dec. 18-19, 1962

132 Ibid., Mar. 3, 1963

133 St. Louis Post-Dispatch, Mar. 28, 1963

134 Newsweek, Feb. 11, 1963

135 St. Louis Globe Democrat, Dec. 5, 1962

136 New York Times, Nov. 16, 1961

137 Saturday Evening Post, Jun. 23, 1963

138 Human Events, Aug. 10, 1963, pg. 9

139 St. Louis Post-Dispatch, Sep. 10, 1962

140 St.Louis Globe Democrat, Dec. 10, 1963

141 Dodd, Congressional Record, Feb. 21, 1963, pg. 2662

142 Ibid., pg. 2663-4

143 Ibid.

144 Ibid.,pg. 2661

145 St. Louis Globe Democrat, Aug. 7, 1963

146 Ibid., Jul. 6, 1963

147 Ibid., Mar. 8, 1963

148 Congressional Record, Aug. 10, 1962, pg. 15093-4

149 St. Louis Post-Dispatch, Aug. 5, 1963

150 Kennedy, Message To Senate On Test Ban Treaty, St. Louis Post-Dispatch, Aug. 8, 1963

151 St. Louis Post-Dispatch, Nov. 28, 1961

152 Ibid.

153 Ibid.

154 Ibid., Aug. 12, 1963

155 Ibid., Jan. 12, 1961

156 Washington Star, Jul. 12, 1963

157 Kennedy, Message To Senate On Test Ban Treaty, St. Louis Post-Dispatch, Aug. 8, 1963

158 Congressional Record, May 31, 1955, pg. A3764

159 Chicago Tribune, Jun. 18, 1962

160 Ibid.

161 Hearings, Military Cold War Education and Speech Review Policies, Senate Armed Services Comm., June 4, 1962, Part 6, pg. 2805

162 Lenin, Selected Works, Vol. VIII, pg. 298

163 St. Louis Post-Dispatch, Sep. 18, 1955

164 Goldwater, Why Not Victory? pg. 150 and jacket

165 Chicago Tribune, Jun. 17-18, 1962

166 Ibid.

167 Ibid.

168 Human Events, Sep. 22, 1961, pg. 623

169 Morton, Congressional Record, Feb. 22, 1963

170 Congressional Record, Feb. 6, 1962, pg. A882

171 Harlan Cleveland, WRC-TV, Dec. 22, 1962, 6-6:30 PM EST

CHAPTER 5

How Has It Happened?

1 Report, Communist Indoctrination—Its Significance To Americans, Major Wm. E. Mayer, U.S. Army Psychiatrist, pg. 14-5

2 Ibid., pg. 11-12

3 J. Edgar Hoover, Communist Illusion and Democratic Reality, Dec. 1959, pg. 10-1

4 Report, Communist Indoctrination, Major Wm. Mayer, pg. 7, 29-31

5 Ibid., pg. 30

6 Ibid., pg. 33-4

7 Ibid., pg. 39-41

8 Ibid., pg. 22

9 Ibid., p, pg. 18-9

10 Ibid., pg. 12
11 Ibid., pg. 28
12 Ibid.
13 Ibid., pg. 6
14 Ibid., pg. 38
15 J. Edgar Hoover, Congressional Record, Oct. 10, 1962, pg. A7547
16 Illegitimacy, U.S. Dept.of Health, Education and Welfare, Apr. 1960, Table 2, pg. 10

CHAPTER 6
Education

1 The Tablet, Aug. 11, 1959
2 Dworkin, Dewey On Education, pg. 19-32
3 Ibid., pg. 22
4 Ibid., pg. 25
5 America's Future, 1956
6 Gordon, What's Happened To Our Schools?, pg. 16
7 Ibid.
8 Schlesinger, The Age of Roosevelt, pg. 156, 176, 563
9 British Fabian Society, 49th Annual Report, 1932
10 Report, Special House Committee To Investigate Tax Exempt Foundations, 83rd Congress, 1954, pg. 137, 153
11 Ibid., pg. 137
12 The New Republic, Jul. 29, 1936, pg. 343
13 Progressive Education, April 1932, pg. 261-2
14 Ibid.
15 Ibid.
16 Counts, The Soviet Challenge To America, pg. 324
17 Counts, Foreword to translation of New Russia's Primer, Ilin, Houghton, 1931
18 Ibid.
19 Counts, Dare The Schools Build A New Social Order, pg. 28-9
20 Hearings, Special House Committee To Investigate Tax-Exempt Foundations, 83rd Congress, 1954, pg. 482
21 Rugg, The Great Technology, pg. 32
22 Ibid., pg. 271
23 Ibid., pg. 258
24 Report, Spec. Comm. To Investigate Tax-Exempt Foundations, 83rd Cong. pg. 150
25 Ibid.
26 Frontiers of Democracy, Dec. 15, 1942, pg. 75-81
27 Report, Spec. Comm. To Investigate Tax Exempt Foundations, 83rd Cong. pg. 154
28 Ibid.
29 Ibid., pg. 155
30 Ibid., pg. 156
31 See pages 255
32 The Social Frontier, Feb. 1936, pg. 134-5
33 Ginn and Company, 1950
34 Harcourt, Brace and Company, 1950
35 Harper & Brothers, 1951
36 Allyn and Bacon, 1951
37 D.C. Heath & Company, 1948
38 D.C. Heath & Company, 1951
39 The New Our New Friends, Scott, Foresman & Co., pg. 156-9
40 Ibid., pg. 159
41 Report, President's Commission on High Education, 1947, Vol. III, pg. 48
42 UNESCO, Towards World Understanding, Vol. I, pg. 6
43 Harper and Company, 1955
44 NEA Journal, April 1946, pg. 175
45 Hoover, Speech, Freedoms Foundation Awards Ceremony, Valley Forge, Pa., Feb. 22, 1962, reprinted, Congressional Record, Mar. 1, 1962, pg. 2906
46 Henry Holt and Co., 1951
47 McGraw-Hill Book Co., 1952
48 See Chapter 3
49 Morris, No Wonder We Are Losing, pg. 3-19
50 Ibid., pg. 17
51 Congressional Record, Oct. 10, 1962, pg. 21831-2
52 Sweezy vs. New Hampshire, 354 US 234 (1957)
53 Slochower vs. Board of Education of New York, 350 US 551 (1956)
54 The Pasadena Story, NEA Commission For Defense Of Democracy Through Education, Jun. 1951, pg. 23
55 See page 159-162

56 Editorial, Tulsa World, Mar. 27, 1962

57 Editorial, Tulsa Tribune, Apr. 26, 1962

CHAPTER 7
Subverting Our Religious Heritage

1 Oxnam, Personalities In Social Reform, pg. 99

2 Bundy, Collectivism In the Churches, pg. 97-8

3 Oxnam, Personalities In Social Reform, pg. 76-7

4 Bundy, Collectivism In The Churches, pg. 101

5 Oxnam, Personalities in Social Reform, pg. 73-4

6 Investigation of Communist Activities In New York City Areas, Part VI, HCUA, Jul. 7, 1953, pg. 2075-7

7 Guide To Subversive Organizations, HCUA, Dec. 1, 1961, pg. 107

8 St. Louis Post-Dispatch, Sep. 25, 1961

9 Investigation of Communist Activities In N.Y., HCUA, Part VI, Jul. 7, 1953, pg. 2075-7

10 Ibid., Part VII, pg. 2169

11 Ibid., pg. 2177

12 A Yearbook of the Church and Social Service In The U.S., 1916, Federal Council of Churches, pg. 23

13 Investigation of Communist Activities In The New York Area, HCUA, Jul. 7, 1953, Part VI, 2092

14 Testimony of Bishop G. Bromley Oxnam, HCUA, Jul. 21, 1952, pg. 3725

15 Issues Presented By The Air Reserve Training Manual, Hearings, HCUA, Feb. 25, 1960, pg. 1303

16 Ibid., pg. 1288

17 The Communist Party Line, J. Ed Hoover, SISS, 1961

18 Study Conference on Churches and World Order, National Council of Churches, Cleveland, Ohio, Oct. 30, 1953

19 Fifth World Order Study Conference, Cleveland, Ohio, Nov. 18-21, 1958

20 Statement, General Board, National Council of Churches, Feb. 22, 1961

21 Ibid.

22 Presbyterian Life, Apr. 1, 1968

23 110 Government Place, Cincinnati 2, Ohio

24 Hearings, Issues Presented By the ARTM, HCUA, Feb. 25, 1960, pg. 1303-4

25 Congressional Record, March 3, 1960, pg. 3981

26 The Holy Bible, Revised Standard Version, Isaiah 7:14

27 Christian Century, Mar. 15, 1961

28 Ibid.

29 Ibid., Mar. 7, 1962, pg. 286

30 Adult Student, Sep. 1962, pg. 14-38

31 Adult Student, General Board of Education, The Methodist Church, Sep. 1962, pg. 15

32 Ibid., pg. 20

33 Ibid., pg. 20-21

34 Ibid., pg. 23

35 Surprising Beliefs of Our Young Ministers, Redbook, August 1961

36 Workers With Youth, Gen. Board of Education, The Methodist Church, Sep. 1962, pg. 5

37 Ibid.

38 Morrell, Of Bread And Circuses, Facts Forum, Feb. 1956

39 The Rightist Crisis In Our Churches, Look, Apr. 24, 1962

40 Speech, Communism and Religion in the U.S., Wm. Sullivan, Asst. Dir., FBI, Dallas, Texas, Oct. 19, 1961

41 Communist Propaganda and the Christian Pulpit, J. Edgar Hoover, Christianity Today, Oct. 24, 1960

42 Ibid.

CHAPTER 8
The Press, Radio and TV

1 Trohan, Human Events, Dec. 5, 1961; Oct. 20, 1961 pg. 705

2 See pages 33-34, 63-66

3 N.Y. Times News Service, St. Louis Post-Dispatch, Jan. 25, 1962

4 Ibid.

5 Ibid.

6 Ibid.

7 See pages 63-66

8 The Wanderer, Sep. 27, 1962, pg. 4

9 Guide to Subversive Organizations, HCUA, Dec. 1, 1961, pg. 121

10 Ibid.,pg. 61

11 Select Committee to Investigate Tax-Exempt Foundations, 82nd Congress, Dec. 23, 1952, pg. 725

12 Hearings, Military Cold War Education and Speech Review Policies, Senate Armed Services Committee, 87th Congress, Part IV, pg. 1491

13 See page 163-164

14 Who's Who In America, 1961

15 Ibid.

16 Romerstein, Communism and Your Child, pg. 98

17 Petition of Clemency to President Kennedy for Carl Braden and Frank Wilkinson, Christmas 1961

18 New York Times, Jan. 2, 1962

19 Ibid., Feb. 22, 1962

20 Romerstein, Communism and Your Child, pg. 99

21 See page 48-51

22 See page 58-59

23 National Review, Nov. 4, 1961

24 Donovan, Eisenhower, The Inside Story, pg. 247-49

25 Chicago Tribune, Oct. 10, 1947 quoted by Hughes, Prejudice and The Press, pg. 86

26 Hughes, Prejudice and the Press, pg. 14-15

27 Ibid., pg. 285

28 Ibid., pg. 33

29 Buckley, McCarthy And His Enemies, pg. 141; Congressional Record, Nov. 14, 1951

30 Monthly Bulletin, John Birch Society, Apr. 1, 1961, pg. 6

31 Ibid.,pg. 10-11

32 Church News, official publication of the Mormon Church, Mar. 16, 1963

33 Report, Senate Factfinding Subcommittee on Un-American Activities, California State Legislature, June 1963, pg. 37

34 Ibid., pg. 42-3

35 Ibid., pg. 61-2

36 Pourade, New Disturbing Journalistic Era Opens, Human Events, Oct. 13, 1961, pg. 673-78

37 Ibid., pg. 673

38 Human Events, Apr. 7, 1961, pg. 213

39 Fabian News, Oct. 1909, pg. 78, quoted in Keynes at Harvard, pg. 46

40 Shafer, The Turning Of The Tides, pg. 2

41 Congressional Record, Jan. 11, 1962, pg. A76

42 Ibid., pg. A76, A81, A82

43 Ibid.,pg. A70

44 Ibid.

45 Ibid.

46 Ibid.

47 NEA Journal, Mar. 1935, quoted, Bending The Twig, pg. 55-6

48 Lattimore, Ordeal By Slander, quoted, Human Events, Feb. 17, 1961, pg. 111

49 Human Events, Feb. 17, 1961, pg. 111

50 Ibid.

51 Ibid.,pg. 110

52 See page 119-120

53 Human Events, Oct. 20, 1961, pg. 692

54 Smith, The State of Europe, quoted, National Review, Dec. 31, 1962

55 Smith, The State Of Europe, pg. 393

56 Ibid., pg. 395-6

57 Smith, Last Train From Berlin, quoted, National Review, Dec. 31, 1962

58 National Review, Dec. 31, 1962, pg. 511

59 Human Events, Feb. 10, 1962, pg. 109

60 National Review, Jul. 3, 1962, pg. 473

61 Human Events, Jul. 14, 1961, pg. 446

62 St. Louis Globe Democrat, Jan. 13, 1962

63 See page 206-207

64 Reprinted by Human Events, Aug. 11, 1961, pg. 525

65 St. Louis Globe Democrat, Feb. 22, 1961

66 St. Louis Post-Dispatch, Oct. 3, 1962

67 United Press International News Wire, Sep. 30, 1962, 11:23 PM CDT

68 Speech, Brig. Gen. Clyde Watts, USA (Ret), Alton, Ill. Apr. 28, 1963

69 See pages 49-50, 58-59, 63-66

70   Hunter, An Analysis of the Editorial Policies of The St. Louis Post-Dispatch, Dec. 3, 1961
71   Ibid., Appendix I, pg. 21-42
72   Ibid., pg. 42-51

CHAPTER 9
Mental Health

1   Chisholm, Psychiatry, February 1946
2   Ibid.
3   Chisholm, Speech, Conference on Education, Asilomar, Calif., Sep. 11, 1954
4   Psychiatry, Feb. 1946
5   Ibid.
6   Mental Health and World Citizenship, Int. Cong. On Mental Health, London, 1948, pg. 8
7   Psychiatry, February 1946
8   Overstreet, The Great Enterprise, pg. 110
9   Ibid., pg. 115
10 Psychiatry, February 1946
11 Ibid.
12 See page 222
13 A Draft Act Covering Hospitalization Of The Mentally Ill, Section 6a
14 Ibid., Sec. 9b, Sec. 9f
15 Ibid., Sec. 9f
16 Maisel, Reader's Digest, Feb. 1962, pg. 98
17 Ibid.
18 DeToledano, Seeds Of Treason, pg. 272
19 Telegram Tribune, San Luis Obispo, Calif., Mar. 14, 1957
20 Report, The Bang-Jensen Case, Senate Internal Security Sub- committee, Sep. 14, 1961, pg. 1, 3, 8-17
21 Ibid., pg. 3, 27-39
22 Ibid., pg. 43
23 Ibid., pg. 17
24 Congressional Record, May 17, 1962, pg. 8065-8071
25 Ibid.
26 See page 215-216
27 Washington (D.C.) Star, Oct. 7, 1962
28 Ibid.
29 Hearing, Court of Federal Judge Chas. Clayton, Nov. 20-21, 1962
30 Yearbook of Neurology-Psychiatry for 1958-59, pg. 369
31 Ibid.
32 Preface, International Conciliations, Mar. 1948
33 Law Enforcement Looks At Mental Health, Law And Order, March, 1916, page 25-6
34 Boroff, Coronet, August 1961
35 Ibid.,
36 Ibid.
37 Life, Sep. 21, 1962
38 Congressional Record, Oct. 10, 1962, pg. 21835
39 Ibid.
40 Congressional Record, Oct. 10, 1962, pg. 21837-38
41 Life, Sep. 21, 1962
42 Ibid.

CHAPTER 10
The Organized Labor Movement

1   Lenin, Leftwing Communism, An Infantile Disorder, pg. 38
2   Hearings, Special Committee on Un-American Activities, 75th Congress, 3rd Session, Vol. II, pg. 1659
3   Ibid.
4   Ibid. Vol. I, pg. 248-251
5   Congressional Record, Sep. 22, 1950, pg. A6831
6   Report, Interlocking Subversion, SISS, Jul. 30, 1953, pg. 5
7   Congressional Record, Sep. 22, 1950, pg. A6831
8   Hearings, Communism In Labor Unions, HCUA, 80th Congress, 1st Session, pg. 51-52
9   The Worker, June 3, 1962
10 Ibid.
11 Foreword, The Naked Communist, Skousen
12 Gompers Statement, Jan. 22, 1917, Human Events, Mar. 10, 1961
13 Shafer, The Turning Of The Tides, pg. 2
14 Gompers, speech, 1903, Human Events, Dec. 22, 1961, pg. 874
15 Partisan Review, May-June 1947, Cong. Record, Feb. 6, 1962, pg. A881
16 Ibid., pg. A883
17 Hearings, Special Committee On

Un-American Activities, 78th
Cong., Appendix, Part IX, pg. 261-6
18 Congressional Record, Feb. 6, 1962,
pg. A883
19 COPE Manual, How To Win
20 See page 82
21 Morris, No Wonder We Are Losing,
pg. 196-9
22 Ibid.
23 Report, 100 Things You Should
Know About Communism, HCUA,
pg. 81
24 Ibid.
25 Hearings, Communist Infiltration
in the U.S. Government, 1953,
HCUA, pg. 1649-84
26 Burnham, The Web of Subversion,
p. 66
27 Report, Interlocking Subversion in
Government Departments, SISS,
Jul. 30, 1953, pg. 40-3

CHAPTER 11
The Tax-Exempt Foundations

1 Spec. Comm. To Investigate Tax-Exempt Foundations, 82nd Cong. (Cox
Comm.)
2 Spec. Comm. To Investigate Tax-Exempt Foundations, 83rd Cong.
(Reece Comm.)
3 Report, Reece Committee, Dec. 16,
1954, pg. 1-4
4 Fosdick, The Story of the Rockefeller
Foundations, pg. 29
5 See page 162
6 Keppel, The Foundation: Its Place
In American Life, pg. 107
7 Hearings, Reece Committee, 1954,
pg. 475
8 Report, Reece Committee, pg. 85-7
9 Hearings, Reece Committee, pg. 945
10 Report, Reece Committee, pg. 117
11 Ibid., pg. 118
12 Ibid.,pg. 120, 135-41, 149
13 Ibid., pg. 137
14 Ibid., pg. 154-6
15 Ibid.
16 Ibid., pg. 156-7
17 Hearings, Reece Committee, pg.
934
18 Report, Reece Committee, pg. 32
19 Ibid., pg. 185
20 Ibid.
21 Report, Interlocking Subversion,
SISS, Jul. 30, 1953, pg. 6
22 Report, Reece Committee, pg. 41,
pg. 179-80
23 See page 68-75
24 Report, Reece Committee, pg. 180
25 Ibid., pg. 175
26 American Legion Post 140, 3905
Powers Ferry Road, Atlanta, Ga., $1
per copy
27 Report, Reece Committee, pg. 200-1
28 Ibid., pg. 186
29 Prospects For America, Rockefeller
Bros. Panel Reports, pg. XXIV, 466-
7
30 Ibid.,pg. 39
31 Ibid.,pg. 46
32 Report, Reece Committee, pg. 111-4
33 Ibid.
34 Daily News, Philadelphia, Pa., Aug.
7, 1962
35 Report, Reece Committee, pg. 186-7
36 Ibid., pg. 186
37 Ibid., pg. 137
38 Ibid., pg. 136
39 Ibid., pg. 41

CHAPTER 12
Economics and Government

1 Mill, Essay On Representative
Government
2 Congressional Record, Oct. 10, 1961
3 Harris, Saving American Capitalism
4 Shaw, Intelligent Woman's Guide To
Socialism and Capitalism, pg. 94
5 Thomas, A Socialist's Faith, pg. 117
6 Harrod, Life Of John Maynard
Keynes, pg. 462
7 Veritas, Keynes At Harvard, pg.
86-87
8 Strachey, Contemporary
Capitalism, pg. 310
9 Ibid.,pg. 287-288
10 Ibid.,pg. 284
11 Keynes At Harvard, pg. 34-35
12 Toledano and Lasky, Seeds of
Treason, pg. 236
13 Goldwater, Conscience of a Conservative, pg. 25
14 Chase, A New Deal, pg. 163

15 Who's Who In America, 1961

16 Report, Interlocking Subversion, SISS, Jul, 30, 1953, pg. 44

17 Ibid.

18 Ibid.

19 Ibid., pg. 4

20 Hearings, House Select Committee To Investigate Certain Statements of Dr. William Wirt, 73rd Congress, 2nd Session, April 10 and 17, 1934

21 Ibid.

22 Ibid.

23 Ibid.

24 Ibid.

25 Ibid.

26 Ibid.

27 Ibid.

28 Ibid.

29 Ibid.

30 Ibid.

31 Hearings, Interlocking Subversion, SISS, June 23, 1953, pg. 823-40

32 Committee On Government Operations, U.S. Senate, July 23, 1956

33 Ibid., pg. 43, 160, 343, 345

34 Wilbur and Hyde, The Hoover Policies, quoted by Lyons in The Herbert Hoover Story, pg. 305-06

35 Lyons, The Herbert Hoover Story, Chapters 19-20

36 Ibid., pg. 307

37 Ibid.

38 Ibid., pg. 308

39 Ibid., pg. 292

40 Garrett, The People's Pottage, pg. 7

41 Ibid., pg. 11

42 A.L.A. Schechter vs. U.S., 295 US 495 (1935)

43 Gordon, Nine Men Against America, pg. 14

44 Schechter vs. U.S., Carter vs. Charter Coal Co., 298 US 495 (1936) U.S. vs. Butler, 297 USI (1936)

45 Gordon, Nine Men Against America, pg. 15

46 Ibid., pg. 16-25

47 A. B. Kirschbaum vs. Walling, 316 US 517 (1942)

48 Wickard vs. Filburn, 317 US 131 (1942)

49 Hearing, Limitation Of Appellate Jurisdiction of The U.S. Supreme Court, SISS, Feb. 19-21, 25-28, 1958, Appendix IV, Part II

50 Gordon, Nine Men Against America

51 Congressional Record, June 26, 1962

52 Manuel Enterprises Case, Congressional Record, June 26, 1962, pg. 10944

53 Chart, Congressional Record, May 2, 1962, pg. 7028-31

54 Ibid.

55 Ibid.

56 Speech, reprinted in Root's Brainwashing In The High Schools, pg. 205-07

57 Ibid.

58 Ibid.

59 Congressional Record, Sep. 22, 1950, pg. A6832

60 Ibid.

61 Ibid., Jan. 16, 1962, pg. A192

62 Morris, No Wonder We Are Losing, pg. 174-6

63 Aims of the ADA, Part II, Los Angeles Times, Sep. 4, 1961

64 Adams, First Hand Report, pg. 31-2

65 Taft, How I Lost The Nomination, Human Events, Dec. 2, 1959

66 Public Debt of the U.S., 1870-1962, Treasury Dept., The World Almanac, 1963

67 The New York Times, Jan. 18, 1960

68 Congressional Record, Oct. 5, 1962

69 Goldwater, Conscience of a Conservative, pg. 66

70 Congressional Record, Apr. 8, 1957

71 Public Debt of the U.S., 1870-1962, Treasury Dept., The World Almanac, 1963

72 The ADA: Its Impact on The New Frontier, Part I, Los Angeles Times, Sep. 3, 1961

73 Congressional Record, Feb. 6, 1962, pg. A881

CHAPTER 13

Internationalism

1 Washington, Farewell Address, 1796

2 Report, Spec, Comm. To Investigate Tax-Exempt Foundations, Dec. 16, 1954, pg. 169

3 Hearings, Military Cold War Educa-

tion, Sen. Armed Service Comm., Apr. 4, 1962, pg. 1474

4 Ibid.

5 Congressional Record, Jul. 28, 1945

6 Report, Interlocking Subversion, SISS, Jul, 30, 1953, pg. 6- 10; Foreign Relations of the U.S., The Conference at Malta and Yalta, 1945, Dept. of State, pg. 44, 58, 794

7 As quoted, Widener, Behind The UN Front, pg. 57

8 Congressional Record, Mar. 1, 1962, pg. 2937

9 Hearings, Activities of U.S. Citizens Employed By The UN, SISS, Dec. 1952

10 Document AT/DEC/32, UN Administrative Tribunal, Sep. 1, 1953

11 Morris, No Wonder We Are Losing, pg. 154

12 Report, The Bang-Jensen Case, SISS, Sep. 14, 1961, pg. 16

13 Ibid., pg. 17

14 Ibid., pg. 21

15 Ibid.

16 See page 70-74

17 St. Louis Globe Democrat,Feb. 22, 1963

18 Ibid.

19 Report, U.S. Foreign Assistance, Jul. 1945-Jun. 1961, Agency for International Development, Mar. 21, 1962, pg. 9, 12, 13, 17, 20, 24, 25, 31

20 Lane, I Saw Poland Betrayed, pg. 67, 68, 102

21 Report, Interlocking Subversion, SISS, Jul. 30, 1953, pg. 10-12

22 See page 71

23 Newsweek, Nov. 13, 1961

24 Speech, Upsala, Sweden, May 1962

25 New York Times, Oct. 5, 1961

26 Congressional Record, Jan. 15, 1962, pg. 198

27 Ibid., Jan. 15, 1962; Apr. 11, 1962

28 Ibid., Jan. 15, 1962

29 Ibid.

30 Ibid.

31 Ibid.

32 Ibid.

33 Annual Report of the Council on Foreign Relations, 1960, pg. 57-70

34 Report, Spec. House Comm. To Investigate Tax-Exempt Foundations, 1954, pg. 176

35 Ibid., pg. 177

36 Smoot, The Invisible Government, Dan Smoot Report, Vol. 7, Nos. 24-31

37 References to CFR membership in this chapter, except as noted, are based on membership rosters published in the CFR Annual Reports for 1960 and 1961.

38 Encyclopedia Britannica, 1959, Vol. 22, pg. 705-12

39 Smoot, The Invisible Government, pg. 168-71

40 Congressional Record, Feb. 6, 1962, pg. A883

41 Ibid.

42 Time, Mar. 16, 1942

43 Fed. Council of Churches, 1946 Report, pg. 240-6, as quoted, Bundy, Collectivism in the Churches, pg. 174-7

44 Ibid., pg. 175

45 See pages 140-143

46 Congressional Record, Feb. 6, 1962, pg. A883

47 Prospects For America, Rockefeller Bros. Panel Reports, pg. 39

48 Schlesinger, The Big Decision— Private Indulgence or National Power, pg. 13

49 Bloomfield, A World Effectively Controlled By The UN, ARPA- IDA Study Memo No. 7, Mar. 10, 1962, Dept. of State Contract SCC 28270, Feb. 24, 1961

50 Congressional Record, Feb. 23, 1954, pg. 2014ff

51 Ibid.

52 Public Debt of the U.S., 1870-1962, U.S. Treasury, The World Almanac, 1963

53 Report, U.S. Foreign An Assistance, Agency for Inter. Dev., Mar. 21, 1962

54 See pages 193-194

55 Campaigne, American Might and Soviet Myth, pg. 27-8

56 Ibid., pg. 31-2, and Gutierrez, The Tragedy of Bolivia, pg. 57-74

57 Stalin, Marxism and the National Colonial Question, pg. 114-5

58 St. Louis Globe Democrat, Jul. 6, 1963

59 Ibid.

60 Cong. Abraham Multler, (D-NY), HR 6900, 87th Congress
61 Bess, Silent Weapon of the Cold War, Saturday Evening Post, Oct. 18, 1958
62 Ibid.
63 See page 49
64 Gutierrez, The Tragedy of Bolivia, pg. 71
65 Ibid. pg. 75
66 Constitution of the United States, Article VI, Par. 2
67 3 Dall 199, as quoted, MacBride, Treaties vs. the Constitution, pg. 41
68 252 US 416 (1920)
69 315 US 203 (1942)
70 Congressional Record, Feb. 23, 1954, pg. 2014ff
71 Ibid.
72 Treaty Against Genocide, quoted, MacBride, Treaties vs. the Constitution, pg. 22
73 U.S. Constitution, Amendments, I, VI
74 Congressional Record, Jan. 28, 1954, pg. 899
75 The 1954 Bricker Amendment, Section One
76 St. Louis Post-Dispatch, May 26, 1962
77 Joint Declaration Against War Propaganda, Par. 1, 2, 5
78 Statute of the International Court of Justice, Article 59
79 Ibid. Article 60
80 Charter of the United Nations, Article 94
81 See pages 111-117

CHAPTER 14
What Can You Do?

1 Patrick Henry, Liberty of Death Speech, Virginia House of Burgesses, 1775
2 Walter, How To Fight Communism, HCUA,88th Congress
3 Hoover, Letter To Law Enforcement Officials, Apr. 1,1961
4 Hoover, Communist Illusion and Democratic Reality, Dept. of Justice, Dec. 1959
5 Walter, How To Fight Communism, HCUA
6 Ibid.
7 Peters, Manual on Organization, Communist Party, USA, pg. 57
8 Hall, Political Parties and the 1964 Elections, The Worker, Jun. 23, 1963
9 Ibid.
10 St. Louis Globe Democrat, Jul. 15, 1963
11 St. Louis Post-Dispatch, Jul. 19, 1963
12 Basler, Collected Works of Abraham Lincoln, Vol. I, pg. 201-3
13 Hoover, Speech to DAR, Apr. 22, 1954, as quoted: Report, Spec. Comm. To Investigate Tax-Exempt Foundations, 83rd Congress, Dec. 16, 1954, pg. 114
14 Hoover, Letter to Law Enforcement Officials, Mar. 1, 1960

CHAPTER 15
In The 25 Years Since...

1 The Holy Bible, King James Version
2 See Chapters 16 and 18
3 Evans, The Panama Canal Treaties Swindle, Signet Books, 1986, pg. 14
4 See Chapter 17
5 See Chapter 19
6 See Chapter 23

CHAPTER 16
Soviet Might—American Made

1 The Holy Bible, King James Version
2 The Columbus Dispatch, Apr. 13, 1989, pg. 3A
3 Report, Joint Economic Committee, U.S. Congress, Sep. 14, 1987 as quoted in The New American, Oct. 26, 1987, pg. 5
4 St. Louis Post-Dispatch, Apr. 11, 1988, pg. 2B
5 Ibid.
6 The New American, Oct. 26, 1987, pg. 5
7 Ibid., pg. 6
8 The Columbus Dispatch, Apr. 13, 1989, pg. 3A
9 Washington Times, Apr. 27, 1989, pg. 1

10 Ibid., Dec. 27, 1987, pg. 1E

11 Washington Times, Apr. 11, 1988, pg. 1; Mar. 29, 1989, pg. C3; Dec. 27, 1988, pg. A9; St. Louis Post-Dispatch, Apr. 14, 1988; Washington Times, Mar. 17, 1988, pg. C5; New York Times, Mar. 28, 1988

12 St. Louis Post-Dispatch, Dec. 9, 1989, pg. C1

13 Washington Times, Aug. 5, 1987, pg. A7; Nov. 9, 1987; Feb 2, 1988, pg. 1

14 Annual Report, Export-Import Administration, FY 1981, pg. 167-173

15 Ibid., pg. 174-178

16 Washington Times, Jul. 2, 1987; Dec. 6, 1987, pg. A3

17 Ibid., Feb 2, 1988, pg. 1

18 Ibid., Nov. 9, 1987, pg. A4

19 Ibid., Jul. 2, 1987, pg. A4

20 Congressional Record, October 24, 1973

21 Palo Alto, CA Times, Feb. 24, 1968

22 Los Angeles Times, Nov. 26, 1966

23 Ibid., Dec. 18, 1966

24 San Francisco Examiner, May 4, 1969, pg. 9

25 Oakland Tribune, Sep. 15, 1969

26 Industrial Research & Development, Jul. 1980, pg. 5

27 Ibid. pg. 60

28 Washington Times, Jul. 21, 1989, pg. A7

29 Ibid.

30 Ibid.

31 Proceedings of the Naval Institute, Aug. 1983, pg. 73-74

32 Los Angeles Times, Oct. 30, 1976; Dallas Morning News, November 23, 1983; Los Angeles Daily News, January 12, 1984; Wall Street Journal, Apr. 10, 1984

33 Dallas Morning News, Nov. 23, 1983

34 Los Angeles Times, Oct. 30, 1976

35 Washington Times, Jun. 3, 1988, pg. 1

36 Ibid., Sep. 15, 1986, pg. 6A

37 Schlafly, Washington Times, Nov. 15, 1988

38 Federal Register, May 29, 1981

39 Wall Street Journal, Jan. 21, 1983

40 Ibid., Jan. 20, 1983

41 Washington Times, Aug. 5, 1987, pg. C10

42 Ibid.

43 Ibid.

44 Ibid., Jul. 25, 1988, pg. A5

45 Ibid, Aug. 5, 1987, pg. C10

46 New York Times, Mar. 28, 1988

47 St. Louis Post-Dispatch, Apr. 9, 1988

48 Ibid., May 3, 1989, pg. 1

49 Los Angeles Herald Examiner, Oct. 10, 1983

50 Ibid.

51 St. Louis Post-Dispatch, Aug. 11, 1987, pg. 1

52 Howard Phillips, Issues and Strategy Bulletin, Sep. 21, 1987

53 Washington Times, Dec. 11, 1987, pg. 1

54 Ibid., Apr. 11, 1988, pg. 1

55 Ibid., Apr. 14, 1988, Dec. 27, 1988, Mar. 29, 1989

CHAPTER 17
The Treaty Traps

1 U.S. Government Printing Office, Washington, DC, 1964

2 Helsinki Accords, Articles VII & VIII, Dept. of State Bulletin, Sep. 1, 1975

3 Ibid., Article I

4 Ibid., Articles I-IV and VI

5 Special Report No. 34, Department of State, June 1977, pg. 5, 6

6 Ibid., pg. 8

7 Ibid.

8 Treaty Between The US and the USSR on Limitations of Anti-Ballistic Missile Systems, 1972, Reprinted: Congressional Record, Feb. 4, 1988, pg. S711-713

9 Quoted by Sullivan, The Bitter Fruit of SALT, pg. 22

10 Ibid., pg. 1

11 Ibid., Article III

12 St. Louis Post-Dispatch, Dec. 3, 1987, pg. 3

13 St. Louis Post-Dispatch, Dec. 3, 1987, pg. 1

14 Hearings, Military Implications of SALT II Treaty, Senate Armed Services Committee, Oct. 9-16, 1979, pg. 1327

15 Ibid., pg. 943, 1194, 1201, 1211

16 Ibid., pg. 1178
17 Ibid., pg. 1142, 1157, 1194
18 Ibid., pg. 1177
19 Ibid., pg. 973
20 Protocol to SALT II Treaty, Article II, Heritage Foundation Arms Control Handbook, pg. 163
21 St. Louis Post-Dispatch, Oct. 2, 1987, pg. 11A
22 Hearings, Military Implications of the SALT II Treaty, pg. 1180
23 INF Treaty, Congressional Record, Feb. 4, 1988, pg. S692
24 New York Times, Mar. 30, 1988, pg. A26
25 Associated Press, The Boston Globe, pg. 3
26 Ibid.
27 USA Today, Jul. 24-26, 1987, pg. 1
28 St. Louis Post-Dispatch, May 24, 1988, pg. 3B
29 Ibid.
30 St. Louis Post-Dispatch, Aug. 25, 1987, pg. 1
31 New York Times, Dec. 12, 1987
32 Washington Times, Dec. 10, 1987, pg. 1
33 St. Louis Post-Dispatch, Nov. 22, 1987
34 Washington Times, Feb. 22, 1988, pg. A3
35 Biography, Frank Carlucci, Who's Who In America, 1986-87
36 Ibid.
37 Ibid.
38 Cited by Weiss and Lehman in Beyond Salt II Failure; Praeger, NY, 1981
39 New York Times Magazine, Apr. 12, 1959, pg. 2

CHAPTER 18

The War In Vietnam

1 St. Louis Globe Democrat, Mar. 23, 1967
2 Ibid., Jan. 27, 1967
3 Ibid.
4 Ibid.
5 St. Louis Globe Democrat, Sep. 13, 1967
6 Ibid., Sep. 15, 1967
7 Associated Press, Atlantic City, N.J. Press, Jun. 29, 1967
8 St. Louis Globe Democrat, May 13, 1967
9 Ibid.
10 Ibid.
11 Ibid., Aug. 2, 1967
12 Ibid.
13 St. Louis Globe Democrat, Jun. 13, 1972
14 Ibid.
15 Ibid.
16 St. Louis Post-Dispatch, Mar. 30, 1975, pg. 1
17 Ibid.
18 New York Times News Service, St. Louis Post-Dispatch, Mar. 30, 1975, pg. 14A
19 Daily World, Oct. 4, 1975, pg. 2
20 Daily World, Dec. 28, 1973
21 Ibid.
22 America's Future, 514 Main Street, New Rochelle, N.Y., 1988
23 AIM Report, April-A, 1983, pg. 2
24 Lichter & Rothman, The Media Elite, 1986, pg. 15
25 Ibid.
26 The Powers That Be, pg. 491 as quoted by Lichter & Rothman, pg. 17
27 New York Review of Books article, quoted AIM Report, April-B 1983, pg. 4
28 AIM Report, February-B 1986.
29 The Media Elite, pg. 15
30 Podhoretz, Why We Were In Vietnam, pg. 125 as quoted in Passport Magazine, May-June 1988, pg. 6
31 Quoted by Brownfield, How Media Bias Distorts Our View of the World, pg. 18
32 AIM Report, February-B 1986, pg. 1-2
33 Ibid.
34 Film, Hanoi Hilton, Columbia Pictures, quoted Passport Magazine, May-June 1988, pg. 6
35 Newsweek, May 5, 1969, pg. 120
36 Daily World, May 15, 1979
37 Ibid.
38 Ibid.
39 Ibid.
40 Ibid.
41 Official Program, Memorial Ser-

vice, Dr. Sidney L. Jackson, May 10, 1979

42 Obituaries published May 8 & 9, 1979 in four newspapers

43 St. Louis Globe Democrat, Mar. 23, 1967

CHAPTER 19
No Internal Security

1 Washington Times, Jul. 30, 1981, pg. 20

2 Human Events, Aug. 3, 1985, pg. 7

3 Washington Times, Jul. 30, 1987

4 Human Events, Aug. 3, 1985, pg. 7

5 St. Louis Post-Dispatch, Sep. 15, 1988, pg. 12A

6 Washington Times, Jan. 29, 1988, pg. A3

7 St. Louis Post-Dispatch, Sep. 15, 1988, pg. 12A

8 Ibid.

9 St. Louis Sun, Nov. 5, 1989

10 New York Times, Oct. 13, 1989

11 Guide To Subversive Organizations and Publications, House Document No. 398, 87th Congress, 2nd Session, Apr. 12, 1962, pg. 121

12 Senate Document 117, Apr. 23, 1956, pg. 91

13 Powell, Covert Cadre, Green Hill Publishers, 1987, pg. 58n

14 New York Times, Oct. 13, 1989

15 Powell, Covert Cadre, pg. 96

16 Ibid., pg. 15

17 Ibid., pg. 16-17

18 Ibid., pg. xiii

19 Ibid., pg. xvii

20 Ibid., pg. 13

21 Ibid., pg. 26

22 Ibid., pg. 19-20

23 Ibid., pg. 26

24 Ibid., pg. 43

25 Ibid., pg. 39

26 Ibid., pg. 29

27 Paragraph 3 of the Settlement Agreement, Quoted Ibid., pg. 79

28 Human Events, Aug. 3, 1985, pg. 7

29 Ibid.

30 Ibid.

31 Ibid.

32 Ibid.

33 Obituary, Washington Times, May 12, 1987, pg. 5A

34 St. Louis Post-Dispatch, Oct. 2, 1987, pg. 19A

35 Ibid.

36 Washington Times, Aug. 11, 1987, pg. D3

37 Ibid.

38 Washington Times, Jul. 3, 1987, pg. D3

39 Ibid.; St. Louis Post-Dispatch, Jul 29, 1987, pg. 3B

40 Washington Times, Aug. 11, 1987, pg. D3

CHAPTER 20
Why Our Leaders Betray Us

1 Speech, Dean Rusk, World Affairs Conference, International Union of Electrical, Radio and Machine Workers, Washington, DC, Feb. 25, 1964

2 Partisan Review, May-June 1947, Reprinted, Congressional Record, Feb. 6, 1962, pg. A881-3

3 Ibid.

4 Remarks by the President, Texas A&M Graduation, May 12, 1989, Transcript, Office of the White House Press Secretary, pg. 2-3

5 St. Louis Post-Dispatch, Jan. 30, 1967

6 Ibid.

7 State of the Union Message, Jan. 13, 1967

8 Atlantic City NJ Press, Jun. 26, 1967

9 New York Times, Jun. 26, 1967

10 Gorbachev, Perestroika, pg. 60-61

11 International Affairs, Aug. 1986, pg. 3, 4 & 5

12 Ibid., pg. 10

13 Ibid.

14 Ibid., pg. 6, 10

15 Ibid., pg. 6

16 St. Louis Post-Dispatch, Jan. 17, 1966

17 St. Louis Globe Democrat, Jan. 15, 1966

18 St. Louis Post-Dispatch, Jan. 24, 1966

19 Philadelphia Daily News, Jul. 1, 1965

20 St. Louis Globe Democrat, Jun. 8, 1966

21 Ibid., Jul. 20, 1965

22 Washington Times, Jun. 27, 1989, pg. F3

23 St. Louis Globe Democrat, Jul. 17, 1965; St. Louis Post-Dispatch, Dec. 14, 1965

24 St. Louis Post-Dispatch, Dec. 14, 1965; Jun. 6, 1966

25 Ibid., Dec. 14, 1965

26 U.S. News & World Report, Aug. 21, 1961

27 Report, Crimes of Khrushchev, House Committee on Un-American Activities, Part I, pg. 7; Part II, pg. 2

28 Washington Times, Feb. 23, 1989, pg. A6

29 Report, Gorbachev, Perestroika: The Revolution Continues, Supreme Soviet, USSR, Nov. 2, 1987, pg. 55

30 See Chapter 19

31 Quoted, Perloff, The Shadows of Power, Western Islands, 1988, pg. 208

32 Ibid.

33 Ibid., pg. 8

34 Ibid., pg. 169

35 St. Louis Post-Dispatch, Nov. 24, 1988, pg. 1

36 Washington Times, Nov. 18, 1988, pg. F4

37 Ibid.

38 Ibid.

39 Schlesinger, Partisan Review, May-June 1947, Reprinted Congressional Record, Feb. 6, 1962, pg. A881

40 Washington Times, Dec. 1, 1989, pg. A4; Human Events, Dec. 9, 1989, pg. 2

41 Humanist Manifestoes I and II, Prometheus Books, Buffalo, 1973

42 Ibid., pg. 16-17

43 Ibid., pg. 3-4

44 Ibid., pg. 24-31

45 Servant Books, 1986.

46 Adler and Adler Publishers, 1987

47 America's Future, 514 Main Street, New Rochelle, N.Y., 1988, 24 pages, $1

48 Ibid., pg. 6

49 Ibid., pg. 7

50 Philadelphia Inquirer, May 3 & 4, 1988, pg. 1; St. Louis Post-Dispatch, May 10, 1988, pg. 1

CHAPTER 21
How the CPUSA Manipulates Congress

1 Leninism and the World Revolutionary Working-Class Movement, pg. 169, Progress Publishers, Moscow

2 Gus Hall, The Revolutionary Process, Report to 19th National Convention, CPUSA, New Outlook Publishers, 1969, pg. 8

3 Gus Hall, Speech, International Meeting of Communist and Workers' Parties, Moscow, 1969, pg. 427-428, Peace and Socialism Publishers, Prague, 1969

4 Political Affairs, January 1987, pg. 3-10

5 Ibid., pg. 9-10

6 People's Daily World, Dec. 24, 1987, pg. A9

7 New York Times, Dec. 8, 1988

8 U.S. Postal Circulation Statement, People's Daily World, Oct. 3, 1987

9 Lenin, Collected Works, Vol. 33, pg. 227, Quoted, World Marxist Review, August 1972, pg. 133

10 Quoted by Gus Hall, Lame Duck In Turbulent Waters, pg. 43, New Outlook Publishers, New York, 1972

11 Gus Hall, Report to Central Committee CPUSA, Dec. 12, 1981, pg. 91, 95

12 Budenz, The Techniques of Communism, Henry Regnery Co., Chicago 1954

13 Ibid., pg. 136

14 Ibid., pg. 136-137

15 Ibid., pg. 146

16 Gus Hall, Lame Duck, pg. 37

17 Ibid., pg. 37-38

18 Ibid., pg. 48-49

19 Ibid., pg. 53-54

20 People's Daily World, Jan. 15, 1987, pg. 16A

21 Ibid., Feb. 15, 1989, pg. 1

22 Sworn testimony, Hearings, Communist Activities in the Chicago Area, Part 2, pg. 3767, HCUA, 1952; Hearings, Communist Penetration

of Vital Industries-Chicago, pg. 583-584, HCUA, 1959

23 Ravines, The Yenan Way, Scribner's, New York, 1951, quoted in SISS Report, Southern Conference Educational Fund, Inc. 1955, pg. 83

24 New York Times, Dec. 8, 1988

25 Philbrick & Bales, Communism and Race In America, Bales Books, Searcy, AR, 1965, pg. 13

26 Letter, Majority Leader Stationery, House of Representatives, Mar. 20, 1984 reprinted, The Aker Foreign Information Service, P.O. Box 4206, Woodbridge, VA 22194, May 1985

27 Ibid.

28 Philbrick & Bales, pg. 13

29 SISS, Hearings, Scope of Soviet Activity in the United States, Sep. 5, 1956, pg. 3003-3025 as reprinted in For The Skeptic, The Bookmailer, New York, 1959, pg. 131-132

30 Ibid., pg. 137-154

31 Ibid.

32 Hall, Lame Duck, pg. 23

33 Leninism and the World Revolutionary Working Class Movement, pg. 120, Progress Publishers, Moscow 1971

34 Hall, Lame Duck, pg. 37-41.

35 Gus Hall, Report to the Central Committee, CPUSA, Dec. 12, 1981, pg. 95

36 Political Affairs, February 1982, pg. 33

37 Ibid.

38 Daily World, Nov. 4, 1983, pg. 6D

39 Ibid., Nov. 11, 1983, pg. 4D

40 Ibid., Mar. 10, 1984, pg. 4D

41 Ibid., pg. 8D

42 Ibid., May 7, 1985

43 Ibid.

44 People's Daily World, Feb. 3, 1989, pg. 1

45 Lenin On Peaceful Coexistence, Articles and Speeches, Scientific Socialism Series, Moscow, 1971

46 Political Affairs, March 1986, pg. 10

47 Hall, 1988 Elections: Unity: The Only Way, pg. 79,

48 Ibid. pgs., 83 & 85

49 People's Daily World, Feb. 15, 1989, pg. 4A

50 Ibid., Dec. 24, 1987, pg. 3

51 Ibid., Dec. 22, 1987, pg. 3A

52 Political Affairs, December 1987, pg. 10

53 Ibid., pg. 11

54 Ibid. pg. 10

CHAPTER 22

Communist Influence– How Do They Get It?

1 Hyde, Dedication and Leadership, Notre Dame Press, pg. 18

2 Hall, Unity—The Only Way, pg. 89

3 Methvin, The Riot Makers, pg. 138, Arlington House, New Rochelle, 1970

4 Political Affairs, March 1986, pg. 13

5 Daily World, May 15, 1979

6 Jackson on Drtina, Sidney Jackson Papers, Kent State University Archives

7 Budenz, The Techniques of Communism, pg. 301

8 Smith, Biography, Sidney Jackson Papers, KSU Archives, Sep. 19, 1979

9 Obituary, Daily World, May 15, 1979

10 Hyde, Dedication and Leadership, Notre Dame Press, pg. 10, 11, 18

11 Information Digest, Sep. 27, 1985, pg. 267-270

12 Letter, Jan. 23, 1979, Sidney Jackson Papers, KSU Archives

13 Information Digest, Sep. 27, 1985, pg. 269

14 Ibid., pg. 268

15 Stormer, The Death of a Nation, pg. 26, Liberty Bell Press, Florissant MO, 1968

16 Testimony, Hoover, House Appropriations Subcommittee, Feb. 16, 1967, pg. 619

17 New York Times, Jul. 22, 1964

18 Luce, Road To Revolution, pg. 9, quoted Stormer, The Death of a Nation, pg. 24-25

19 Report of Cuyahoga County Special Grand Jury, Aug. 9, 1966

20 Associated Press, St. Louis Globe Democrat, Aug. 3, 1967

21 Ibid.

22 New York Post, Jun. 15, 1967

23 St. Louis Post-Dispatch, Sep. 15, 1967

24 St. Louis Globe Democrat, Aug. 3, 1967

25 St. Louis Post-Dispatch, Jul. 25, 1967

26 Ibid., Jul. 26, 1967

27 St. Louis Globe Democrat, Aug. 19, 1967

28 Ibid., Aug. 9, 1967

29 Ibid.

30 Ibid., Aug. 9-14, 1967, distributed by North American Newspaper Alliance, Inc.

31 Ibid., Aug. 12, 1967

32 Quoted by J. Edgar Hoover, Statement on 17th National Convention CPUSA, SISS, Jan. 26, 1960, pg. 6

33 Ibid., pg. 7

34 Hoover, Testimony, House Appropriations Subcommittee, Feb. 16, 1967, pg. 619

35 Ibid. 1964, quoted, U.S. News & World Report, May 4, 1965

36 Ibid., 1967, pg. 619

37 St. Louis Post-Dispatch, Jan. 19, 1989, pg. 1A, 1B

38 Washington Times & St. Louis Post-Dispatch, Sep. 4 & 5, 1989, pg. 1 all editions

39 Human Events, Aug. 27, 1966

40 Ibid.

41 Ibid.

42 Ibid., Nov. 18, 1967

43 St. Louis Post-Dispatch, Aug. 4, 1967

44 Ibid., Aug. 5, 1967

45 Human Events, Aug. 5, 1967

46 St. Louis Post Dispatch and Lousiville Courier Journal, Aug. 13, 1967

47 Ibid.

48 Congressional Record, Feb. 8, 1967, pg. A544

49 Ibid., Nov. 14, 1967, pg. H15180

50 Ibid., pg. H15189

51 U.S. News & World Report, Jan. 31, 1966

52 The Federal Government and the Non-Profit Sector, The Urban Institute, Washington DC, 1981, 57 pages

53 Washington Times, Jul. 13, 1989, Sep. 14, 1989

54 Midwest Distributors Catalog, Fall 1984, Kansas City KS 66119

55 Political Affairs, June 1983, pg. 38-40; December 1984, pg. 38;Daily World, Jan. 7, 1984; People's Daily World, Feb. 24, 1987, pg. 11A; Jun. 24, 1987, pg. 9A

56 Hoover, Report, Communist Target Youth, HCUA, Washington DC, 1961, pg. 1, 10

57 Ibid., pg. vii

58 World Magazine, People's Daily World, May 11, 1989, pg. 13

59 Ibid., pg. 12

60 Ibid., pg. 13

61 Ibid.

62 St. Louis Post-Dispatch, Jul. 20, 1987, pg. 6A

63 Jul. 25, 1989

64 Pages E 4717-4725

65 Soviet Active Measures in the U.S., 1986-87, The Security and Intelligence Foundation Reprint Series, Arlington VA, July 1988, pg. 10

66 Ibid. pg. 10-11

67 Ibid., pg. 13

68 Reader's Digest, January 1983, pg. 120-125

69 Ibid., pg. 120-121

70 Ibid., pg. 125

71 Koshy, Does Marxism Presuppose Atheism?, Ecumenical Press Service, 89.02.45, pg. 1-2 Feb. 21-18, 1989

72 Ibid., 88.09.36, pg. 1-2, Sep. 18-14, 1988

73 Ibid. pg. 2

74 Ibid., 89.07.28, Jul. 21-25, 1989

75 Hall, Speech, Election '84 Roundup: The Communist View, New York, Nov. 16, 1984, pg. 9

76 Daily World, Jul. 25, 1981

77 World Magazine, People's Daily World, Jun. 25, 1987, pg. 11A; Nov. 17, 1988, pg. 12-13

78 NEA Journal, December 1967, pg. 34, quoted Blumenfeld, NEA: Trojan Horse in American Education, The Paradigm Co., Boise, ID, pg. 161

79 Quoted, Blumenfeld, pg. 169

80 Ibid., pg. 172

81 Quoted, The Blumenfeld Education Letter, August 1988, pg. 1

82 Quoted, Blumenfeld, Trojan Horse, pg. 241

83 See Chapter X

84 The Security and Intelligence Foundation Reprint, July 1988, pg. 8-10

85 Ibid., pg. 9

86 Daily World, Dec. 17, 1985, pg. 2D; People's Daily World, Nov. 12, 1987, pg. 22A

87 Ibid., Oct. 21, 1982, pg. 4

88 Ibid., Mar. 25, 1981, pg. 4

89 Ibid., Mar. 25, 1981

90 Political Affairs, May 1987, pg. 34-38

91 Hall, Report, 1988 Elections: Unity—The Only Way, 24th National Convention, CPUSA, 1987, pg. 85

92 McVey, View Points, MSLC, January 1987, pg. 1

93 Ibid., pg. 2

94 1989 PDW Fund Drive Report, People's Daily World, Jun. 22, 1989, pg. 22

95 I Corinthians 5:6

CHAPTER 23
Conquest Without War

1 Kozak, How Parliament Can Play A Revolutionary Role In The Transition To Socialism, Report, House Committee on Un-American Activities, Dec. 30, 1961

2 Ibid., pg. 1

3 Ibid.

4 Mager & Katel, Conquest Without War, pg. 57; Kozak, HCUA Reprint, pg. 11

5 This Week, Oct. 29, 1961

6 Kozak, HCUA Reprint, pg. 8, 32

7 pg. 227-228

8 Ibid., pg. 228

9 Kozak, HCUA Reprint, pg. 7

10 Ibid., pg. 25

11 Ibid., pg. 43-44

12 Ibid., pg. 27

13 Ibid., pg. 35

14 Associated Press, Memphis Commercial Appeal, quoted and pictured in film, Communist Encirclement, Harding College, 1961

15 Kozak, HCUA Reprint, pg. 13

16 World Marxist Review, February 1974, pg. 28

17 Ibid., footnote, pg. 28

18 Ibid. pg. 28

19 Political Affairs, Dec. 1987, pg. 17

20 Ibid.

21 Ibid., pg. 21

22 Kozak, HCUA Reprint, pg. 31

23 Political Affairs, Jun. 1989, pg. 34

24 Quoted, Yakushevsky, Lenin's Two Tactics Of Social Democracy in the Democratic Revolution, Progress Publishers, Moscow, 1988

25 Dorsey, Report, Nation States, Party States And International Law, 1983, pg. 135-136

26 Political Affairs, Jan. 1989, pg. 6

27 St. Louis Post-Dispatch, Oct. 23, 1986, pg. 3B

28 USA Today, Jul. 28, 1988, pg. 1B

29 Political Affairs, December 1987, pg. 19

30 Information Digest, 2805 St. Paul St., Baltimore, MD, 21218, Dec. 2, 1988, pg. 273

31 People's Daily World, Nov. 12, 1988, pg. 2A

32 Ibid., Nov. 15, 1988, pg. 2A

33 Political Affairs, Jan. 1989, pg. 5

34 Information Digest, Dec. 2, 1988, pg. 273

35 Kozak, HCUA Reprint, pg. 32

36 Kozak, HCUA Reprint, pg. 24

37 Lenin, Collected Works, Moscow 1964, Vol. V, pg. 430-431

38 Political Affairs, March 1972, pg. 5

39 Human Events, Aug. 5, 1989, pg. 1

40 Ibid.

41 Chicago Tribune, Aug. 2, 1989, pg. 1

42 Human Events, Aug. 5, 1989, pg. 1 & 7

43 Political Affairs, July 1984, pg. 9

44 Hall, Working Class USA: The Power and the Movement, International Publishers, New York, 1987, pg. 171, 311, 377

45 Kozak, HCUA Reprint, pg. 20-21

46 Federal Communications Commission, Report No. 4846, Dec. 13, 1968, pg. 116

47 Ibid., pg. 2

48 Congressional Record, Nov. 14, 1973

49 St. Louis Post-Dispatch, Aug. 3, 1989, pg. 1

50 Briefing Paper, Avirgan and Honey vs. 29 Defendants, pg. 1, 4, 6

51 New York Times, Mar. 17, 1989; ABA Journal, August 1989, pg. 34

52 Ibid.

53 Falwell letter, Sep. 21, 1989; USA Today, Jun. 17, 1988, pg. 2A; CWA Newsletter, October 1989;Washington Times, Nov. 2, 1989, pg. A5; Human Events, Nov. 25, 1989, pg. 15

54 Political Affairs, November 1984, pg. 10

55 Ibid., pg. 13

56 Ibid., pg. 14

57 Gus Hall, Main Report, 24th National Convention, Communist Party, USA, August 1987, pg. 81

58 Political Affairs, Sep./Oct. 1988, pg. 13, 15

59 Ibid., pg. 13

60 Ibid., pg. 12, 16

61 Kozak, HCUA Reprint, pg. 25, 43

62 Lenin, Collected Works, Vol. 29, pg. 108; Vol: 28, pg. 466; Vol. 35, 4th edition , pg. 108

63 Stalin, Stalin's Works, Vol. 10, pg. 378

64 Washington Times, Apr. 12, 1989, pg. 1

65 All discussed and documented in earlier chapters.

66 St. Louis Post-Dispatch, Oct. 11, 1988, pg. 11A

67 Washington Times, Apr. 5, 1989, pg. B5

68 Kozak, HCUA Reprint, pg. 35

69 Burns, Power To Lead, pg. 189

70 The News Leader, Springfield, MO, Mar. 8, 1989, pg. 1B

71 St. Louis Post-Dispatch, Mar. 20, 1988

72 Philadelphia Inquirer, Sep. 9, 1989, pg. 7C

73 Washington Times, Jan. 13, 1989, Op Ed Page

74 Ibid.

75 Ibid.

76 Reprinted, The Phyllis Schlafly Report, Box 618, Alton, IL, September 1987

CHAPTER 24
Why Communism Kills

1 TIME Magazine, Jun. 12, 1989, pg. 26

2 Ibid.

3 Chicago Tribune, Jun. 12, 1989, pg. 1

4 Quoted, Christian Anti-Communism Crusade newsletter, Aug. 1, 1989

5 Hearing, Communist Persecution of Churches in Red China and Korea, HCUA, pg. 3

6 Ibid., pg. 4

7 Ibid., pg. 31

8 Ibid., pg. 31-32

9 Dooley,. Deliver Us From Evil, pg. 98

10 Ibid.

11 Ibid., pg. 101

12 Quoted, Hoover, Masters of Deceit, pg. 184

13 The Blade, Toledo, Ohio, Oct. 14, 1966

14 Marx, The Communist Manifesto, Washington Square Press, 1964, pg. 85-86

15 Gorbachev, Perestroika: The Revolution Continues, Report to the Supreme Soviet, Nov. 2, 1987, Northern Neighbors edition, pg. 16

16 The Reader's Digest, February 1977, pg. 228

17 Christian Anti-Communism Crusade, P.O. Box 890, Long Beach CA 90801

18 The Readers' Digest, February 1977, pg. 245, 249

19 Ibid., pg. 237

20 Schwarz, pg. 10

CHAPTER 25
Know Your Enemy

1 Sun Tzu, The Art of War

2 Marx & Engels, The Communist Manifesto, Washington Square Press, 1964, pg. 87

3 Ibid., pg. 94

4 The Manifesto, pg. 88

5 Ibid., pg. 88

6 Congressional Record, Oct. 10, 1962

7 Scott Foresman & Co., 1968

8 Ibid., pg. 10, 14-16

9 Workbook, The Family You Belong

To, Turner- Livingston Reading Series, pg. 11

10 Ibid., pg. 15

11 Ibid., pg. 25

12 Marx, The Communist Manifesto, pg. 87-88

13 Ibid., pg. 89

14 Land of the Free, A History of the United States, Benziger Brothers, 1966, pg. 106

15 Our Nation From Its Creation, Prentice-Hall, 1966, pg. 41-42

16 Page 43

17 First Grade Social Studies Curriculum Guide, Contra Costa County Schools, 1963, pg. xiii

18 Ibid., pg. xvii

19 Ibid., pg. 38

20 Rieff, The Triumph of the Therapeutic, Harper & Row, 1966

21 Ibid., pg. 2

22 Ibid., pg. 156

23 Ibid., pg. 156-159

24 Ibid., pg. 159-160

25 Ibid., pg. 160-161, 187

26 Pages 6 & 7

27 Page 9-11

28 Page 7

29 Page 9

30 Pages 8,10

31 Pages 12-13

32 Engels, The Origin of the Family, Private Property and the State, International Publishers, 1942, pg. 63-67

33 Emblem of Freedom: The American Family in the 1980s, Carolina Academic Press, pg. 101

34 The Communist Manifesto, pg. 92

35 Barton, The Myth of Separation, Wallbuilders, 1989, pg. 11-12

36 Ibid., pg. 55, 62

37 Ibid., pg. 50

38 Ibid., pg. 76

39 McDowell and Beliles, America's Providential History, Providence Press pg. 222

40 Grant, Trial and Error—The ACLU and Its Impact On Your Family, pg. 154

41 30th Anniversary Reunion Book, Harvard Class of 1905, quoted in Congressional Record, May 23, 1952 and Grant, Trial and Error, pg. 154.

42 Report, The Coming Nuclear Attack on Christianity—A Report on The ABA Seminar on Tort and Religion, Shelby Sharpe, 500 Throckmorton St., Ft. Worth TX 76102

43 Marx, Communist Manifesto, pg. 87

44 Ibid., pg. 91

45 Engels as quoted by Lenin, The State and the Revolution, International Publishers, 1932 & 1943, pg. 8-9, 15-16

46 One World, The monthly magazine of the World Council of Churches, October 1989, pg. 17

47 Hyde, Dedication and Leadership, University of Notre Dame Press, 1966

CHAPTER 26

The Basis For Victory

1 People's Daily World, Jun. 17, 1987

2 Ryle, Five Christian Leaders, pg. 10-11

3 Robinson, Proofs of a Conspiracy, 1796

4 Ryle, pg. 11

5 Letters of John Newton, pg. 7

6 Ryle, pg. 17-18

7 Cyclopedia of Biblical, Theological & Ecclesiastical Lectures, pg. 18

8 Quoted by Bready, This Freedom Whence?, pg. 95

9 Ibid., pg. 96-97

10 Ibid., pg. 97

11 Ibid., pg. xv

12 Quoted, Nation Under God, pg. 24

13 Maxfield, Revival in America, pg. 283

14 Ibid.

15 Quoted, Magruder, American Government, 1952, pg. 13

16 Bready, pg. 342

INDEX

To Keep You Up-to-date On World Events
John Stormer periodically issues a newsletter...

UNDERSTANDING THE TIMES

Understanding The Times, **published by Liberty Bell Press, P.O.Box 32, Florissant MO 63032,** features periodic reports on activities of the Communist Party as discerned from screening their official publications and reports to members. Significant news developments in foreign policy, politics, education, religion and economics are culled from leading newspapers and twenty weekly and monthly newsletters. A wealth of material is analyzed and put into proper perspective.

For A Free Sample Copy, Write or Return This Coupon Now!

NAME: _____

ORGANIZATION (If any): _____

ADDRESS: _____

CITY: _____ STATE: _____ ZIP: _____